Submission Fighting Techniques

Steven S. Iverson

© 2001 Spartan Submissions, Inc.

Fayetteville, NC

All rights reserved.

Published in the United States of America.

No part of this book may be reproduced in any form or by any electronic or mechanical means, including information storage and retrieval devices or systems, without prior written permission from the publisher.

Author: Steven S. Iverson

ISBN 0-9714133-1-2

Library of Congress Control Number: 2002101125

WARNING !

Any type of submission fighting or grappling is a potentially dangerous sport. The techniques described in this book are for sport competition. You should only practice these techniques under the supervision of an experienced, trained professional. Anyone who is not considered a legal adult should only practice these techniques under adult, professional supervision.

Grappling and submission fighting are physical sports requiring physical fitness on the part of the participant. You should condition your body physically through strength training and aerobic conditioning before participating in any type of submission training. You should consult a physician before training with any of the techniques presented in this manual.

When implementing the techniques in this manual, the person applying the technique has a responsibility to implement the technique in a manner that does not harm the defender. You should never employ these techniques to completion of the move, you only apply enough pressure to elicit the submission. If you are in doubt as to if you are harming the defender, stop the technique immediately.

The defender of a submission technique also has a responsibility during training. The defender must know his physical limitations and be ready to submit to protect himself. It is better to protect yourself from permanent injury that try and tough out a technique and hope your body will withstand the attack.

All participants in submission fighting must understand what their techniques can potentially cause in damage. Neck cranks can hyper-extend the cervical spine and damage the spinal column, the vertebrae and cartilage. Arm and knee bars, squeeze locks and levers, can damage the ligaments and bursa sacks of the targeted joint. Heel hooks and ankle cranks can damage the ligaments and meniscus of the knee. Hip locks, ankle locks and wrist locks can damage the ligaments of the targeted joint. Shoulder cranks and locks can tear the muscles of that complicated joint.

Spartan Submissions, Inc. and the author are not responsible for any injuries sustained from practicing these techniques.

PREFACE

It is the intent of this book to present the interested reader with a variety of submission techniques from different fighting positions. In this book, techniques are kept as realistic as possible. However, it is more important to illustrate the technique to the reader than show actual competitors fighting. As a consequence, some techniques may appear unrealistic. Take the concept and principles of the techniques and then apply them to your own fighting style.

This book is not a complete work on submission fighting. It is a very specific book. It describes offensive, no gi, submission techniques. There is a great deal to successful submission fighting including conditioning, takedowns, reversals, body positioning, combinations, tactics, and strategy. This is just one piece of the puzzle; please accept it for its limitations and for what it intends to accomplish.

The author of this book is not an expert on submission fighting and does not pretend to be so. It is expected that the reader may know many of these techniques or may know variations of these techniques. Keep what is useful and discard what is not. Alter these techniques to fit your style; improve on them and make yourself a better fighter.

A great deal of work and care was put into this book. There are almost nine hundred pictures with over two hundred and fifty submission techniques from a score of positions. Enjoy this book and learn from its limitations and errors. It is a worthwhile work which, hopefully, meets the expectations and demands of the readers.

Contents

Warning, iii

Preface, iv

Chapter: 1 Submissions From Standing

Neck Cranks, 2 - 4

Chokes, 5 - 7

Ankle Locks, 8 - 9

Knee Bars, 10 - 13

Arm Bars, 14 - 17

Forearm Lock, 18

Shoulder Crank, 19

Squeeze Lock, 20

Groin Stretch, 21

Chapter 2: Submissions From the Closed Guard

Closed Guard Explanation, 23

Neck Cranks, 24 - 25

Chokes, 26 - 30

Arm Bars, 31 - 40

Shoulder Cranks, 41 - 44

Squeeze Lock, Arm, 45

Wrist Lock, 46

Chapter 3: Submissions From The Open Guard

Open Guard Explanation, 48

Choke, 49

Foot Attacks, 50 - 53

Knee Bars, 54 - 55

Knee Lever, 56

Arm Bars, 57 - 58

Squeeze Lock, Arm, 59

Chapter 4: Submissions In The Closed Guard

Neck Cranks, 61- 62

Chokes, 62 - 65

Foot Attacks, 66 - 67

Chapter 5: Submissions In The Open Guard

Foot Attacks, 69 - 74

Knee Bars, 75 - 78

Squeeze Lock, Leg, 79

Groin Stretch, 80

Chapter 6: Submissions From The Half Guard And In The Half Guard

Half Guard explanation, 82

From Half Guard

    Knee Lever, 83

    Knee Bar, 84

    Ankle Crank, 85

In Half Guard

    Ankle Crank, 86

    Knee Bar, 87

    Squeeze Lock, Leg, 88

    Knee Lever, 89

Chapter 7: Submissions From The Mount And In The Mount

Mount Explanation, 91

From The Mount

    Neck Cranks, 92 - 93

    Chokes, 94 - 100

    Shoulder Crank, 101

    Arm Bars, 102 - 105

    Knee Lever, 106

 In the Mount

    Knee Lever, 107

    Heel Hook, 108

    Ankle Locks, 109 - 110

Chapter 8: Submissions From Modified Mount

Modified Mount Explanation, 112

Neck Cranks, 113

Chokes, 114 - 116

Arm Bars, 117 - 119

Shoulder Cranks, 120 -121

Squeeze Lock, Arm, 122

Forearm Lock, 123

Hip Lock, 124

Chapter 9: Submissions From Reverse Mount

Reverse Mount Explanation, 126

Shoulder Crank, 127

Arm Bar, 128

Ankle Crank, 129

Chapter 10: Submissions From Side Control

Side Control Explanation, 131

Neck Cranks, 132 - 134

Chokes, 135 - 137

Arm Bars, 138 - 140

Forearm Lock, 141

Shoulder Cranks, 142 -143

Knee Bars, 144 - 145

Hip Locks, 146 - 147

Foot Attacks, 148 - 154

Chapter 11: Submissions In Side Control

Neck Crank, 156

Chokes, 157 - 159

Arm Bars, 160 & 162

Shoulder Crank, 161

Chapter 12: Submissions From Scarf Hold, In Scarf Hold, And From Modified Scarf Hold

Scarf Hold Explanation, 164

From Scarf Hold

    Neck Cranks, 165 - 166

    Chokes, 167 - 171

    Shoulder Crank, 172

    Arm Bars, 173 - 174

In Scarf Hold

    Choke, 175

    Arm Bar, 176

Modified Scarf Hold Explanation

    Arm Bars, 178 & 180

    Shoulder Crank, 179

Chapter 13: Submissions From Knee On Stomach

Knee On Stomach Explanation, 182

Cradle, 183

Choke, 184

Arm Bars, 185 - 187

Knee Bar, 188

Chapter 14: Submissions From Knee On Chest

Knee On Chest Explanation, 190

Neck Crank, 191

Choke, 192

Arm Bar, 193

Shoulder Crank, 194

Chapter 15: Submissions Against Referee's Position And In Referee's Position

Referee's Position Explanation, 196

Against Referee's Position

    Neck Cranks, 197 - 198

    Chokes, 199 - 203

    Arm Bars, 204 - 207

    Squeeze Lock, Arm, 208

    Knee Bar, 209

    Knee Levers, 210 -214

    Foot Attacks, 215 - 218

    Groin Stretch, 219

From Referee Position

    Knee Bar, 220

Chapter 16: Submissions From Rear Mount And In Rear Mount

Rear Mount Explanation, 222

From Rear Mount

    Neck Cranks, 223 - 225

    Chokes, 226 - 228

    Arm Bars, 229 - 230

    Squeeze Locks, 231 - 232

    Shoulder Crank, 233

    Shoulder Lock, 234

In Rear Mount

    Ankle Cranks, 235 - 237

    Ankle Lock, 238

Chapter 17: Submissions From North/South And In North/South

N/S Explanation, 240

From N/S

    Neck Cranks, 241 - 242

    Chokes, 243 - 245

    Shoulder Crank, 246

In N/S

    Arm Bar, 247

    Choke, 248

Chapter 18: Variations of Triangle Choke, Arm Bar, Knee Bar, And Foot Attacks

Triangle Choke Explanation, 250

    Arm Assists, 251

    Shoulder Cranks, 253

    Foot Attacks, 254

Arm Bar Explanation, 255

    Arm Bar Variations, 256 – 257

    Wrist Lock, 258

    Shoulder Cranks, 259

    Squeeze Lock, Arm, 260

Knee Bar Explanation, 261

    Knee Bar Variations, 262

    Squeeze Lock, Leg, 263

Foot Attacks, 264 - 269

Chapter One

Standing Submissions

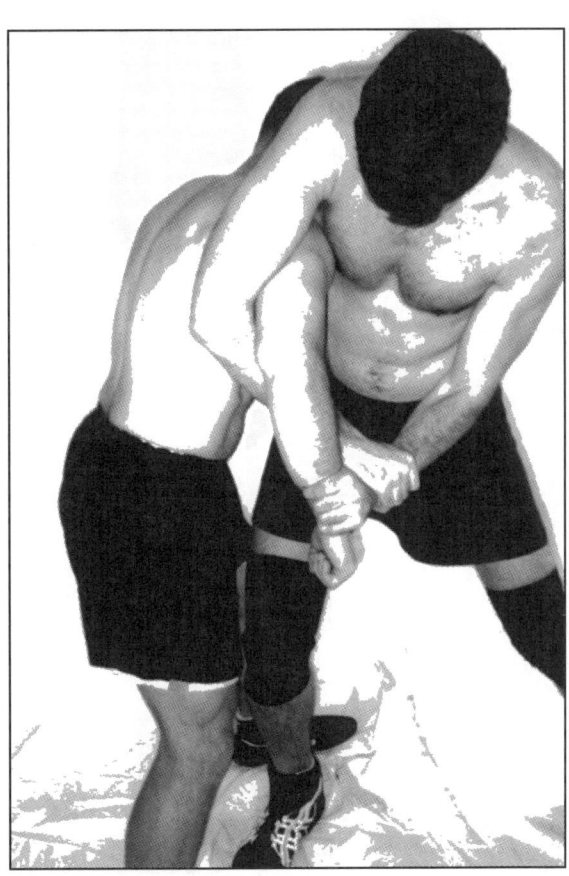

NECK CRANK *Crucifix*

Set up your opponent by hooking one arm behind his neck and controlling his arm.

Snap his head down and hook your arm over his head and under his arm as shown. (This picture is from the opposite angle)

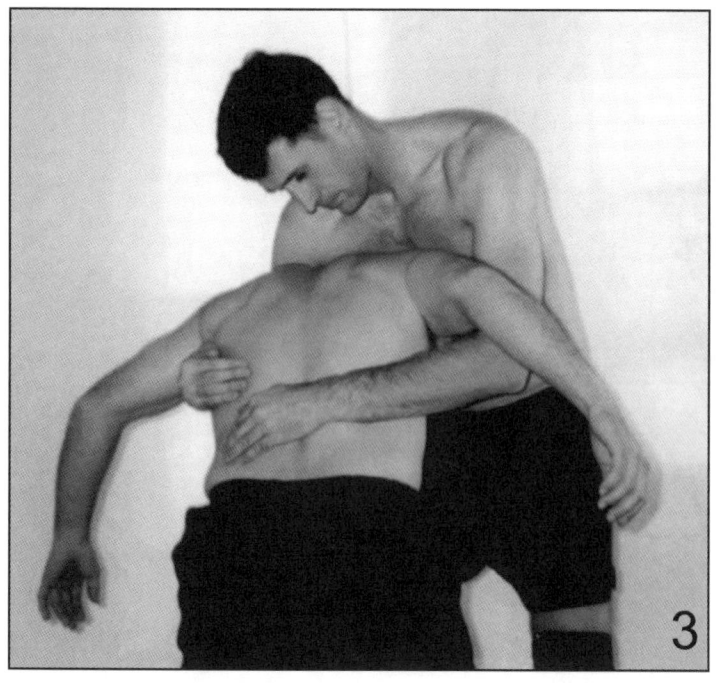

Hook your other arm under his so that both of your arms are hooked under his.

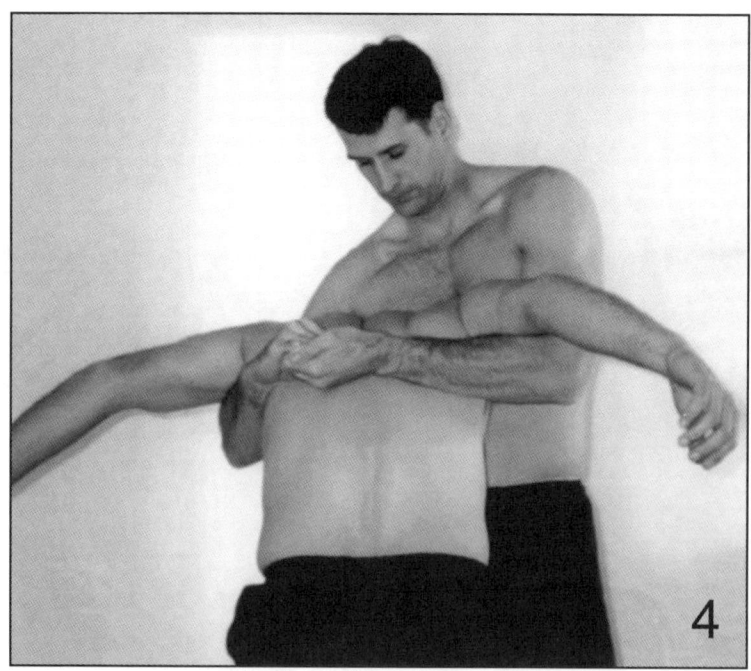

Clasp your hands and drive them upwards while pressing down on his neck with your armpit. This pressure will force his neck downwards, hyperextending his cervical spine for the submission.

NECK CRANK *Figure Four Lock*

Set up your opponent with one arm clasping the back of his neck. Ensure your hips and feet are far enough back to give his head room to travel when you snap it downwards. (Left)

Snap his head downwards and with the same arm slide your wrist across his jaw, forcing his chin to turn to the side as shown. (This picture is from the opposite angle) (Right)

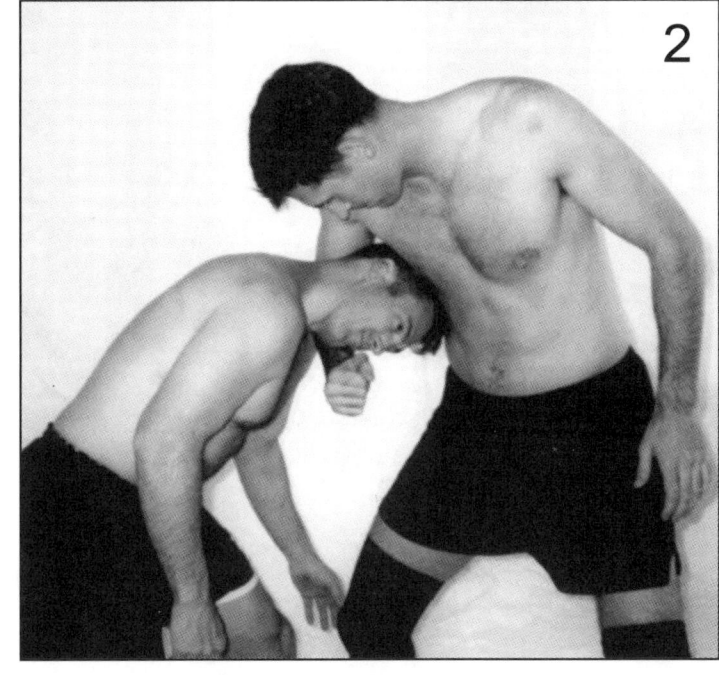

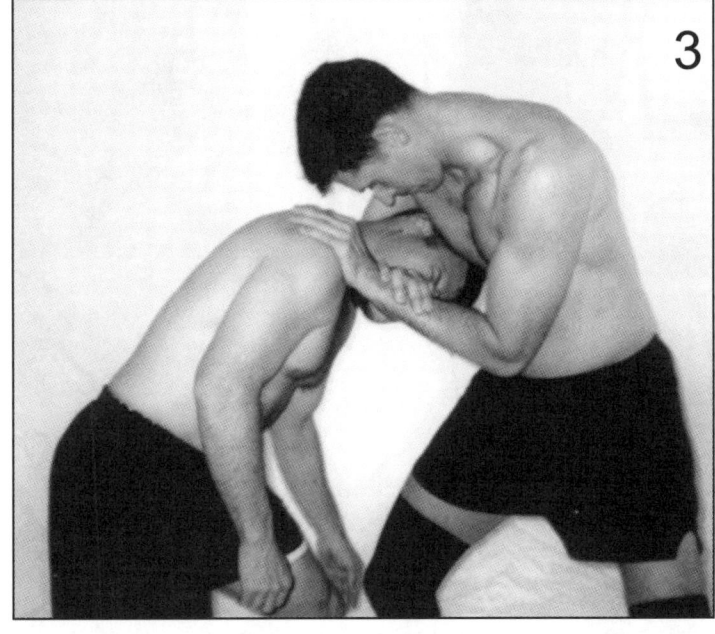

Place your free arm on his shoulder and grab it at the wrist with your attacking arm. Notice how your opponent's head is trapped under your attacking arm's shoulder and armpit. Push up with your arm across his chin while pushing his head down with your armpit. This will hyper-extend the cervical spine until he submits. (Left)

NECK CRANK *Underarm Hold*

1. You have your opponent set up in a side bear hug. (Left)

Reach over his head and across his neck with your rear, attacking arm. (Right)

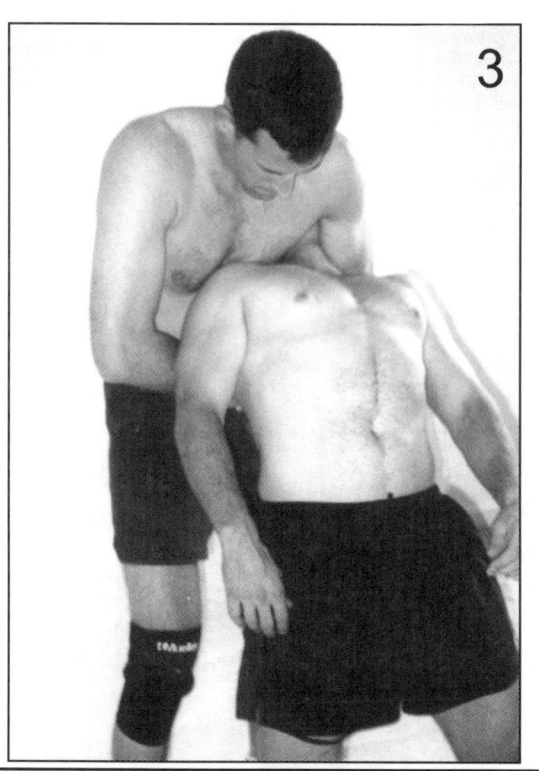

Clasp your hands together behind his back, securing his head and neck under your attacking arm's armpit. Arch your back and drive your hands into the base of his neck for the submission. This move will hyperextend his cervical spine for the submission. (Left)

CHOKE *Kata Gatame*

Set your opponent up with one arm hooking the back of his neck. Your other arm is cupped behind the elbow of his arm.

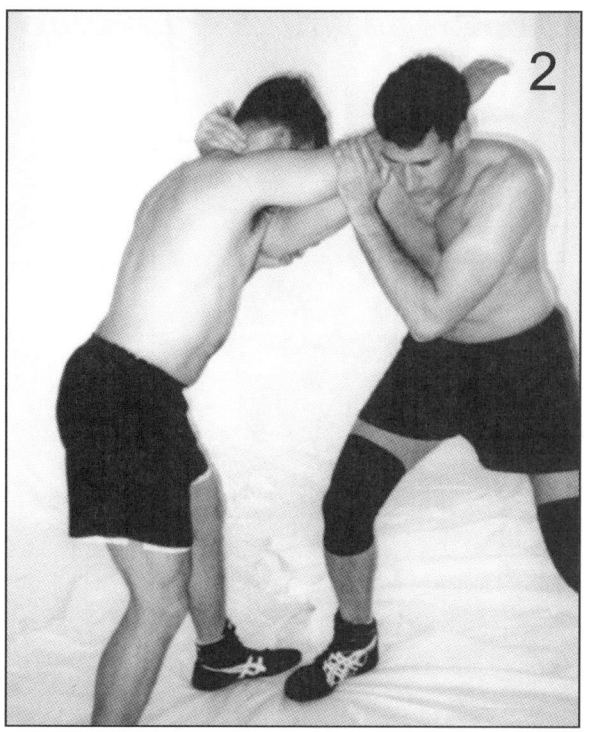

Snap his head forwards, duck under his arm and push it across his face as shown. Your other arm remains hooked behind his head. (This picture is taken from the opposite angle)

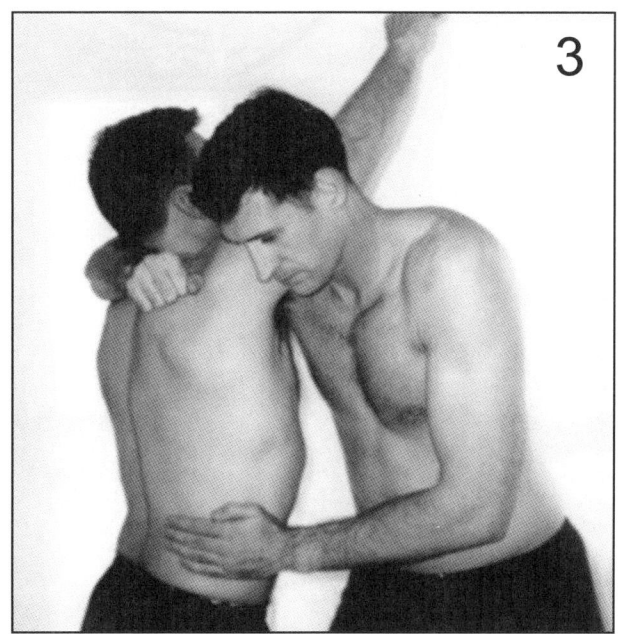

Hug yourself to him with your hooked arm and drive your head forwards, trapping his arm between his head and yours.

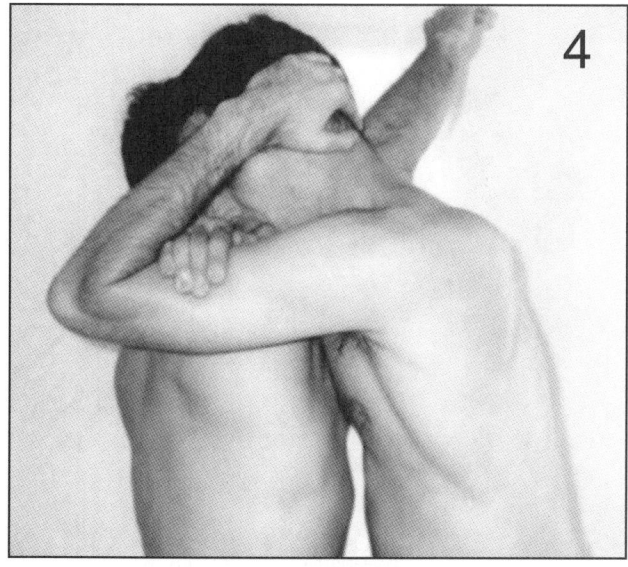

Your attacking arm grabs your other, locking arm at the biceps; place your locking hand on the back of your own head. Drive the blade of your attacking forearm into the base of his neck. Also, drive your shoulder forward into his neck and contract the muscles of your attacking arm. This will crank his neck and cut off his carotid arteries for the submission.

CHOKE *Shoulder Variation*

Hook your attacking arm behind his neck and trap his head between your arm and your shoulder.

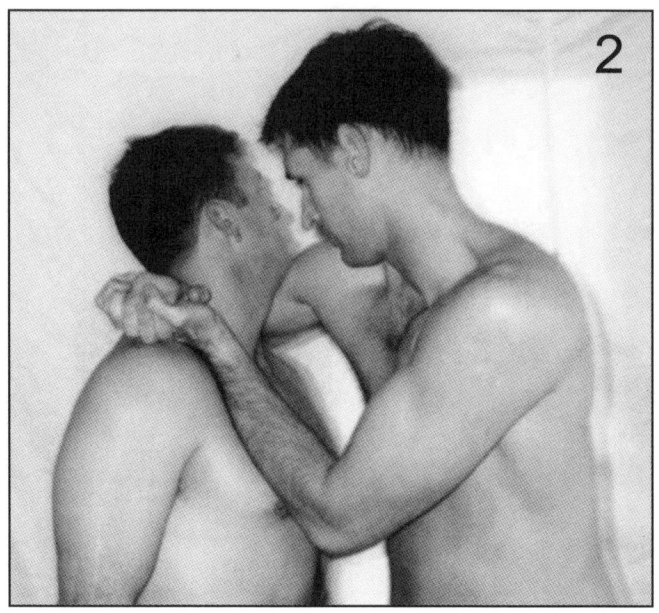

Clasp your attacking hand with your locking hand and place your locking arm against his chest as shown.

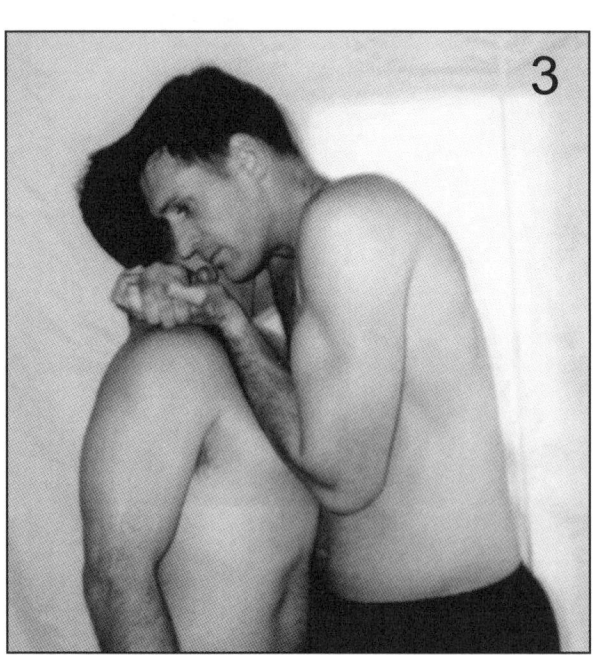

Drive your shoulder into his throat while driving the blade of your attacking forearm into the base of his neck. The pressure from your shoulder will choke him.

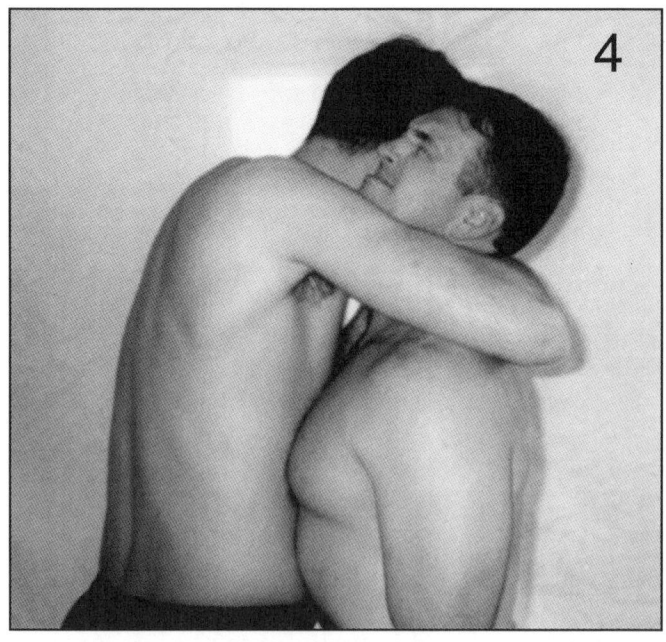

This is the same step from the opposite side. Driving the blade of your forearm into his neck will also crank his neck for a submission.

CHOKE *Guillotine*

Set your opponent up with one hand hooked behind his neck.

Snap his head forwards and place your arm over the back of his neck as shown.

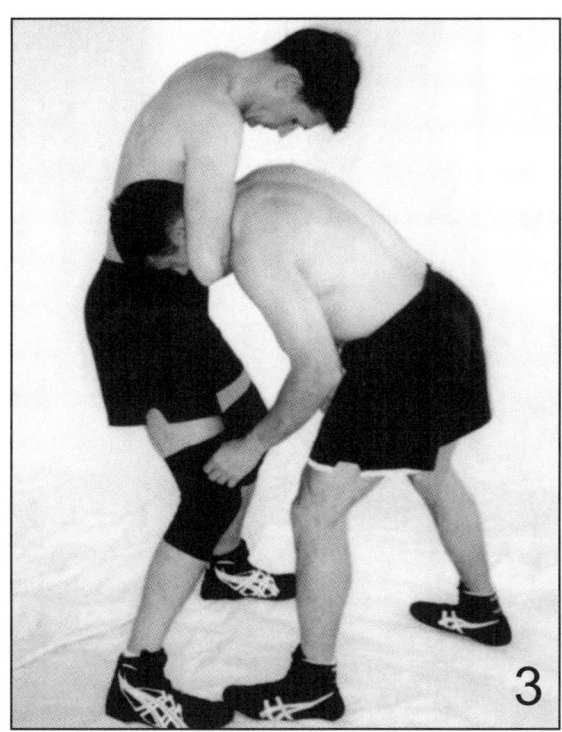

Wrap your attacking arm across his throat and under his chin. Grab your attacking arm at the wrist with your other, locking arm.

Here it is from the other side. Pull up with your choking forearm, driving the blade of your forearm into his throat; arch your back and push his head downwards with your armpit. This choke crushes his esophagus for the submission.

DROP TO AN ACHILLES LOCK

Set up your opponent by placing your leg across his opposite thigh/waist area. Your near arm is hooked under his near arm. (Above)

Drop to your side and place your free leg behind his far leg as shown. Your body weight will bring him forwards as you maintain your under hooked arm. (Top Right)

Secure his exposed ankle with your free arm. (Right)

Gain control of his leg with yours in preparation for your ankle attack. (Bottom Right)

Secure his targeted foot under your armpit. Drive the blade of your attacking forearm up and into his Achilles tendon while arching backwards for the submission. (Bottom)

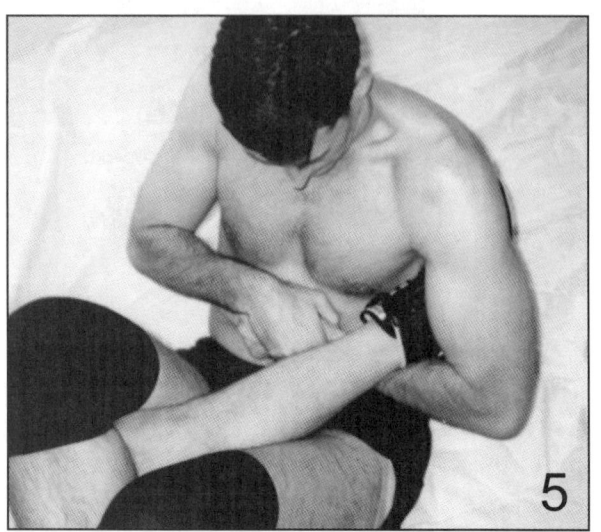

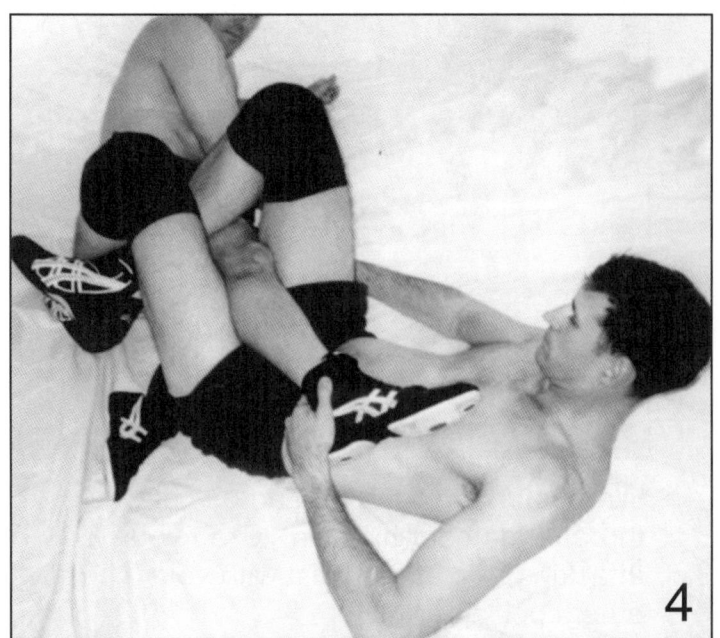

ANKLE PICK TO AN ANKLE LOCK

Set your opponent up with an arm hooked around the back of his neck. Notice how he has his weight over his forward leg.

Snap his head downwards and grab his exposed leg at the ankle.

Bring his leg upwards and hug it as shown. Drive your shoulder into his knee and twist your body, driving his body weight over his trapped leg, dumping him onto the ground.

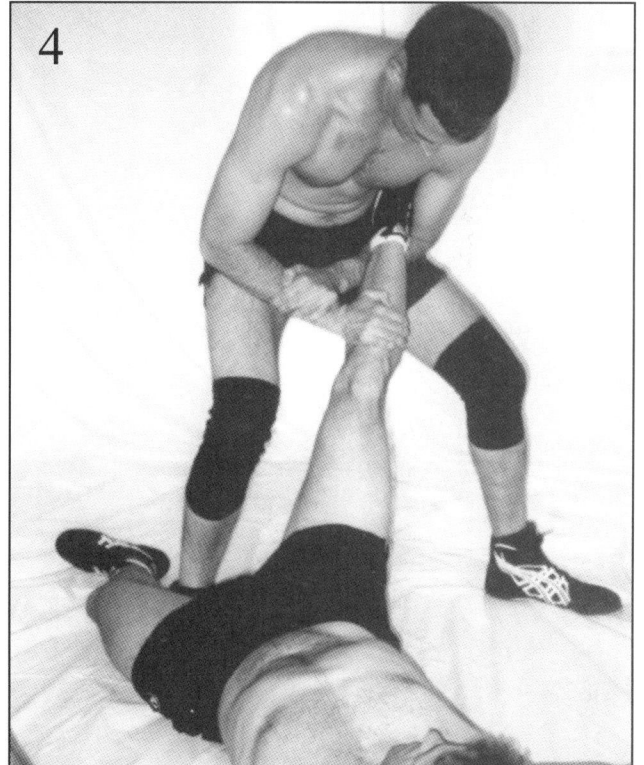

Secure an ankle lock, figure fouring your arms as shown. Arch your back and look upwards as you hyper-extend his foot at the ankle for the submission. You can also sit down and submit your opponent from that position.

DROP TO A KNEE BAR

Set up your opponent as shown. Secure a grip on his lat muscle and hook your near leg between his.

Place your arm on the ground for balance and hook your other leg as shown. Rotate your hips backwards using your arm for assistance, and topple him backwards over your straightened leg.

You have fallen in a manner so that your legs are already locked around his targeted leg. As you can see, your opponent's trapped leg is vulnerable to a variety of attacks.

Rotate your hips onto his knee cap and grab his leg at the ankle. Hug his leg tightly to your chest and arch your hips forwards to hyper-extend his leg at the knee for the submission.

ROLLING KNEE BAR

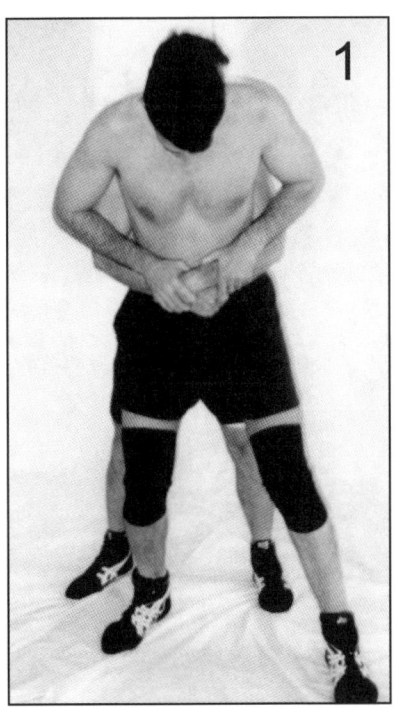

Your opponent is set up securing you around the waist. Grab him at the wrists. (Above)

Lean forwards and cup his ankle with one hand while maintaining your grip on his wrist with your other hand. (Above Right)

Roll forwards, maintaining your hold on his ankle, hooking your inside leg on is buttocks. (Right)

Hook your other foot on his hip/back area. Roll forwards until you are on your back. (Bottom Right)

You'll end up with his leg trapped as shown. Hug his leg, arch your hips forwards, and hyper-extend his leg at the knee for the submission. (Below)

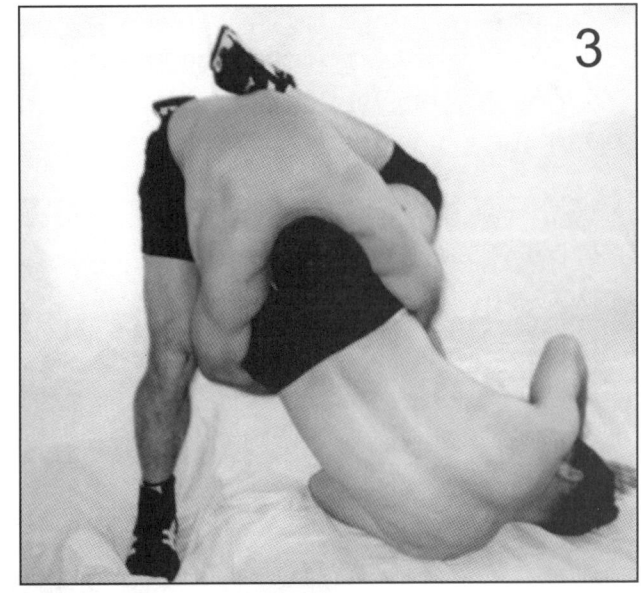

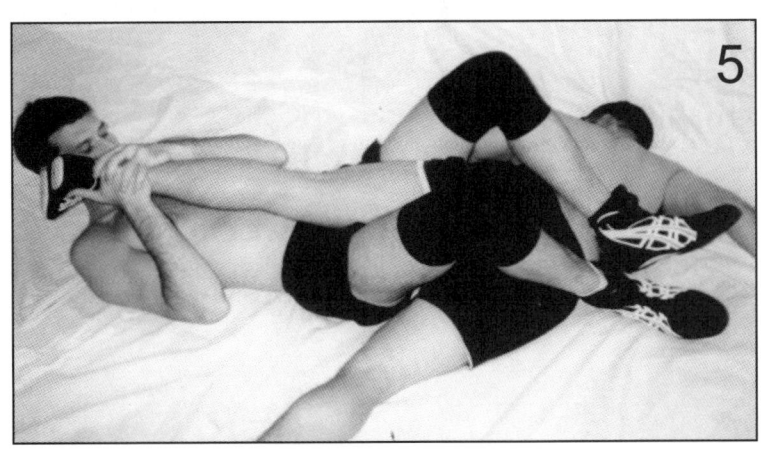

ROLLING KNEE BAR

Your opponent is set up as shown. Grab him on his lat muscle with your arm.

Lean forwards and grab him at the ankle. Your body weight is forwards in preparation to roll.

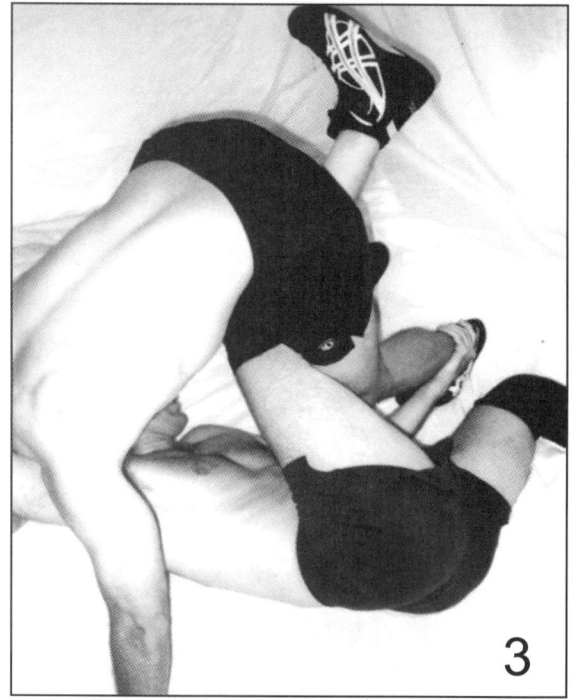

Roll forwards over your shoulder, bringing him over with you. This is your body positioning as you hit the ground. Maintain your grip on his ankle and drive him forwards with your leg that is hooked between his.

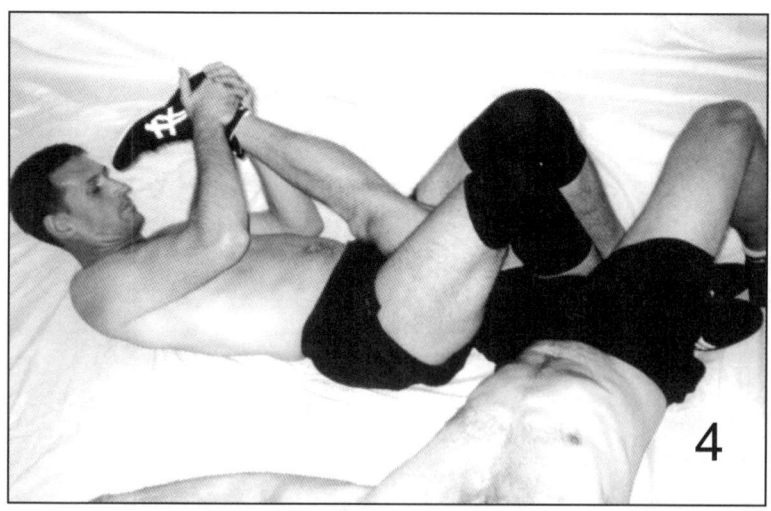

You will finish rolling with you both on your backs. Hug his leg, arch your hips, and hyper-extend his leg at the knee for the submission.

KNEE BAR *Sitting*

Your opponent is set up behind you and he may, or may not, have you in a bear hug Ensure you are straddling one of his legs.

Reach down with both arms and cup both of your hands behind the heel of his targeted leg.

Pull up with both of your arms while forcing your hips backwards. This will cause him to fall backwards. Maintain control of his leg with both hands.

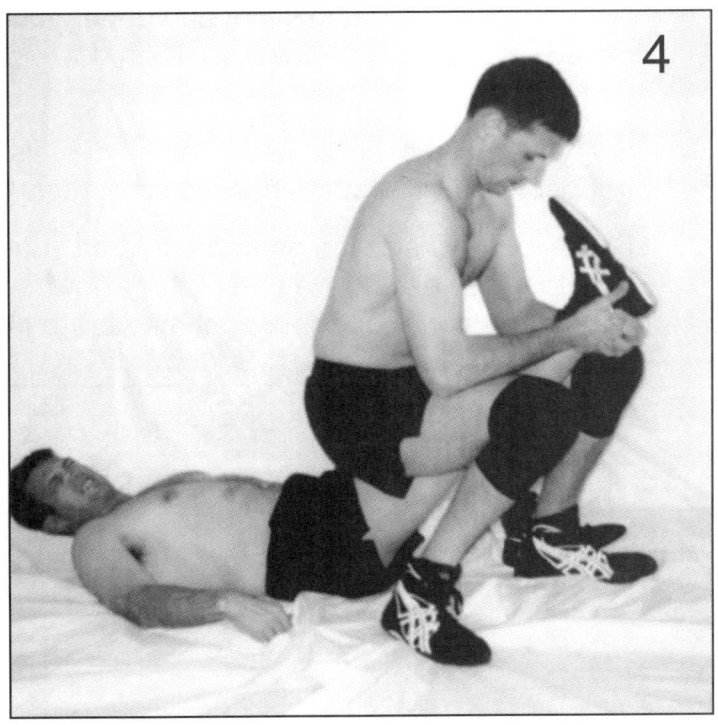

Maintain a good base and sit slightly above his knee cap, closer to his groin. Pull straight up on his heel while sitting on his knee to hyperextend his leg at the knee for the submission.

STANDING ARM BAR *Cross Leg Variation*

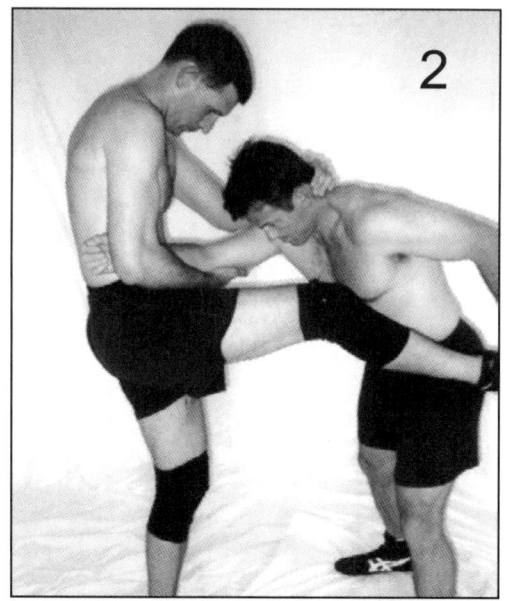

Set up your opponent by grabbing his elbow and behind his head. (Above)

Place your leg across his midsection as depicted. (Top Right)

Sit down right next to his foot and under your raised leg. As you sit down, pull him down with you. (Right)

Swing your leg over his head and secure his trapped arm with both hands. (Bottom Right)

Drive your heels to the ground and arch your hips to hyper-extend his arm at the elbow for the submission. Your opponent may fall to his back or remain standing. (Bottom)

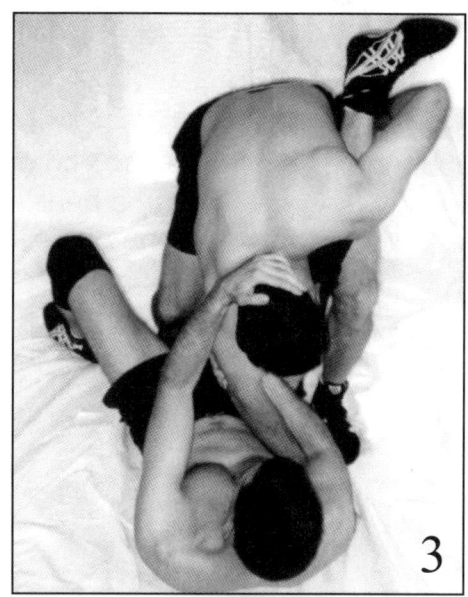

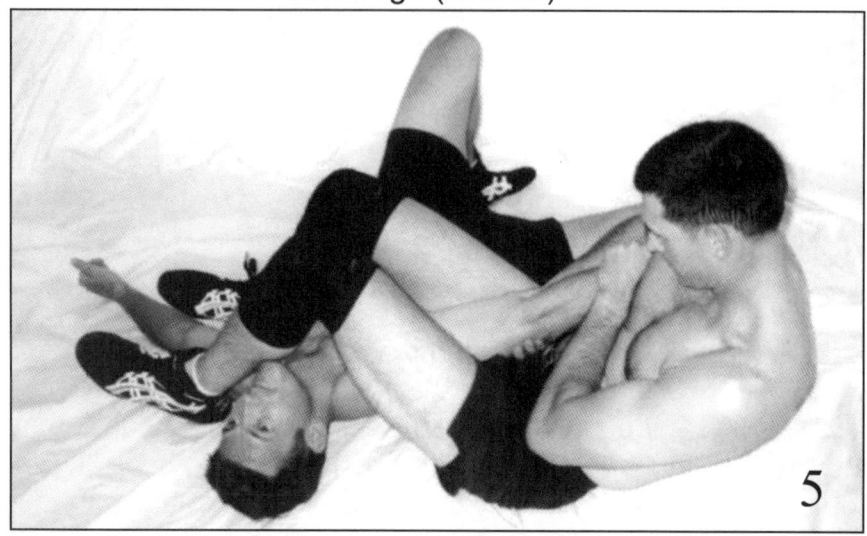

STANDING ARM BAR *Knee Variation*

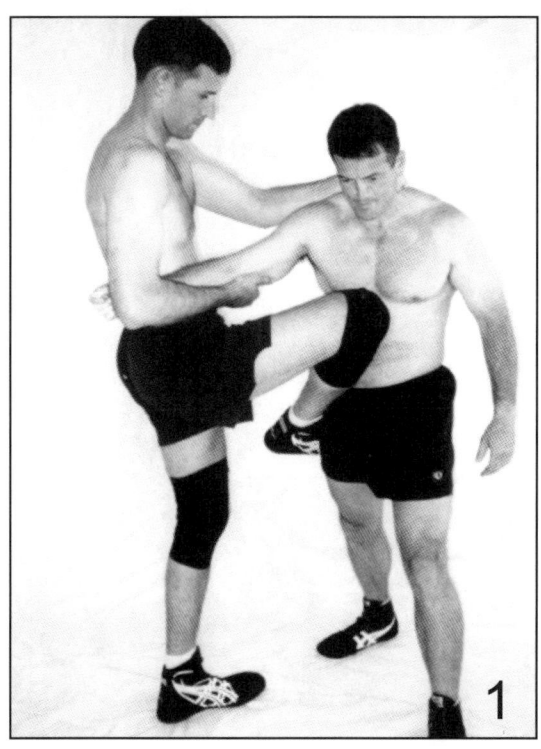

Set up your opponent by hooking the back of his head and his arm at the elbow. Place your knee against his midsection.

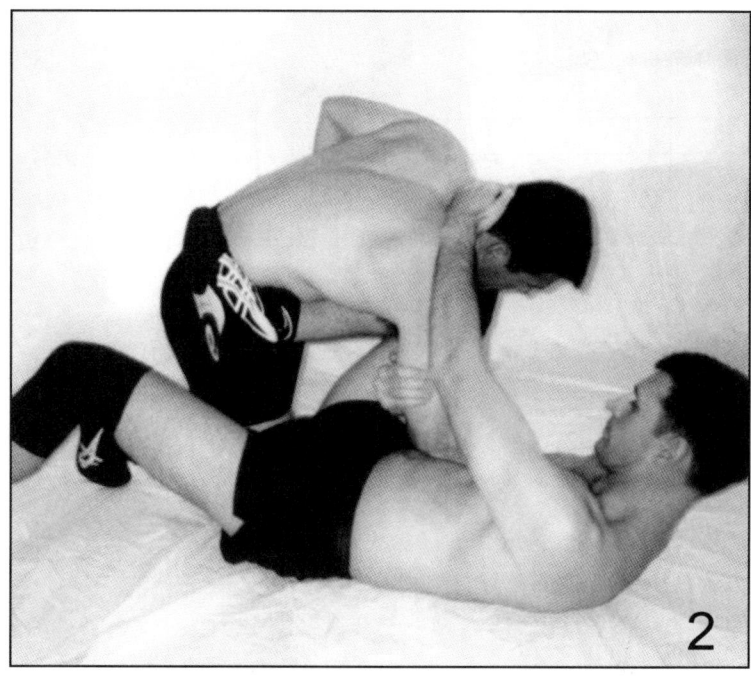

Sit straight down under his trapped arm, pulling him down with you. Ensure your opponent does not place his knee on your groin. (This picture is from the opposite angle)

Now that his weight is forwards, swing your leg over his head. Secure his trapped arm with both hands.

Squeeze your knees together, drive your feet to the ground and arch your hips forwards. This will hyper-extend his arm at the elbow for the submission.

ARM BAR *Figure Four Lock*

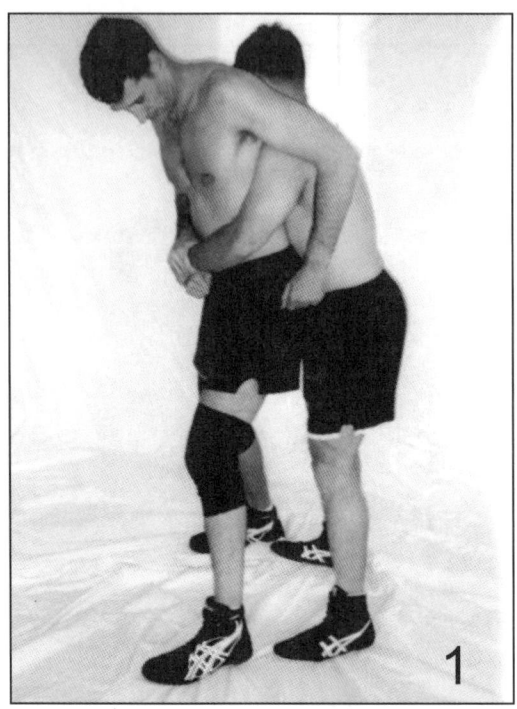

Your opponent is behind you and has you in a bear hug with your arms free.

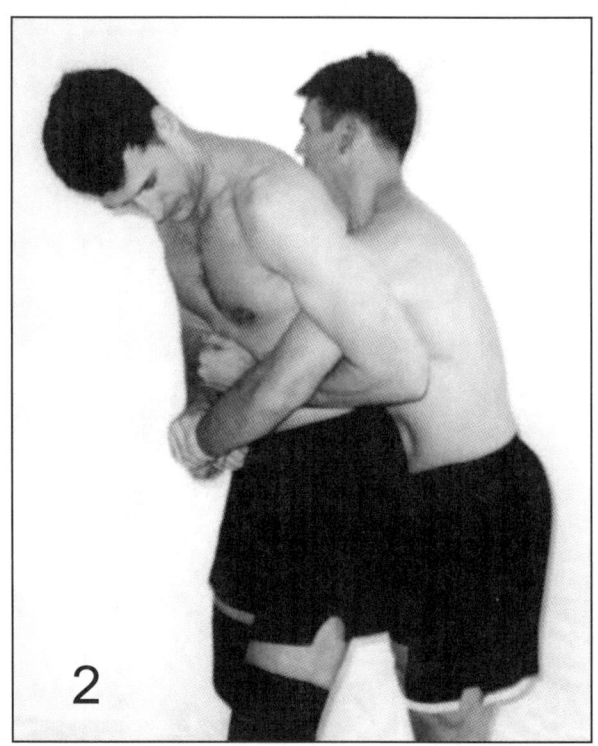

Wrap your attacking arm around his arm as depicted.

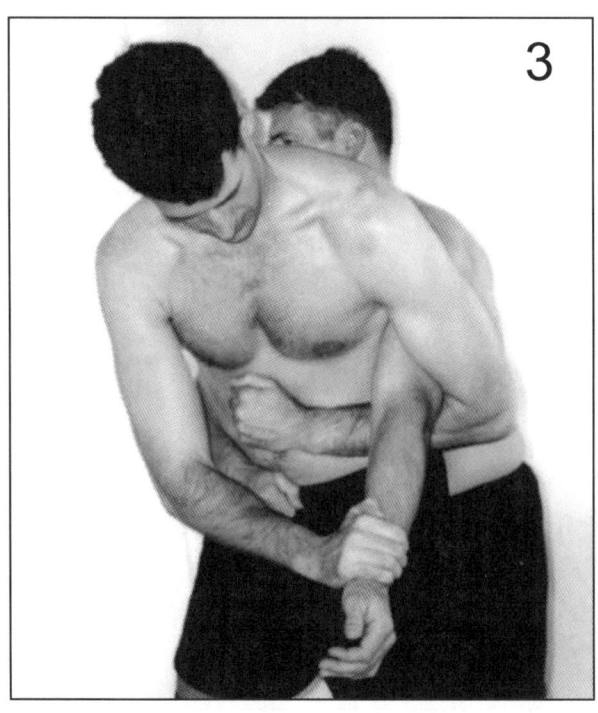

Grab his trapped wrist with your free, locking arm. Keep your attacking arm tightly wrapped around his arm.

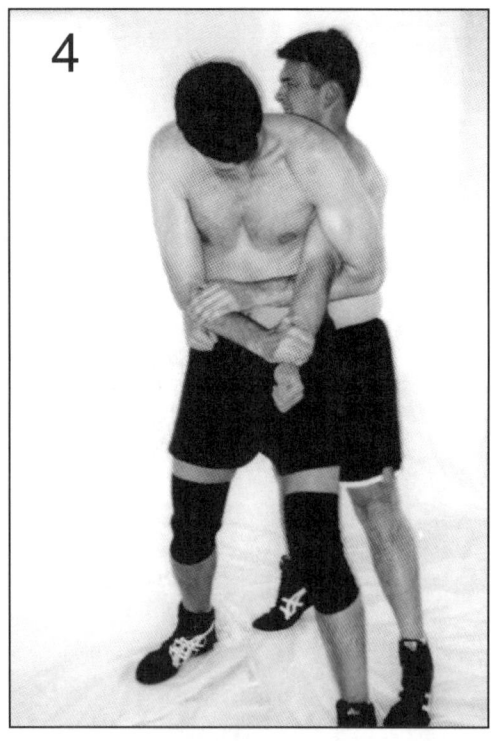

Ensure that your attacking arm crosses his arm just above or on his elbow and grab your other forearm. Pull up with your attacking arm while pushing down with your locking arm, hyper-extending his arm at the elbow.

ARM BAR *Elbow Lock*

Your are tied up with your opponent, controlling his targeted arm at the elbow, ensuring distance between you.

Swim through with your attacking arm, wrapping up his arm from the inside and securing his arm at the elbow.

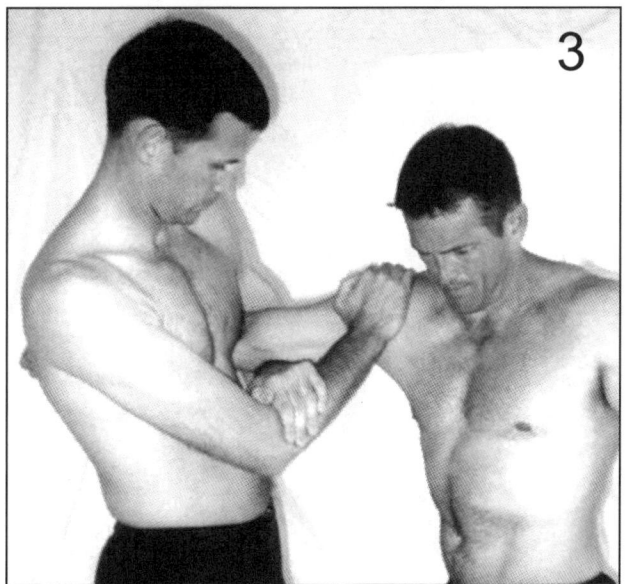

Grab your own locking arm at the forearm making a figure four lock. Place your locking arm on his trapped shoulder. Ensure that your attacking arm is on his elbow or just above it, closer to his shoulder. For the submission, arch your back, pull up with your attacking arm while pushing down on his trapped shoulder to hyper-extend his arm at the elbow.

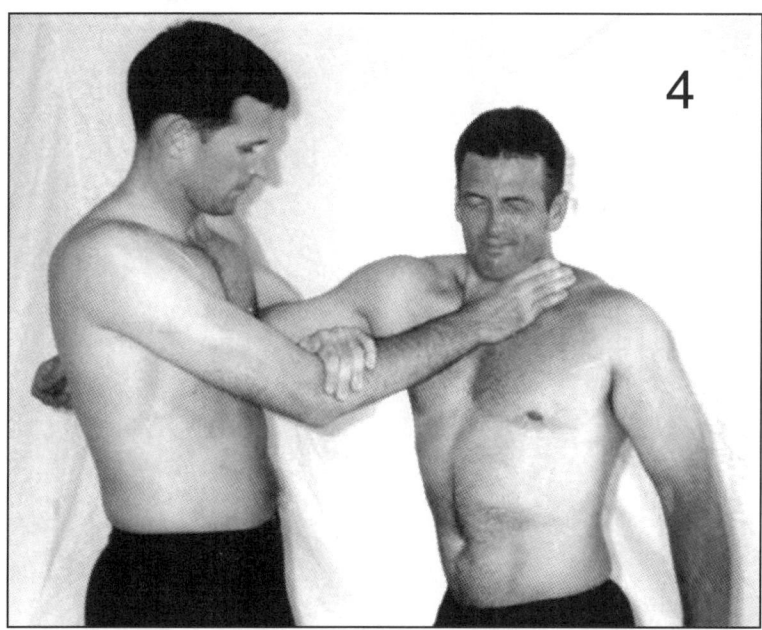

As an alternate grip, you can place your locking hand against his throat. This can aid in keeping his upper body away from yours and extending out his arm.

FOREARM LOCK

Set up your opponent, securing an arm as shown.

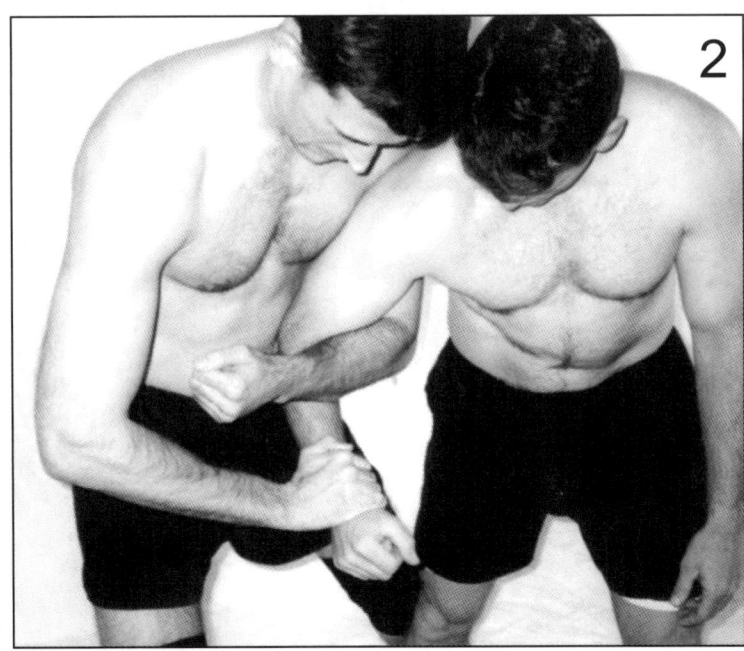

Hug his arm tightly at the elbow with your attacking arm and prepare to trap his arm with your other, locking arm.

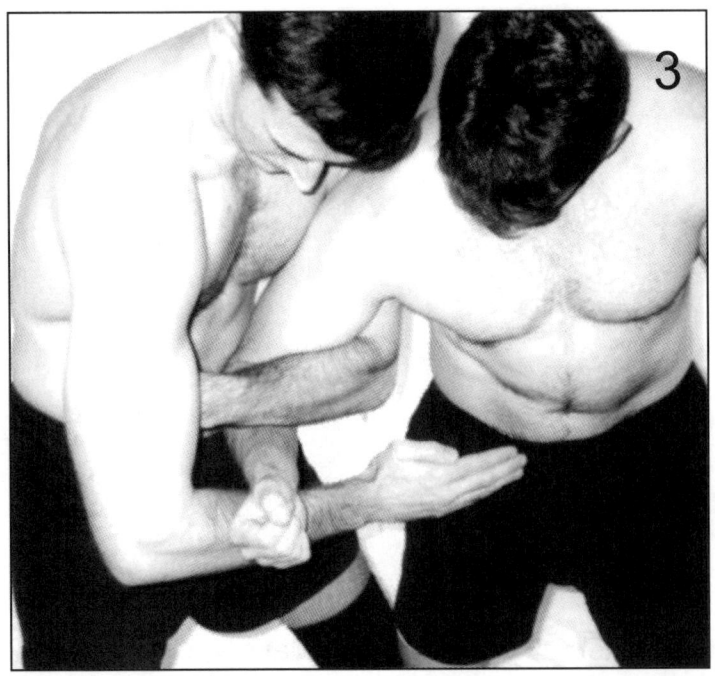

Maintain control of his arm with your attacking arm and place the hand of your attacking arm under your armpit. Secure his arm at the wrist with your locking arm. Ensure his palm is facing up.

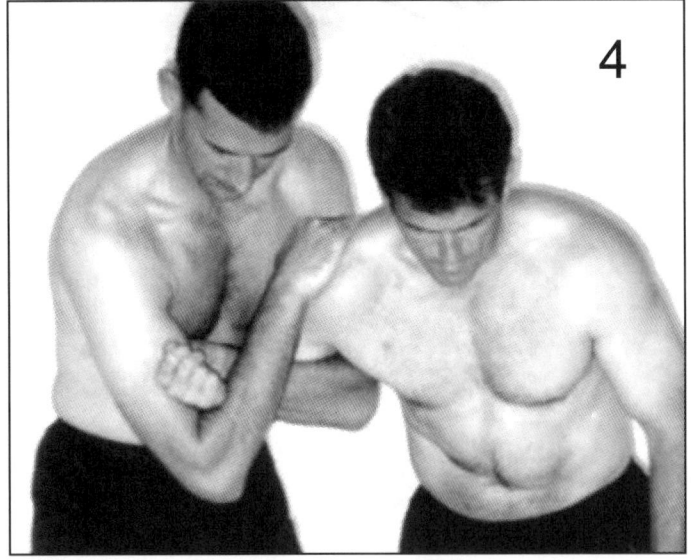

Hook your locking arm on his own shoulder, trapping his arm. Drive the blade of your attacking arm into his forearm. Your other, locking arm, hooked on his shoulder, pulls up to help drive his forearm into the blade of your attacking forearm. The submission is from the pain of driving the relatively narrow blade of your forearm into the wider bones of his forearm.

SHOULDER CRANK *Drop Key Lock*

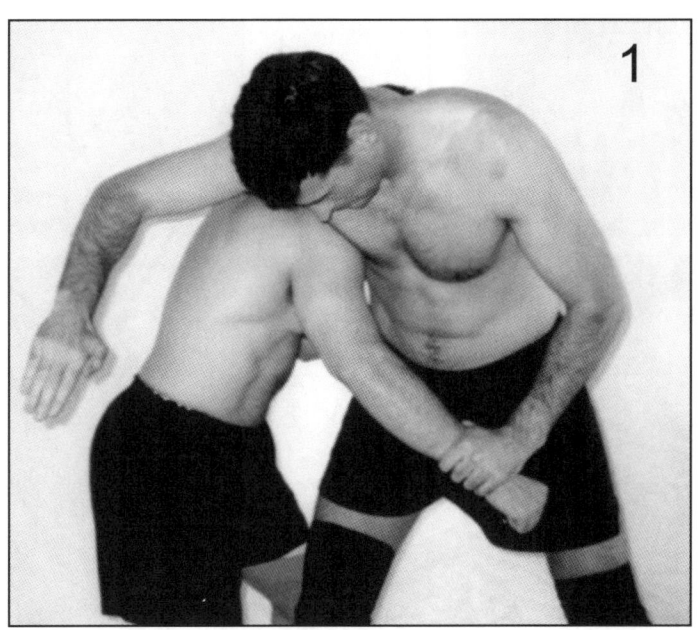

Your opponent is set up as shown. You have your opponent's arm secured at the wrist. Reach over his head with your other arm.

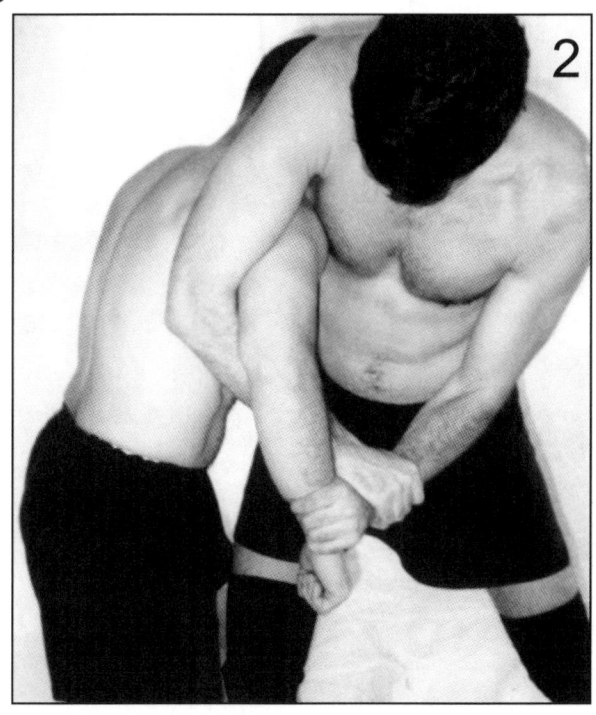

Reach over his upper arm and under his forearm, securing your other arm at the wrist, forming a figure four lock.

Place the heel of your foot across his far foot. Twist his trapped arm towards his head and sit down directly under his trapped arm. (Opposite angle)

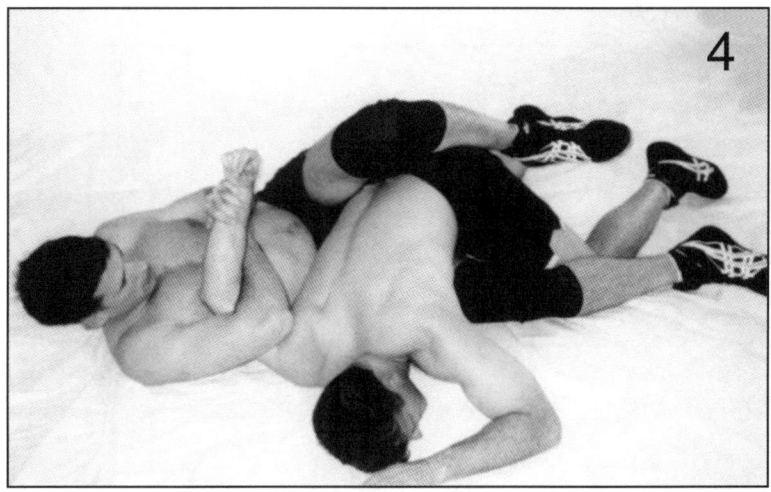

Your opponent will fall forwards. Place your top leg over his back to prevent him from rolling forwards. Twist his captured arm towards his head, attempting to place his wrist on the ground next to his head. This movement uses his bent arm as a lever to torque his shoulder for the submission.

SQUEEZE LOCK *Nutcracker*

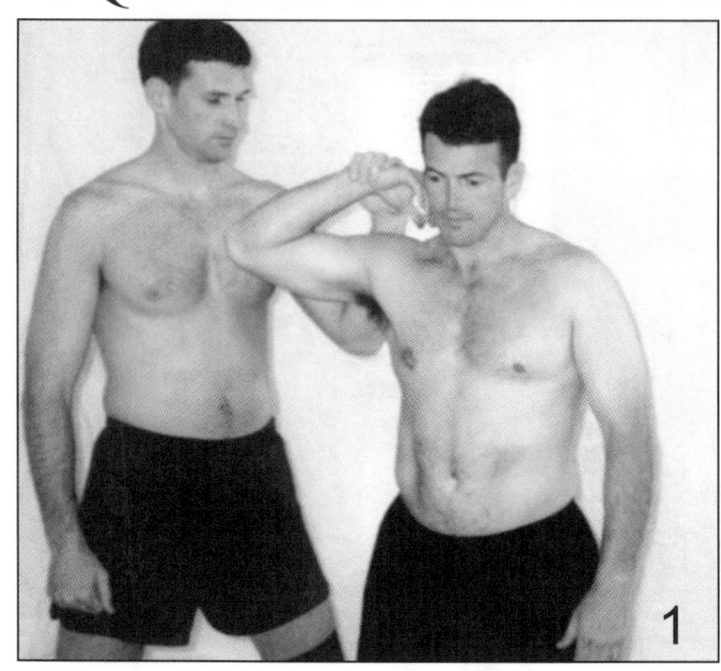

Secure your opponent's arm at the wrist as shown. (Left)

Squat under his arm and drive your shoulder against his triceps, maintaining your hold on his wrist. (Right)

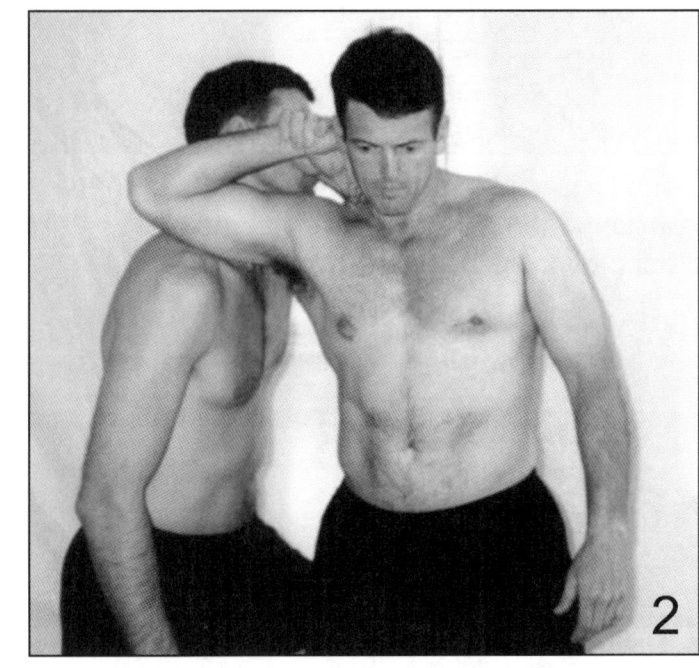

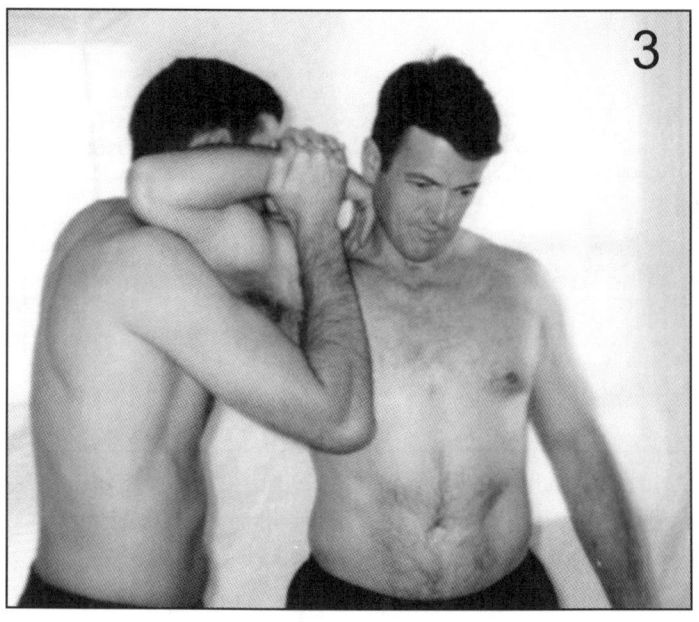

Grab his wrist with both hands. Pull his wrist down and towards his shoulder while you push up with your shoulder. This will hyper-flex his arm at the elbow for the submission; the pain on his elbow is intense. (Left)

GROIN STRETCH *Banana Split*

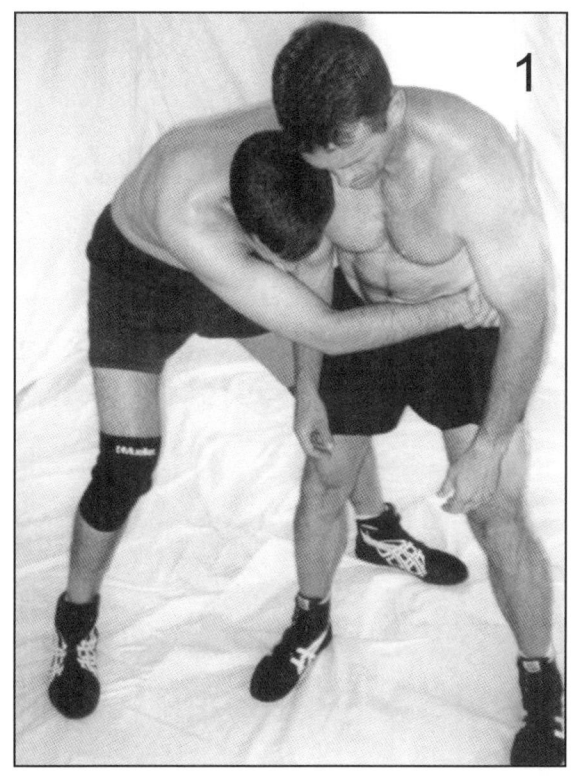

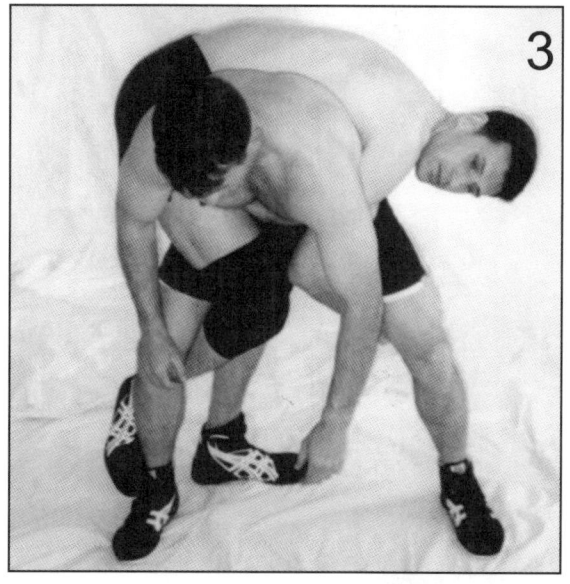

Your opponent is set up in a side bear hug. (Above)

Lace your leg around his near leg, stepping over his thigh and hooking your foot around his lower leg. (Top Right)

Reach across his back and grab his far leg, bear hugging his upper thigh. (Right)

Swivel your hips away from him and drop your weight backwards, bringing him to the ground. (Bottom Right)

Straighten your entangled leg and arch your back, straightening your upper body and stretching his groin. He will submit before his groin tears. Note alternate leg control. (Bottom)

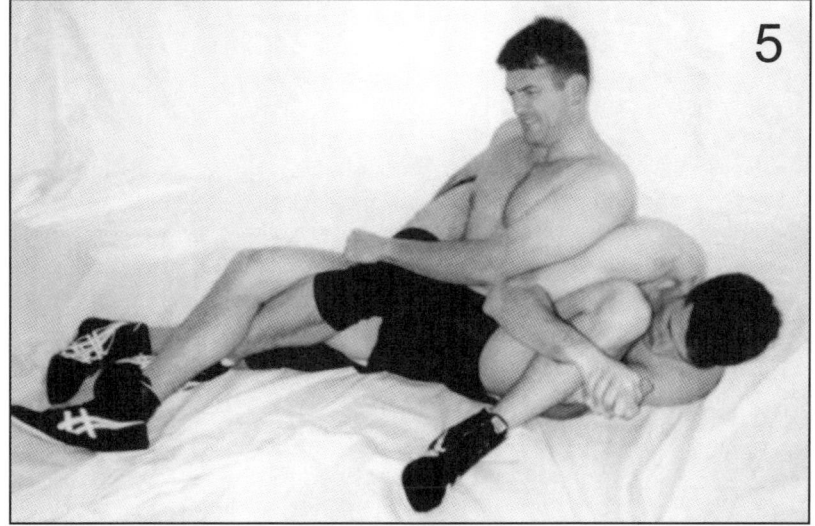

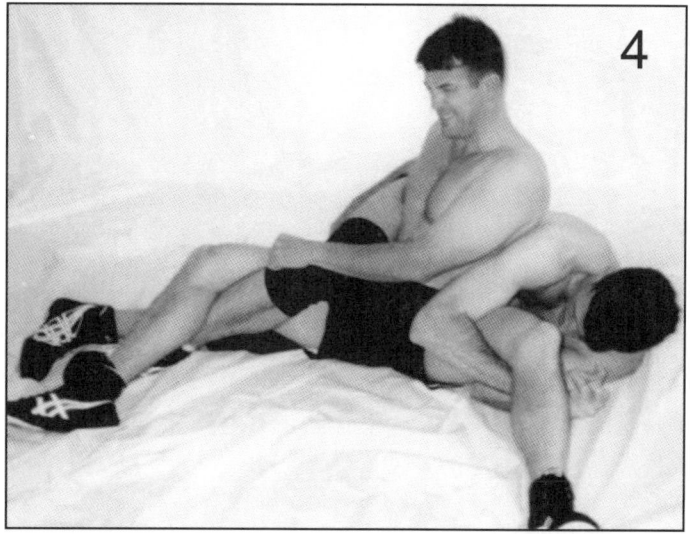

Chapter Two
Submissions From The Closed Guard

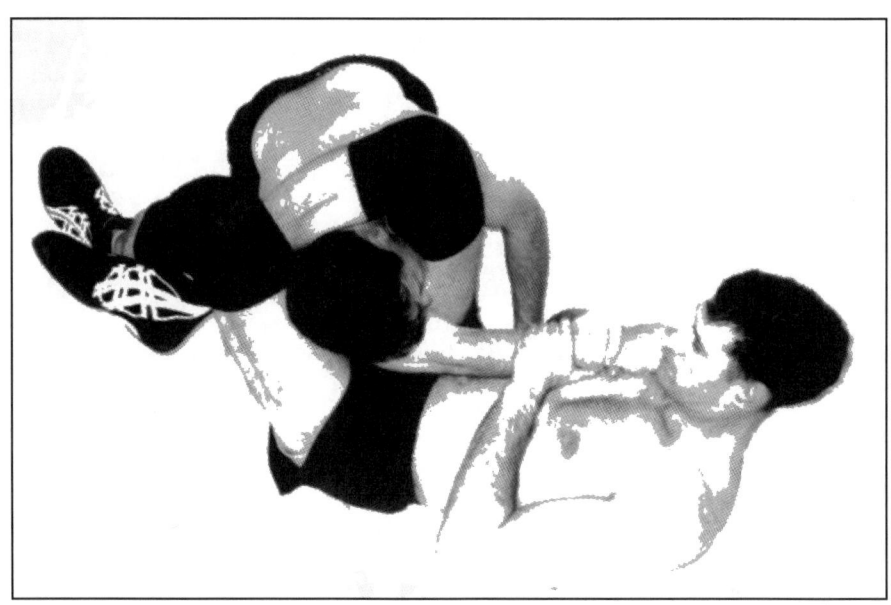

The Closed Guard

Your opponent is pulled forwards into your guard. He has the most options when he can sit back and work on breaking your guard.

Your legs are wrapped tightly around his body and your feet are locked, making it difficult for him to break your guard.

You have an arm hooked under his. This limits his striking ability, keeps him forwards in your guard, and helps set him up for reversals and counter-attacks.

Your head is pressed tightly against his head, limiting his ability to strike your face. Also, you can use an arm to control his head. If you control his head, you control his body.

NECK CRANK *Figure Four Lock*

Your opponent is forwards in your guard and you are securing the back of his neck.

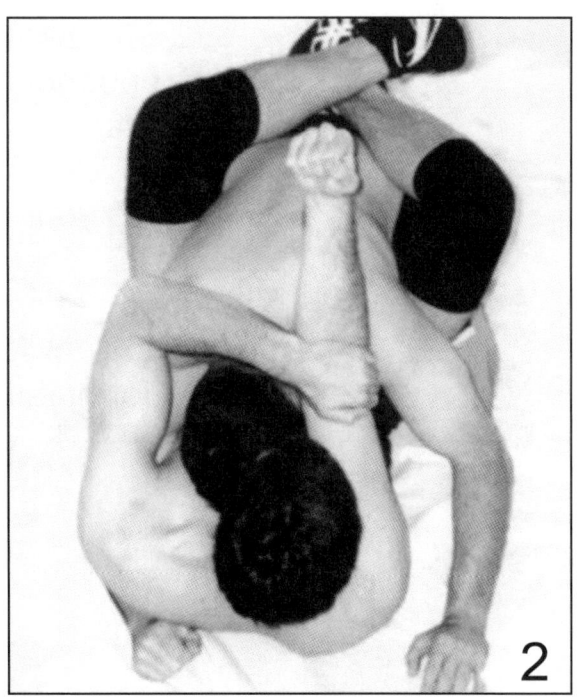

Your attacking arm is hugging the back of his neck; grab your other, locking arm at the biceps.

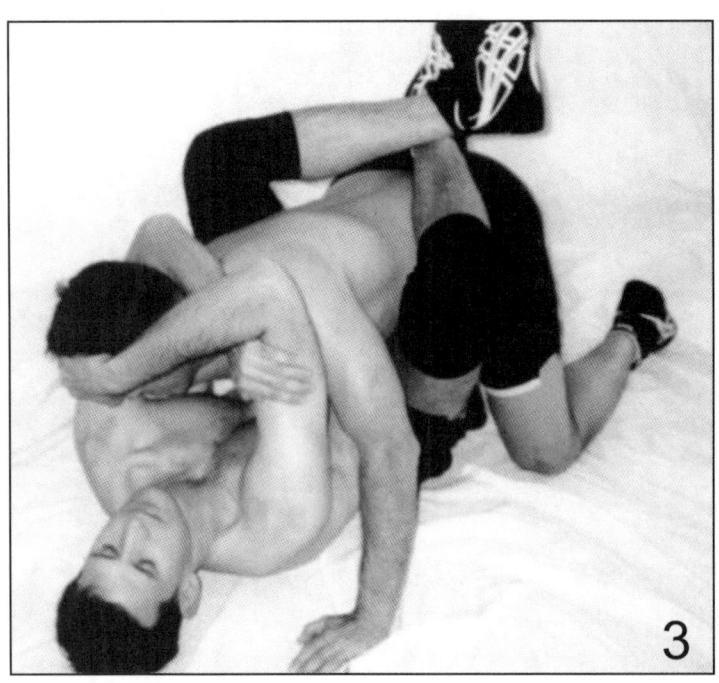

Place your locking hand on his forehead. The higher on his forehead you grasp, the more leverage you will have for this move.

Pull him in tight into your own body, placing your head against his. Drive the blade of your attacking forearm into the base of his neck while you push forwards on his forehead with your locking hand. This will hyper-extend his cervical spine for the submission.

NECK CRANK *Crucifix*

Your opponent is forwards in your guard and you are controlling his head as shown.

Hook your arm over his neck and under his arm, trapping his head under your armpit.

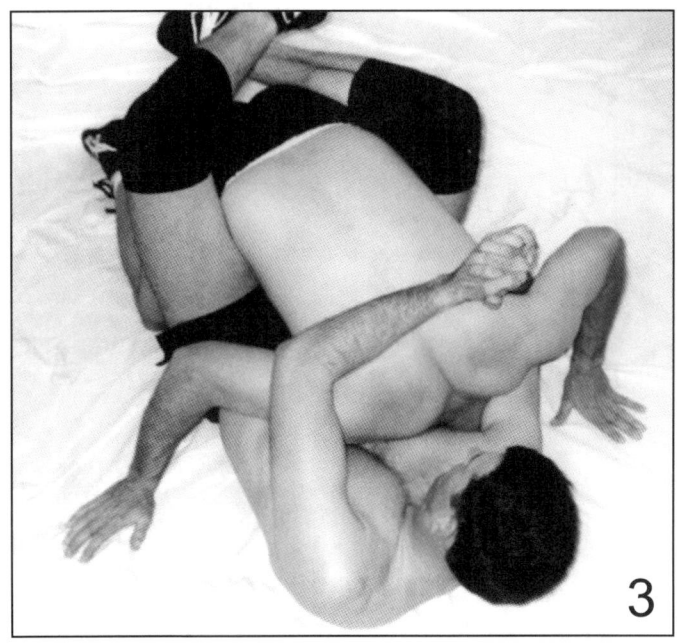

Clasp your hands behind his back and pull upwards with your hands while driving your armpit downwards on the back of his head. Push your legs straight out. This will hyperextend his cervical spine for the submission.

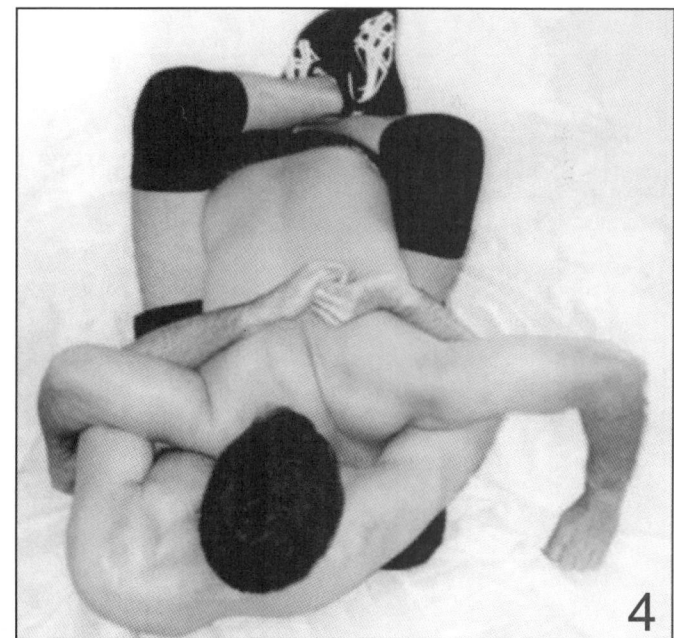

Here is a variation of the same technique; note that both of your arms are under hooked. This is a tighter hold and takes a lot of slack out of his spine. Use the same motion for the submission.

CHOKE *Scissors*

Your opponent is forwards in your guard and you are controlling his head as shown.

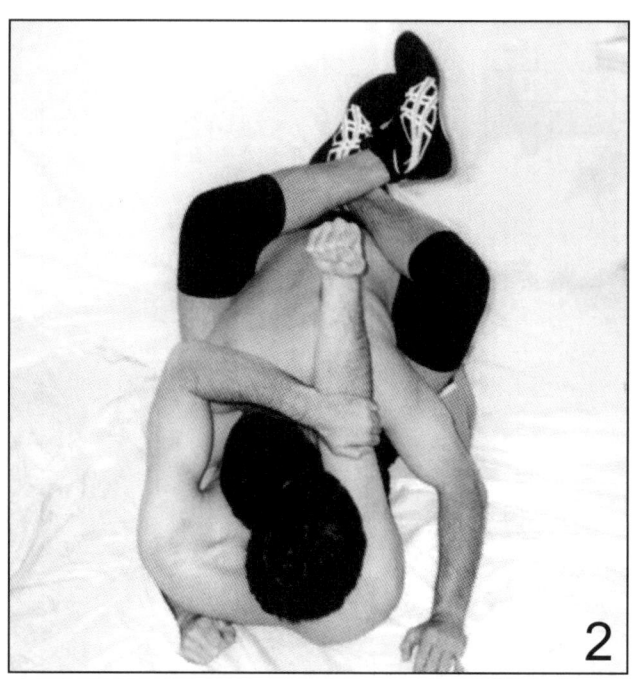

Your locking arm is hugging the back of his neck; grab your attacking arm at the biceps.

Place your attacking arm across his throat.

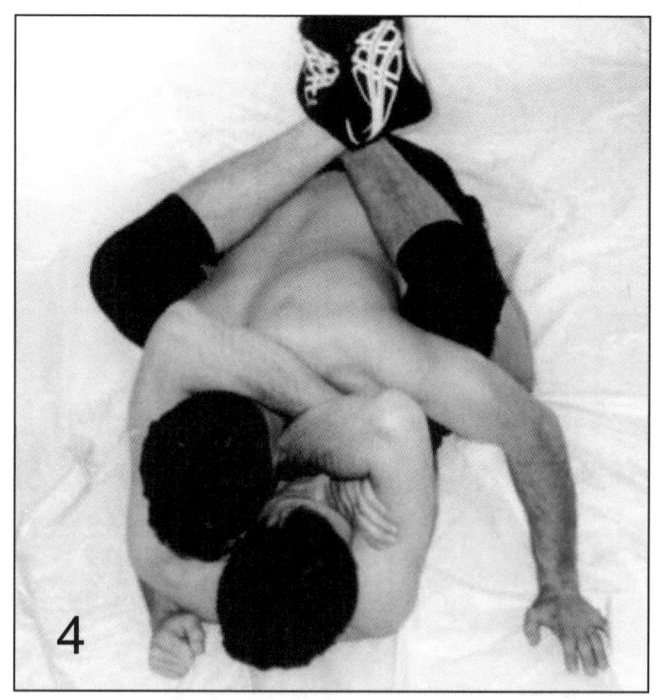

Pull your opponent into yourself, placing your head tightly against his. Drive the blade of your locking arm into the base of his neck while you drive the blade of your attacking arm into his throat. This will crush his esophagus for the submission.

CHOKE *Guillotine*

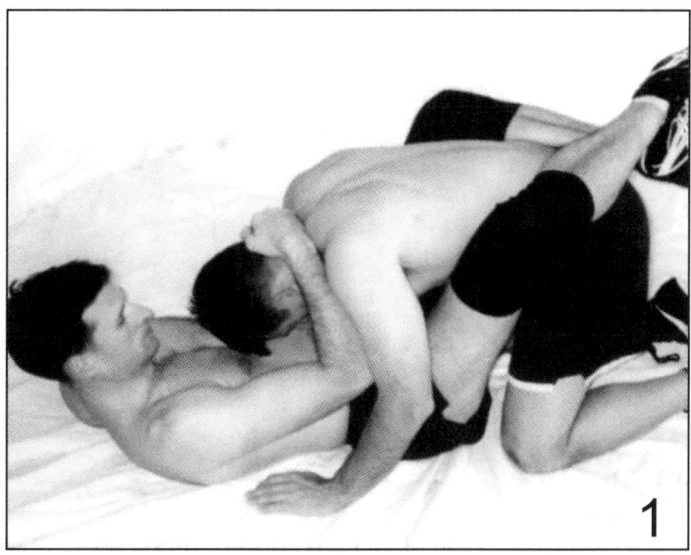

Your opponent is forwards in your guard and you are controlling his head. Your hips are back so you can sit up and you have the space to attack his neck.

Slide your hips away from him and sit up. While you are doing this, snap his head down and then reach over his neck as shown.

Bring your attacking arm under his chin and across his throat. Grab your attacking arm at the wrist with your other, locking arm as shown. (This picture is from the opposite angle)

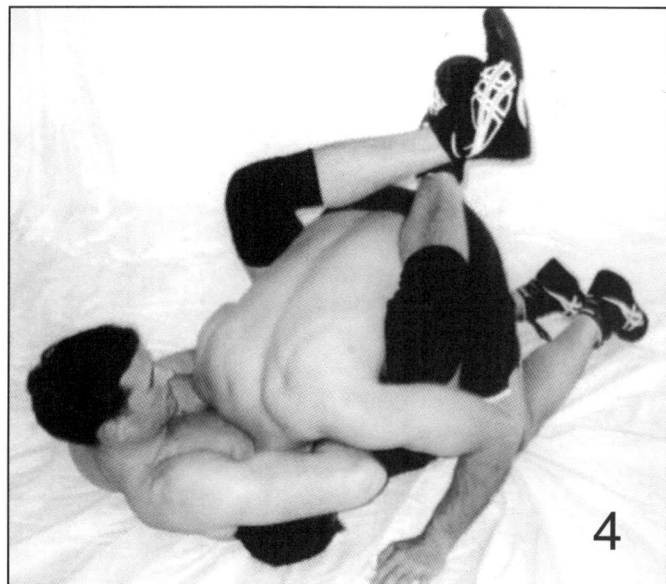

Push your legs straight out and pull the blade of your attacking forearm up against his throat. This choke crushes the esophagus for the submission.

CHOKE *Kata Gatame*

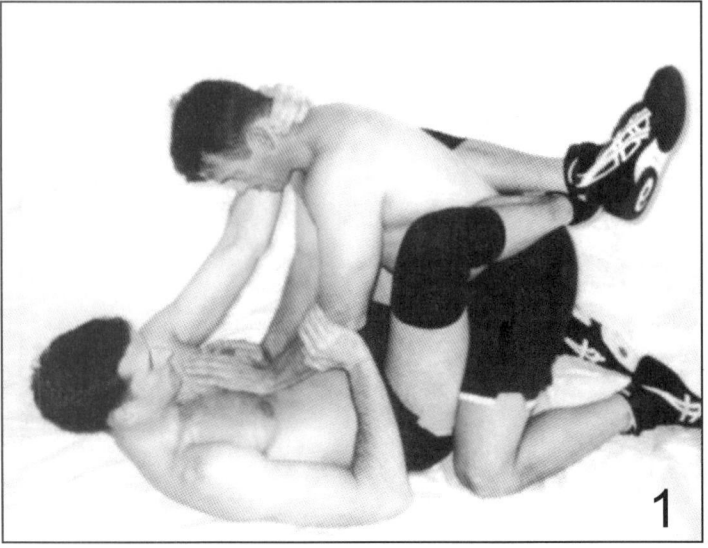

Your opponent is sitting up in your guard. You are controlling his head and his arm as shown.

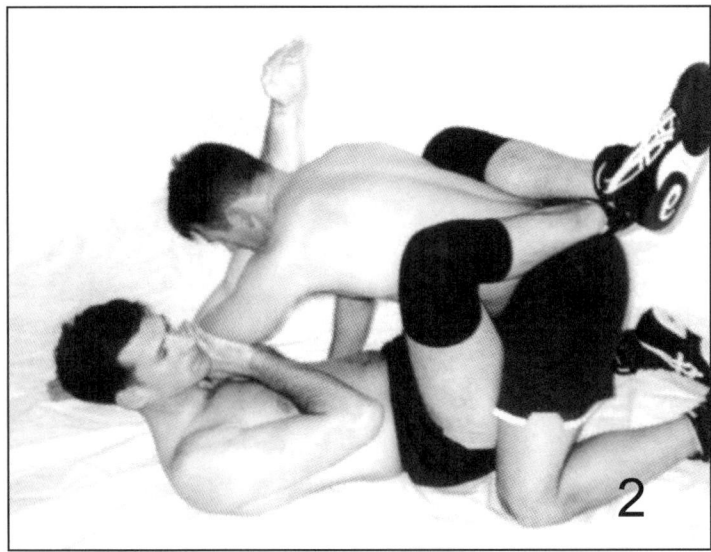

Push his arm across your body and reach up with your hand that was controlling his neck. You can sit up into him to help bring his body into yours.

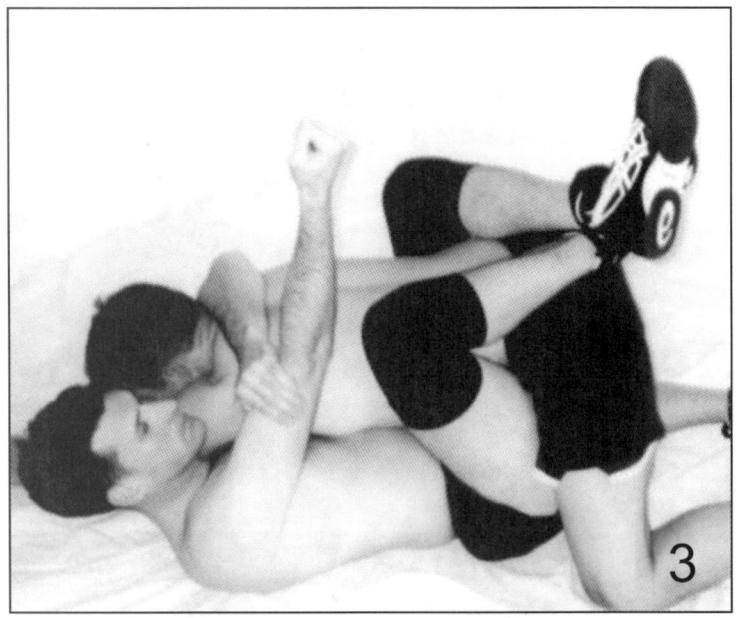

Hug the back of his head with your attacking arm and grab your locking arm at the biceps. Notice how his arm is trapped between your head and his own.

Grab the back of your head with your locking arm and press your head tightly against his. Drive the blade of your attacking arm into the base of his neck while contracting the muscles of your attacking arm. This is a blood choke and cuts off the carotid arteries running along his neck. You can also crank the base of his cervical spine.

CHOKE *Modified Kata Gatame*

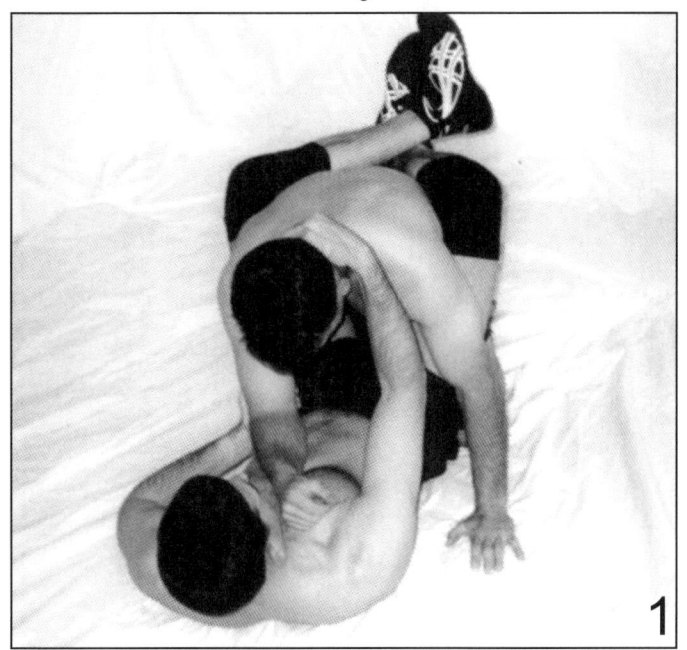

Your opponent is sitting up in your guard and you are controlling his head and arm as shown.

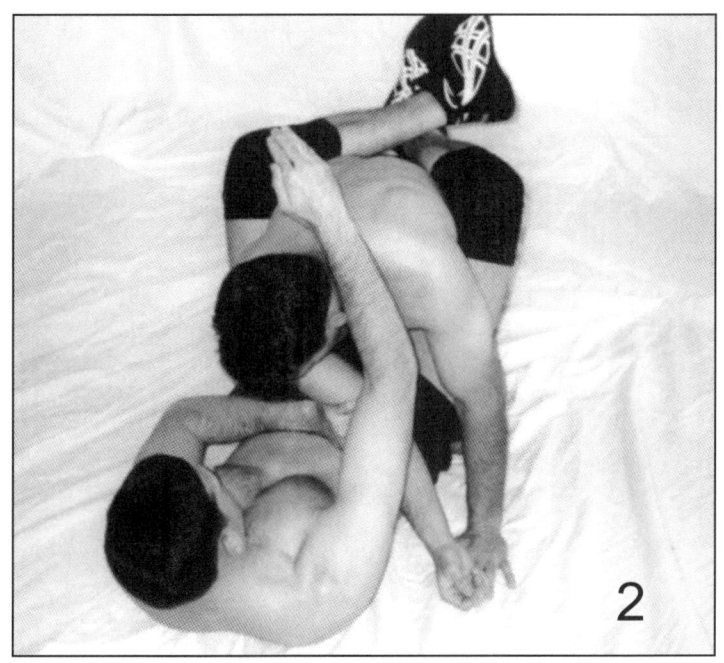

Push his arm across your chest and reach up with your arm that was controlling his head.

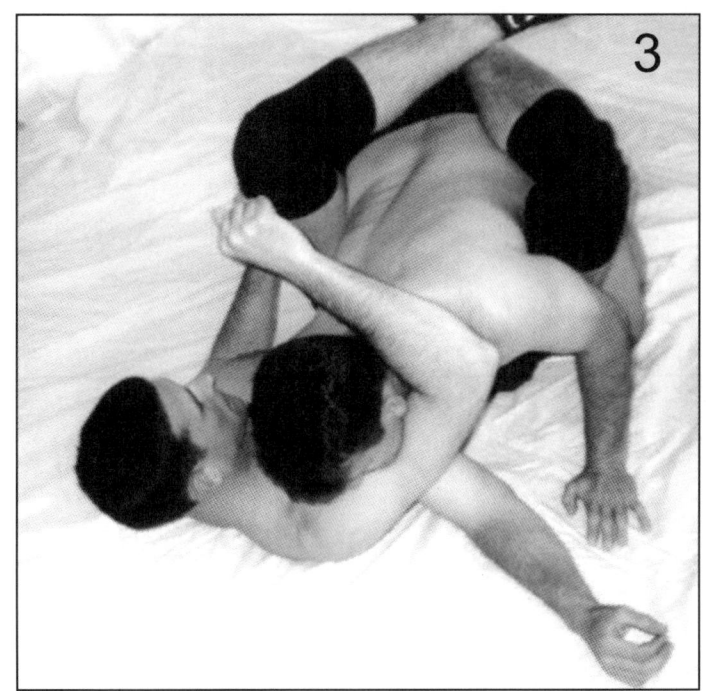

Hug the back of his neck with your attacking arm, trapping his arm between your chest and his.

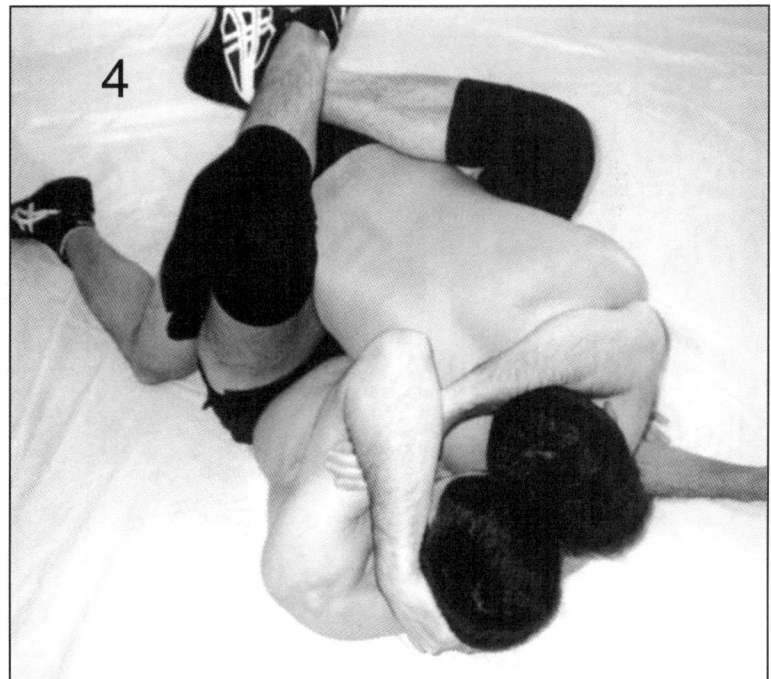

Grab your locking arm at the biceps and place your locking arm on the back of your head. Drive your head against his and contract the muscles in your attacking arm. This a blood choke and cuts off the carotid arteries in his neck for the submission. You may be able to crank his neck as well.

CHOKE *Triangle*

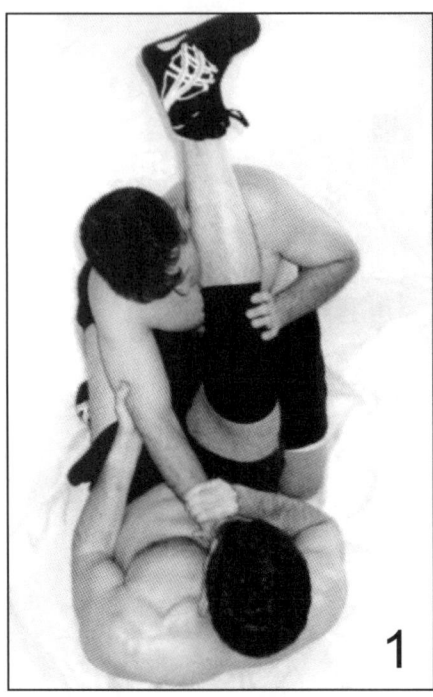

1. Your opponent is attempting to pass your guard. He is sitting back and has your leg over his shoulder. You are controlling one of his arms as shown.

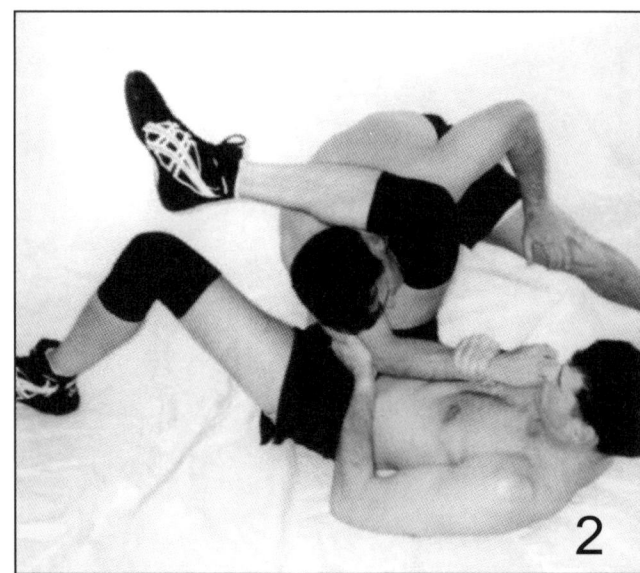

2. Rotate your body at the hips so you are now perpendicular to his body. Drive your attacking leg forwards against his neck while pulling his arm, in the opposite direction, against his own throat.

3. Hook your locking leg over your attacking leg, making a figure four lock. Maintain control of his arm.

4. Squeeze your knees together to place pressure against the sides of his neck. Also, keep his arm tight against his own throat. This is a blood choke and cuts off his carotid arteries in his neck.

ARM BAR

Your opponent is set up in your guard, sitting back with an arm across your chest. Secure his arm at the elbow and wrist as shown.

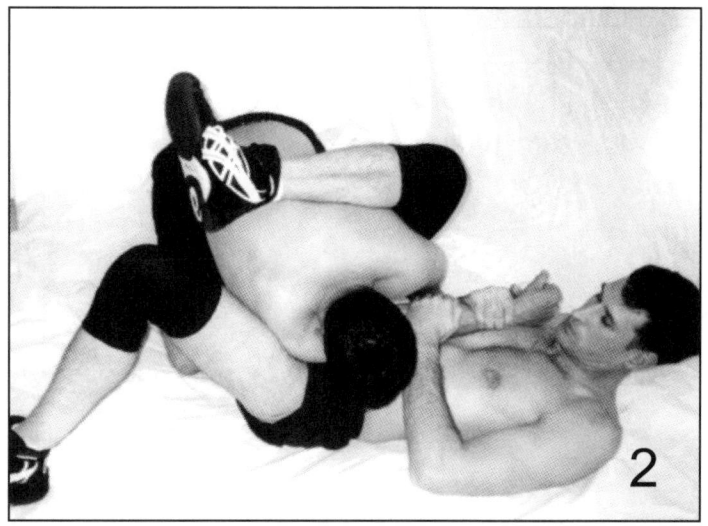

Pivot on your hips so that you are perpendicular to his body. Bring your leg across his shoulders and pull his arm across his body.

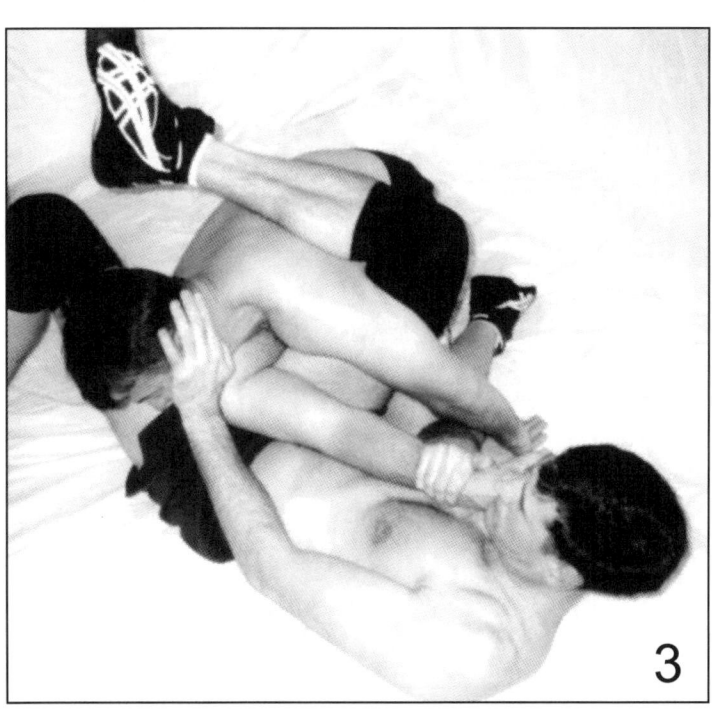

Push his head away from you, giving your bottom leg room to swing over it. Push the heel of your top leg downwards to help prevent him from escaping. Maintain control of his wrist.

Swing your leg over his head. Squeeze your knees together and drive your heels to the ground. Keep his arm tight against your chest and drive your hips upwards to hyper-extend his arm at the elbow for the submission.

ARM BAR *Underarm Variation*

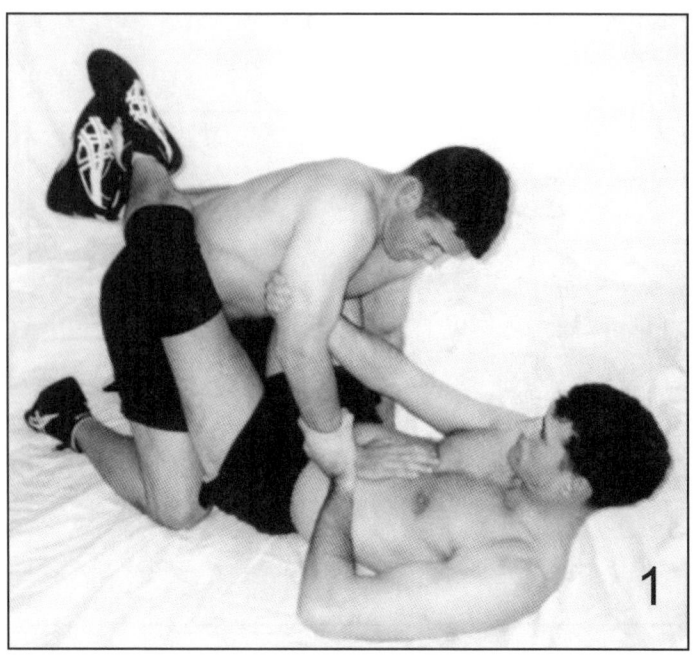

Your opponent is sitting back in your guard as shown. Control his arm at the wrist and reach under his arm and grab him under the triceps.

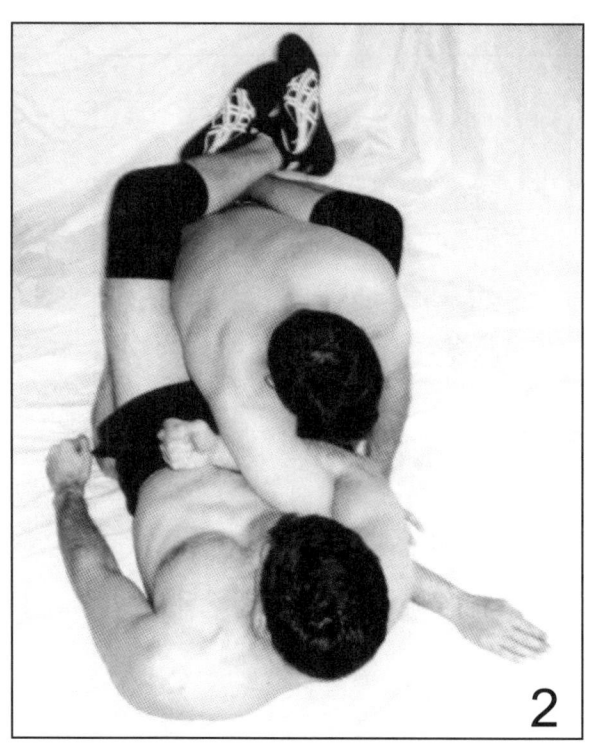

Push his arm across your body and pull his arm down and under your armpit, securing it tightly.

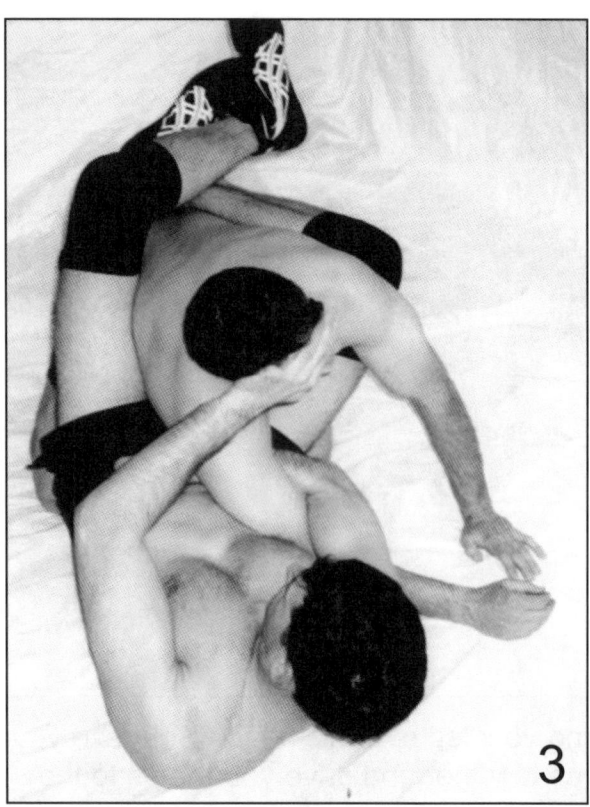

Push his head away from you in preparation for swinging your leg over it.

Swing your leg over his head, squeeze your knees together, drive your heels to the ground, and arch your hips to hyper-extend his arm at the elbow. Because of the underarm grip, there is very little play in his arm and submission is quick.

ARM BAR *With Leg Under hook*

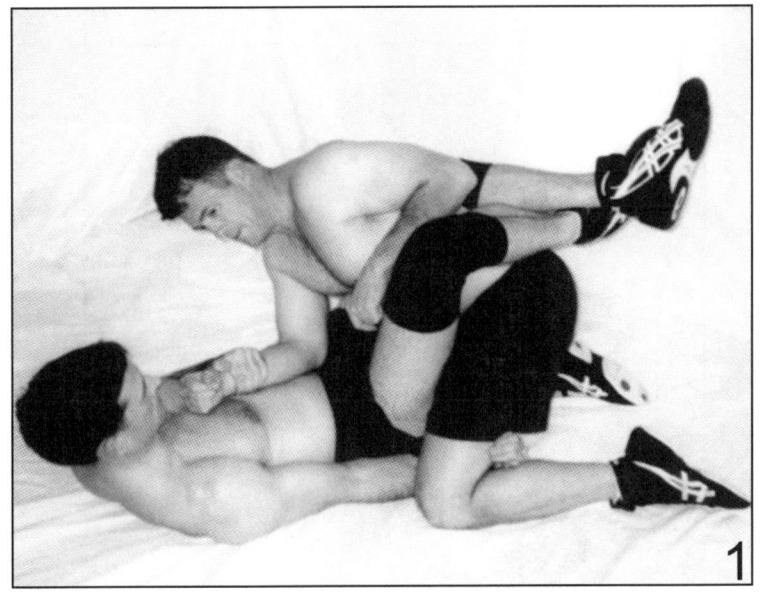

Your opponent is sitting back in your guard as shown. One of his legs is positioned forwards. Control his arm and hook his leg behind the knee with an underarm grip.

Pull yourself into his hooked leg and rotate your hips so that your body is perpendicular to his. Swing your leg over his head while maintaining control of his arm.

Drive your heels to the ground until he lands on his back. You are maintaining control of his arm and leg. Under hooking his leg helps to remove his base and limits his ability to reposition; all of which aids in placing him off balance.

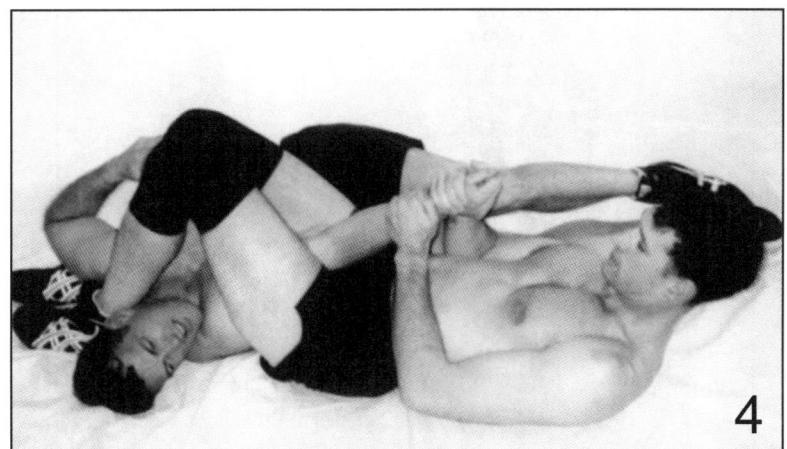

Secure his arm with both hands, squeeze your knees together, and arch your hips to hyper-extend his arm at the elbow for the submission.

ARM BAR *Leg Scissors*

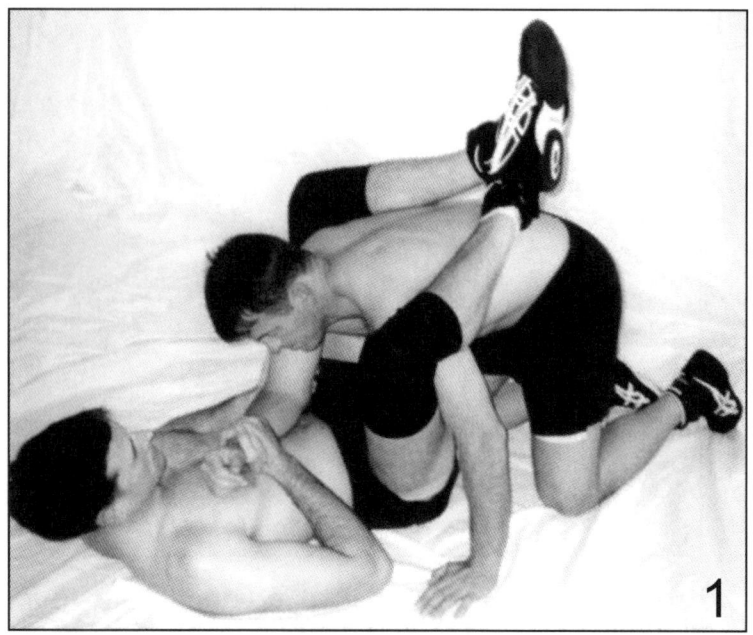

Your opponent is set up with one arm out in an attempt to pass your guard. You are controlling his other arm with both hands at the elbow and wrist.

Rotate your body at the hips so you are 45 degrees to his body. Maintain control of his arm and squeeze your legs together to control his head.

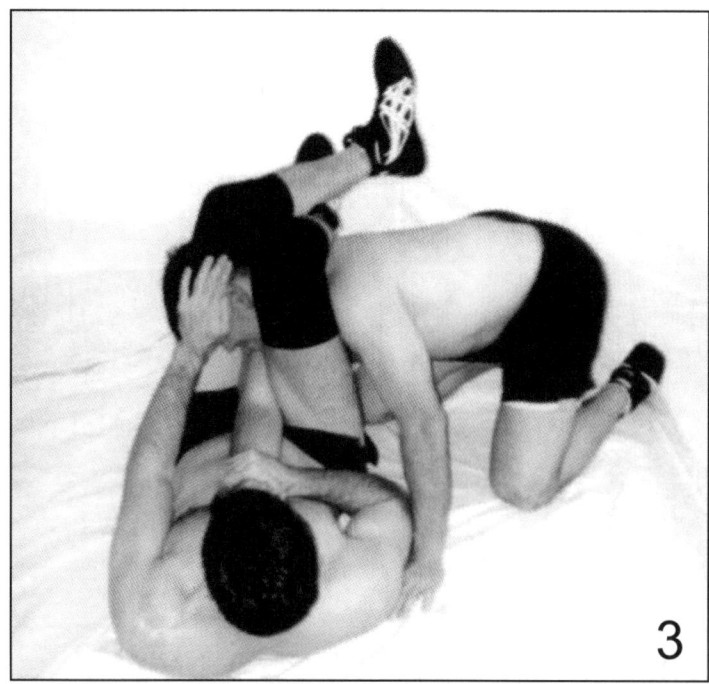

Push his head away from you in preparation for placing your leg across his face.

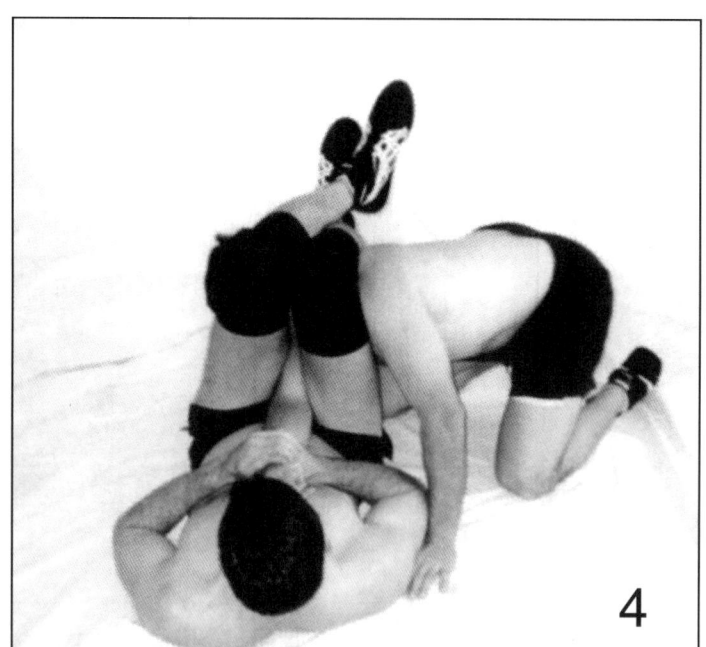

Place your leg across his face as shown. Push your legs straight out and arch your hips to hyper-extend his arm at the elbow for the submission.

ARM BAR *Double Arm Variation*

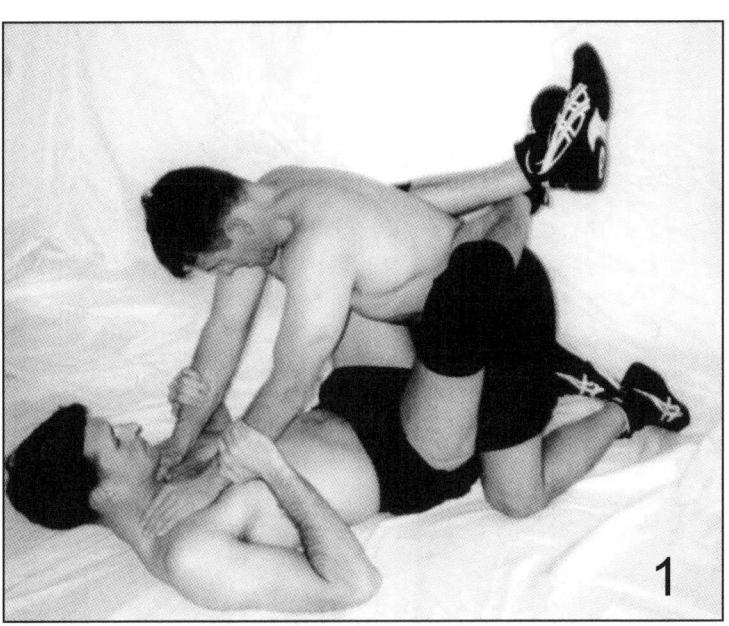

Your opponent is in your guard, on his knees and with both arms placed on your chest.

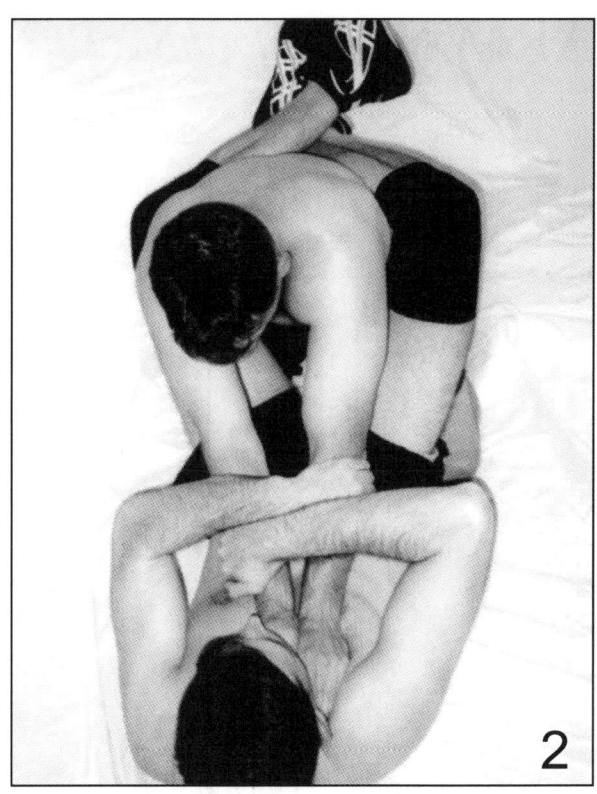

Grab both of his arms at the elbows and squeeze them together.

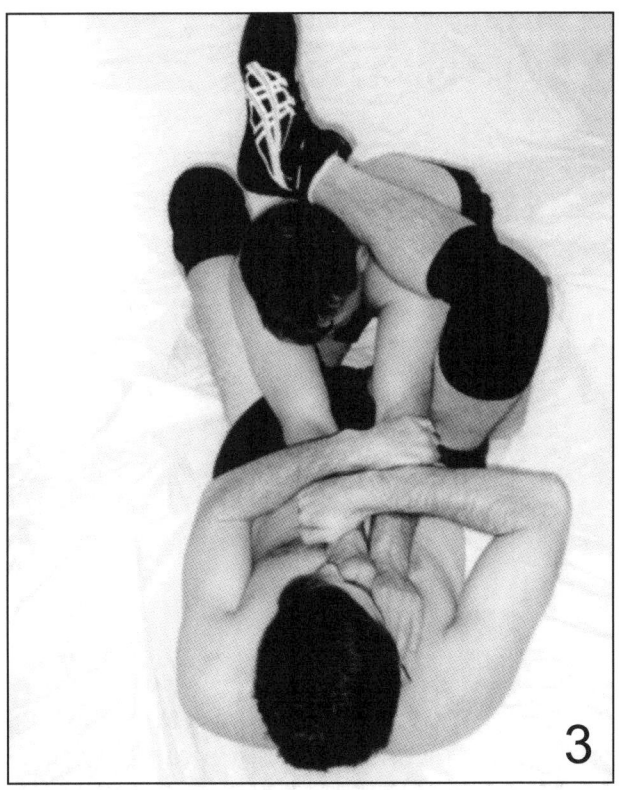

Place one leg across the top of his shoulder while maintaining a tight grip on his arms.

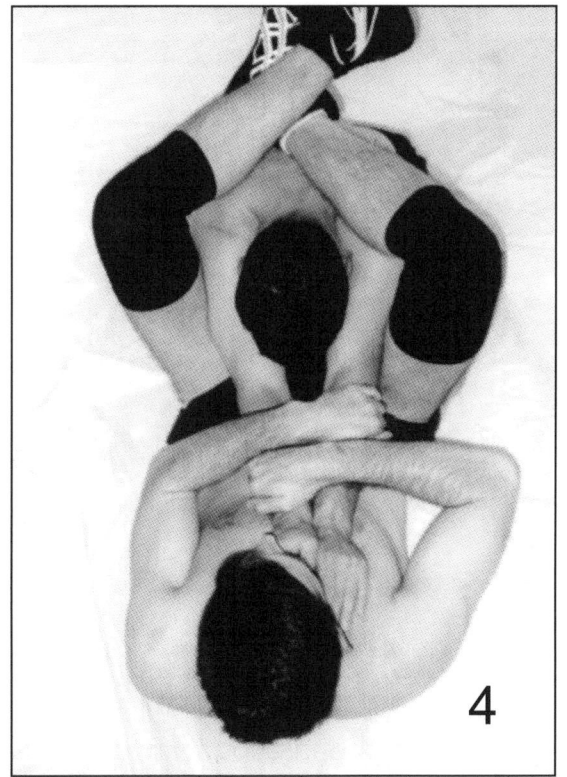

Place your leg across his other shoulder and hook your ankles with each other. Push down with your heels and arch your hips to hyper-extend both arms at the elbow for the submission.

ARM BAR *Double Elbow lock*

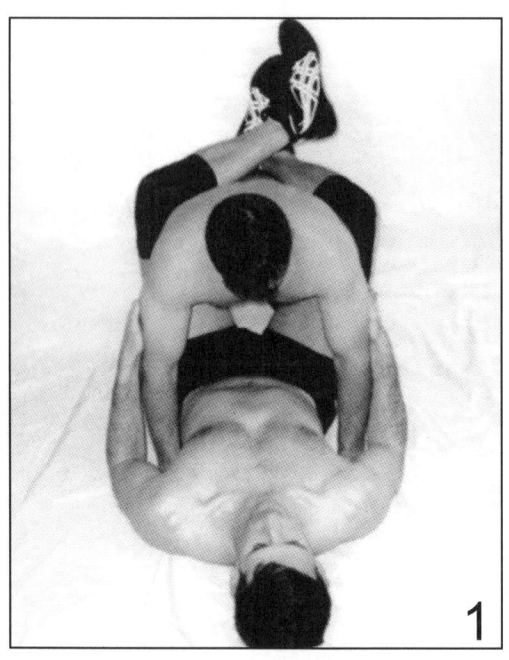

1. Your opponent is in your guard with both hands placed on the ground.

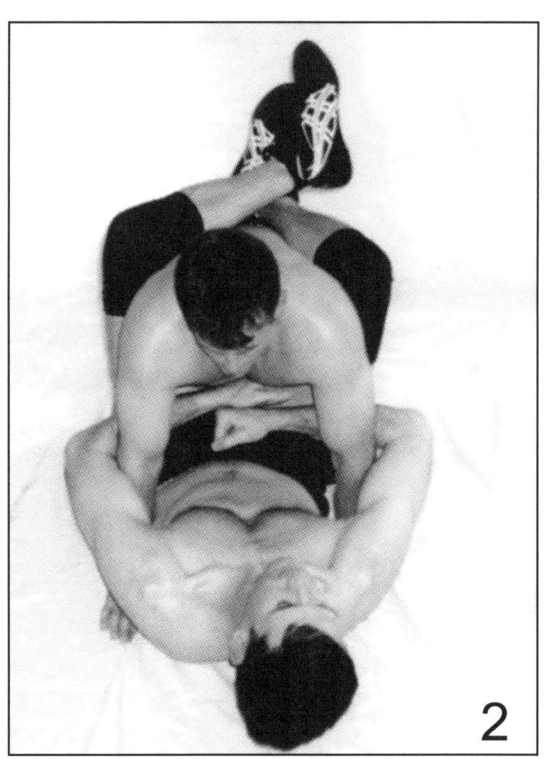

2. Hook both of your arms around his, above his elbows.

3. Grab one of your wrists and pull his arms towards you in preparation for repositioning your feet.

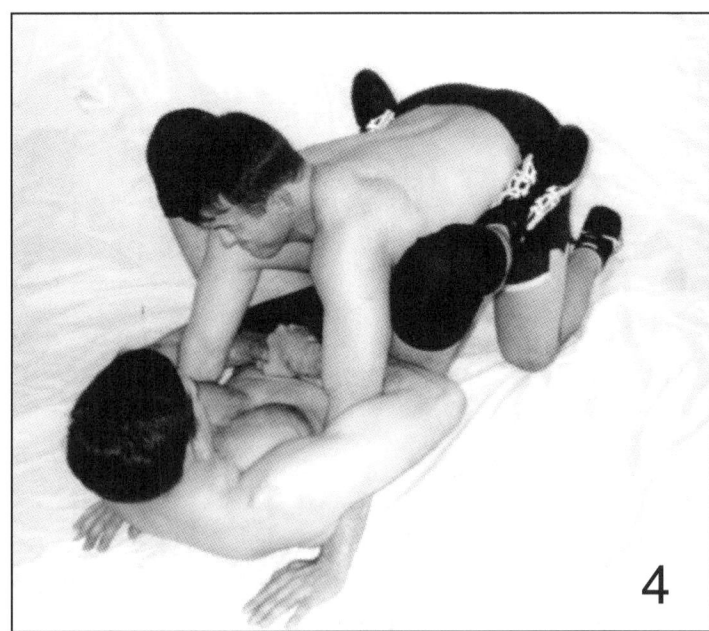

4. Place both of your feet on his hips and push him away from you. Ensure that your arms are directly on or are slightly above his elbow joints; drive your forearms against his elbows. This hyper-extends his arms at the elbows for the submission.

ARM BAR *Elbow Lock*

Your opponent is set up with an arm placed on the ground. Control his arm at the elbow as shown.

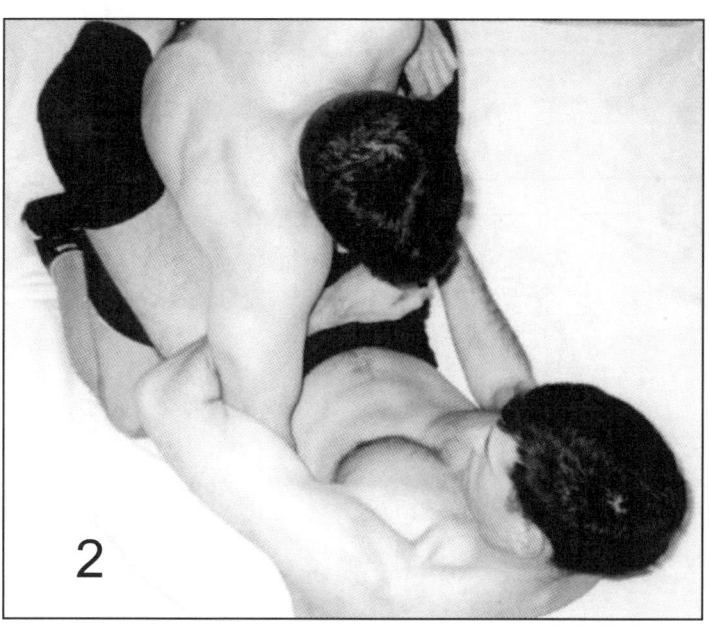

Hook your arm around his targeted arm and above the elbow.

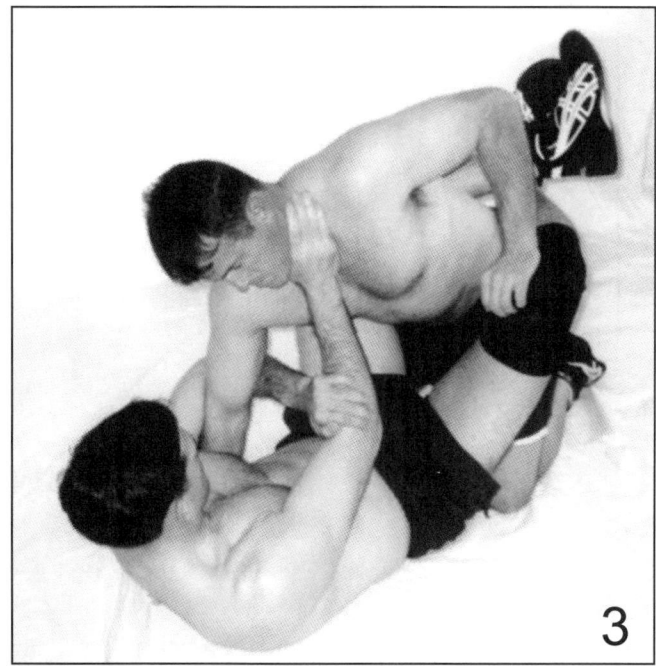

Drive your other hand against his throat and grab your arm at the biceps, forming a figure four lock.

Drive your hand against his throat and pull your other arm against his trapped arm at the elbow, using your figure foured arms for leverage. This will hyper-extend his arm at the elbow for the submission.

ARM BAR *Elbow Lock With Entangled Leg*

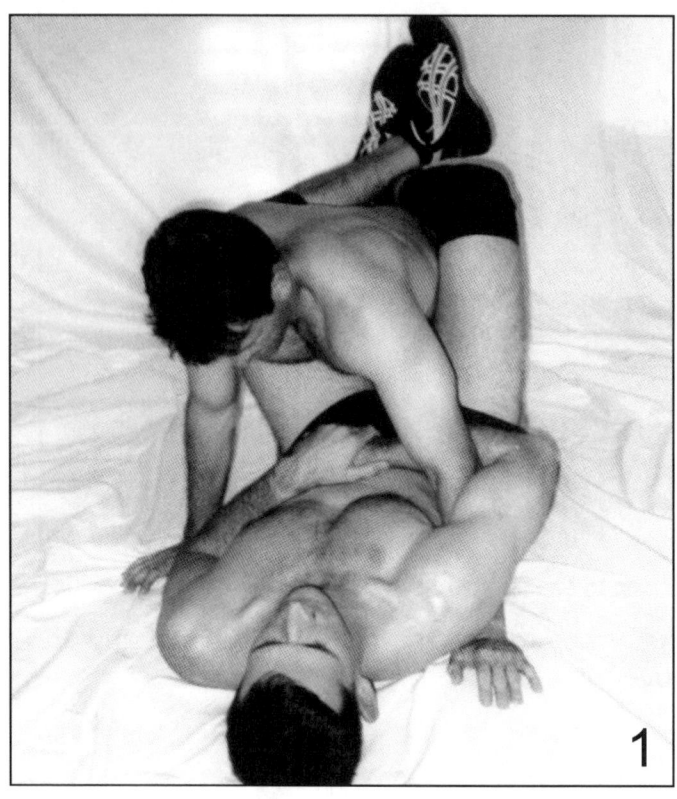

Your opponent is sitting back in your guard and has posted an arm on the ground. Secure this arm as shown, ensuring that your arm is above his elbow or directly on it. (Left)

Place your same side leg across his face, maintaining a tight grip on his trapped arm. (Right)

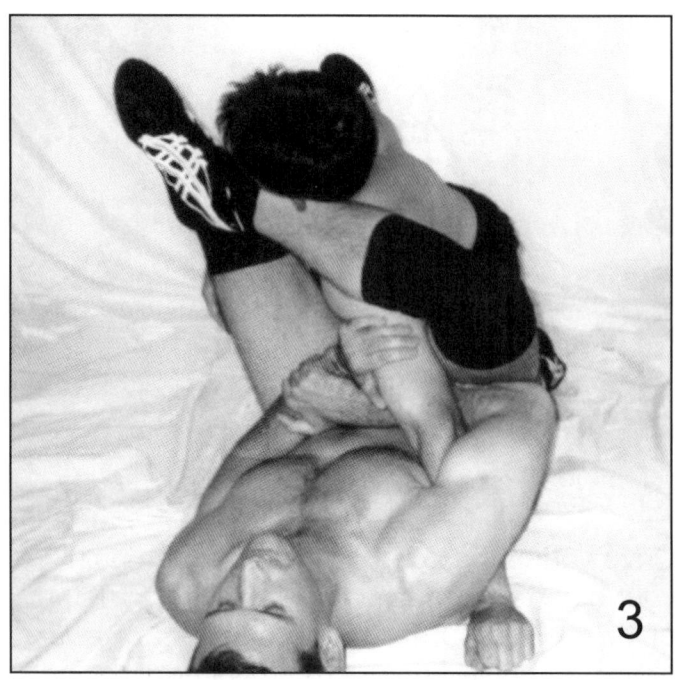

Establish a figure four grip on his arm as shown. Drive your entangled leg away from you and across his face and drive your forearm against his elbow. Hyper-extend his arm at the elbow for the submission. (Left)

ARM BAR *Straight Arm With Leg Assist*

Your opponent is forwards in your guard and he has one arm placed over your shoulder. You are controlling his head and arm as shown.

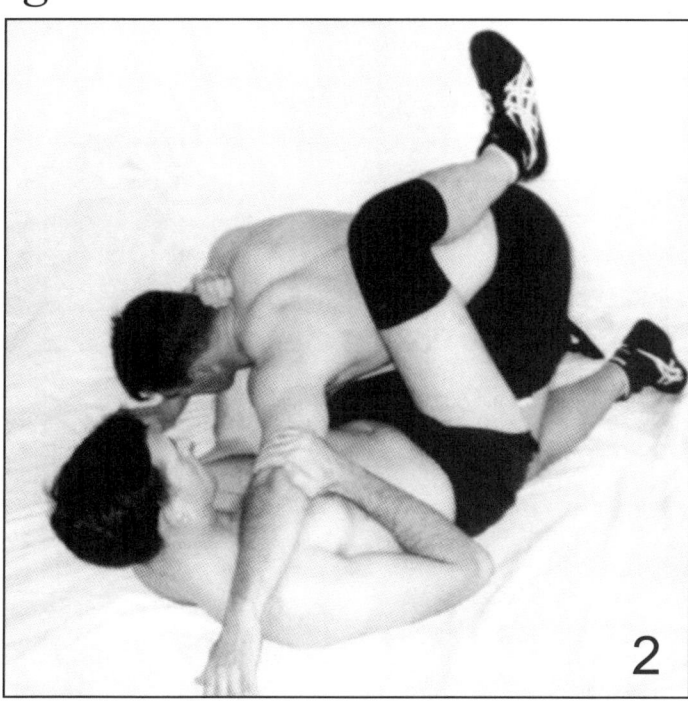

Rotate your hips to the side, towards his trapped arm, and maintain control of his arm and head.

Rotate your hips out to the side and slide your top leg on top of his shoulder, helping to trap his arm. Place the foot of your bottom leg on his far hip. Keep control of his arm, trapping it between your head and shoulder.

Squeeze your knees together, trapping his shoulder and pinning him to the ground. Secure his arm at the elbow with both hands. Pull down with both arms and raise your shoulder to hyperextend his arm at the elbow for the submission.

ARM BAR *"X" Variation*

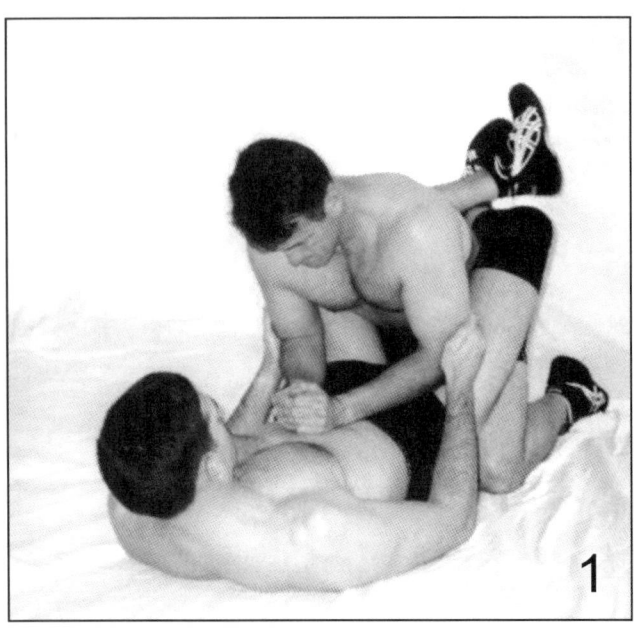

Your opponent is sitting back in your guard with both arms on your midsection. Secure his arms at the elbows as shown.

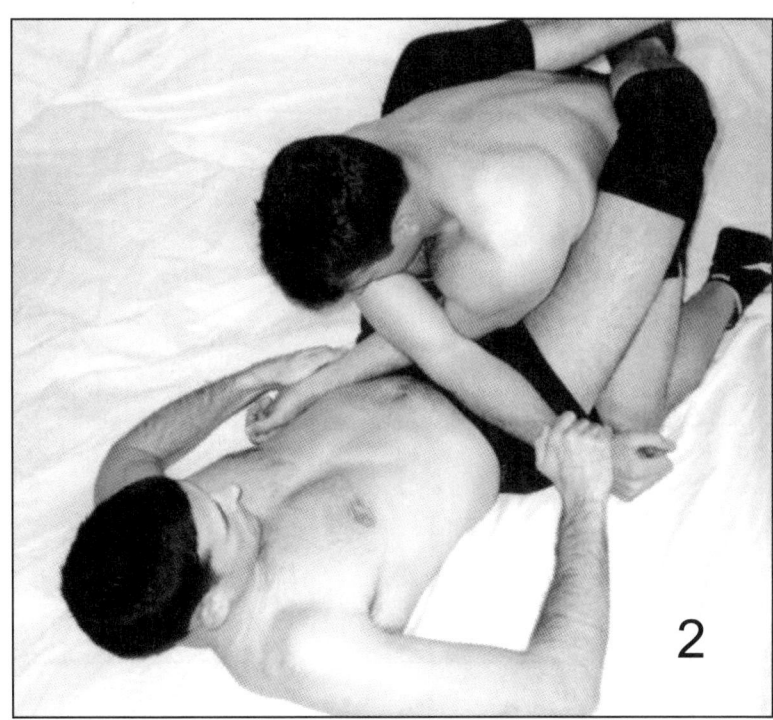

Push his elbows towards each other until his arms cross. Then, secure his wrists and continue to pull his arms across each other.

Bring both of your legs up high across his shoulders and drive your heels towards the ground. Control his top arm at the wrist, arch your hips, and hyper-extend his top arm at the elbow for the submission.

Also, you can place your leg over his head to trap his arms as shown. When you arch your hips you are now placing pressure on both elbows for the submission.

SHOULDER CRANK *Key Lock*

Your opponent is leaning forwards in your guard. He has an arm posted on the ground. Slide your hips away from him and reach past his head and over his trapped arm. Secure his arm at the wrist with your other arm as shown.

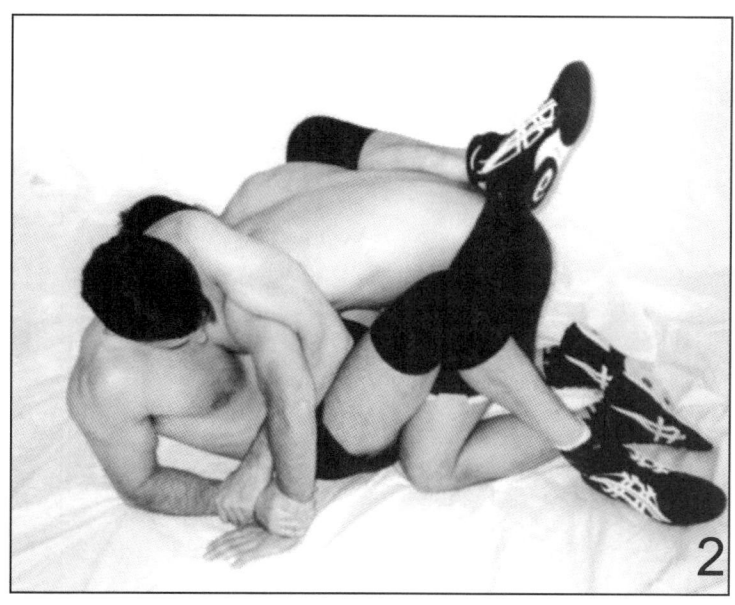

Grab your own arm at the wrist, making a figure four lock.

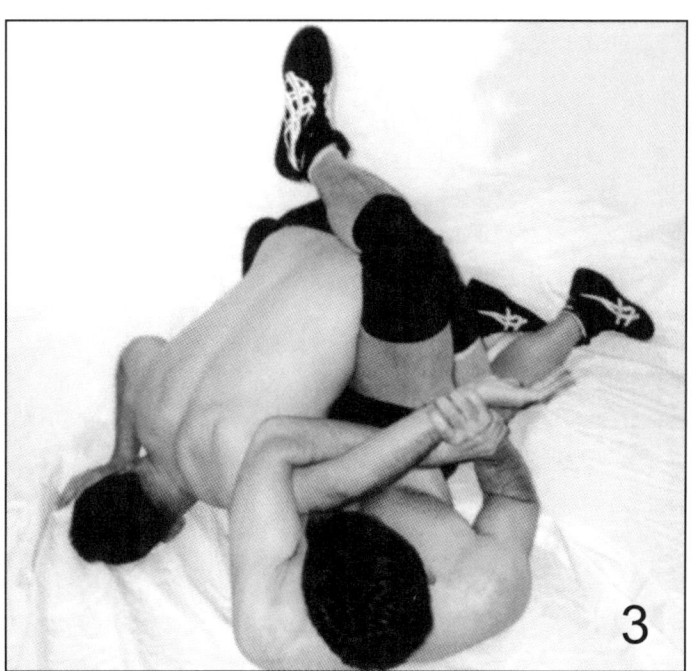

Slide your hips out from under him and to the side. Maintain your grip on his trapped arm and rotate your upper body so his head and shoulder are pinned to the ground.

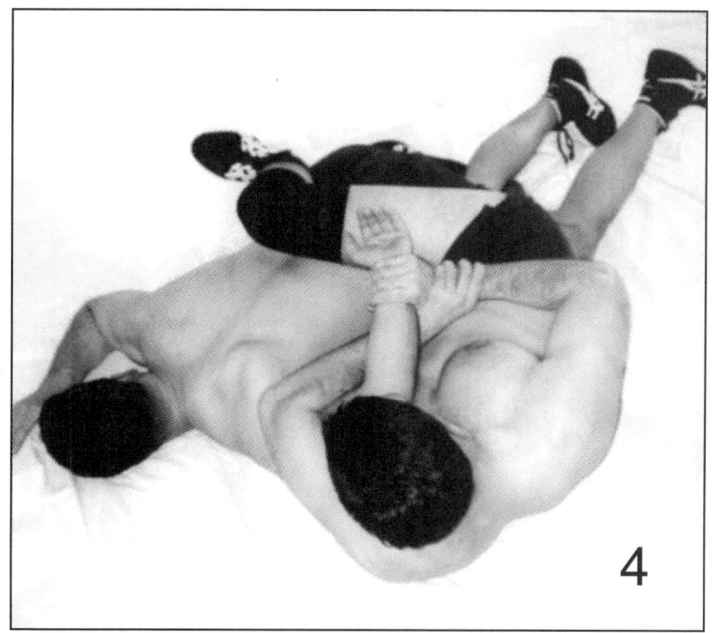

Place your top leg across his back so he can not roll forwards and out of the lock. Rotate his trapped arm in an attempt to place his wrist next to his own head. This will use his bent arm as a lever to torque his shoulder for the submission.

SHOULDER CRANK *With Leg Assist*

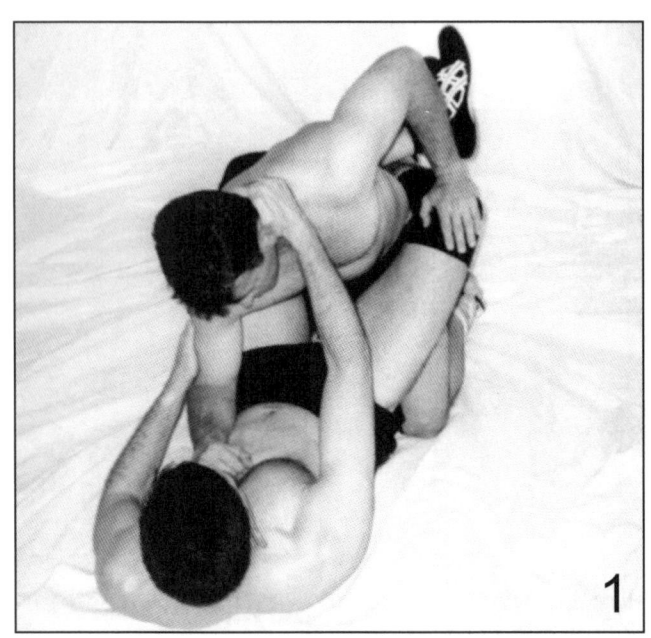

Your opponent is set up in your guard with an arm on your chest as shown.

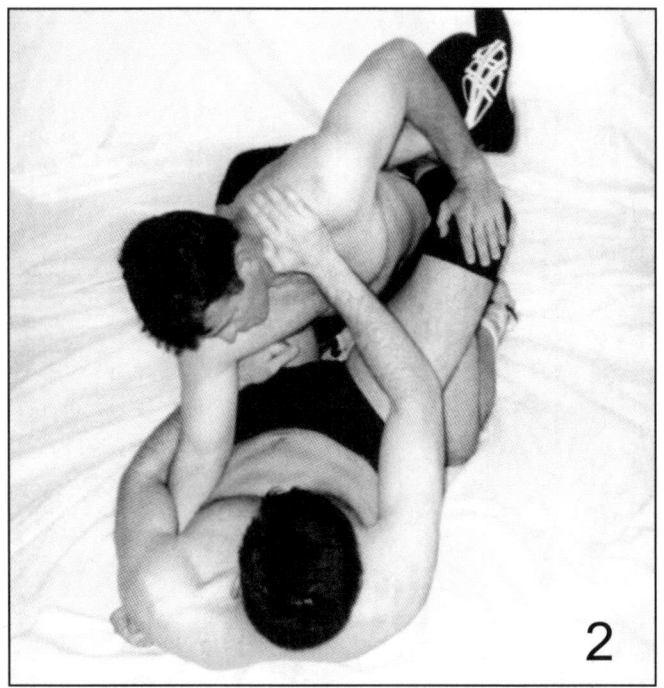

Hook your arm under his, trapping it. Use your other arm to keep his upper body away from your own, in preparation for swinging your leg over his head.

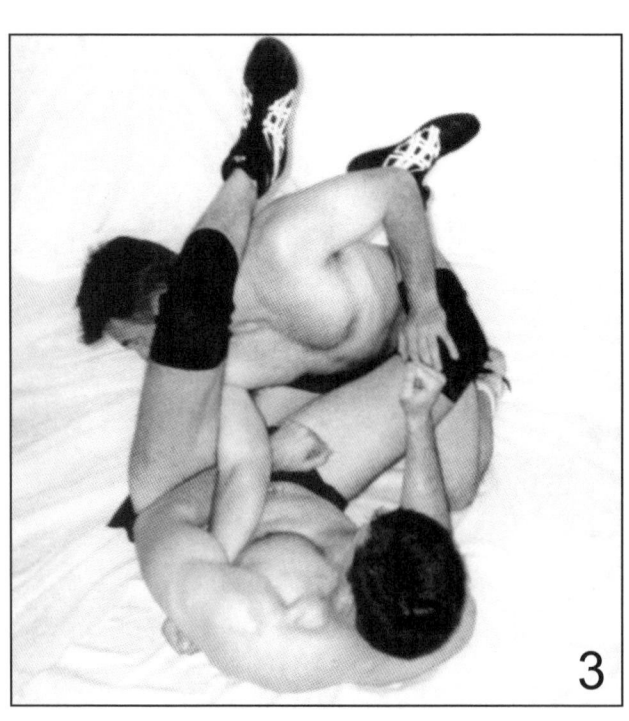

Swing your leg over his head while maintaining your under hooked arm.

Secure a figure four lock on his trapped arm. Squeeze your knees together and drive your heels towards the ground. Crank his shoulder by attempting to push his trapped elbow to the ground, near his head. This uses his bent arm as a lever to torque his shoulder for the submission.

SHOULDER CRANK *From A High Guard*

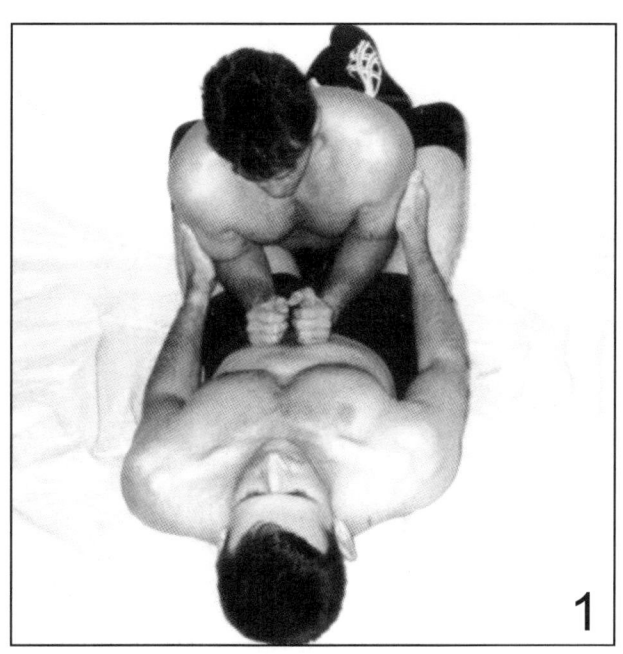

Your opponent is set up, sitting back in your guard with both arms on your midsection.

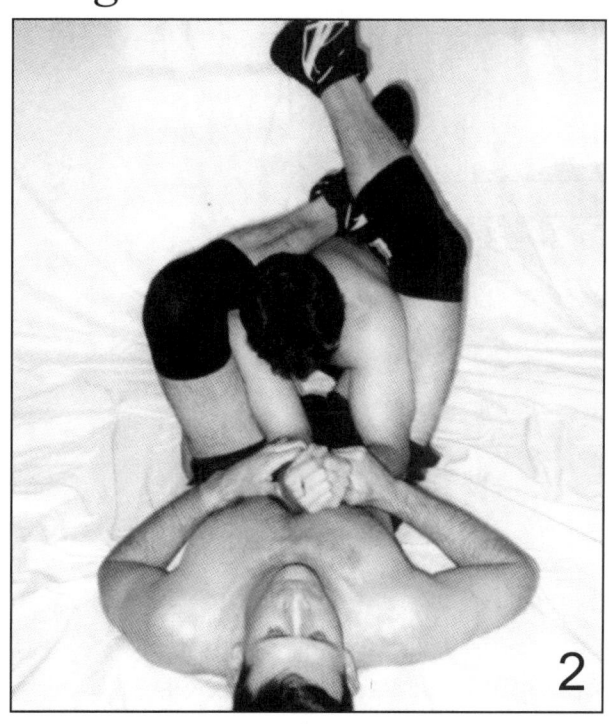

Secure a high guard with one leg hooked over his shoulder.

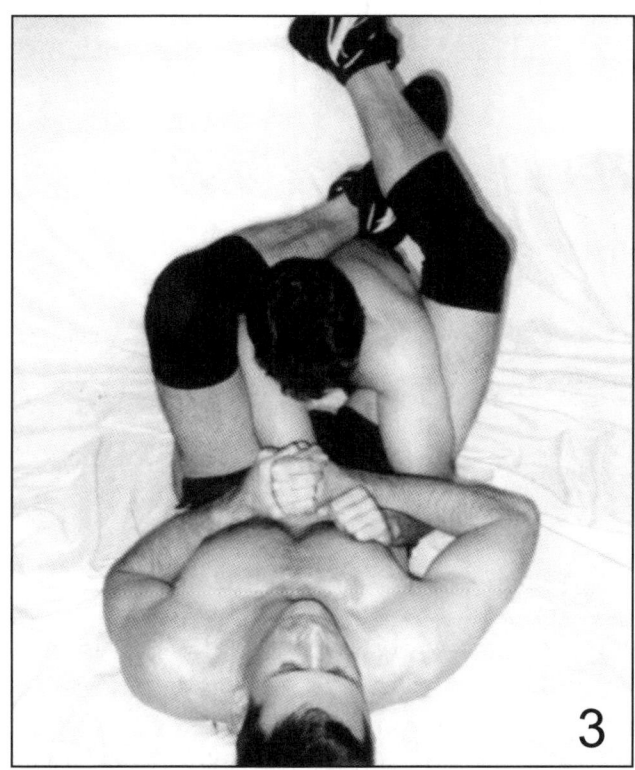

Secure his trapped arm at the wrist with both hands. This is the same arm that has your leg over its shoulder.

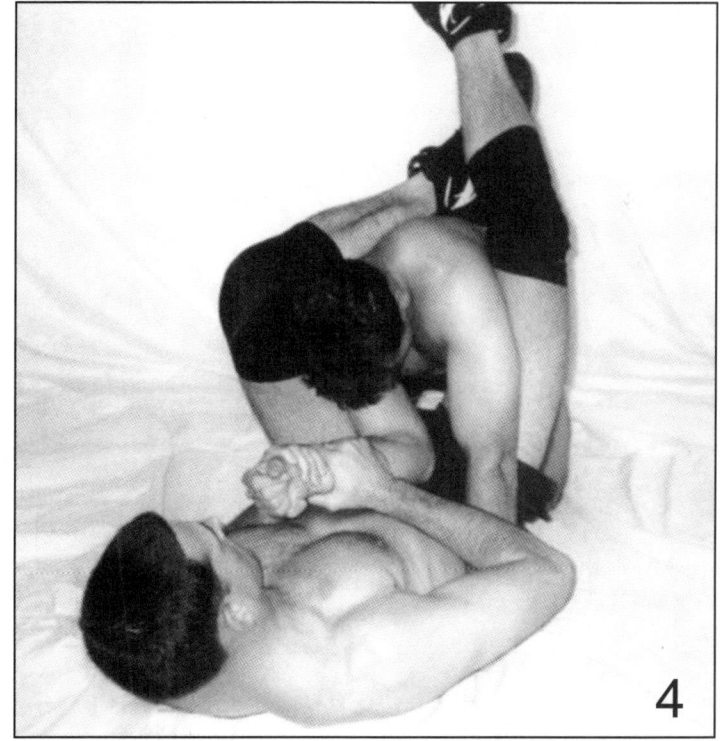

Push your leg into him, at the shoulder. Push his arm in the opposite direction. Note how his arm is at a right angle. This uses his bent arm as a lever to torque his shoulder for the submission.

SHOULDER CRANK *With Legs*

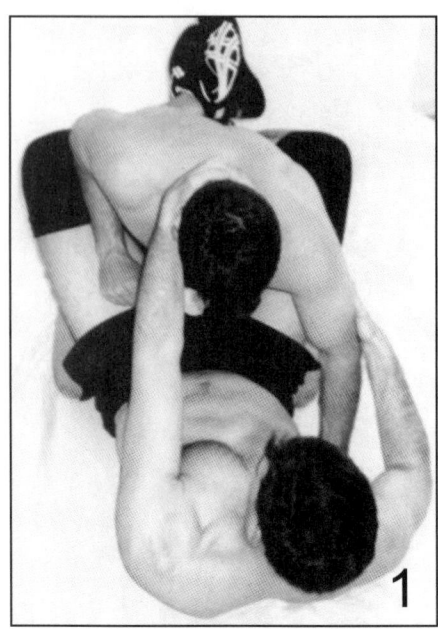

Your opponent has an arm posted on the ground; you are controlling his head with one arm and his posted arm with your other one.

Release your guard with your legs, maintaining a downwards pull on his head, and swing your leg up and behind his trapped arm. Rotate your hips away from him; you are spinning your body until your head is where your feet used to be and your feet are where your head used to be.

Rotate your hips away from his body and continue to drive your leg forwards, driving him forwards and to the ground.

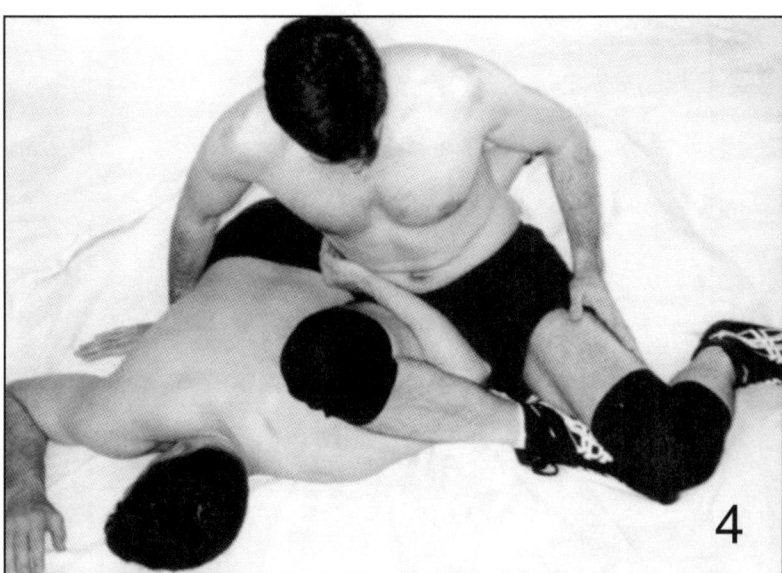

Continue to rotate your body and driving his body forwards at his trapped arm until he is pinned on the ground. Place your arm across his back so he can not roll forwards and out of the lock. Drive your hips forwards and come to your knees in an attempt to place his wrist on the ground near his head. This uses his bent arm as a lever to torque his shoulder for the submission.

SQUEEZE LOCK

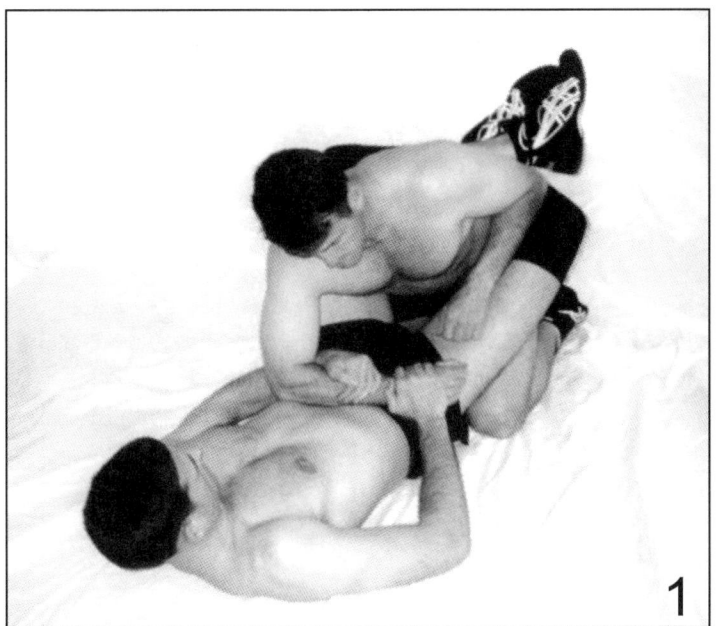

Your opponent has an arm placed on your midsection. Secure his arm as shown with an arm hooked under his forearm and one securing his wrist.

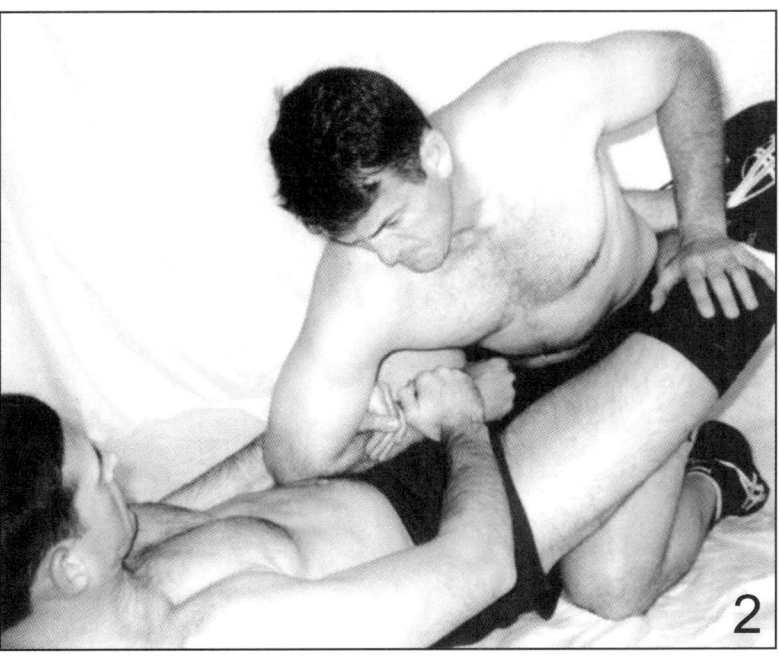

Pull on his forearm with the under hooked hand and push with the other, rotating his wrist towards himself and your groin.

Maintain control of his arm. Break your guard and swing your attacking leg over his arm, trapping his arm between your leg and your groin.

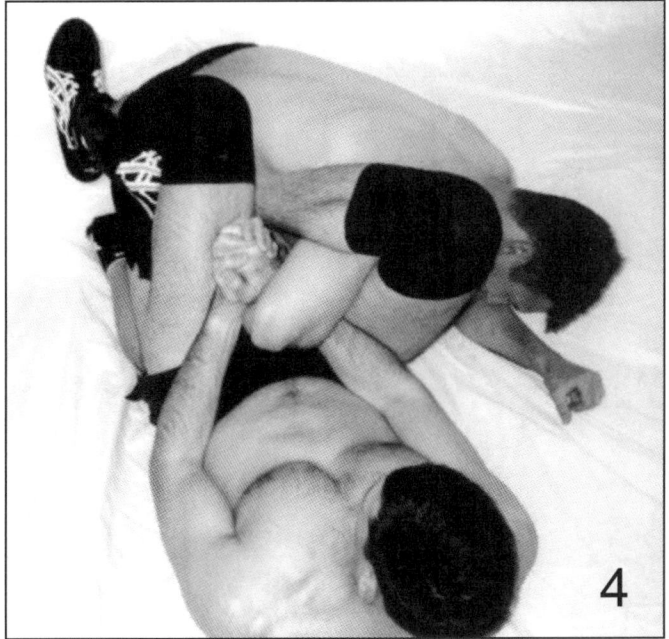

Hook your attacking leg under your locking leg as shown. Clasp your hands together and pull the blade of your forearm into the joint of his arm at the elbow. This puts enormous pressure on his biceps where it inserts at the joint and threatens to separate his arm at the elbow. He will submit from the pain.

WRIST LOCK

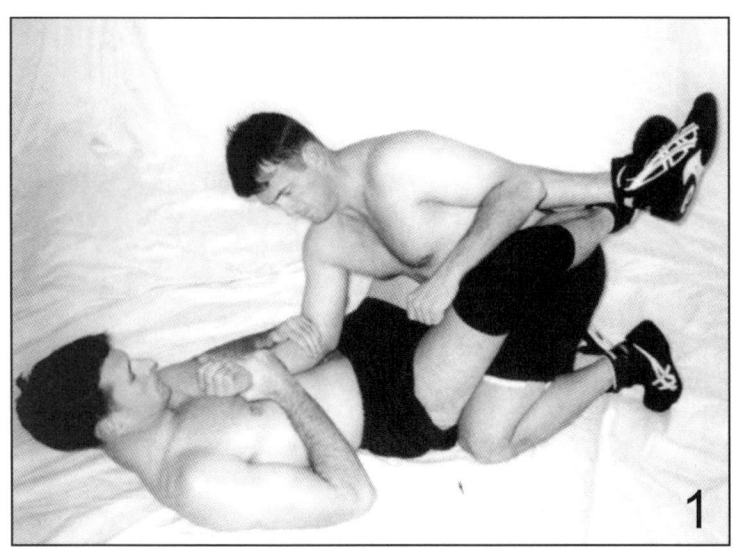

Your opponent has an arm placed on your chest. Secure his arm with both hands so that his arm is facing palm up.

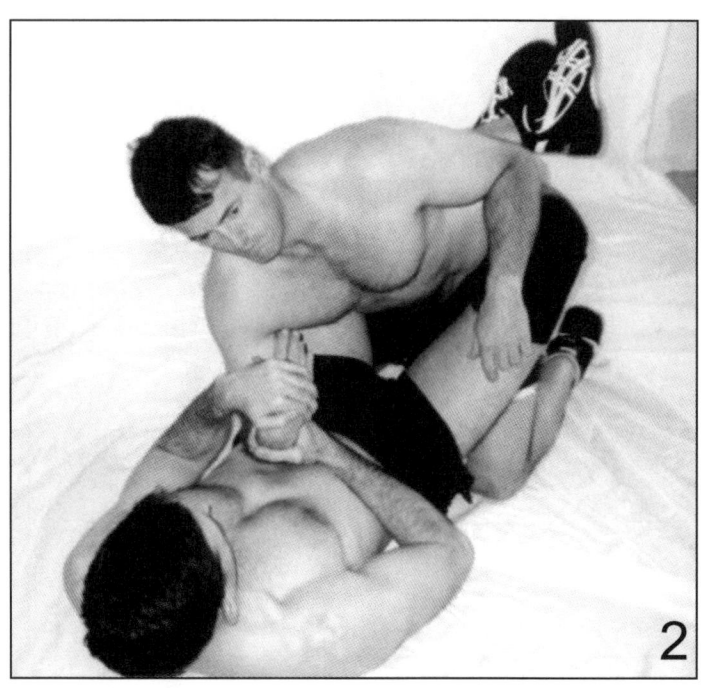

Secure his arm at the wrist with one hand and grasp the back of his trapped hand with your other, attacking arm.

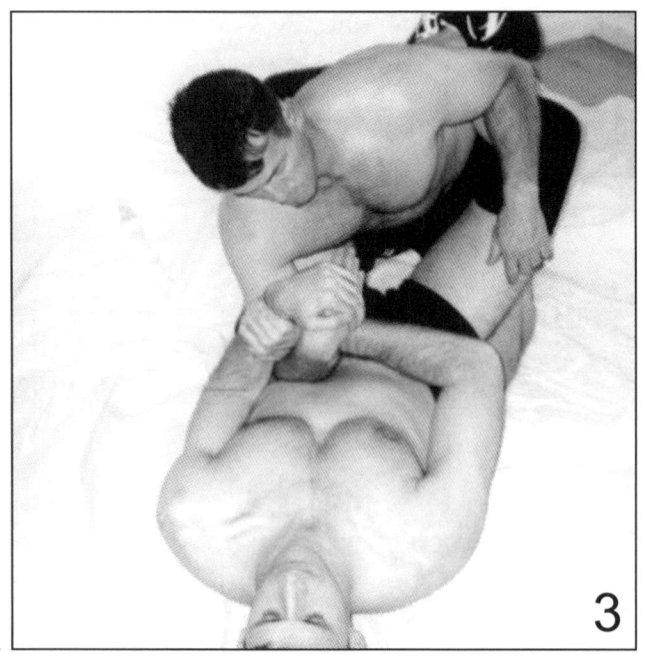

Grab your attacking arm at the wrist with your other, locking hand, forming a figure four lock as shown.

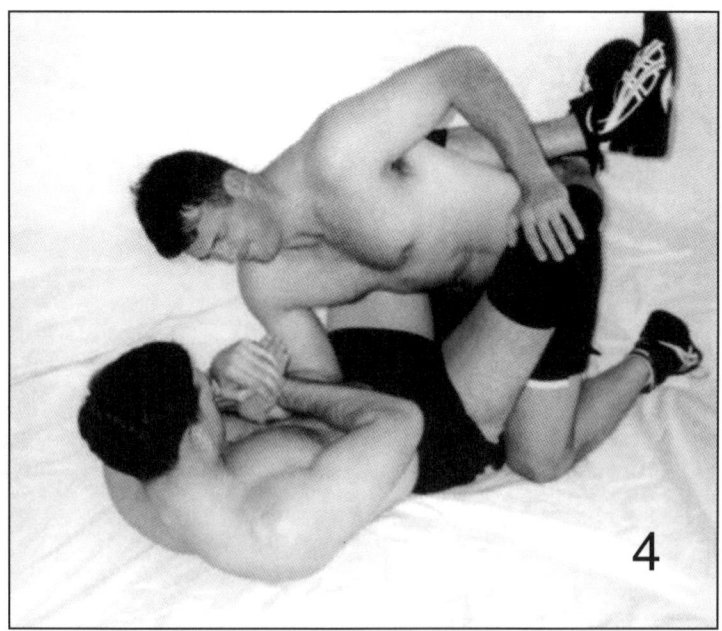

Hug his trapped arm tightly against your chest with your locking arm. Use your attacking hand and the leverage from your locking hand to push his wrist down and away from you. This motion hyper-flexes his wrist for the submission.

Chapter Three
Submissions From the Open Guard

The Open Guard

Use your legs to trap his in order to control his body movement and set him up for an attack.

Use your legs to create space and keep your opponent away from you or to set him up for a reversal.

Your hips are positioned so that you have distance between you and your opponent. You have room to maneuver and reposition.

Use your arms to control his arms or to control his legs. You have to use your whole body to effectively attack your opponent and to maintain an effective defense.

CHOKE *With Shin*

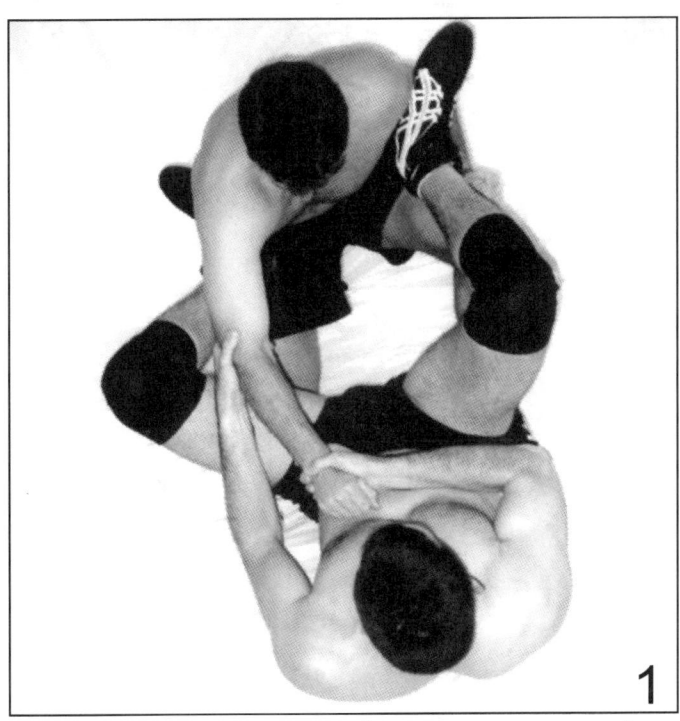

Your opponent is set up in your open guard. You have one foot on his biceps and the other on his hip; you are controlling his near arm.

Place your attacking leg across across his throat and hook your foot against the back of his head. Maintain control of his arm.

Grab the back of his head with your arm and pull his neck tight against your shin.

Grab the back of his head with your other hand. To apply the choke, push your shin away from you and into his neck and pull both of your hands towards you, driving his neck against your shin. This choke cuts off his air by crushing his esophagus.

HEEL HOOK

Your opponent is set up as shown. Note how he has stepped over one of your legs. Control his targeted leg at the ankle with your hand.

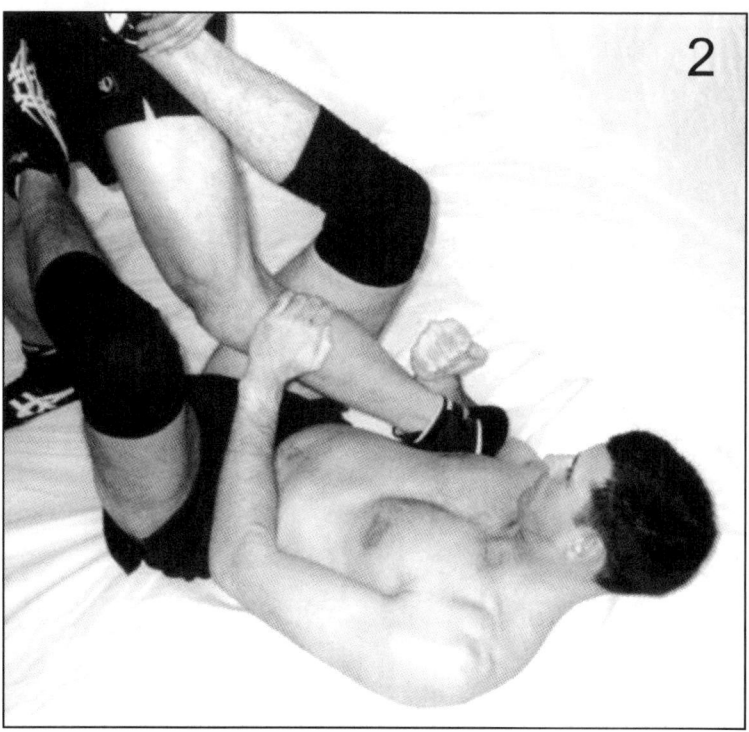

Scoop his heel with the crook of your arm. Use your other arm to help control his leg.

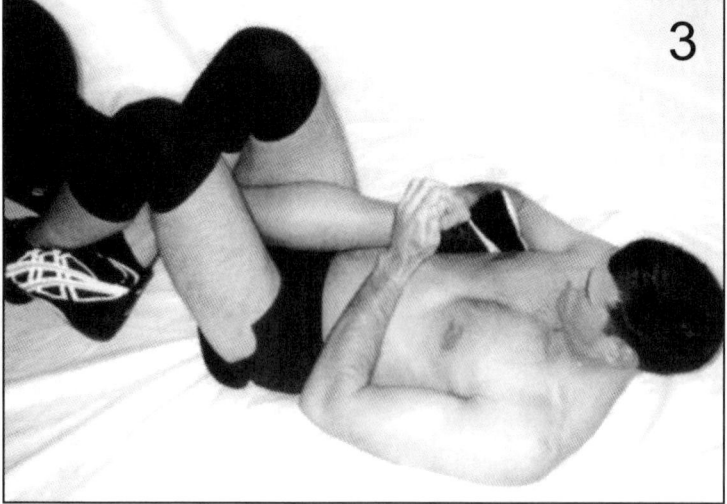

Gain control of his legs with your own to prevent his escape from the attack. Hook his heel in the crook of your arm and clasp your hands together. Twist your upper body, cranking his foot. This move uses his foot as a lever to torque his knee for the submission.

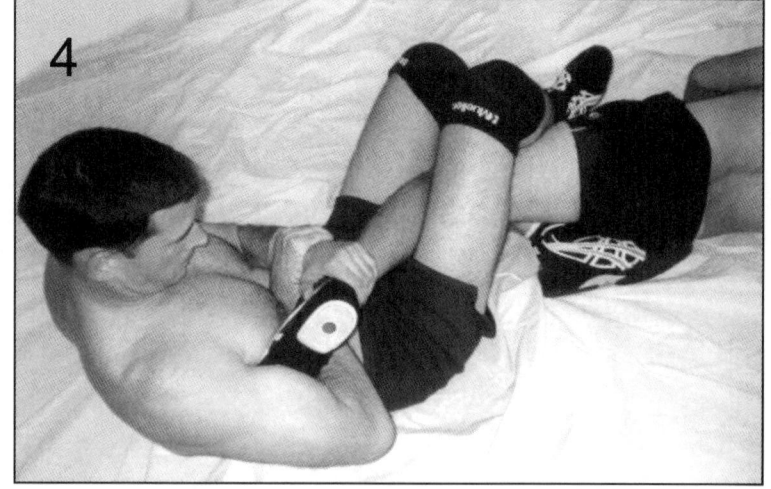

If your opponent is able to spin with the heel hook and stall your attack, simply reposition your legs and your hold on his foot and crank his foot in the opposite direction to torque his knee for the submission.

HEEL HOOK *From A Takedown*

Your opponent has one leg placed over yours. Secure his near leg at the ankle with your hand and at the upper thigh with your entangled leg.

Hook your other leg behind his far knee with your instep.

To take your opponent down, push both of your legs straight away from you. Your entangled leg pushes him backwards while your hand and other foot prevent him from stepping back and balancing himself.

Position your legs in a figure four lock as shown to protect your feet from attack. Hook his trapped leg at the heel and clasp your hands. Twist your upper body and torque his knee for the submission.

ANKLE LOCK

1. Your opponent has a leg placed over yours. Secure his leg at the ankle and place your far leg on his far hip.

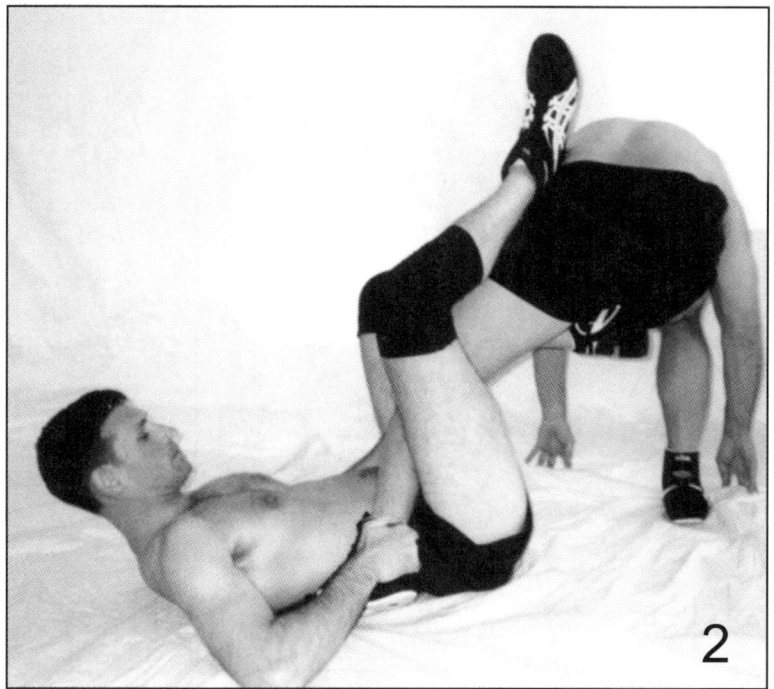

2. To take your opponent down, push him straight back over his trapped leg. Your far leg pushes on his far hip and your entangled leg pushes straight back over his near hip.

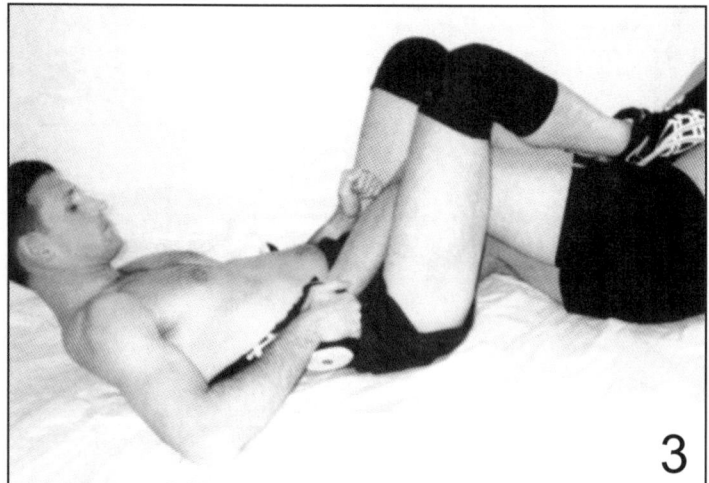

3. Secure his trapped leg by squeezing your knees together. Secure a good grip on his leg with your hands to prevent his escape.

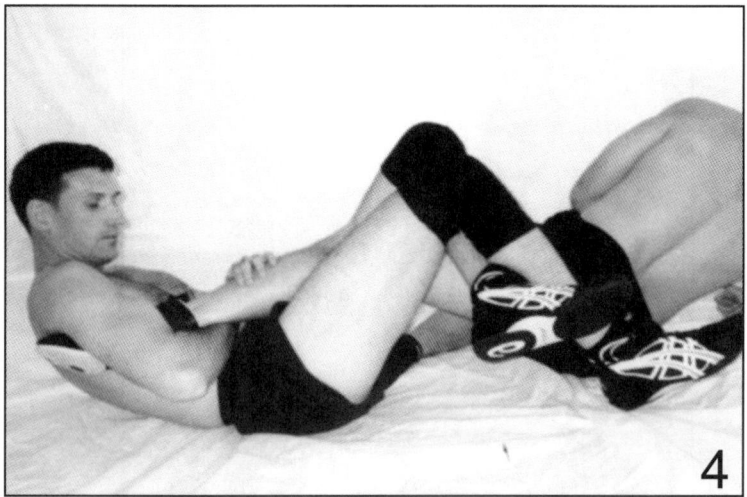

4. Reposition your feet to protect them from attack. Hook his foot under your armpit and establish a figure four lock on his shin. Arch your back and look skywards while you push downwards on his shin with your hands and at his knee with your legs. This will hyper-extend his foot at the ankle for the submission.

ANKLE LOCK *From A Takedown*

Set up your opponent with a foot on his hip and his far biceps. One arm is securing his leg at the ankle. (Top)

Switch your legs positioning so your top foot is on his hip and your bottom is hooking the back of his far heel. (Top Right)

Push him at the hip with your top leg to push him over. (Right)

Bring your bottom knee under his leg. Secure his foot under your armpit with a figure four lock. (Opposite angle) (Bottom Right)

Bring your top leg up and squeeze your knees together. Arch your back and hyper-extend his foot at the ankle for the submission. (Bottom)

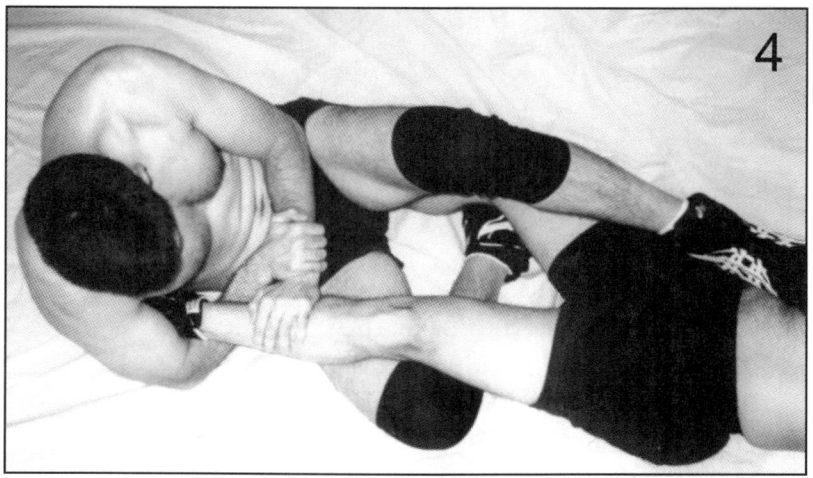

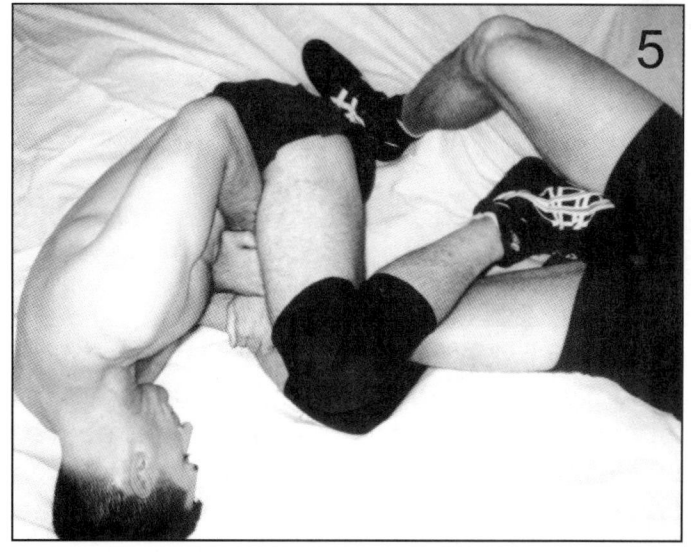

KNEE BAR

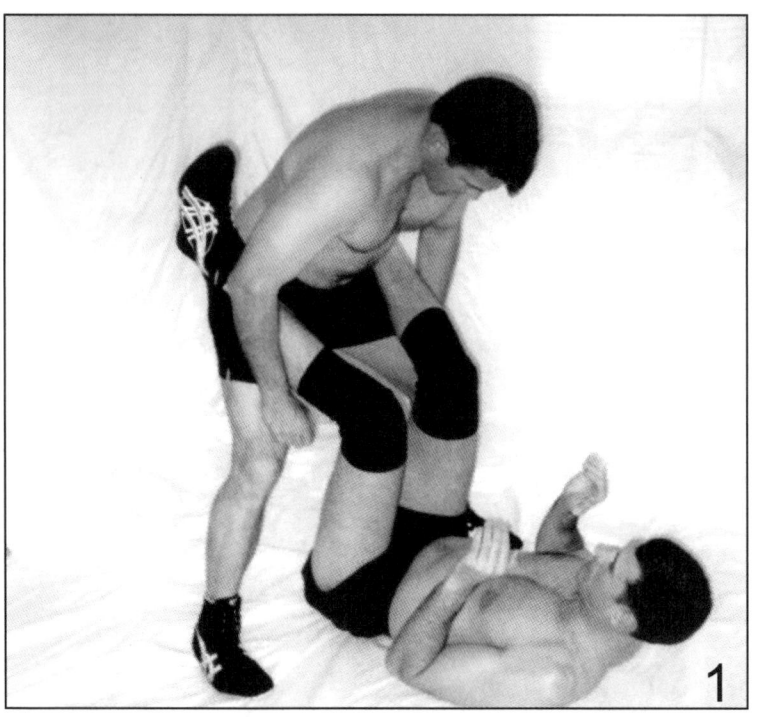

Your opponent is set up with both of your legs outside of his hips. You have space between his hips and yours so that you can reposition.

Hook behind his ankle with an underhand grip, palm facing you. Rotate your hips away from his trapped leg and place your knee on the inside of his as shown.

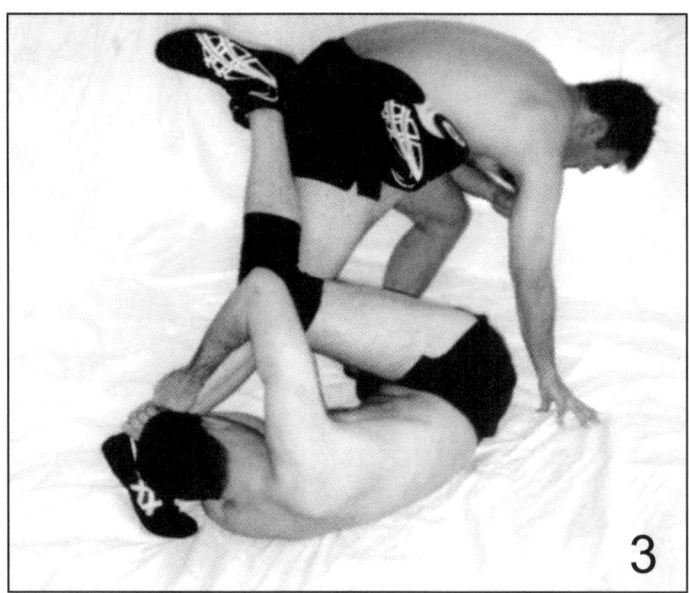

Swing your far leg over his trapped leg and place your heel on his buttocks. Grab his trapped leg with your other hand. Push his buttocks with your top foot and drive your hips forwards, toppling him forwards.

You have ended in a position where you are bear hugging his leg. Keep his leg hugged tightly to your chest and ensure your hips are placed just above his knee, closer to his groin. Drive your hips forwards and drive your top heel downwards to hyper-extend his leg at the knee for the submission.

KNEE BAR *Sit Up*

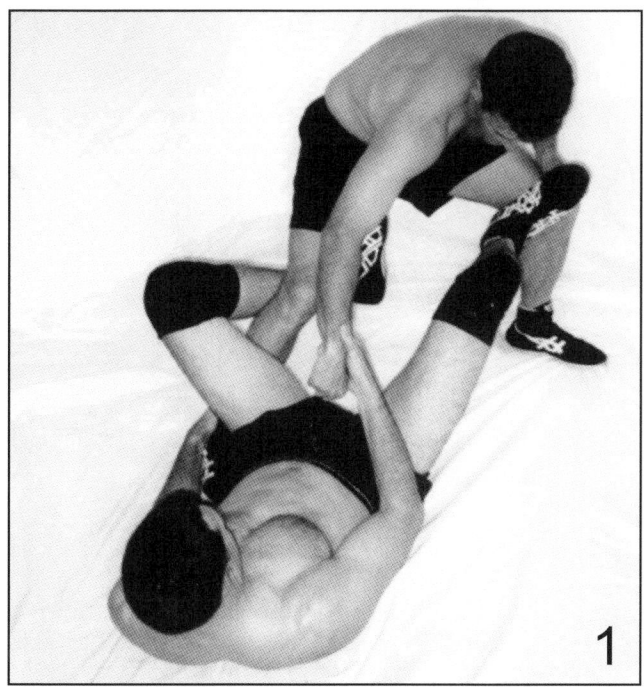

Your opponent is set up in your open guard. You have his near leg secured at the ankle with your hand and and at the knee with your entangled leg. Your other leg is creating space by pushing on his far knee.

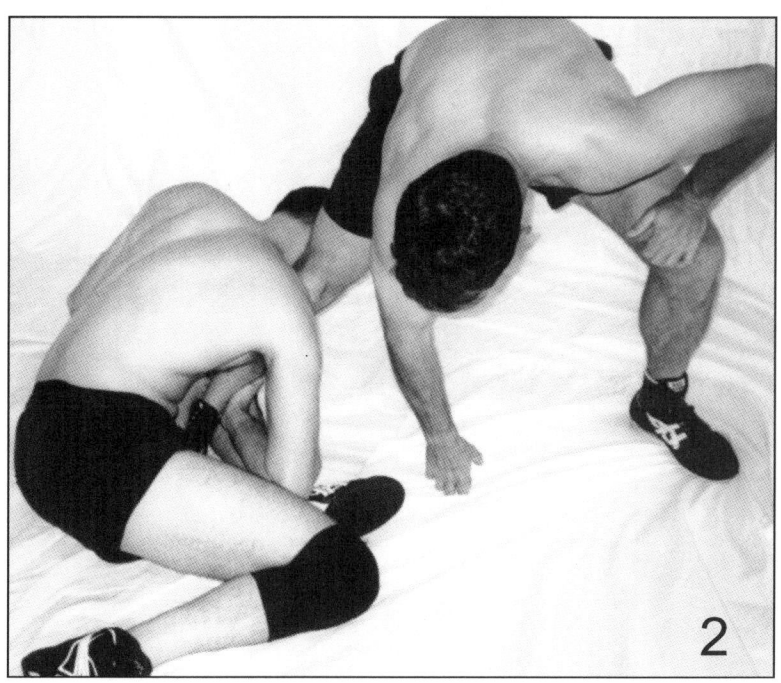

Sit into him and hug his knee. Your entangled leg is flat on the ground, hooking behind his ankle, and your shoulder is driving into his knee.

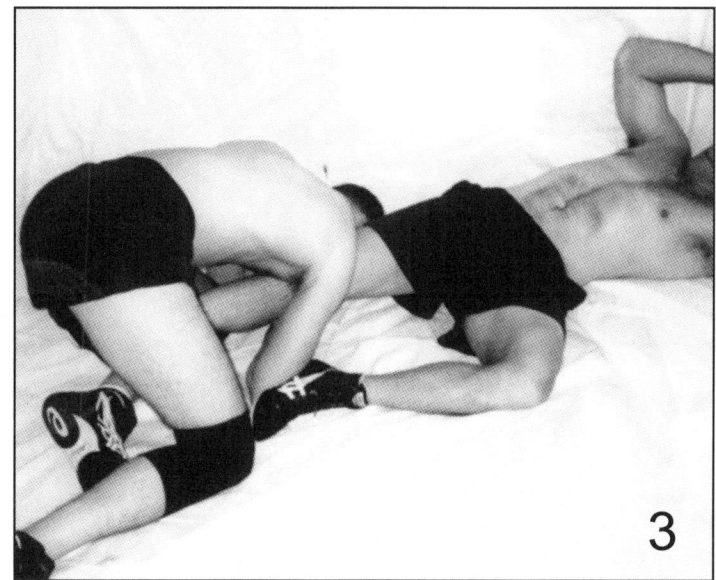

To take him down, drive your shoulder forwards while maintaining your leg hooked behind his ankle. Your shoulder forces him backwards and your hooked leg prevents him from stepping backwards and balancing.

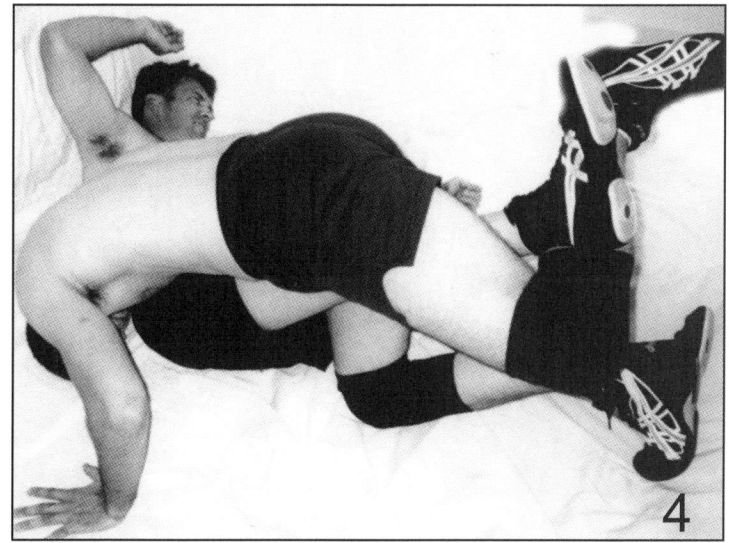

Maintain your leg hooked behind his trapped foot. Ensure that your groin is slightly above his knee cap, closer to his groin. Lift your entangled leg up and drive your hips into him to hyperextend his leg at the knee for the submission. (This picture is from the opposite angle)

KNEE LEVER

Your opponent is set up with one leg through your legs. Gain control of his targeted leg with your own leg and control his foot at the heel. Your other leg is posted on his far knee, keeping his legs apart.

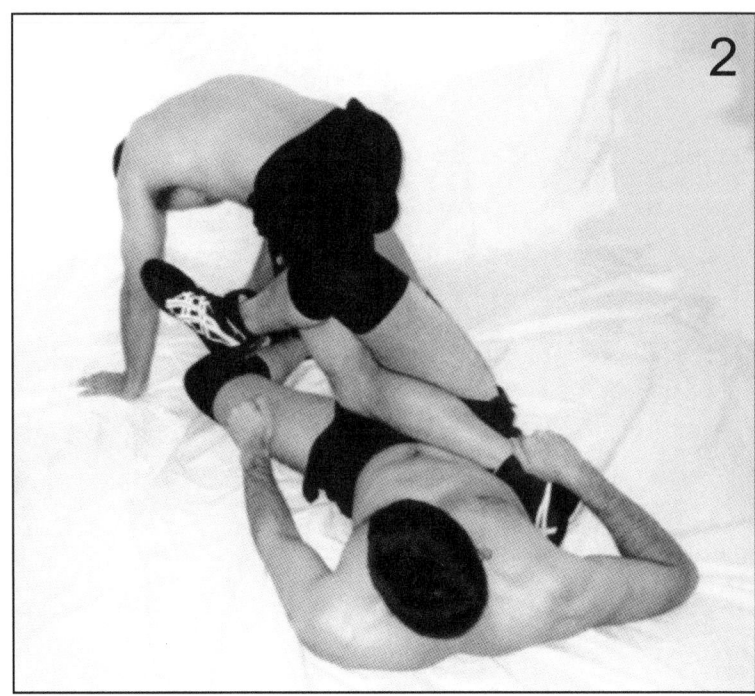

Bring your near leg across his and turn your hips towards his trapped leg and push off on his far knee, driving him off balance.

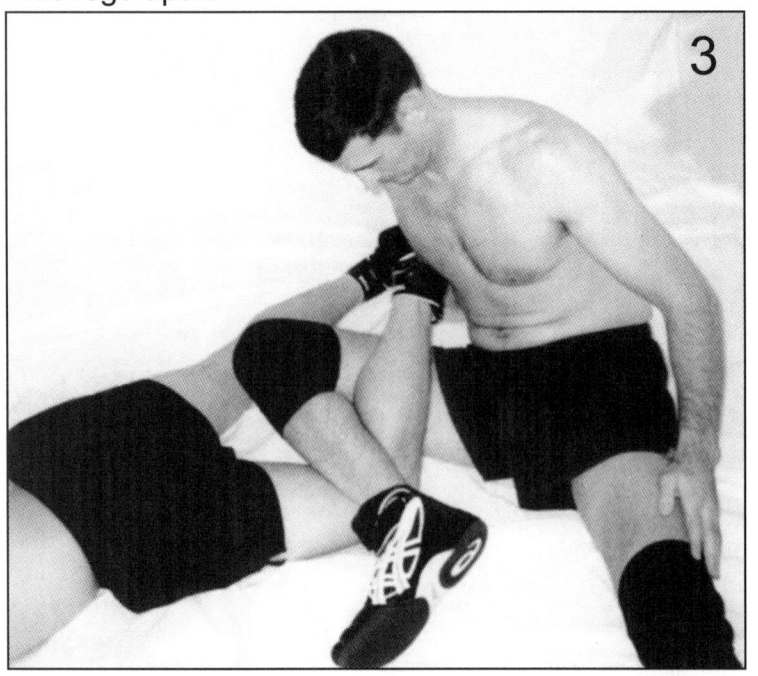

As your opponent falls to the ground, keep your pressure on his trapped leg. Bring your hips away from him and sit up while hooking your leg behind his knee.

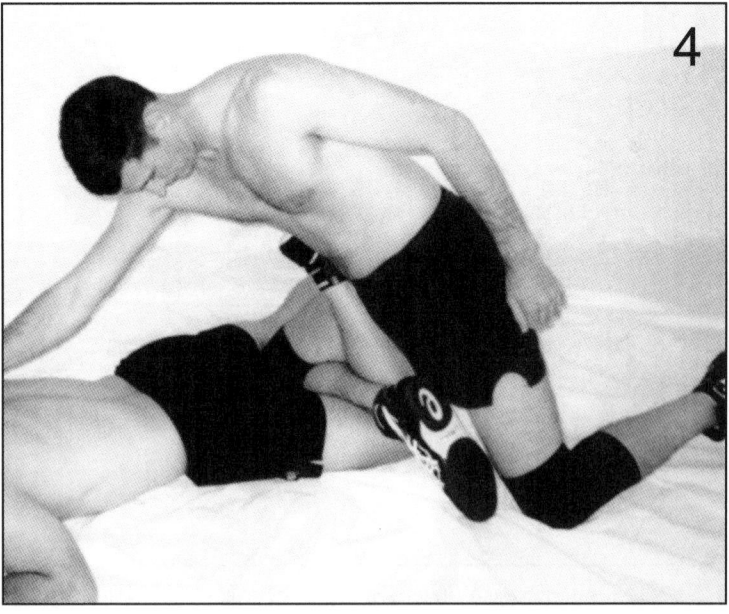

Sit up towards him, driving your hips forwards. Try to force his heel to his buttocks. This movement will attempt to separate his knee joint. He will submit before his heel reaches his buttocks.

ARM BAR

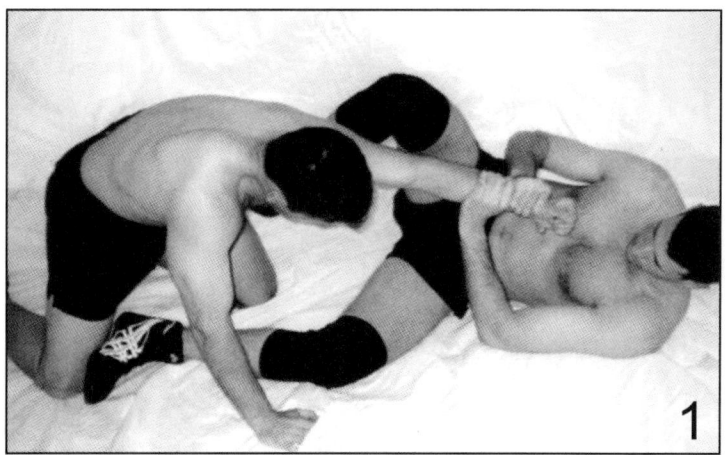

Your opponent is set up in your open guard. Your top foot is planted on his hip. Your bottom foot is planted on his knee. You have control of his arm as shown. You are pushing away with your legs and pulling in with your arms in order to stretch his body out and expose his arm.

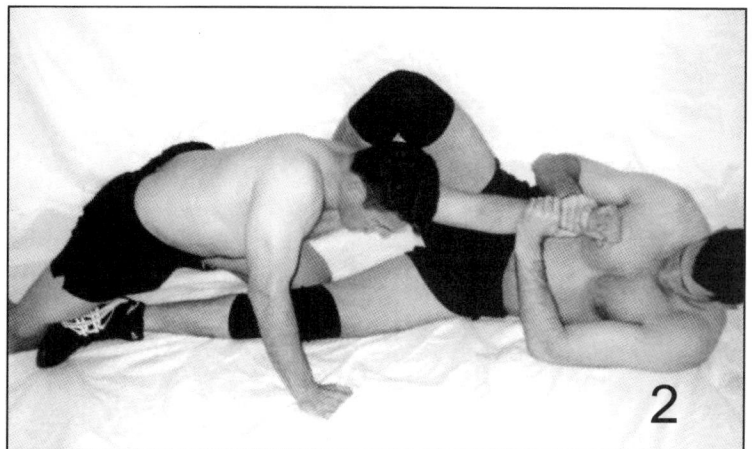

Push his knee back with your bottom leg so that he is off balance.

Place your top leg over his trapped arm and across his face.

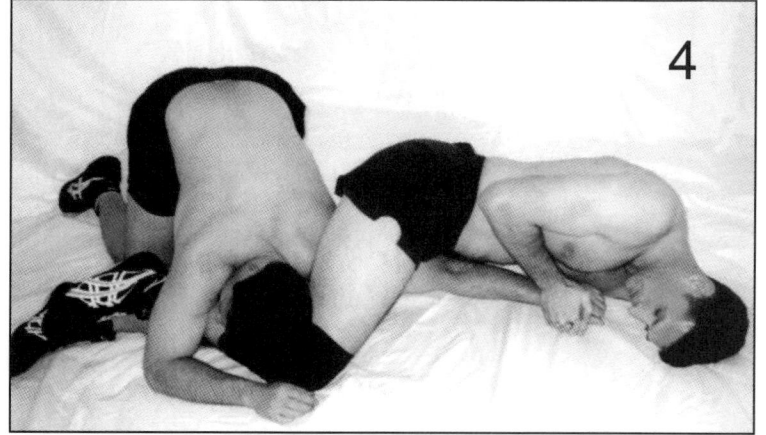

Rotate your hips so that you now have your groin tight against his arm. Ensure that your hips are close to his shoulder. Squeeze your knees together to help isolate and control his arm. Secure his arm at the wrist and arch your hips forwards to hyper-extend his arm at the elbow for the submission.

ARM BAR *With Leg Scissors*

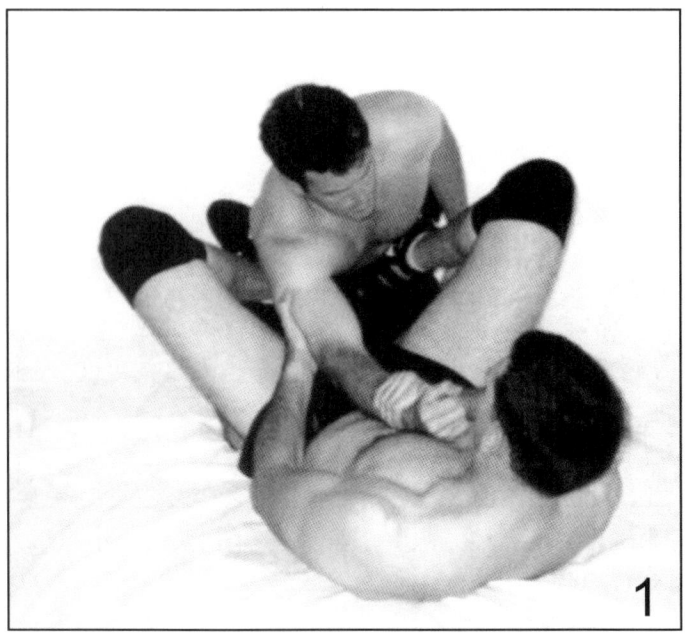

Your opponent is set up with both of your feet planted on his hips. You are controlling one exposed arm at the wrist and elbow as shown.

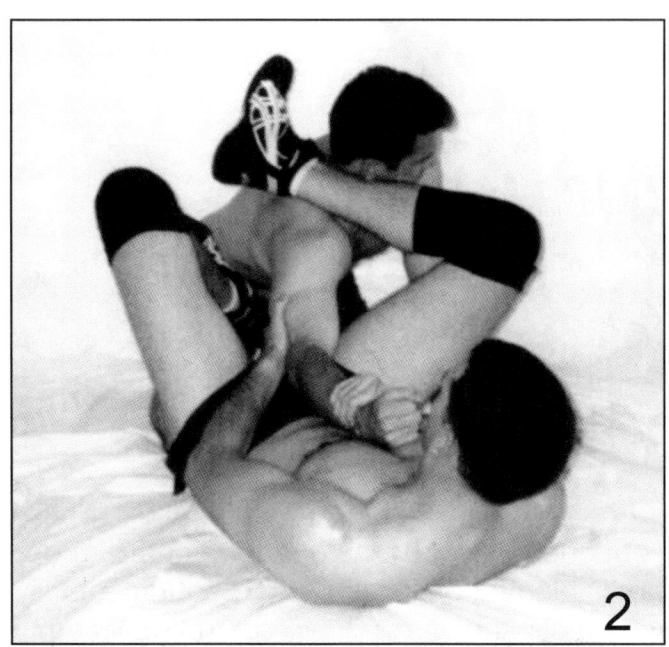

Bring your leg across his face and drive his head away with your shin.

Bring your remaining leg across his face and over your other leg, obtaining a scissors lock on his head. Maintain control of his arm.

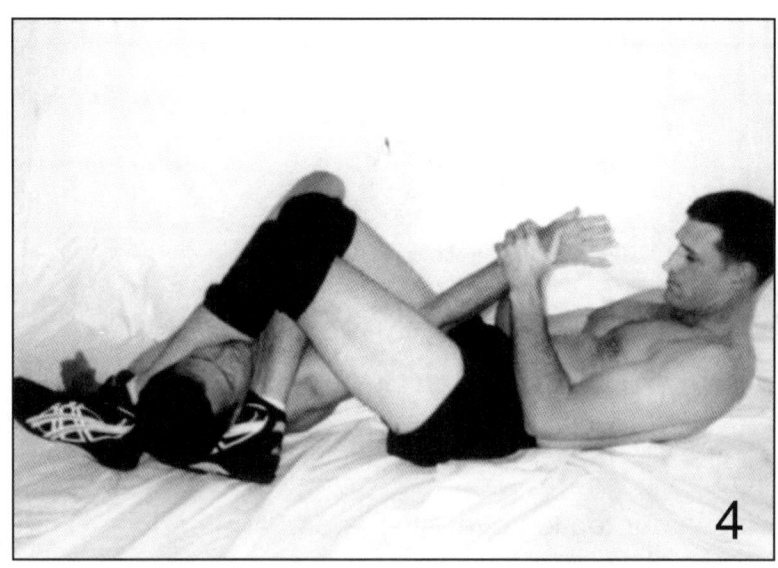

Drive your heels to the ground, pinning his head to the ground. Drive your hips forwards and hyperextend his arm at the elbow for the submission.

SQUEEZE LOCK

1. Your opponent is set up with one of your feet planted on his hips, controlling his distance. You are controlling one of his arms at the wrist. You have your other leg entangled over his targeted arm as shown. (Left)

Pull his trapped arm towards you and grab his trapped arm behind his triceps. (Right)

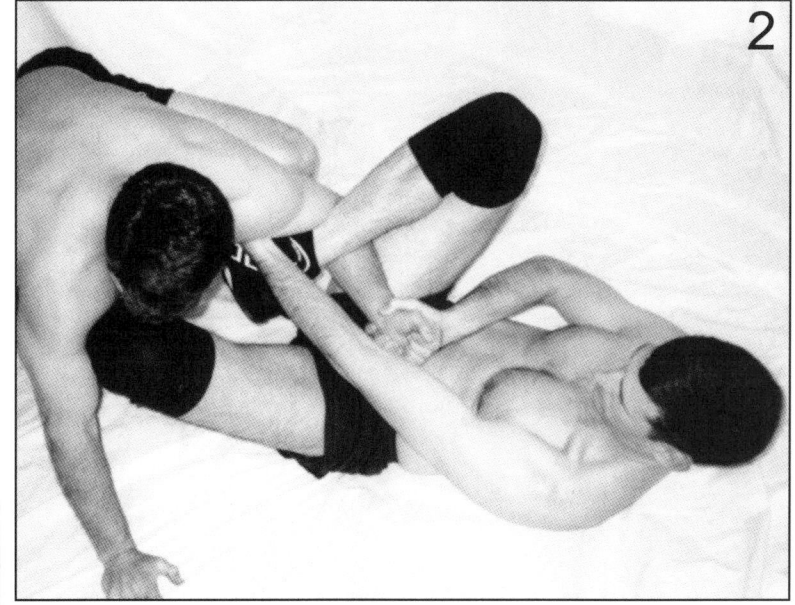

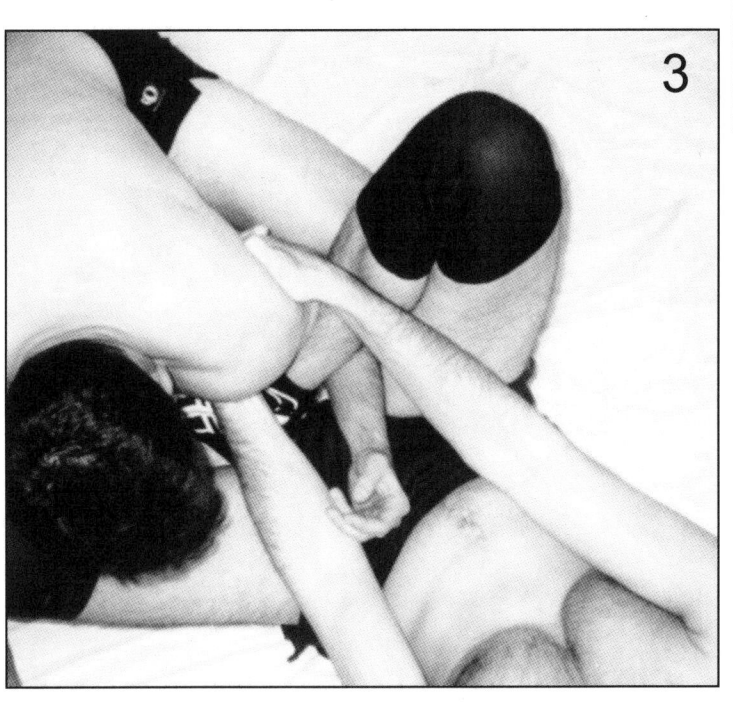

Grab his arm behind the triceps with your other arm. His arm is now trapped with his forearm against your groin and with your shin driving into his arm at the joint. To submit, drive your shin forwards while pulling his arm into your shin with both of your arms. This movement threatens to separate his elbow at the joint and also puts pressure on his biceps where it inserts at the joint. (Left)

Chapter Four
Submissions In The Closed Guard

NECK CRANK *Can Opener*

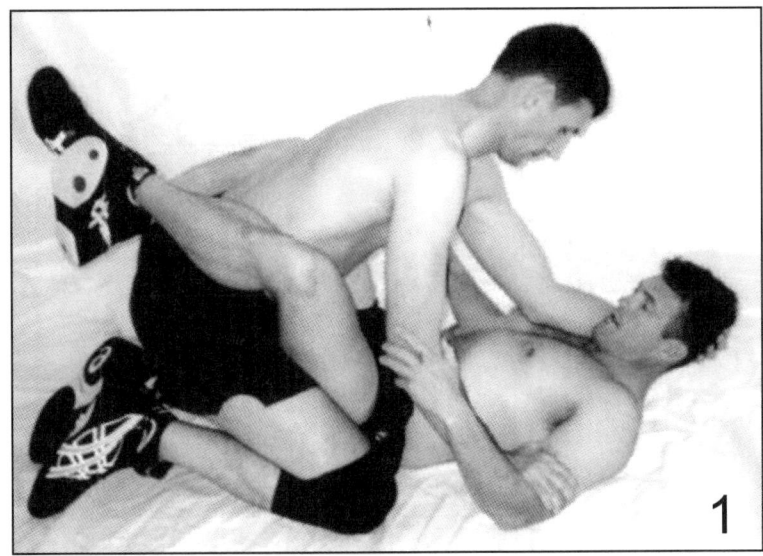

You are forwards in his guard with one arm hooked behind his head. Your other arm is controlling is arm at the biceps.

Place your other arm behind his head as shown, cradling his head in your forearms and hands.

Ensure your elbows are close together and driving into his chest to prevent his escape. Pull up with your hands, forcing his head forwards.

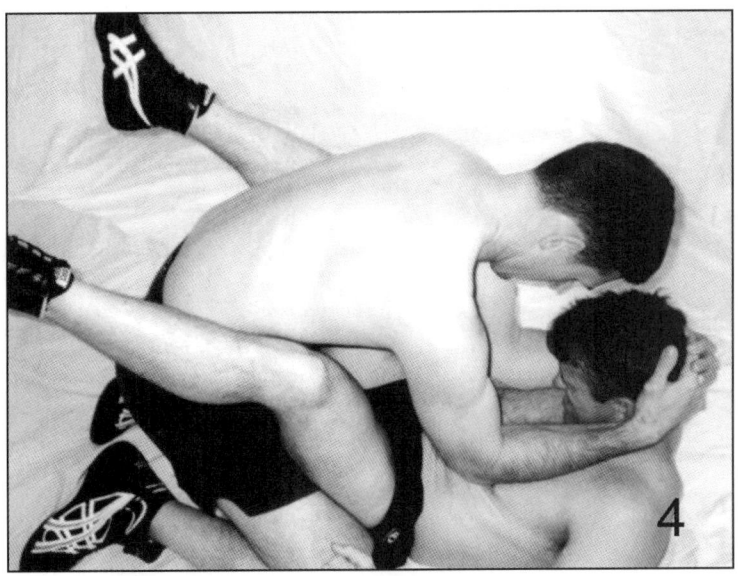

The higher up on his head that you have your grip, the more leverage you have. Continue to crank his head and hyper-extend his cervical spin until he submits. He will often split his legs to relieve the pressure on his spine, offering an opportunity to pass his guard.

NECK CRANK *Figure Four Lock*

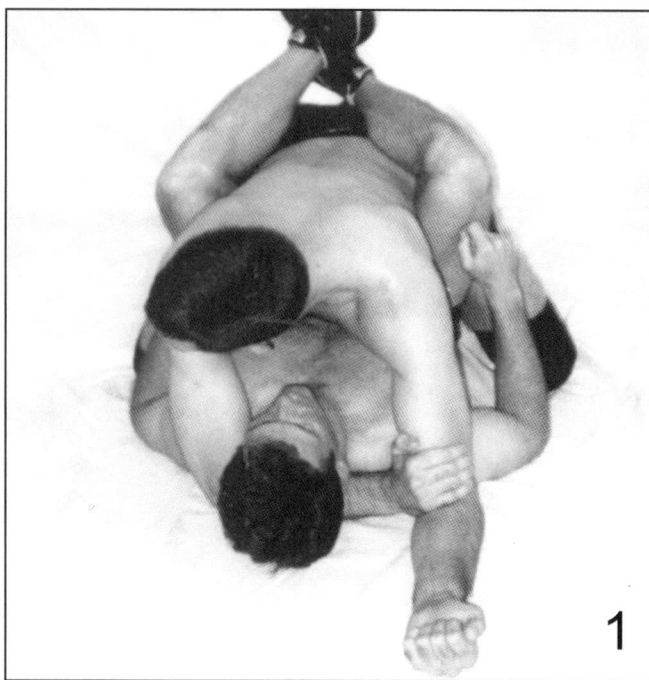

1. You are forwards in your opponent's guard. Your attacking arm is wrapped behind his neck and you are grabbing the biceps of your locking arm.

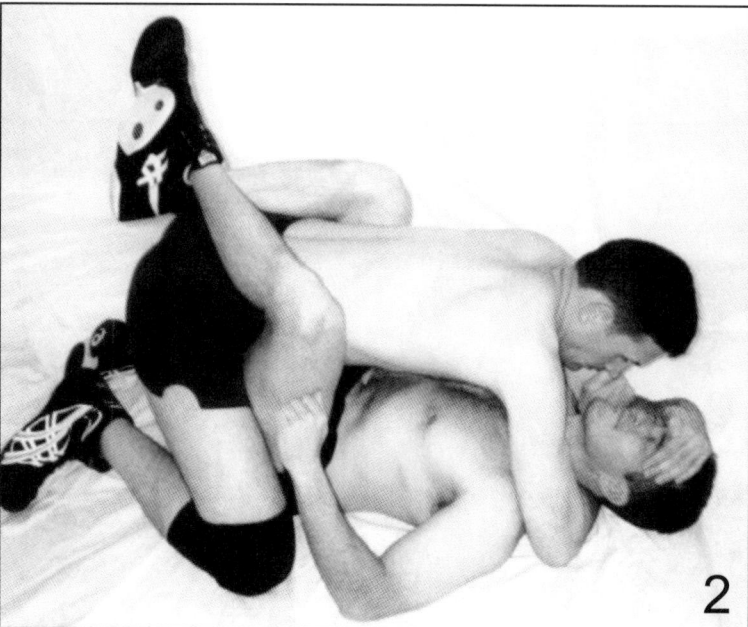

2. Place your locking hand on his forehead; the higher up you are the more leverage you will have. To crank, drive the blade of your attacking forearm into the base of his neck while pushing down on his forehead with your other hand, hyper-extending his cervical spine for the submission.

CHOKE *Forearm Variation*

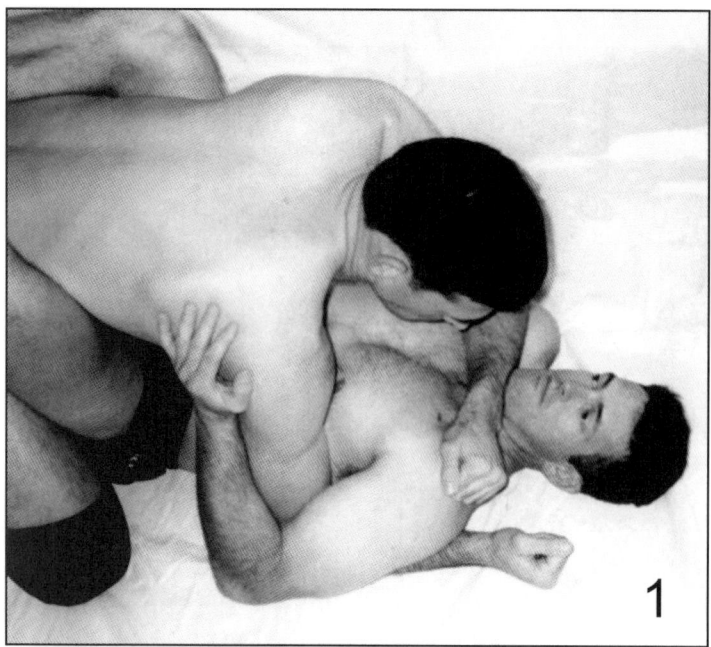

1. You are forwards in your opponent's guard. One arm is hooked under his arm and the other, attacking arm is across his throat.

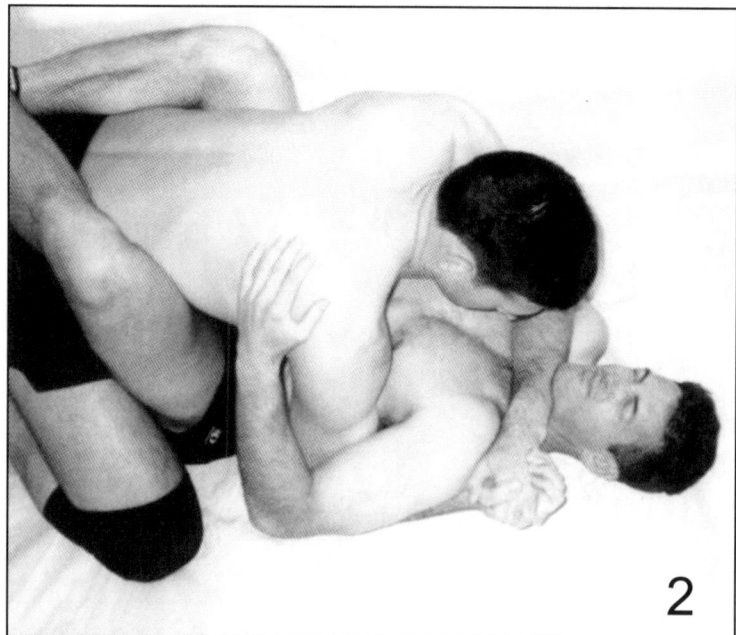

2. Clasp your hands together, ensuring your hands are pressed against the ground. Drive your attacking elbow to the ground, forcing the blade of your forearm into his throat. This will cut off his air by crushing his esophagus.

CHOKE *Scissors Variation*

You are forwards in your opponent's guard with your locking arm behind his neck and grasping your attacking arm at the biceps.

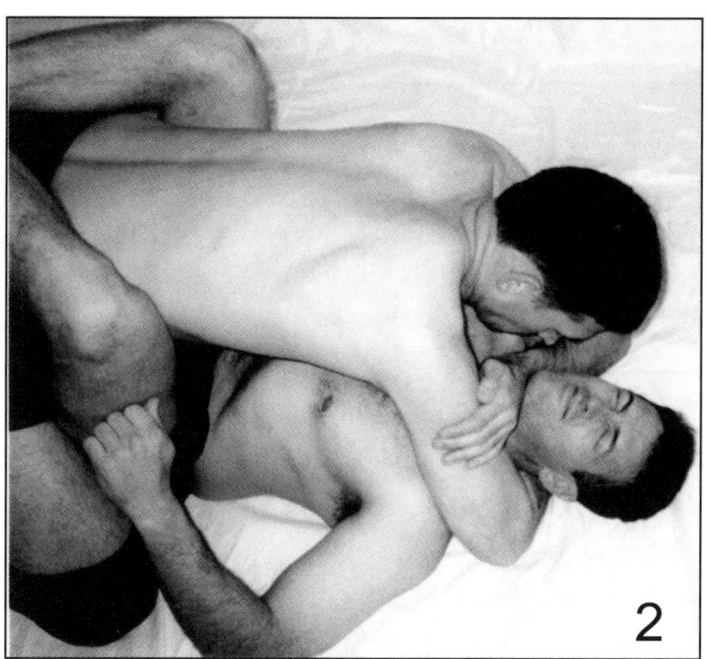

Place your attacking arm across his throat. Drive the blade of your locking arm upwards into the base of his neck while driving the blade of your attacking arm downwards into his throat, crushing his esophagus for the submission.

Forearm Variation With Entangled Arm

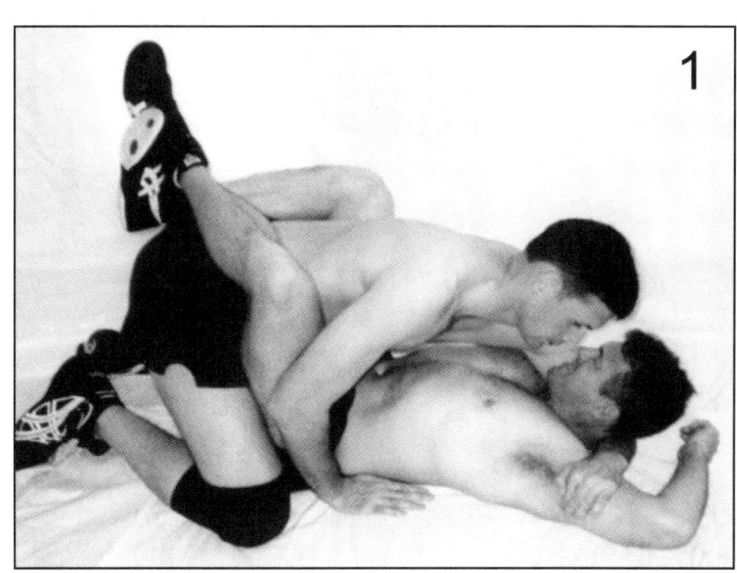

You are forwards in your opponent's guard. Your locking arm is under his neck and securing his arm at the triceps as shown.

Bring your attacking arm across his throat and grab your locking arm at the triceps. Drive your attacking elbow towards the ground, crushing his esophagus for the submission.

CHOKE *Kata Gatame*

You are forwards in your opponent's guard. Your attacking arm is wrapped behind his neck. Secure his exposed arm in preparation for pushing it across his body. (Left)

Push his arm across his body and trap it between his head and your own. Grab your locking arm at the biceps as shown, keeping your head tight against his arm. (Right)

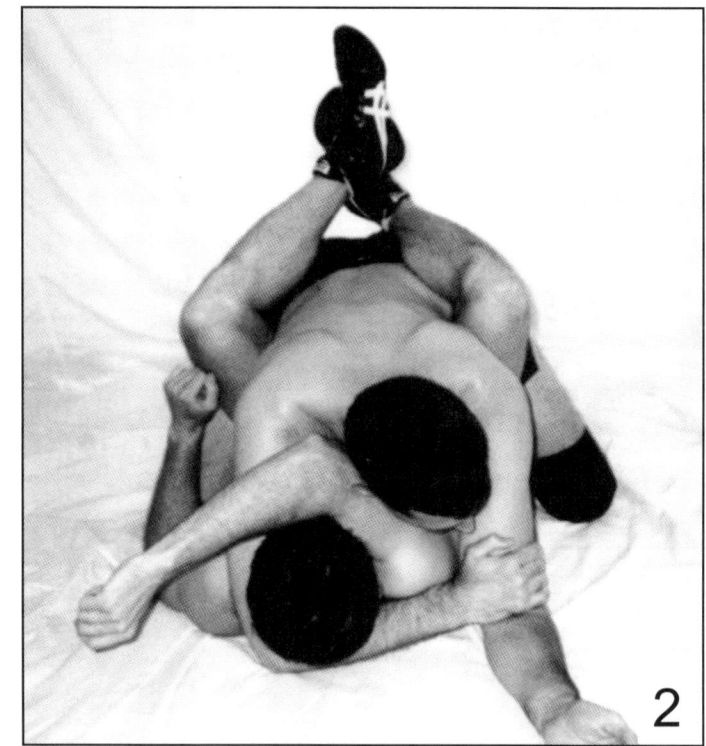

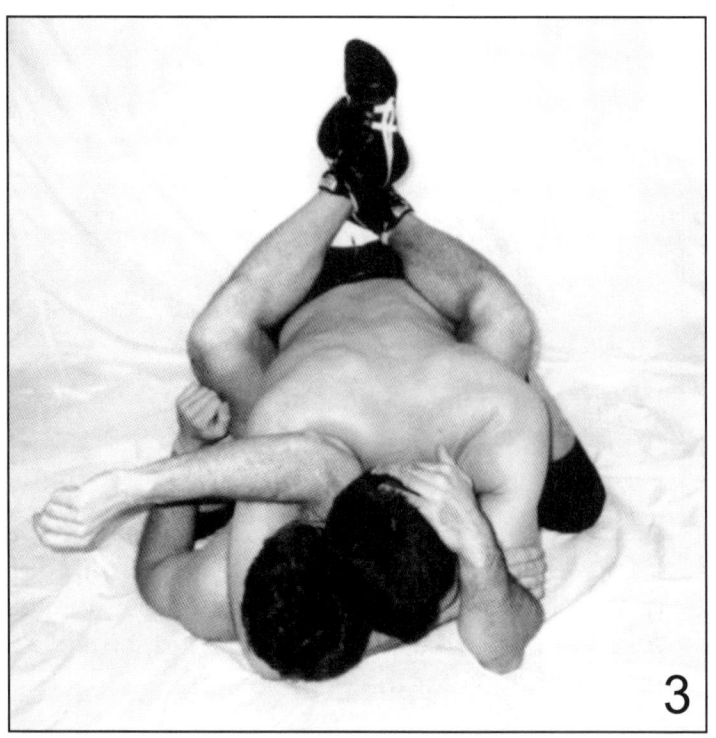

Grab your own head to lock in the hold. Drive the blade of your attacking forearm upwards and into the base of his neck. Contract the muscles of your attacking arm and drive your head against his. This will cut off the carotid arteries in his neck. Also, your attacking arm driving into the base of his neck can crank his cervical spine for the submission. (Left)

CHOKE *Modified Kata Gatame*

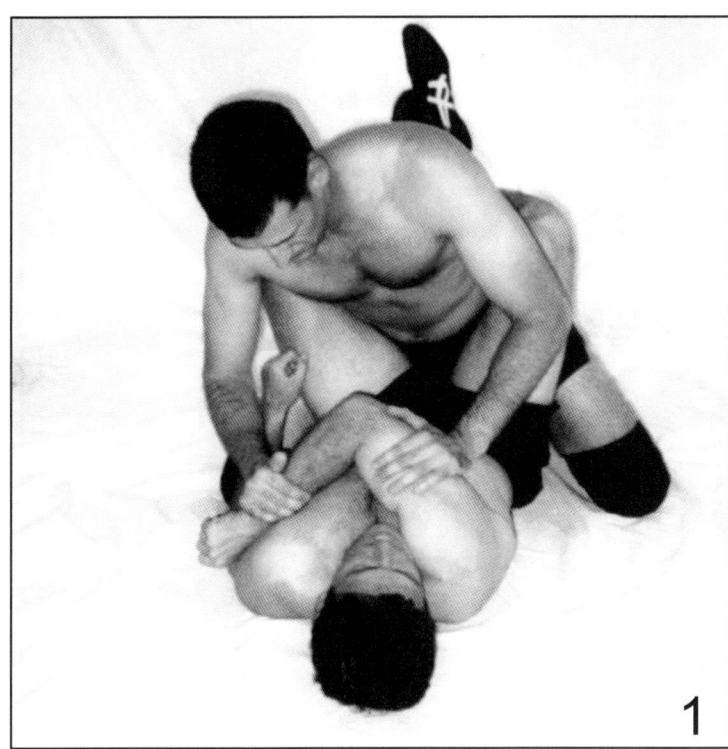

This technique is very similar to Kata Gatame. Drive your opponent's exposed arm across his chest as shown. (Left)

Place your attacking arm over his arm and behind his neck, trapping his arm between his body and yours. Grab your other, locking arm at the biceps. (Right)

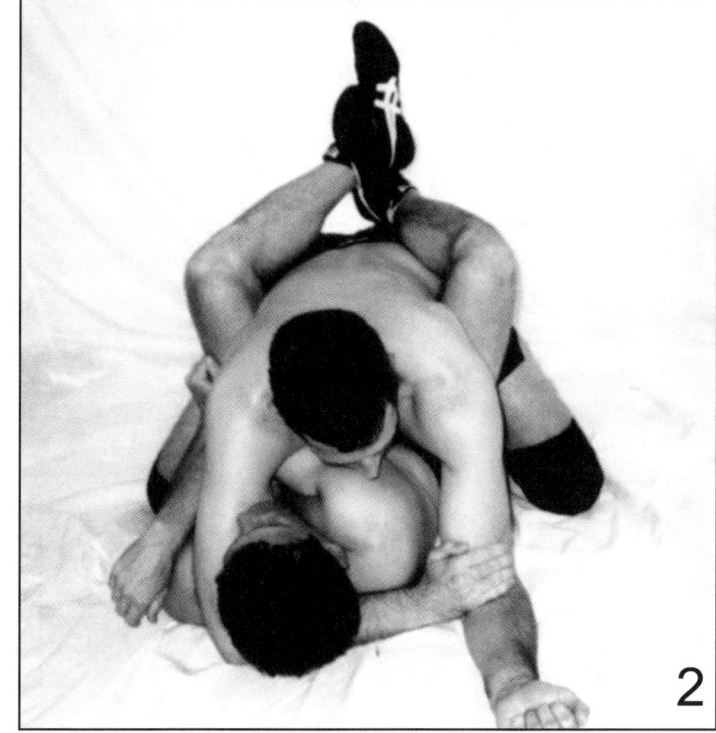

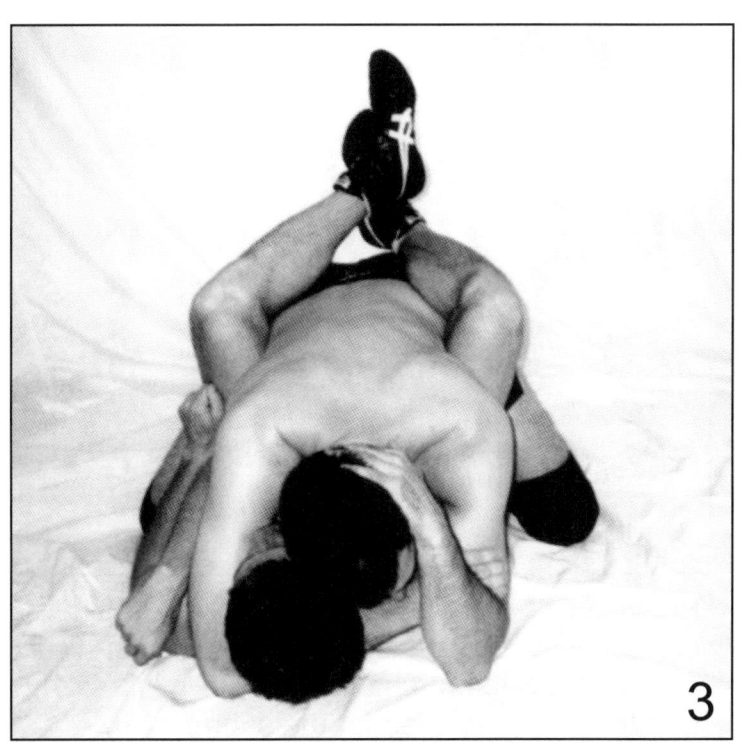

Grab your own head to lock in the technique. Drive the blade of your attacking forearm into the base of his neck and contract the muscles of your attacking arm. Keep your head placed tightly against his. This technique will crank his neck and cut off the blood flow in his carotid arteries for the submission. (Left)

ANKLE CRANK

You are in your opponent's guard. You have your knee pushing against his tailbone.

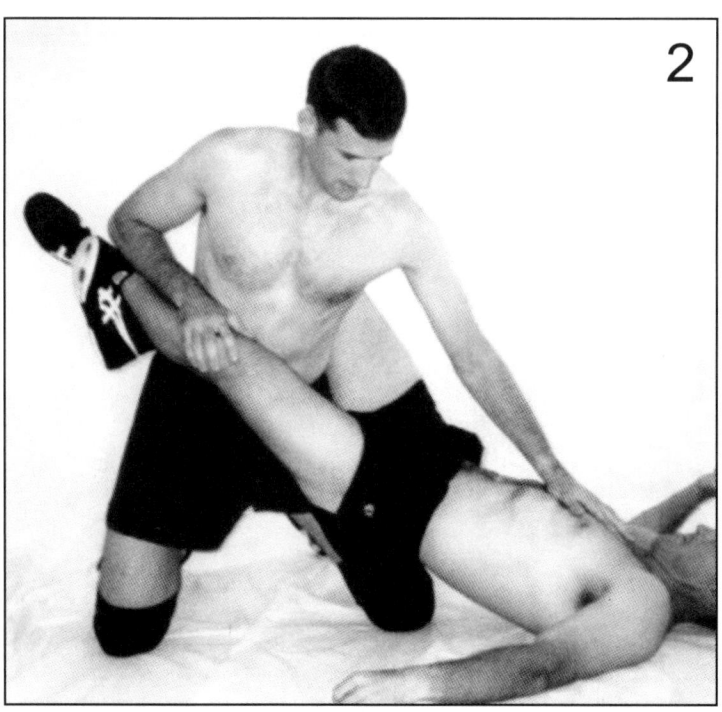

Twist your body so that you are sideways in his guard and push off with your knee, coming up to your knees.

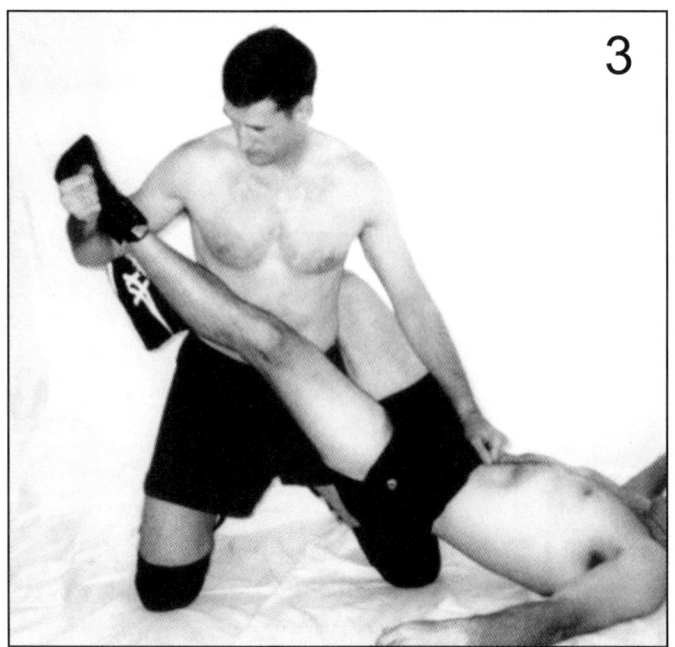

Hook your arm under his top foot, breaking his guard.

Press your knee against his far, free leg to help control his body positioning. Reach under his foot and grab it with both hands as shown. Crank his foot to torque his knee for the submission.

ANKLE LOCK *Step Over*

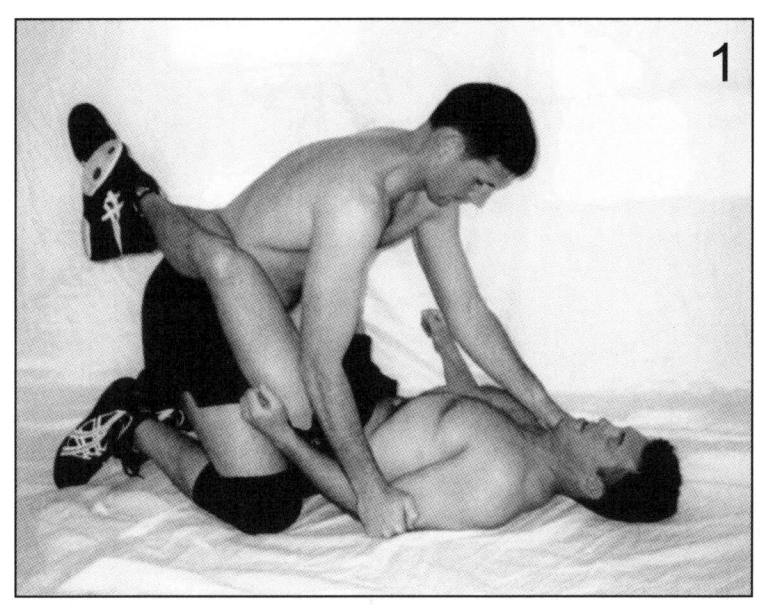

You are sitting back in your opponent's guard.

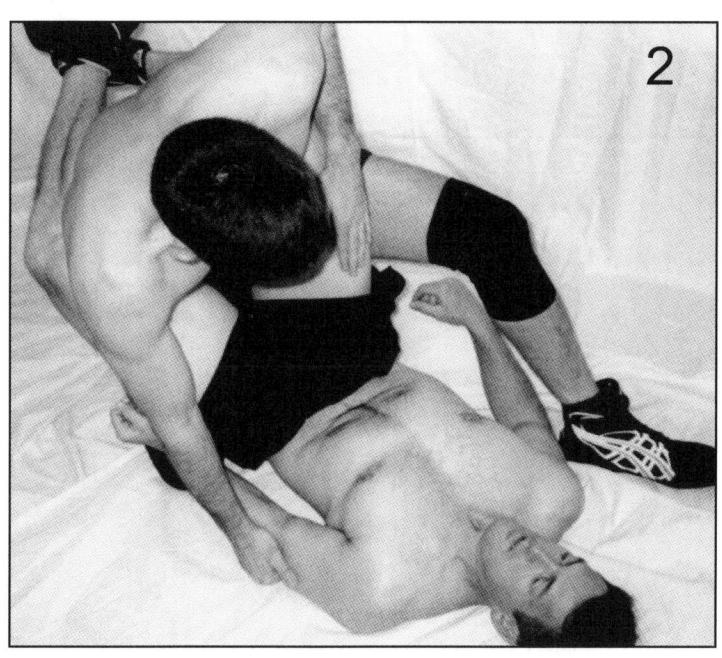

Bring you leg up in preparation for stepping over his body. Secure his targeted leg with your same side arm. Secure his arm at the elbow so he can not post out and stop your step over.

Step over with your leg, turning him over onto his stomach. You are maintaining control of his targeted leg with your arm as shown.

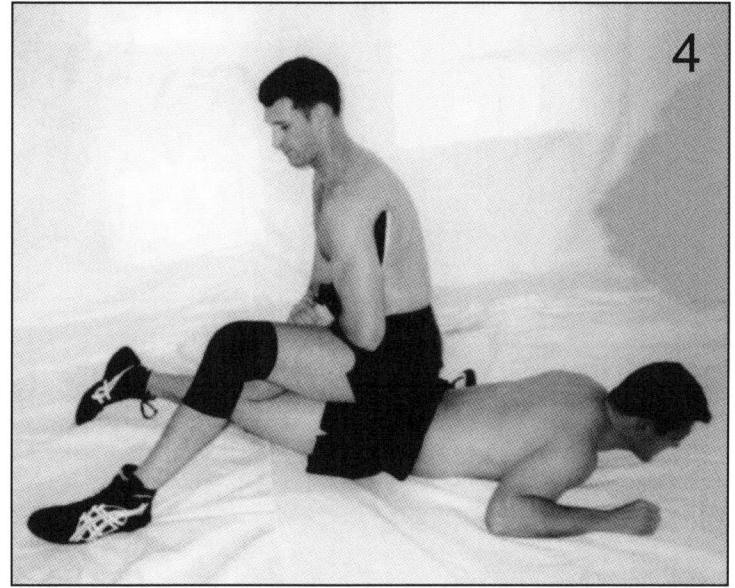

You can finish him with a variety of moves but, here, finish with an ankle lock. Secure his foot under your armpit with a figure four lock and sit firmly on his buttocks, keeping him pinned to the ground. Arch backwards and hyper-extend his foot at the ankle for the submission.

Chapter Five

Submissions In The Open Guard

HEEL HOOK

You are in your opponent's open guard with his legs on your hips.

Keep a good, wide base and squeeze your legs together at the knees, forcing his legs together as shown.

Keep his legs pinned together and secure his targeted leg, hooking his heel with your forearm.

Secure his heel by clasping your hands together. While keeping his legs pinned, turn your upper body and use his ankle as a lever to torque his knee for the submission.

HEEL HOOK *From A Sweep*

You are in your opponent's guard and he is trying to reverse you with a sweep, bringing his leg across your body. (Left)

Spread your base to prevent the reversal and hook his exposed foot at the heel with your forearm as shown. (Right)

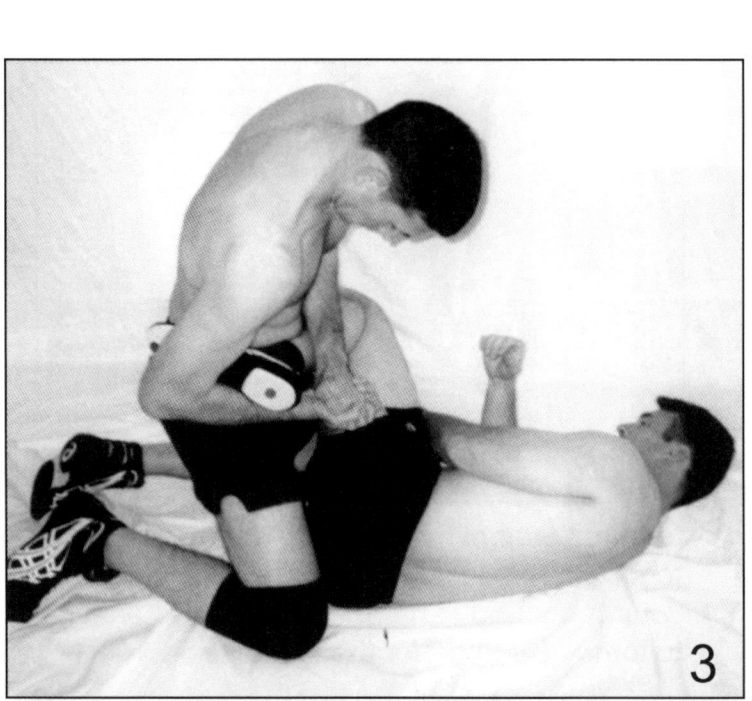

Keep a good base and lock in the technique by clasping your hands. Turn your upper body towards his knee, using his foot as a lever to torque his leg at the knee for the submission. (Left)

ACHILLES LOCK *Standing And Sitting*

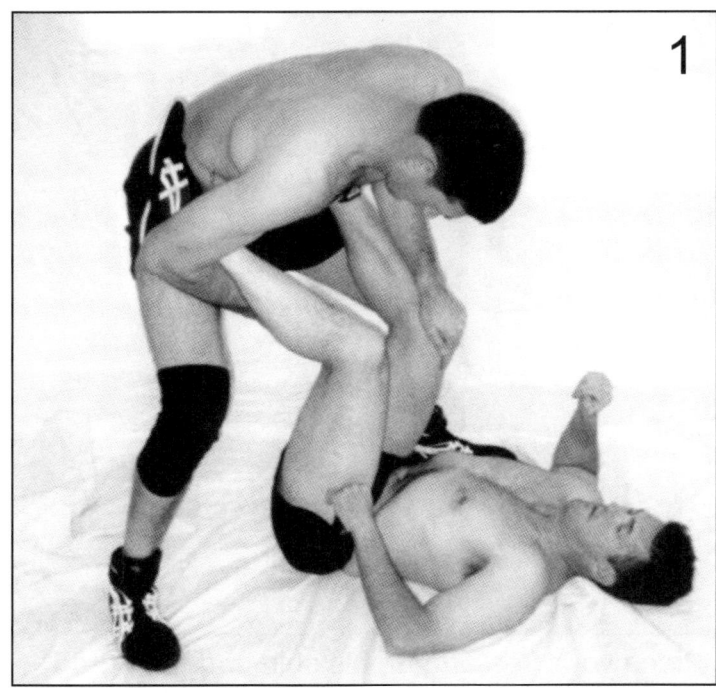

Your opponent has his legs split and you have a foot secured with one of your arms.

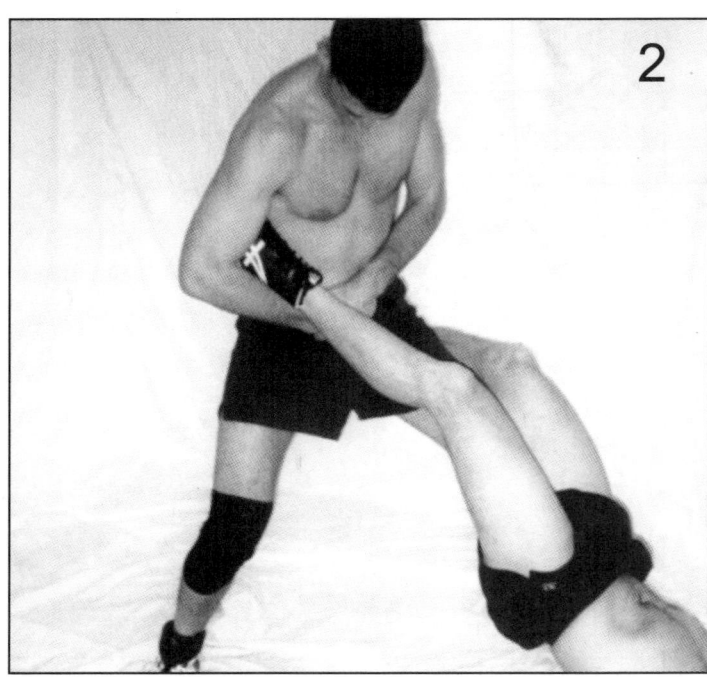

Clasp your hands together to secure the technique. Arch backwards and drive the blade of your forearm upwards, into his Achilles tendon. This is a pain submission.

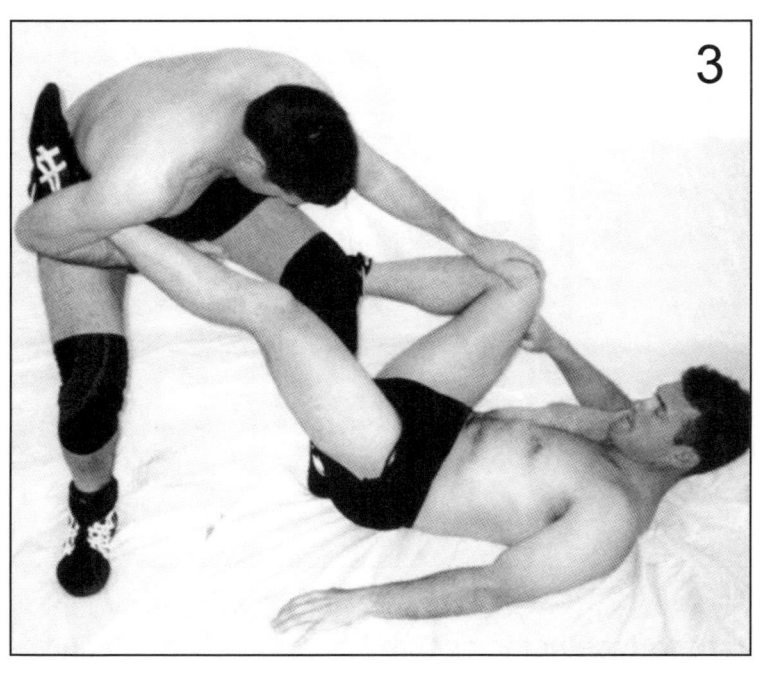

Or, hold his trapped foot securely under your arm. Place your foot at the base of his tailbone and control his free leg in preparation for sitting back.

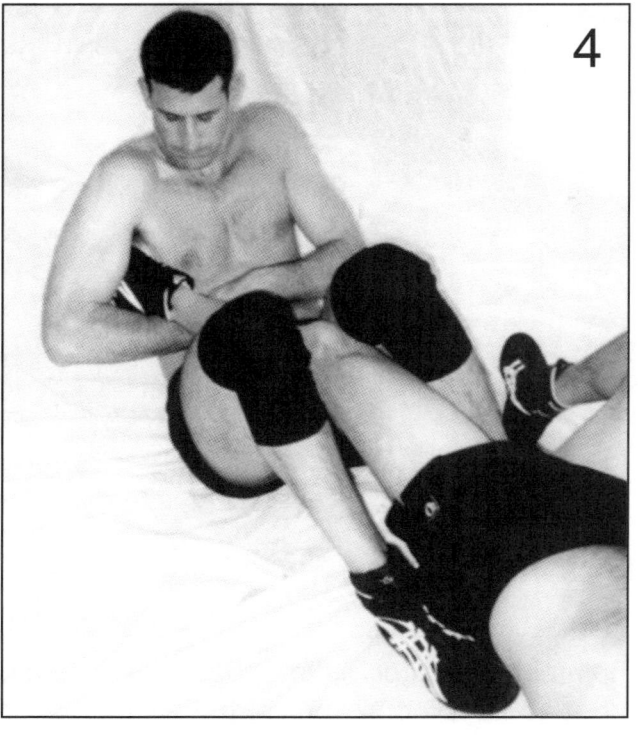

Sit back and squeeze your knees together, securing his trapped leg. Clasp your hands together and drive the blade of your forearm upwards and into his Achilles tendon for the submission.

ANKLE LOCK *Standing And Sitting*

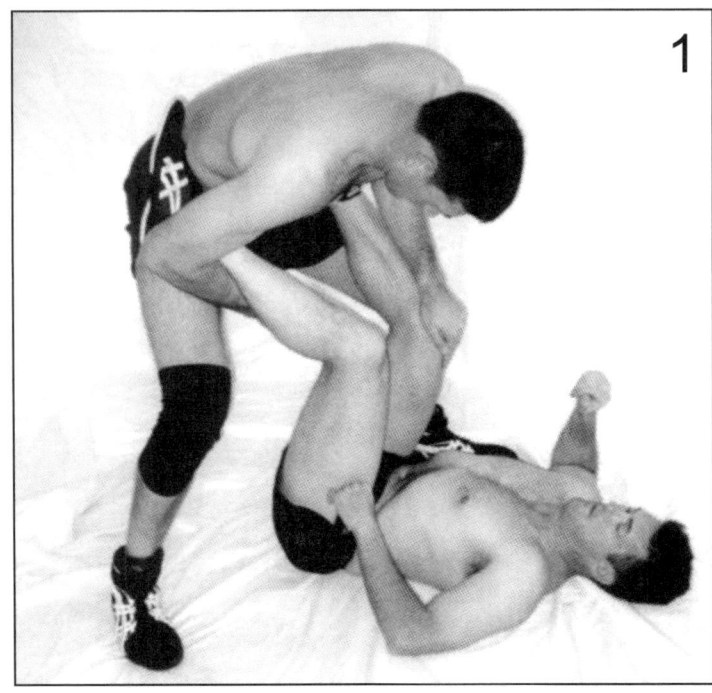

You have one of your opponent's feet trapped with your arm as shown.

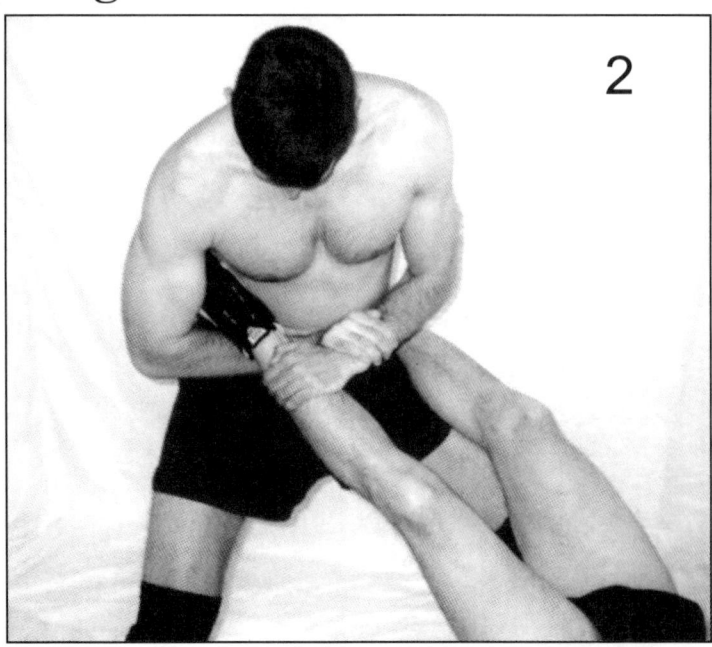

Place your free arm on his shin and then grab your wrist with your other arm, forming a figure four lock. Arch backwards while pushing downwards on his shin to hyper-extend his foot at the ankle for the submission.

Or, maintain control of his trapped foot and place your foot at his tailbone and control his free leg in preparation for sitting down.

Sit away from your opponent and squeeze your knees together to secure his leg. Secure a figure four lock on his leg as shown. Arch your back and push down on his shin to hyper-extend his foot at the ankle for the submission.

ANKLE CRANK *Spin Variation*

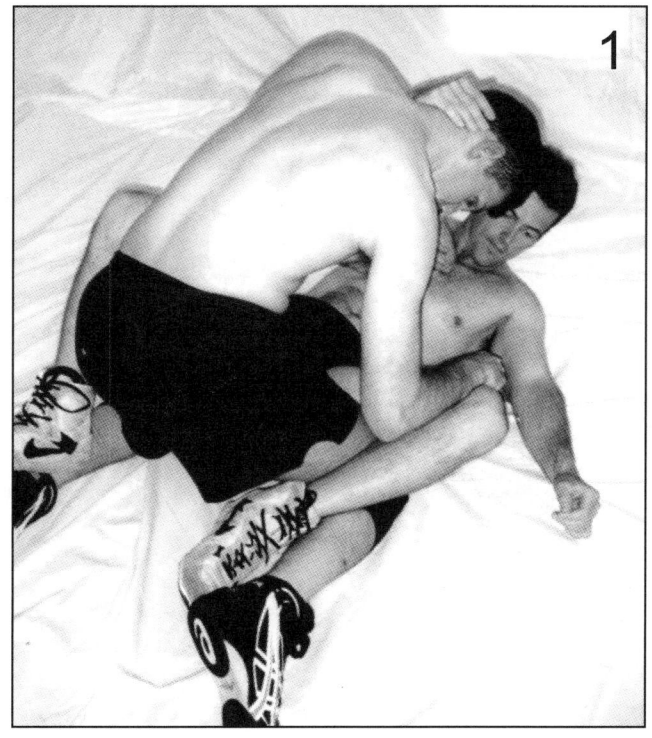

You have broken your opponent's guard. His leg is placed over yours and you are controlling his targeted leg with your arm.

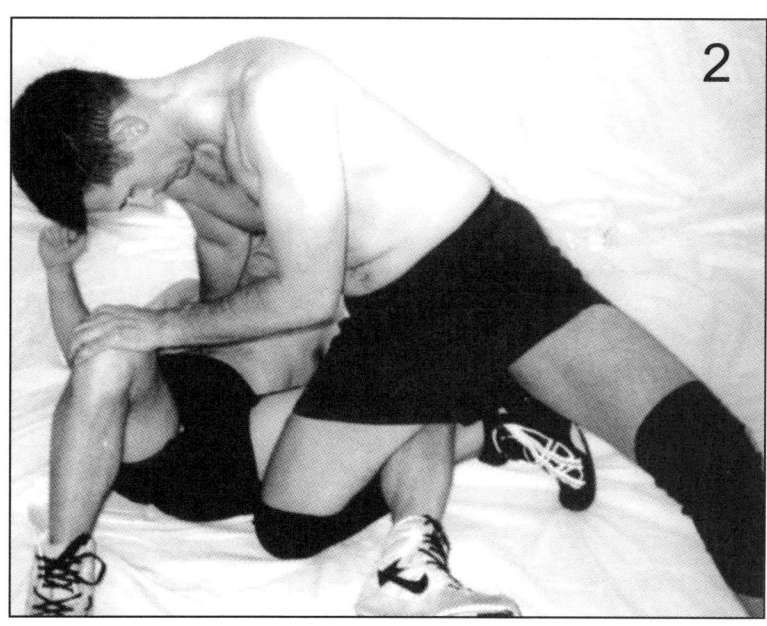

Pivot on your knee, turning your back to your opponent and trapping his targeted leg between your hamstring and calf.

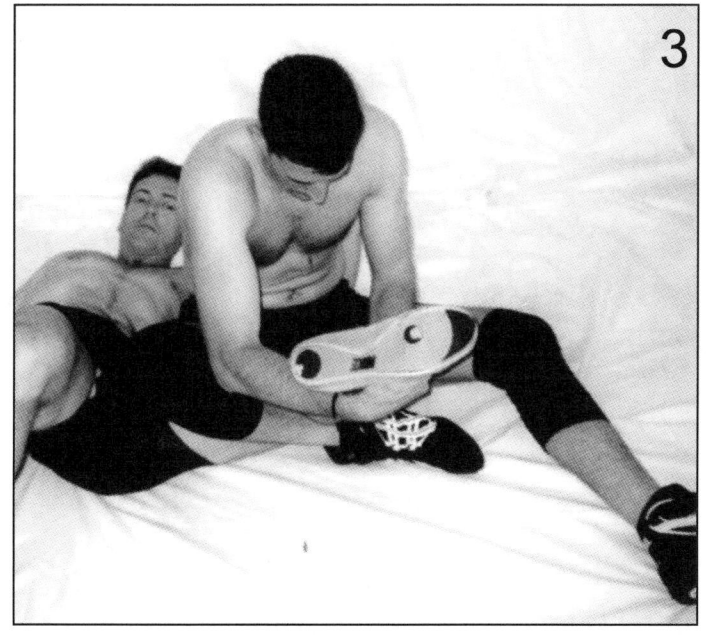

Secure his foot with both hands. Lean forwards to prevent a choke. Place your weight on his upper thigh near his hip, pinning him to the ground.

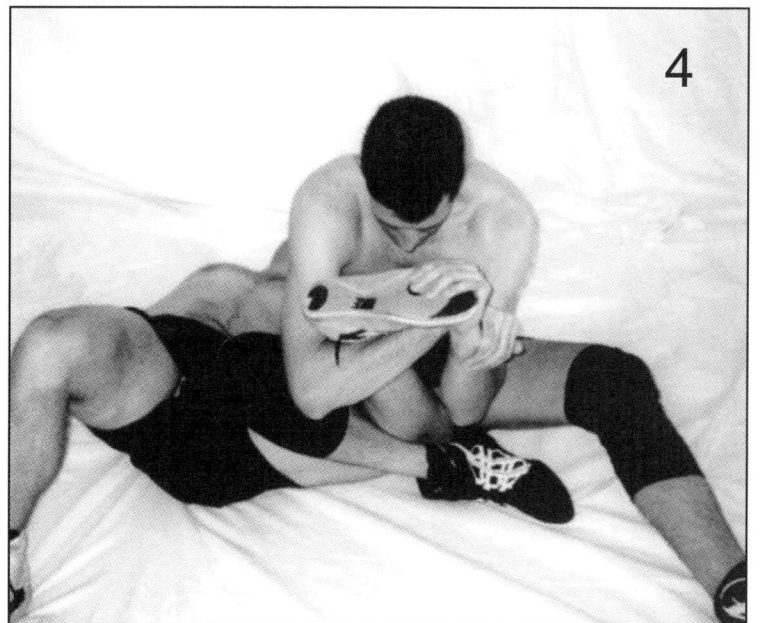

Secure a figure four lock on his foot. One hand is on his toes while the other traps his ankle and grabs your other hand at the wrist. Rotate his toes downwards for the submission. This will use his foot as a lever to torque his leg at the knee for the submission.

ANKLE CRANK

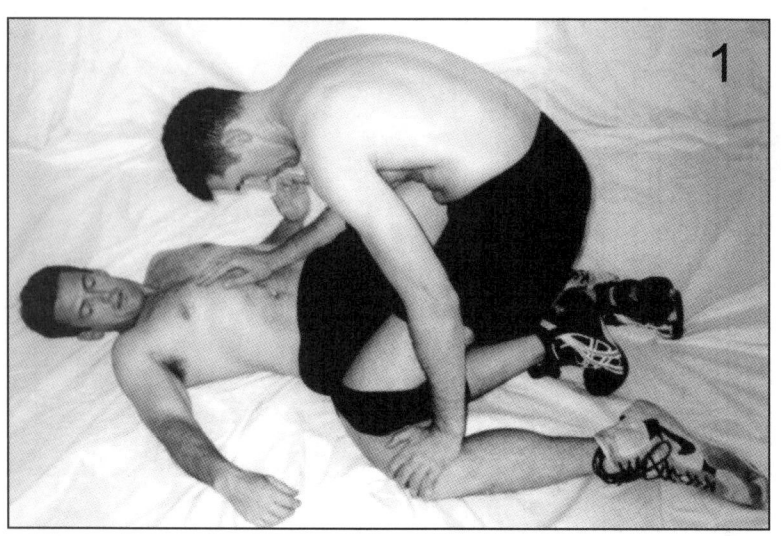

You have broken your opponent's guard and have pinned one of his legs to the ground with your knee and hand as shown.

Drive your other knee across his trapped leg, placing your shin across his upper thigh, near his hip, pinning him to the ground. Bring your other knee back so that you are now straddling his targeted leg.

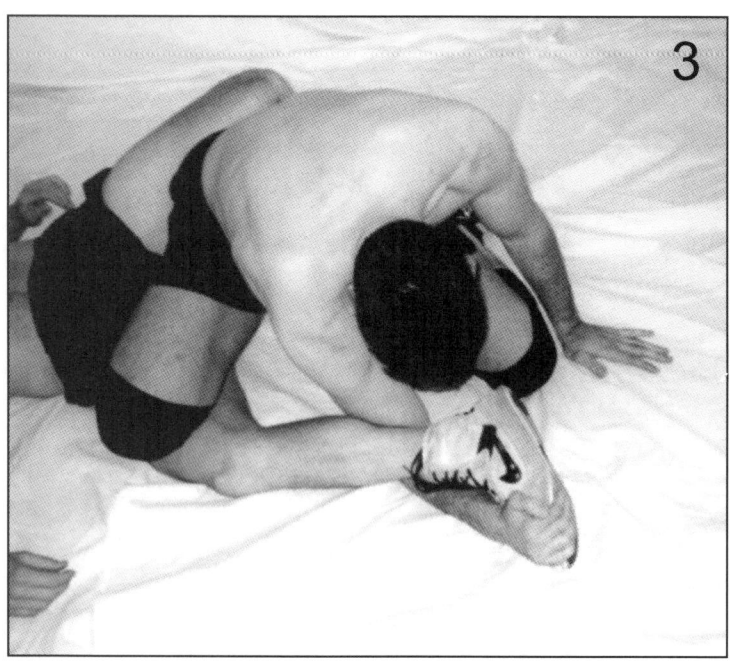

Reach under his shin and grab his foot near his toes and on his instep.

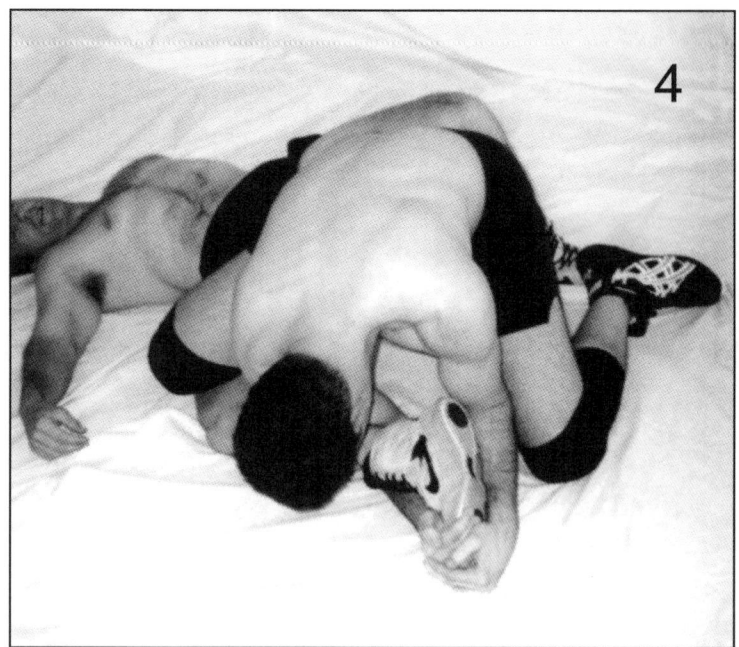

Grab his foot at the toes with your other hand and pull his toes towards you. This will use his foot as a lever to torque his leg at the knee for the submission.

KNEE BAR *From An Ankle Lock*

You have your opponent's leg trapped as shown. You may apply a variety of foot attacks from this position or transition to a knee bar. (Left)

Bring your leg back so your knee is propped underneath his calf, close to his ankle. Your other leg remains over his leg, near the top of his knee. (Right)

To execute the technique, drive your knee that is under his calf upwards; you can assist by pulling up on his ankle with your hand. Lean towards him and drive your other leg downwards, you can grab him behind the neck to help pull yourself into him. This movement puts pressure on his leg at the knee and threatens to hyper-extend his leg for the submission. (Left)

KNEE BAR *Step Over*

You have secured one of his legs at the foot and you are controlling his other, pushing it towards the ground.

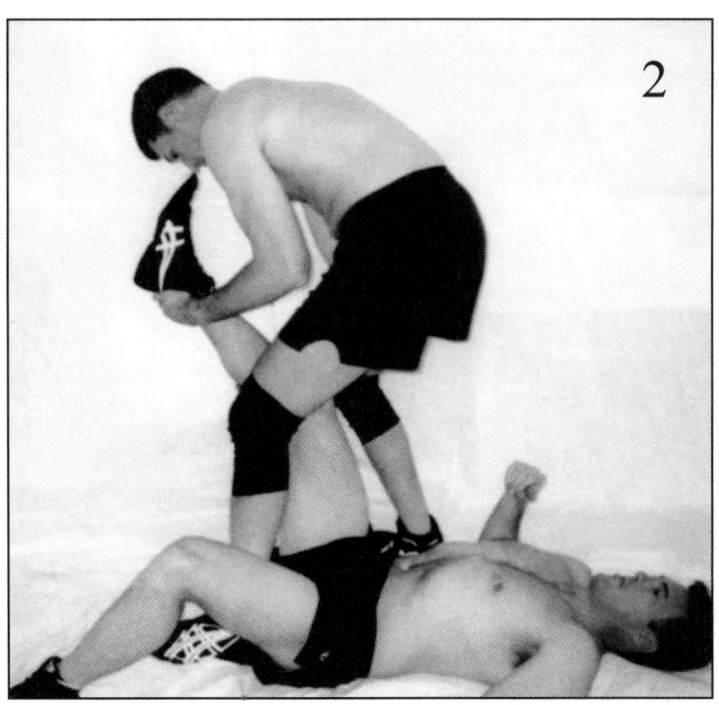

Step through his legs and maintain your control of his foot. You are now straddling his leg and have your back towards him.

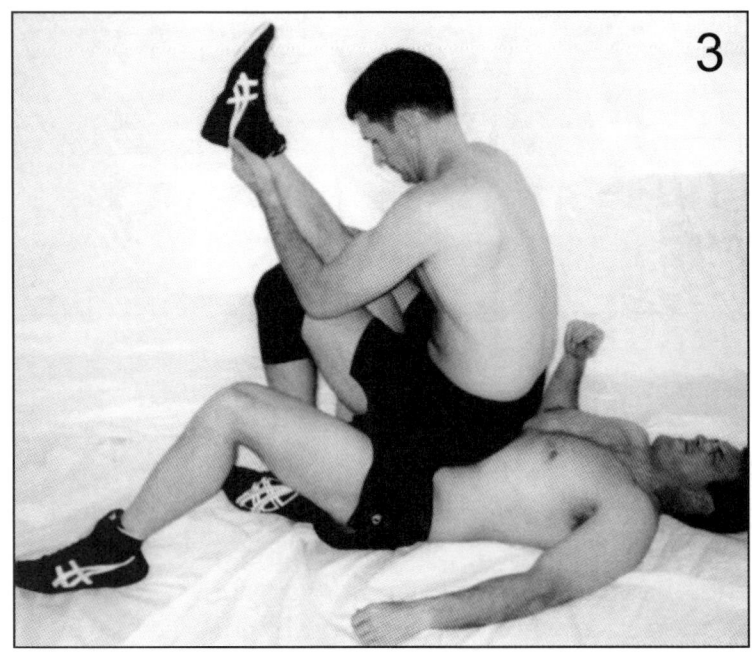

Hug his leg with both arms and sit down on his groin, keeping your own groin as close and tight to his upper leg as you can. (Ideally, you want to stay as low and close to his groin as you can when you step through.)

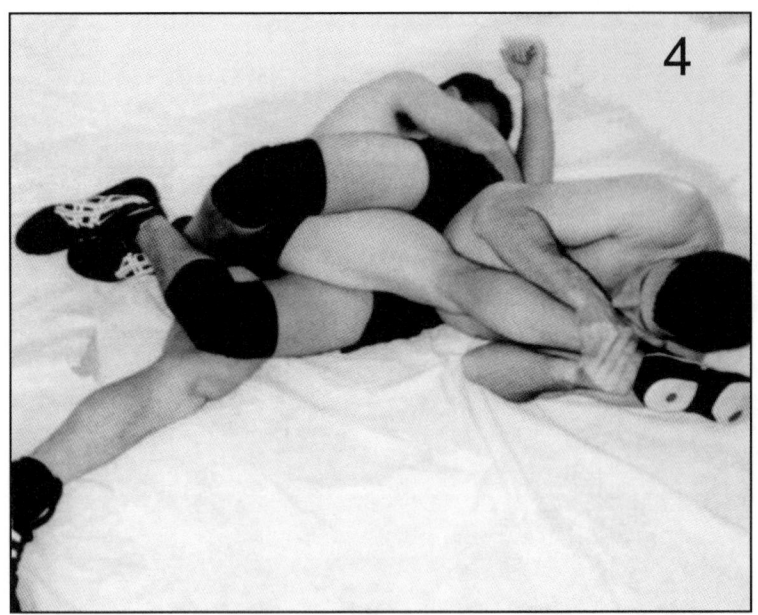

Fall across his body and onto your side, pinning him to the ground. Ensure your groin is just above his knee cap, closer to his groin. Drive your heels into his buttocks, hug his foot tight to your chest, and arch your hips forwards. This will hyper-extend his leg at the knee for the submission.

DOUBLE KNEE BAR

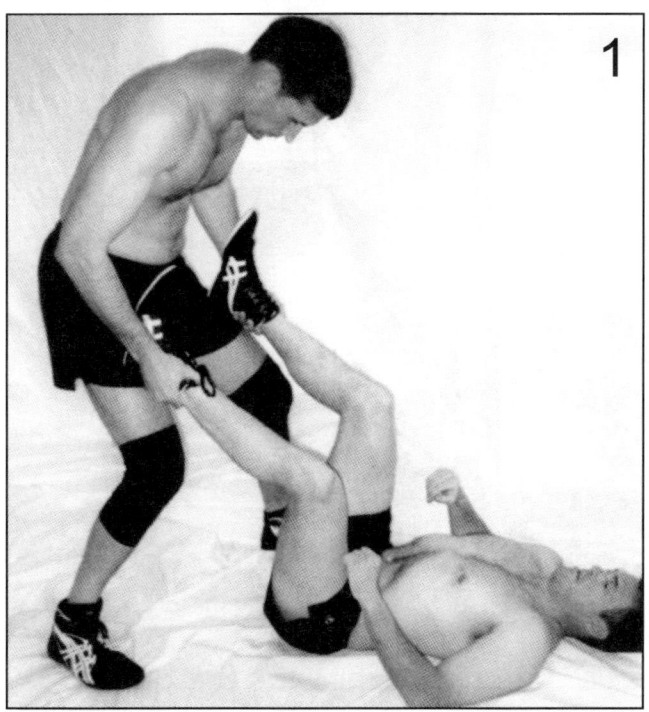

You have some distance between you and your opponent and you are controlling his feet at the ankles as shown.

Hug his feet, squeezing them together, and place them over your shoulder.

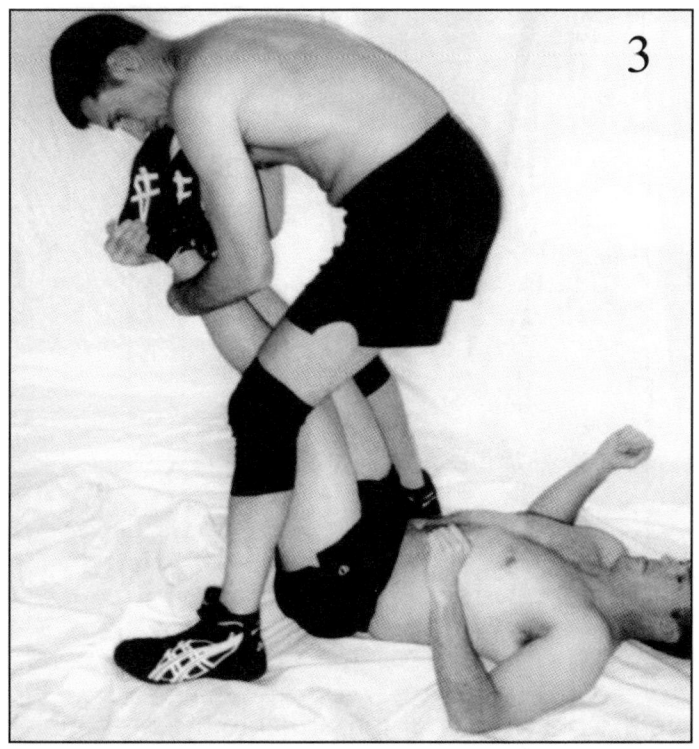

Step over his legs so that you are now straddling his legs and have your back towards him.

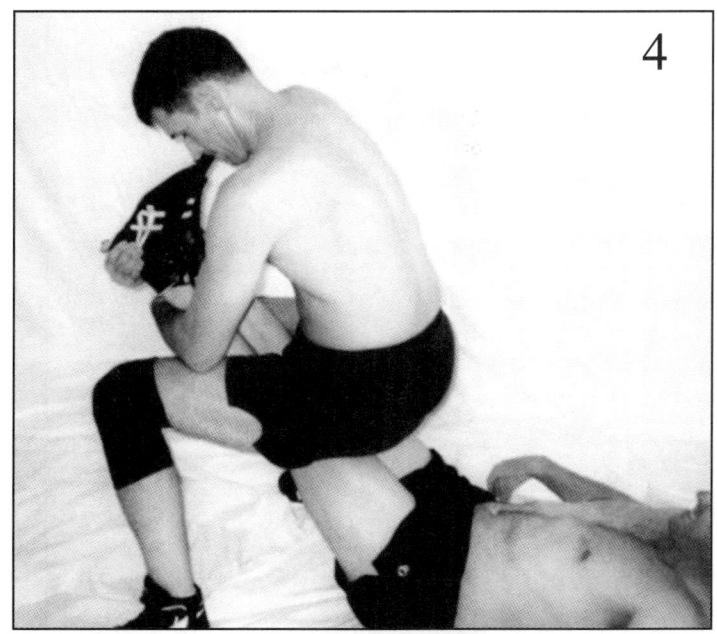

Sit just above his knee caps, closer to his groin. Maintain your hug on his feet, holding them at the ankles. Drop your hips and place weight on his legs while pulling up at his ankles. This will hyper-extend his legs at the knees for the submission.

KNEE BAR *Straight Knee*

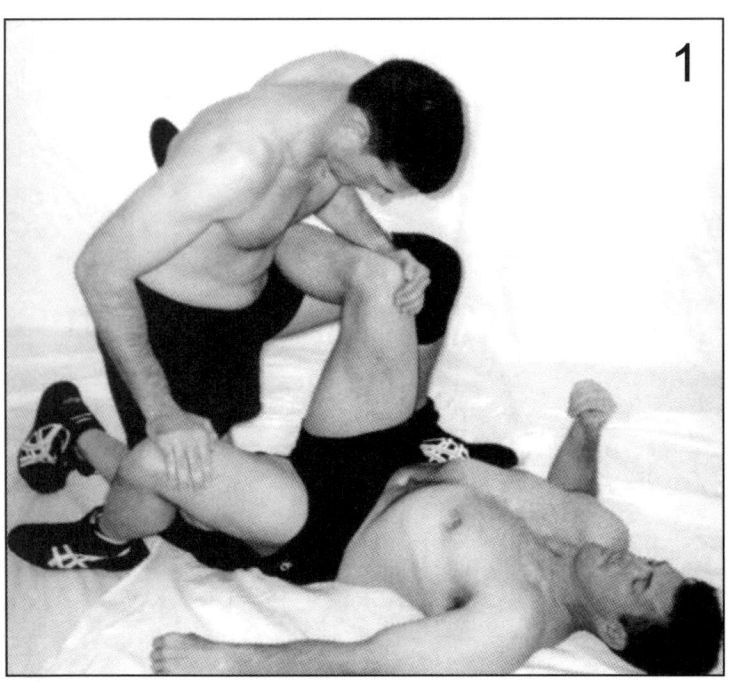

You are controlling one of your opponent's legs, pushing it towards the ground. His other leg is draped over your leg as shown.

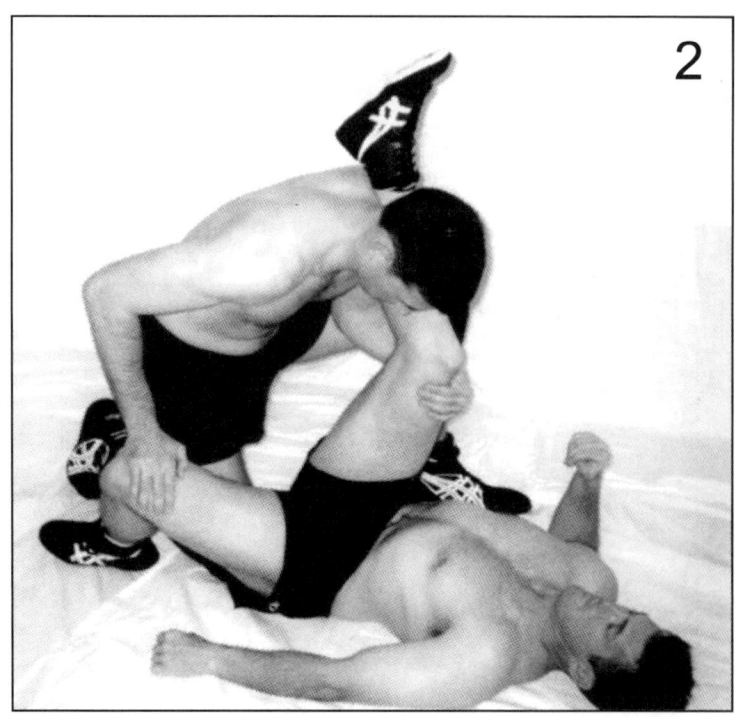

Reach under his raised leg and place it on your shoulder while maintaining control of his other leg.

Drive your knee over his free leg and pin it to the ground.

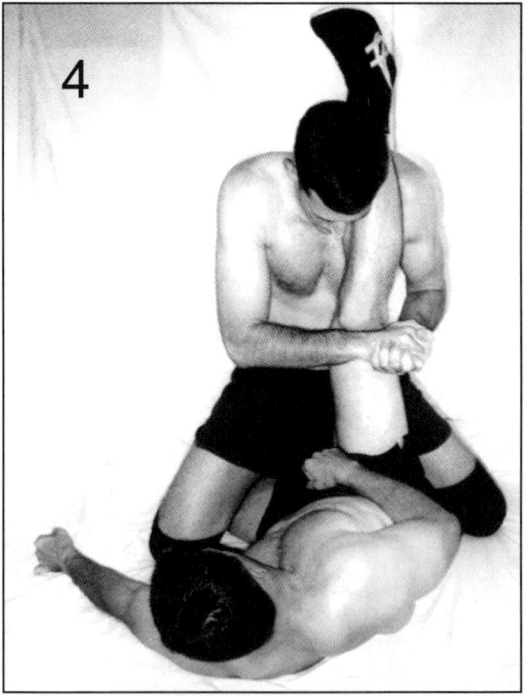

Drive the blade of your forearm into the area just above his knee cap. Push your shoulder forwards, straightening out his leg. Continue to push with your shoulder and pull with your arms until you hyper-extend his leg at the knee for the submission.

SQUEEZE LOCK

Secure his leg with your arm going under his leg at the knee joint. (Left)

Step over with one leg, placing it across his groin. Place the other leg over his ankle and sit back, securing his leg as you sit. Notice how his leg is trapped between your legs. (Right)

Hook your foot behind your other leg's knee. Ensure that your attacking forearm is pulled deeply and tightly into his knee. If it is not deep enough, the technique will be ineffective. Squeeze your knees together and try to drive his heel to his buttocks. Pull up with your hands and drive the blade of your forearm into his knee joint until he submits. (Left)

GROIN STRETCH

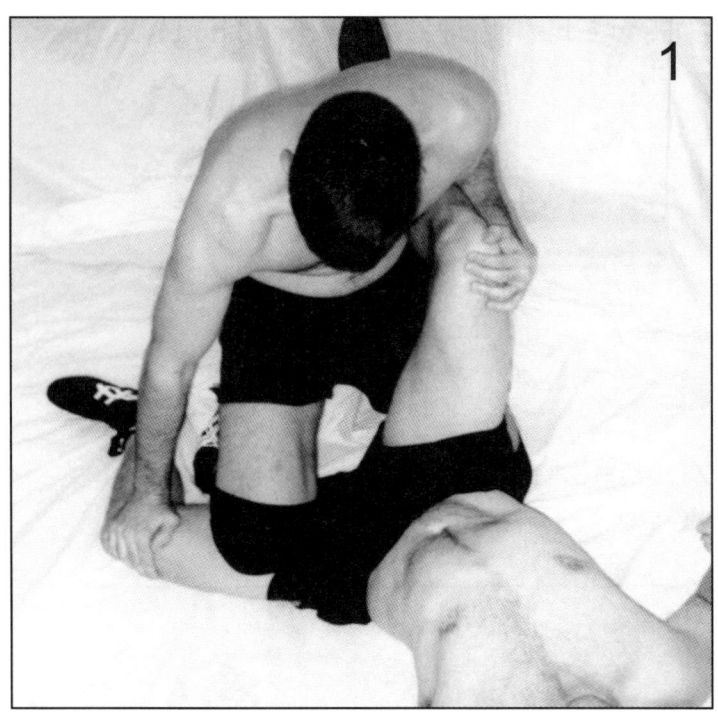

Pin one of your opponent's legs to the ground with your knee and hand as shown.

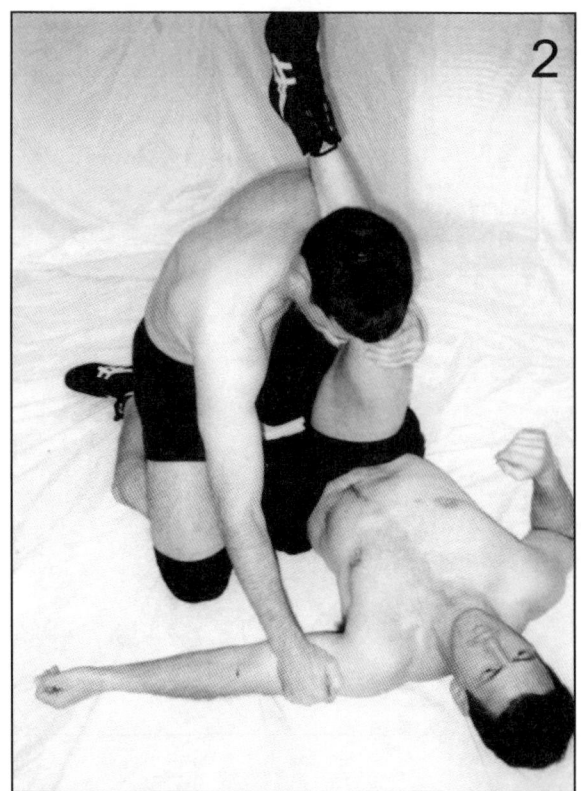

Drive your knee over his leg and pin his leg to the ground. Reach under his free leg so it is on your shoulder.

Turn your hips so that you are facing across his body. Hook a hand behind his neck and the other on his shoulder.

Drive your shoulder forwards and try to place his knee besides his own head. Unless he is exceptionally flexible, you will put pressure on his groin muscles, threatening to tear them, for the submission.

Chapter Six

Submissions From The Half Guard And In The Half Guard

Half Guard

You are controlling your opponent's leg so he can not mount you. Also, he can not post with this leg if you try to reverse him on that side.

Your arm is hooked under his. This prevents him from attacking your legs and allows you to escape and take his back.

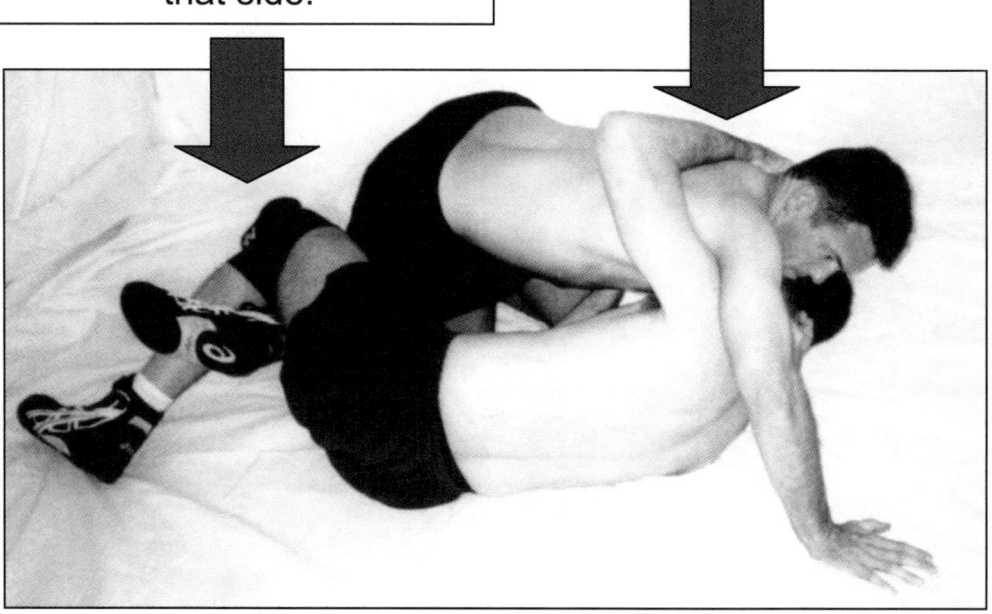

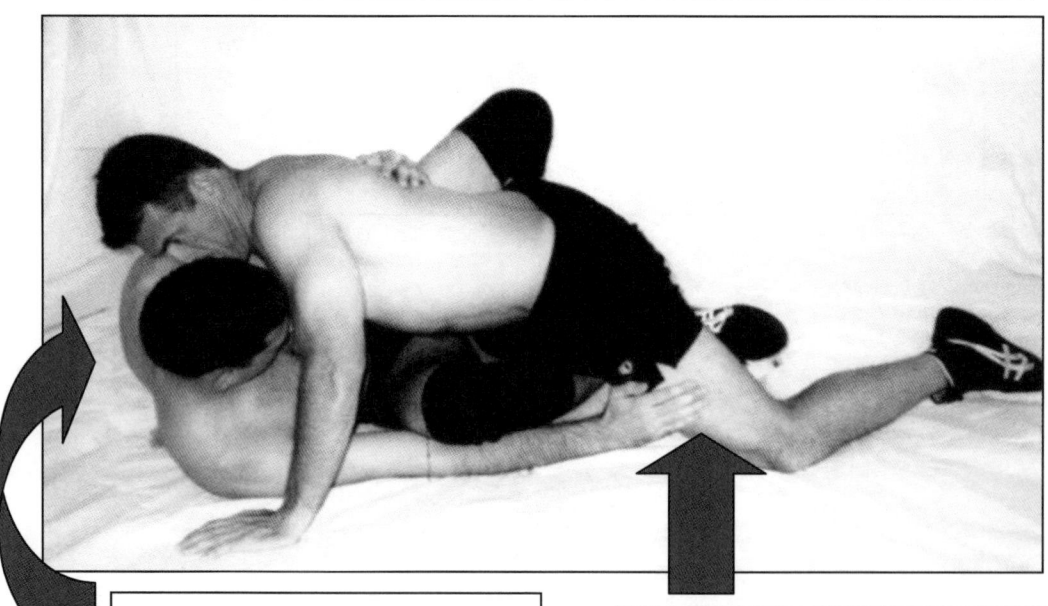

Your head is in tight to his body, making it difficult for him to attack your neck and control your body positioning.

You can try and roll your opponent to the side, forcing him to post out with his arm and leg. When he posts, bring him back into your full guard.

KNEE LEVER

You have your opponent in the half guard. There is space between the two of you.

Secure his arm at the wrist and the elbow.

Bring his arm across your body and then reach under his arm, bypassing his upper body.

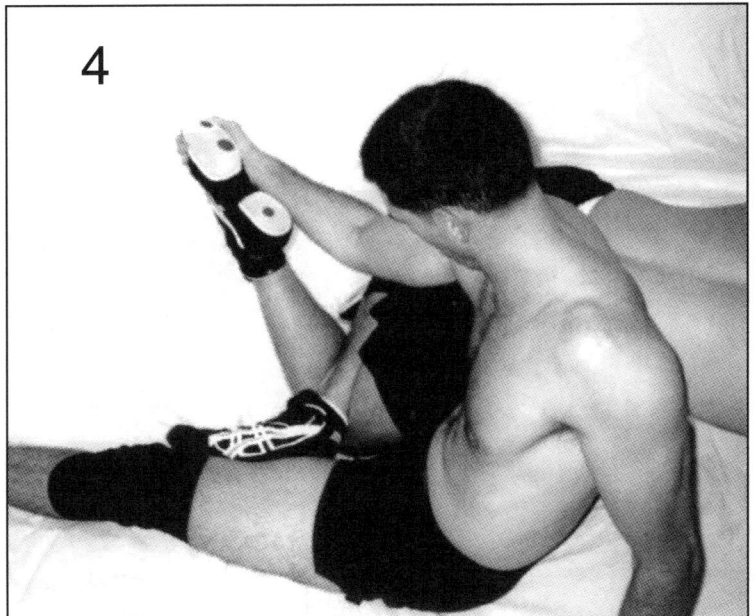

Grab his trapped leg at the foot. Pull his foot forwards, attempting to place his heel against his own buttocks. Keep your shin firmly against the back of his knee and deep in his joint. Pull until he submits or his knee separates at the joint.

KNEE BAR

Grab your opponent under his arms and drive him forwards and over your head.

Place your near arm between his legs.

You are essentially bear hugging his leg. Ensure your groin is slightly above his kneecap, closer to his groin. Plant your feet firmly on the ground, trapping his lower leg. Arch your hips to hyperextend his leg at the knee for the submission.

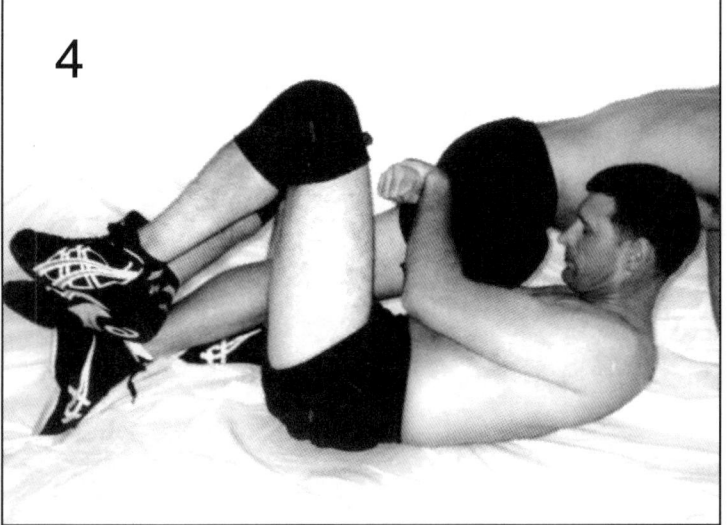

People with shorter legs can plant both feet on the ankle of his targeted leg. Drive your feet downwards on his lower leg while you arch your hips for the submission.

ANKLE CRANK

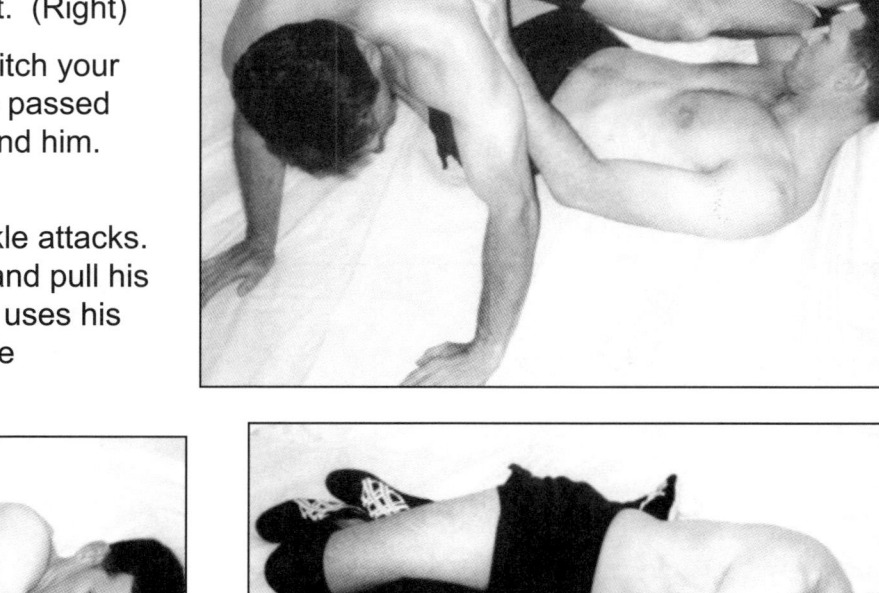

You have your opponent in half guard. (Top)

Push his arm across his body. (Top Right)

Hook your arm under his leg at the foot. (Right)

Bring his leg over your body as you switch your hips and rotate to your side. You have passed yourself between his legs and are behind him. (Bottom Right)

You can finish him with a variety of ankle attacks. Here, grab his instep with both hands and pull his toes down and towards his body. This uses his foot as a lever to torque his knee for the submission. (Bottom)

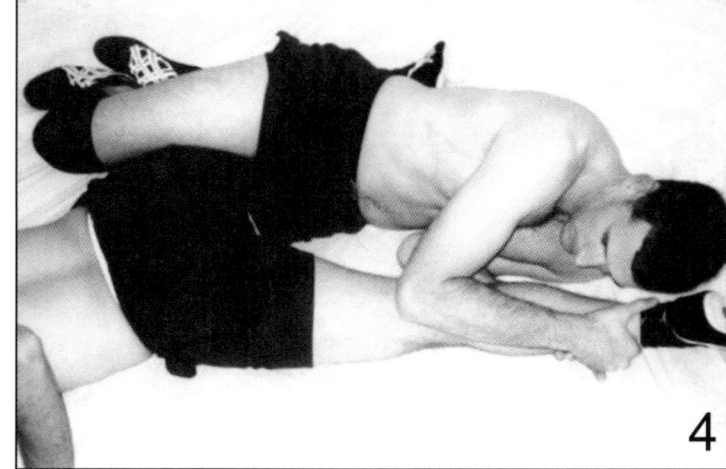

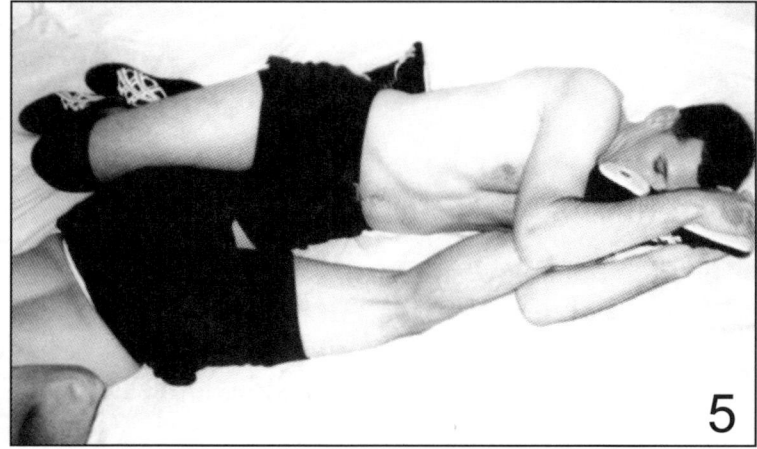

85

IN HALF GUARD – ANKLE CRANK

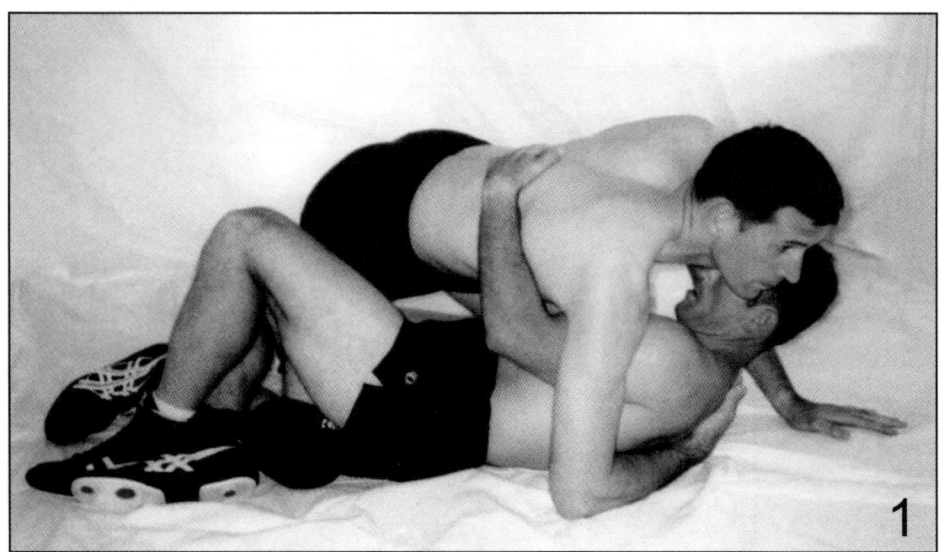

Your opponent has you in his half guard. (left)

Control his head and push his arm across his body. (Right)

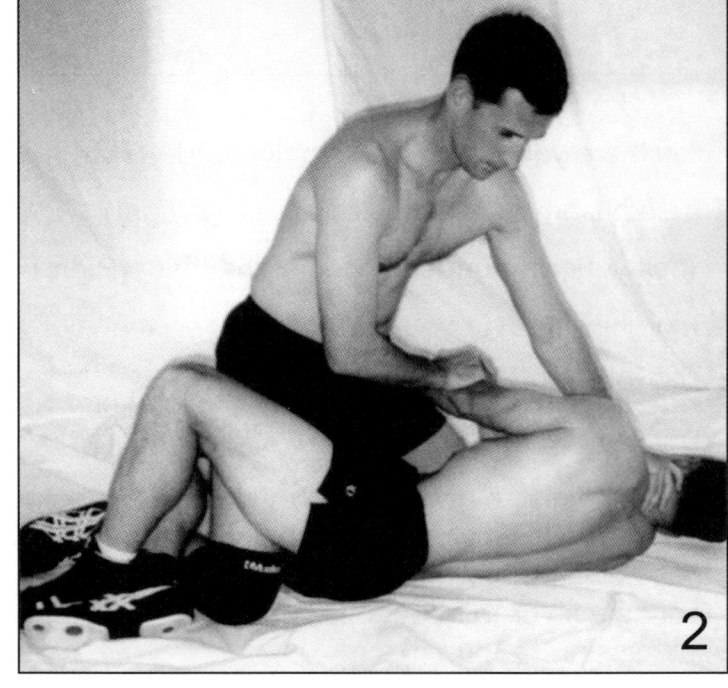

Reach back and grab his heel and the blade of his foot near his toes. Pull up on his heel and push down on his blade, using his foot as a lever to torque his knee for the submission. (Left)

KNEE BAR

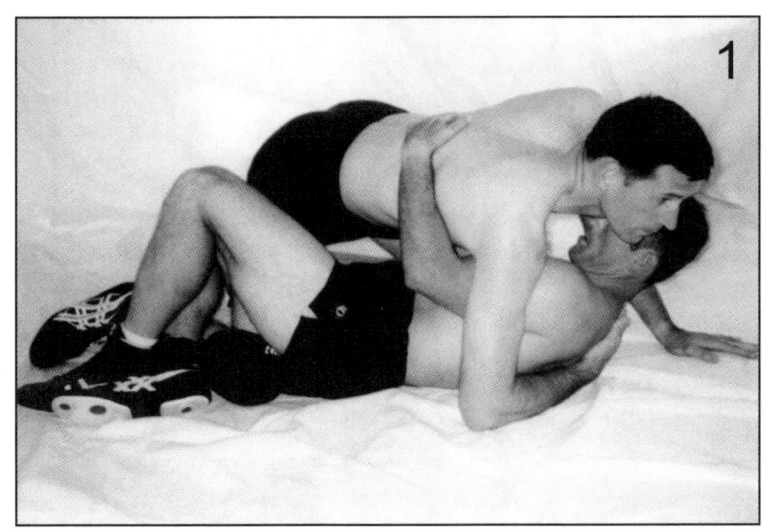

Your opponent has you in his half guard.

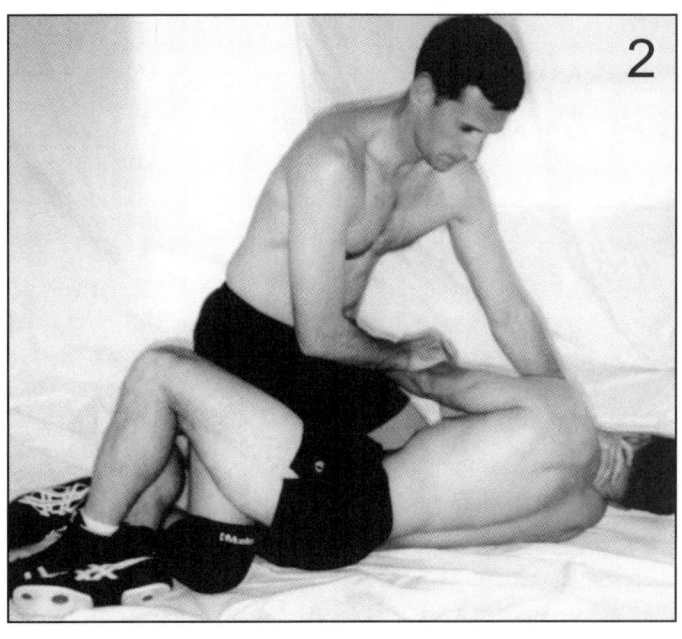

Control his head and push his arm across his body.

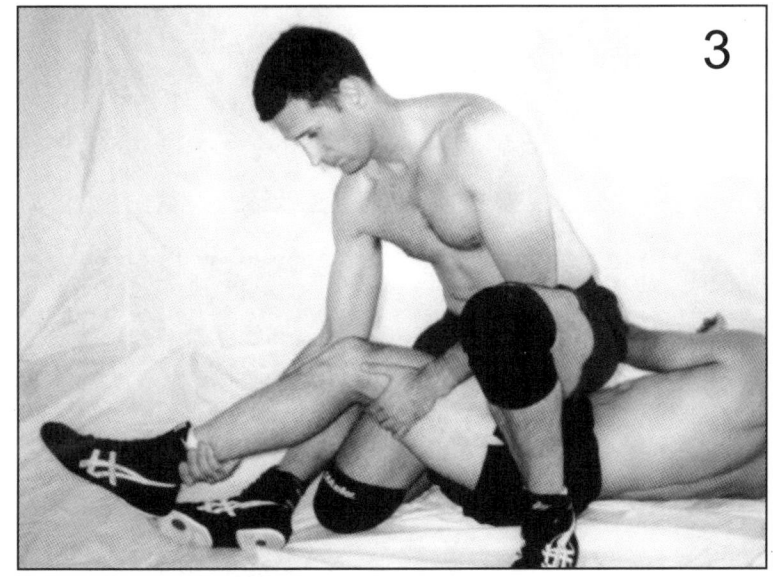

Step over his body and secure his targeted leg.

Fall to your side with his leg secured tightly. Drive your feet into his buttocks, arch your hips, and pull his foot into your chest. This hyper-extends his leg at the knee for the submission.

SQUEEZE LOCK

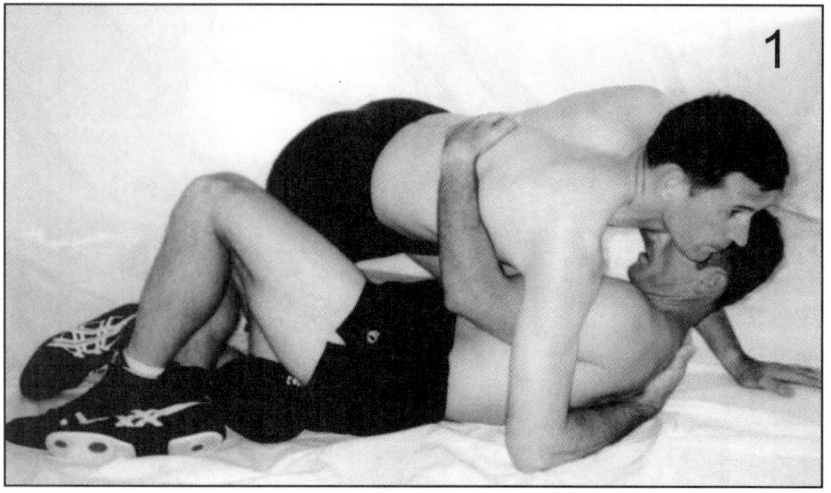

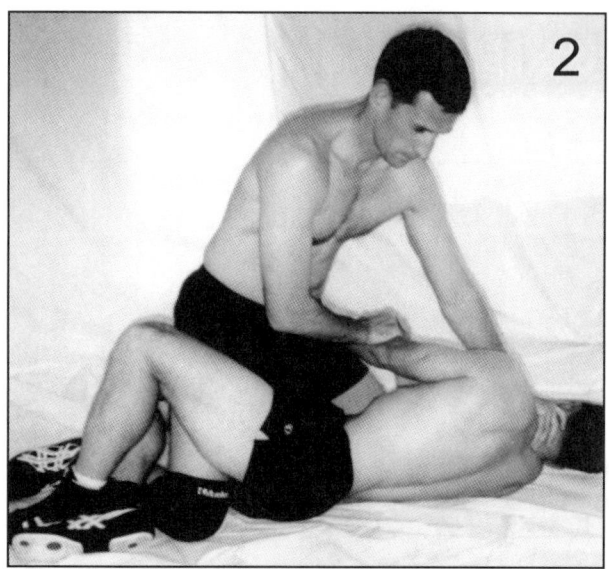

Your opponent has you in his half guard. (Top)

Control his head and push his arm across his body. (Top Right)

Step over his body and secure his leg behind his knee. (Right)

Bring your leg over his shin; maintain your grip behind his knee. (Bottom Right)

Hook the foot of your leg behind the knee of your other leg, trapping his leg. Squeeze your knees together and attempt to place the heel of his trapped foot to his own buttocks. Clasp your hands and pull the blade of your forearm up and into his knee joint. This move attempts to separate his knee joint for the submission. (Bottom)

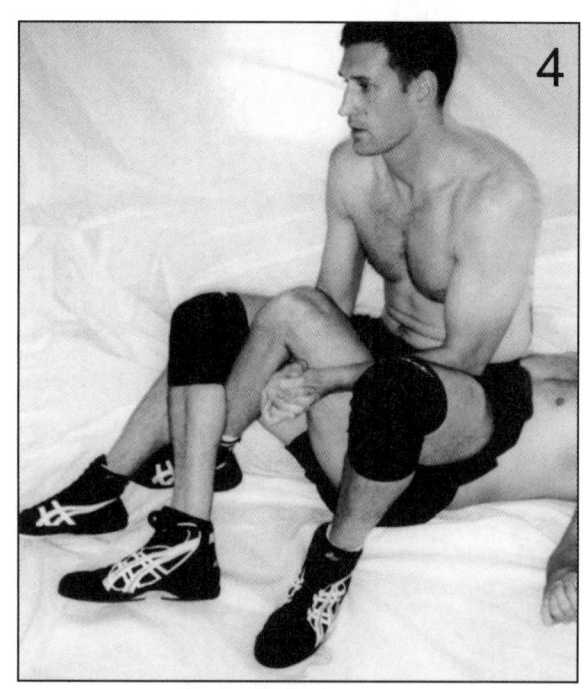

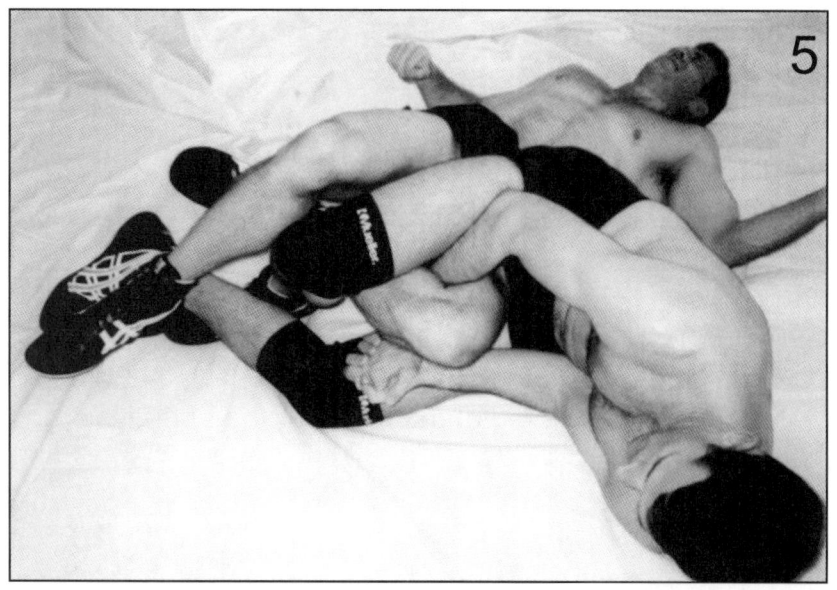

KNEE LEVER

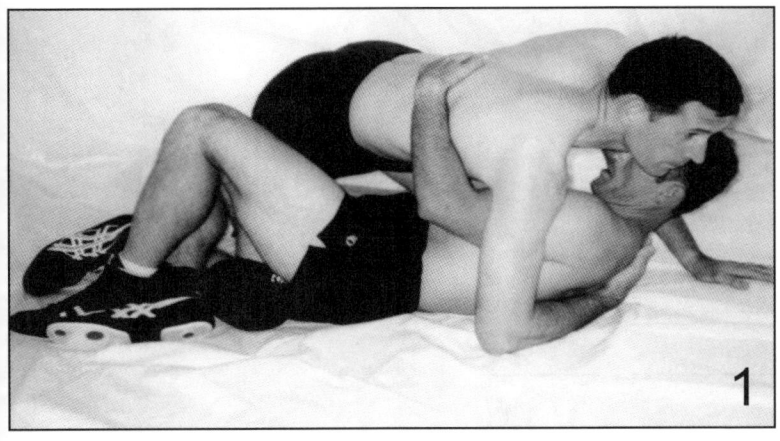

Your opponent has you in his half guard.

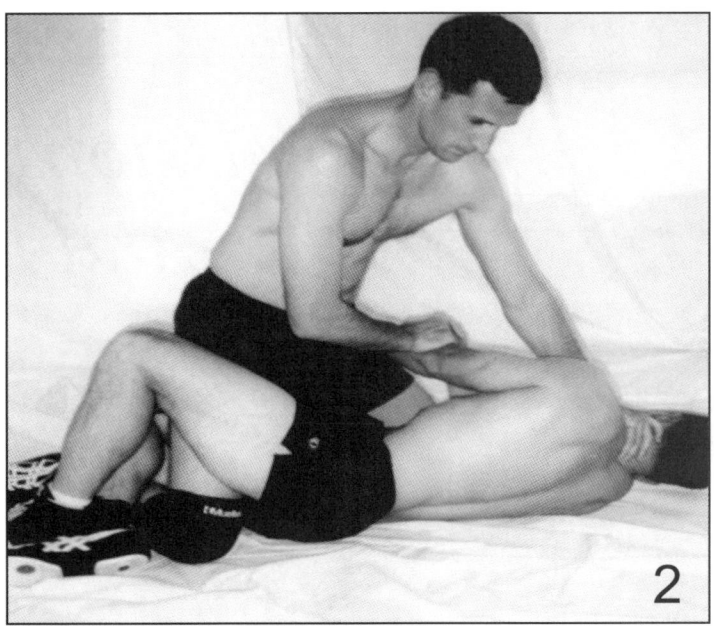

Control his head and push his arm across his body.

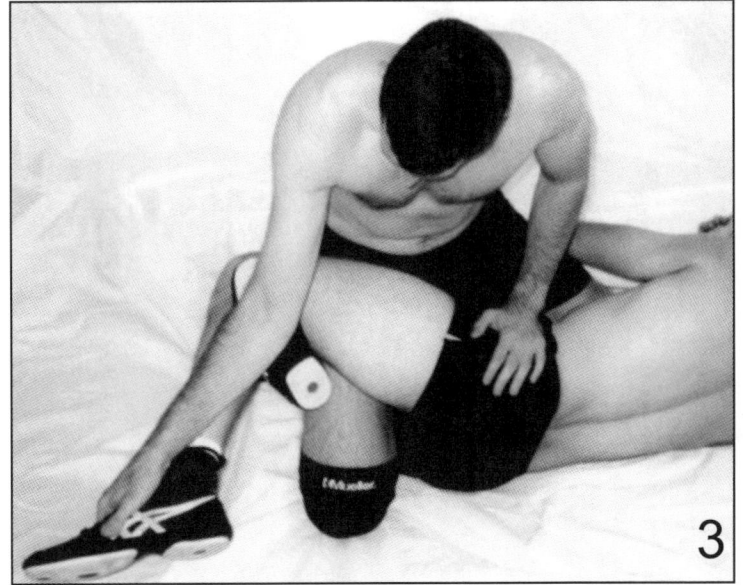

Secure his targeted foot at the instep. Ensure that your elbow is placed against the sole of his other foot to help prevent him unhooking his legs.

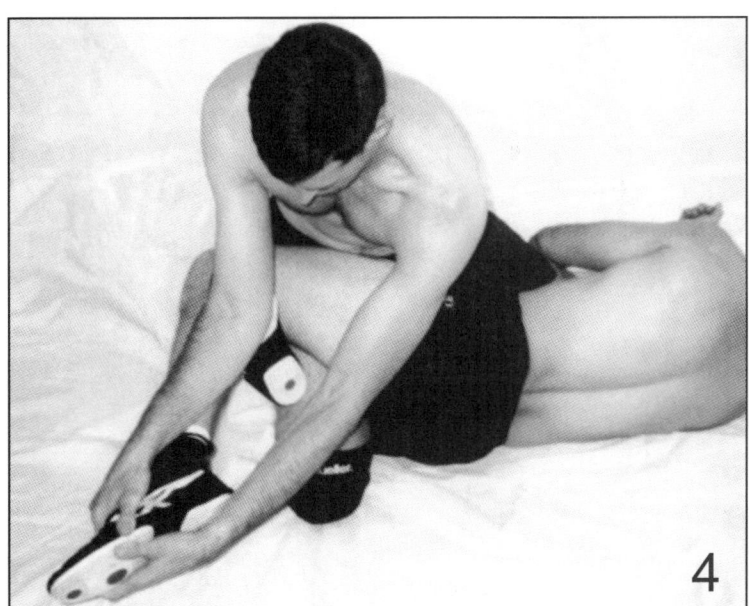

Grab his foot with your other arm and pull his foot backwards, attempting to place the heel of his foot against his buttocks. This technique attempts to separate the knee joint for the submission.

Chapter Seven
Submissions From The Mount And In The Mount

The Mount

The person who is mounted must ensure he keeps a stable base for he may be reversed relatively easily if he is not technically sound.

Keep your head tight to his and press your chest against his. This pins him to the ground and gives you a low center of gravity.

Keep your hips low so that you have a low center of gravity. This will make it harder for him to reverse you.

You can post out with either arm to keep your balance and maintain your position. You can use this arm to attack his arms if he exposes them.

You can hook your feet under his legs to make it harder for him to bridge or push you off of him. Keep the insteps of your feet against the ground; this prevents you from injuring a knee if you get rolled to the side.

NECK CRANK *Figure Four Lock*

You are mounted on your opponent and you have your attacking arm wrapped behind his neck. (Left)

Grab the biceps of your other, locking arm. (Right)

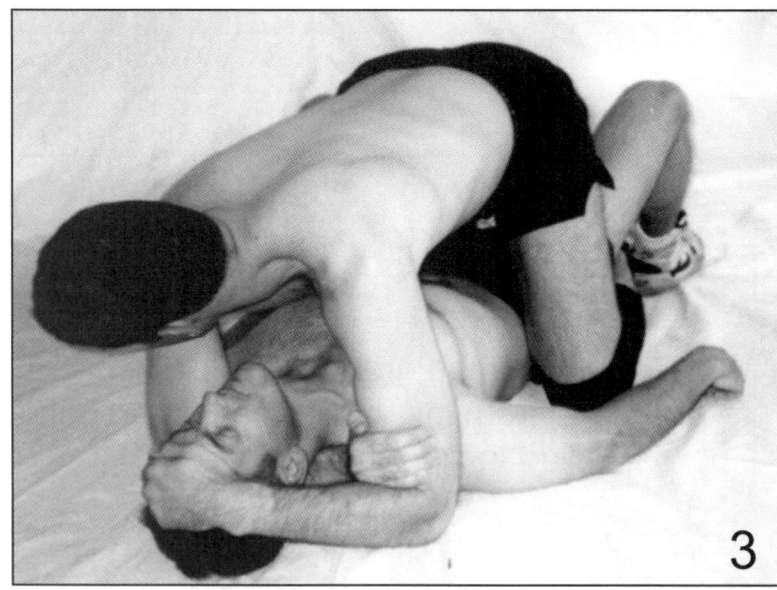

Place your locking hand on his forehead. The higher on his head you are, the more leverage you have. Drive the blade of your bottom, attacking forearm into the base of his neck and push down on his forehead. This will hyper-extend his cervical spine for the submission. (Left)

NECK CRANK *Crucifix*

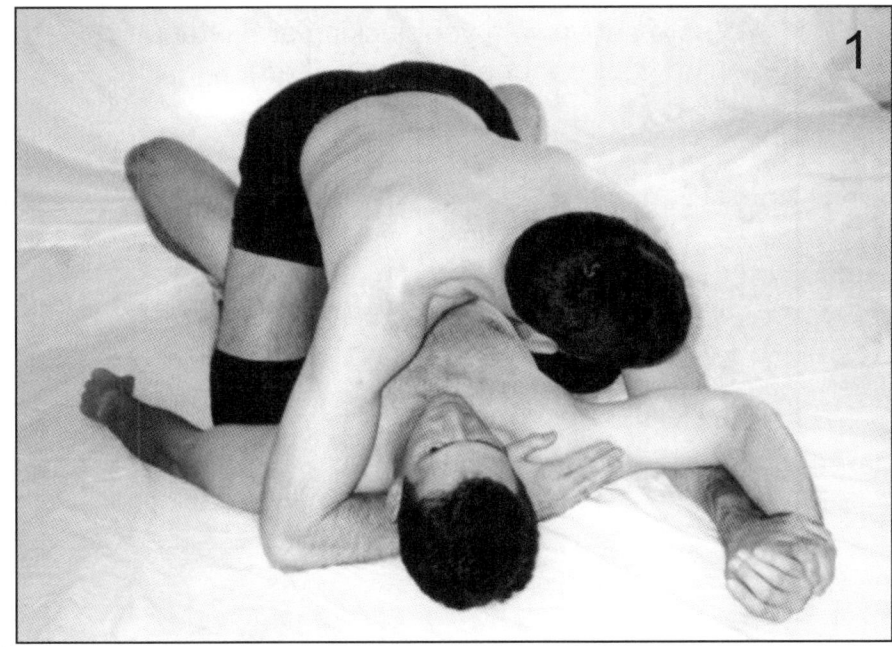

1\. You are set up with one arm wrapped behind your opponent's neck and you are controlling his arm as shown. (Left)

Place your attacking arm behind his neck and hook it arm under his armpit. (Right)

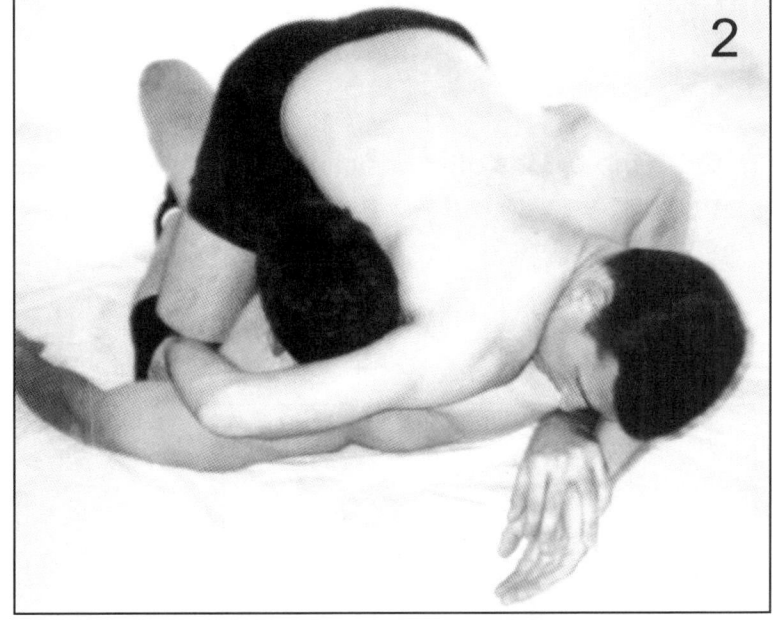

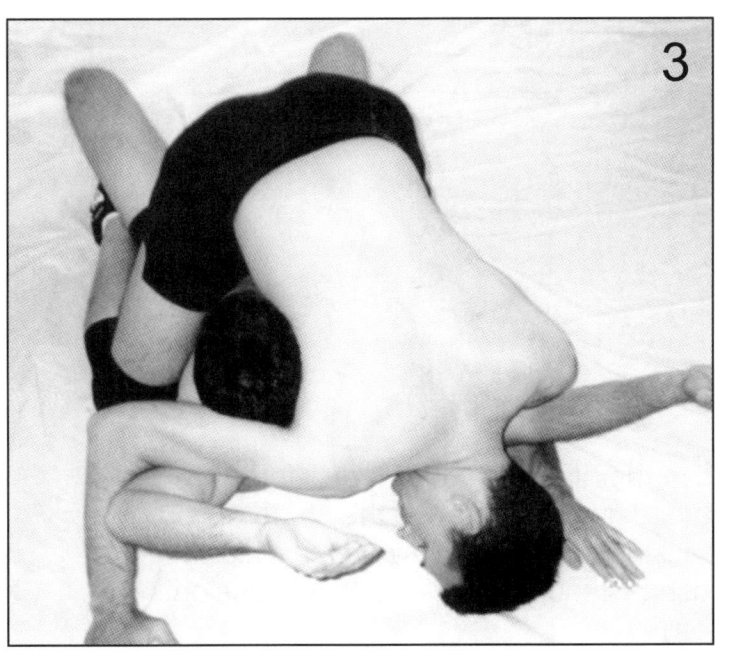

Both of your arms are hooked under his arms, between his armpits and his elbows. Slide your hands forwards while you push his trapped head in the opposite direction with your armpit and shoulder. This will hyper-extend his cervical spine for the submission. (Left)

CHOKE *Scissors*

You are set up with your locking arm wrapped behind your opponent's neck. (Left)

Grab the biceps of your other attacking arm. (Right)

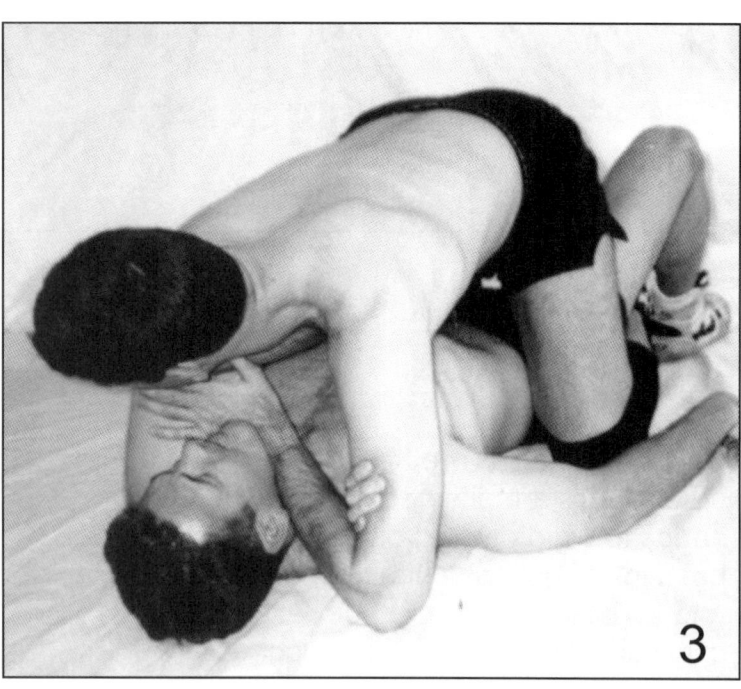

Drive the blade of your locking forearm upwards while you drive the blade of your attacking forearm downwards. This will crush his esophagus for the submission. (Left)

CHOKE *Forearm with Under hook*

You have your opponent set up with one arm hooked under his as shown.

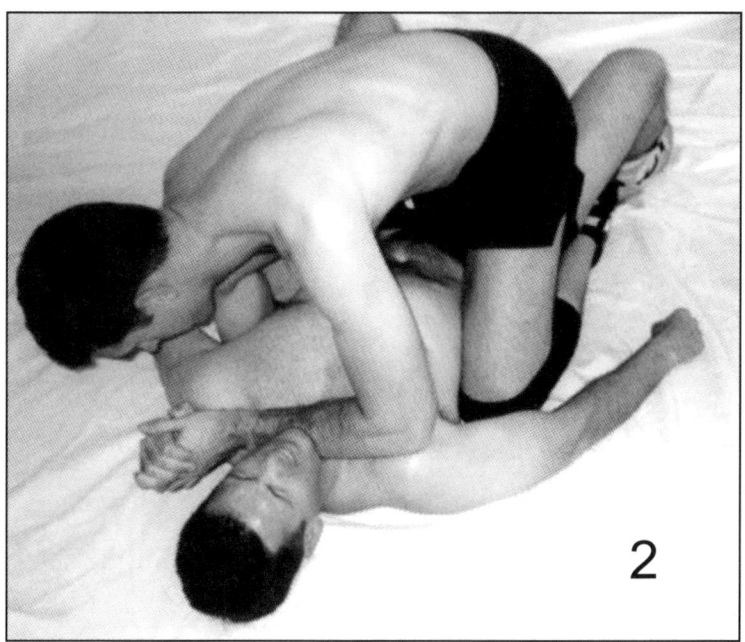

Clasp your hands together and keep them pressed to the ground. Drive your attacking elbow to the ground, forcing the blade of your forearm into his esophagus for the submission.

Entangled Arm Variation

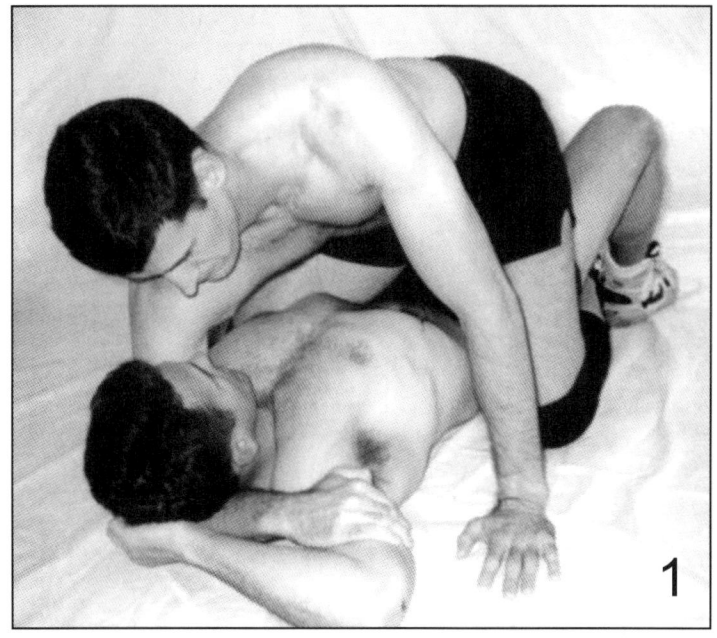

You have an arm entangled behind your opponent's neck and are trapping his arm at the triceps as shown.

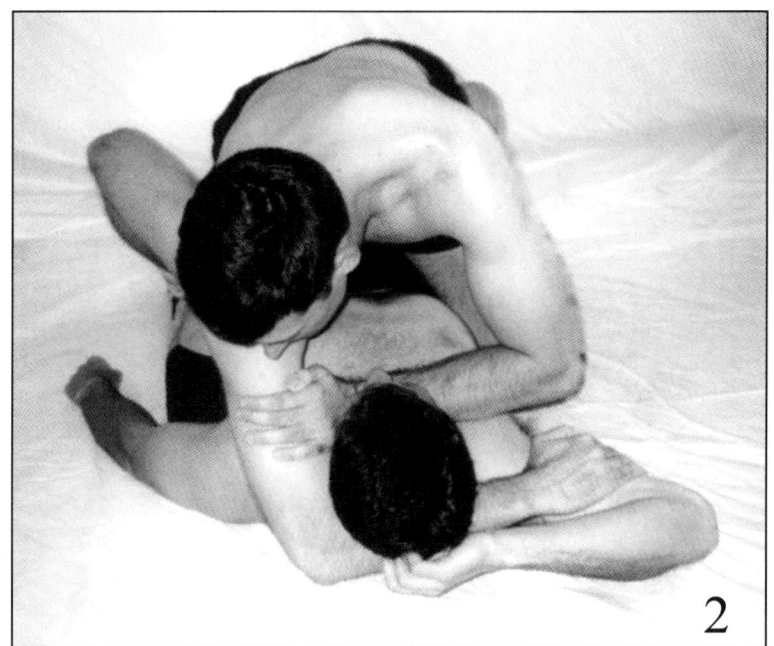

Grab your own arm at the biceps. Drive the blade of your bottom forearm upwards while driving the blade of your top forearm downwards. This will crush his esophagus for the submission.

CHOKE *Guillotine*

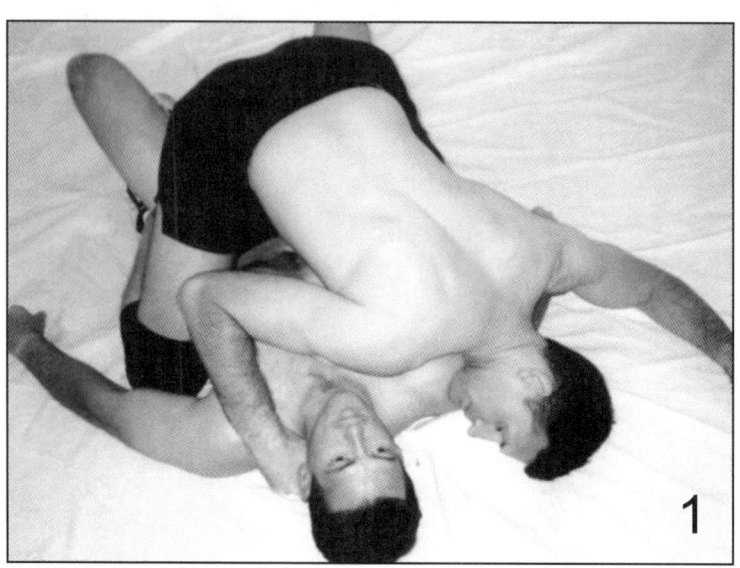

You are set up keeping your base low.

Place your attacking arm behind his neck and bring your forearm across the front of his throat.

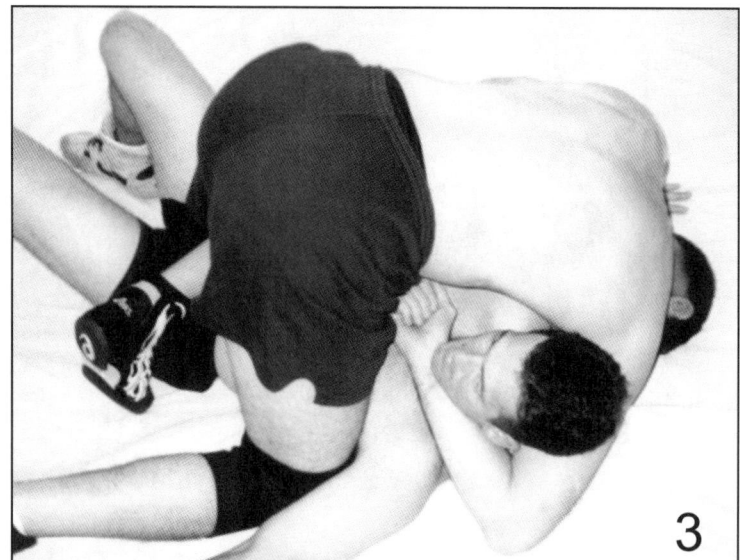

Bring your far leg across his stomach so your shin is pinning him to the ground. Place the weight of your upper body on your head for balance in preparation for sinking the choke.

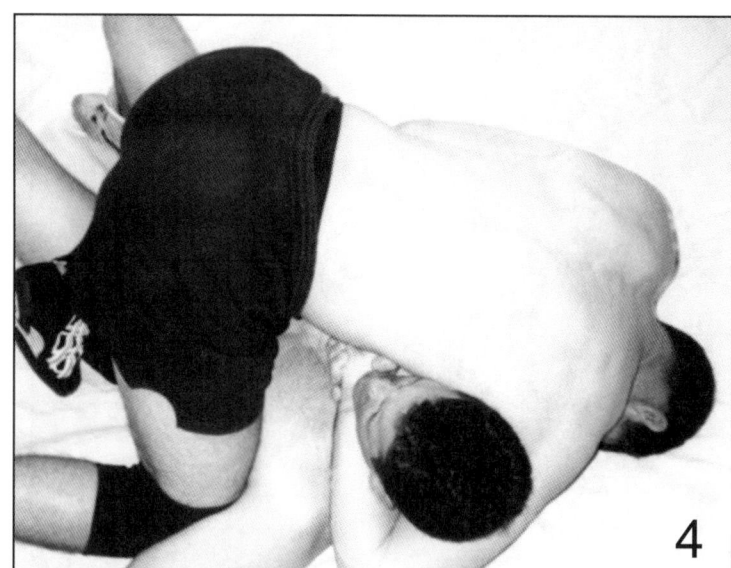

Grab the wrist of your attacking arm and pull the blade of your attacking forearm into his throat for the submission.

CHOKE *Triangle*

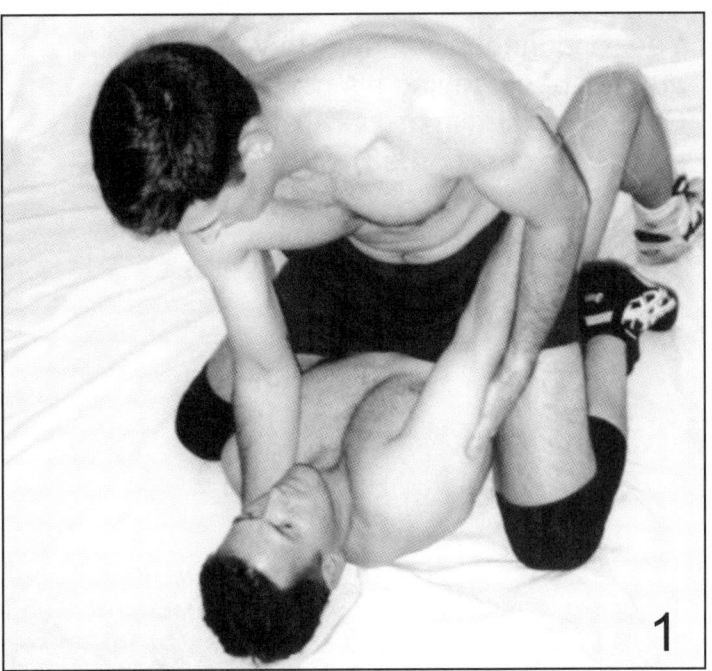

1

You are mounted high on your opponent with your knees under his armpits. You are controlling his head and one arm as shown. He has his other arm under your leg.

2

Maintain control of him with your arms and place your attacking leg behind his neck.

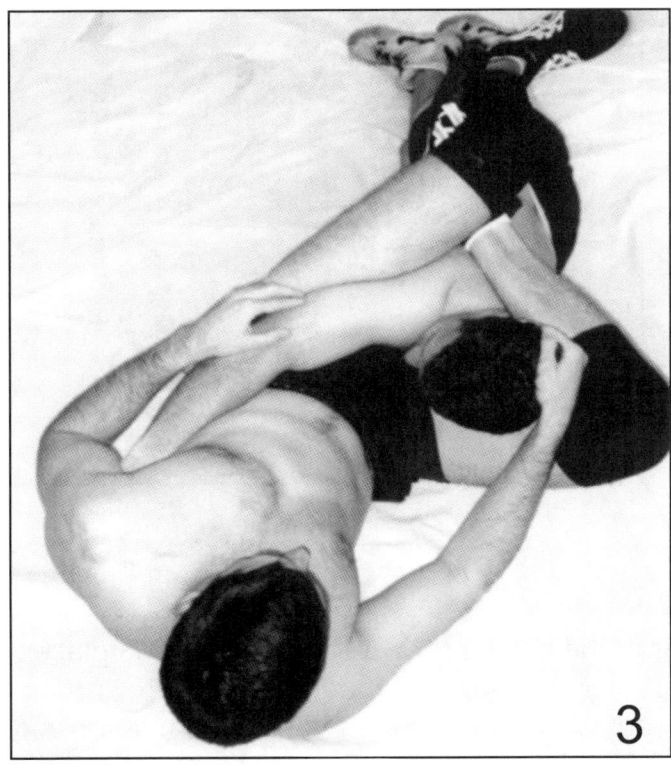

3

Roll to your side so you are now on the ground and hook the foot of your attacking leg behind the knee of your other, locking leg.

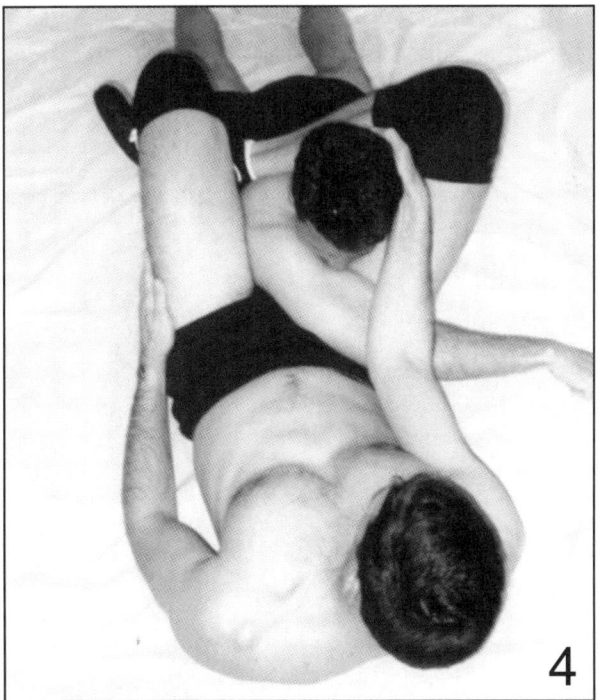

4

Place his arm across his own neck, pull down on the back of his head, and squeeze your knees together. This is a blood choke and will cut off his carotid arteries. Pulling down on his head may cut off his airway, also.

CHOKE *Kata Gatame*

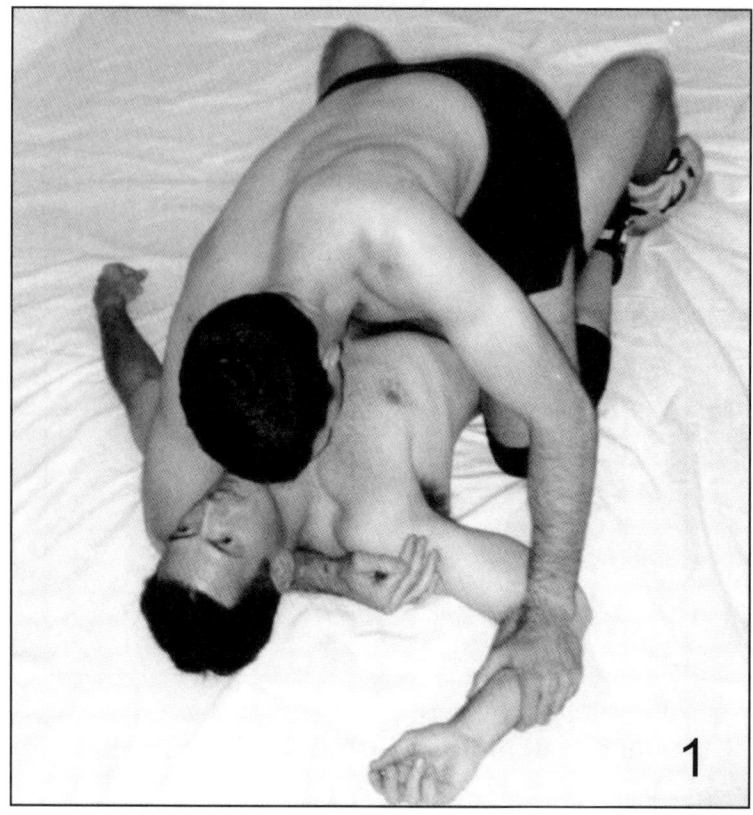

Your opponent is set up with your attacking arm wrapped behind his neck as shown. Control his arm in preparation for pushing it across his chest. (Left)

Push his arm across his chest and place your head tight against him, trapping his arm. (Right)

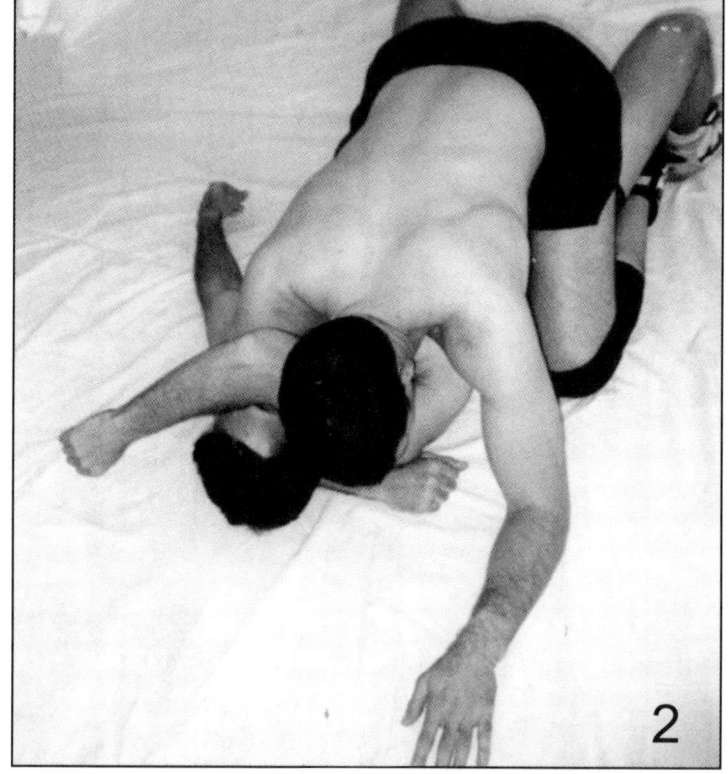

Grab the biceps of your locking arm and place your locking hand on the back of your own head. Drive the blade of your bottom, attacking forearm into the base of his neck and contract the muscles of your arm. This will cut off his carotid arteries and crank his neck for the submission. (Left)

CHOKE *Modified Kata Gatame*

Your opponent is set up with you pushing his exposed arm across his chest. (Left)

Place your attacking arm over his arm and behind his head, trapping his arm between your bodies. (Right)

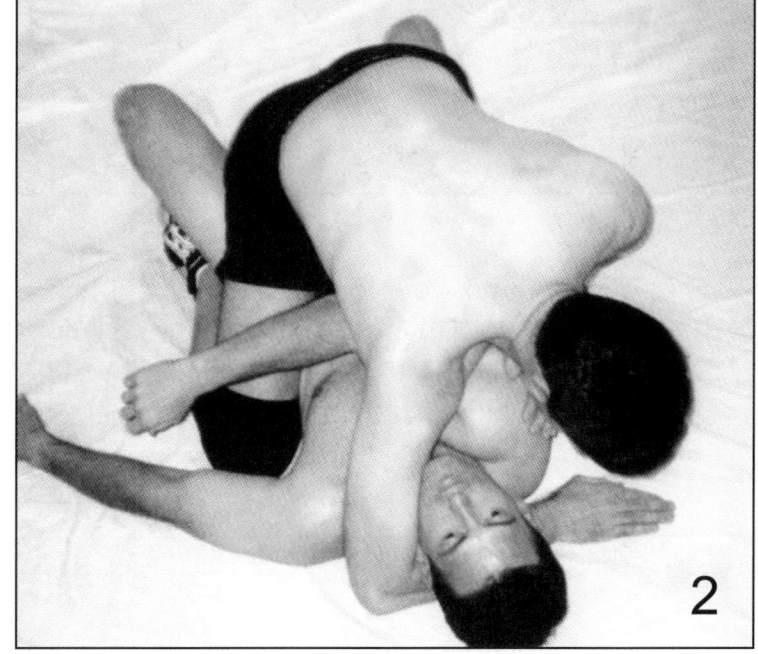

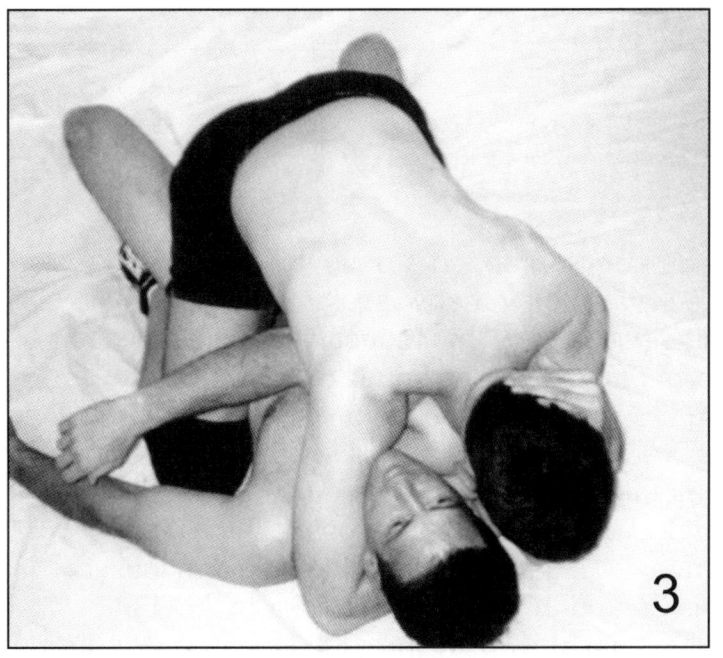

Grab the biceps of your locking arm and grab your own head. Drive the blade of your bottom, attacking forearm into the base of his neck and contract the muscles of your attacking arm. This will cut off his carotid arteries and may crank his neck, as well, for the submission. (Left)

CHOKE *Smother*

Your opponent is set with your arm wrapped behind his neck. (Left)

Grapevine both of your legs and drive your hips downwards, into him. This will give you a better base and help stop him from bridging out of your technique. (Right)

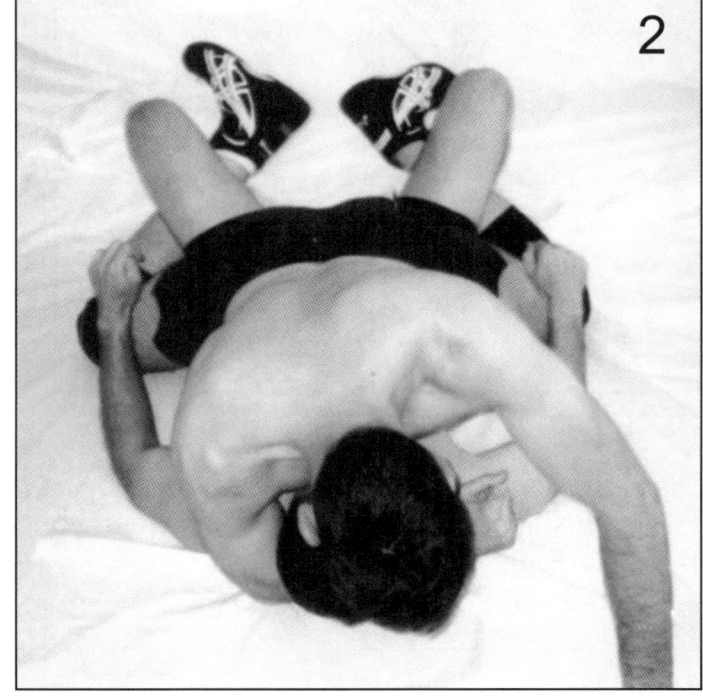

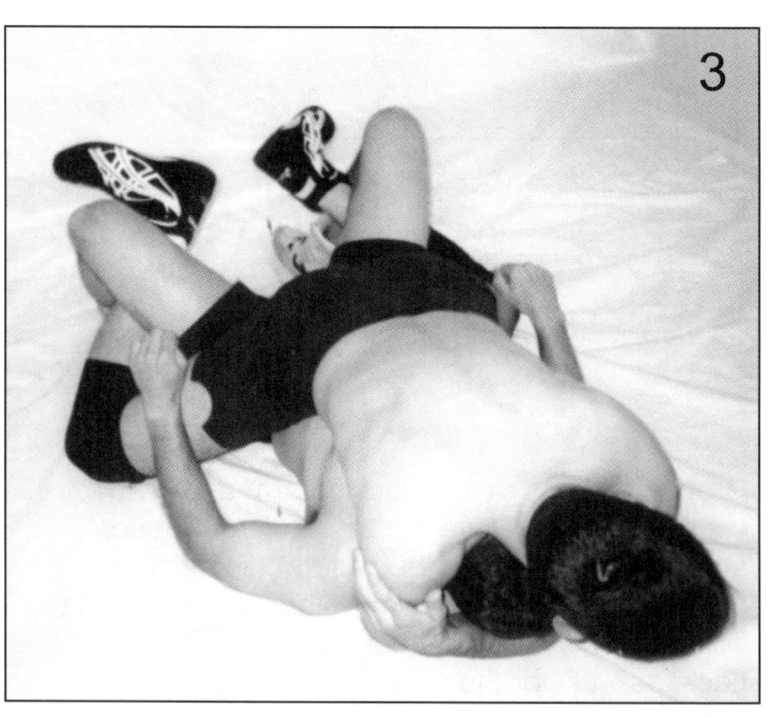

One arm is wrapped around the base of his neck while the other wraps around the top of his head. Place your chest flat against the front of his face and squeeze your arms tightly, pulling his face into your chest. If he is breathing heavily he will submit from being smothered. Also, driving your chest into the bridge of his nose is very painful. You can drive the blade of your bottom forearm into the base of his neck for a neck crank. (Left)

SHOULDER CRANK *Americana / Key Lock*

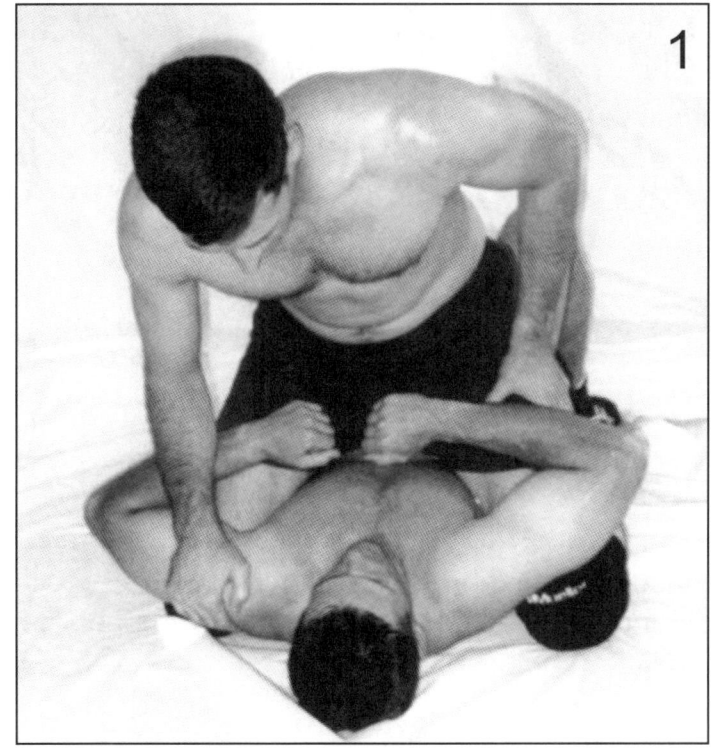

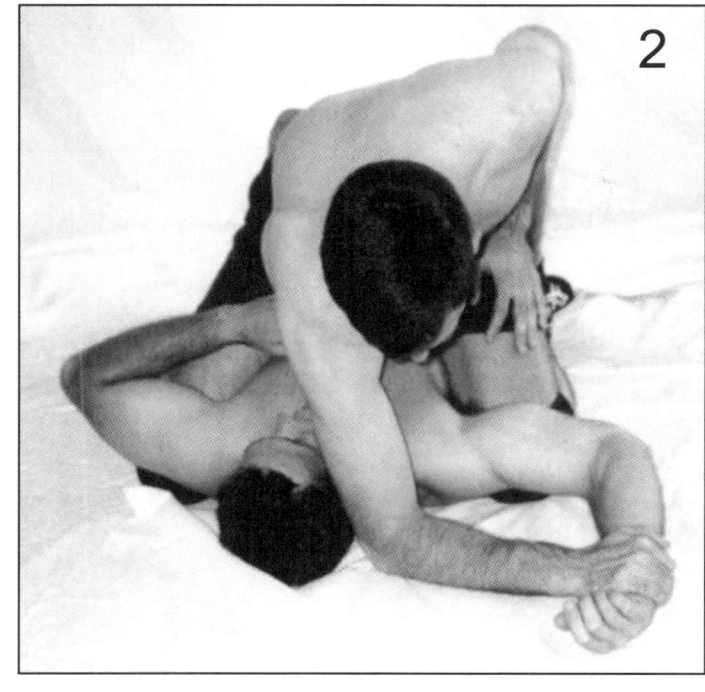

You have your opponent in a high mount, with your knees under his armpits. His arms are forced away from his body, exposing them to attack. (Left)

Reach across and grab his arm at the wrist, pinning it to the ground. Place your elbow tightly against his head. (Right)

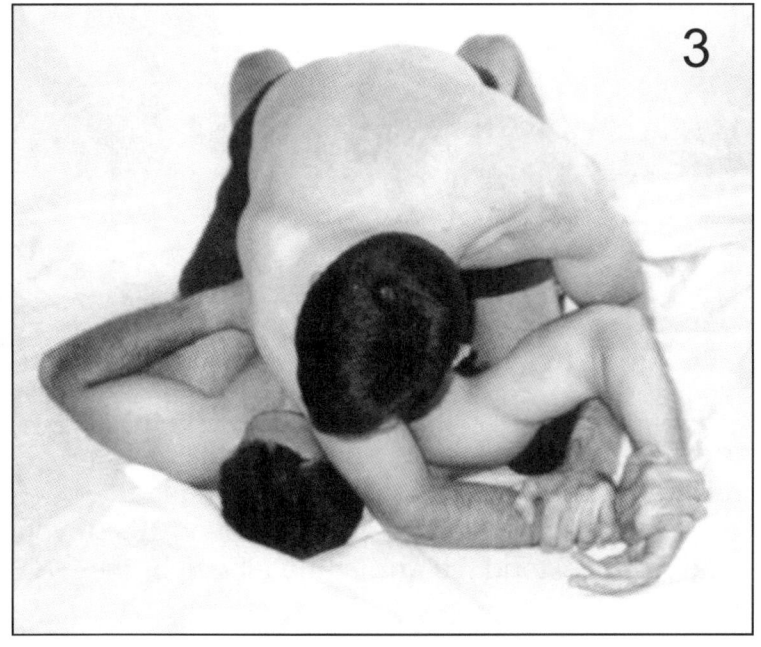

Reach under his trapped arm and grab your own arm at the wrist, forming a figure four lock. Keep his wrist pinned to the ground as you raise his elbow and attempt to place it on the ground by his head. Also, if you slide his trapped elbow closer to his own side first, the more pressure you can exert. This move uses his bent arm as a lever to torque his shoulder for the submission. (Left)

ARM BAR

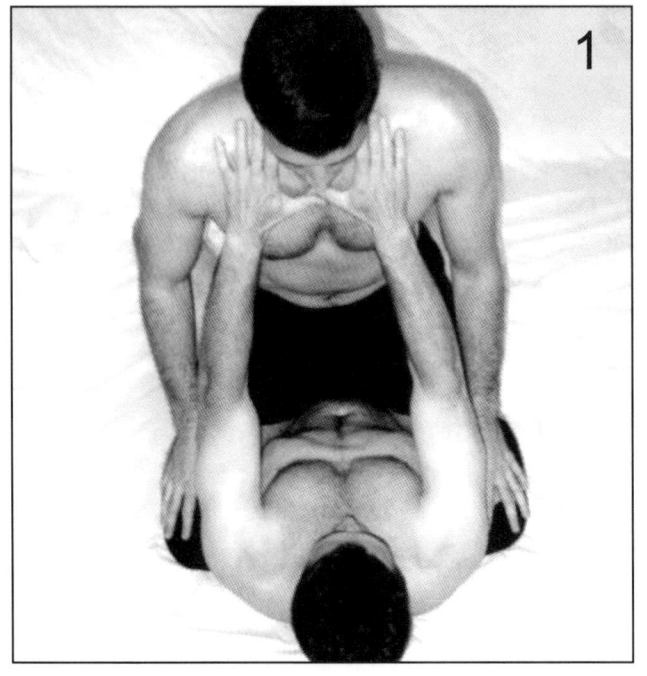

Your opponent is set up, pushing up against your chest.

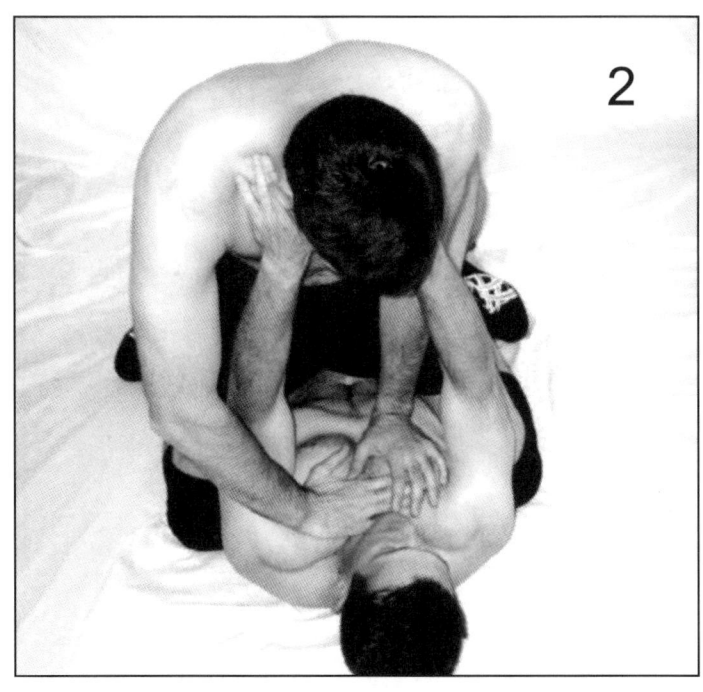

Place one hand on his chest and place the other over his targeted arm and on his upper chest.

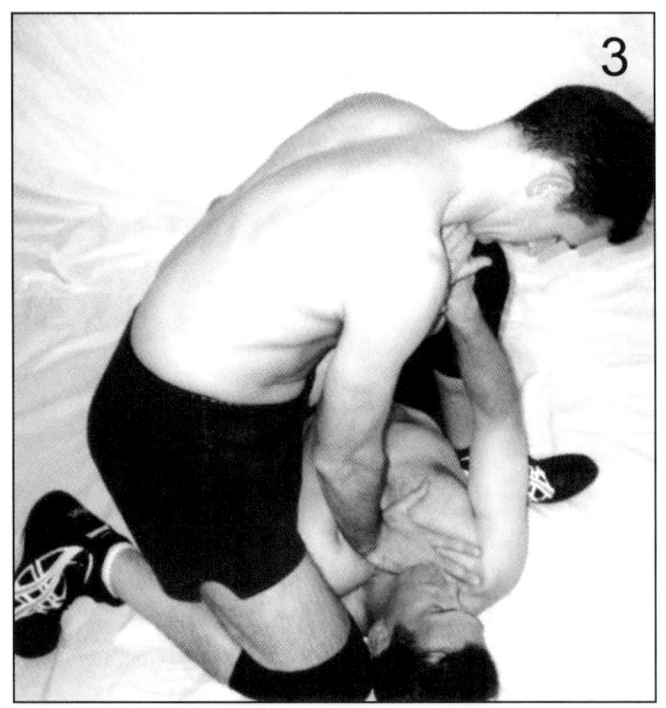

Place your body weight on his chest, pinning him to the ground. Rotate your body and bring your leg towards his head in preparation for sweeping it over his head.

Swing your leg over his head and lay back. You are controlling his arm and your knees are squeezed together. Your feet are driving into the ground. Arch your hips and hyper-extend his arm at the elbow for the submission.

ARM BAR *Straight Arm*

You have your opponent in a high mount, with your knees under his armpits, and he has one arm over your shoulder.

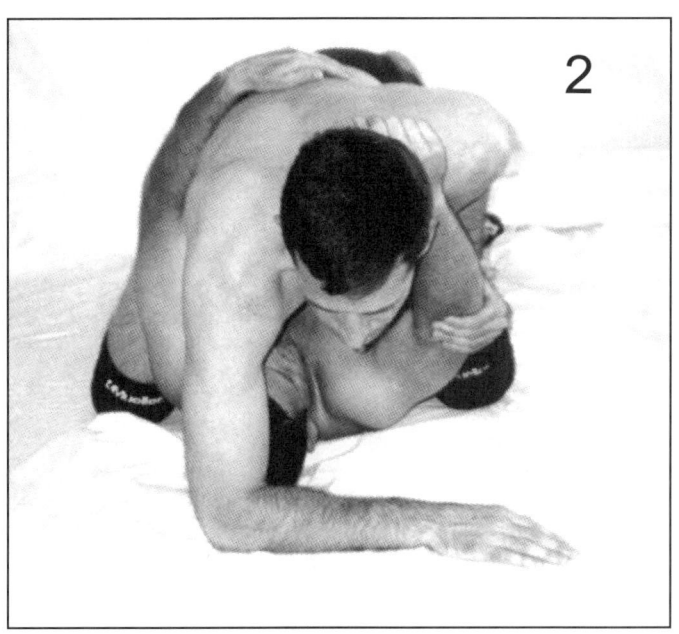

Secure his exposed arm at the elbow.

Maintain pressure on his elbow and step over his head with your knee, driving your shin into his neck. Your other shin goes across his stomach. Balance your weight on your head.

Grab his elbow with both hands and pull his elbow towards your stomach for the submission. This move hyper-extends his arm at the elbow.

ARM BAR *Underarm Variation*

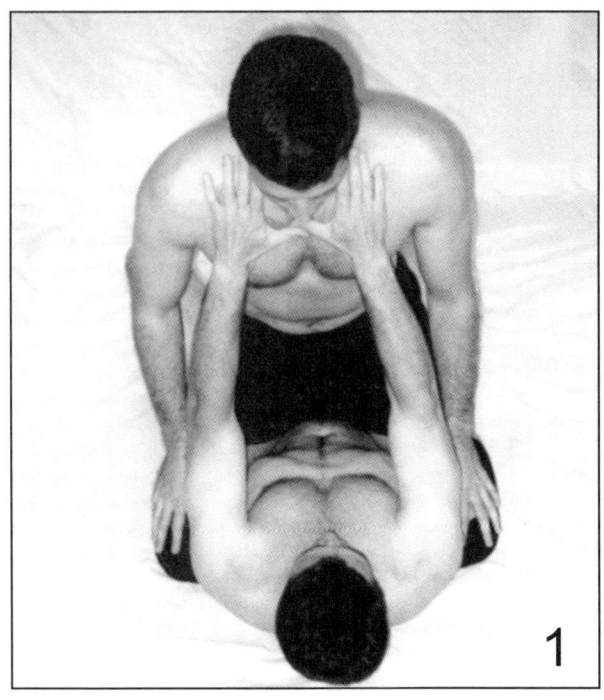

You are set up with your opponent pushing off on your chest.

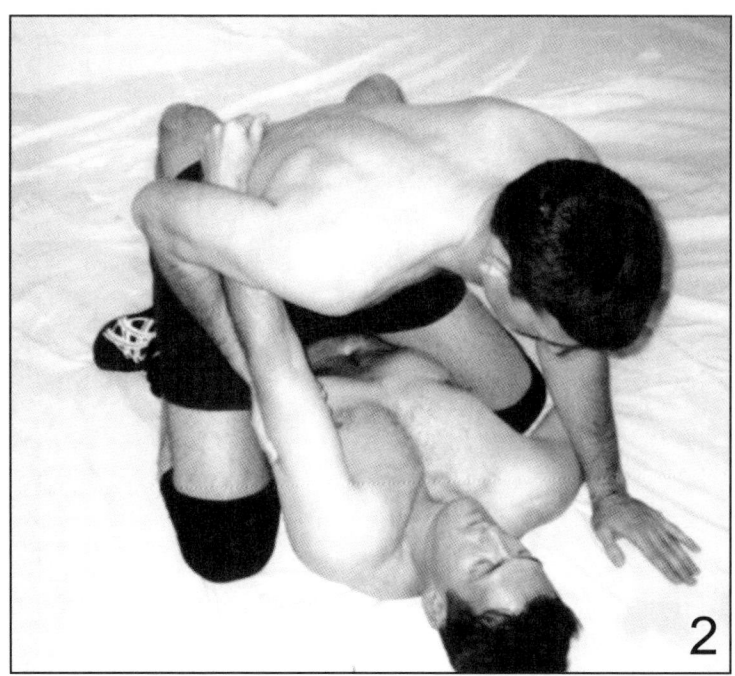

Swim through his targeted arm and wrap it under yours, trapping it under your armpit.

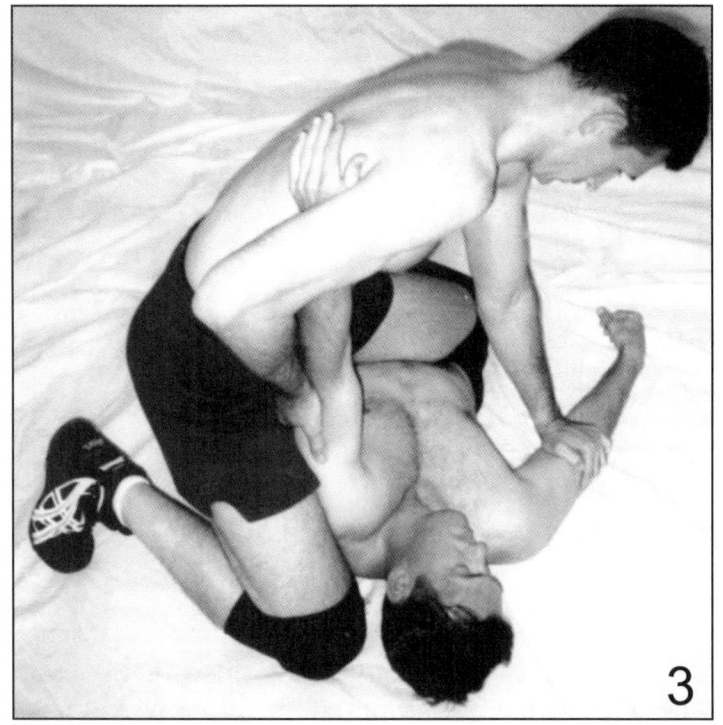

Control his far arm and bring your shin across his stomach and put your weight on his stomach. You have rotated your hips so that you are now perpendicular to his body.

Bring your other knee across his face and drive your weight into his neck/chin. Arch your hips forwards and hyper-extend his arm at the elbow for the submission.

ARM BAR *Roll Over*

Your opponent pushes you to the side in an attempt to escape. (Top)

Grab his arm at the wrist. (Top Right)

Continue your momentum in the direction of the push and pin his wrist to the ground. Place your shin across his stomach. (Right)

Bring your other knee across his head and drive your shin in the back of his neck. Grab his arm at the wrist with both hands and arch your hips forwards while pulling his arm upwards. Ensure that your groin is on or slightly above his elbow, closer to his shoulder. (Bottom Right)

Also, you can bring your leg across his face. Arch your hips forwards and lift up on his wrist to hyper-extend his arm at the elbow for the submission. (Bottom)

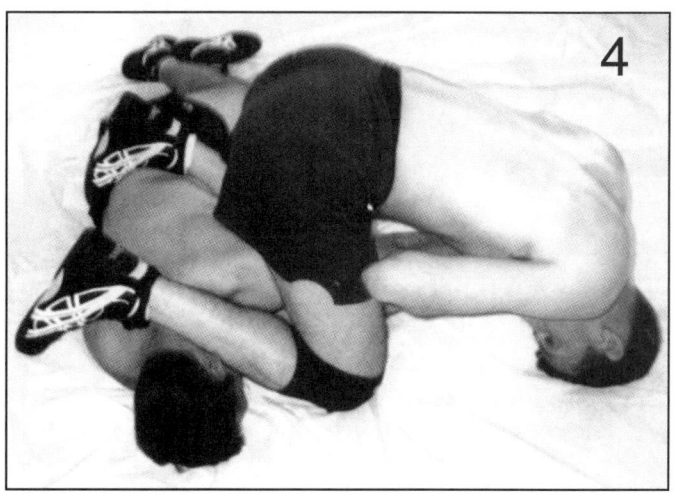

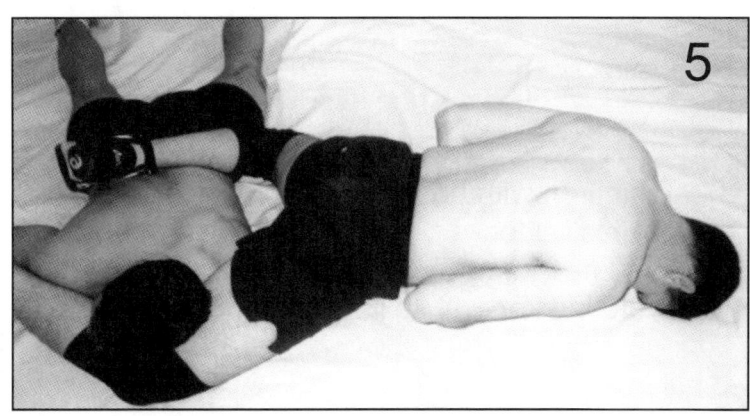

KNEE LEVER

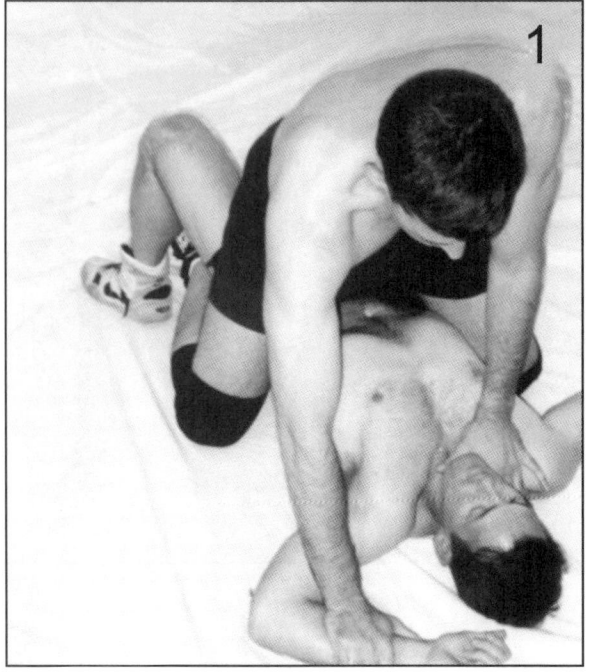

You are mounted on your opponent and are controlling him at the head and arm. You have your leg hooked under his targeted leg as shown.

Reach back and grab his targeted foot.

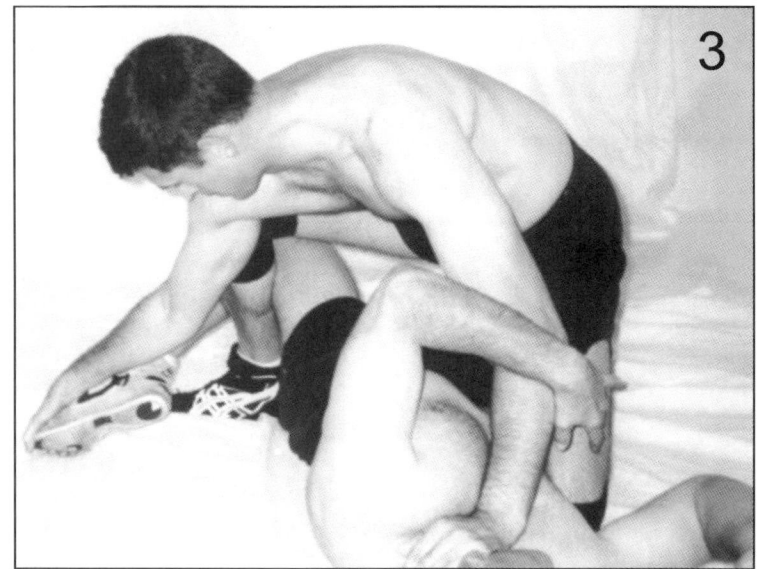

As you pull on his foot, he will roll on his side. Continue to pull your own leg into his knee joint as he repositions. You can put pressure on his neck/head to limit his mobility.

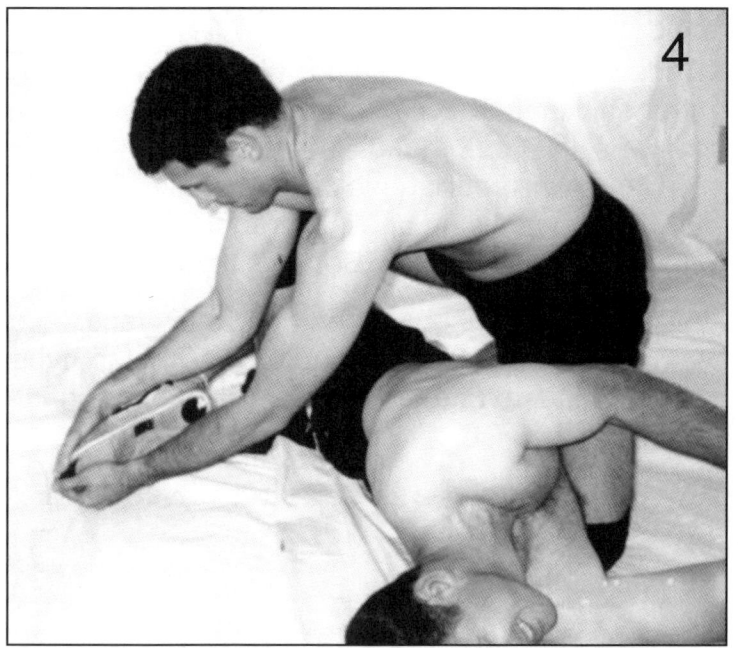

Grab his foot with both hands and try to pull his heel to his buttocks. Keep your own leg deep into his knee joint. This move threatens to separate his knee at its joint for the submission.

ATTACKS IN THE MOUNT – KNEE LEVER

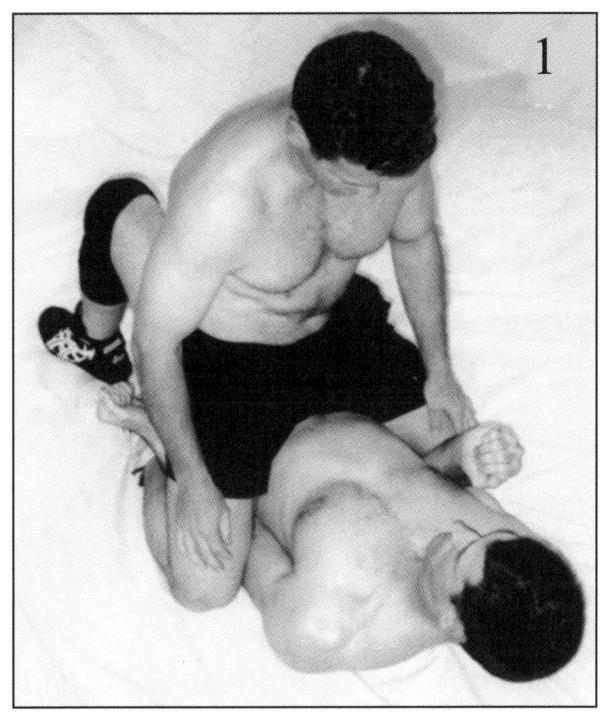

Your opponent has you mounted but you have one arm hooked under one of his legs as shown.

Clasp your under hooked hand with your other arm. This will prevent him from trapping your free arm and give you more strength and leverage in executing the technique. Drive your hips upwards, forcing your opponent to balance out on his hands.

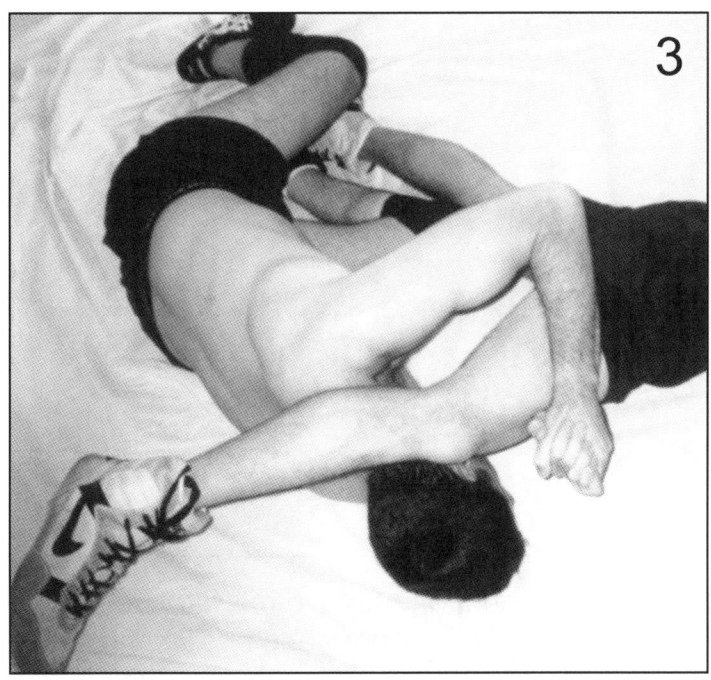

Pull your opponent over your head with your clasped arms as you slide your hips backwards and out from under him. Clasping your hands will also help prevent him from grabbing your arm on the way out.

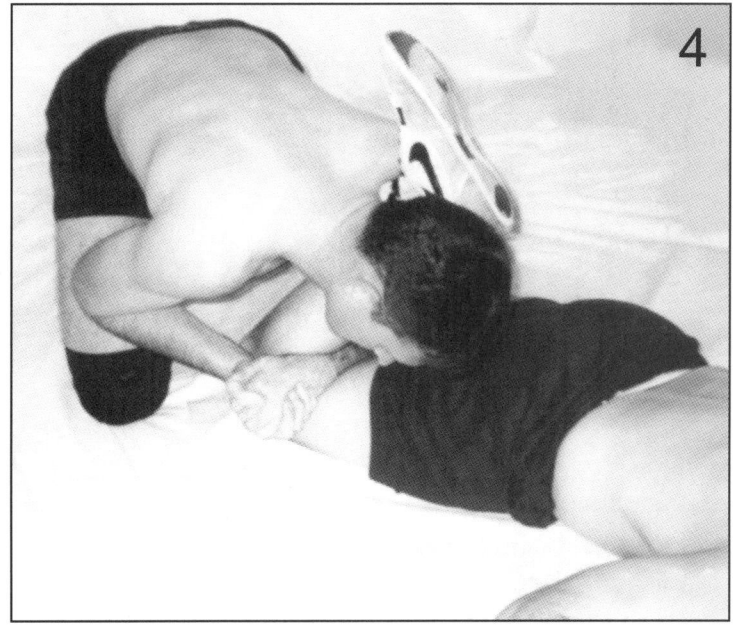

Continue to slide away from your opponent and come to your knees, maintaining your grip on his leg. Pull your forearm tight into his knee joint and drive his heel to his buttocks, with your shoulder, for the submission.

HEEL HOOK

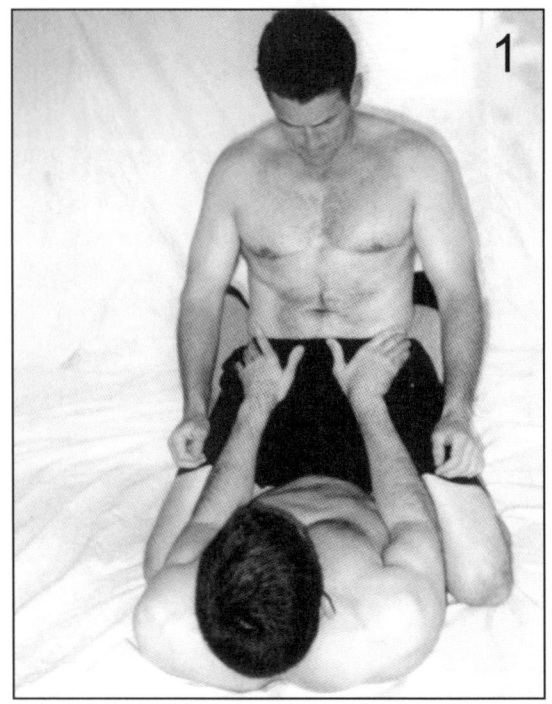

Your opponent is mounted on you and you have placed your hands on his hips.

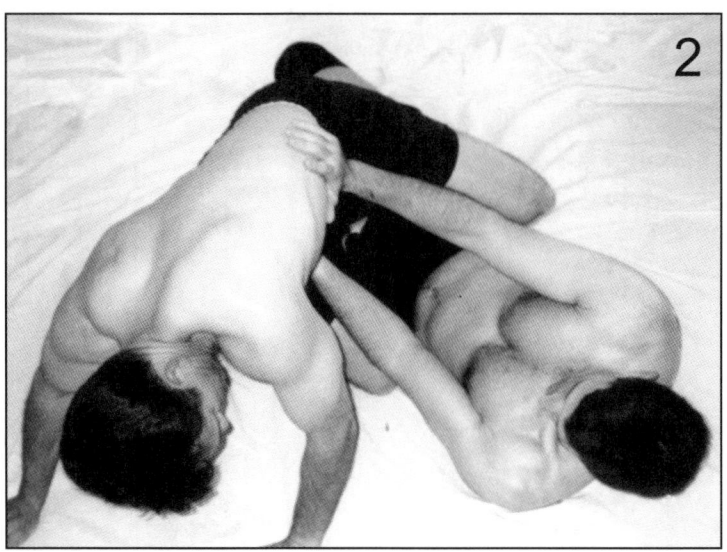

Push him to the side, forcing him to base out and use his hands for balance. You are also turning your hips so that you are on your side.

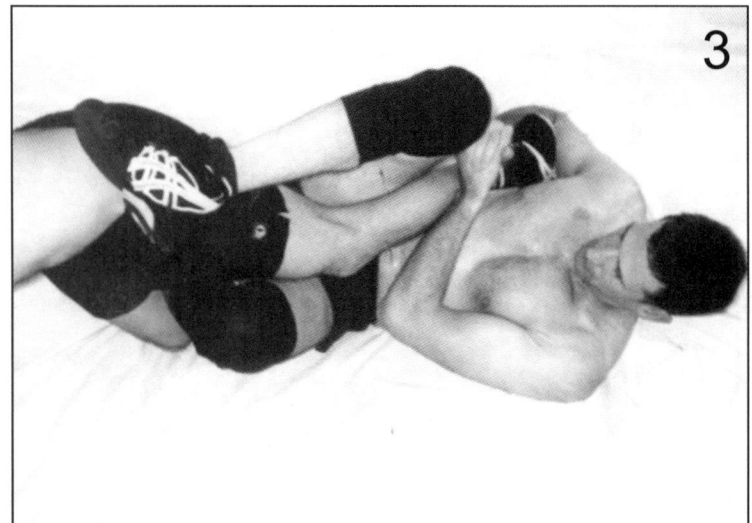

Bring your bottom knee up and drive it between his legs. Also, hook your top leg over his targeted leg and plant it at his hip to help control his body. Secure his heel and turn your upper body towards the ground, using his foot as a lever to torque his leg at the knee for the submission.

If your opponent attempts to roll with the hook and escape, switch your hand positioning and torque his knee in the opposite direction.

ANKLE LOCK

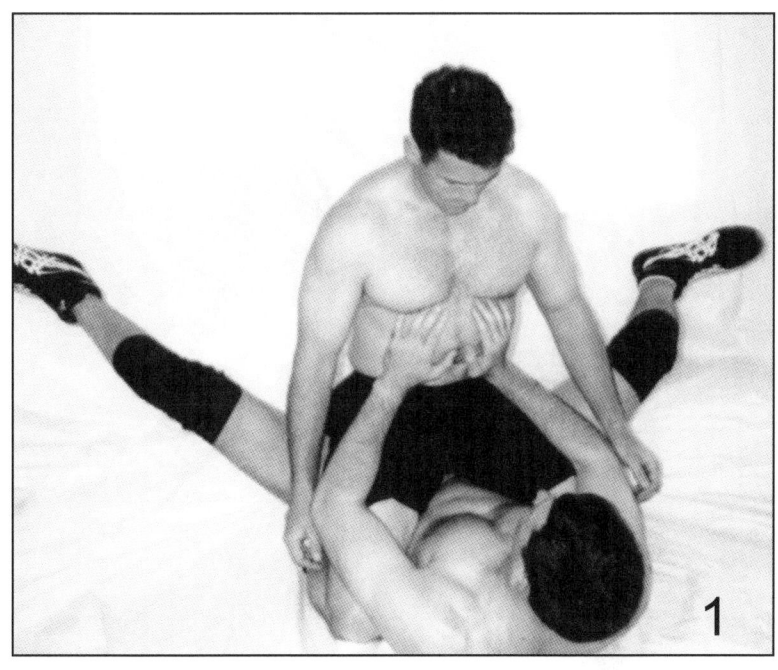

Your opponent is mounted high on you with his knees under your armpits. Place your hands on his lower abdomen to prevent him from leaning forwards. Swing your legs out in preparation for hooking them over his head.

Hook your feet on his chest, the higher up they are located, the more leverage you will have.

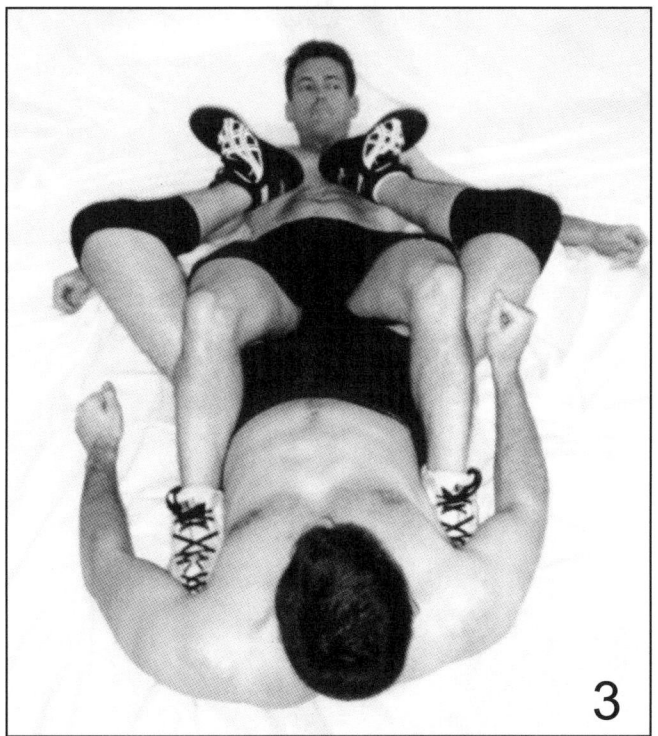

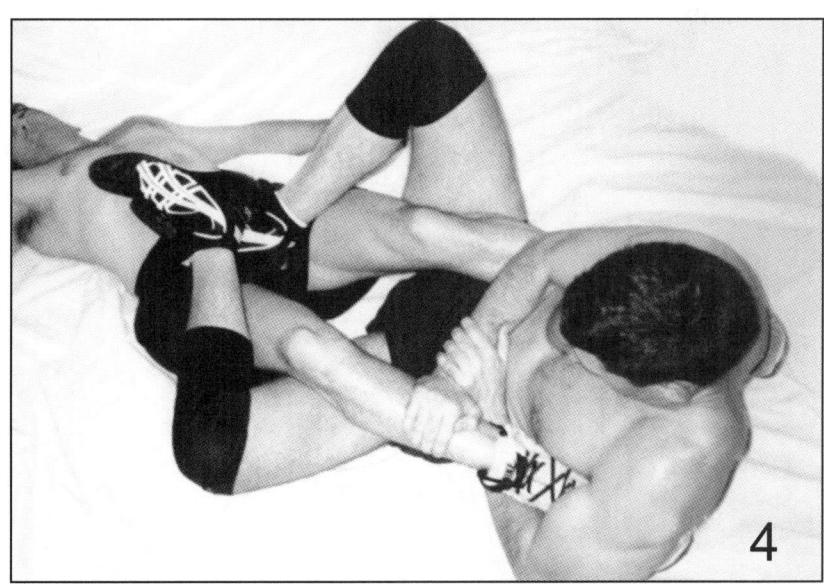

Drive your feet to the ground, driving him backwards and to the ground. If he doesn't fall backwards properly, he may damage the ligaments in his knees as he falls.

You can finish your opponent with a variety of ankle locks. Here, finish him with a standard ankle lock, hyper-extending his foot at the ankle for the submission.

ANKLE LOCK *From A Roll Out*

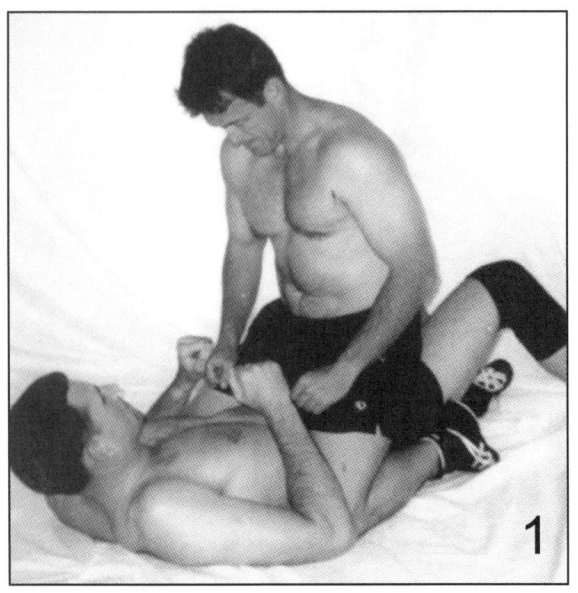

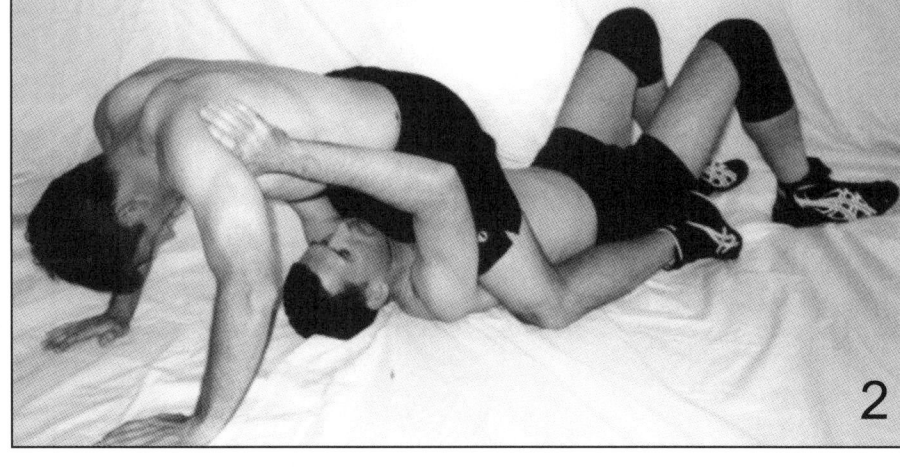

Your opponent is mounted and is sitting up, high on his knees. (Top)

Plant your hands under his armpits and drive him forwards, forcing him to base out with his hands. (Top Right)

Hook both, or one, of your legs under his armpits and roll out backwards. (Right)

Secure one of his legs as you roll out from under him. (Bottom Right)

You can finish him with a variety of moves. Here, finish him with an ankle lock. (Bottom)

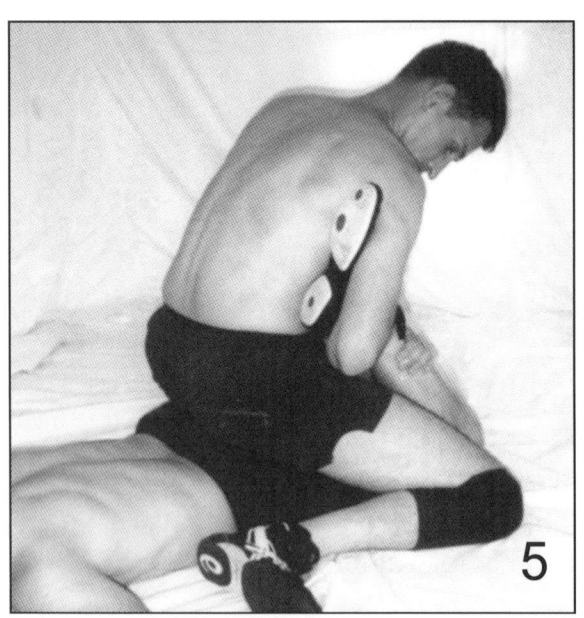

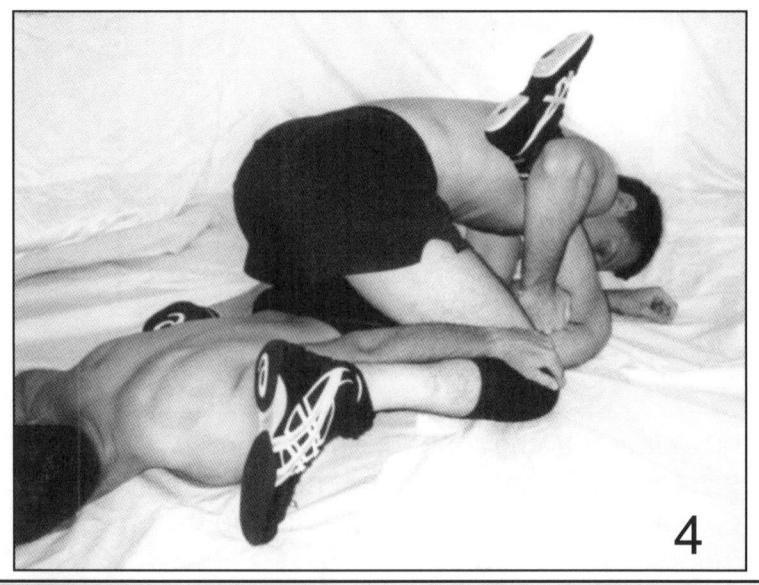

Chapter Eight

Submissions From Modified Mount

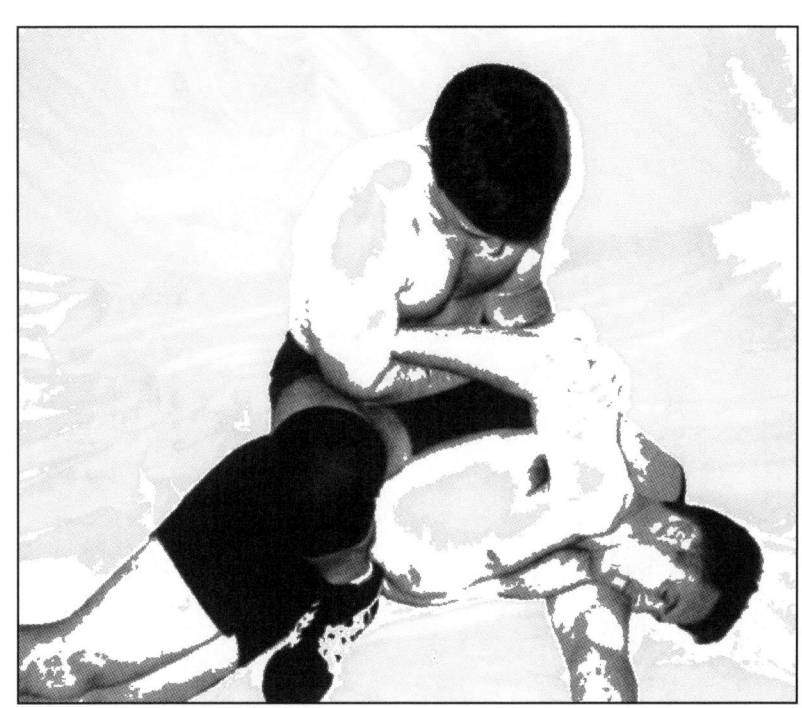

Modified Mount

Essentially, you have your opponent's back. He has limited attack options; his best strategy is to reposition or escape.

Your knee is pressed firmly against his upper back. This prevents him from rolling out of the position. Your hips are low to give you a low center of gravity.

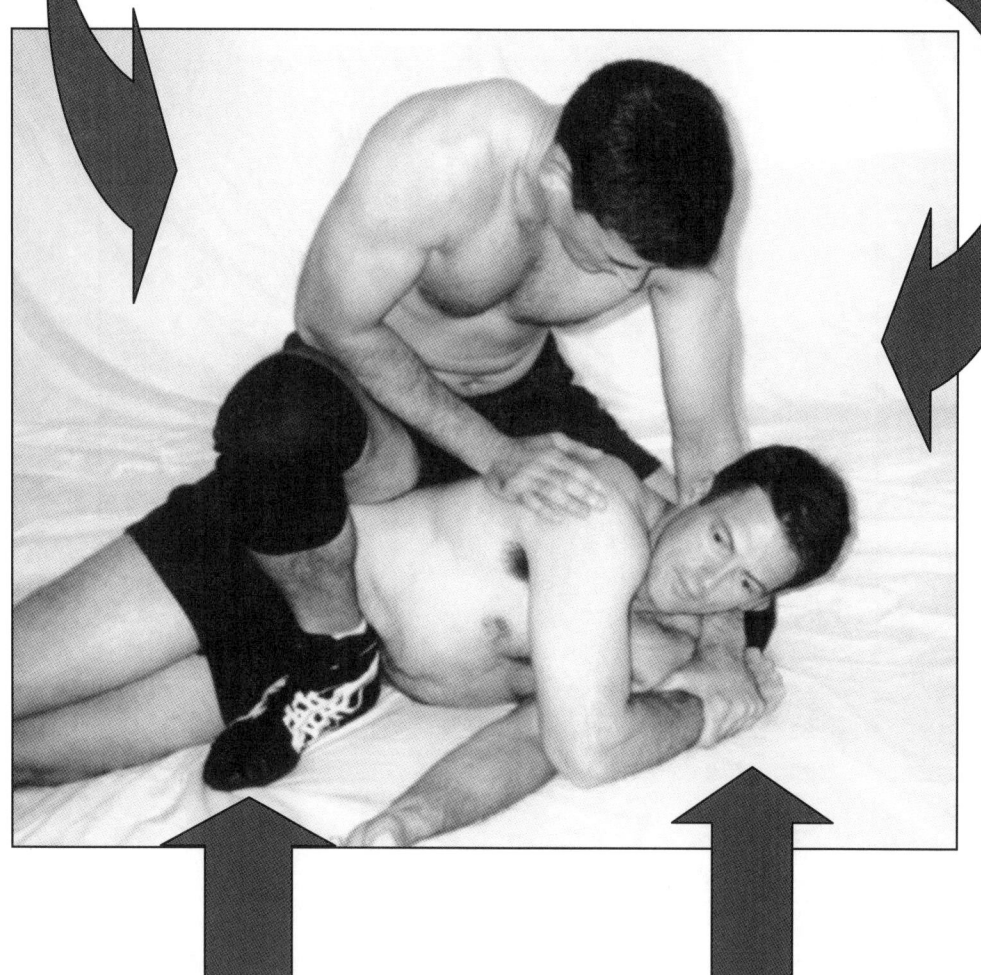

Your leg is firmly pressed against his stomach. This prevents him from rolling out of the position and eliminates the use of his legs.

You are in a good position to control and attack his exposed, top arm and neck.

NECK CRANKS *Bottle Cap*

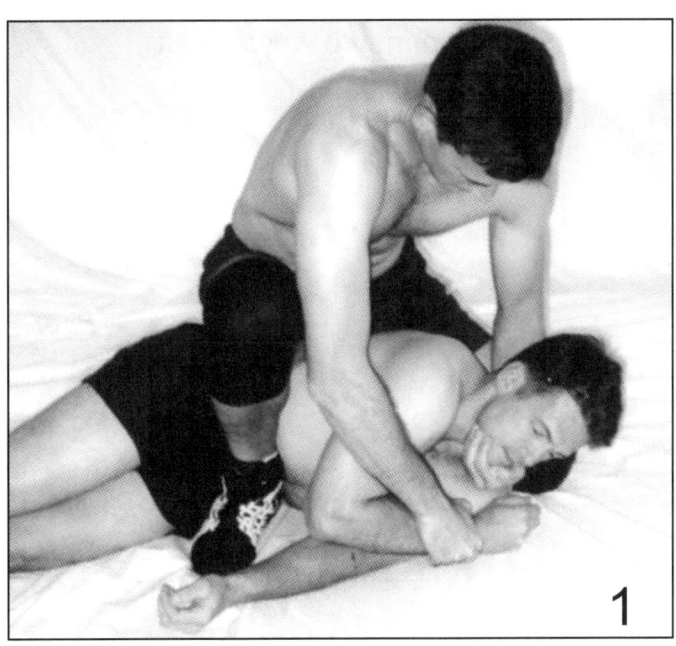

Secure your opponent's top arm and hook your other hand behind his neck and on his jaw as shown.

Plant your hand on the top of his head. Pull with your hand on his jaw and push with your other hand, using his head as a lever to torque his cervical spine for the submission.

Underarm Neck Crank

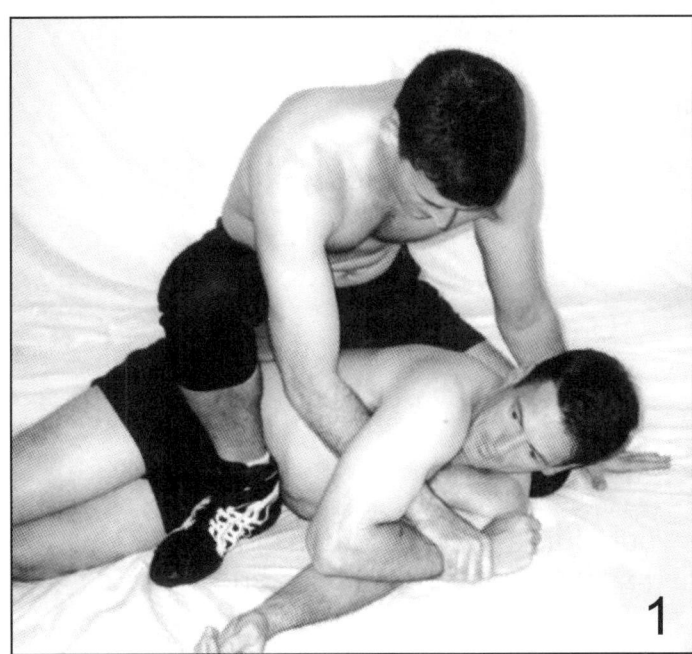

Secure his top arm as shown. Notice how his head is raised off the ground.

Reach across the front of his of head and hook your arm under his chin. Arch your back and hyper-extend his neck backwards for the submission.

CHOKE *Rear Naked Strangle*

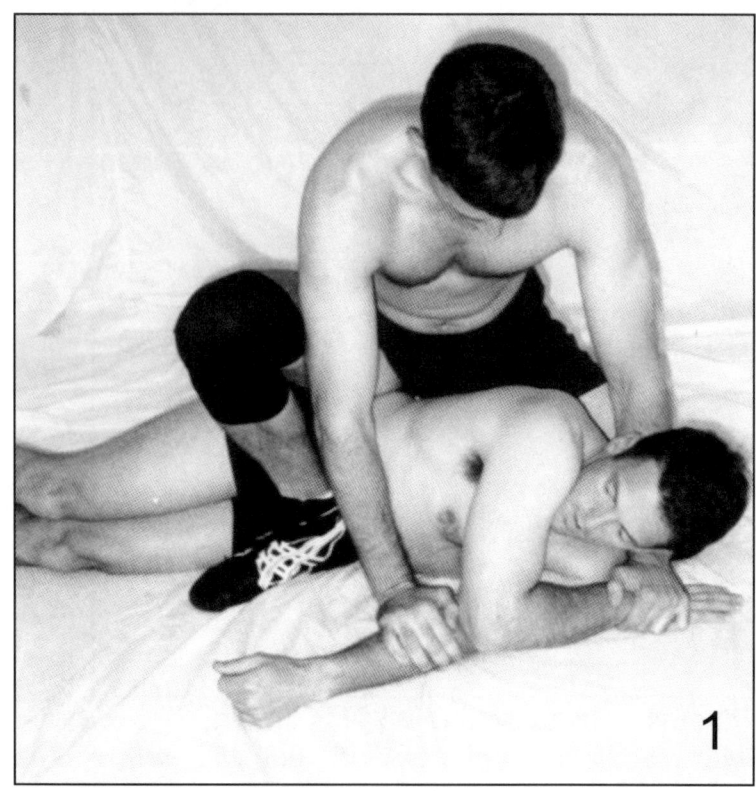

Secure his top arm by reaching behind his head and grabbing his arm at the wrist. (Left)

Bring your other, attacking arm over his trapped arm and across his throat. (Right)

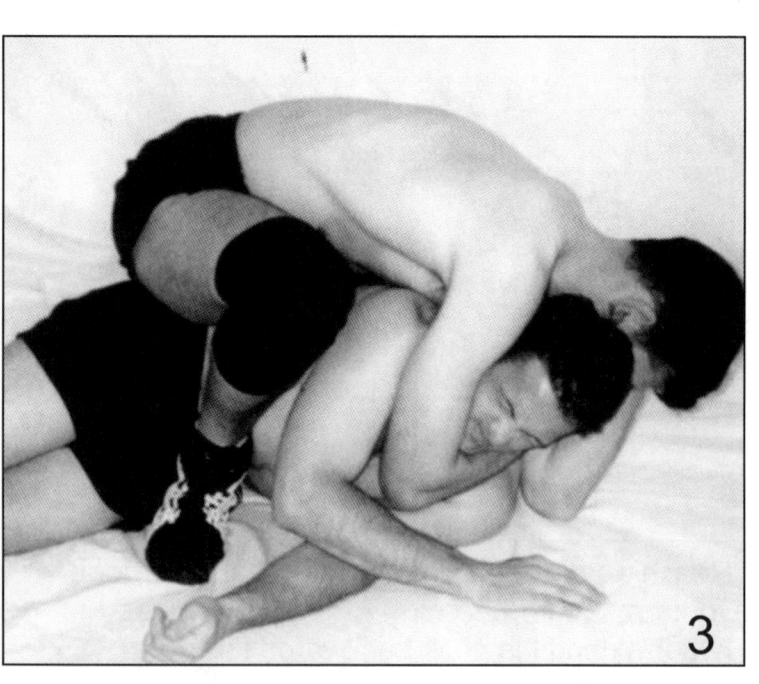

With your attacking arm, grab the biceps of your locking arm that was trapping his arm. Place the hand of your locking arm on the back of your head to lock in the hold. Pull your shoulders to the rear and expand your chest to choke your opponent into submission. (Left)

CHOKE *Kata Gatame*

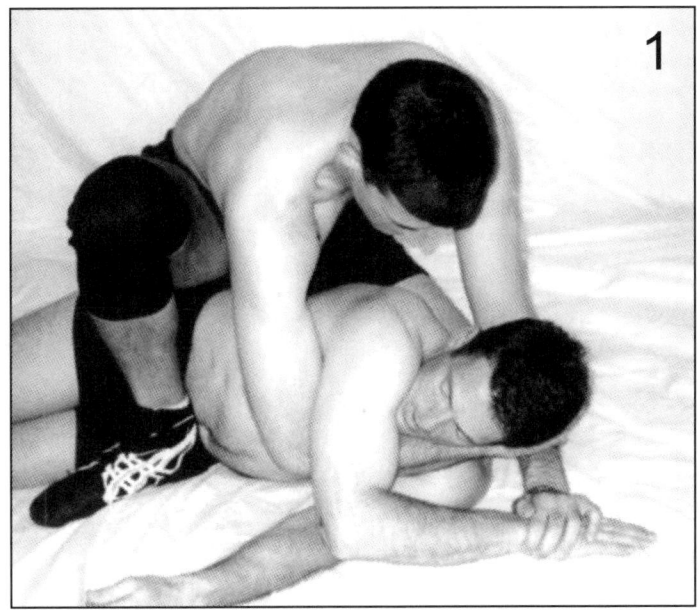

Secure his top arm at the wrist. Slide your other, attacking arm under his trapped arm and across his neck.

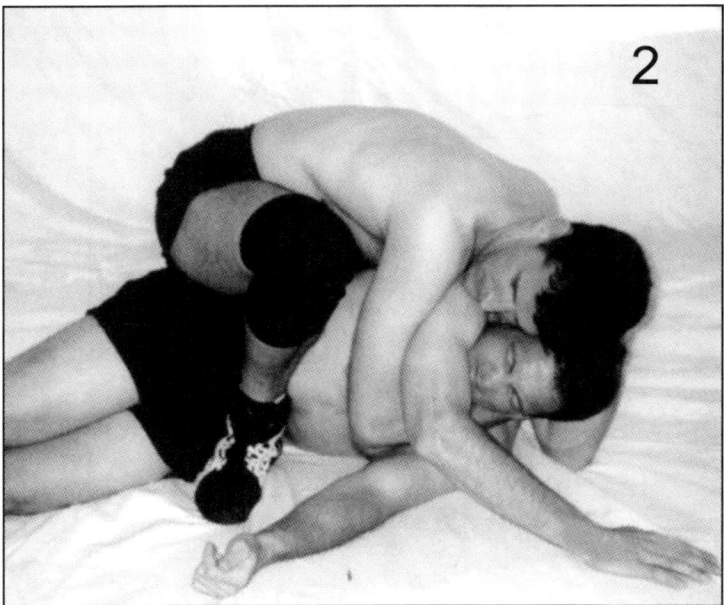

Grab your other, locking arm at the biceps and place your locking hand on the back of your head. Keep your head tight against his. Drive your forearm into the side of his neck and contract the muscles of your attacking arm for the choke.

Paper Cutter

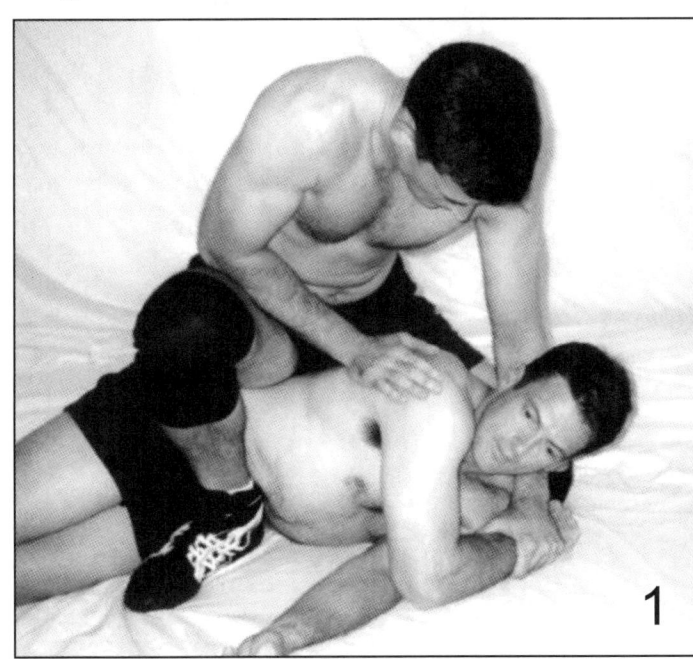

Secure his top arm by reaching behind his head and grabbing his wrist.

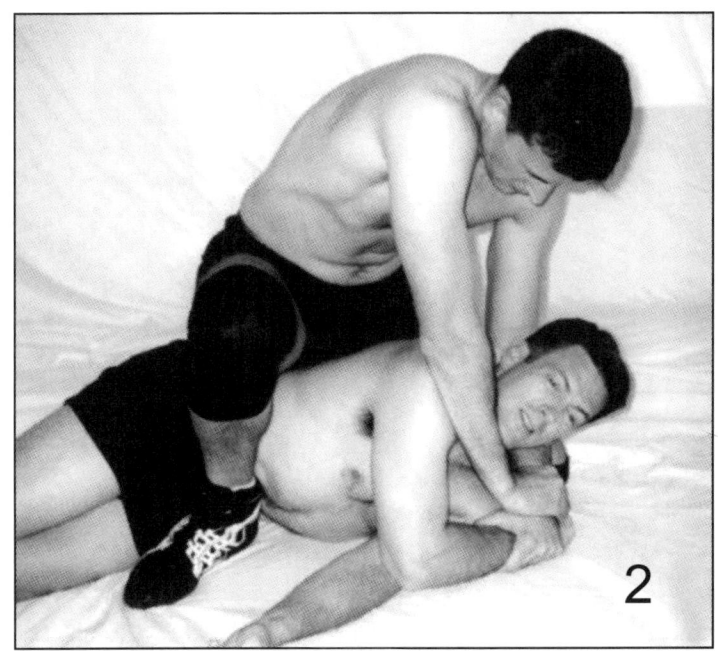

Place your arm across his throat and grab your other arm at the wrist. Drive the elbow of your choking arm to the elbow of your other arm to crush his esophagus for the choke.

CHOKE *Triangle*

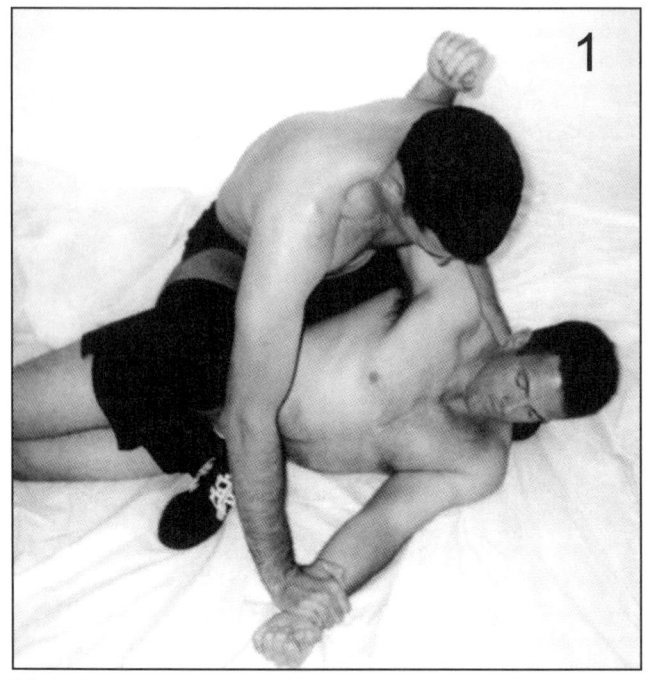

You have your opponent secured; his top arm is under your arm and his bottom arm is pinned at the wrist.

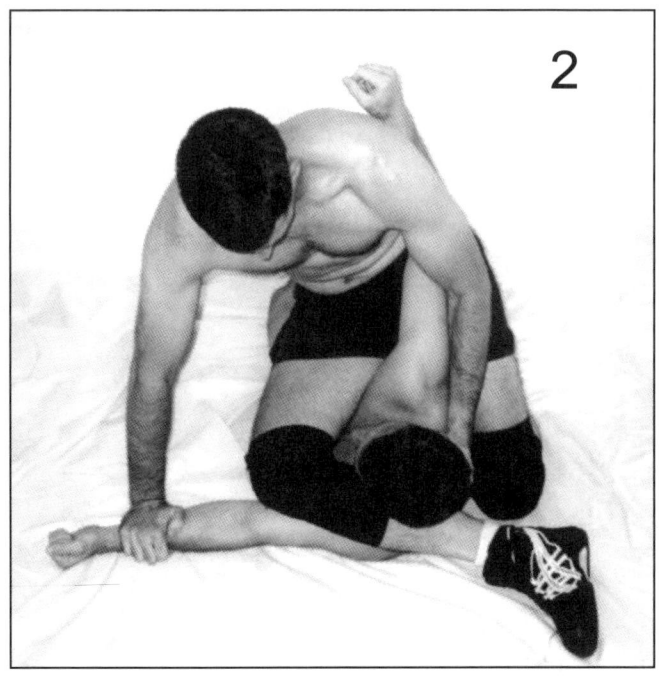

Drive your front leg over his shoulder and behind his neck.

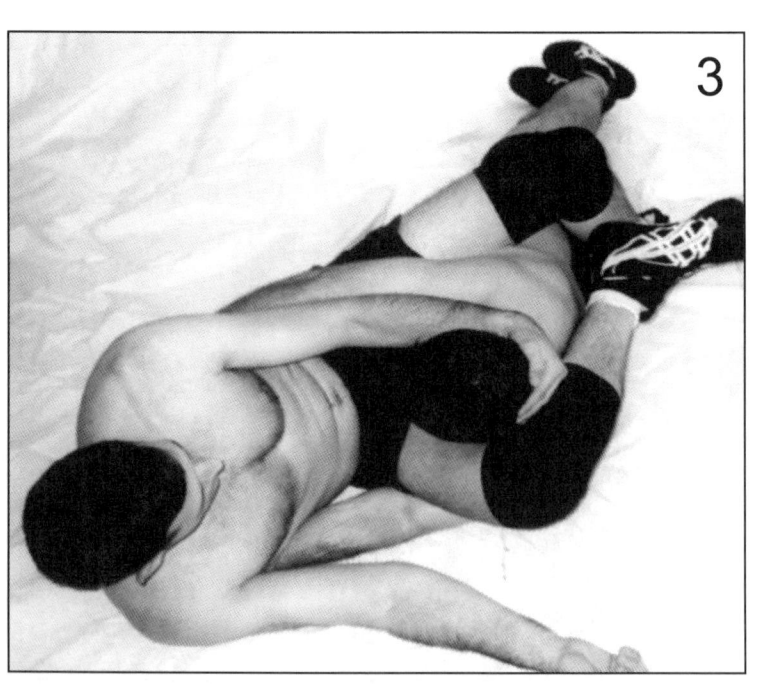

Roll to your side; maintain control of his head as you roll.

Hook your legs in a figure four lock as shown and bring his trapped arm across his own neck. Squeeze your knees together and pull his head forwards for the choke.

ARM BAR *With Figure Four Lock*

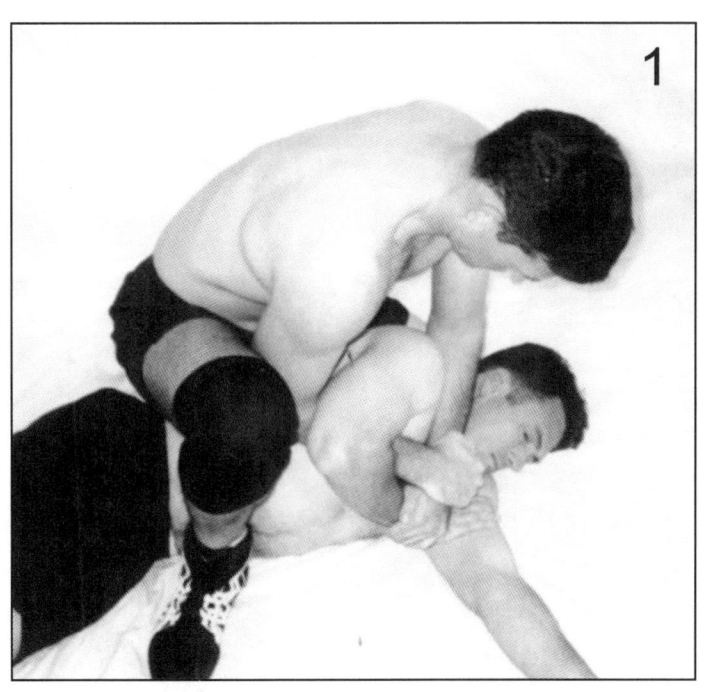

Secure your opponent's arm with a figure four lock as shown.

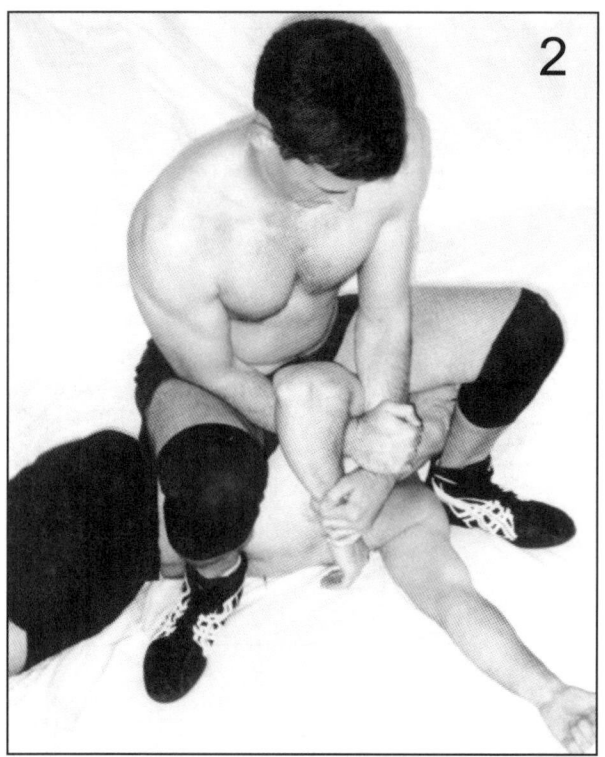

Maintain your grip and bring your rear leg over his head and across his neck.

Sit backwards while maintaining a secure grip on his trapped arm.

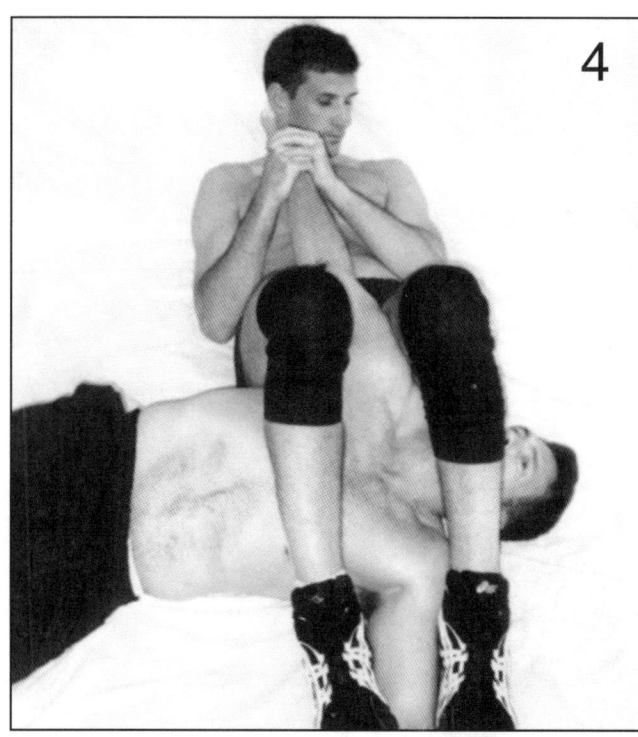

Squeeze your knees together and pull his arm backwards until it straightens. Grab his arm at the wrist, arch your hips, and hyper-extend his arm at the elbow for the submission.

ARM BAR *Elbow Hug*

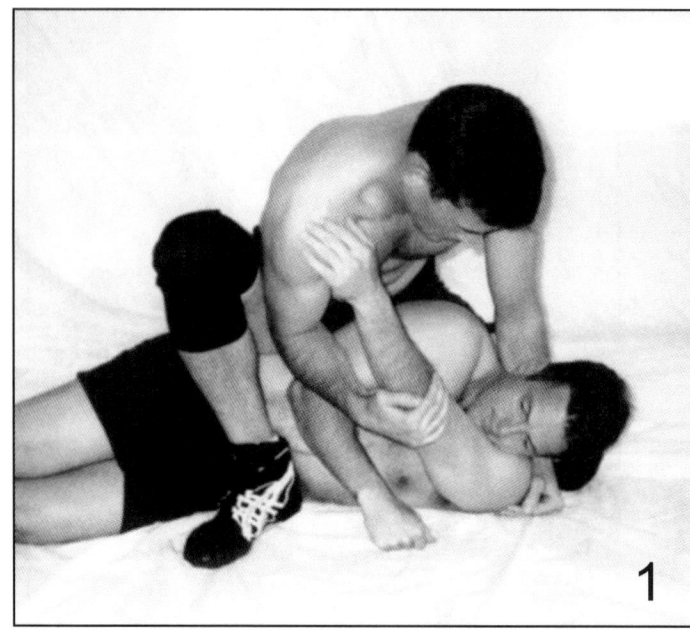

Secure his bottom arm at the elbow. (Left)

Secure his arm at the elbow with your other arm. (Right)

Lean into his arm so that his forearm is resting on your shoulder. Pull in on his elbow with your hands while pushing forwards with your shoulder to hyper-extend his arm at the elbow for the submission. (Left)

ARM BAR *With Leg Under Hook*

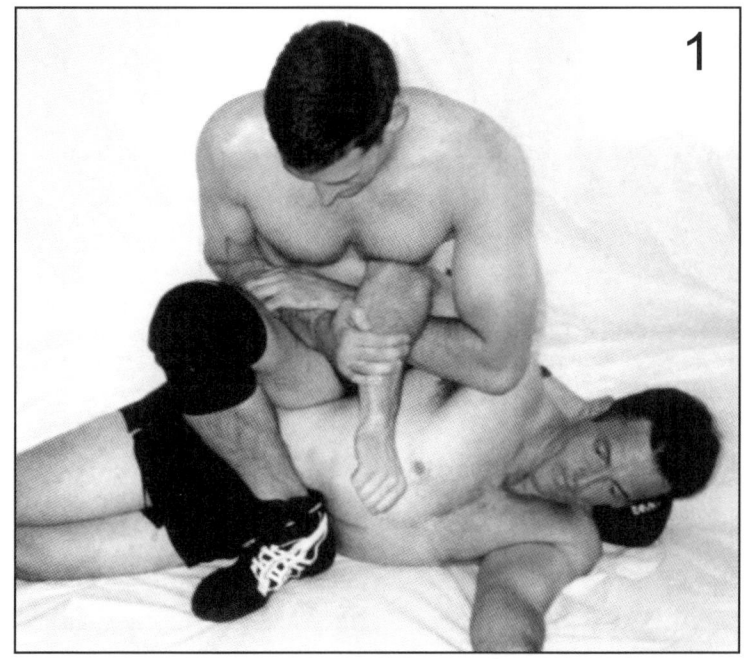

Hook your opponent's top arm securely.

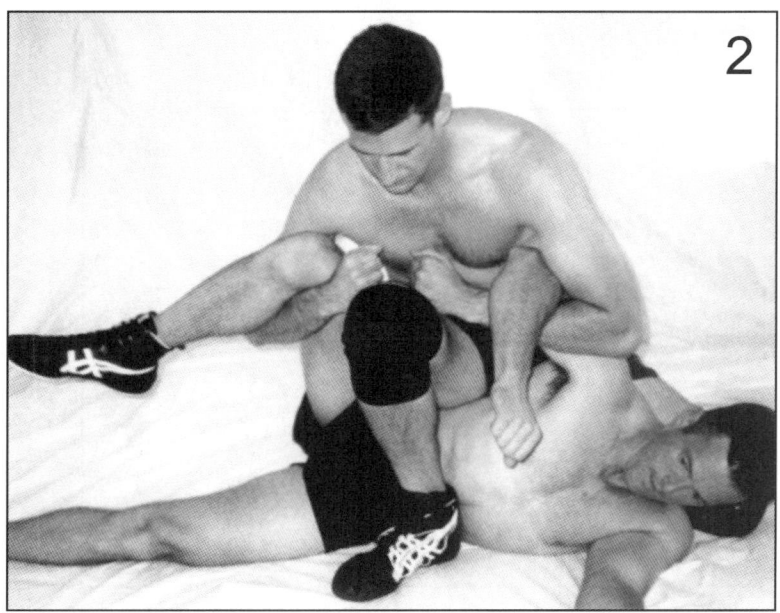

Hook his top leg with your other arm.

Place your rear leg over his head and across his throat. Sit back, hugging both his arm and leg to your chest.

Lay backwards. To submit him, squeeze your knees together and arch your hips to hyper-extend his arm at the elbow. If he tries to straighten his trapped leg he will exert pressure on his own trapped arm.

SHOULDER CRANKS

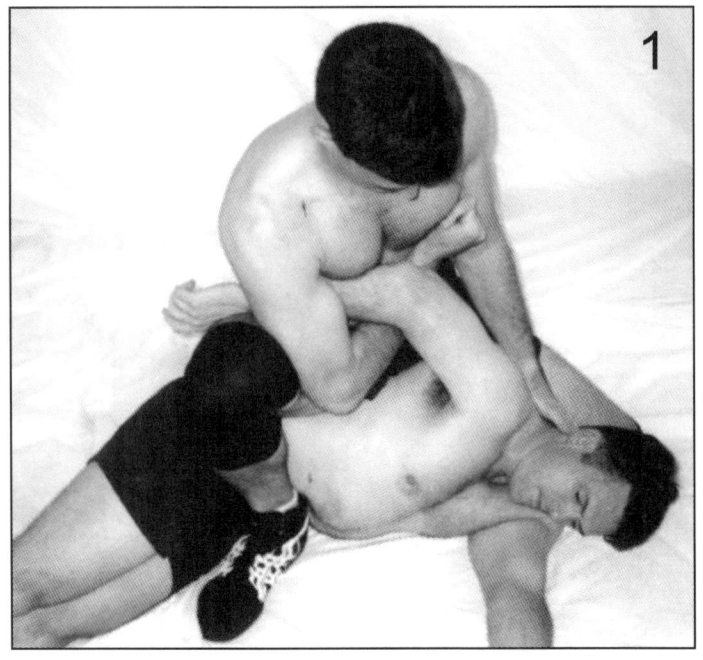

Hook under his top arm and keep it tight to your chest.

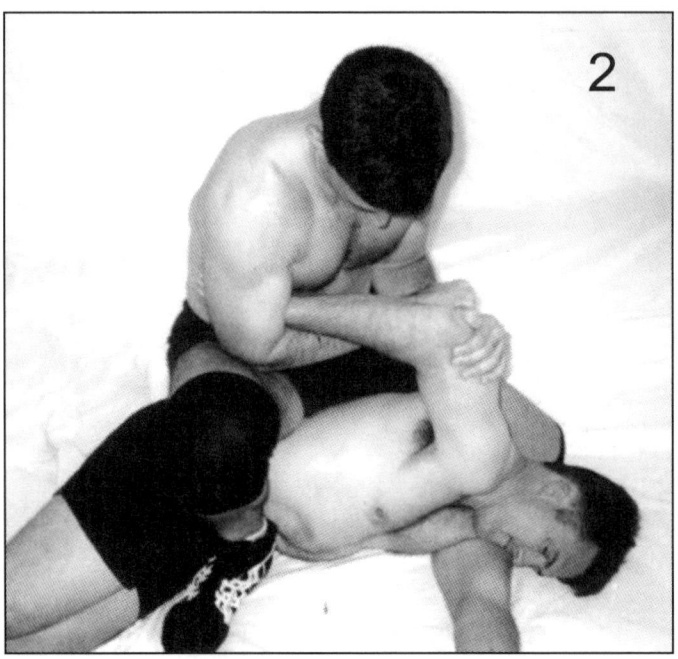

Place your other arm on his elbow and grab this arm at the wrist. Turn your upper body so that his wrist is driven behind his back. You are using his arm as a lever to torque his shoulder for the submission.

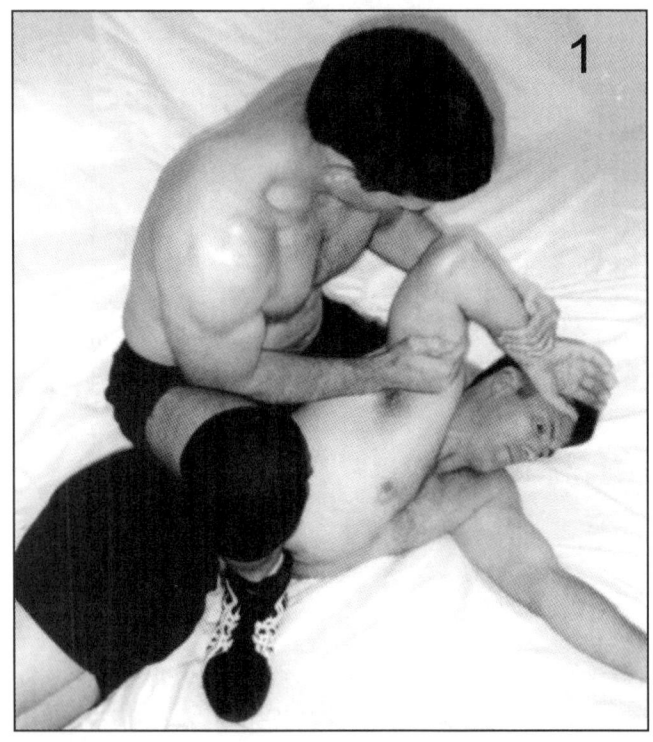

Secure your opponent's arm by bringing it above his head.

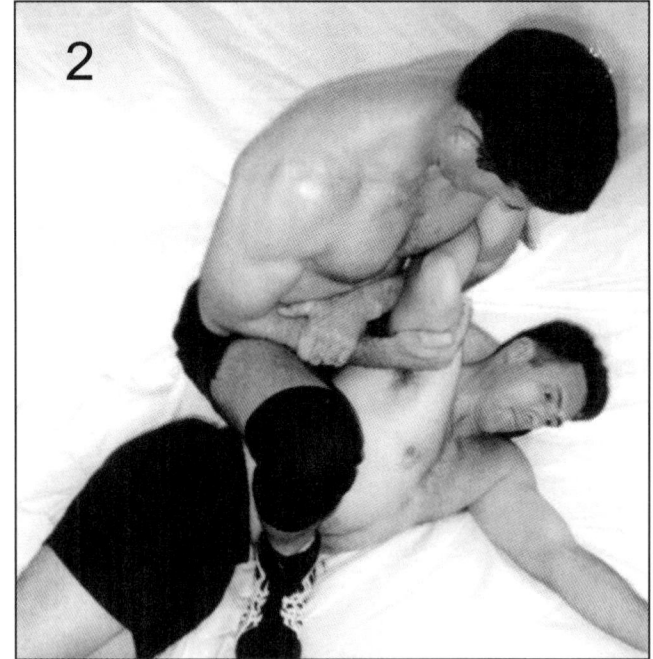

Under hook his arm with your own, place your other hand on his elbow and grab your wrist. With this figure four lock, twist your upper body and drive his wrist behind his back. This uses his arm as a lever to torque his shoulder for the submission.

SHOULDER CRANK *Head Assist*

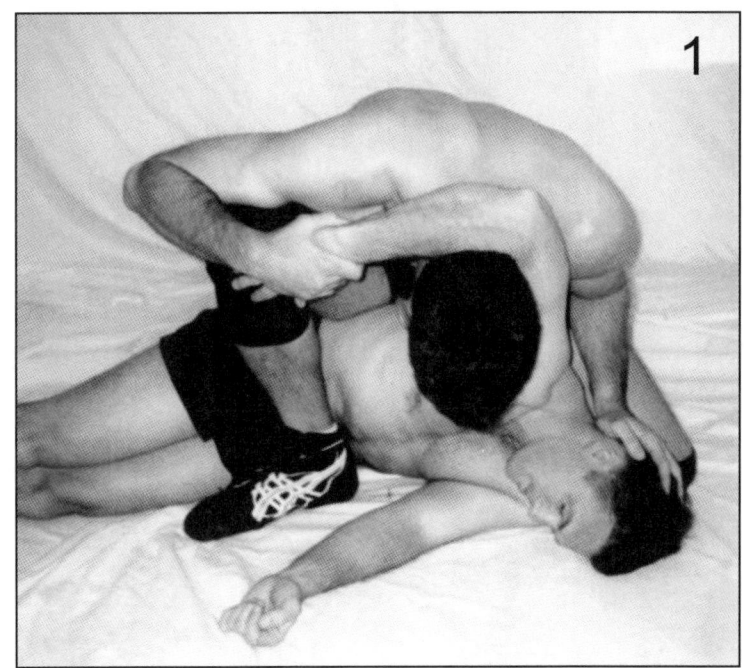

1 Your opponent has his arm over your neck. Grab it at the wrist and keep it tight against your neck. (Left)

Drive your neck upwards and pull down on his wrist with your arm. This will trap his arm and help keep it at a right angle. Turn your upper body to torque his arm. (Right)

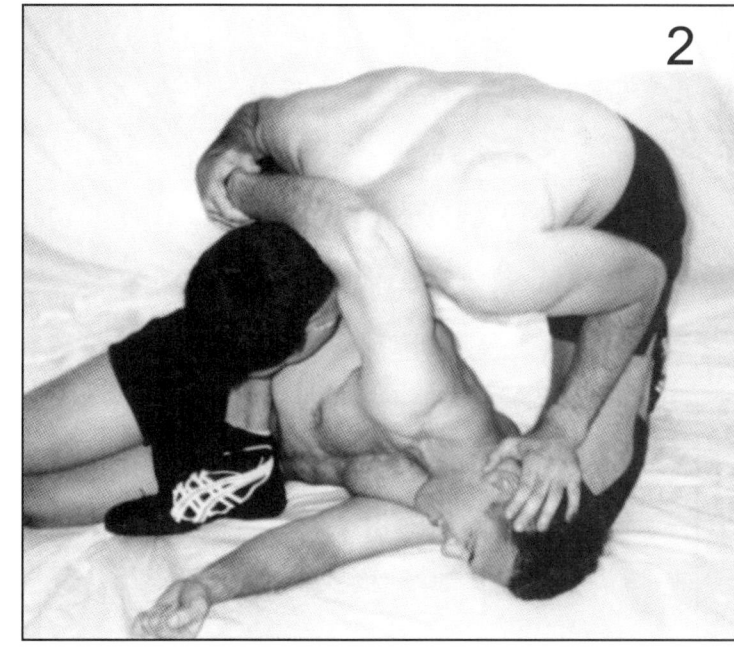

2

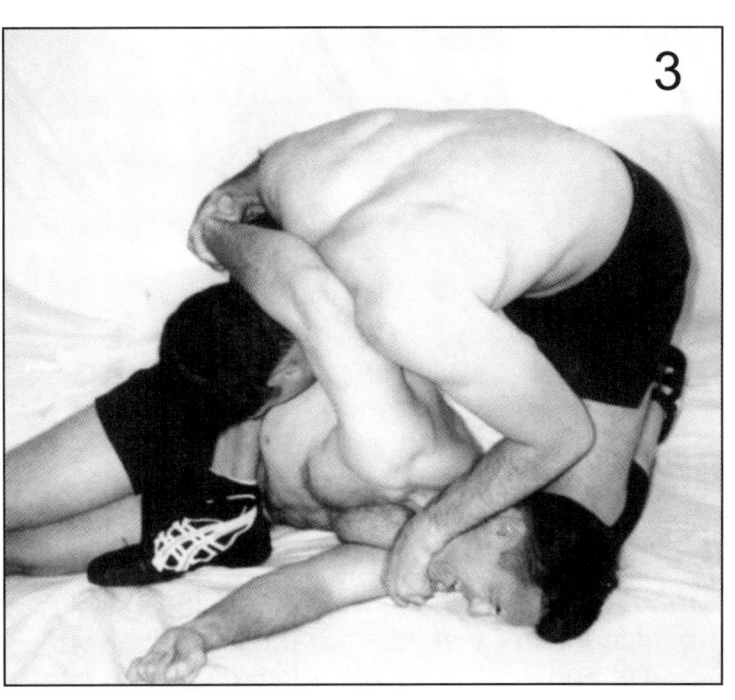

3

You can place the blade of your free forearm across his neck and drive it in to him. This will pin his head to the ground and help control his mobility. Continue to turn your body and bring his wrist towards his back until he submits. (Left)

SQUEEZE LOCK

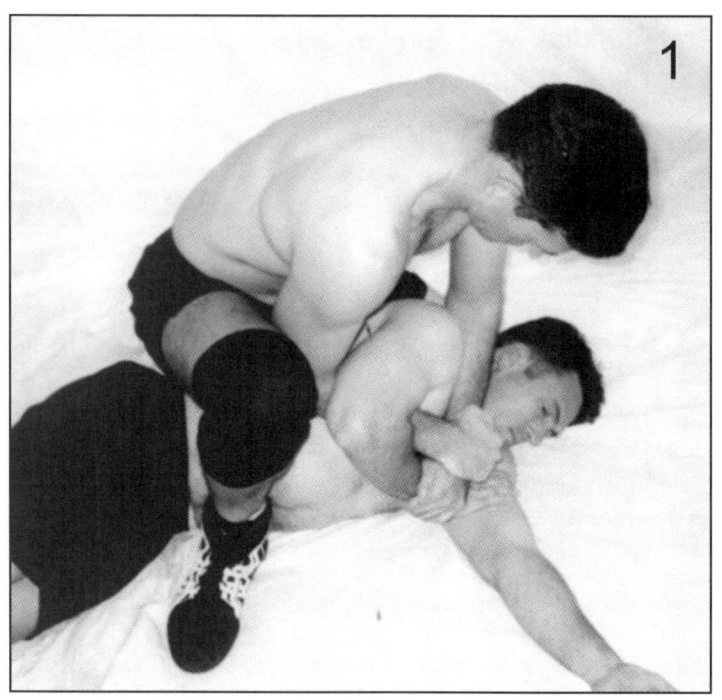

Secure his top arm with a figure four lock as shown.

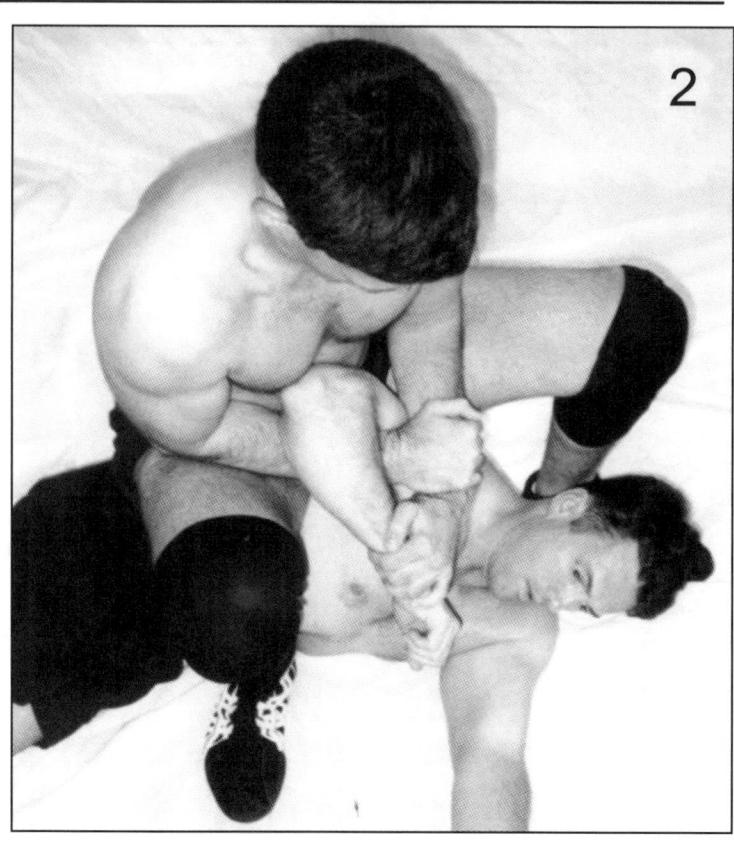

Bring your rear leg up so you are squatting.

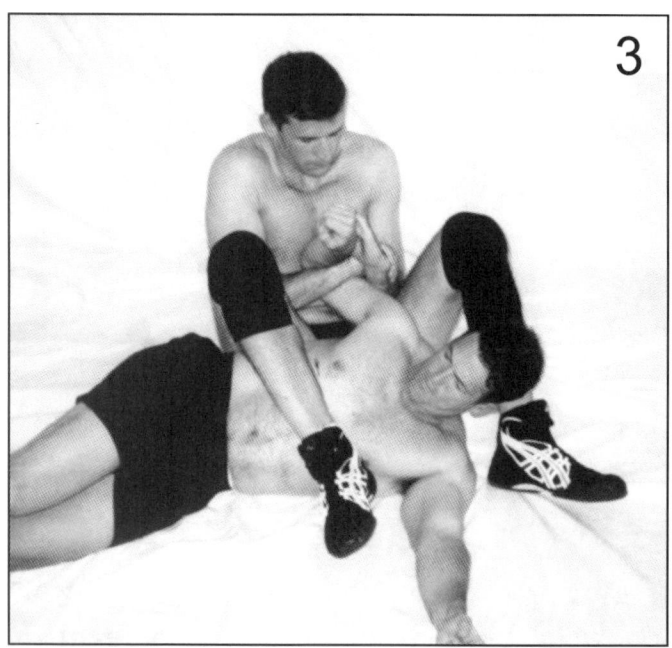

Fall backwards to a sitting position.

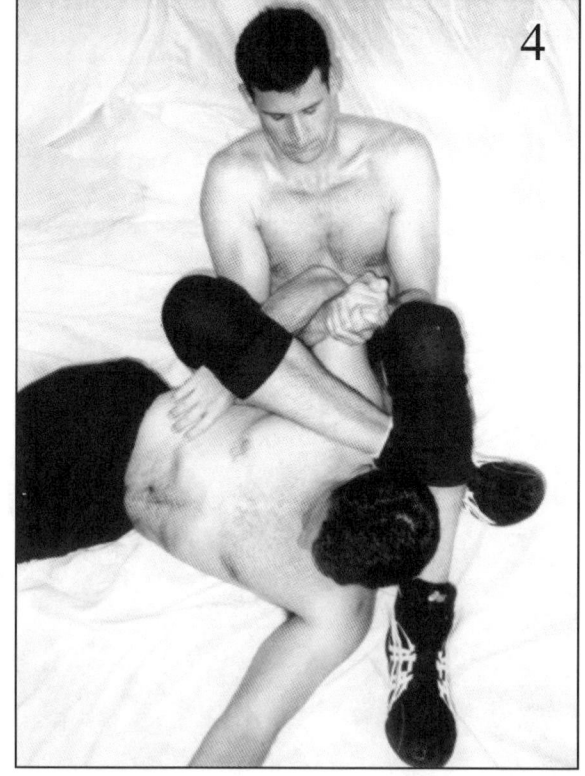

Place your leg across his forearm and lock it behind the knee of your other leg. Clasp your hands and drive the blade of your forearm into his elbow joint for the submission.

FOREARM LOCK

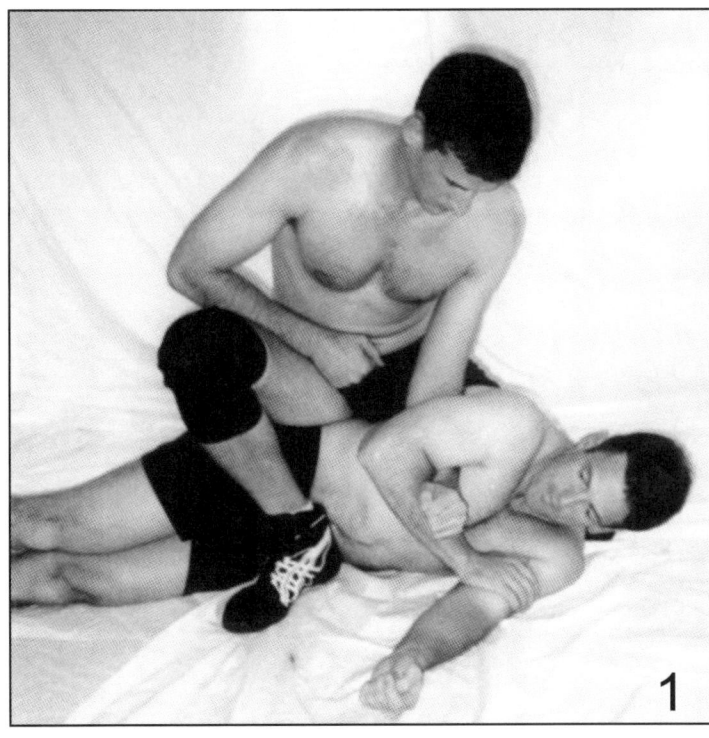

Slide your attacking arm under the biceps of his top arm and over his forearm. (Left)

Place the hand of your attacking arm under your own armpit and hook his wrist with your other, locking arm as shown. (Right)

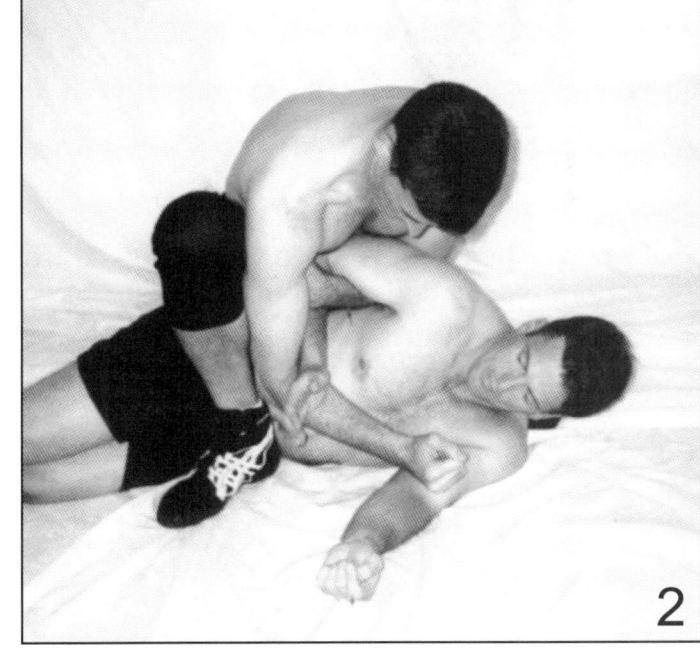

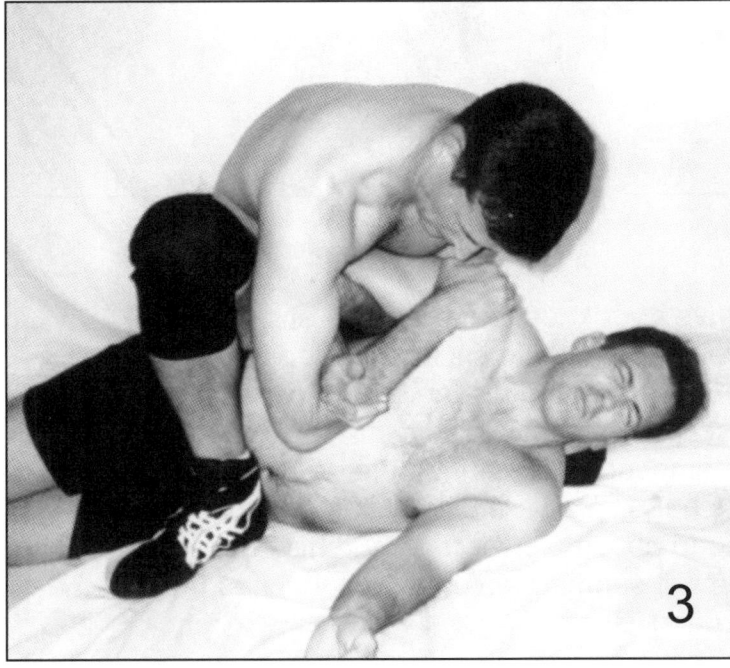

Grab his shoulder with your locking arm so that his targeted arm is trapped securely in your lock. Drive the blade of your attacking forearm into his trapped forearm while pulling up on his wrist with your locking arm. You are driving the relatively narrow blade of your forearm into the relatively wide bones of his forearm. The submission is from pain. (Left)

HIP LOCK

Place your foot between his legs while controlling his upper body. (Left)

Secure a hold on his ankle while keeping his upper body pinned. (Right)

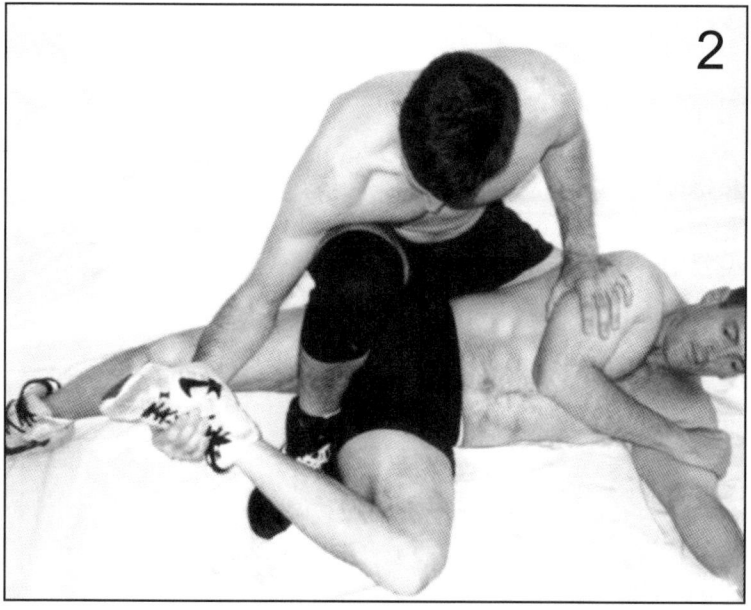

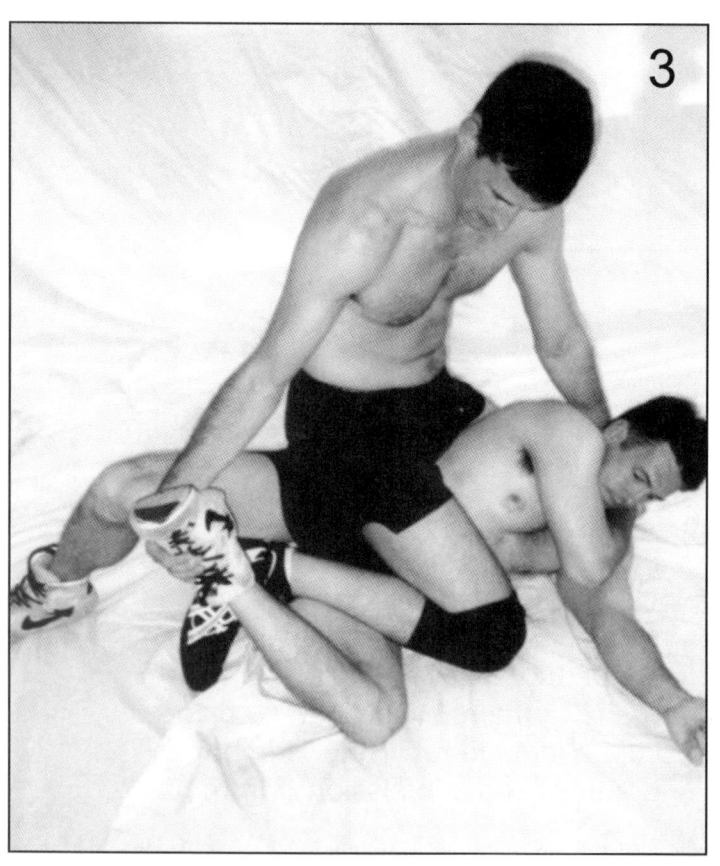

Drive your knee to the ground and place weight on it to pin his trapped leg to the ground. Secure his top arm to help limit his escape options. Pull his foot forwards, attempting to place it on the ground next to his head. You are using his foot and lower leg to act as a lever to torque his hip joint. He will submit before his foot touches the ground. (Left)

Chapter Nine
Submissions From Reverse Mount

Reverse Mount

The weight of your entire body is driving onto his head and neck, pinning him to the ground and limiting his mobility.

Your opponent's arms are vulnerable to a variety of attacks.

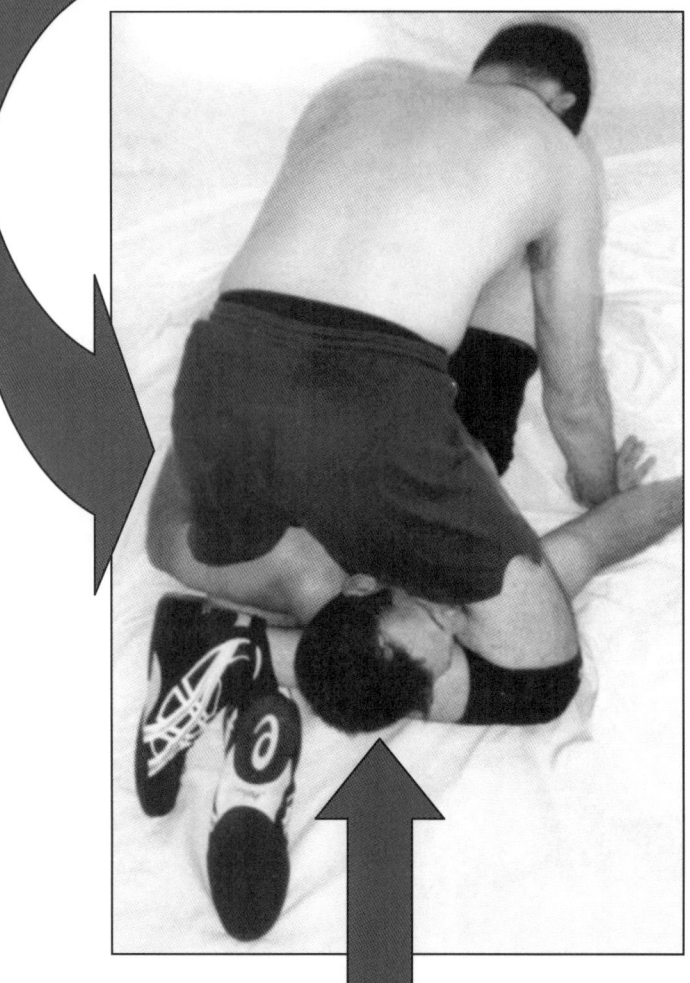

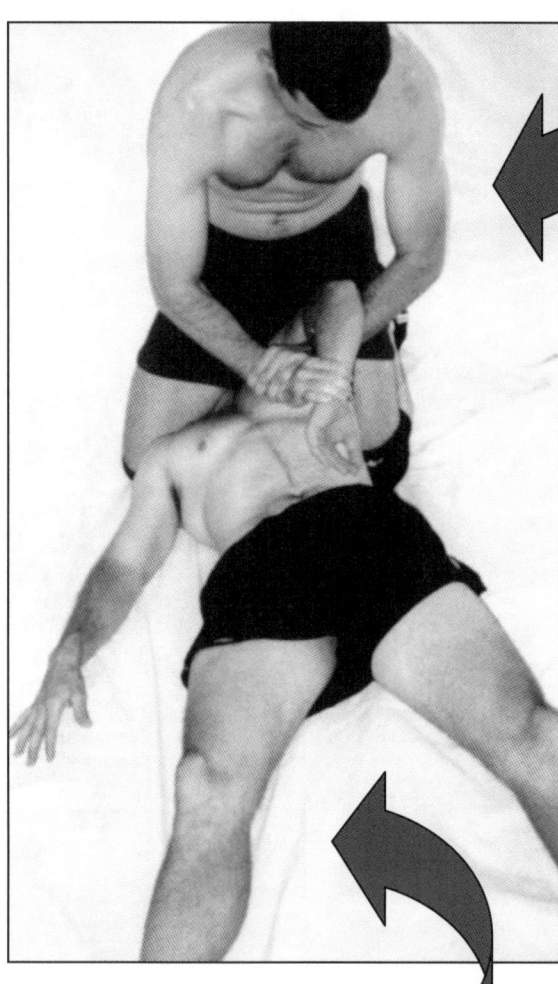

Your opponent has limited vision and can not see what attacks you are mounting against him.

Both of your opponent's legs are exposed to a variety of attacks.

SHOULDER CRANK

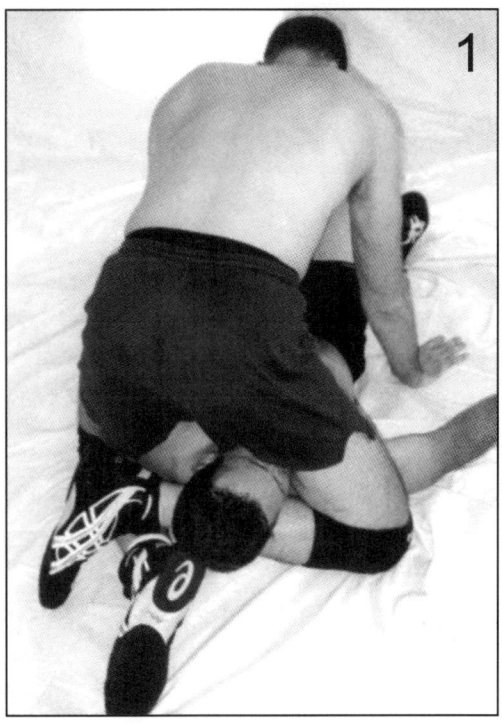

You have your opponent's head trapped in a reverse mount.

Secure an exposed arm at the wrist.

Reach under his arm with your free arm and grab your other arm at the wrist, securing a figure four lock.

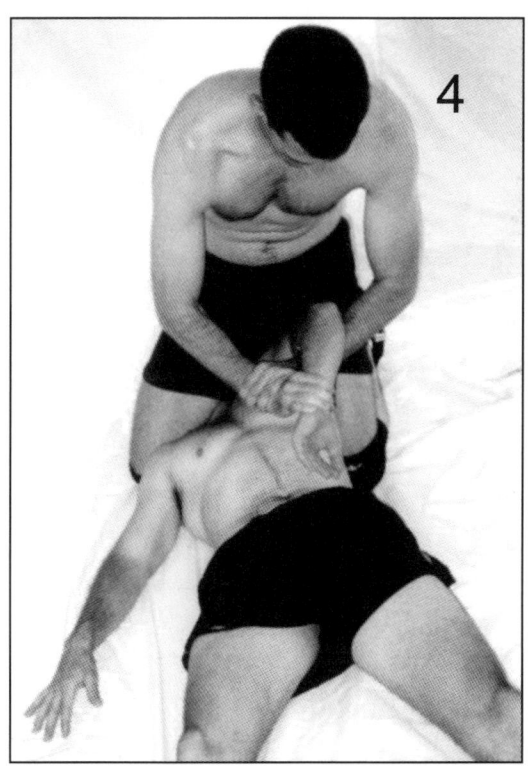

Twist his arm away from his body for the submission. This move uses his bent arm as a lever to torque his shoulder.

ARM BAR *Figure Four Lock*

You have your opponent's head and one arm trapped in a reverse mount.

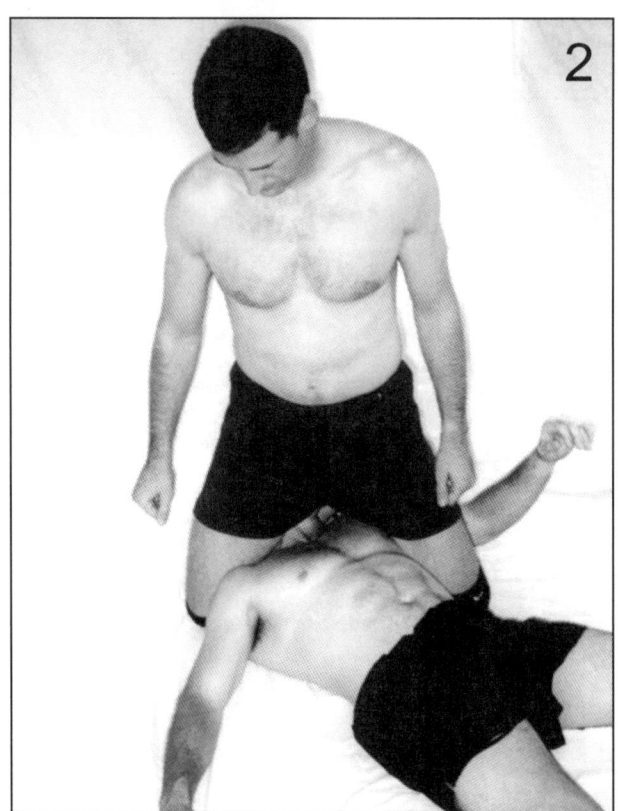

His free arm is isolated and exposed; he has no safe place to put it.

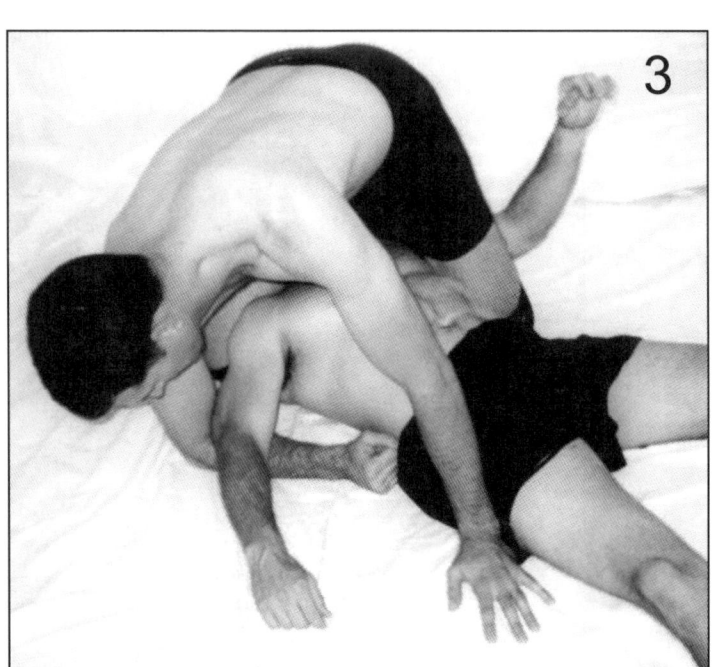

Place your arm under his exposed arm at the elbow.

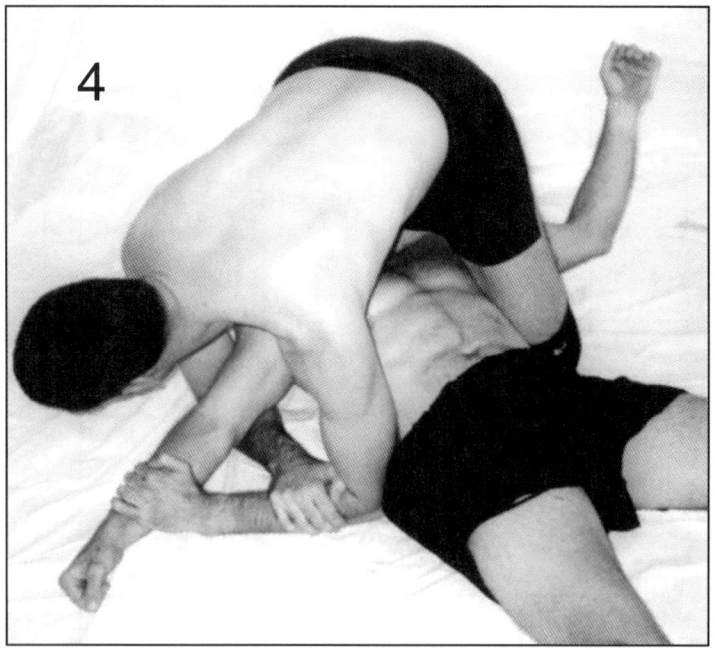

Secure his arm at the wrist and grab your arm at the forearm, forming a figure four lock. To submit him, raise your arm that is under his elbow and push down on his wrist with your other arm. This will hyper-extend his arm at the elbow.

ANKLE CRANK

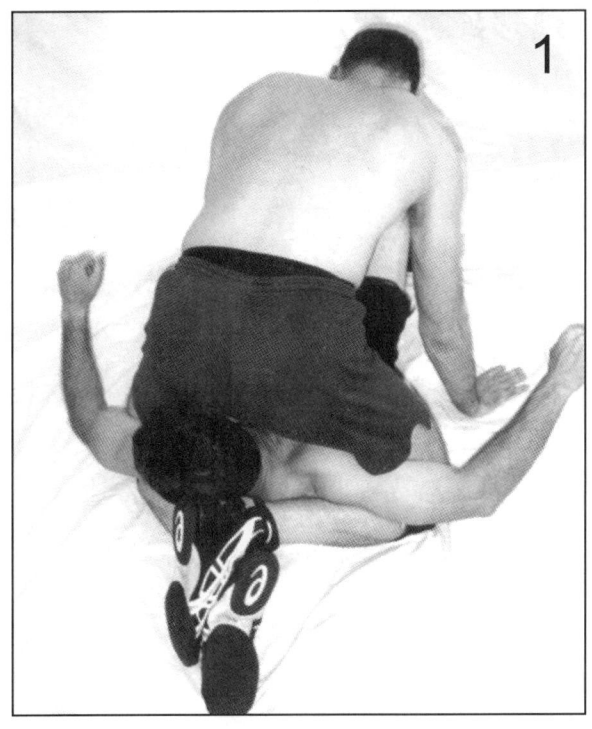

You have both of your opponent's arms and head trapped in a reverse mount.

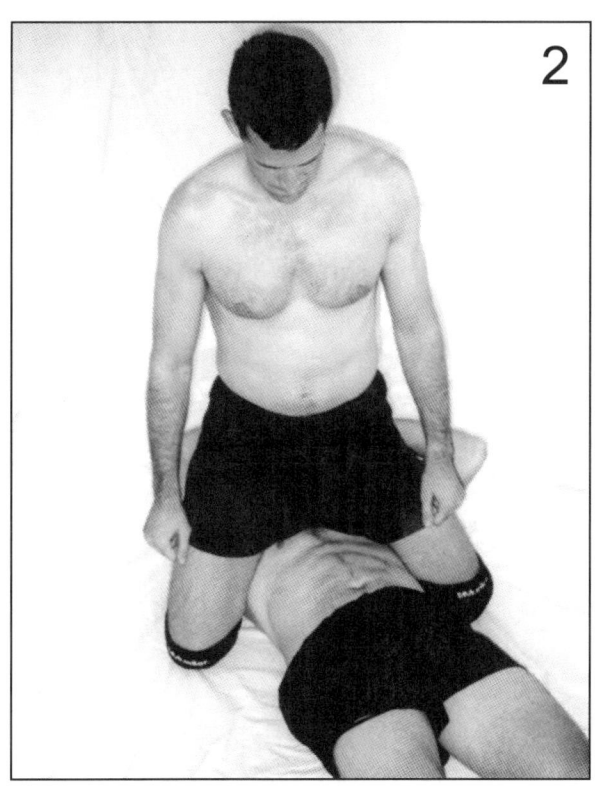

Both of his legs are exposed to attack.

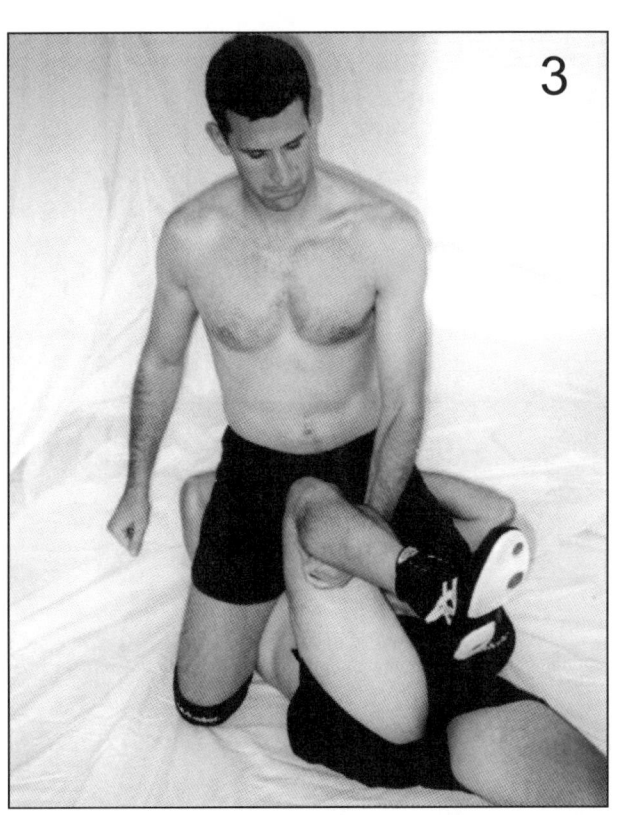

Hook one of his exposed legs under the knee and pull it towards you.

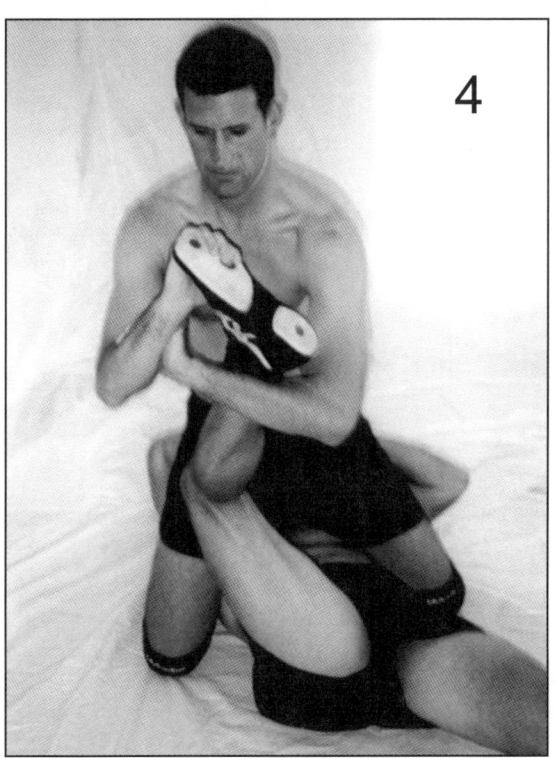

Secure a figure four lock on his foot as shown. Twist his toes away from you while keeping his heel tight against your chest. This uses his foot as a lever to torque his knee for the submission.

Chapter Ten
Submissions From Side Control

Side Control

There are many variations to securing side control. This is just one technique. Change your body positioning to fit your style and the situation.

You have your knees forwards, securing him at his hips and his head. You have your hips low, giving you a low center of gravity and a good base. Your chest is tight against his and your body weight is pinning him to the ground.

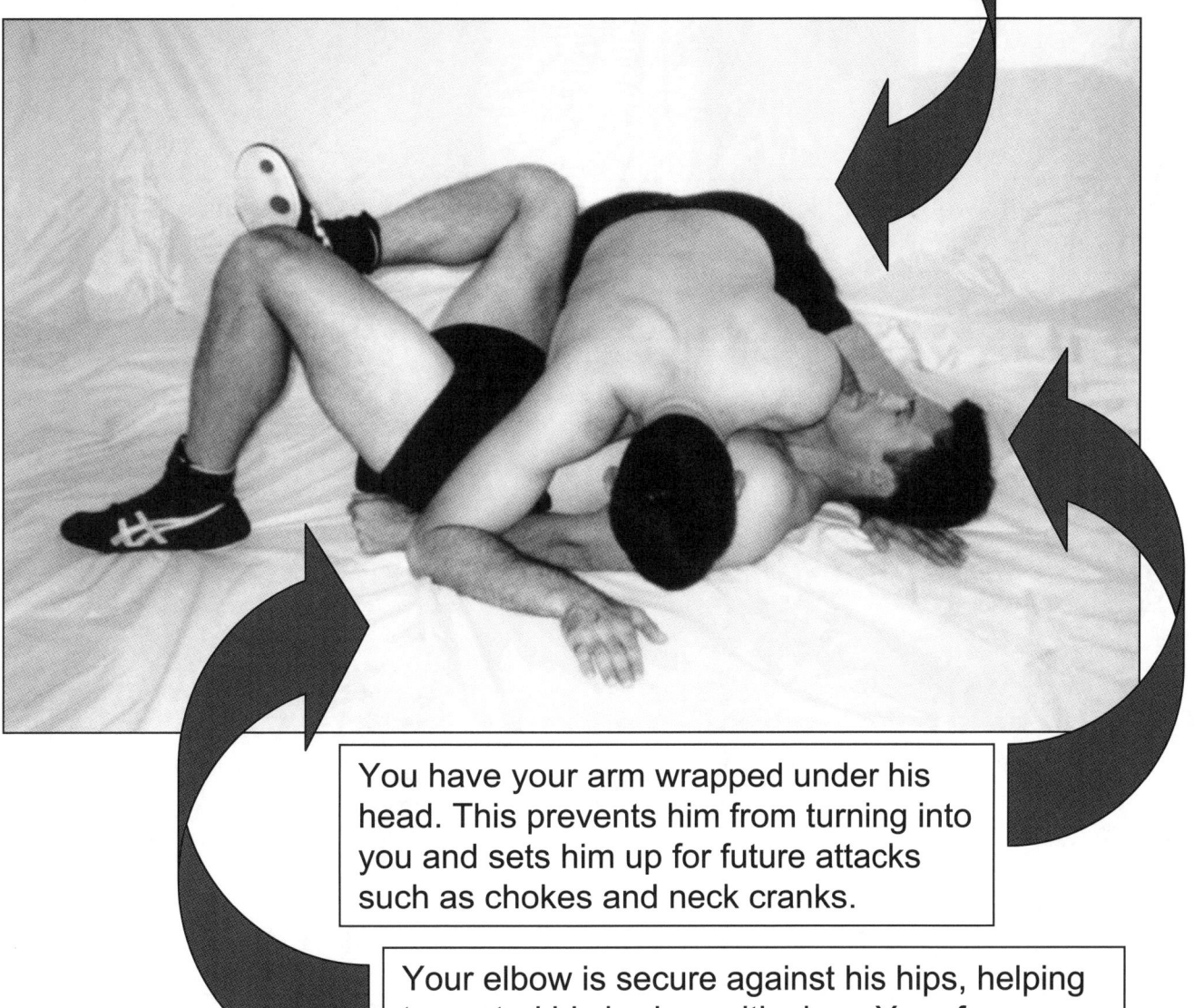

You have your arm wrapped under his head. This prevents him from turning into you and sets him up for future attacks such as chokes and neck cranks.

Your elbow is secure against his hips, helping to control his body positioning. Your forearm is flat helping to secure your base and keep your balance. Your arm is ready to attack his feet and his far arm if he exposes them.

NECK CRANK *Entangled Arm*

1. You have one arm wrapped behind his neck. Your other arm is controlling his far arm.

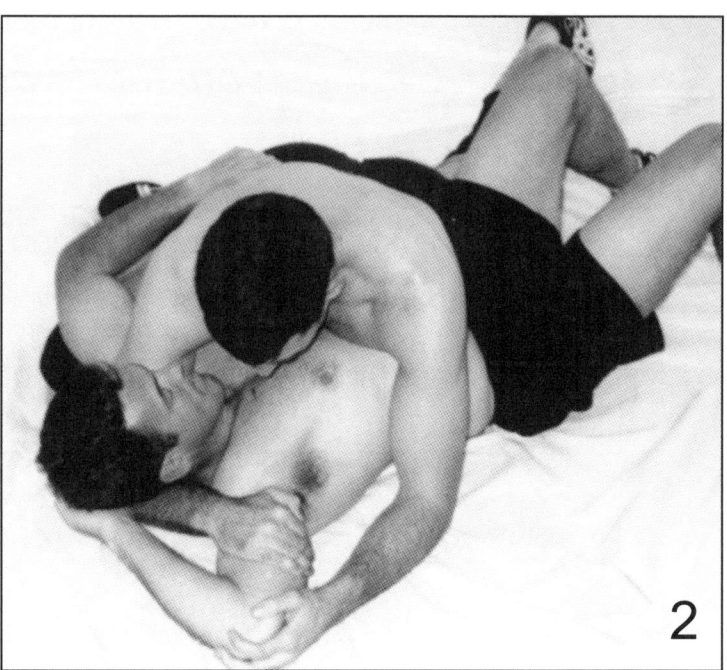

2. Push his far arm towards his head so you can grab it at the triceps with your attacking arm.

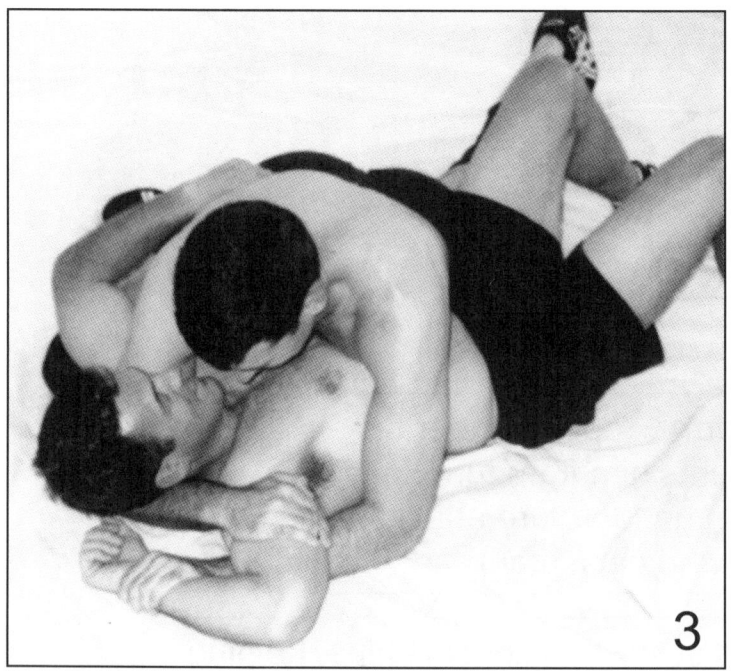

3. Secure his far arm with a grapevine to control it.

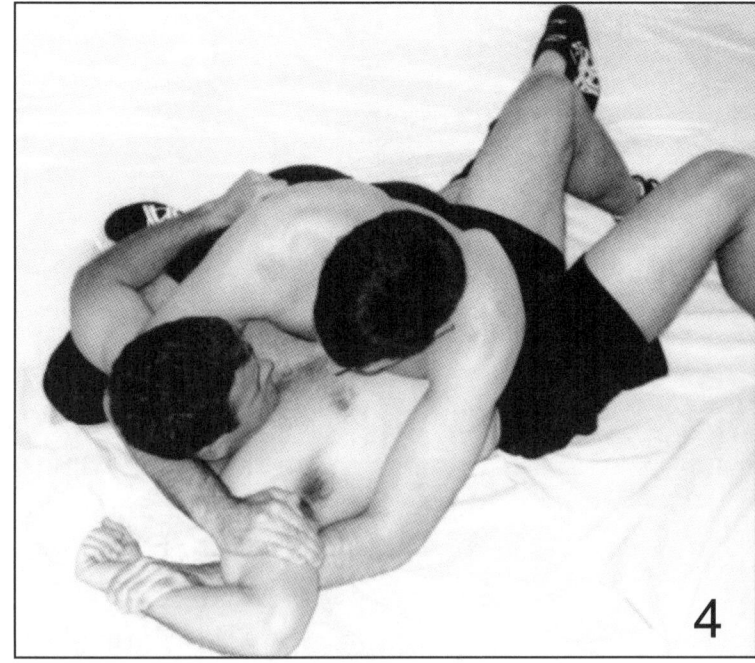

4. To crank his neck, drive the blade of your attacking forearm forwards. This will hyperextend his cervical spine for the submission.

NECK CRANK *Shoulder Variation*

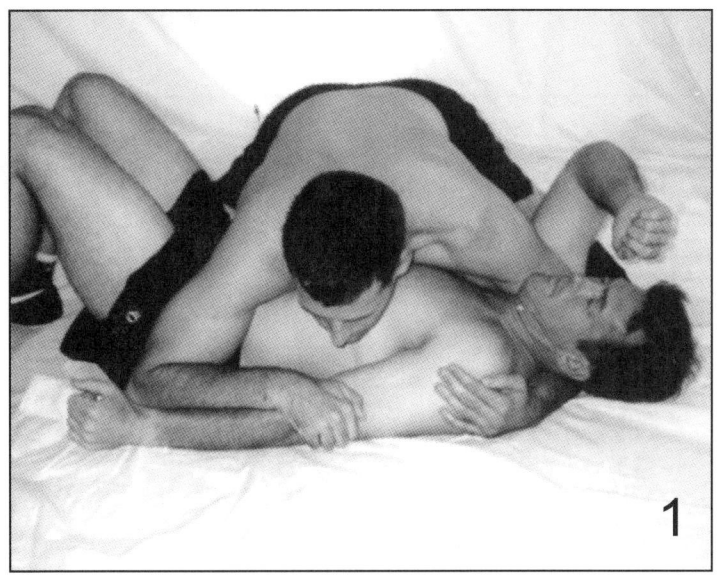

You have one arm cradling his neck and the other is controlling his far arm.

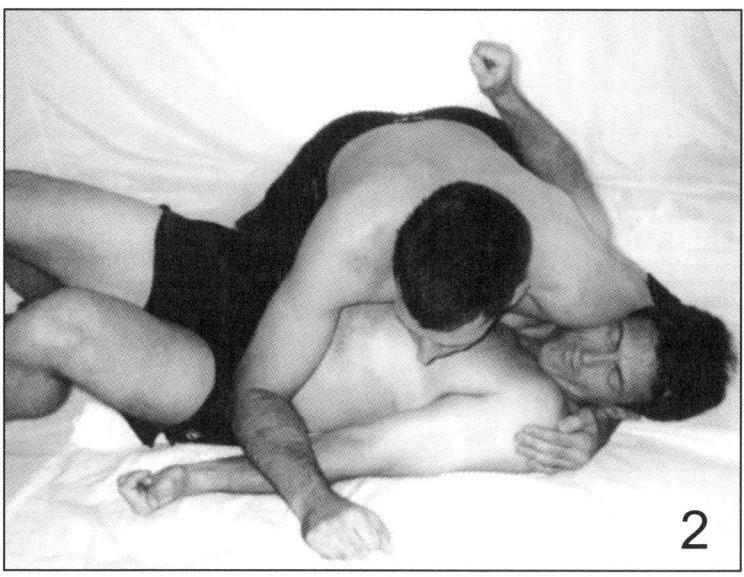

Drive your shoulder into his jaw, turning his head to the side.

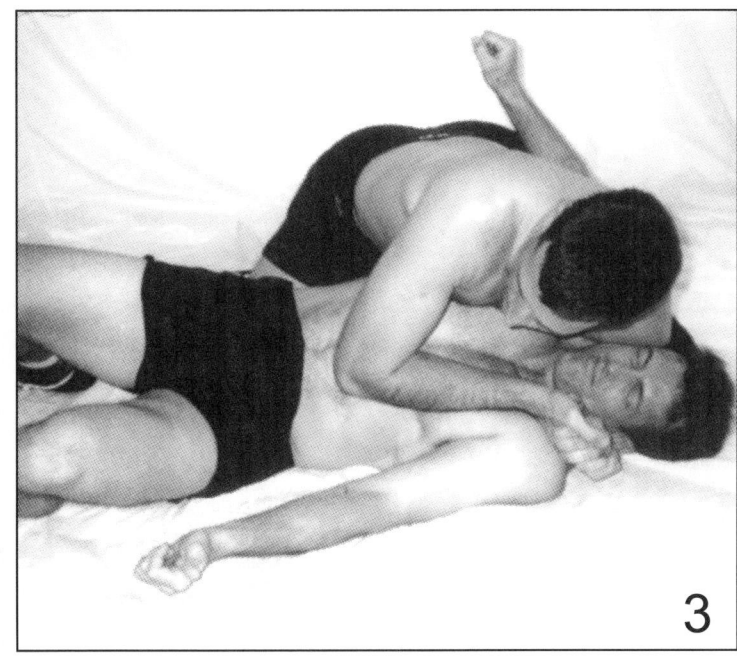

Clasp your hands together just above his shoulder.

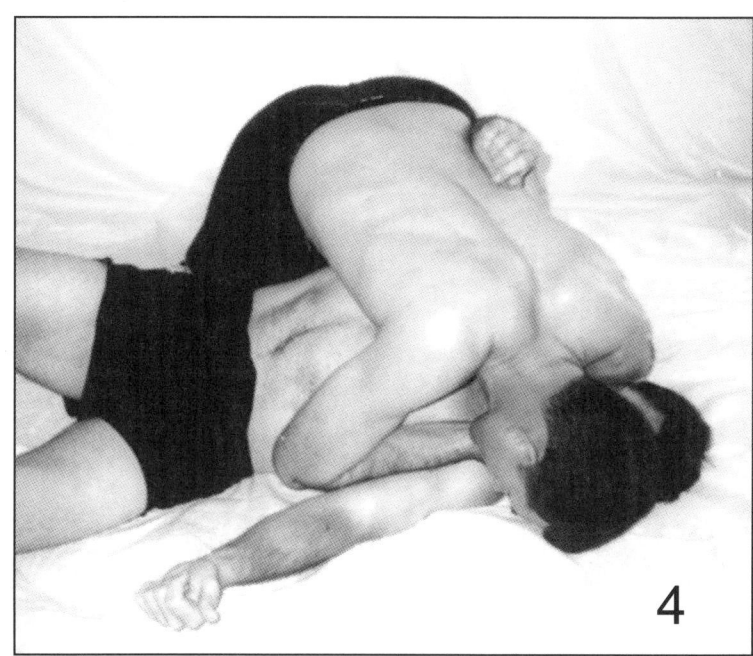

Drive your head to the ground. Push his head to the ground with your shoulder and pull up with the blade of your bottom forearm, driving it into the base of his neck. This exerts pressure on his cervical spine for the submission.

NECK CRANK *Step Over*

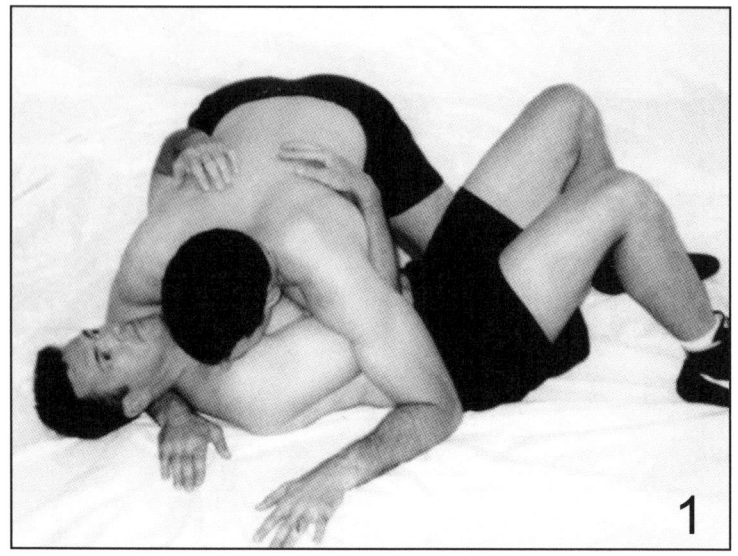

You are set up with your arm under your opponent's head.

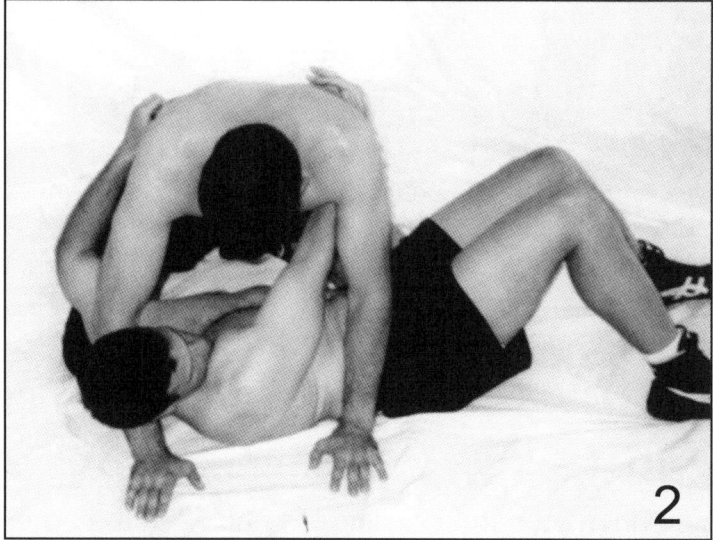

Post on your arm that was under his head, driving his head forwards with your forearm. You are coming to your knees to extend your arm.

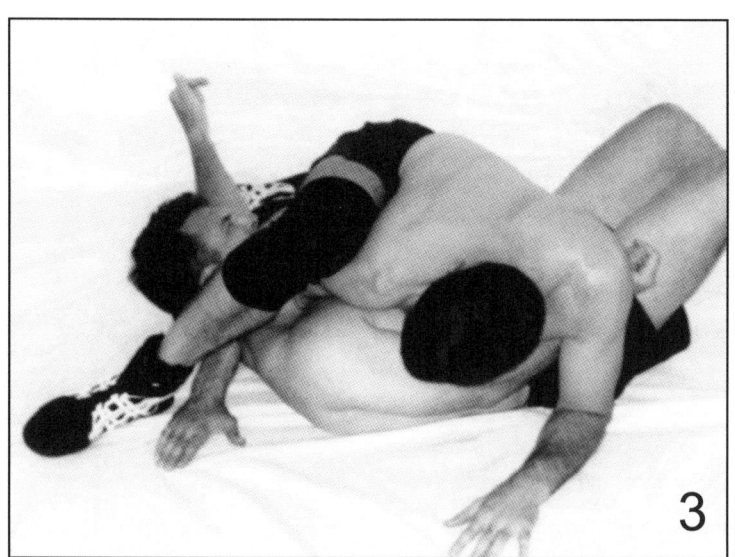

Step over his head with your leg, trapping his head between your arm and leg.

Drive your arm forwards while, simultaneously, driving your leg backwards, catching his head in a scissors lock. This move will cut off his carotid arteries and crank his neck for the submission.

CHOKE *Forearm*

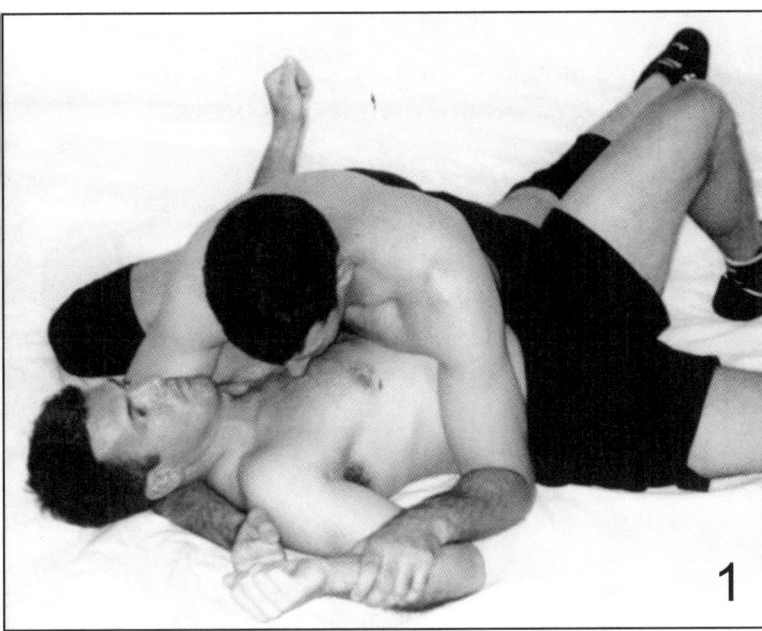

You have your opponent in side control. (Left)

Place your attacking arm across his throat and under his chin. (Right)

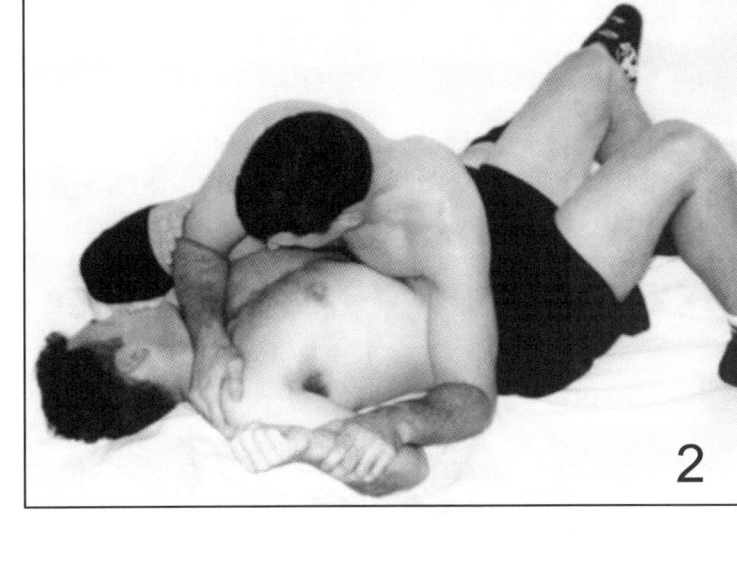

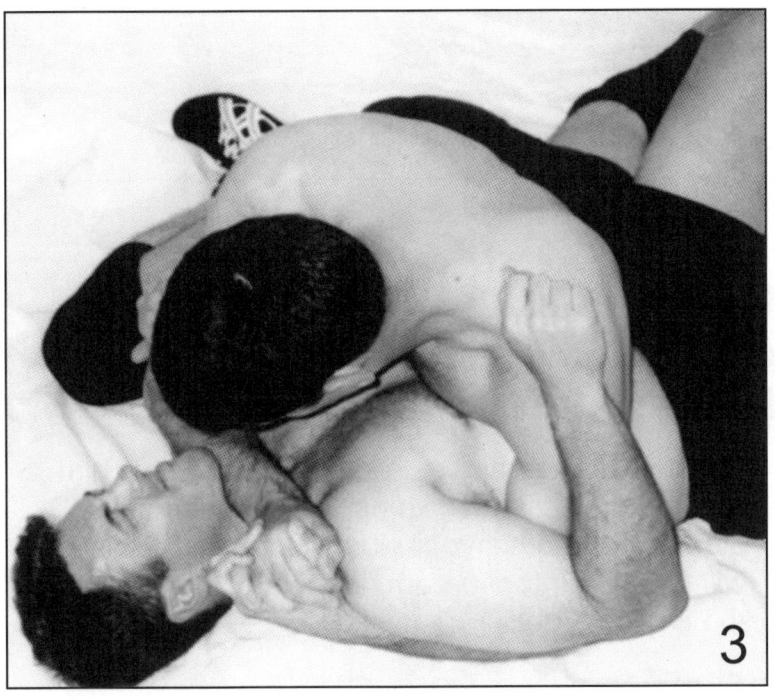

Hook your far arm under his far arm and clasp your hands tightly; keep your hands pressed to the ground. To apply the choke, drive your attacking elbow to the ground and press the blade of your forearm into his esophagus. (Left)

CHOKE *Paper Cutter*

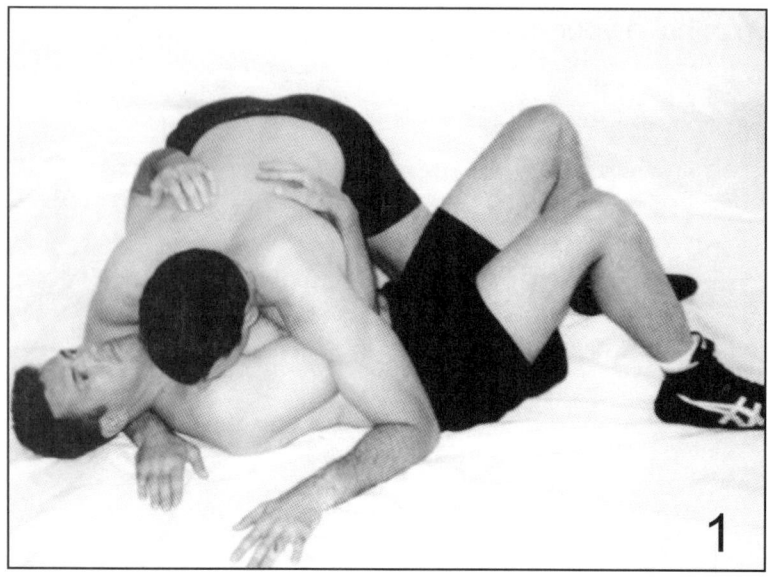

You have side control on your opponent with your arm wrapped under his head. (Left)

Clasp your hands at his far shoulder. Ensure that your top hand is facing palm up when you clasp. (Right)

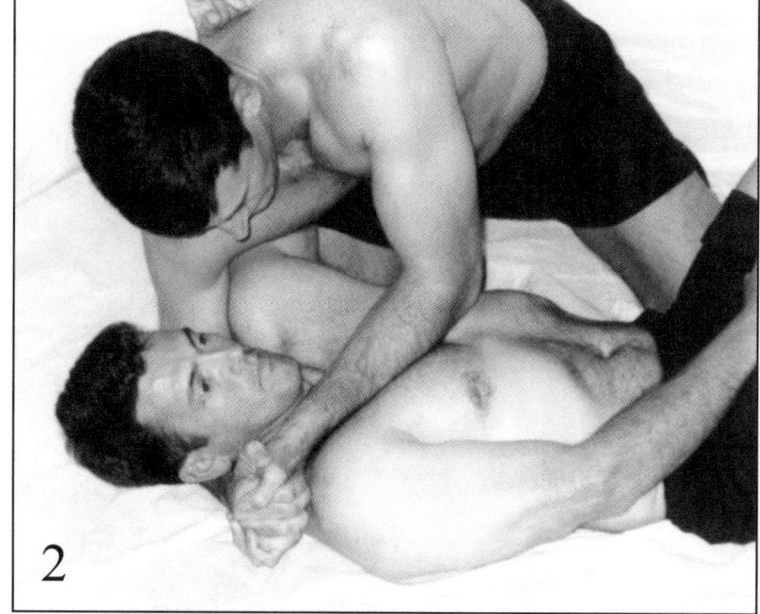

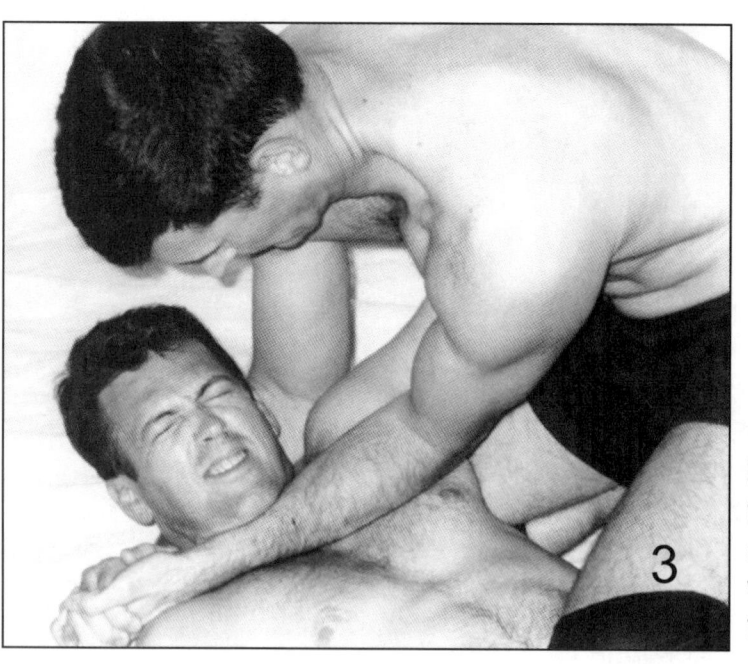

Place your knee across his stomach and pin him to the ground. To choke him, lean towards his stomach and drive your elbows together. This will force your top forearm into his esophagus for the choke. (Left)

CHOKE *Guillotine*

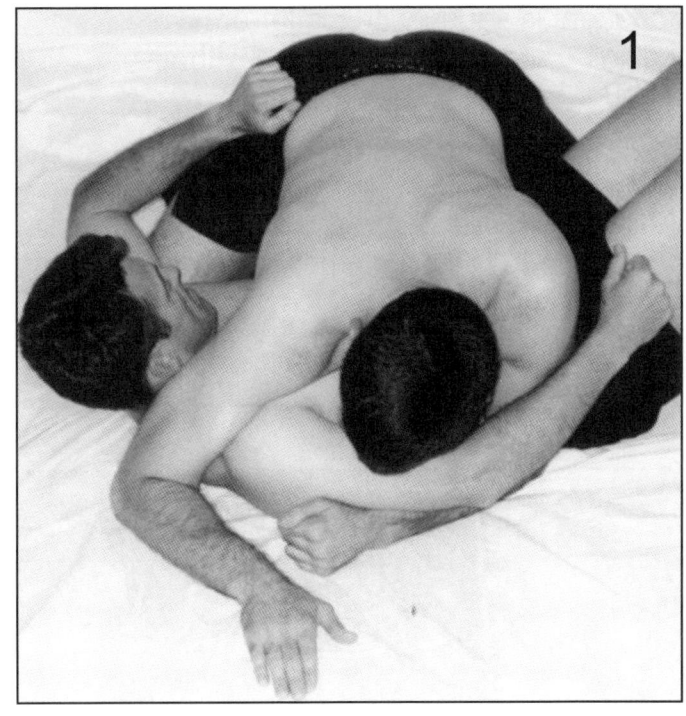

You have your opponent in side control and you have your elbow placed against his head. His head is raised off the ground. (Left)

Hook your attacking arm behind his neck and pull towards you, keeping his head off the ground. (Right)

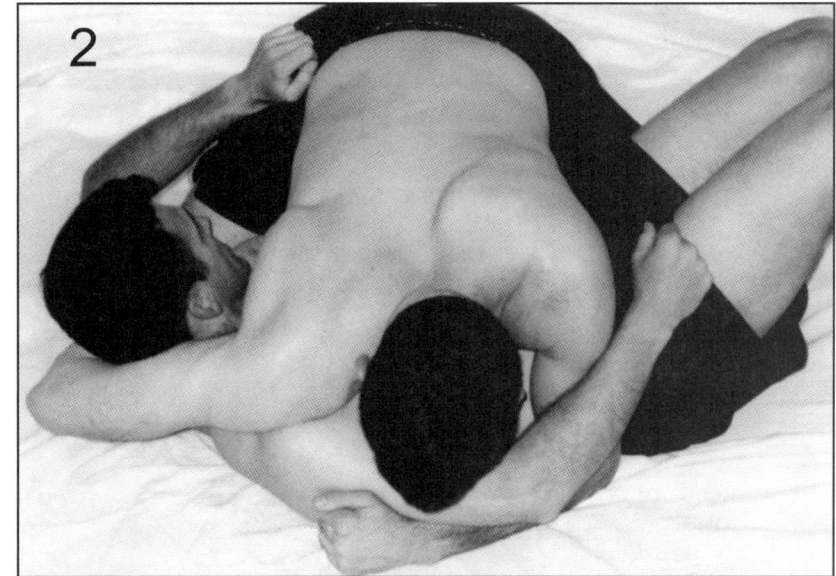

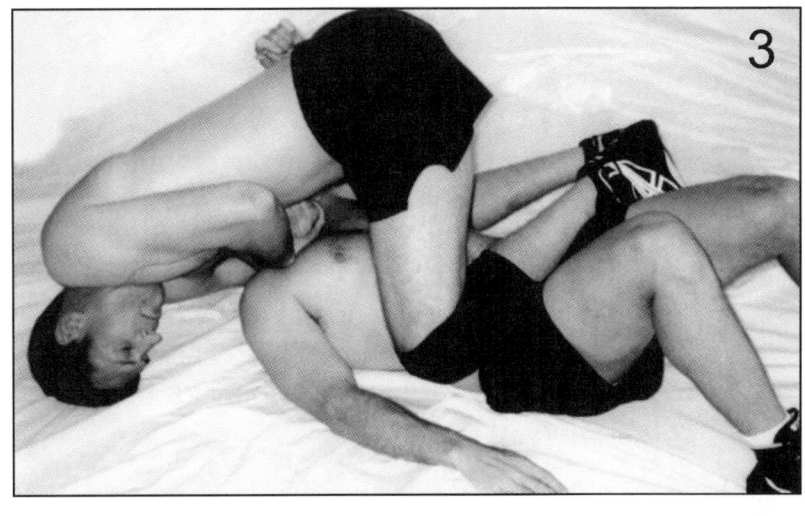

Bring your knee across his stomach. Grab your attacking arm at the wrist with your other arm; ensure that your attacking arm is under his chin. You have your weight balanced on your head, knee, and shin across his stomach. To choke him, pull the blade of your attacking forearm up and into his esophagus for the choke. (Left)

ARM BAR *Figure Four Lock*

Your opponent is set up with his far arm exposed. You are securing his arm with both of yours. (Left)

Secure his forearm while maintaining control of his trapped arm. (Right)

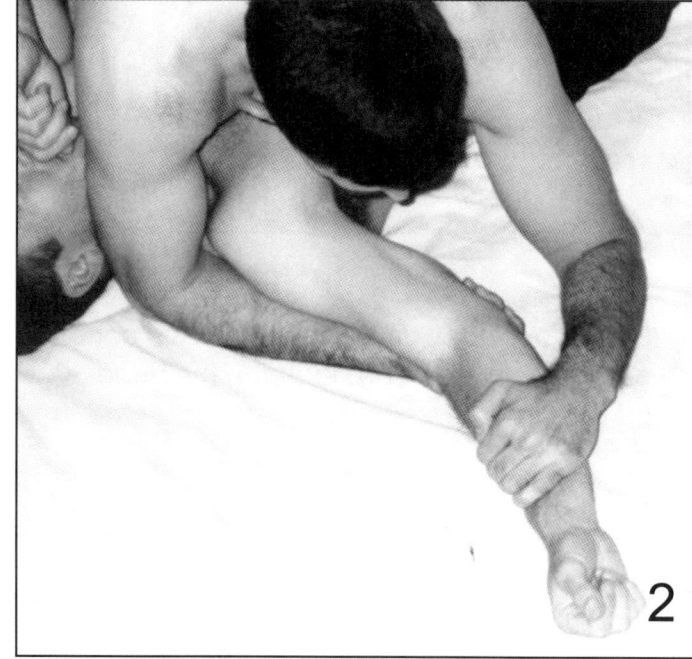

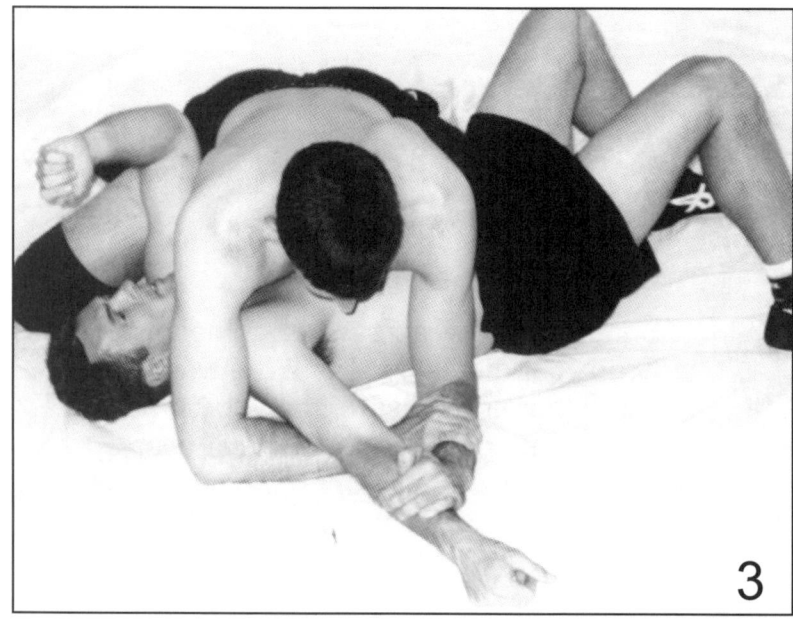

Grab your arm at the wrist, making a figure four lock. Your bottom arm is just above his elbow, closer to his shoulder. Pull up with your bottom forearm, putting pressure above his elbow, while pushing down on his forearm with your other arm. This will hyper-extend his arm at the elbow for the submission. (Left)

ARM BAR *Elbow Hug*

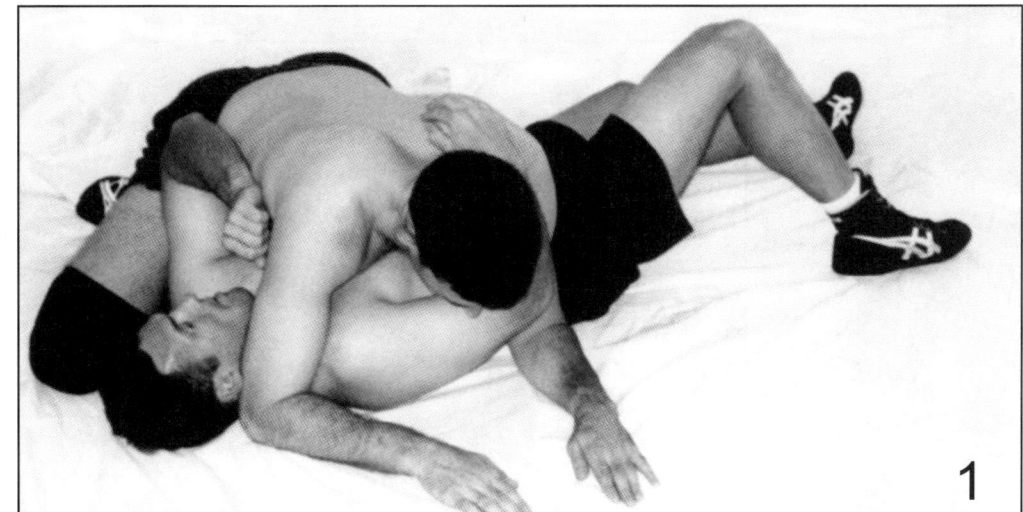

Your opponent is set up with his far arm placed over your shoulder. (Left)

Grab his far arm below the elbow and pull it into you, rotating his body towards you. (Right)

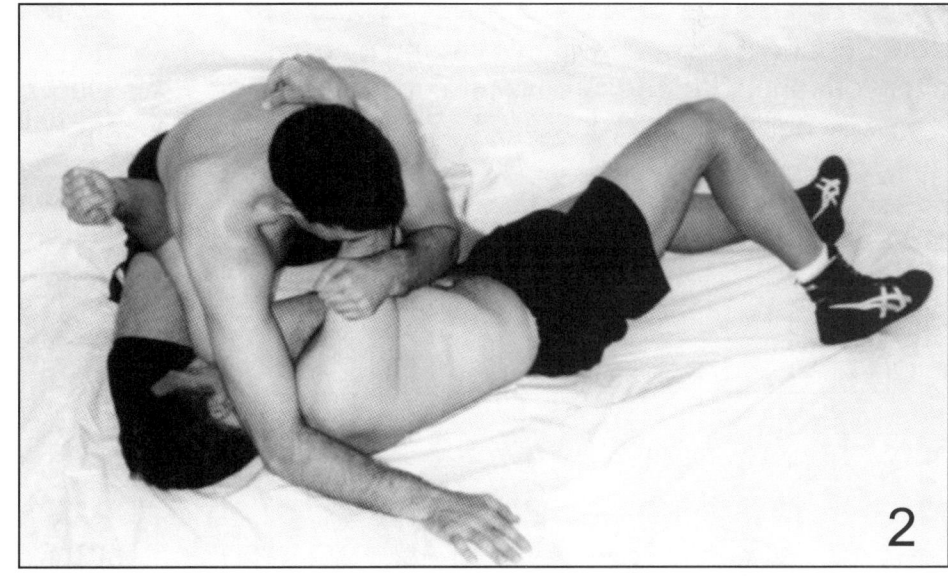

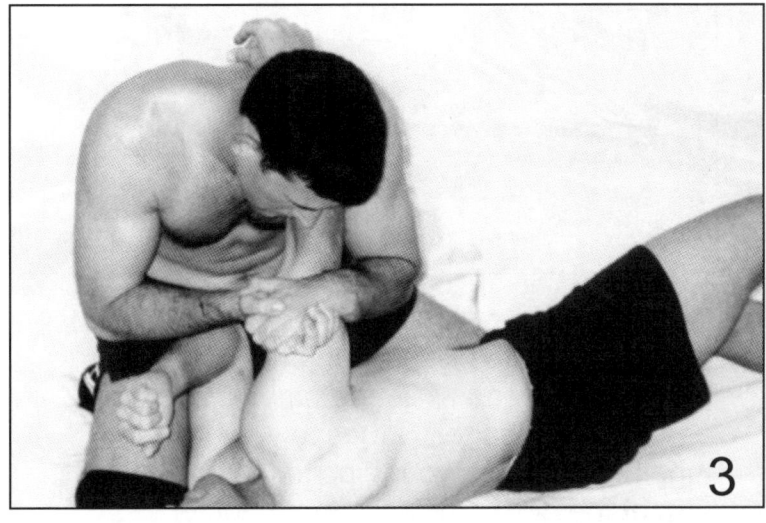

Clasp your hands just above his elbow, closer to his body. Pin his arm to your shoulder with your head. Drive your shoulder forwards and pull his elbow in towards your stomach. This will hyper-extend his arm at the elbow for the submission. (Left)

ARM BAR *Step Across*

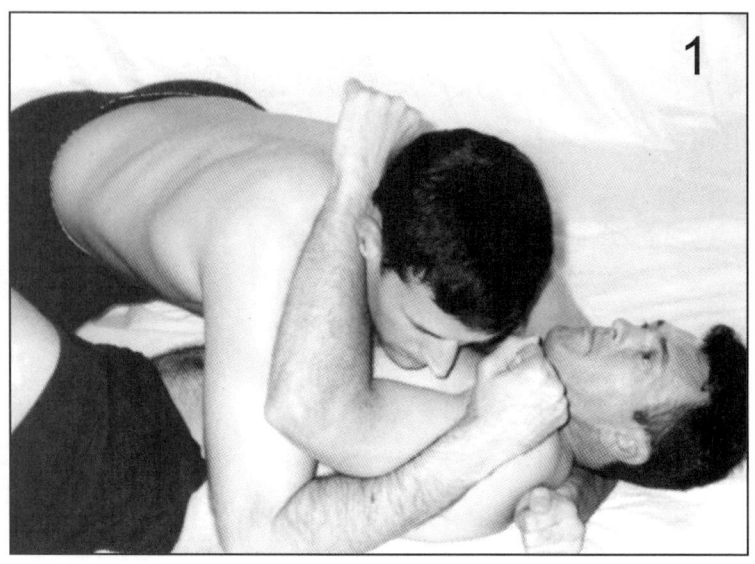

Your opponent is set up with his far arm placed over your shoulder. Secure his arm under the elbow by pulling it towards you.

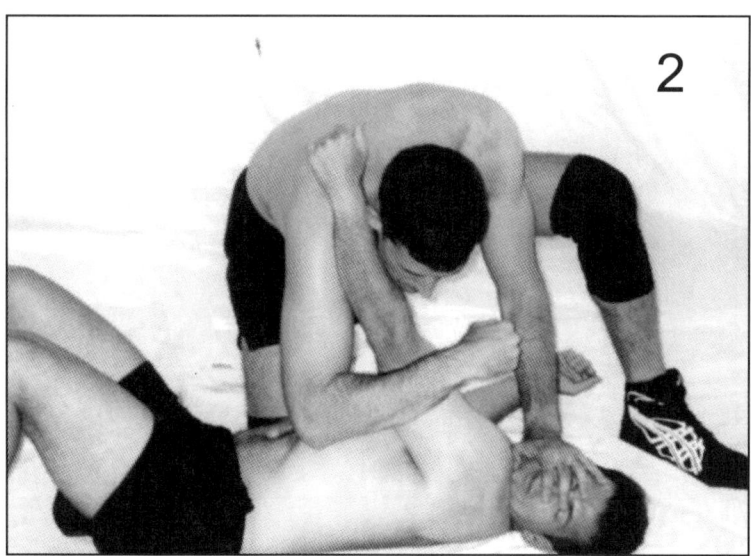

Come up to a knee while maintaining pressure on his elbow, trapping it against your shoulder. Control his head to prevent him from repositioning.

Step across your opponent's body and secure his arm with both of your own. (This picture is from the opposite angle)

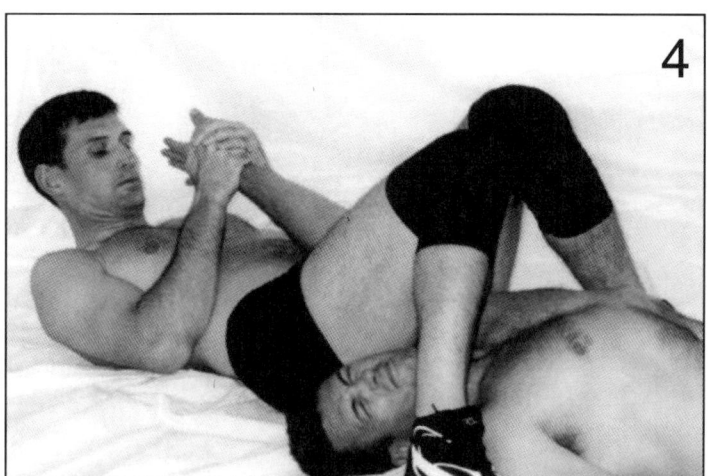

Continue to pivot around your opponent and fall backwards with his trapped arm. One leg is trapping his head while the other is pushing against his ribcage. Squeeze your knees together and arch your hips to hyper-extend his arm at the elbow for the submission.

FOREARM LOCK

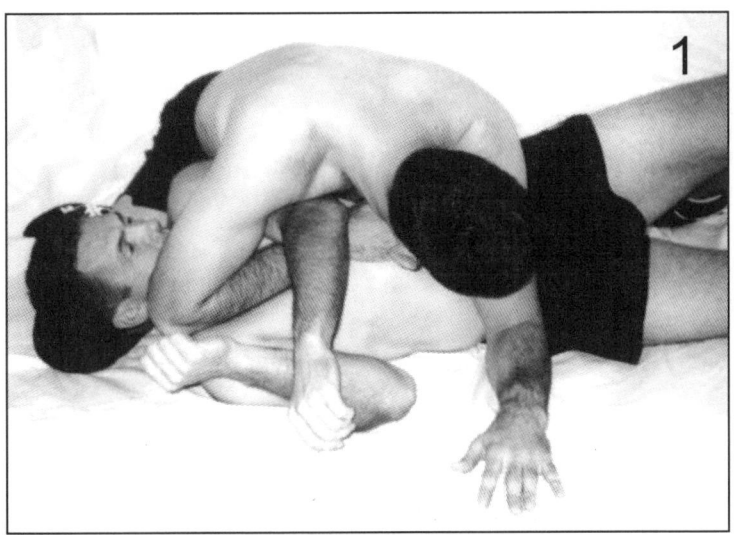

You have your opponent in side control. You have your attacking arm hooked under his near side arm.

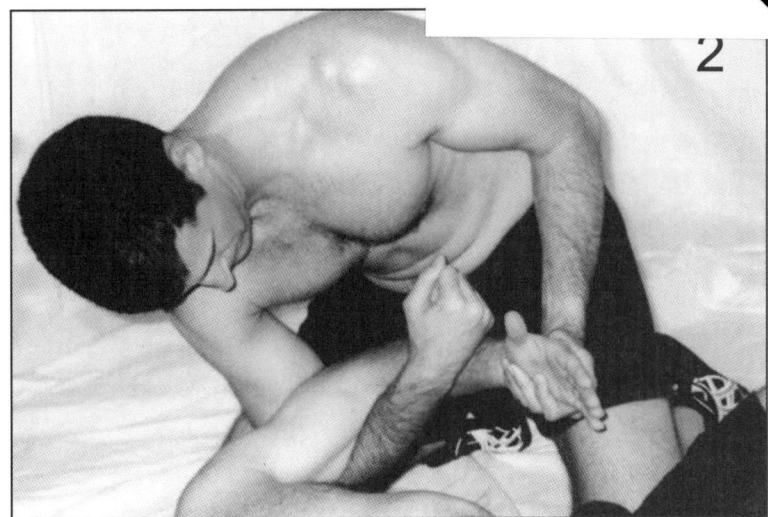

Secure him at the wrist with your other, locking arm.

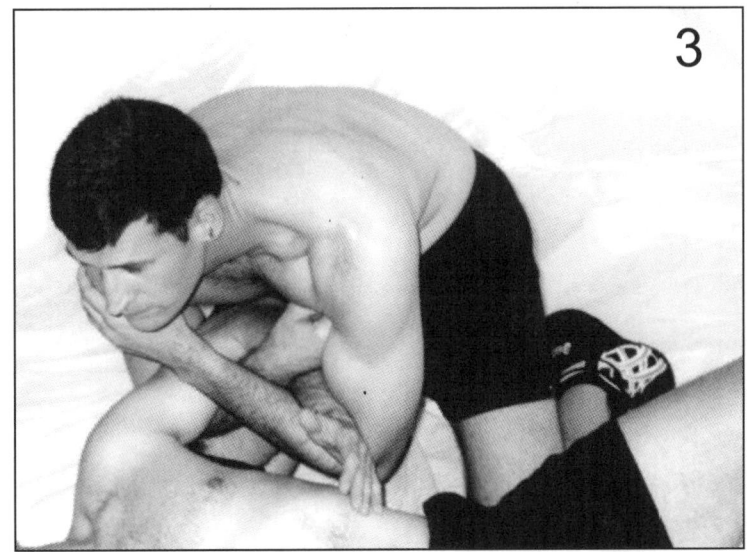

Drive the hand of your attacking arm under the armpit of your locking arm. Grab your attacking arm's shoulder with your locking arm as shown.

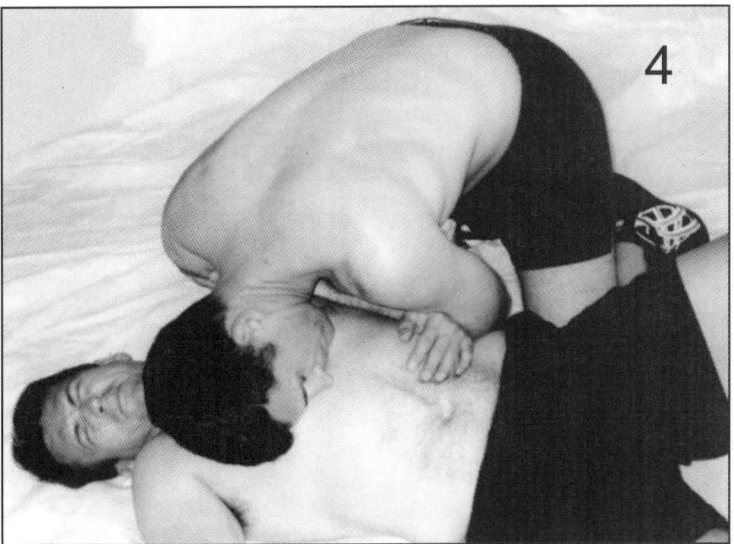

Lean forwards and place your head on your opponent's chest, pinning him to the ground. Drive the blade of your attacking forearm into his trapped forearm. Pull his forearm into your attacking blade with your locking arm. Ensure his hand is palm up for best results. The submission is from the pain of driving the blade of your forearm into the bones of his forearm.

SHOULDER CRANK *Key Lock / Americana*

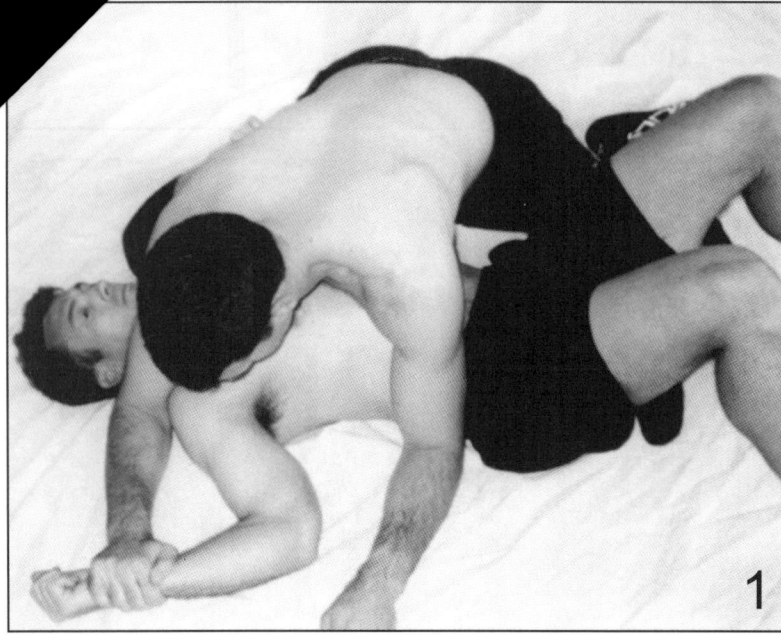

You are securing your opponent's exposed arm at the wrist. Your elbow is tight against his head. (Left)

Take your free arm, reach under his upper arm and grab your other arm at the wrist, making a figure four lock. (Right)

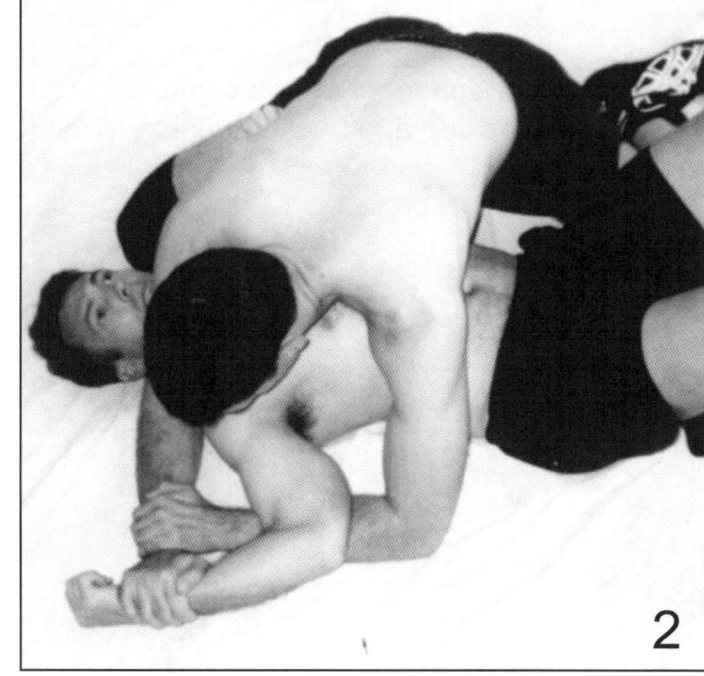

Pull his elbow in close to his side and then rotate his elbow upwards, attempting to place his elbow on the ground next to his head. Keep the wrist of his trapped arm pressed to the ground. This move uses the arm as a lever to torque your opponent's shoulder. He will submit from pain before you tear the muscles of his shoulder. (Left)

SHOULDER CRANK *Reverse Key Lock*

Secure your opponent's exposed, far arm at the wrist. (Left)

Reach under his upper arm with your other arm and grab your wrist, securing a figure four lock and trapping his arm. (Right)

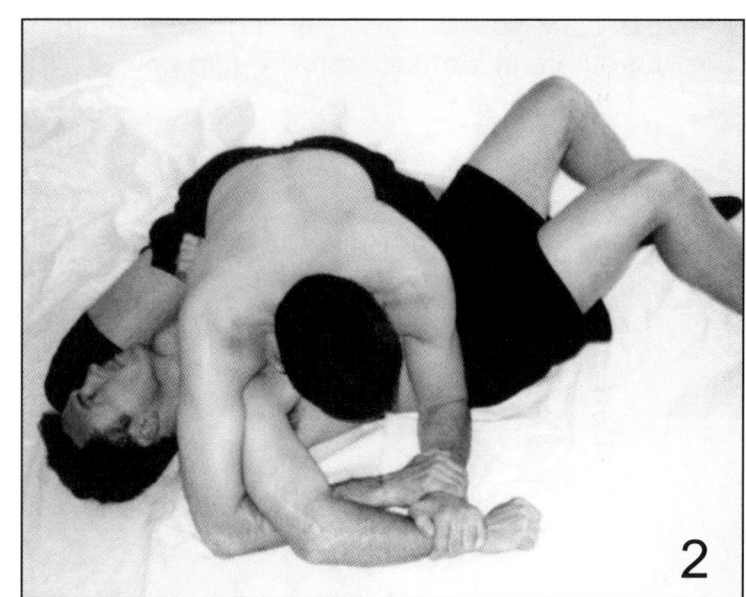

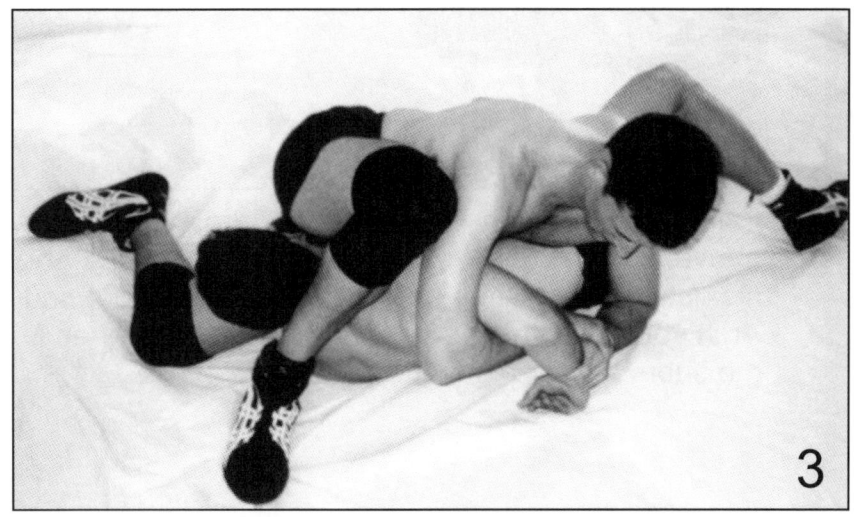

Step over his head with your leg and lift his upper body off the ground. This will give you the space to torque his shoulder. Push his wrist backwards, attempting to place it to your knee. This move uses the arm as a lever to torque your opponent's shoulder for the submission. (Left)

KNEE BAR *Far Leg*

You have your opponent in side control. You have hooked your leg over his near leg; essentially, you are in a modified half guard now.

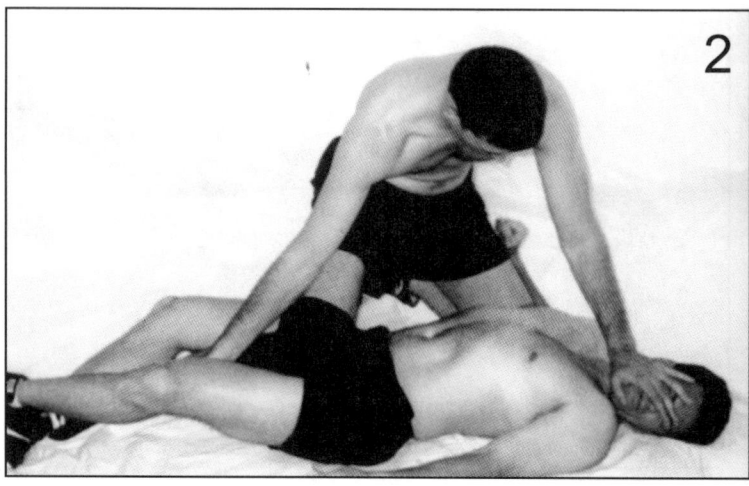

Control your opponent's head to prevent him from repositioning. Hook under his far leg with your free arm. You are preparing to step over his head and attack his far leg.

Step over his body, maintaining a tight grip on his trapped leg. Keep your groin as close to his hip as possible.

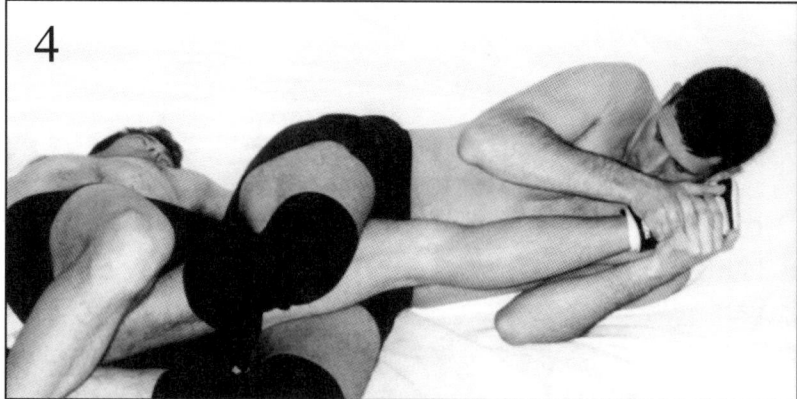

Fall to your side, ensuring that your groin is slightly above his knee, closer to his body. Plant your feet on his buttocks and keep his foot tight against your body. Arch your hips to hyper-extend his leg at the knee for the submission.

KNEE BAR *Near Leg*

You have your opponent in side control. Drive your forearm across his neck to keep his head pinned to the ground. Under hook is near leg with your other arm.

Drive your knee across his stomach and place your weight on it, helping to pin his hips to the ground. Control his far arm.

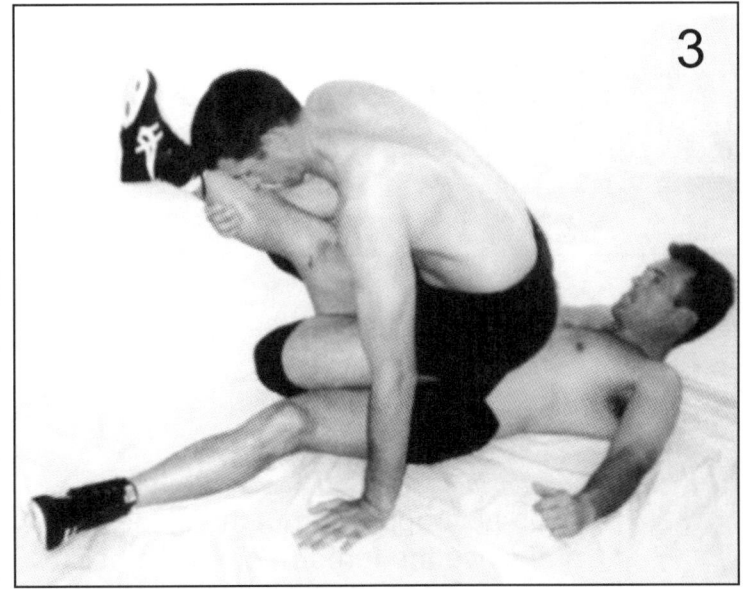

Drive your knee across his stomach and in between his legs. Maintain control of his trapped leg and place your groin as close to his hip as you can.

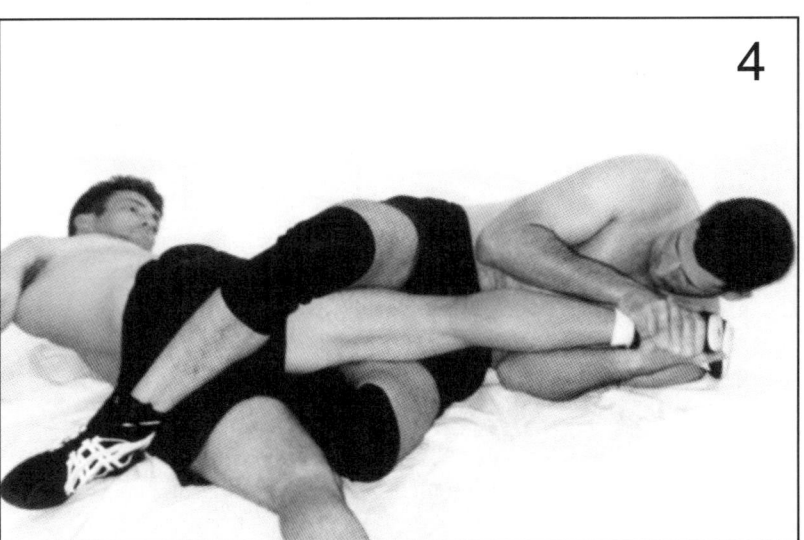

Fall across his body, using his trapped leg and your body weight to pin him to the ground. Hook the heel of your top leg against his buttocks and squeeze your knees together. Secure his foot tightly against your body and arch your hips to hyper-extend his leg at the knee for the submission.

HIP LOCK

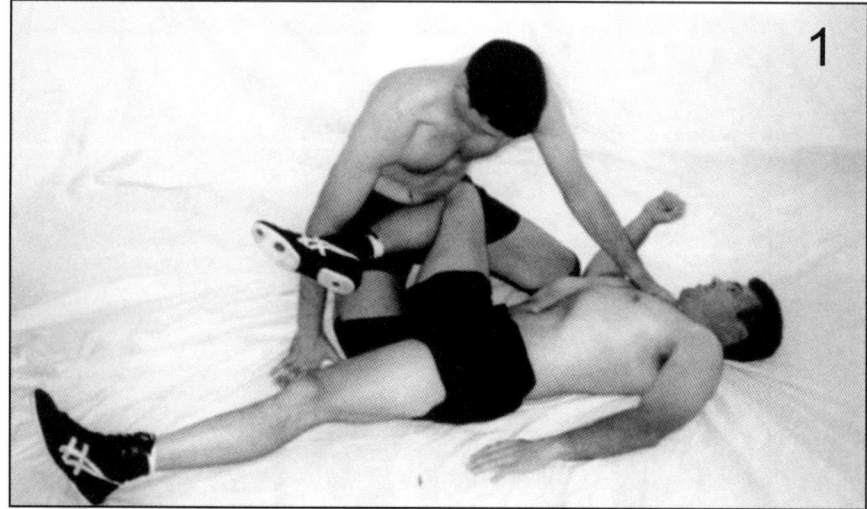

1. You are in side control and your opponent has driven his near knee across your stomach. (Left)

Place your knee over his near knee, trapping his bent leg in between your own legs. (This position is exaggerated to show the details of the positioning) (Right)

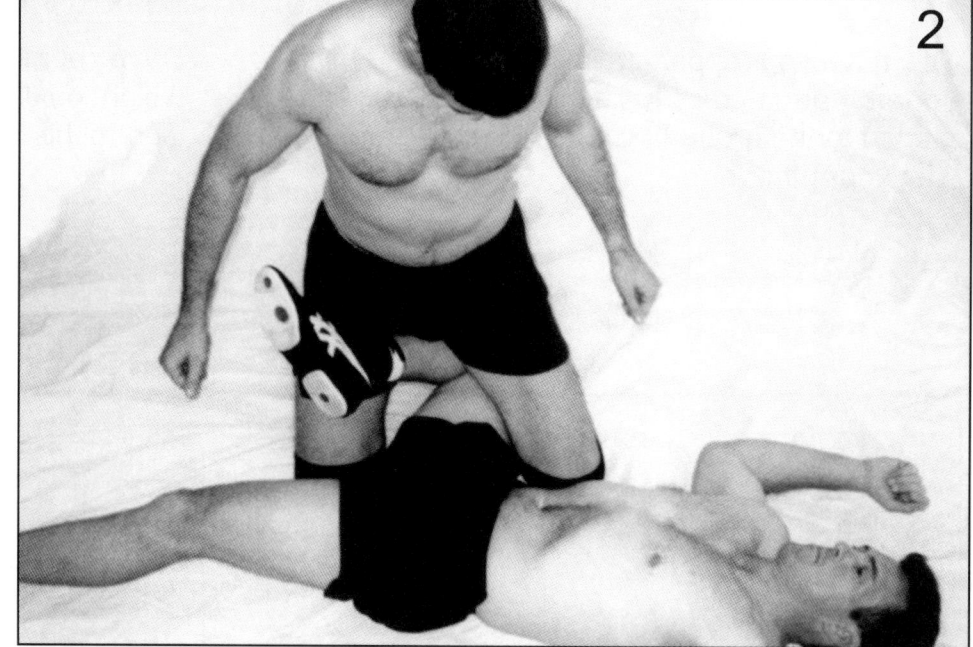

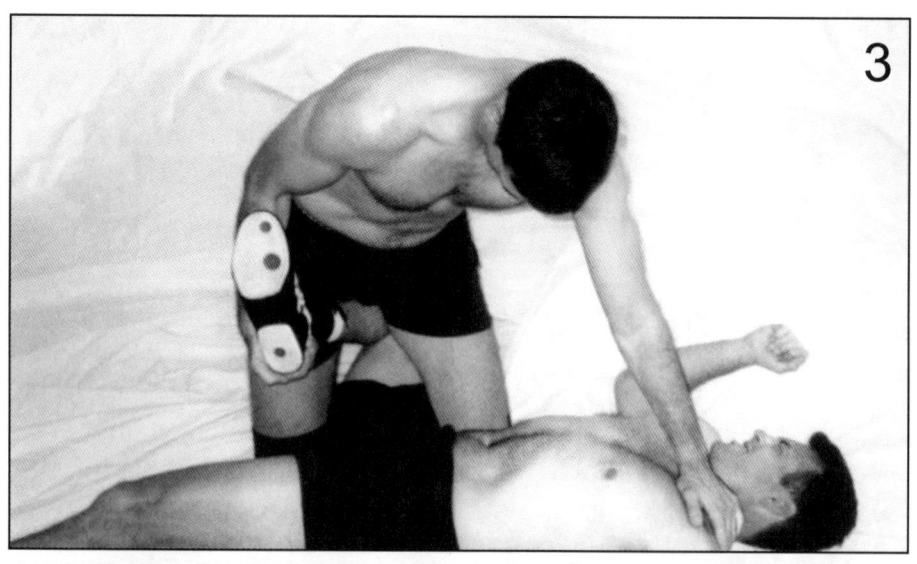

Grab his trapped leg at the ankle and place the forearm of your other arm across his throat and hooked on his shoulder. Push his foot towards his head with your arm while squeezing your knees together. This move uses his bent leg to act as a lever to torque his hip for the submission. (Left)

HIP LOCK *Figure Four Lock*

You have your opponent in side control. His near leg is posted on his knee to prevent you from gaining the mount.

Post one arm on his jaw to pin his head and prevent him from repositioning. Hook over his propped up leg with your other arm as shown.

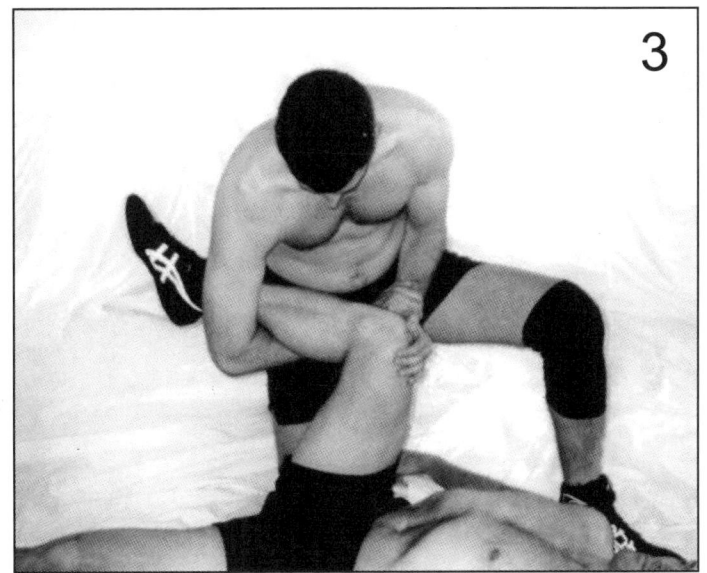

Place one hand on his knee and grab this arm at the wrist, forming a figure four lock to secure his trapped leg.

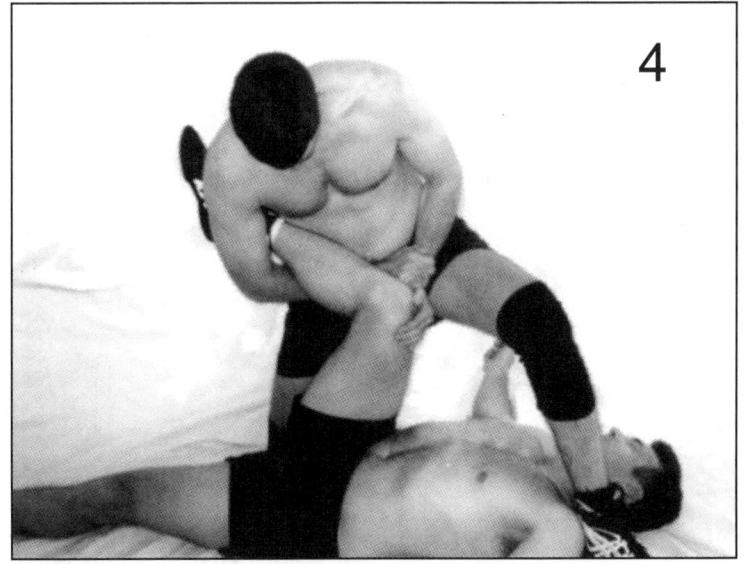

Place your leg over his head and against his neck, pulling his head towards you. Twist your upper body away from him and turn his foot towards your back. This move uses his bent leg as a lever to torque his hip for the submission.

TOE HOLD

You have your opponent in side control and he has his near foot posted on his knee to prevent the mount.

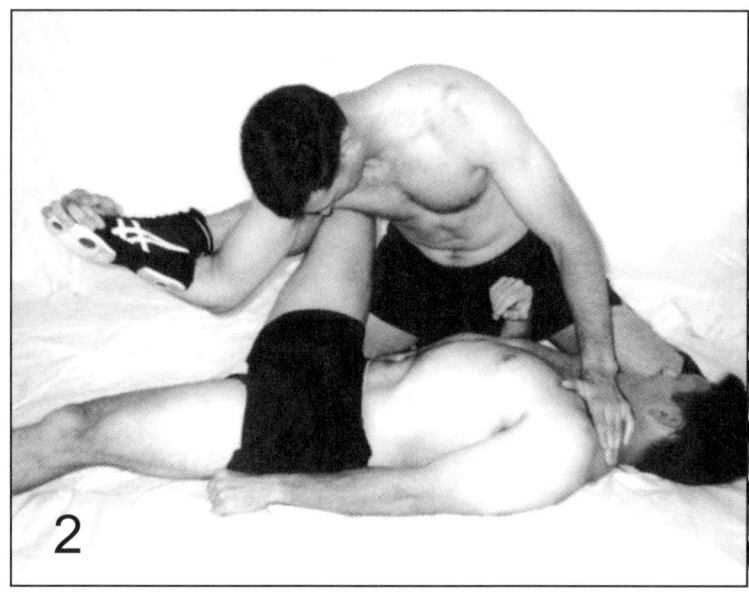

Sit up and control his head with one arm. With the other, reach under his foot and grab his toes.

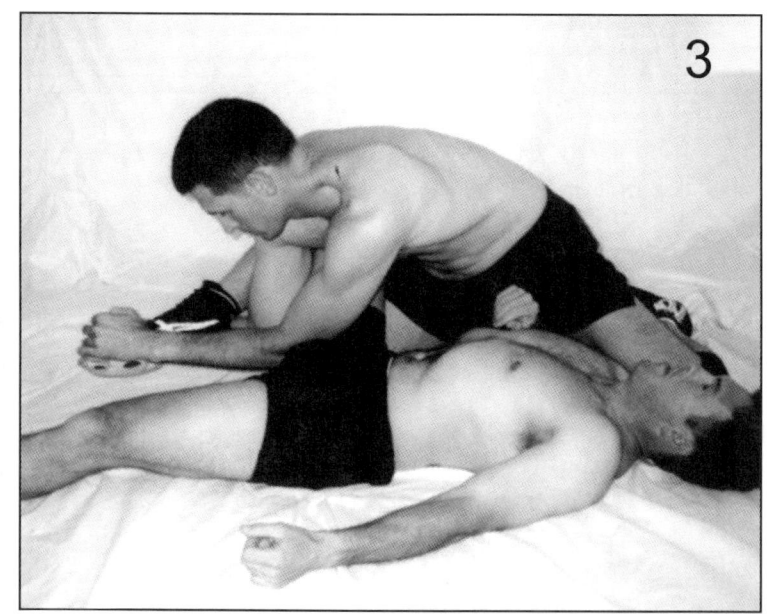

Reach over with your other arm and grab his toes.

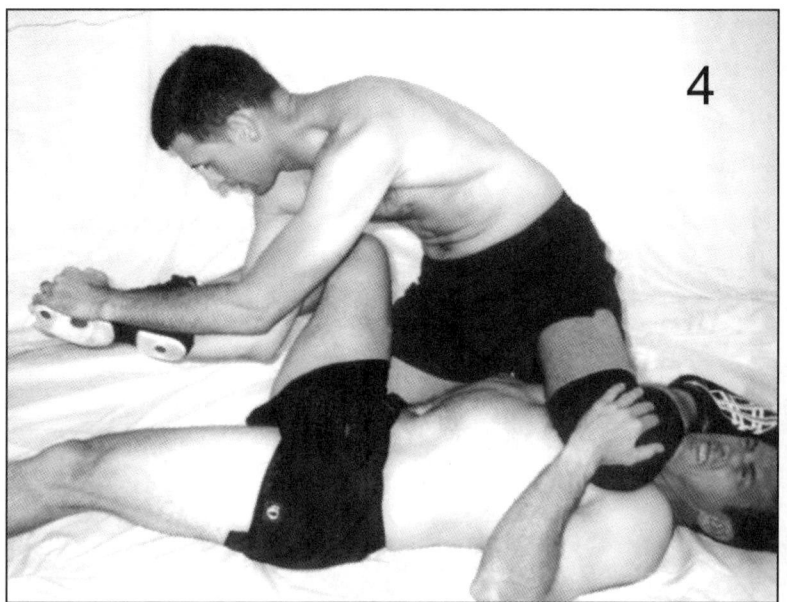

You can place your knee across his face to prevent him from sitting up. Pull his toes towards you, attempting to place them on his buttocks. This move hyper-extends his foot at the ankle for the submission.

ANKLE CRANK *Near Foot*

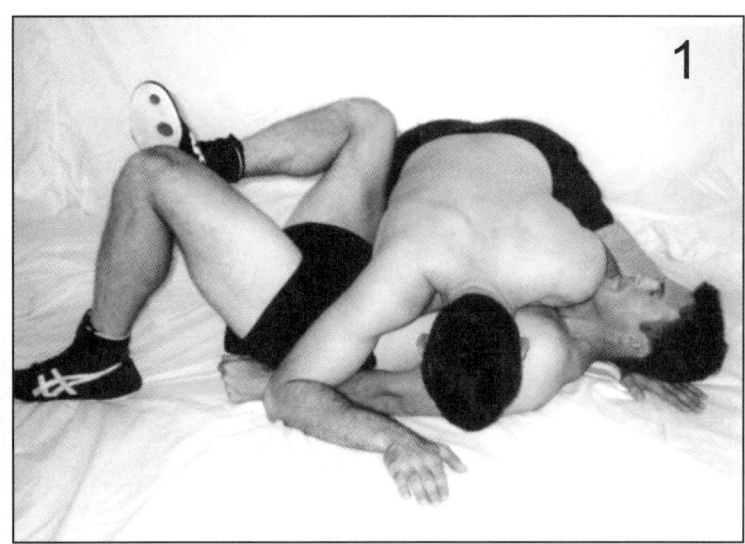

You have your opponent in side control with his near foot posted on his far leg.

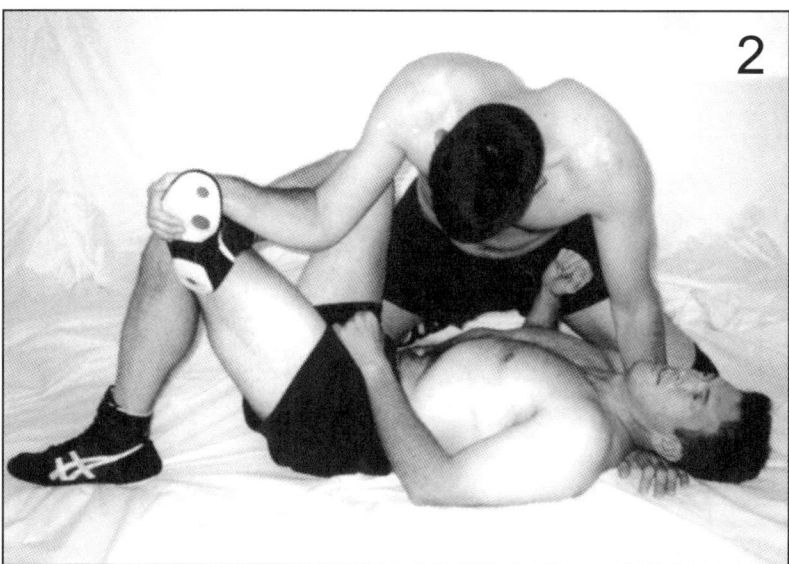

Sit up and reach over his near foot and grab it at the blade. When you grab it, pull it across his far knee so that there is a several inch overhang. Also, keep your elbow lower than his ankle and pressed tightly against his shin.

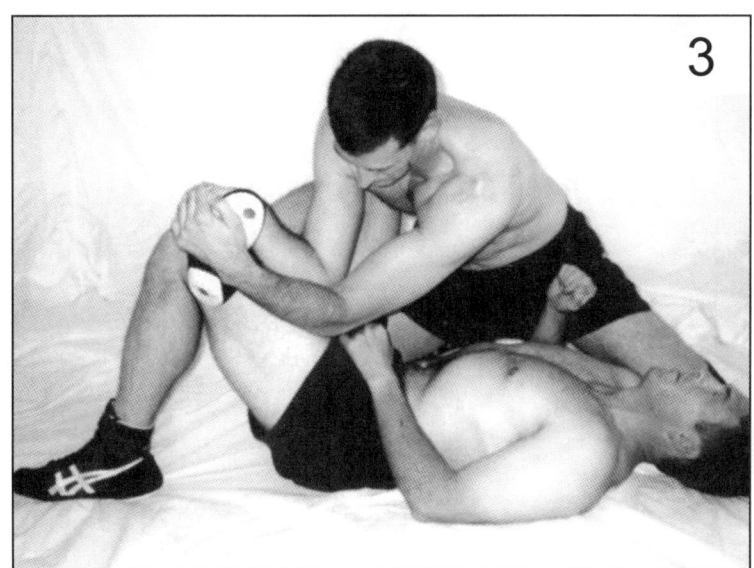

Reach across the sole of his foot with your other arm and grab the blade of his foot.

You can place your knee across his face to help control his upper body. Keep your elbows together and pull down on the blade of his foot. You are using his foot as a lever to torque his knee for the submission.

ANKLE CRANK *Near Foot*

You have your opponent in side control and he has his near foot posted on his far knee.

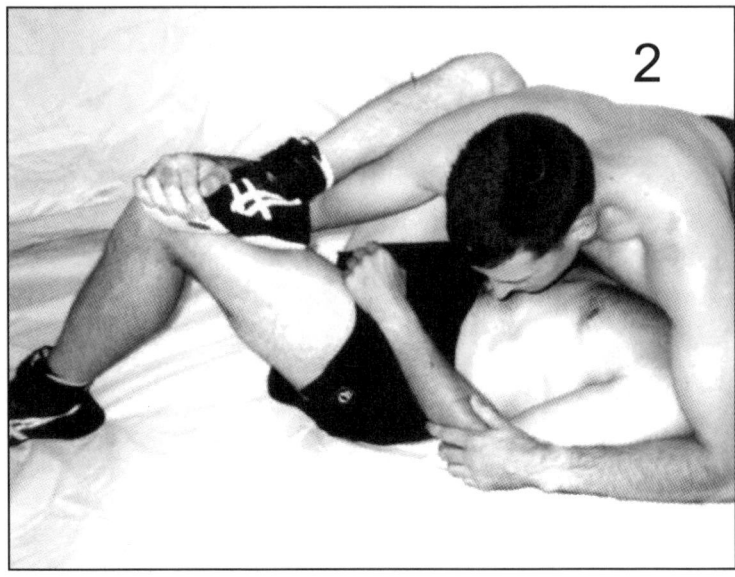

Reach under his foot and grab his instep.

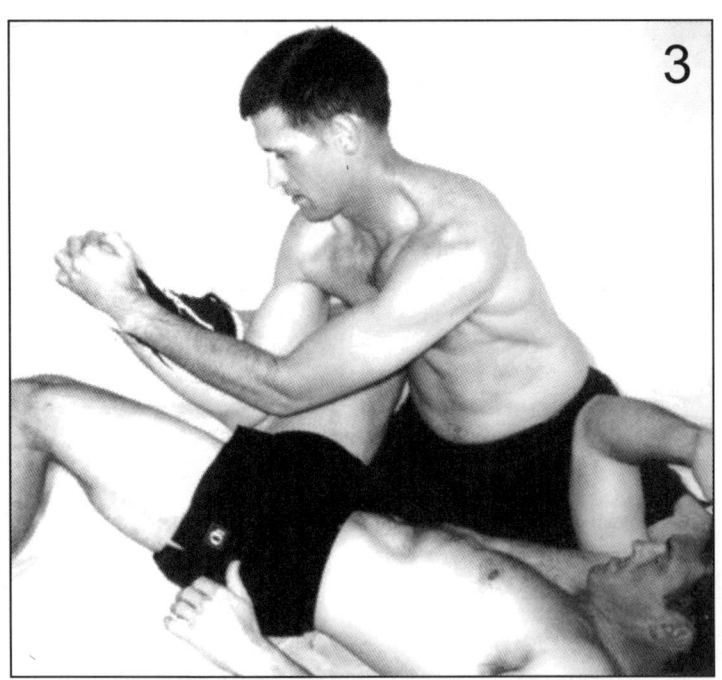

Reach over with your other hand and grab his instep, close to his toes.

You can place your knee across his face to help control his upper body. Pull his toes downwards and twist them towards his head. This move uses his foot as a lever to torque his knee for the submission.

ANKLE CRANK *Far Foot*

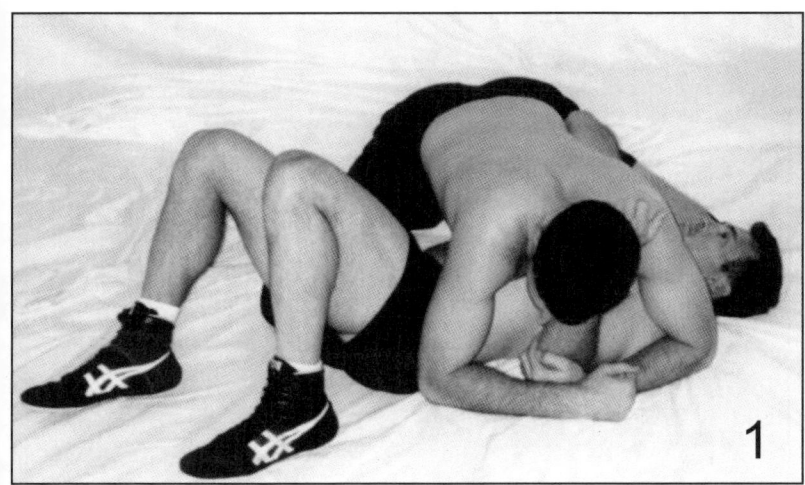

You have your opponent in side control and his far foot is posted close to his buttocks.

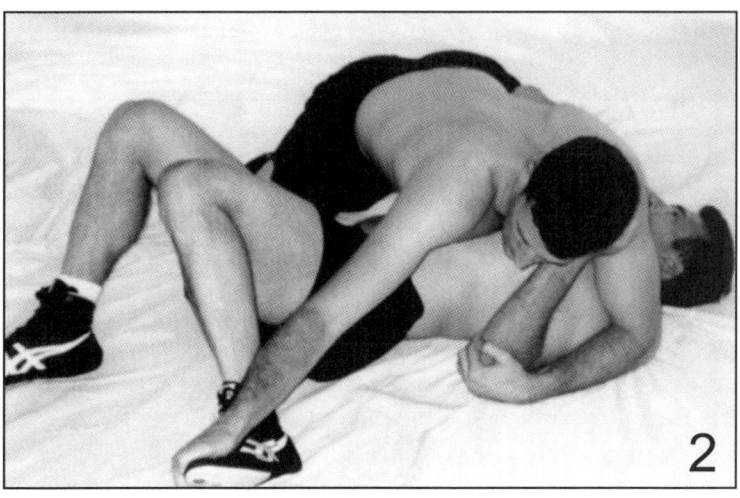

Reach over his foot and grab his instep.

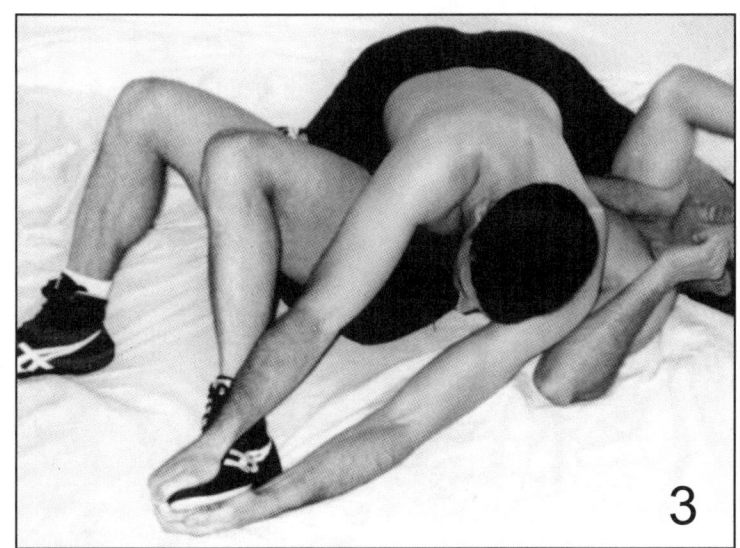

Reach over with your other arm under his foot and at the blade as shown.

You can place your knee across his face to help control his upper body. Post both of your elbows on the ground and pull his instep towards you, keeping his heel pinned to the ground. This move uses his foot as a lever to torque his knee for the submission.

ACHILLES LOCK *Crossed Feet*

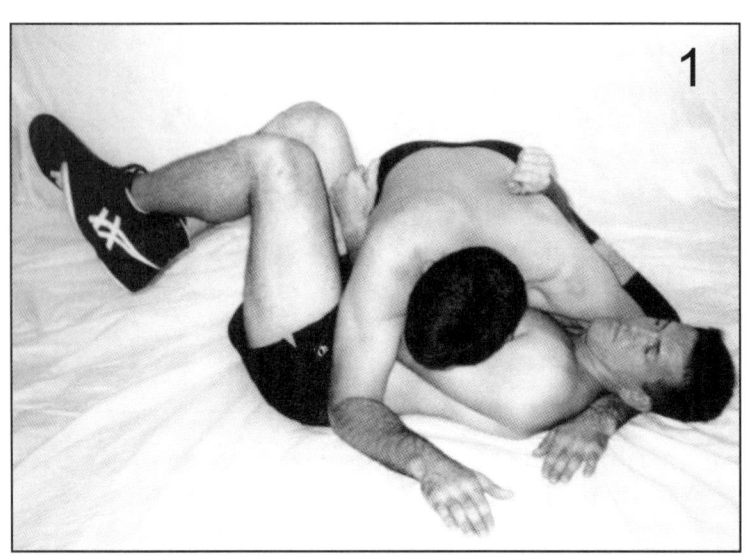

You have your opponent in side control. His feet are crossed as shown.

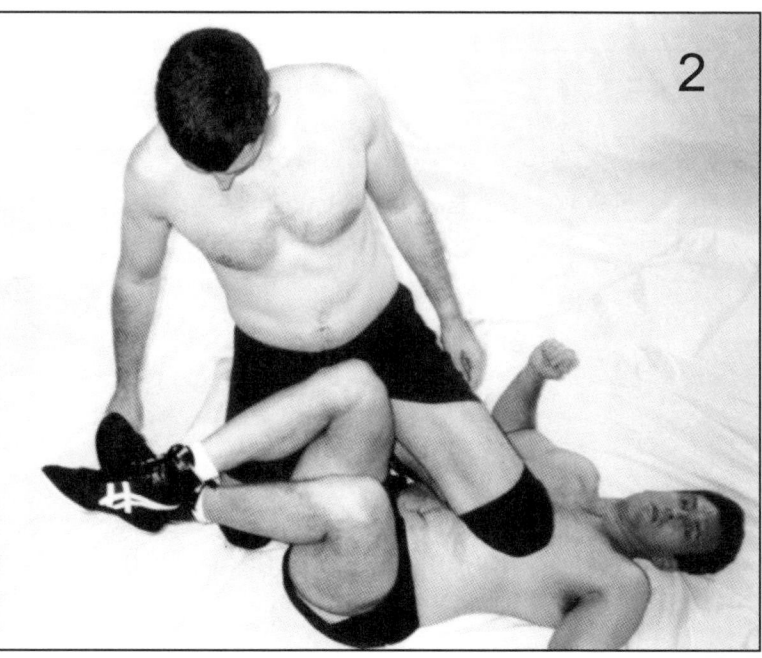

Come to your knees and place one knee across his belly to help control his hips.

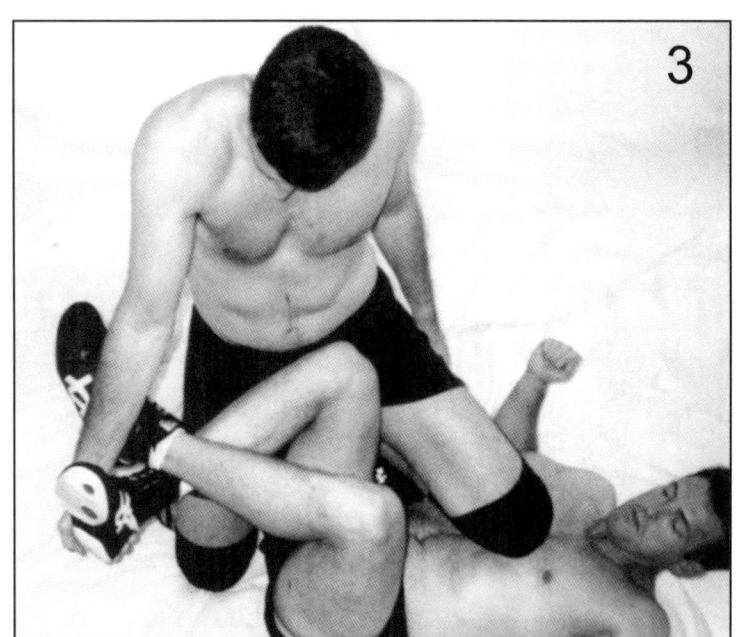

Reach over his top foot and grab his bottom foot on the heel as shown.

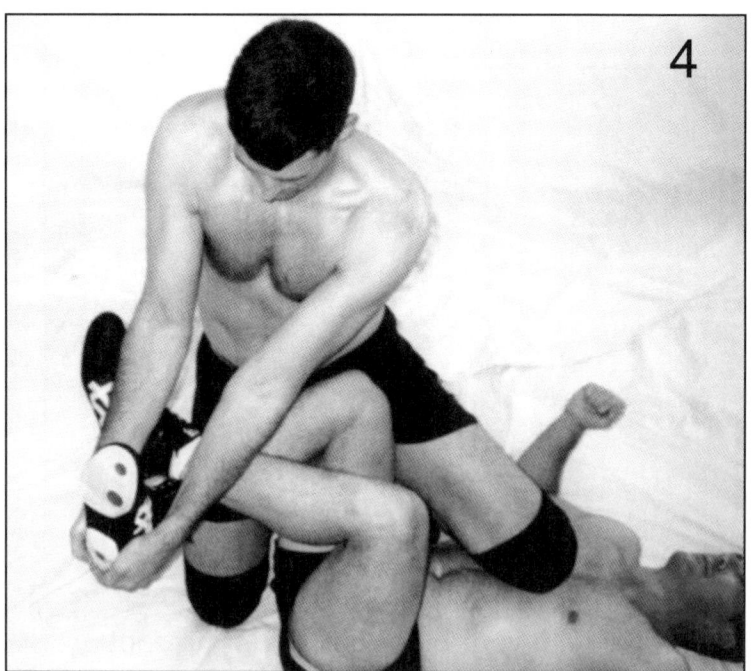

Grab his foot at the ankle with your other arm. Press your elbows firmly against his shin. Press down with your elbows and pull up with your hands for the submission. This move attacks the Achilles tendon of his top leg and puts pressure on the shin bone of his lower leg.

TOE HOLD *Crossed Feet*

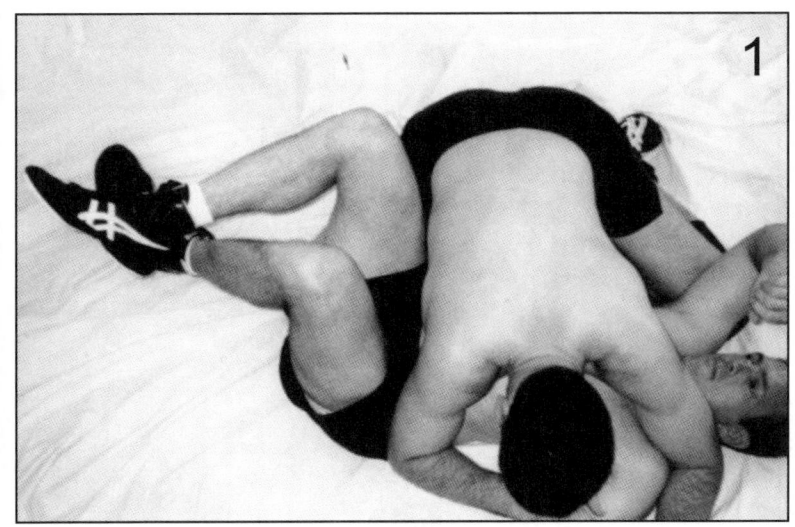

1 Your opponent is in side control with his feet crossed. His near foot is placed over his far foot. (Left)

Reach under his bottom leg and grab his top foot at the instep. (Right)

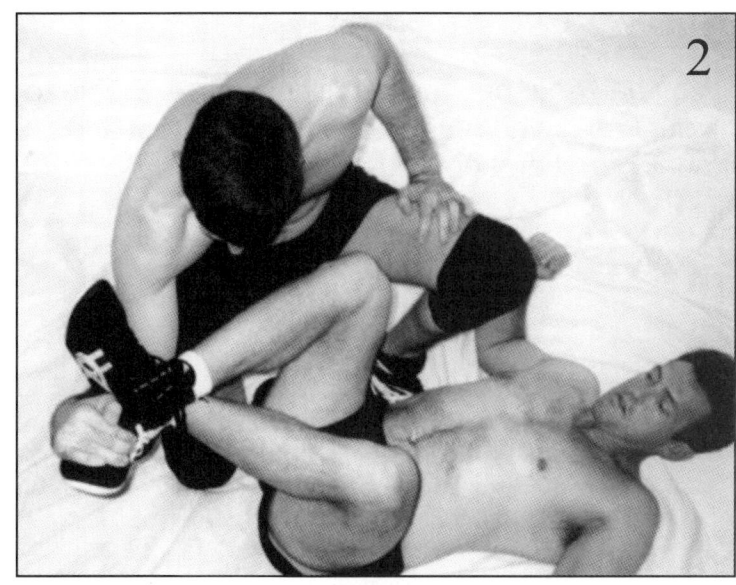

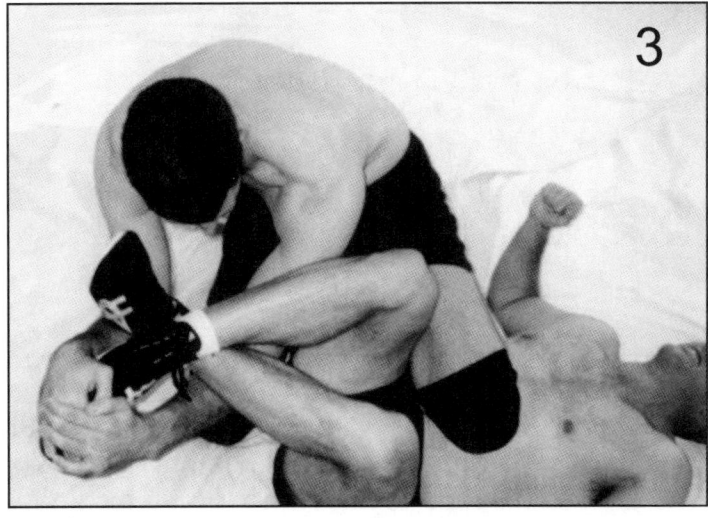

Reach under with your other arm and grab his foot at the instep. Ensure that your forearms are tight against his bottom leg. Pull down on his foot to hyper-extend his foot at the ankle for the submission. (Left)

HEEL HOOK

You had your opponent in side control. Come to your knees and reach under his near foot and hook your hand on his far thigh.

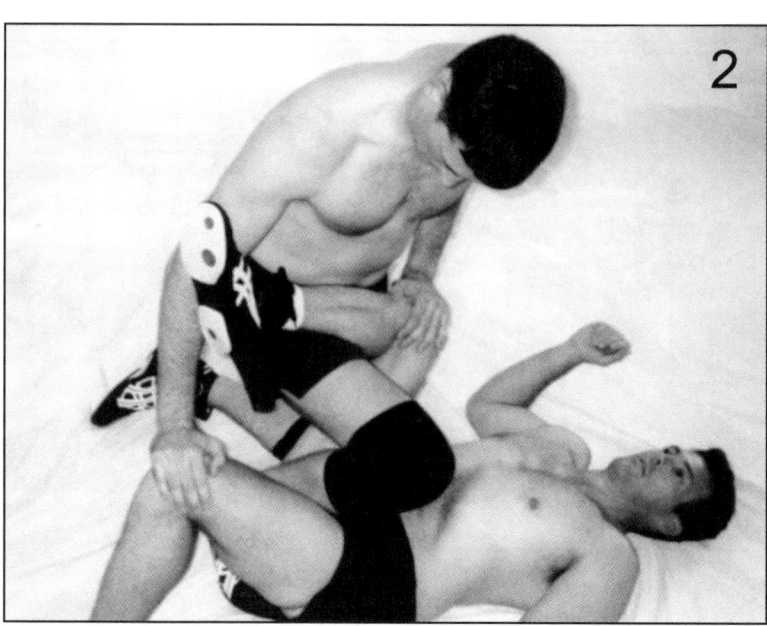

Drive your knee under his targeted foot, across his groin and far upper thigh. Ensure that you control his near leg.

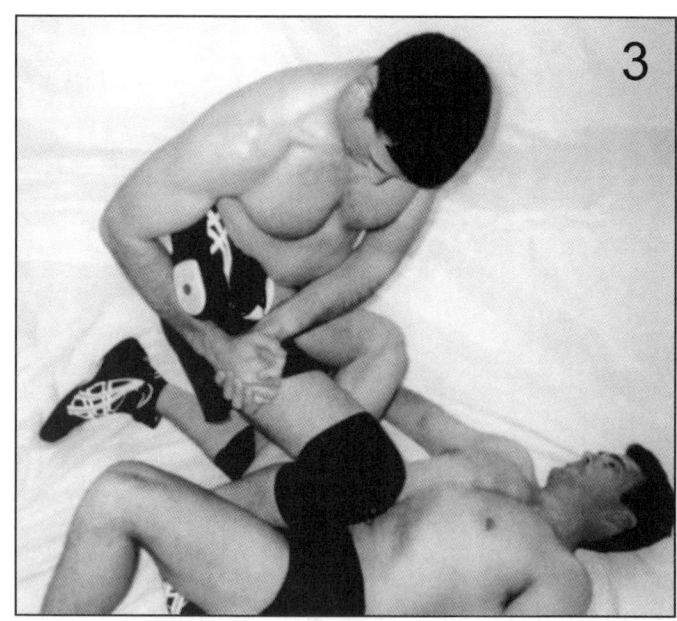

Clasp your hands under his trapped foot and twist your upper body towards his head for the submission.

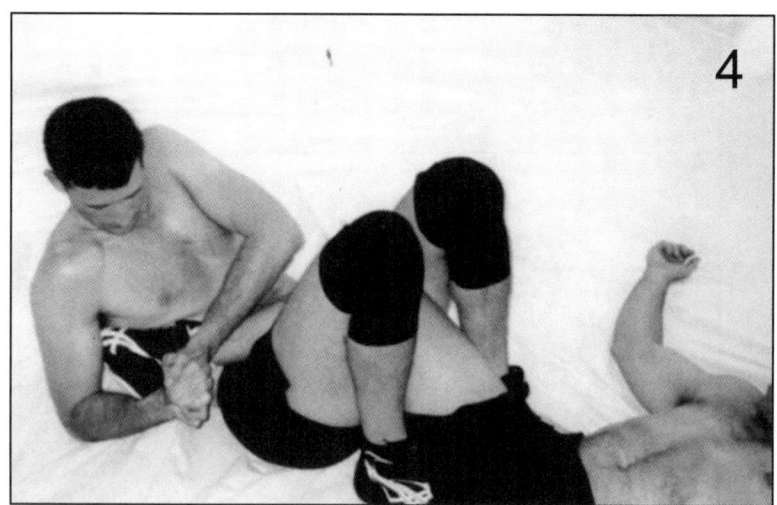

Also, you can fall back and trap his near leg between your knees. Squeeze your knees together and twist your upper body towards his head. This move uses his foot as a lever to torque his knee for the submission.

Chapter Eleven
Submissions In Side Control

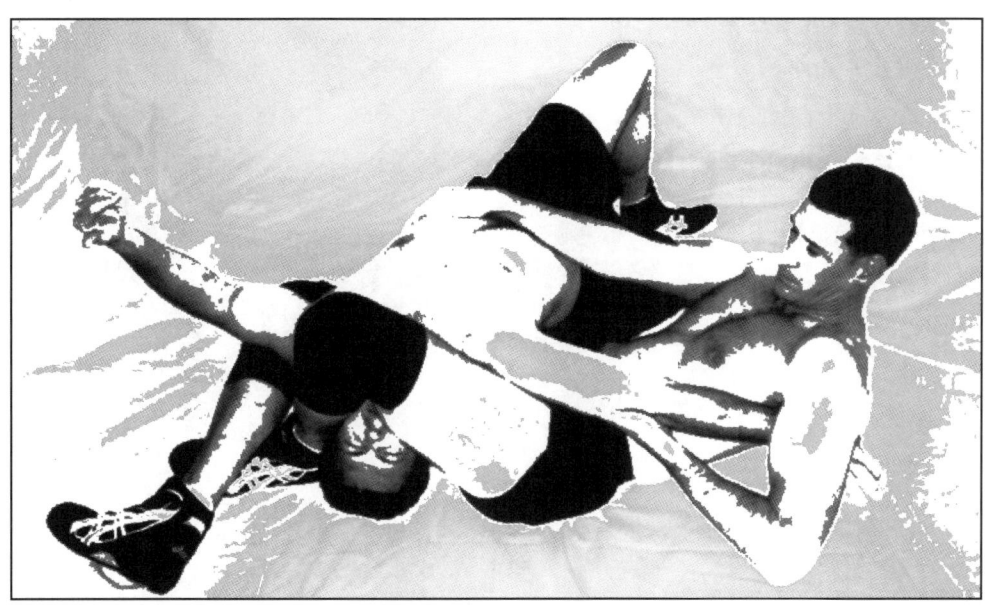

ATTACKS IN SIDE CONTROL *Neck Crank*

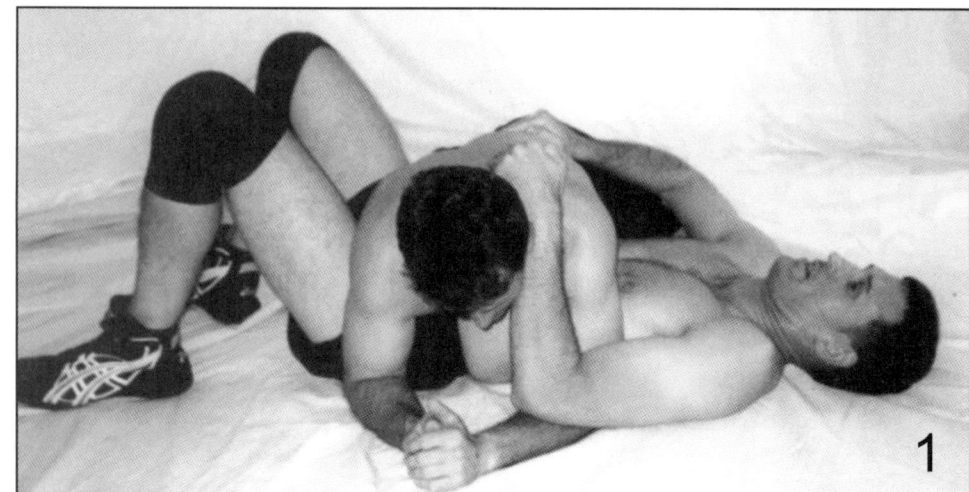

You have both of your arms free; one arm is posted on his neck and the other on his waist. (Left)

Drive your attacking arm across his face, turning his head away from you. Ensure that the blade of your forearm is across his jaw. (Right)

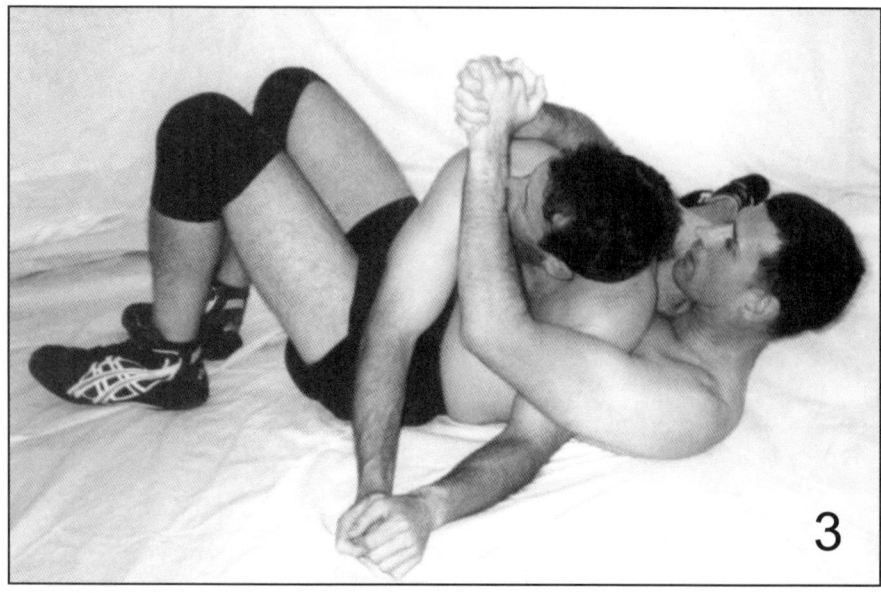

Clasp your attacking arm with your other, locking arm and pull his head backwards, cranking his neck for the submission. (Left)

CHOKE *Kata Gatame*

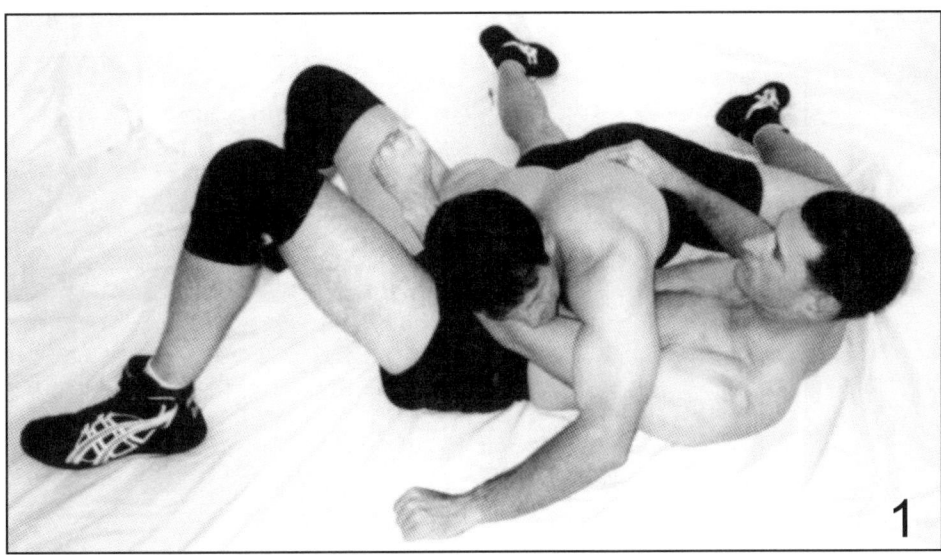

Your opponent is set up with your arm across his far shoulder and his near arm posted out. (Left)

Place your attacking arm around his neck, clasping your locking arm at the biceps. This traps his near arm between your head and his. (Right)

Place your locking hand on the back of your head and press your head against his. Drive the blade of your attacking forearm into the base of his neck and contract the muscles of your attacking arm. This will crank his neck as well as cut off the carotid arteries in his neck for the submission. (Left)

CHOKE *Modified Kata Gatame*

Your opponent has his near arm posted and your arm is across his near shoulder.

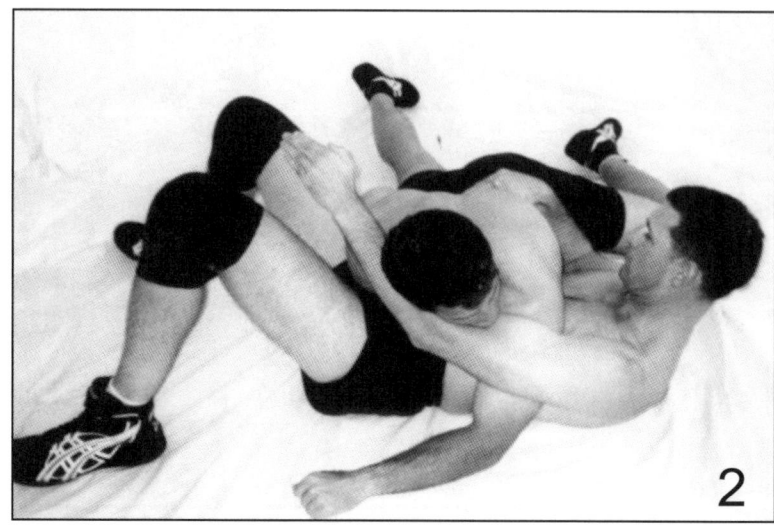

Bring your arm over his head and across his throat, trapping his near arm.

Grab your locking arm at the biceps. This traps his arm between his body and yours.

Place your locking hand on the back of your head and drive your head close to his. Contract the muscles of your attacking arm to cut off his carotid arteries for the submission.

CHOKE *Triangle*

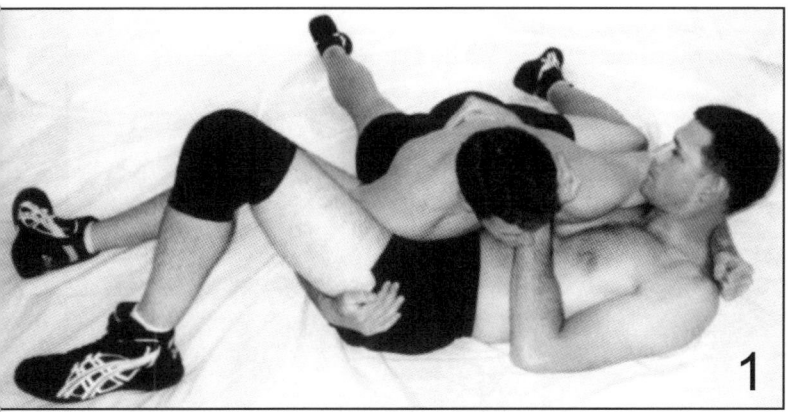

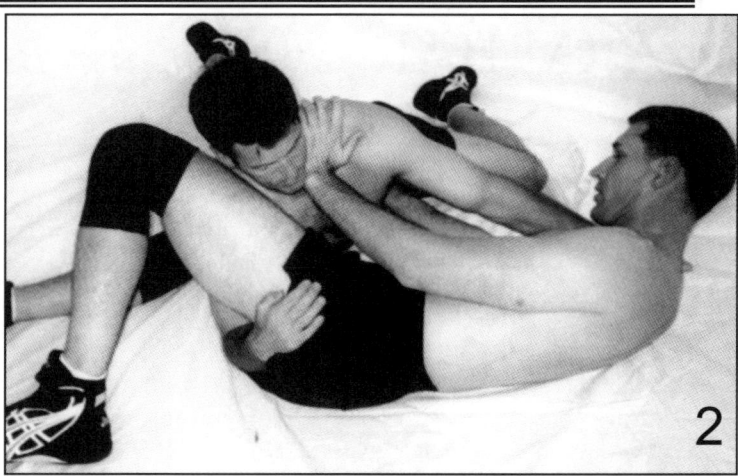

Your opponent is holding you down with one arm between your legs and one behind your neck. (Top)

Push off at his hips and his neck and drive your hips away from him. (Top Right)

Bring your near leg under his body and secure both of his arms. (Right)

Hook your top leg across his shoulders and the top of his neck, pulling him towards you. (Bottom Right)

Lock the foot of your top leg behind your other knee and bring his trapped arm cross his throat. Squeeze your knees together for the choke. (Bottom)

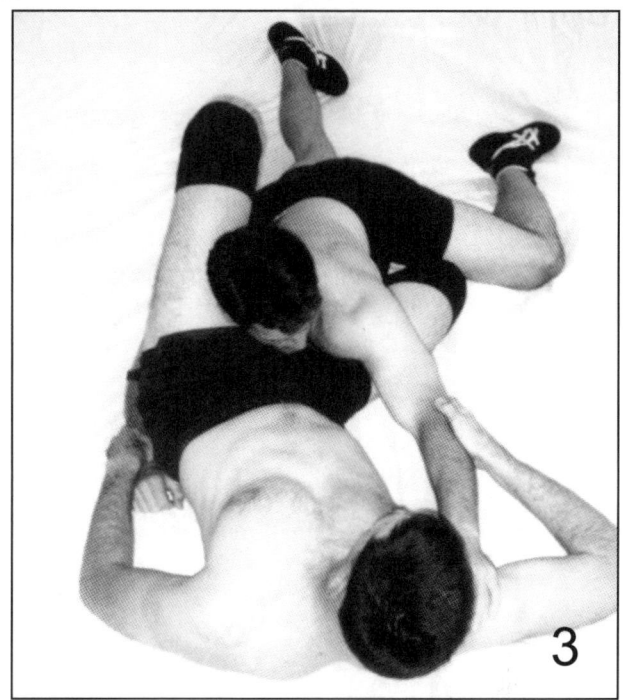

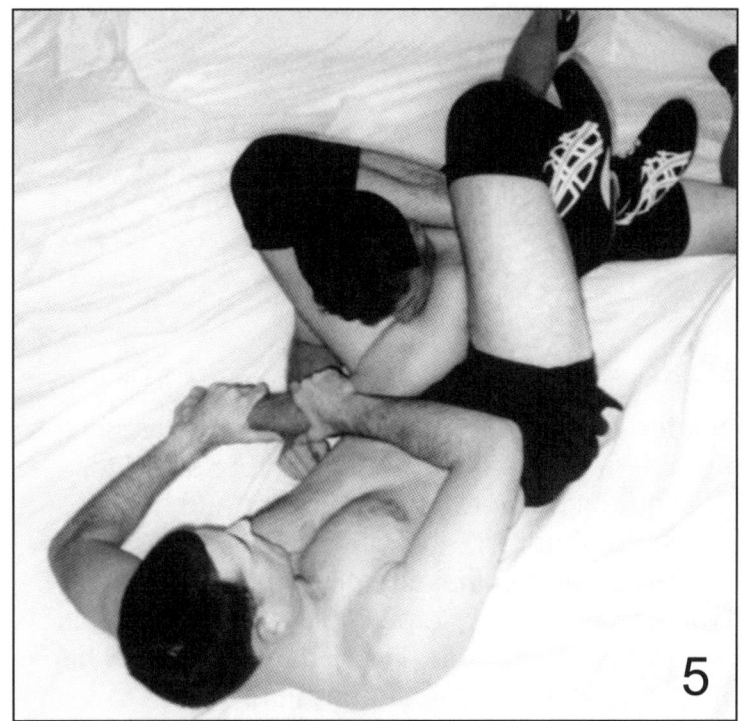

ARM BAR *Straight Arm Bar*

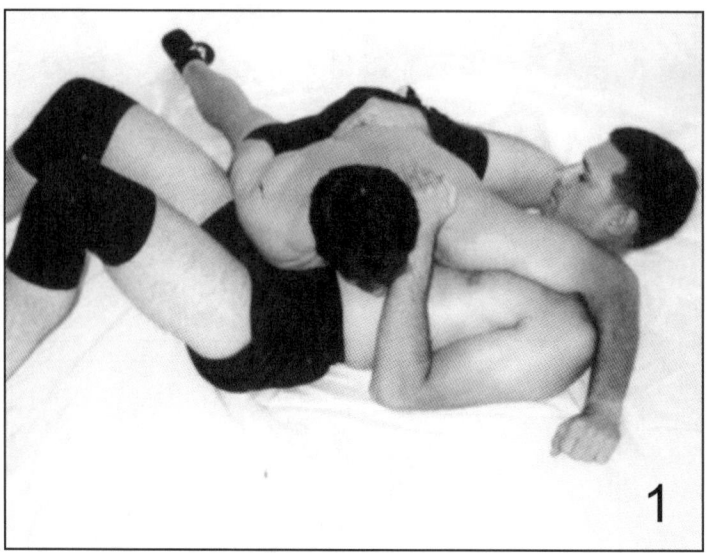

Your opponent is pinning you with one arm securing your hips and one arm across your body.

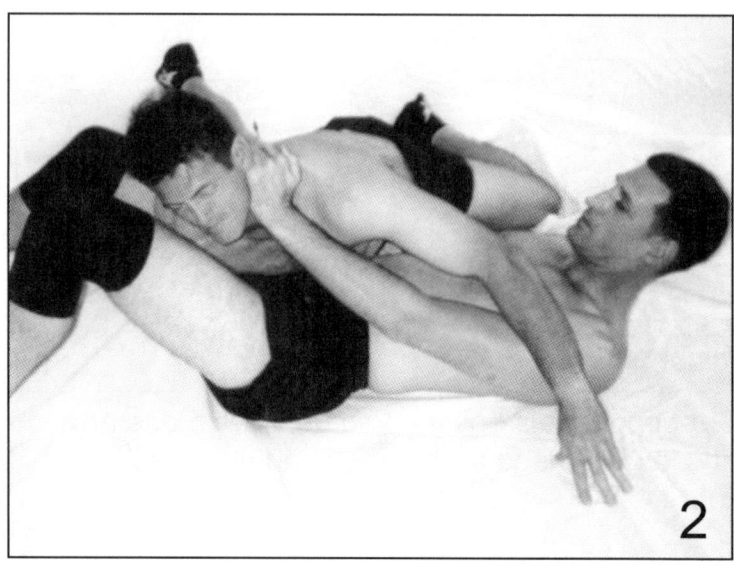

Push him away from you at his neck and his hips.

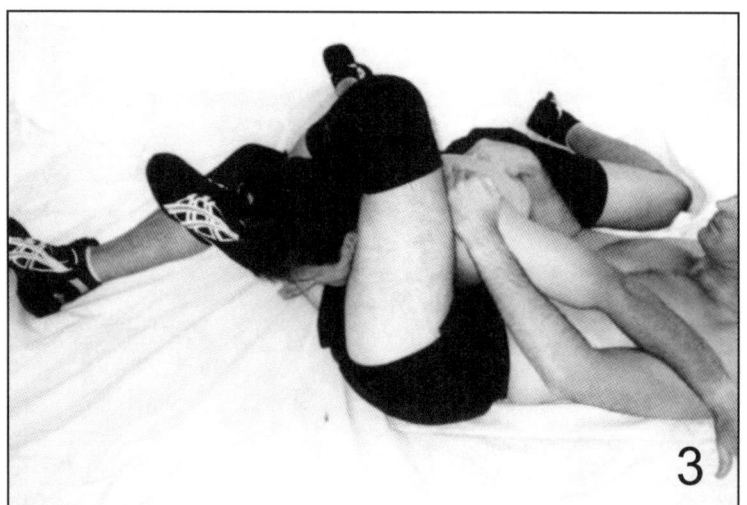

Hook your attacking leg over his head.

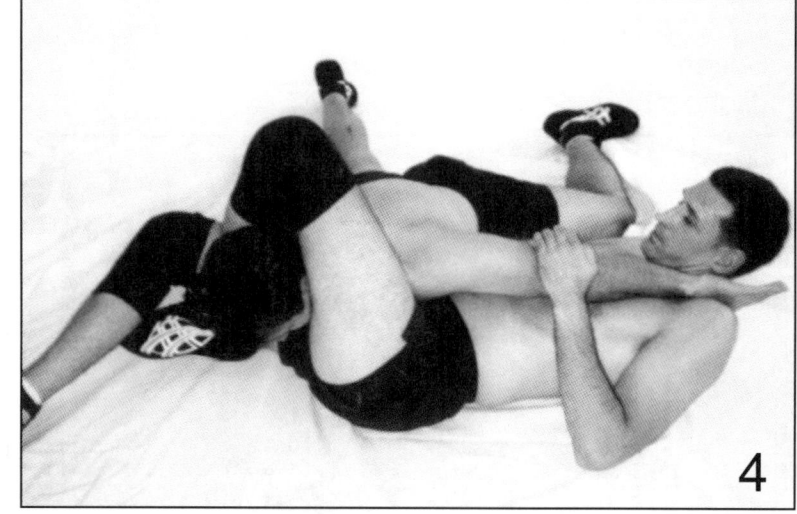

Hook the foot of your attacking leg behind your other knee. Place his arm across your shoulder and secure it between your shoulder and head. Place both hands on the elbow of his exposed arm. Do an abdominal crunch and drive your shoulder upwards while pulling downwards on his elbow with both hands. This will hyper-extend his arm at the elbow for the submission.

SHOULDER CRANK *Key Lock*

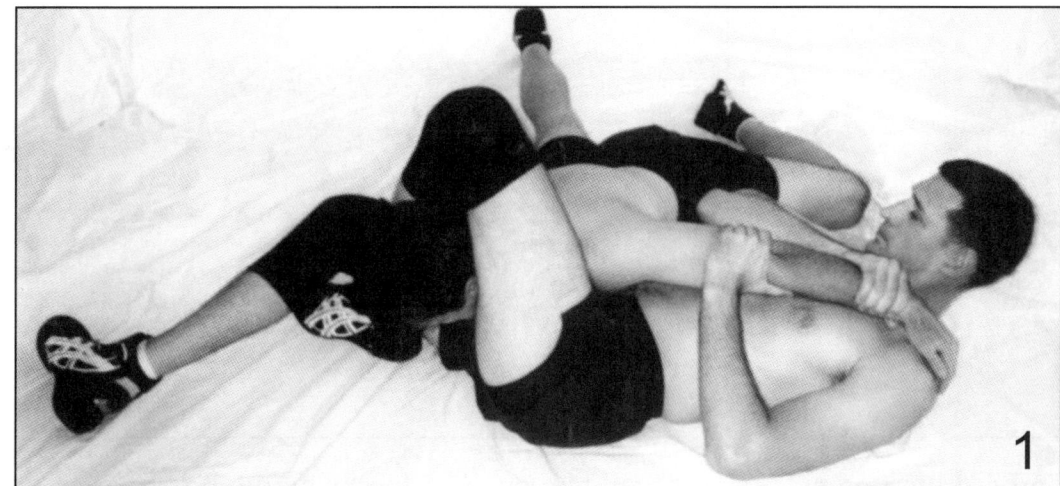

You have your opponent's head trapped with your legs, as in the previous page's technique. Secure his arm at the elbow and the wrist. (Left)

Drive his wrist towards the small of his back, forcing his arm at a right angle. (Right)

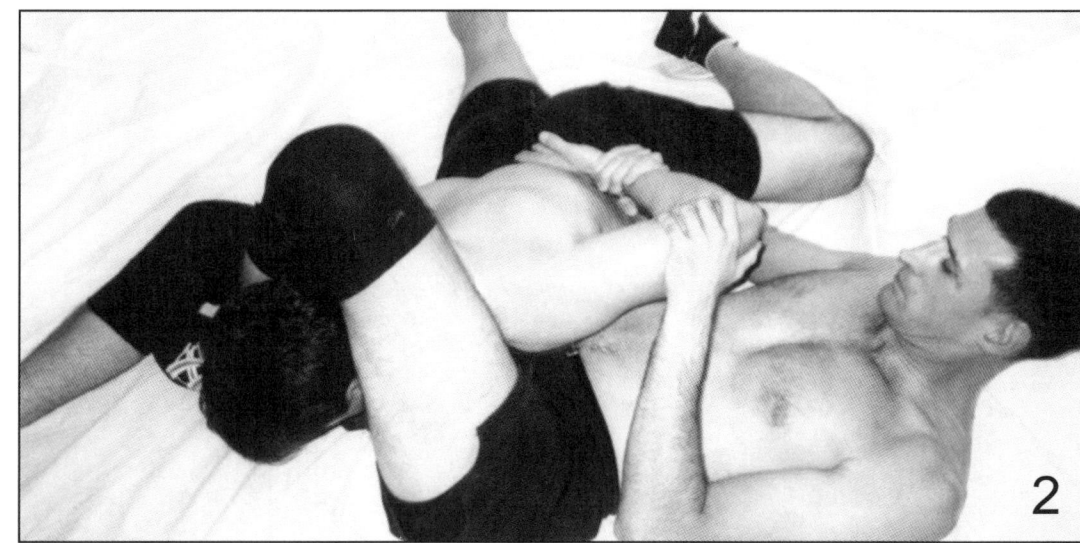

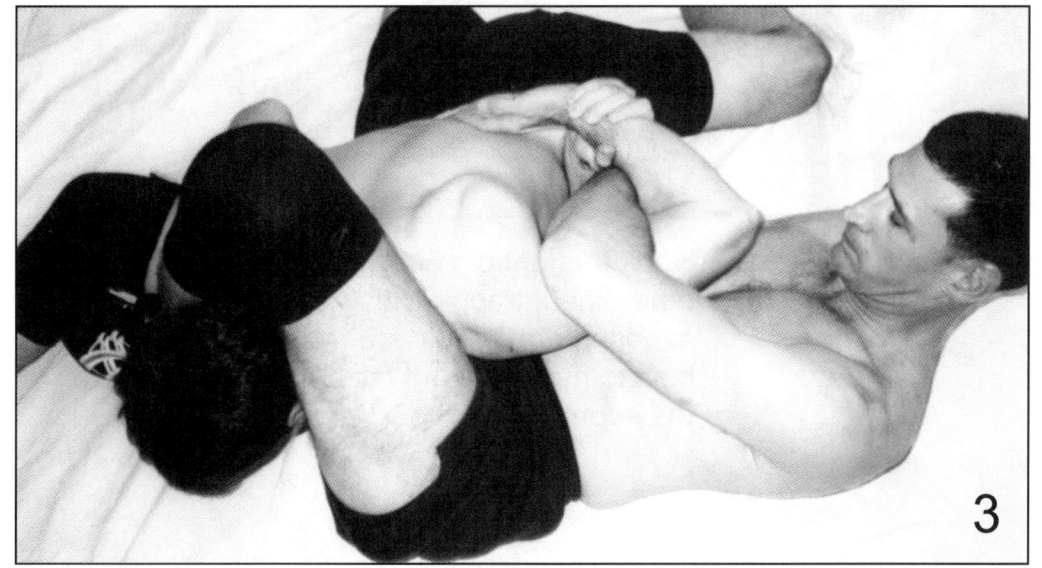

Secure a figure four lock on his trapped arm. Hug his bent elbow tightly to your chest. Attempt to place his wrist next to his head while keeping his elbow firmly in place. This uses his bent arm as a lever to torque his shoulder for the submission. (Left)

ARM BAR

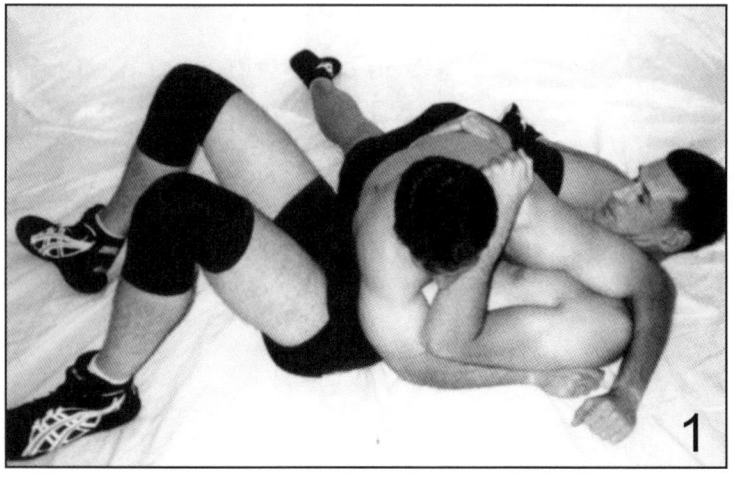

Your opponent has both arms across your body; your arms are posted on his neck and on his waist.

Push him away at the hips and the head.

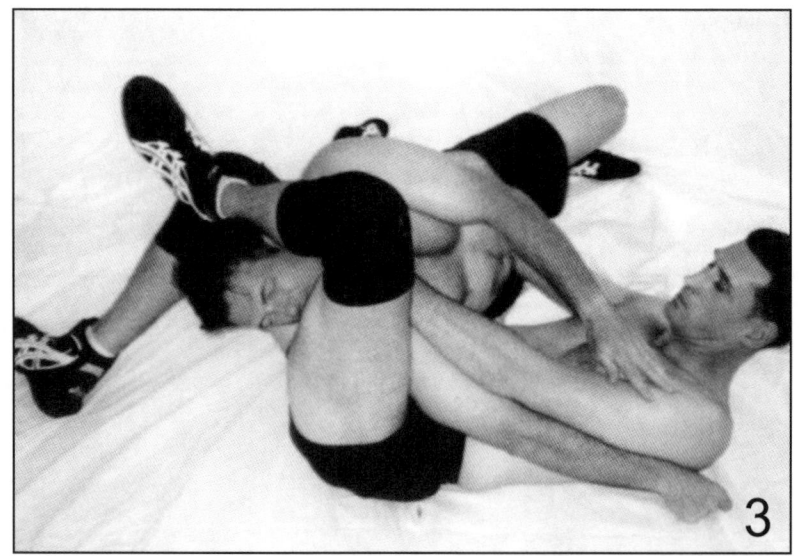

Hook your attacking leg over his head and across his neck.

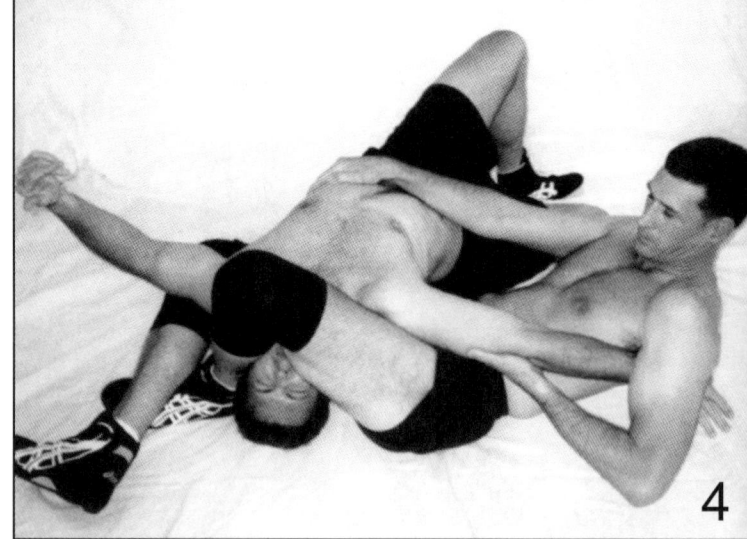

Hook the foot of your attacking leg behind your other knee, trapping his head. Place his exposed arm under your armpit. Arch your hips to hyper-extend his arm at the elbow for the submission.

Chapter Twelve
Submissions From Scarf Hold, In Scarf Hold, And From Modified Scarf Hold

Scarf Hold

This hold allows you to control your opponent with minimal energy output. It allows you to isolate his trapped arm and neck for attacks.

You have his arm secured tightly. Your chest is against his chest, driving your weight into him. Your center of gravity is not directly over his chest but to the side of him, making it difficult for him to bridge you off.

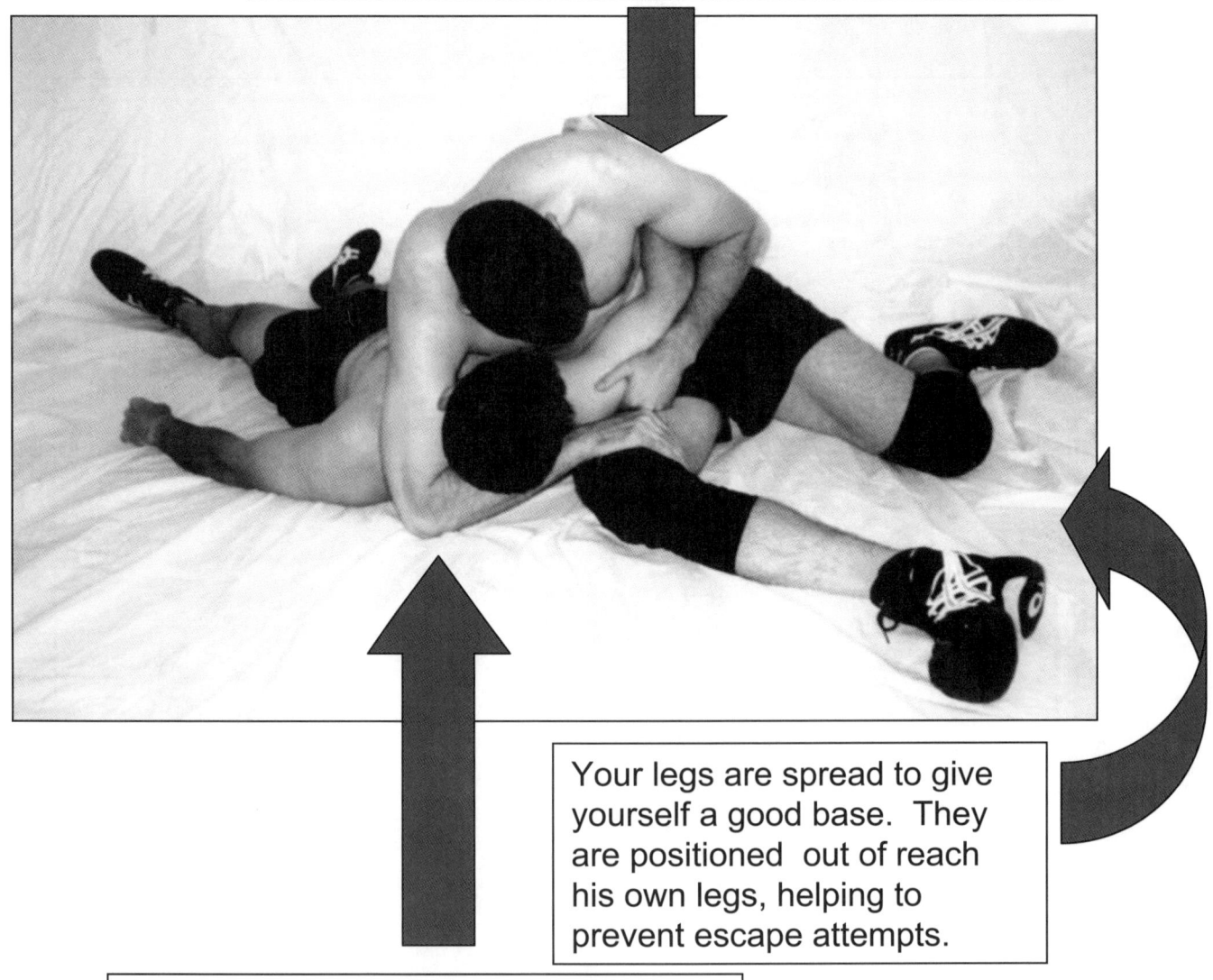

Your legs are spread to give yourself a good base. They are positioned out of reach his own legs, helping to prevent escape attempts.

You have his head secured tightly to help control his body. Your head is close to his and low, helping to prevent counterattacks and keeping your center of gravity low.

NECK CRANK *Modified Can Opener*

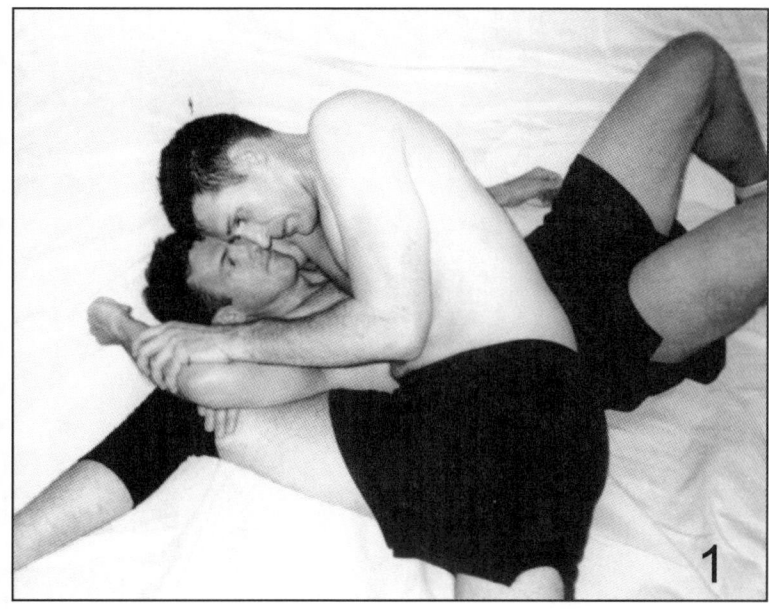

Your opponent has pulled his trapped arm out from under your controlling arm. Control his arm and maintain your position. (Left)

Cradle his head and arm with your free arm. You have trapped his arm between his head and your shoulder. You are essentially hugging his head and trapped arm. (Right)

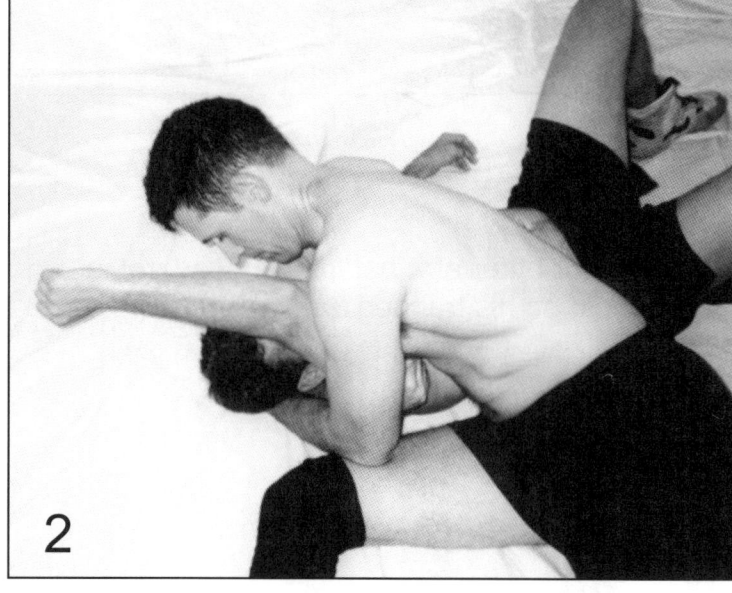

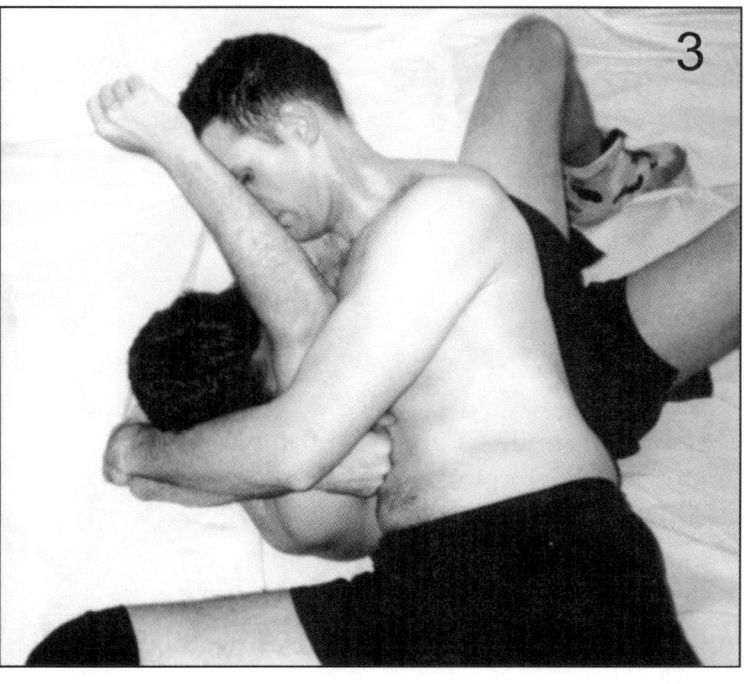

Place your arms tightly around the base of his neck. This technique requires expert weight positioning and looks deceptively easy. You need to crank his neck forwards while keeping sufficient weight on his chest to prevent him from sitting up into you. This move hyper-extends his cervical spin for the submission. Also, you can cut off his carotid arteries for a submission, similar to Kata Gatame. (Left)

NECK CRANK *Can Opener*

You have your opponent in a scarf hold. Lift up on his head with your far arm as shown. (Left)

Wrap your other arm behind his head, releasing your hold on his trapped arm. (Right)

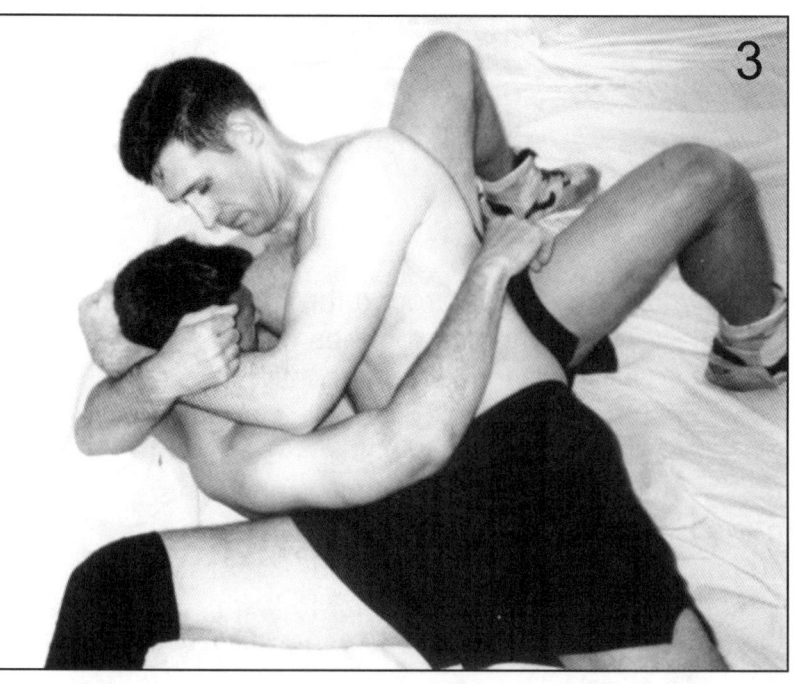

This move requires the right combination of weight balancing to be effective. As you crank his neck towards you, keep enough weight on his chest to prevent him from sitting up into you. This move cranks his cervical spine for the submission. (Left)

CHOKE *Kata Gatame*

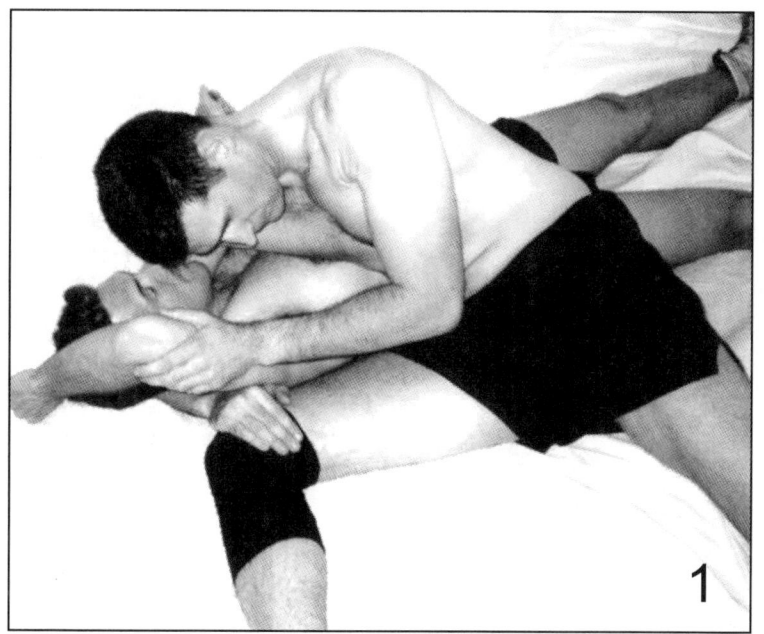

Your opponent has pulled his trapped arm out from your control. Secure his arm at the elbow as shown.

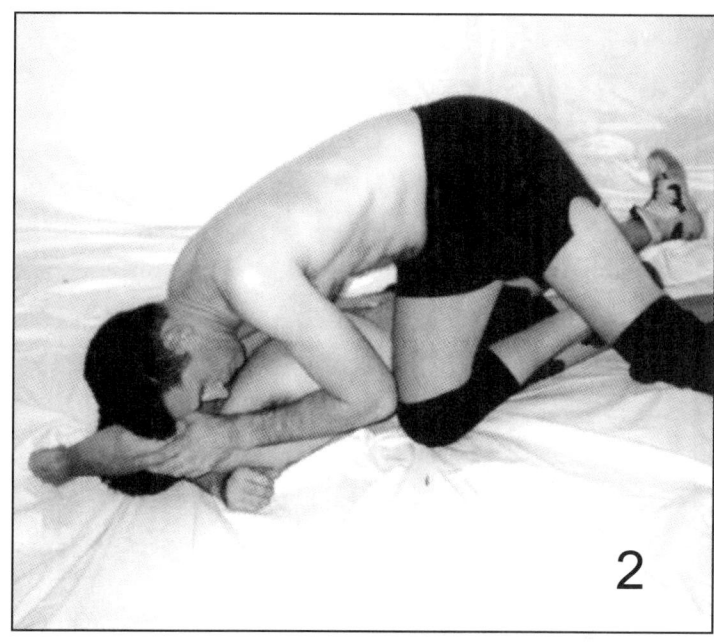

Push his arm tightly against his own head and reposition your body and come to your knees. Your near knee should be tight against his body.

Place your head against his arm, trapping it between your head and his own. Your attacking arm, wrapped around his neck, grabs your locking arm at the biceps. Place your locking hand on the back of your own head.

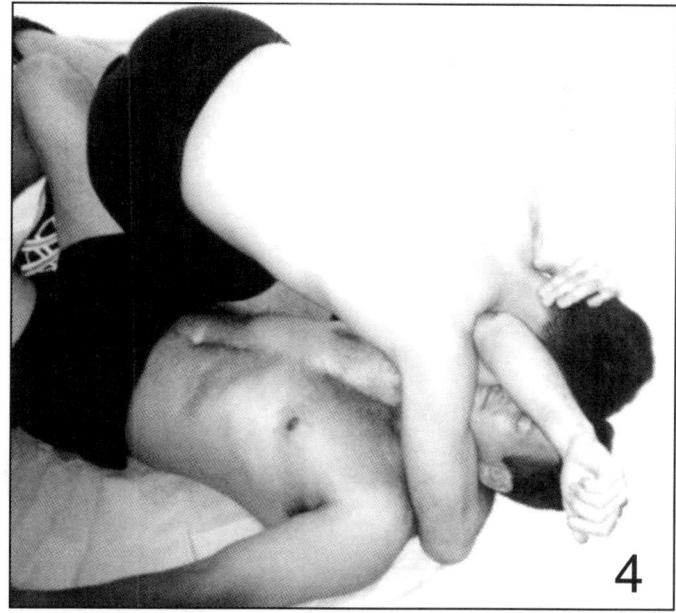

Here's the same position from the other direction. Drive the blade of your attacking forearm into the base of his neck and contract the muscles of your attacking, choking arm. This move will cut off the his carotid arteries and crank his neck for the submission.

CHOKE *Modified Kata Gatame*

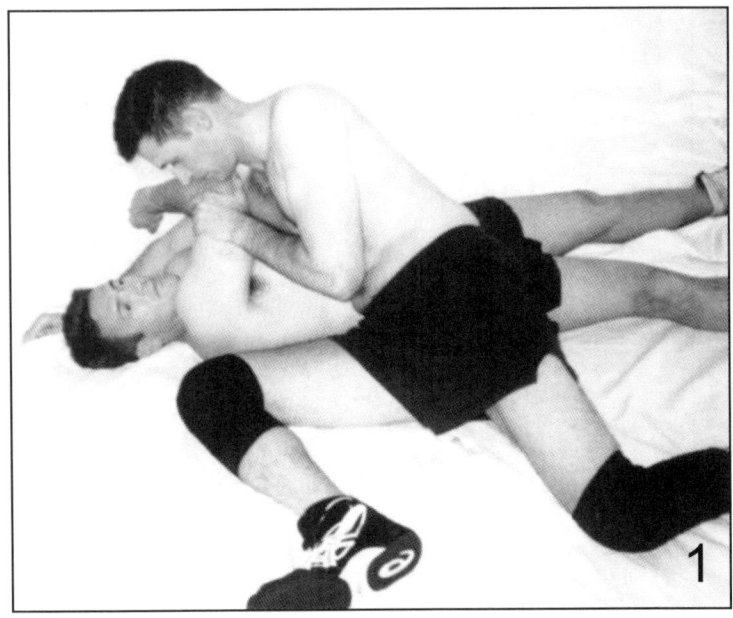

Your opponent has pulled his trapped arm free. Control this arm and push it across his body as shown.

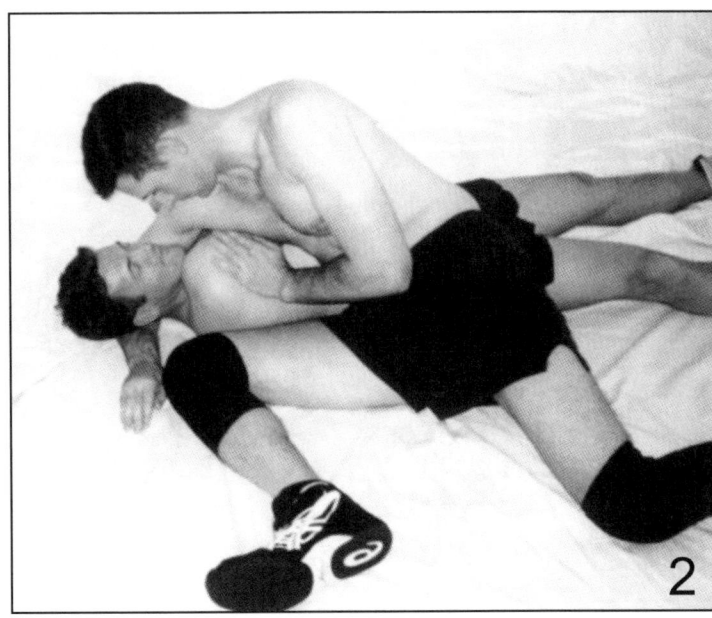

Reach over his arm and behind his neck with your attacking arm, trapping his arm between his body and your own.

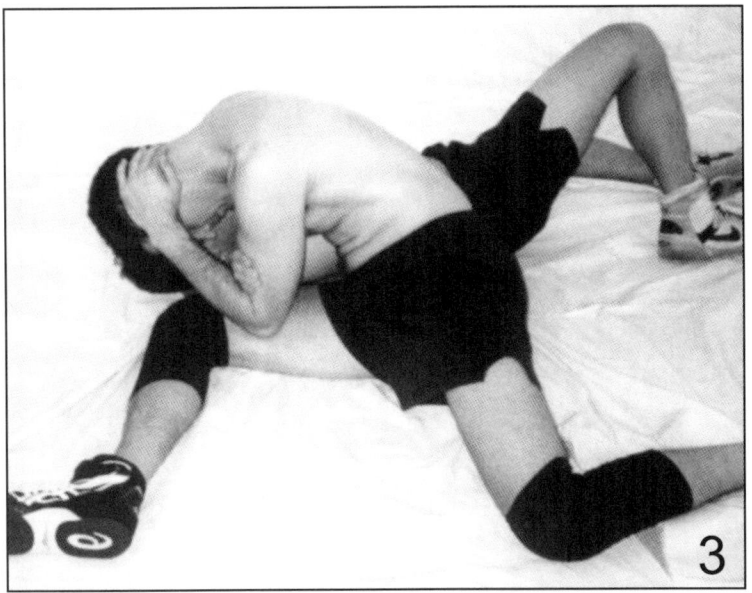

Place the hand of your attacking arm on your locking arm's biceps and grab your own head with your locking hand.

Here is the same position from the opposite side. Drive the blade of your attacking forearm into the base of his neck and contract the muscles of your attacking arm. Also, push your attacking shoulder into his esophagus. This move cuts off his carotid arteries for the submission.

CHOKE *Scissors and Smother*

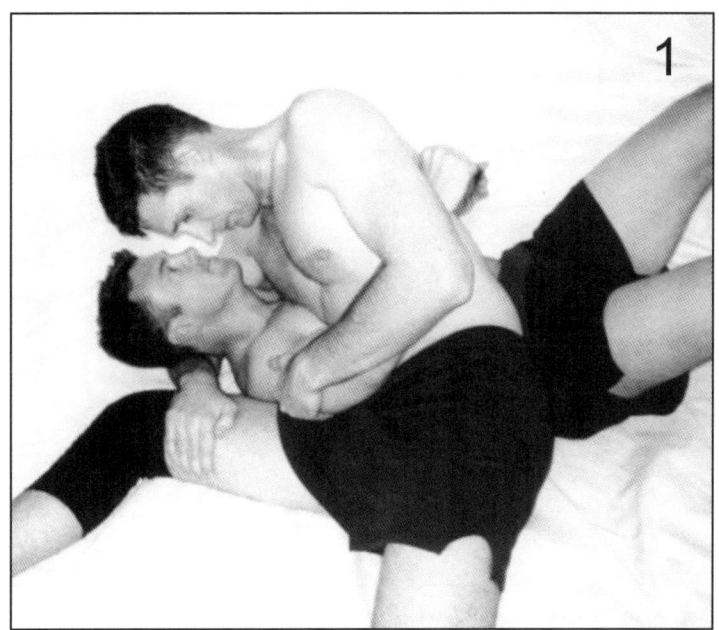

Your opponent is in scarf hold and there is space between his throat and your chest.

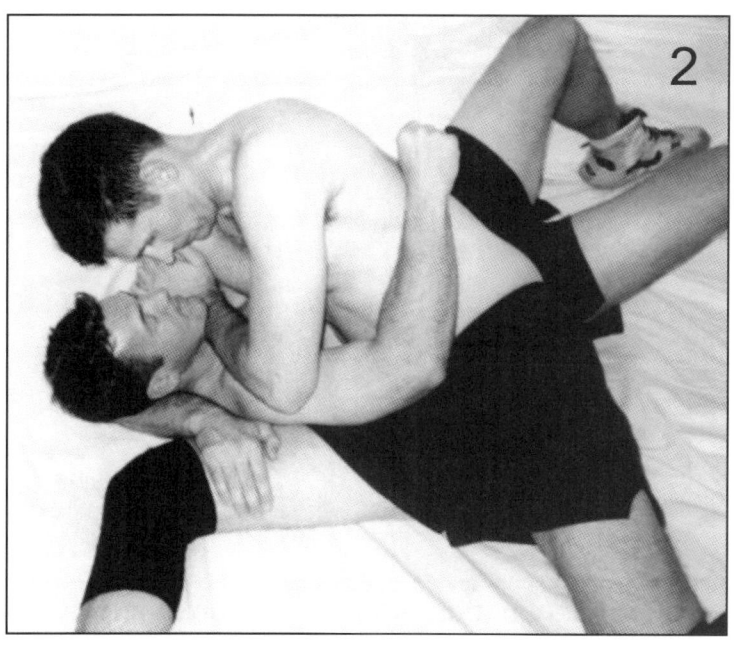

Place the blade of your attacking forearm across his throat and grab your other arm at the triceps.

Grab your attacking arm as shown, locking your arms together. Drive the blade of your top, attacking forearm into his esophagus for the submission.

Smother

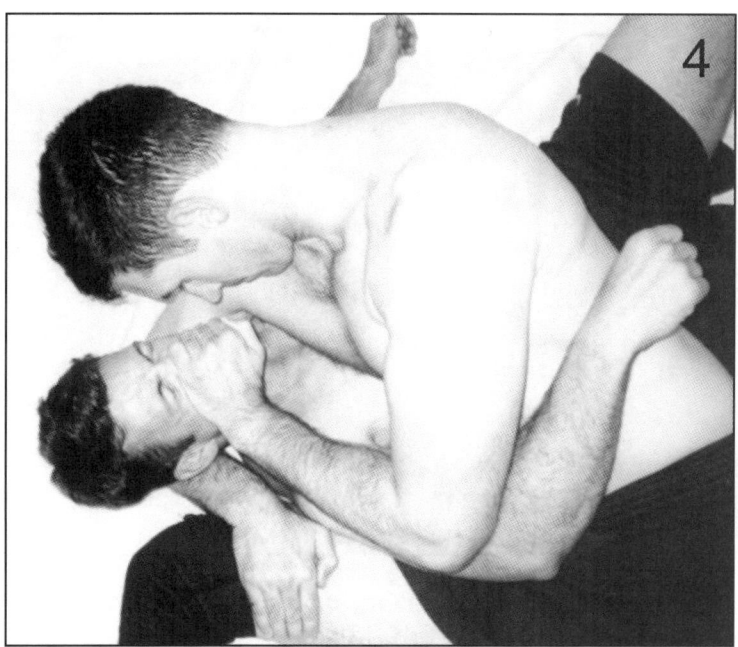

This move is especially effective against someone who has poor breath control, is breathing heavily, or is exhausted. Cover his nose and mouth with your hand, ensure that you have a tight seal so minimal air exchange occurs.

CHOKE *Triangle with Far Arm*

Your opponent brings his far arm up to hook your head in attempt to escape. Grab his arm at the wrist and control it.

Reposition your hips closer to his head and bring your bottom leg under his head.

Bring your far leg over his far arm and his head, trapping his head and arm between your legs.

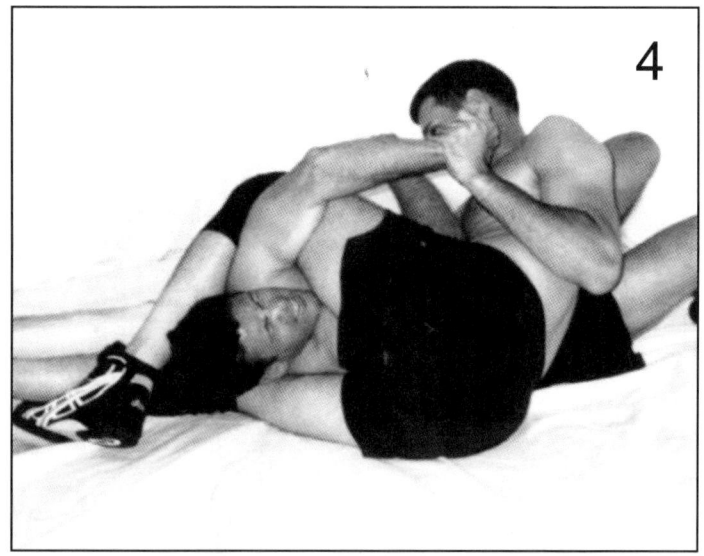

Hook your top leg behind the knee of your bottom leg and squeeze your knees together. Secure his arm at the wrist. You can bring his arm down and across his neck for the triangle choke. Or, you can push his arm away in the other direction and crank his shoulder for the submission.

CHOKE *Triangle with Near Arm*

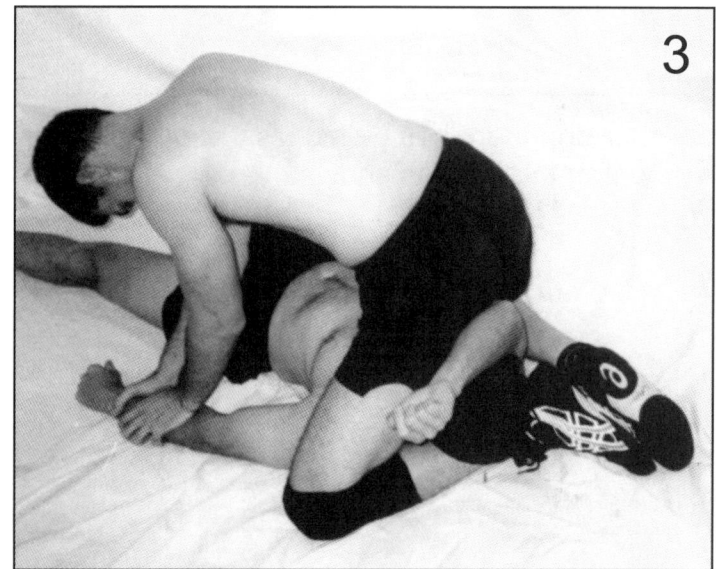

Your opponent has freed his trapped arm; secure it at the wrist. (Above)

Step over with your far leg, trapping his head and near arm. (Above Right)

Sit up to a reverse mount position, trapping his arm and head. (Right)

Rotate your hips and come to your side. Hook the foot of your top leg behind the knee of your bottom leg to make the triangle lock with your legs. (Bottom Right)

Squeeze your knees together and pull his arm across his face for the choke. Or, push his arm away from you, cranking his shoulder for the submission. (Bottom)

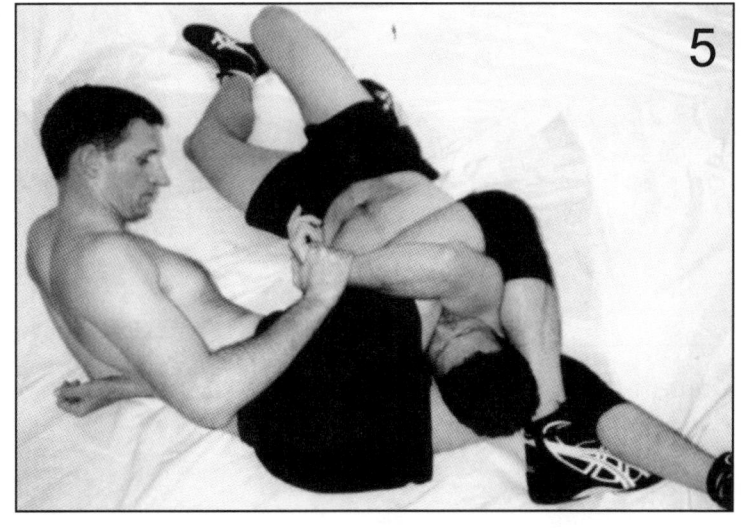

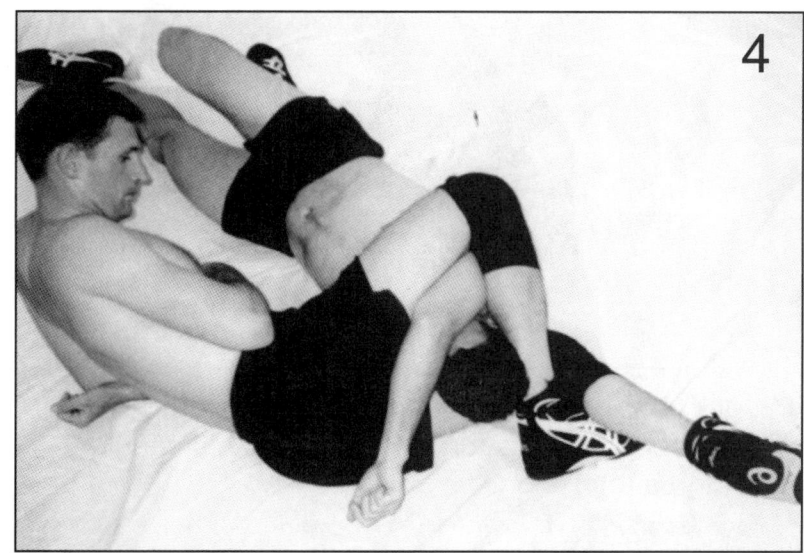

SHOULDER CRANK *With Legs*

Your opponent has pulled his trapped arm free. Control this arm as shown.

Place his arm under your near knee; push your hips forwards, trapping his bent elbow.

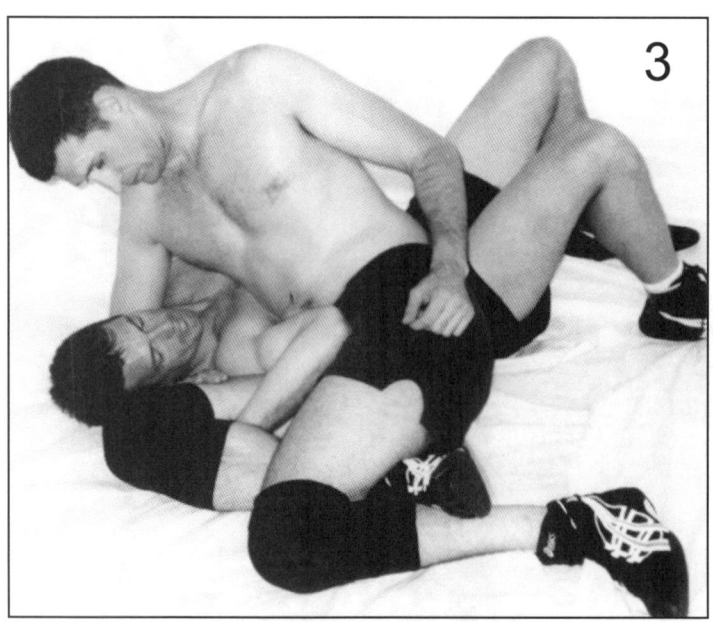

Lock your bottom foot behind your top leg. Sit up and arch your hips forwards to crank his shoulder for the submission.

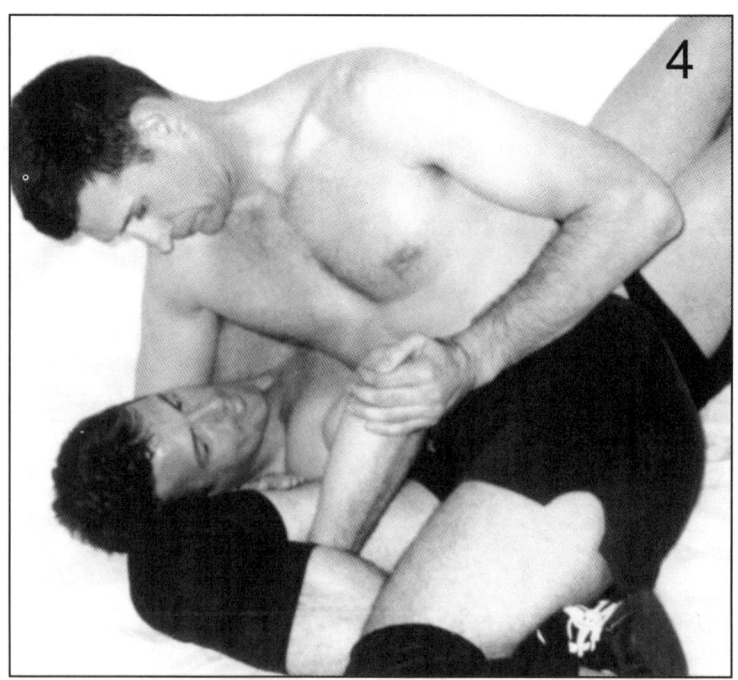

You can also push his arm forwards at the elbow to crank the shoulder.

ARM BAR *With Legs*

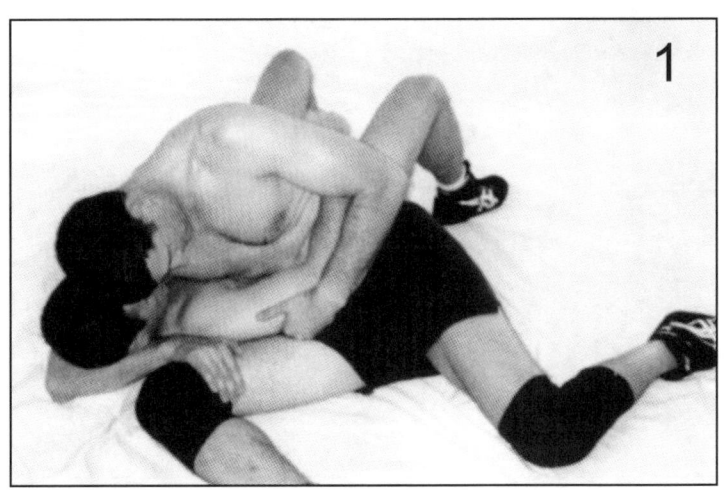

You have your opponent in a secure hold.

He frees his trapped arm and you secure it at the elbow.

Place his arm under your far leg.

To attack his arm, raise your bottom leg while pushing down with your top leg. This hyperextends his arm at the elbow for the submission.

ARM BAR *Step Over*

You have your opponent in a secure hold. Secure his far arm at the biceps as shown. Place your near leg under his head.

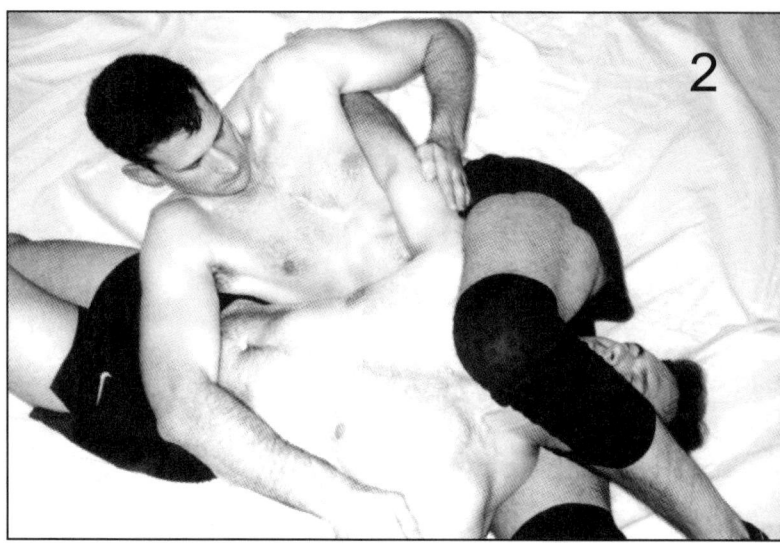

Hook your far leg over his face and across his throat. Maintain control of his trapped arm, keeping it securely under your armpit.

Hook the foot of your top leg behind the knee of your bottom leg. You can extend your legs straight out for a choke if you want to. Securing a lock on his head also helps to pin him to the ground and control his upper body.

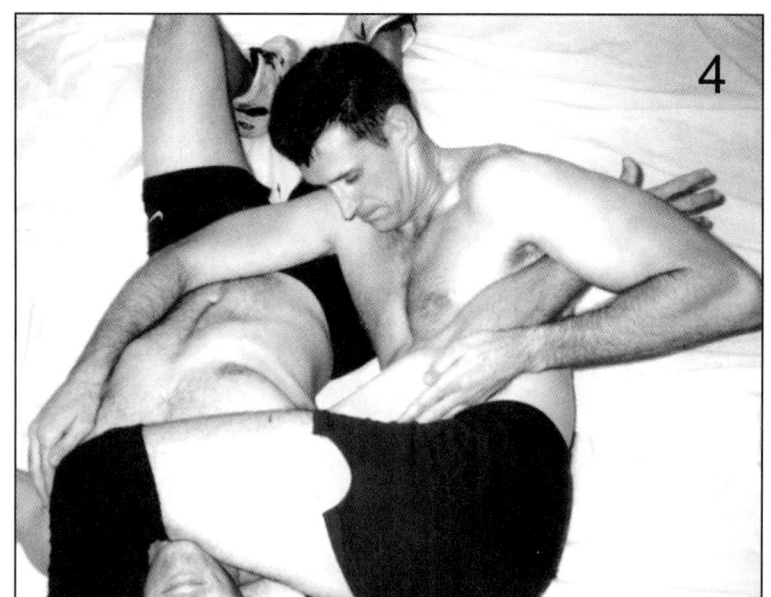

Arch your hips forward and and lean backwards. This will hyper-extend his arm at the elbow for the submission.

IN SCARF HOLD – CHOKE *Kata Gatame*

Your opponent is transitioning into scarf hold and does not have your head secured yet.

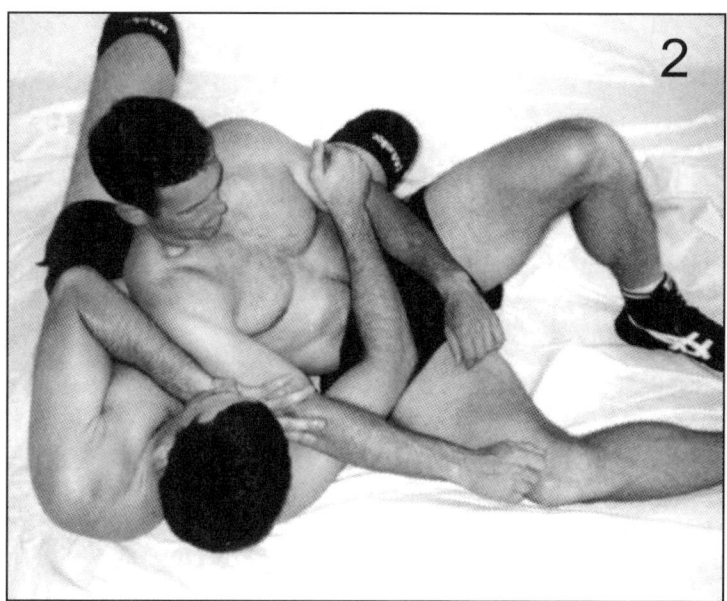

Duck your head and push his arm over and past your head. Grab his far arm at the biceps so that he can not trap it under his far armpit.

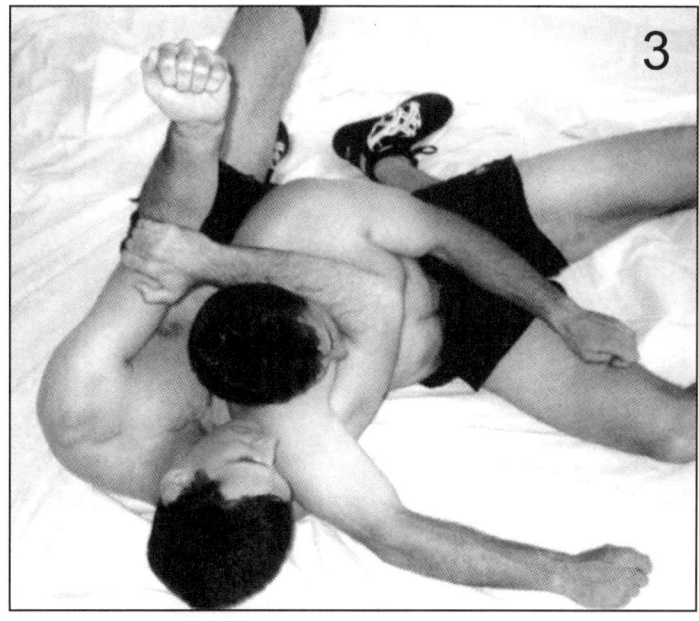

Grab his head and near arm with your attacking arm and grab your locking arm at the biceps.

Slide your hips out from under him so you are taking his back. Hook your top leg over his leg, securing your positioning. Place your locking hand on your head, keep your head close to his, and contract the muscles of your attacking, choking arm. This will cut off his carotid arteries for the submission.

ARM BAR

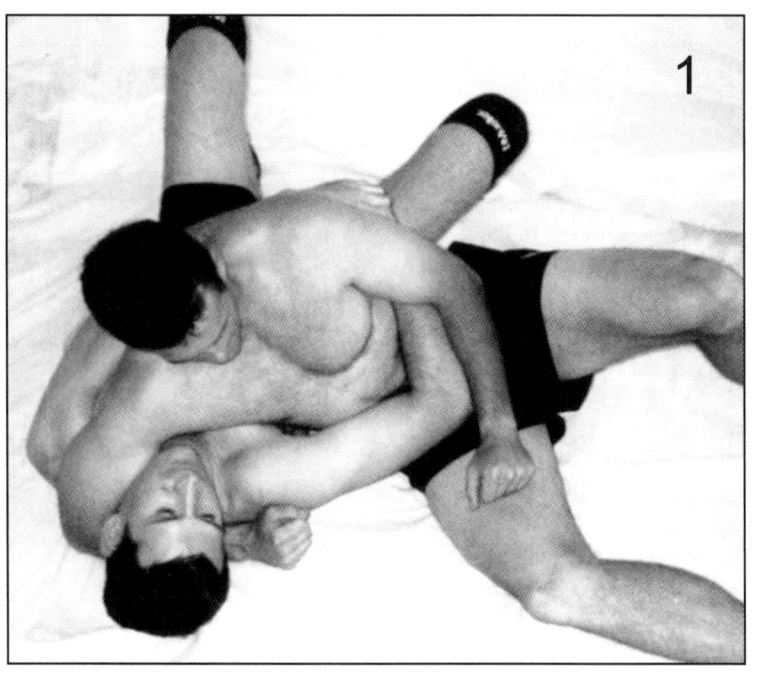

Your opponent has you in scarf hold but he has left his head high.

Hook your free arm over his face, grab his jaw and push his head backwards.

Keep his head pushed away from you as you hook your leg over his head and across his neck. Use your leg to push him onto his back.

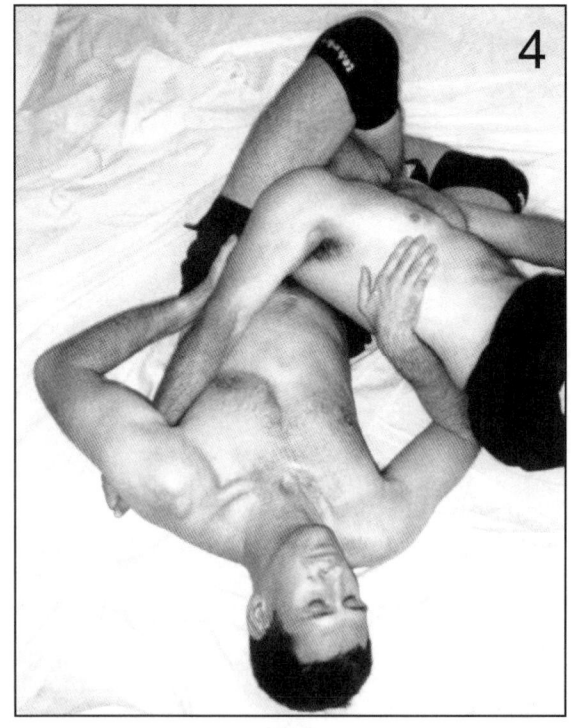

Hook the foot of your attacking leg behind your other knee to secure his head. Place his near arm under your armpit. Push upwards on his elbow and push downwards with your armpit to hyper-extend his arm at the elbow for the submission.

Modified Scarf Hold

You can often transition to this position from side control if your opponent has his arm over your shoulder.

Your head is posted on your hand, trapping his arm which is placed over your shoulder. His arm is isolated and vulnerable to attack.

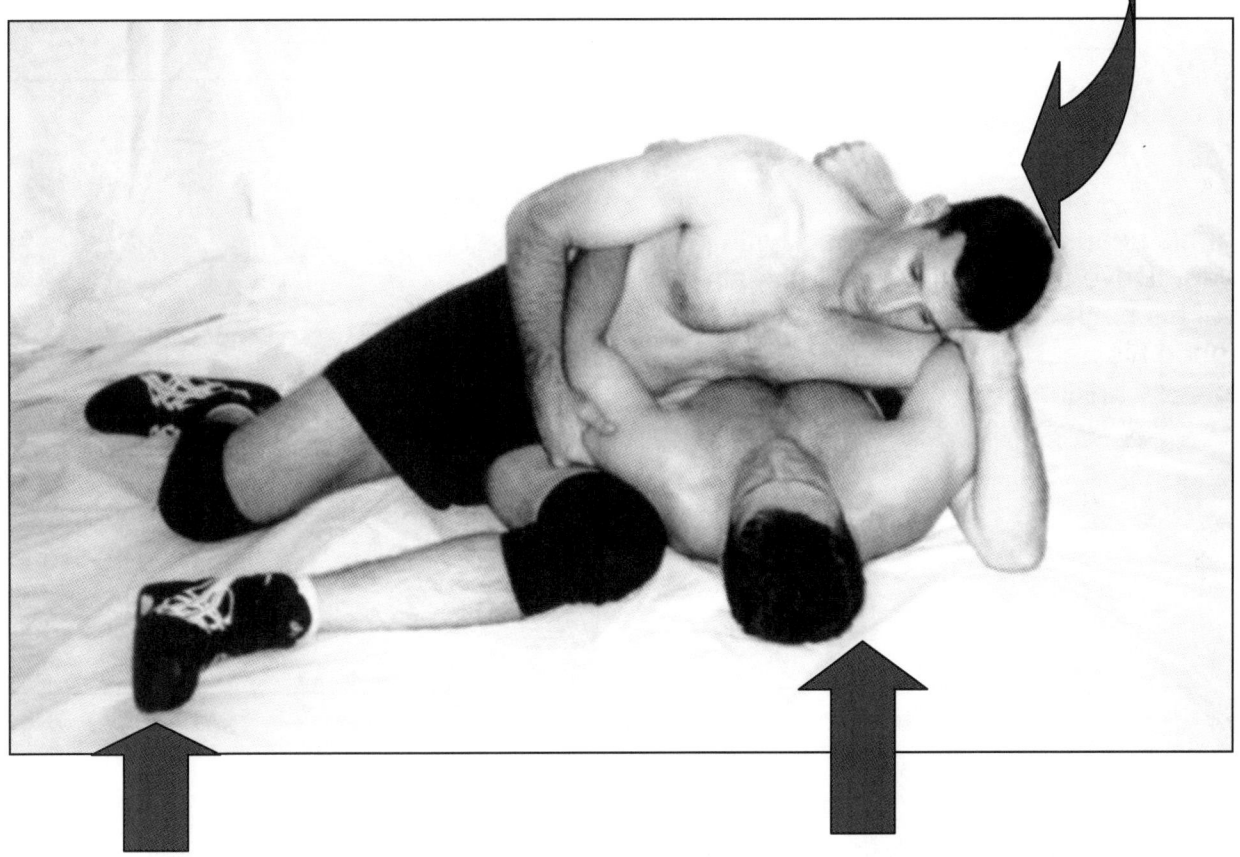

Your legs are spread wide, giving you a good base and making it difficult for you to be reversed.

Your chest is placed on his chest and your body weight is pinning him to the ground.

ARM BAR *Step Over*

1. You have your opponent in modified scarf hold; you are preparing to attack his near arm. (Left)

Step over his head and across his neck with your far leg. Drive the heel of your foot against the side of his neck. By stepping across, you have trapped his near arm between your leg, hips, and body. (Right)

Place your arm in the small of your back, the back of your hand flat against your back. Drive your hips forwards while maintaining pressure against his neck with the heel of your foot. This move hyper-extends his near arm at the elbow for the submission. (Left)

SHOULDER CRANK *Americana*

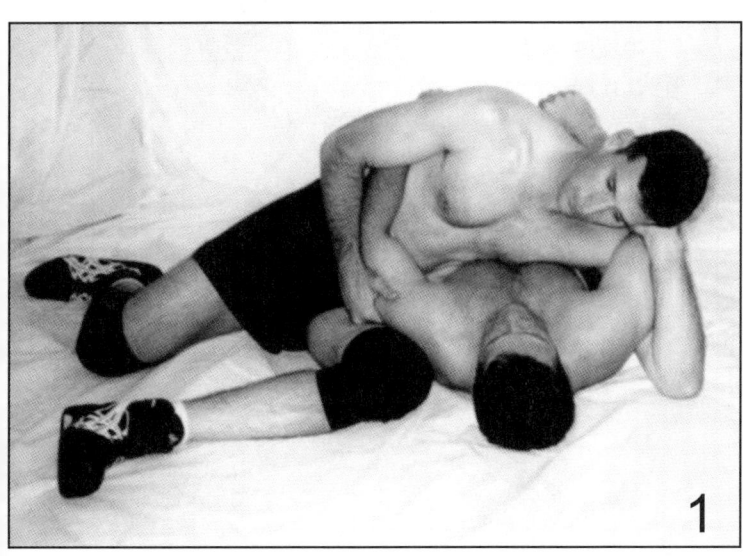

You have your opponent in a secure hold.

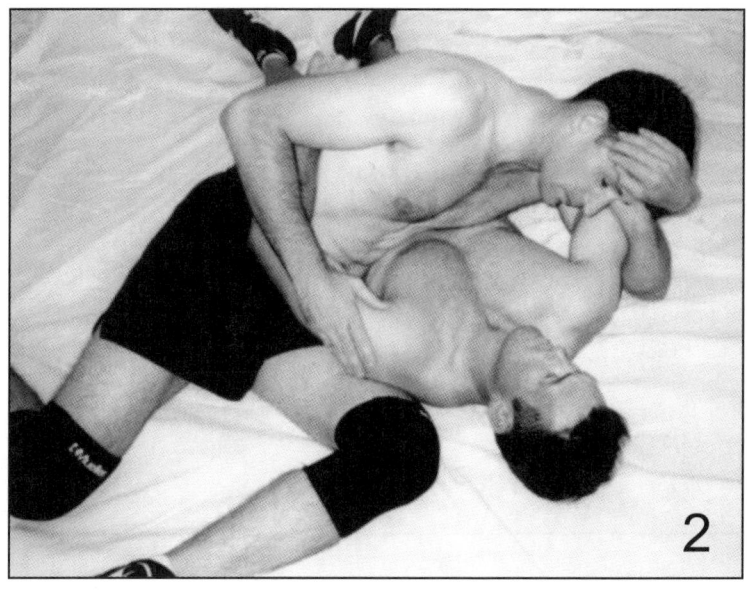

Your opponent attempts to move his far arm, he may try to hook your head to escape.

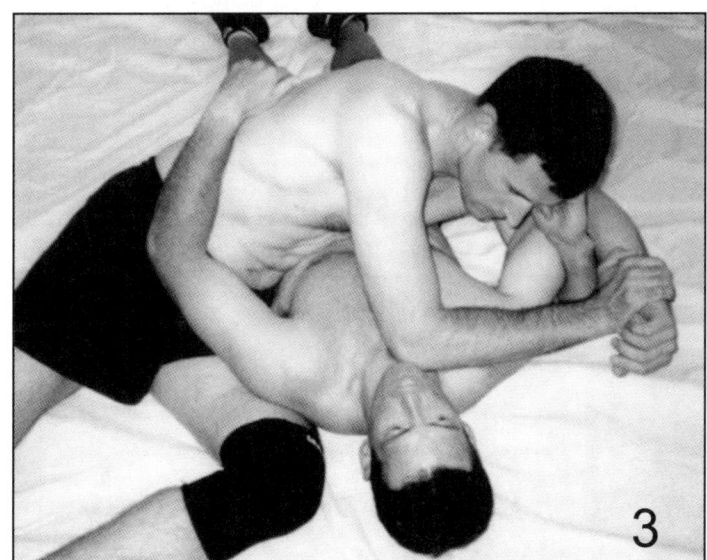

Grab his far arm at he wrist with your free arm and press his arm to the ground.

Secure a figure four lock on his trapped arm. Switch to side control position by turning your hips towards him. Keep his wrist pinned to the ground and raise his elbow to crank his shoulder for the submission.

ARM BAR *Step Across*

You have your opponent securely in a modified scarf hold. (Top)

Step over his head with your far leg, pressing your heel firmly against his neck. (Top Right)

Keep driving your heel into his neck as you hug his far arm and step over his body. (Right)

Rotate your body and stay tight against his arm as you sit on his trapped shoulder. (Bottom Right)

Sit backwards and extend his arm. Squeeze your knees together and raise your hips to hyper-extend his arm at the elbow. (Bottom)

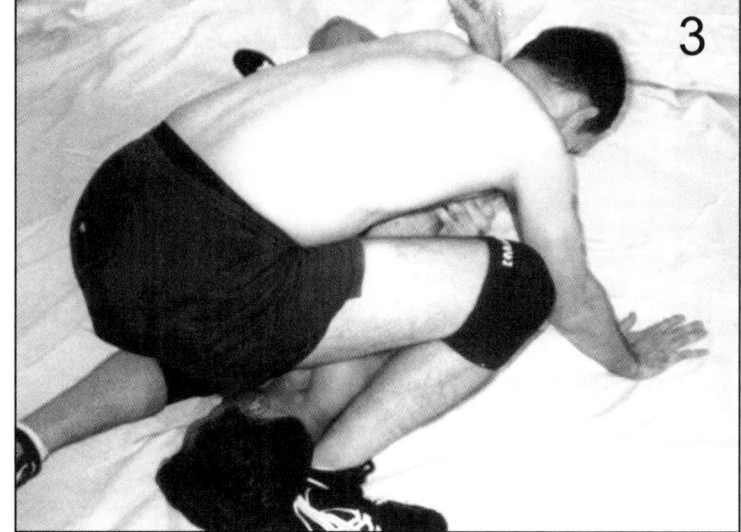

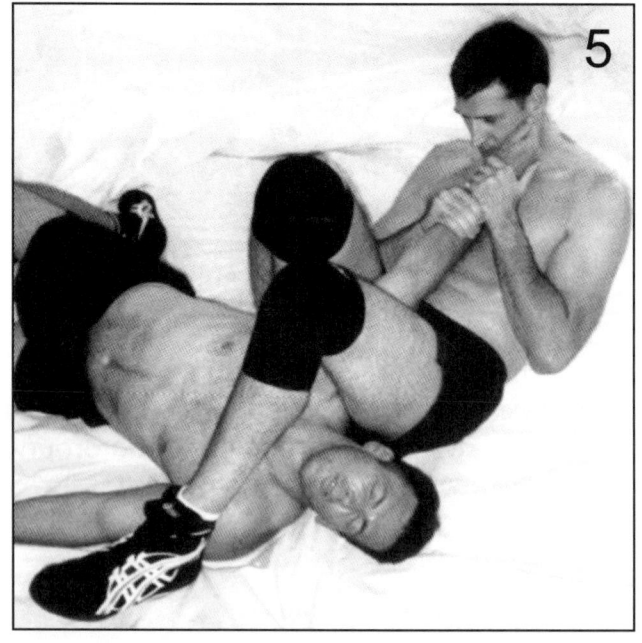

Chapter Thirteen
Submissions From Knee On Stomach

Knee On Stomach

This position lets you pin your opponent with minimal energy and is very painful for him. His attempts to escape often sets him up for successful attacks.

You have a leg hooked and are pulling up on it. This can set his legs up for attacks and helps drive your knee into him

Your leg is far enough away so he can not grab it. This gives you balance and helps drive your knee into him.

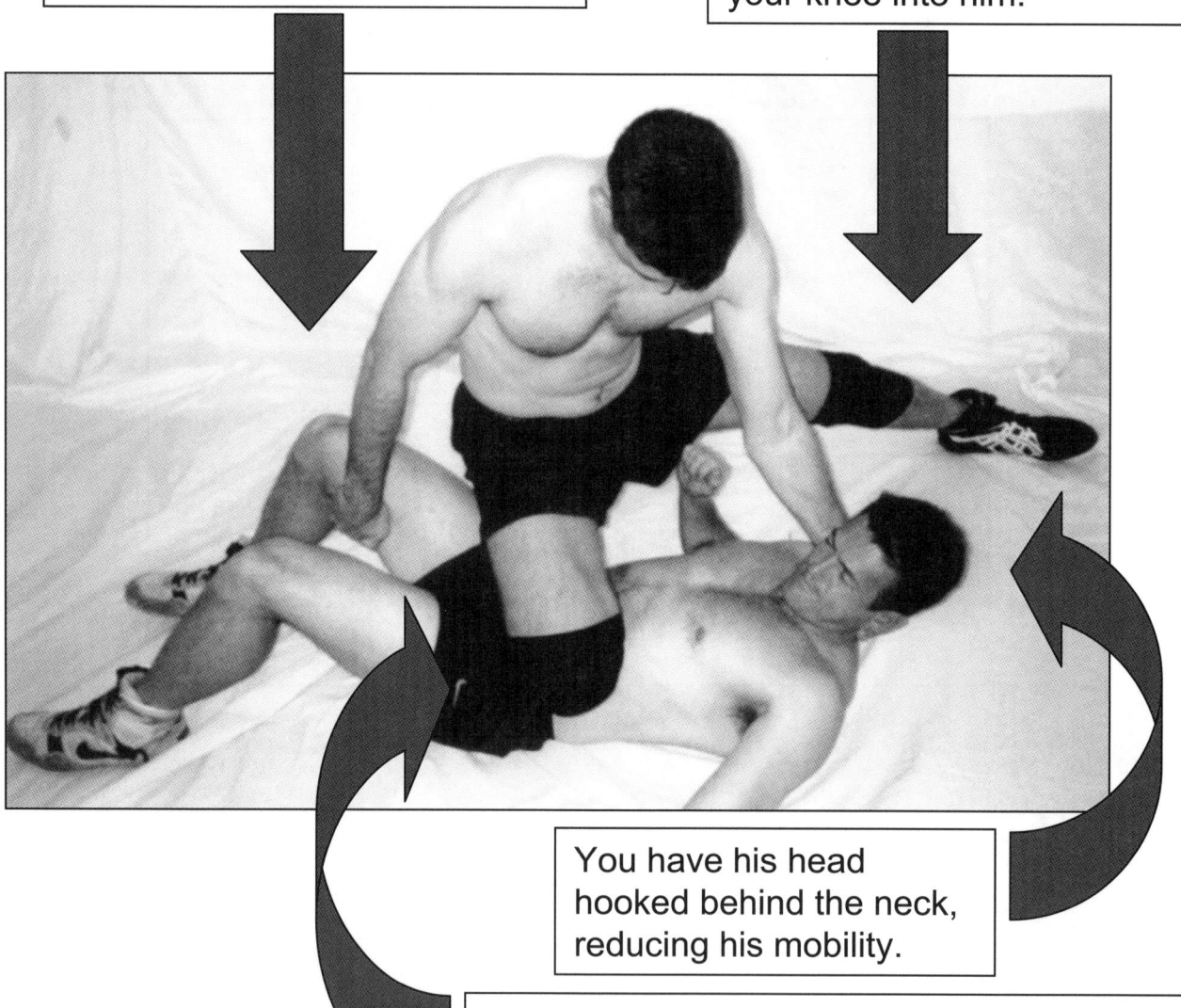

You have his head hooked behind the neck, reducing his mobility.

Your knee is driving down into his stomach or solar plexus, pinning him to the ground. This makes it difficult for him to breath and is painful. You may be able to submit him from this pressure alone.

CRADLE

1. You have your opponent in knee on stomach.

2. Hook your arm under his far leg and bring his leg in tight against your knee on his stomach.

3. Hook your other arm behind his head and pull his head towards your knee on his stomach.

4. Clasp your hands together, putting your opponent in a cradle. You may be able to crank his neck enough for the submission if he is not very flexible. Regardless, drive your knee straight into his solar plexus. The pressure from your knee may cause your opponent to vomit and inhibit his breathing. Maintain pressure until he submits.

CHOKE *Guillotine*

You have your opponent in knee on stomach.

Grab the back of his head with both hands, placing your elbows together and firmly on his chest. You now have your opponent in a can opener; crank his neck until he submits or he may sit up into you to relieve the pressure on his neck.

You crank your opponent's neck and he sits up towards you. Maintain your pressure on his neck and pull him into you.

Wrap your attacking arm over his neck and under his chin, securing a guillotine choke. Grab your attacking arm at the wrist with your other, locking arm. Drive your knee into his stomach and pull upwards with the blade of your attacking forearm for the choke and the submission.

ARM BAR

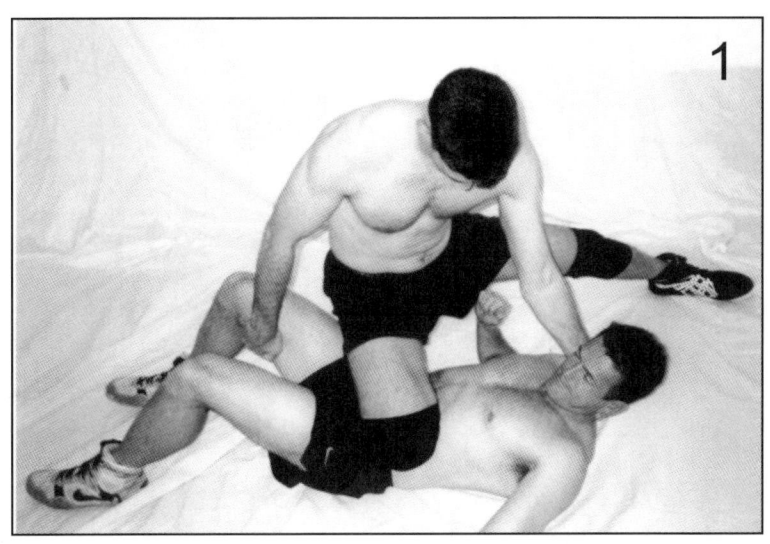

You have your opponent set up in knee on stomach.

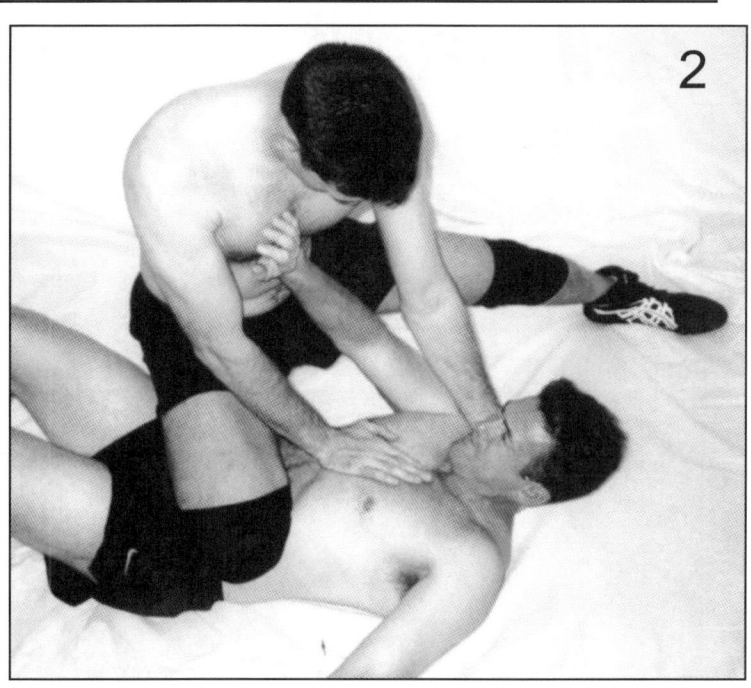

He places his near arm on your chest. Place your far arm on his chest as shown.

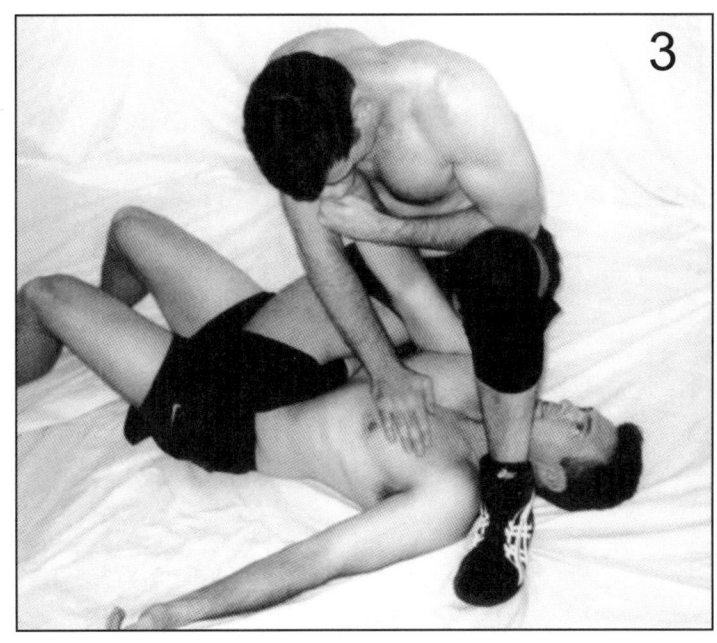

Secure his targeted arm at the wrist and step over his head and across his neck with your far leg.

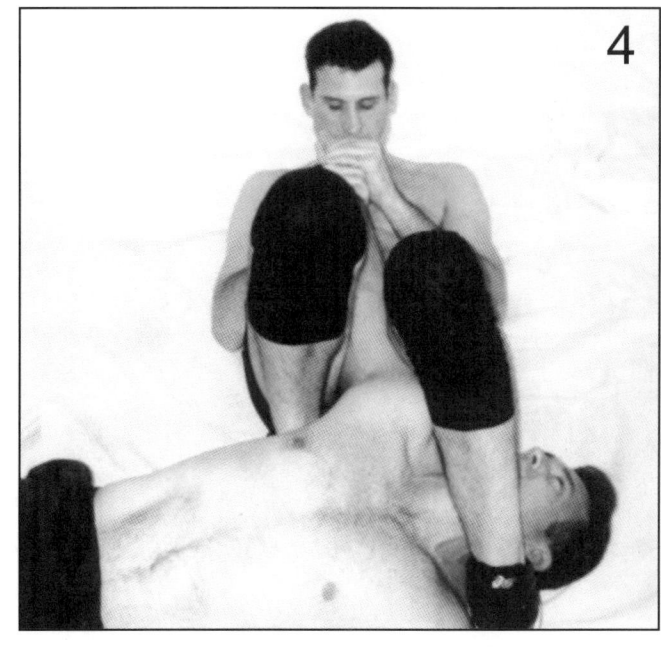

Sit backwards, squeeze your knees together, and arch your hips to hyper-extend his arm at the elbow for the submission.

ARM BAR *Step Across*

You have your opponent in knee on stomach and he pushes off on your knee with his far arm to escape. Hook under his arm and secure him high at the triceps.

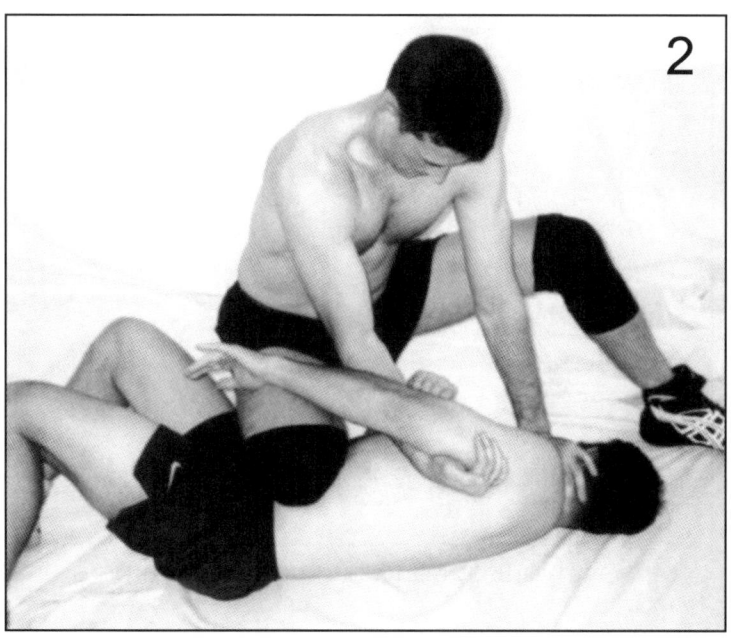

Push down on his jaw to control his head as you lift up his far arm in preparation for stepping over his body.

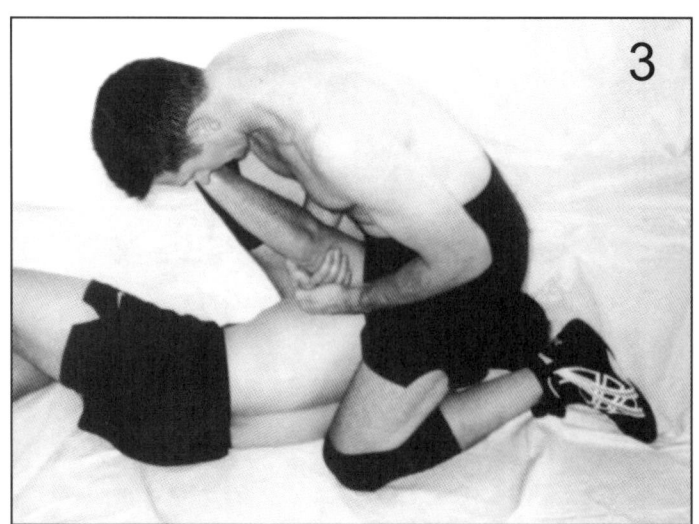

Step over his body with your far leg. Hug his arm tightly to your chest and sit on his trapped arm's shoulder, using your weight to keep him pinned to the ground.

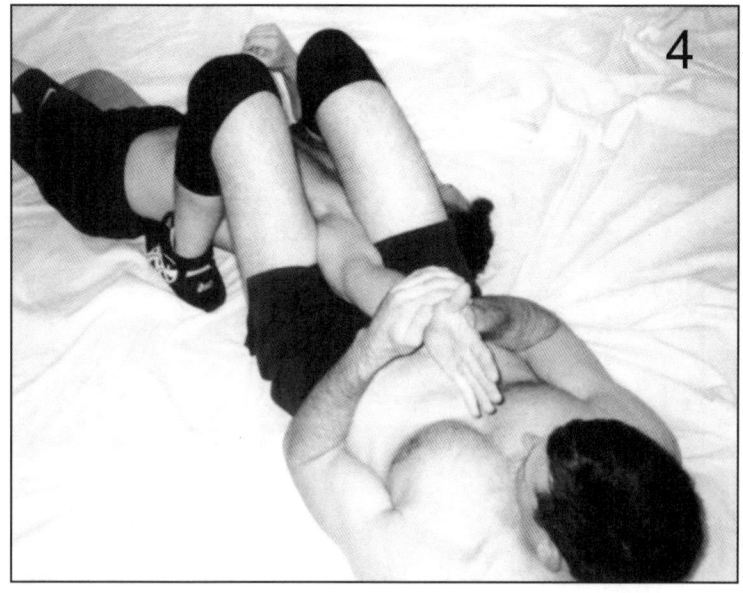

Fall backwards with his trapped arm. Squeeze your knees together and arch your hips to hyperextend his arm at the elbow for the submission.

ARM BAR *Elbow Hug*

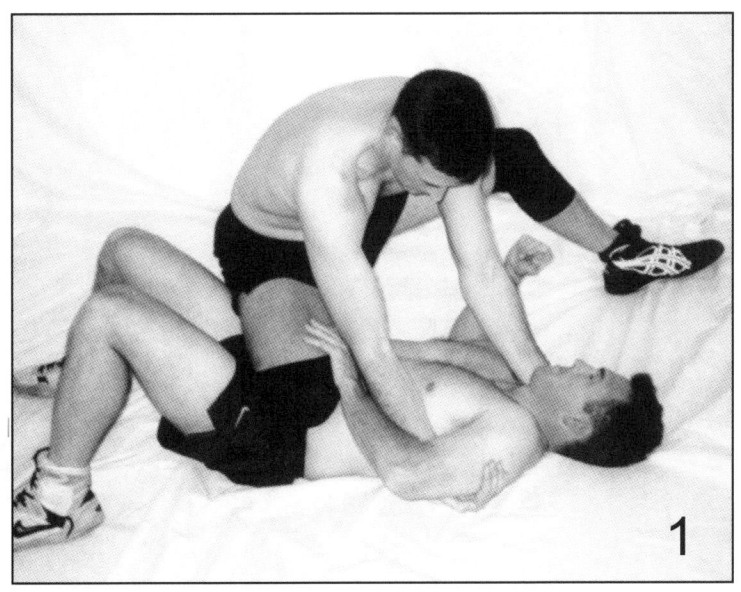

Your opponent is pushing off on your knee with his far arm to escape; you have under hooked his far arm at the triceps.

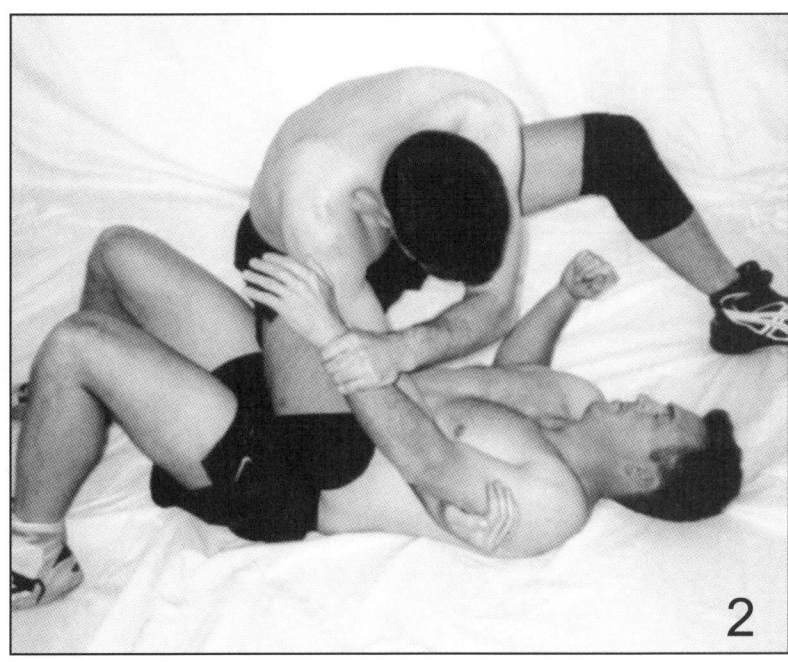

Grab his targeted arm at he wrist with your other arm.

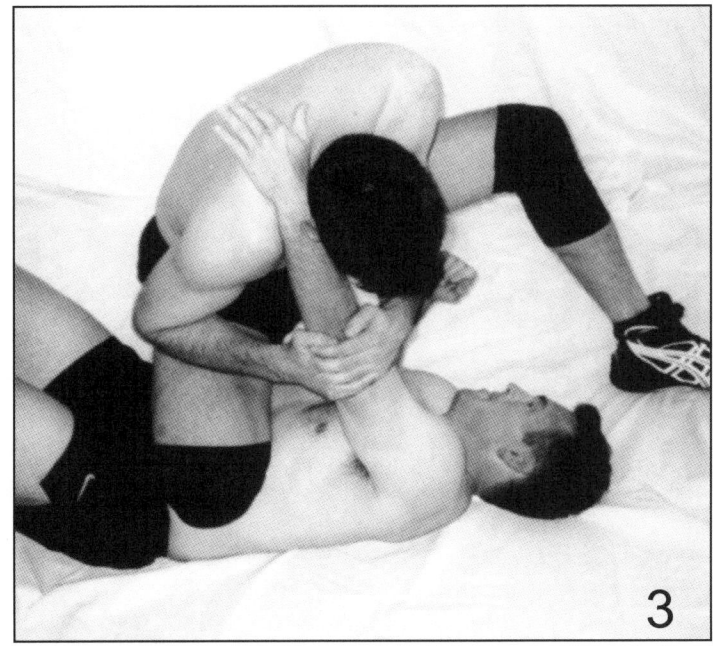

Place his arm against your shoulder and squeeze his arm between your shoulder and your head. Place your hands on his elbow. Drive your shoulder forwards while pulling in with your arms to hyper-extend his arm at the elbow for the submission.

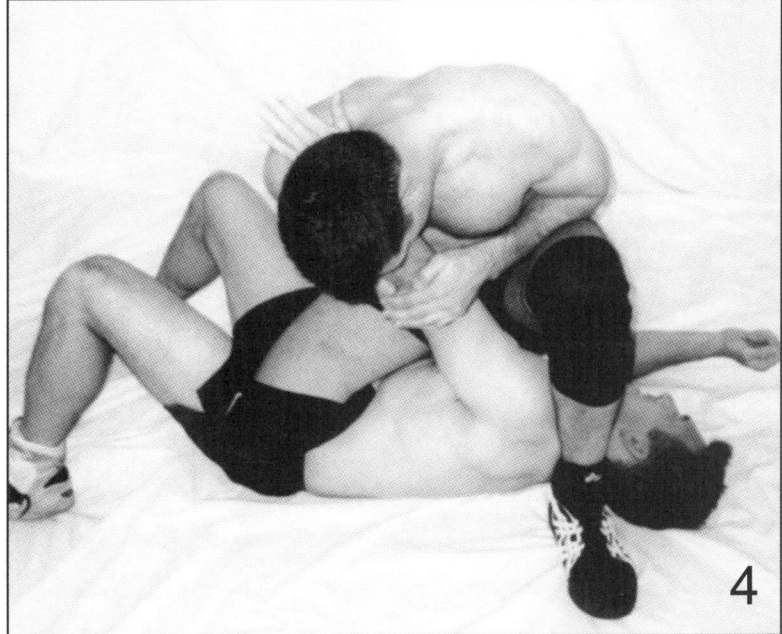

Also, you can step your far leg over his head and against his neck. This traps his arm more securely and allows you to fall forwards, stay in place, or fall backwards and still execute the technique effectively.

KNEE BAR *Far Leg*

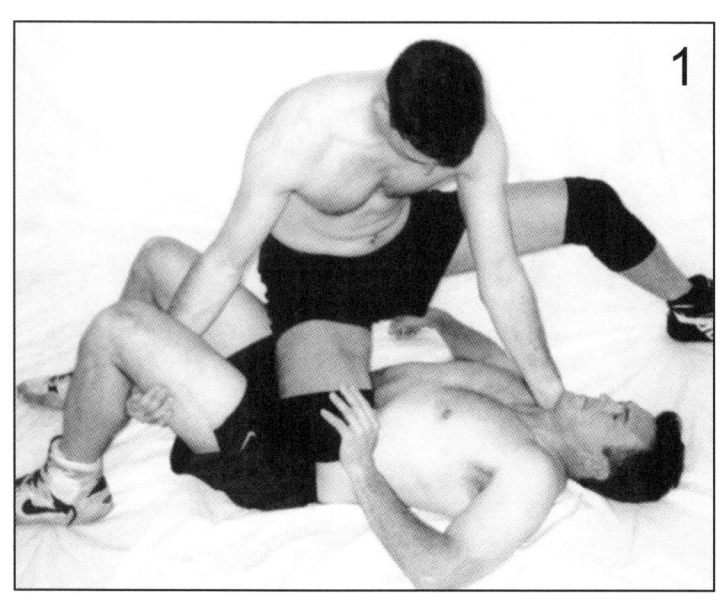

You have your opponent set up with your arm hooked under his far leg.

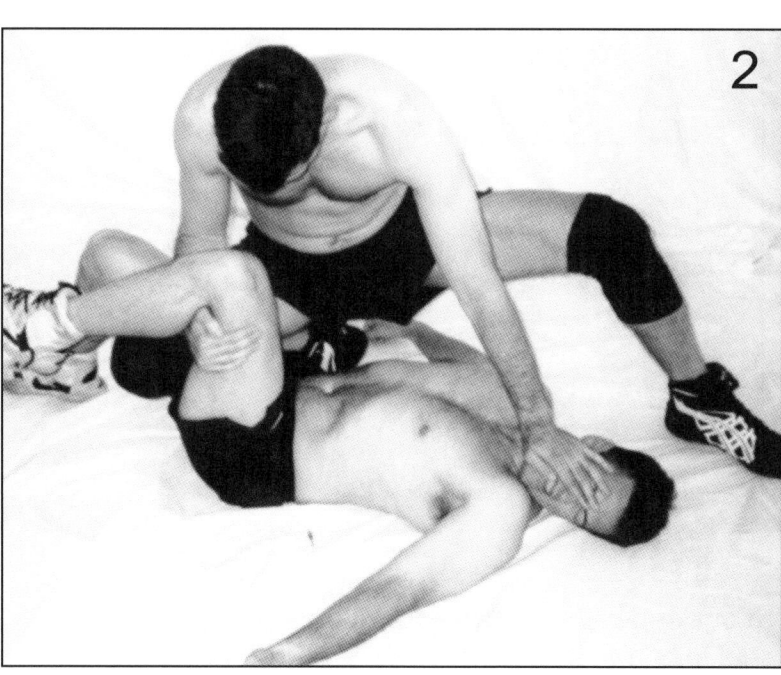

Press down on his jaw to control his upper body, pull up on his targeted leg and slide your knee between his legs.

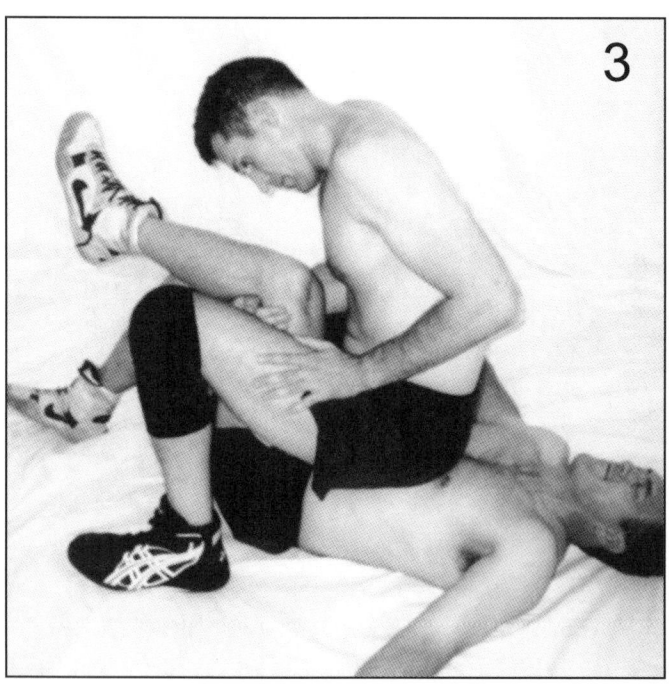

Step over his head and across his body so that you are hugging his trapped leg. Sit as close to his groin as possible to ensure a tight knee bar.

Fall to your side, hug his foot to your chest and arch your hips to hyper-extend his leg at the knee for the submission.

Chapter Fourteen
Submissions From Knee On Chest

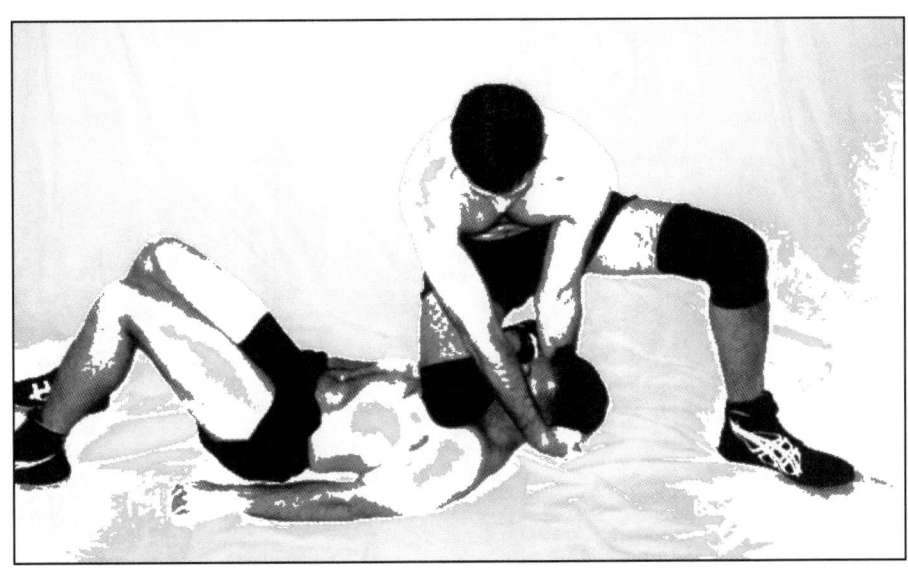

Knee On Chest

This position allows you to drive your body weight into your opponent's solar plexus, which is painful. Also, this position is excellent for eliciting a predictable response from your opponent, setting him up for an attack.

Your leg is posted out so that it can not be grabbed. This leg provides you with balance and helps drive your weight onto your other leg.

You are securing your opponent at his shorts. Push his hips to the ground to control his body positioning and to secure your balance.

Your knee is placed at an angle against his neck and across his chest. You are pulling up on his head to secure your own positioning and help prevent him from escaping. You are driving your knee into his chest.

NECK CRANK *Crucifix*

1. You have your opponent in knee on chest. He tries to pull your knee off with his same side arm. Secure his arm at the wrist and secure his other arm at the biceps.

2. Slide your knee, that is on his chest, forwards and hook your foot under his arm, trapping it behind your knee.

3. Continue to control his arm at the biceps while you lift his head with your free arm.

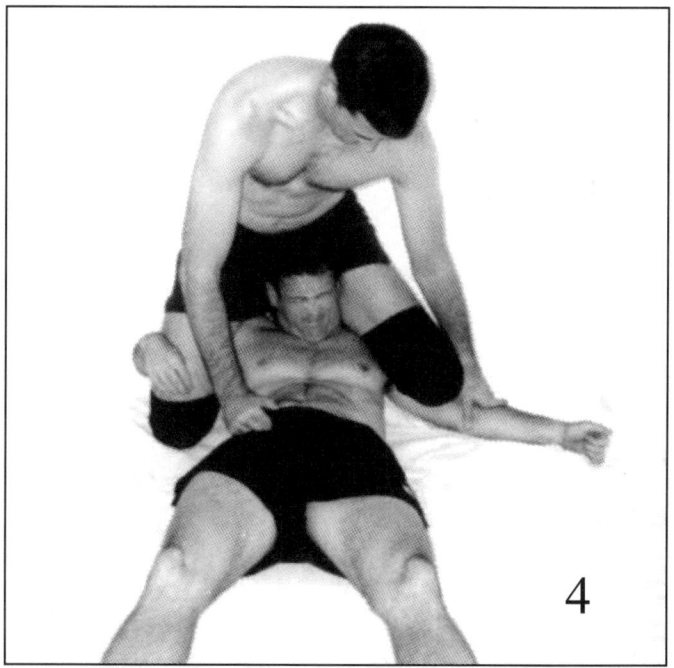

4. Place your groin tightly against the back of his neck and drive your knee over his free arm, at the biceps. You now have both of his arms and his head trapped. Drive your hips forwards to hyper-extend his cervical spine for the submission.

CHOKE *Shin Variation*

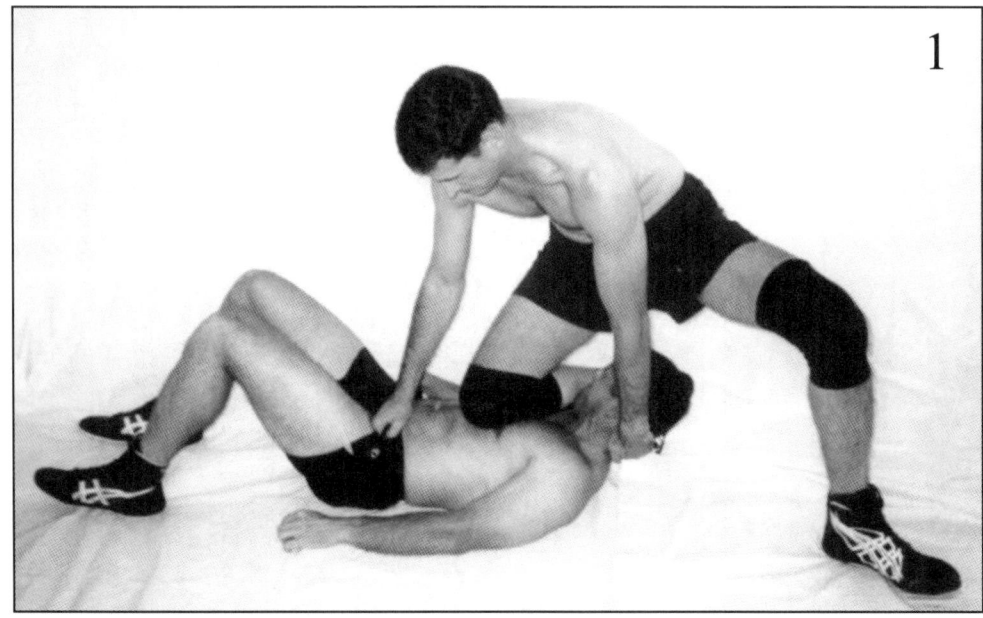

1 You have your opponent in knee on chest. (Left)

Rotate your hips and place your shin across his throat; switch your hand positioning on his head in preparation for the choke. (Right)

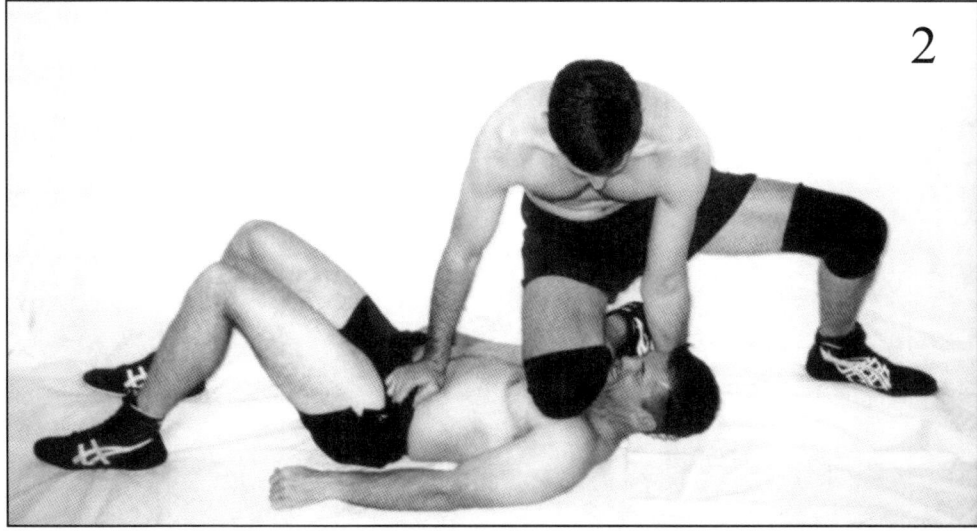

2

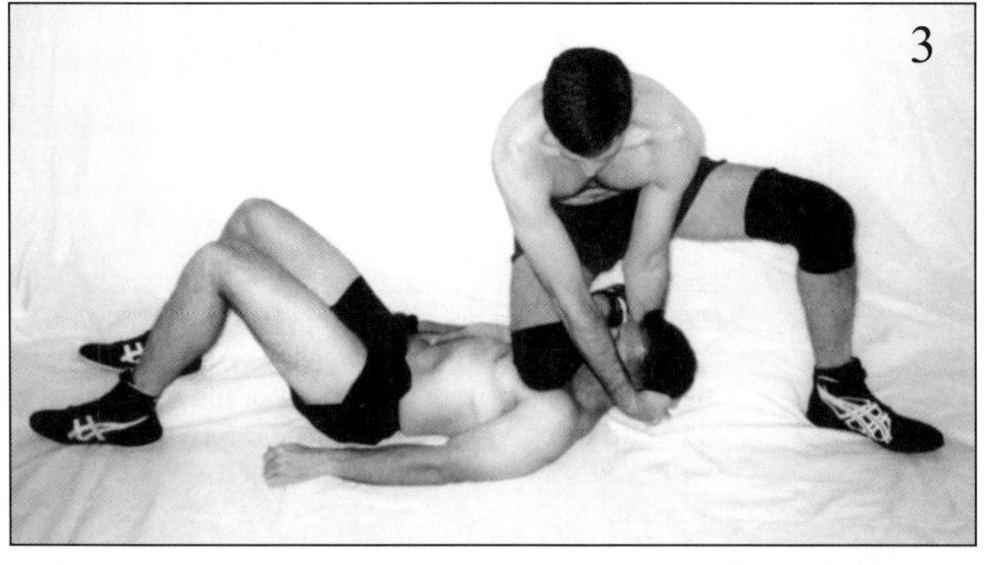

3 Grab the back of your opponent's head with both hands. Drive your knee into his throat while pulling up with both hands. This will crush his esophagus for the submission. (Left)

ARM BAR *Step Across*

Your opponent pushes off on your knee to escape. Hook under his arm at the biceps.

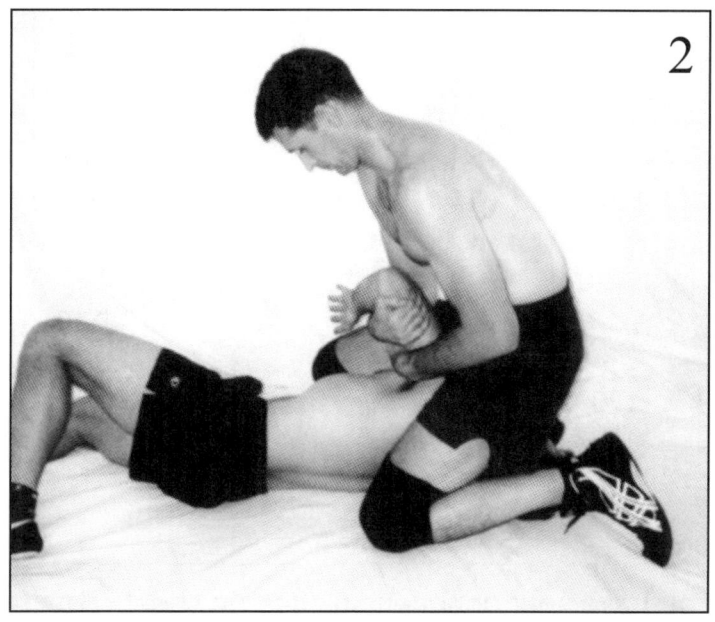

Rotate your far, balancing leg around his back and come to your knees. Hug is trapped arm with both of your arms.

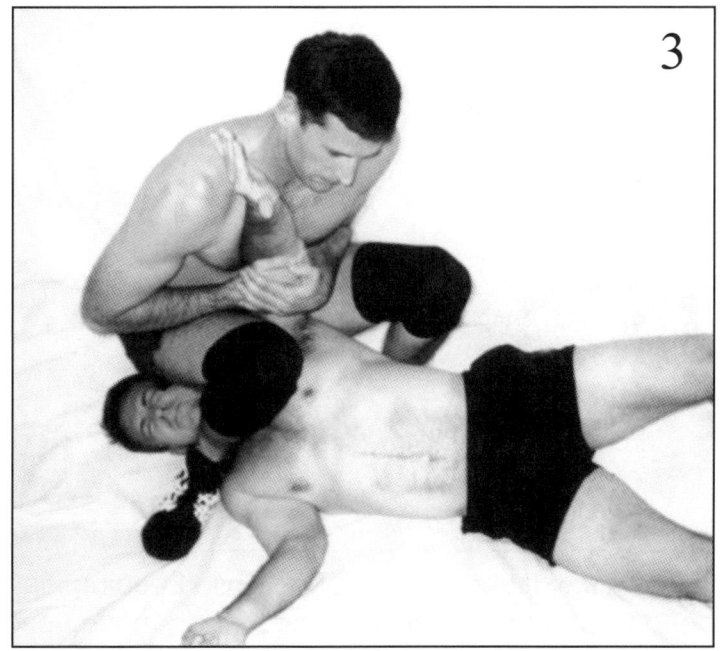

This picture is taken from the opposite angle. Come to your feet and rotate your hips at a 45 degree angle from his body. Maintain control of his arm and keep your groin and hips tight to his shoulder. Notice how your foot is across his throat.

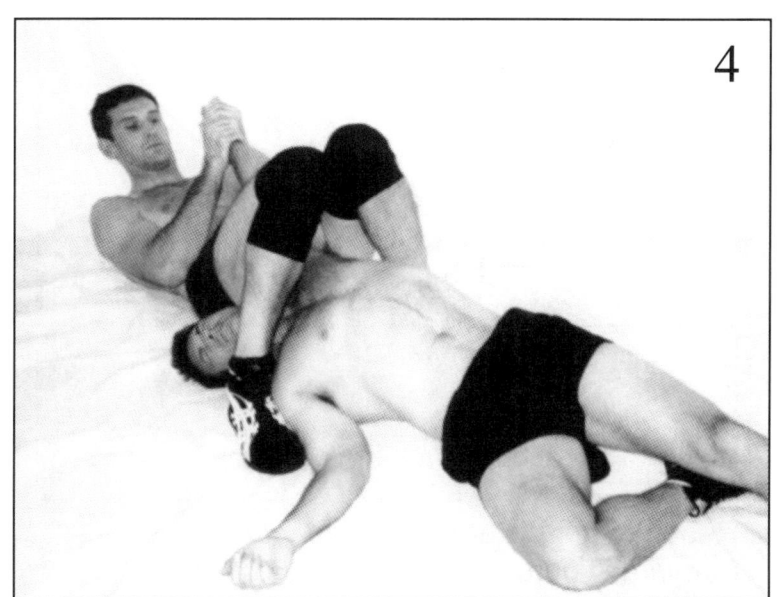

Sit backwards, bringing his trapped arm with you. Squeeze your knees together and arch your hips upwards to hyper-extend his arm at the elbow for the submission.

SHOULDER CRANK

You have your opponent in knee on chest. He is pushing off on your knee in an attempt to escape.

Grab his arm at the wrist.

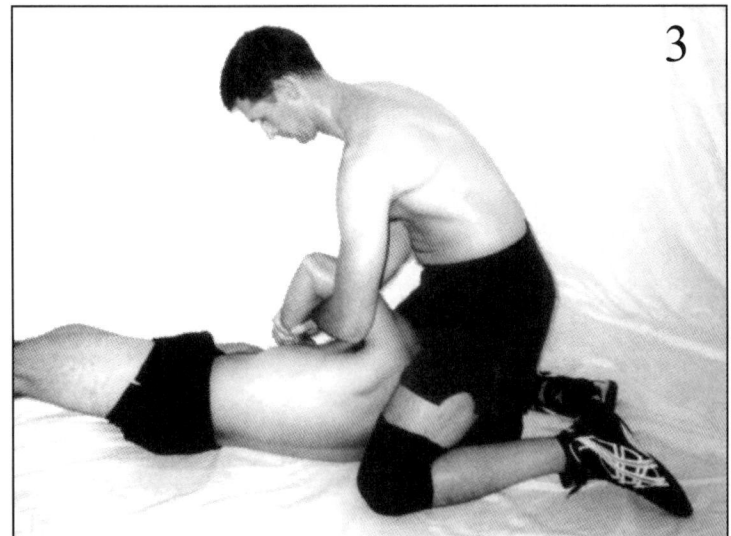

Reach under his arm and grab your own wrist, forming a figure four lock on his arm. Bring your far, balancing leg forward and come to your knees. Notice how you are straddling his head.

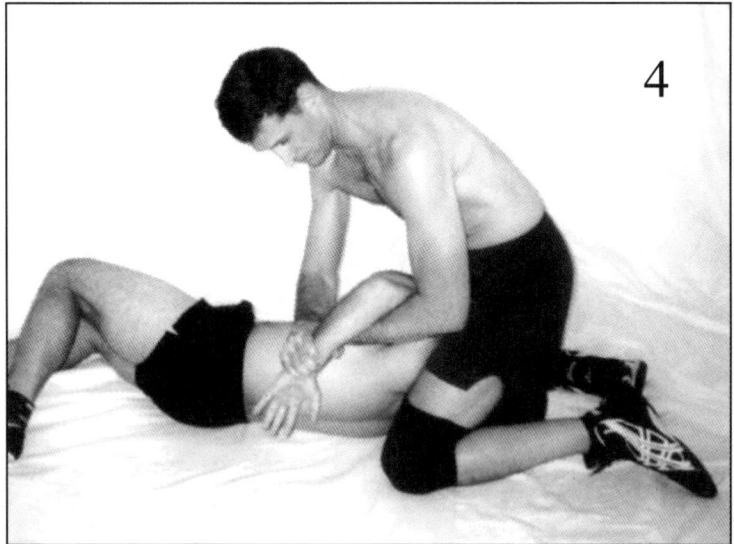

Force his wrist behind his back while keeping his head trapped between your legs. This move uses his bent arm as a lever to torque his shoulder for the submission.

Chapter Fifteen
Submissions Against The Referee's Position And In The Referee's Position

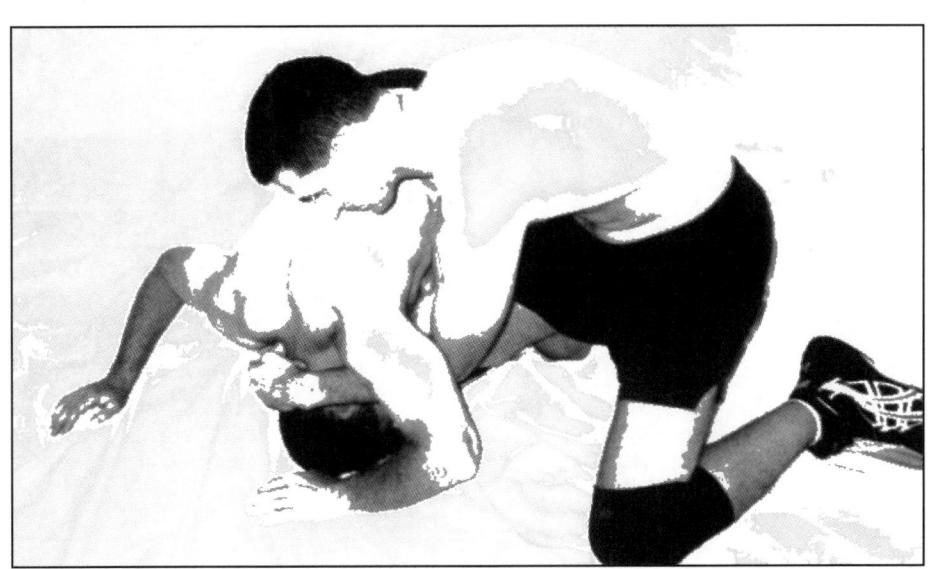

Referee Position

The attacker can try and pin the defender in place while he maneuvers around him. The attacker is looking for opportunities to attack and weaknesses in the defense. The attacker often maneuvers to the defender's rear and attempt to secure a rear mount position.

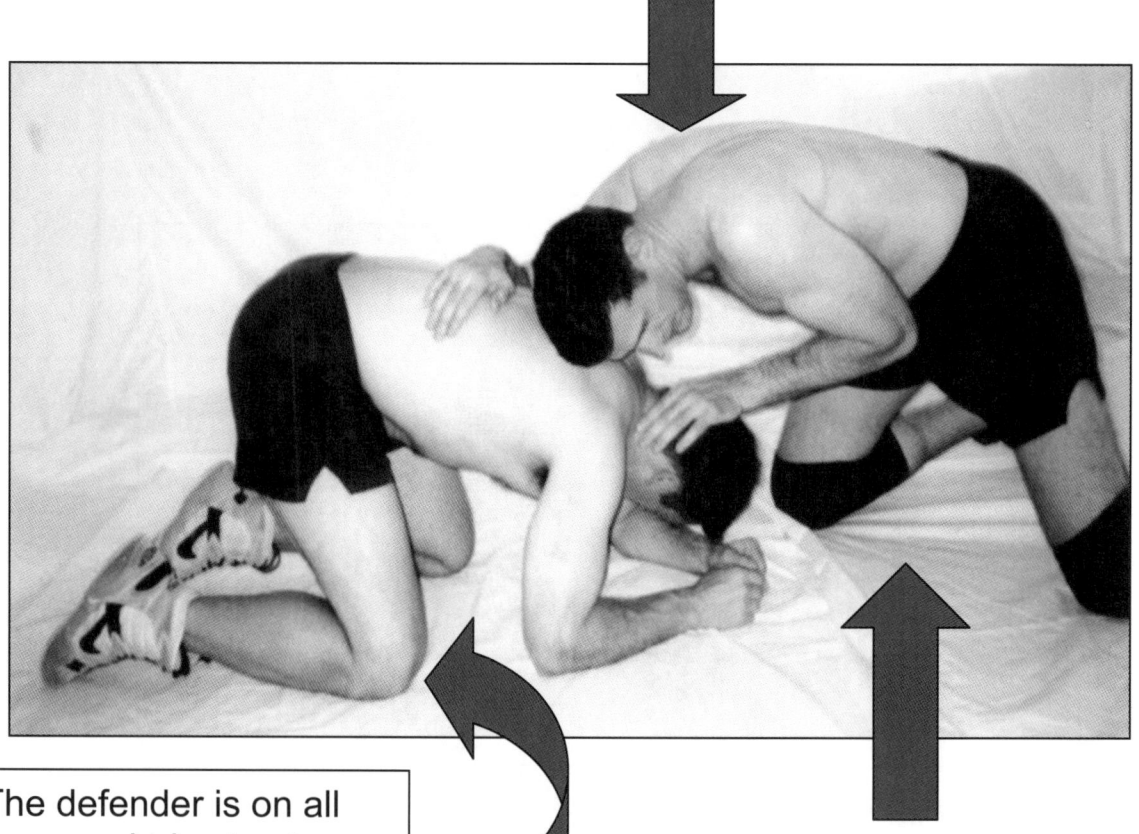

The defender is on all fours and tries to stay low and minimize exposing arms or legs to attack. He can roll forwards to escape or try to reposition if the attacker gives him enough space. This is a defensive position with few opportunities for attack.

There is often a battle for control of the attacker's legs. The attacker tries to keep them away from the defender to maintain his mobility and keep weight on the defender. The defender tries to secure the attacker's legs to reverse him, control his mobility, or obtain a better position.

NECK CRANK *Cross Face*

Your opponent has control of one of your legs and is pulling you into him. (Left)

Bring your same side arm across his jaw, turning his head in the opposite direction of his attack. You can grab his far arm at the triceps for a secure grip.   (Right)

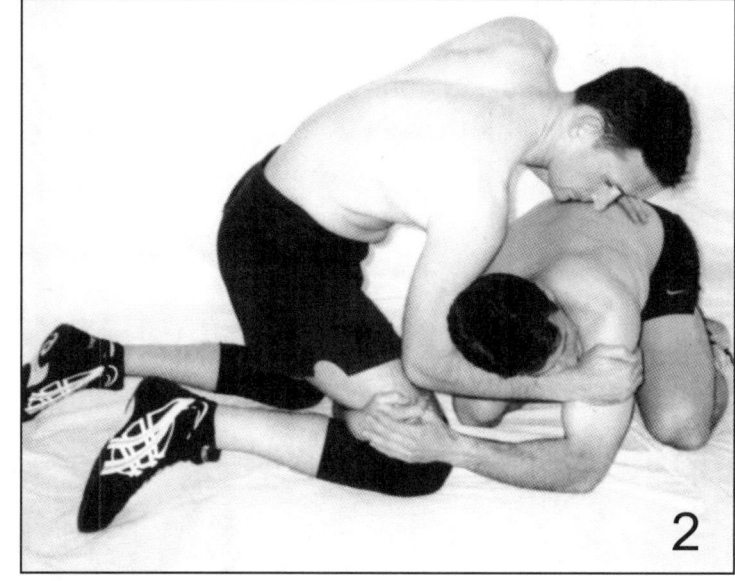

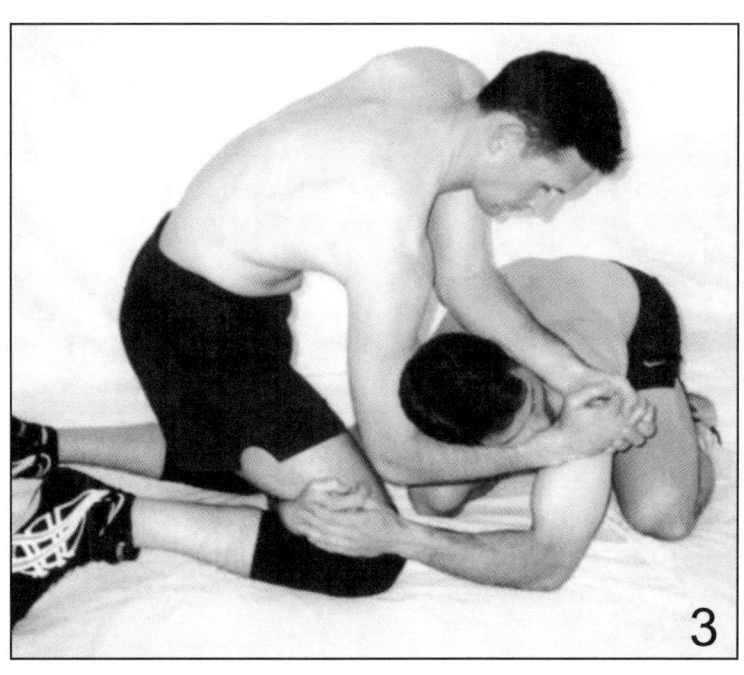

Clasp your hands, keeping his face turned away from you. Squeeze your elbows towards each other, locking his head in a vise-like gripe. Push your top forearm into the base of his neck while pulling your bottom forearm upwards. Turning his head removes most of the flexibility in his cervical spin; when you apply pressure you quickly crank his cervical spine for the submission. (Left)

NECK CRANK *Modified Can Opener*

You are attacking your opponent from his side. He is up high and has space between his body and the ground.

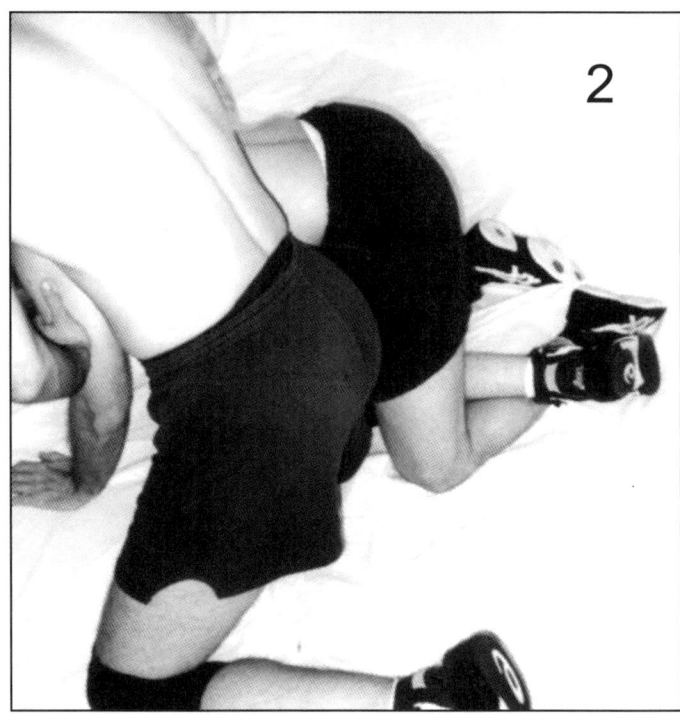

Hook your near leg between his legs and place your foot over the back of his near calf.

Hook your arm under his near arm and over the back of his head, pulling him downwards.

Bring your other arm across his chest and hook the back of his head from the other side. Pull down with both arms to crank his neck for the submission. Your near leg entangled in his prevents him from rolling forwards and out of the crank.

CHOKE

You are attacking your opponent from the front and have control of his head. (Left)

Slide your attacking arm over the back of his neck and under his chin. (Right)

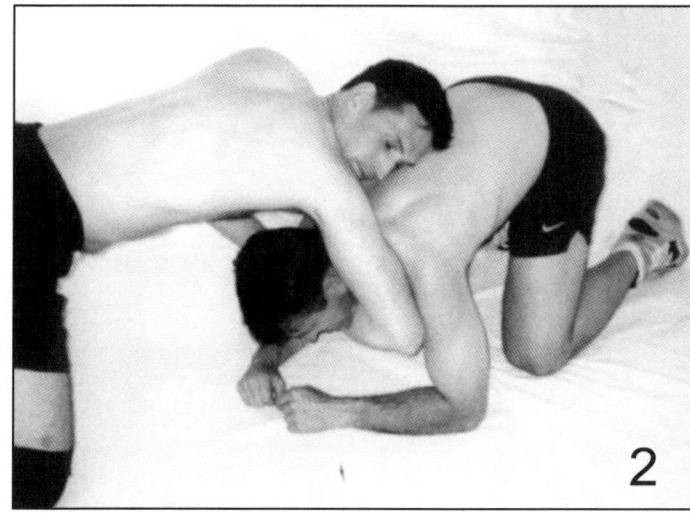

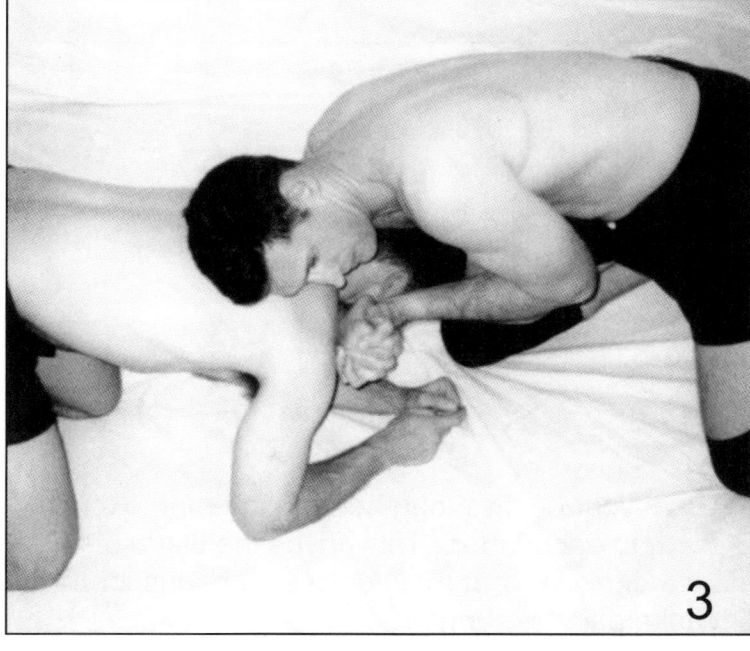

Clasp your hands together to secure the choke. Drive your shoulder into the back of his neck while pulling the blade of your attacking forearm upwards and into his throat. This crushes his esophagus for the submission. (This picture is from the opposite angle.) (Left)

CHOKE *Paper Cutter*

This sequence is exaggerated to show the technique. Place your forearm across his throat and under his chin. Ensure that the palm of your hand is facing you. (Left)

Clasp your hands together as shown. Ensure that the palm of your top arm is facing away from you. (Right)

Drive your elbows together and attempt to touch them to each other. This drives the blade of your choking forearm into his esophagus for the choke and the submission. (Left)

CHOKE *Paper Cutter*

You are attacking your opponent from the side.

Place your near arm across his chest and over his far shoulder.

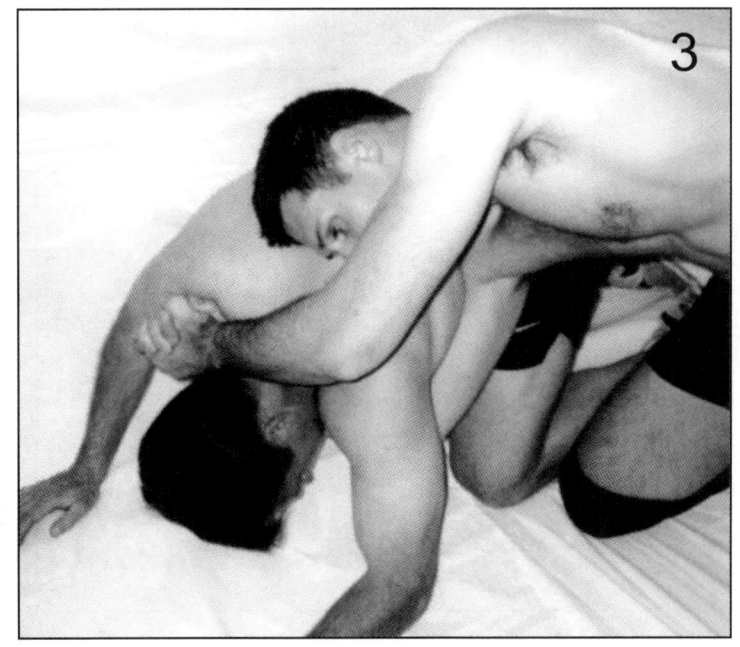

Clasp your hands, placing the forearm of your top arm across the back of his neck.

Attempt to touch your elbows to each other. This will drive the blade of your top forearm into the back of his neck, forcing his head downwards. Your bottom arm will drive upwards, cutting off his air at the esophagus for the submission.

CHOKE *Kata Gatame*

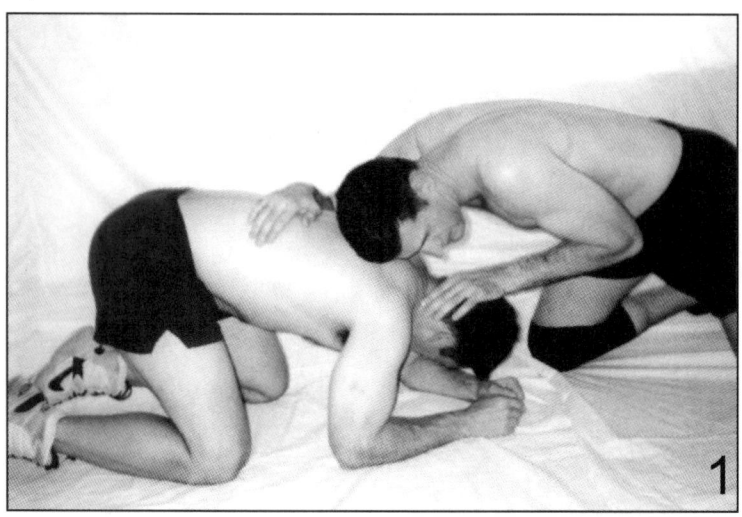

You are attacking your opponent from the front and you have control of his head.

Slide your attacking arm across his head, under his neck, and under his armpit.

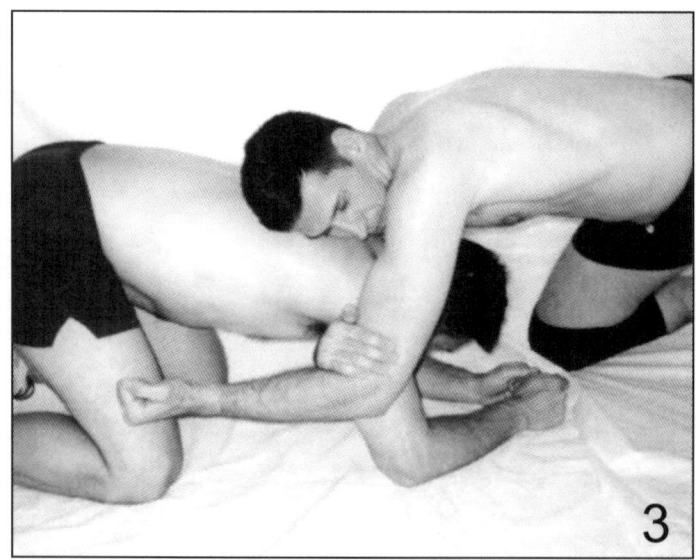

Grab your locking arm at the biceps, trapping his arm against his own head.

Grab your own head with your locking hand. Contract the muscles of your attacking arm and cut off his carotid arteries for the submission.

CHOKE *Triangle*

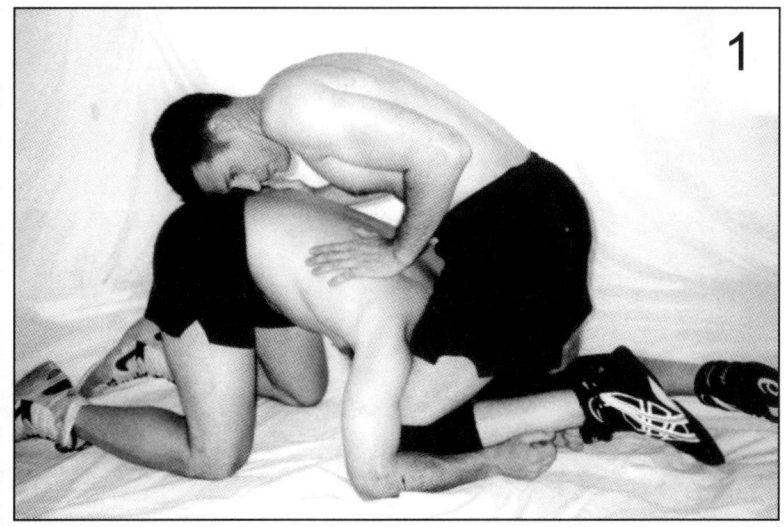

You are attacking your opponent from the front. Drive your left knee deep into his shoulder.

Step over with your other, attacking leg and hook his arm. (This picture is from the opposite angle.)

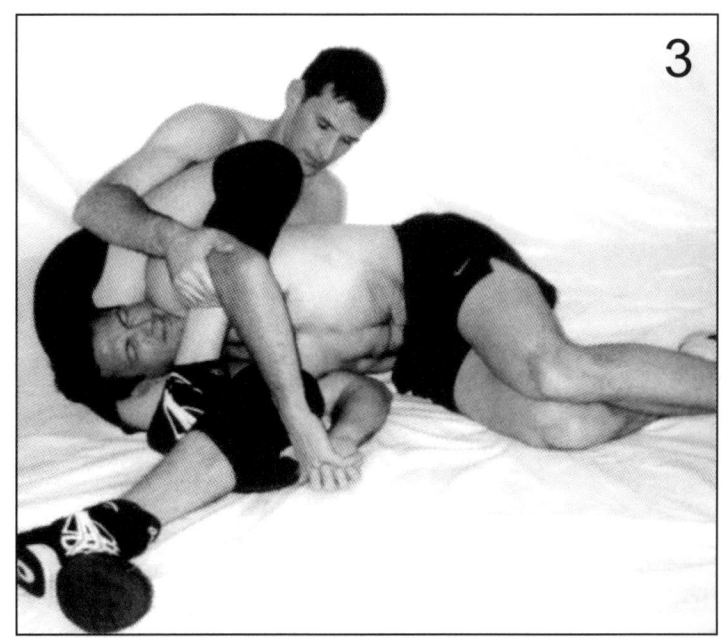

Hook your attacking leg's foot behind your other, locking knee.

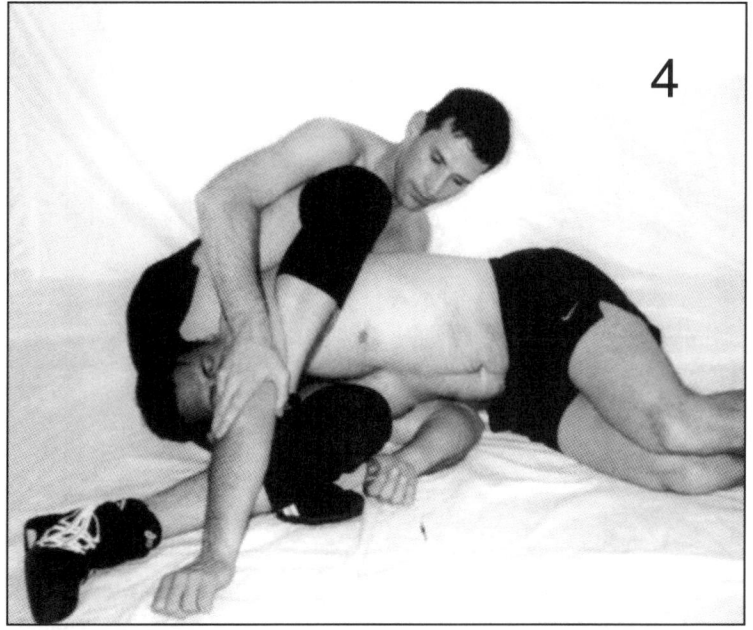

Squeeze your knees together and push his arm across his face at the elbow for the choke.

ARM BAR *With Legs*

Your attacking your opponent from the side and he grabs one of your legs.

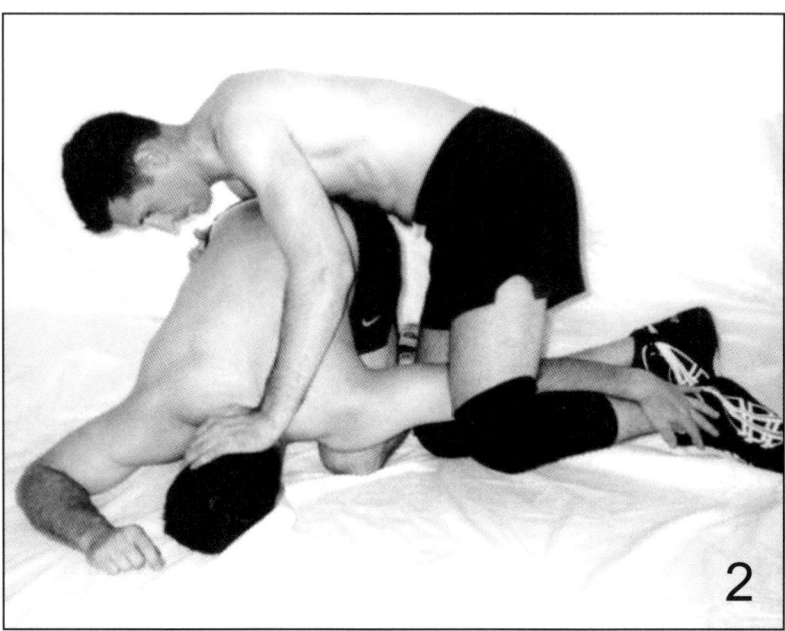

Push his head to the ground and bring your leg to a knee, straightening his arm out.

Hook the foot of your near leg over the calf of your other leg.

Ensure that your groin is just above his elbow, closer to his shoulder. Straighten your legs and arch your hips, hyper-extending his arm at the elbow for the submission.

ARM BAR *Iron Cross*

You are attacking from the side and your opponent grabs your leg. (Top)

Cross your feet, trapping his arm. Secure his far arm and execute a forwards roll, turning your opponent over on his back. (Top Right)

You'll end up like this. Keep a tight hold on his arm with your legs. (Right)

Place his arm under your armpit and arch your back, hyper-extending his arm at the elbow for the submission. (Bottom Right)

Also, you can scissors his head between your legs. Ensure that the medial, inside part of your top knee is against his throat. Extend your legs straight for the choke. (Bottom)

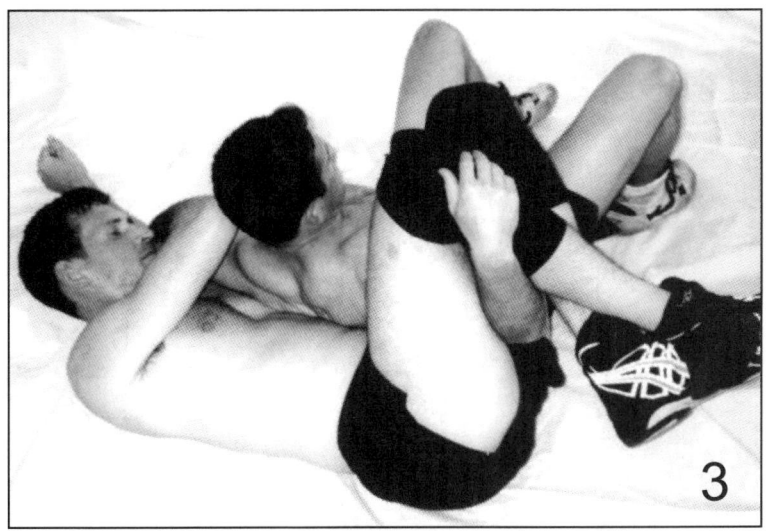

ARM BAR *Step Over With Leg*

You are attacking your opponent from the side and he is up relatively high on his hands and knees.

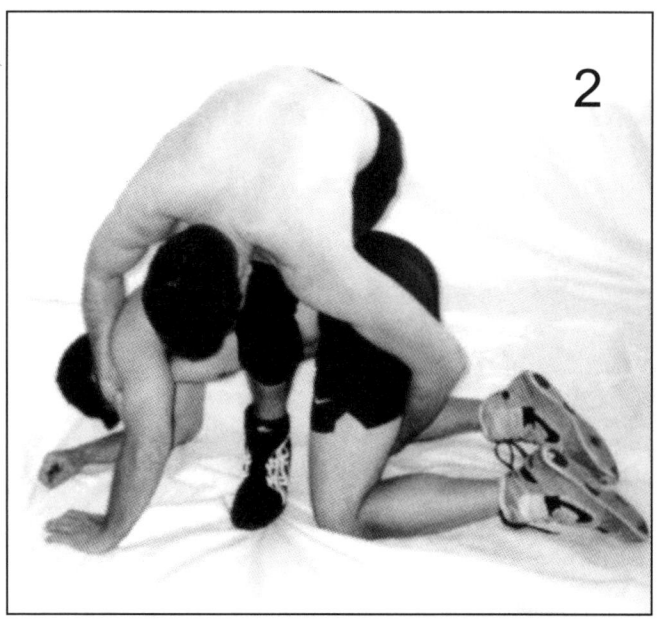

Step over and hook his far arm and far leg. Execute a forwards roll.

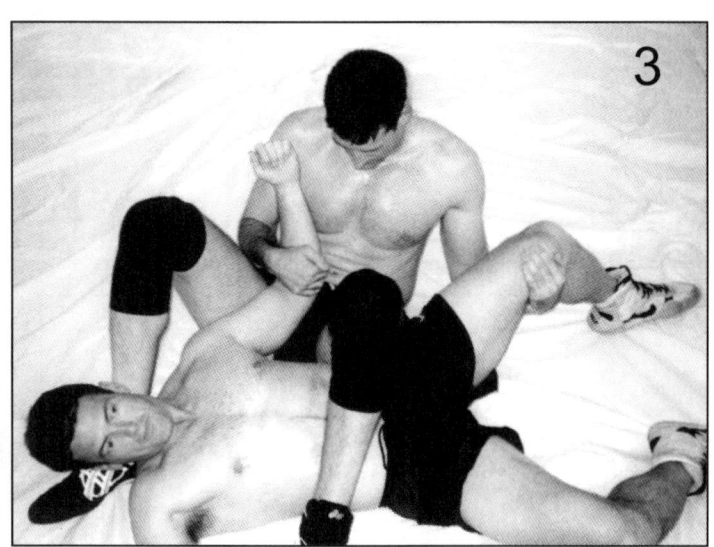

You'll finish your roll on your back with his arm and leg secured.

Place your leg over his neck, squeeze your knees together, and arch your hips to hyper-extend his arm at the elbow. If he tries to straighten his leg, he puts pressure on his own trapped arm.

ARM BAR ¼ *Nelson to an Arm Bar*

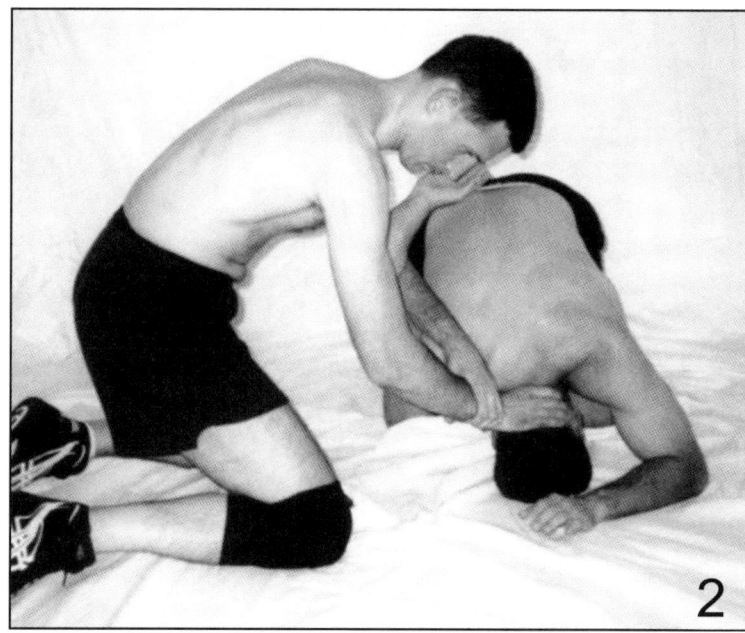

Hook under the biceps of his near arm as shown. (Top)

Place your other hand on the back of his neck and grab this arm at the wrist. (Top Right)

Push down on his head and roll him forwards. Maintain a good grip on his targeted arm as he rolls. (Right)

Bring your knee up against his rib cage and sit backwards as you grab his arm with both hands. (Bottom Right)

Squeeze your knees together, arch your hips, and pull down on his wrist to hyper-extend his arm at the elbow for the submission. (Bottom)

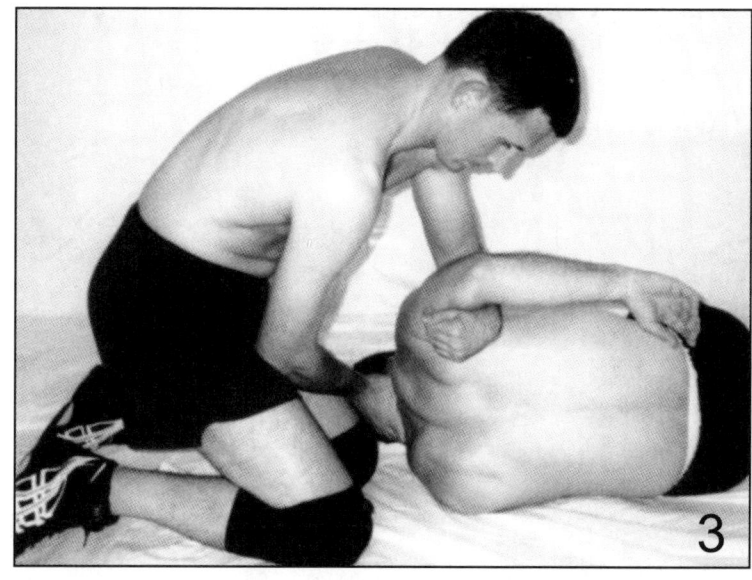

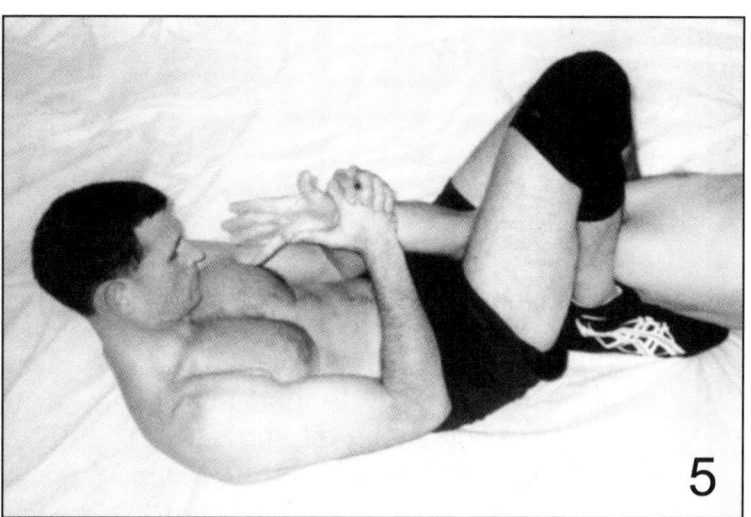

SQUEEZE LOCK *Nutcracker*

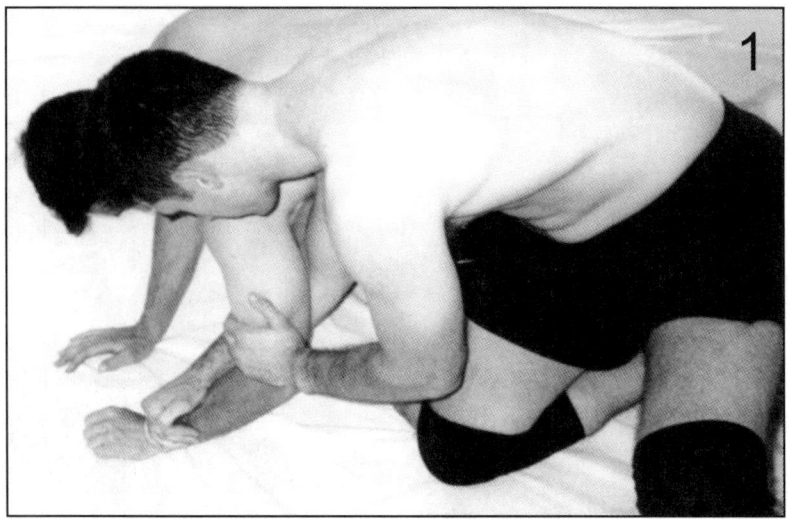

You are attacking your opponent from the side. Control his arm at the elbow and slide your near arm under his armpit. (Left)

Grab his wrist with your near arm and bring your forearm as high into his armpit as you can. Maintain control of his elbow with your other arm. (Right)

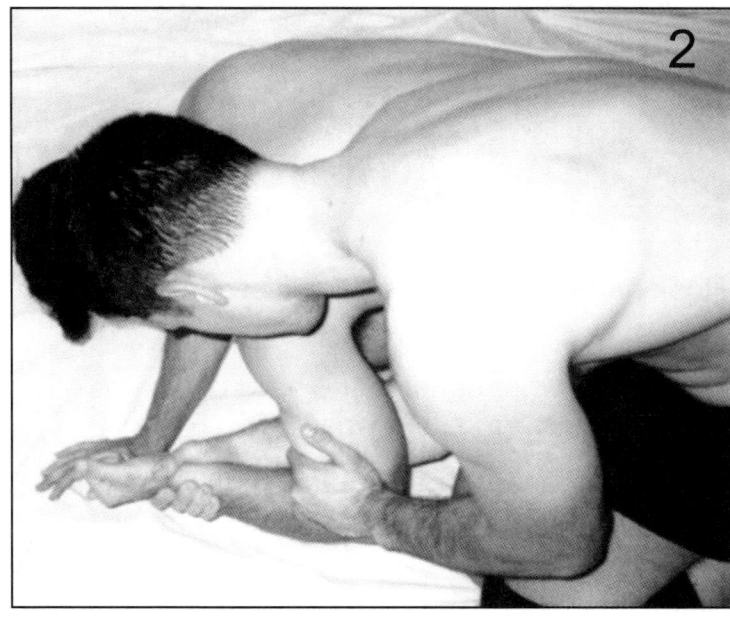

Grab his wrist with both hands and attempt to pull his wrist until it touches his shoulder. Ensure that his palm is facing you. This move attempts to hyper-flex his arm and separate his elbow joint for the submission. (Left)

KNEE BAR *Rolling Knee Bar*

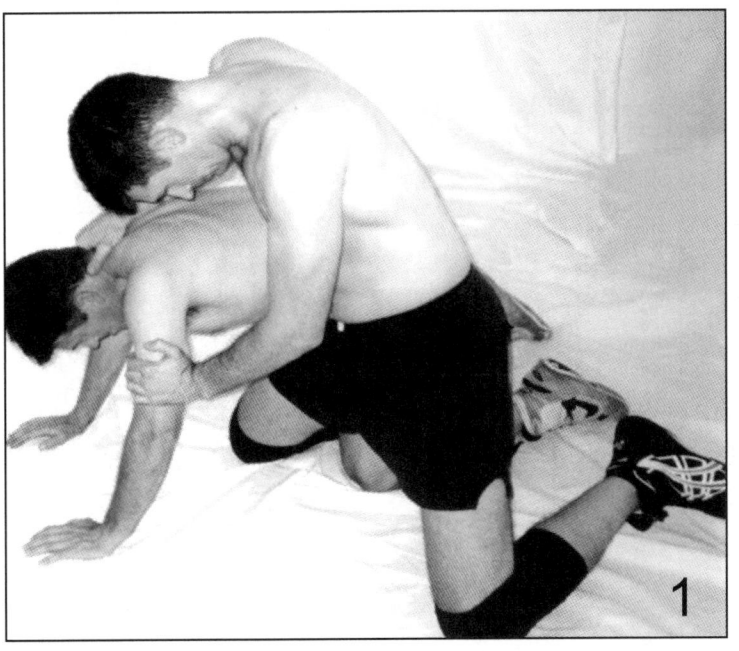

You are attacking your opponent from the side and have placed your near leg between his.

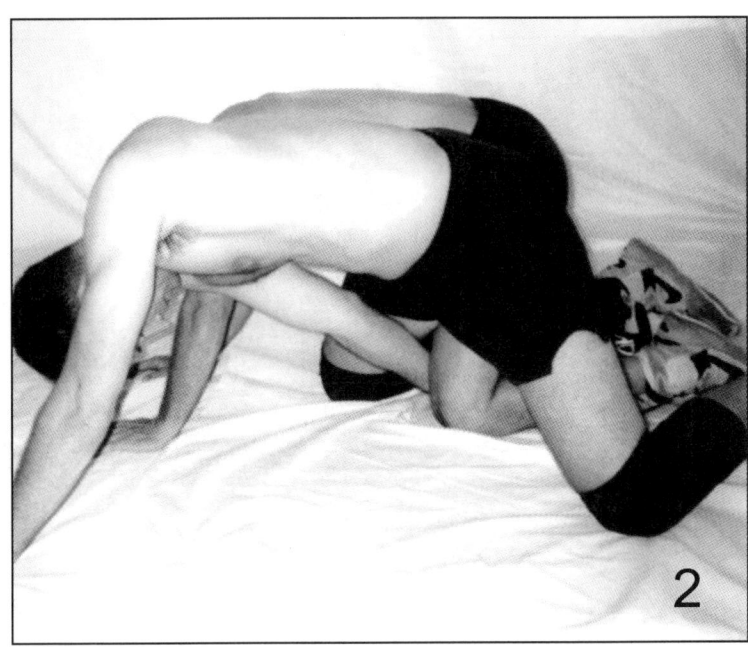

Grab his near leg behind the knee.

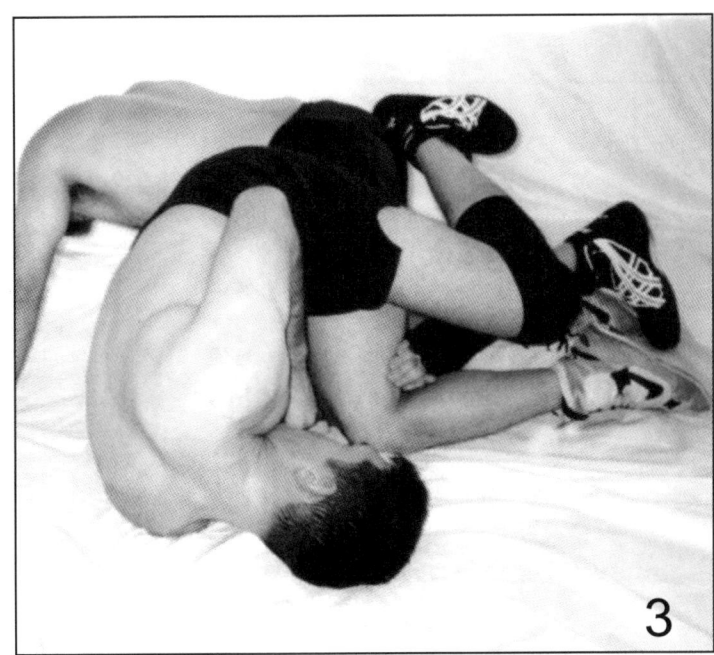

Pull his knee into you as you roll forwards.

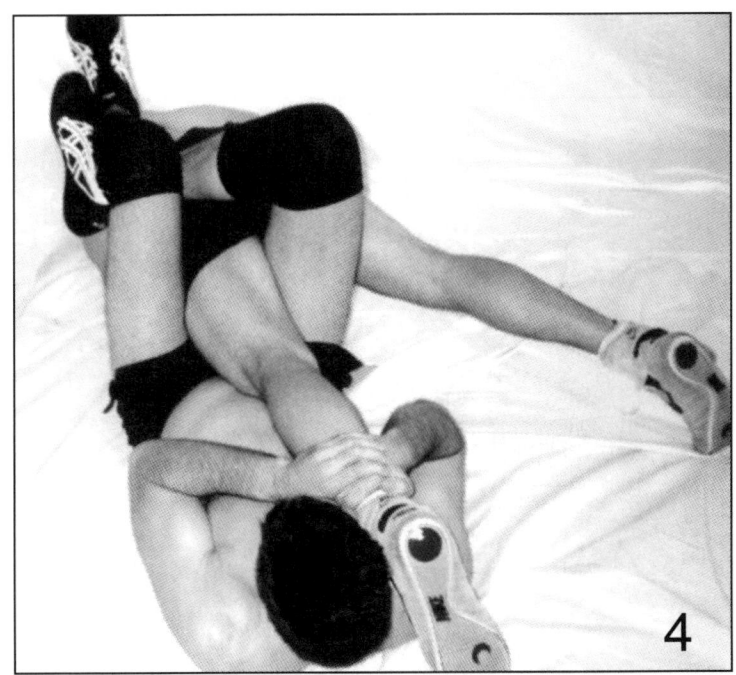

You'll end up hugging his leg when your roll is completed. Drive your heels downwards, arch your hips, and keep his foot tight to your chest to hyper-extend his leg at the knee for the submission.

KNEE BAR *Rolling Knee Bar*

KNEE LEVER *Inside Entangled Leg*

You are attacking your opponent from the rear and have a leg entangled in his, as if you were attempting to take the rear mount position.

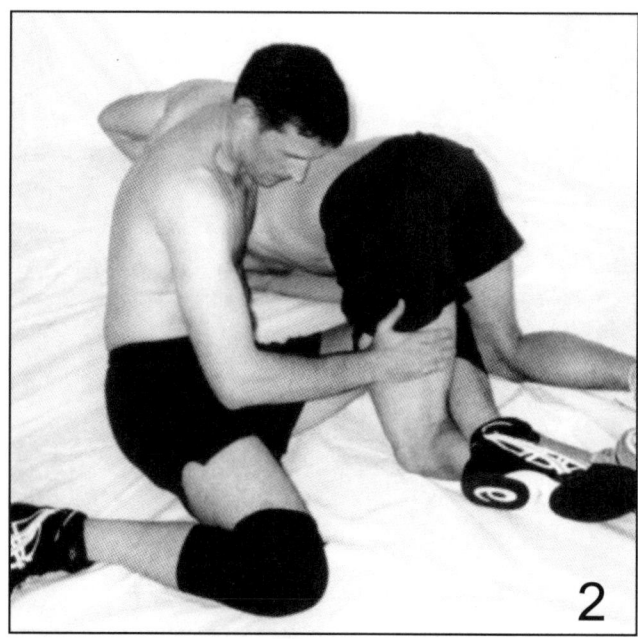

Roll off your opponent and sit on your side, keeping your leg entangled in his targeted leg.

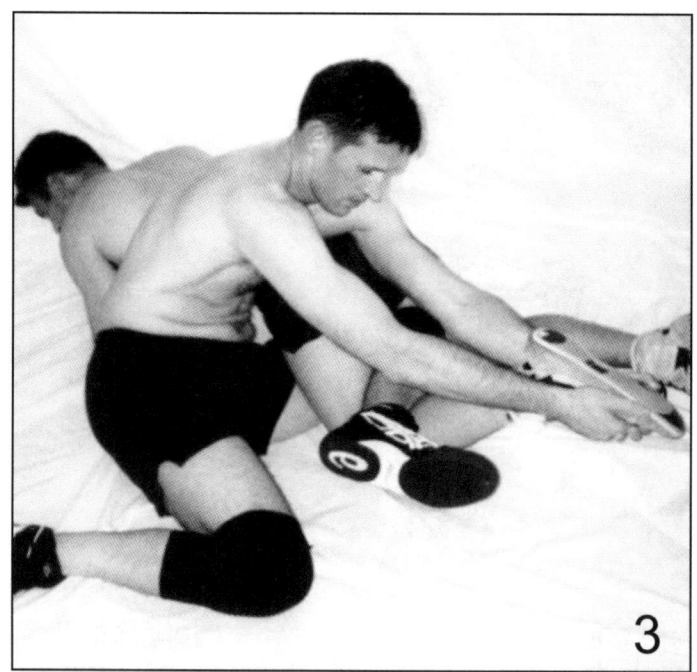

Grab his trapped leg at the foot with both hands.

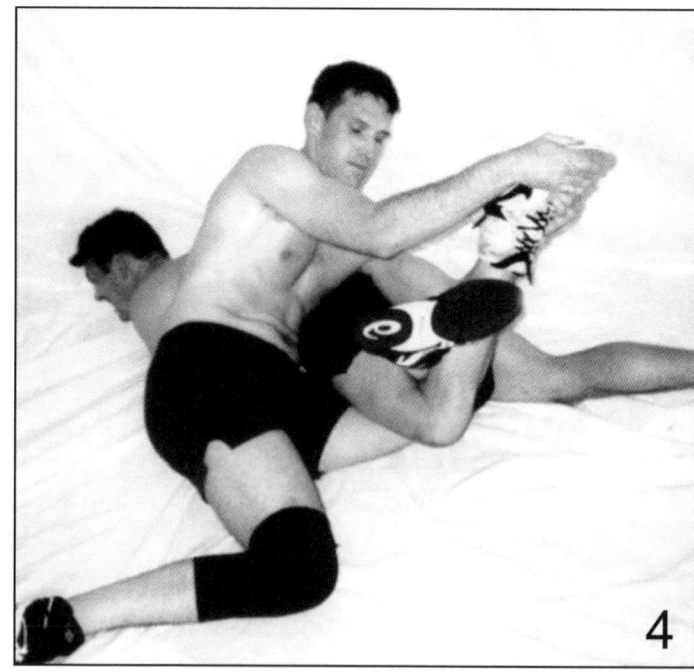

Drive your shin into the back of his knee and attempt to place the heel of his foot against his buttocks. This move attempts to separate his knee joint for the submission.

KNEE LEVER *Entangled Leg*

Your opponent is posted high on his hands and knees. Grab his targeted leg at his foot.

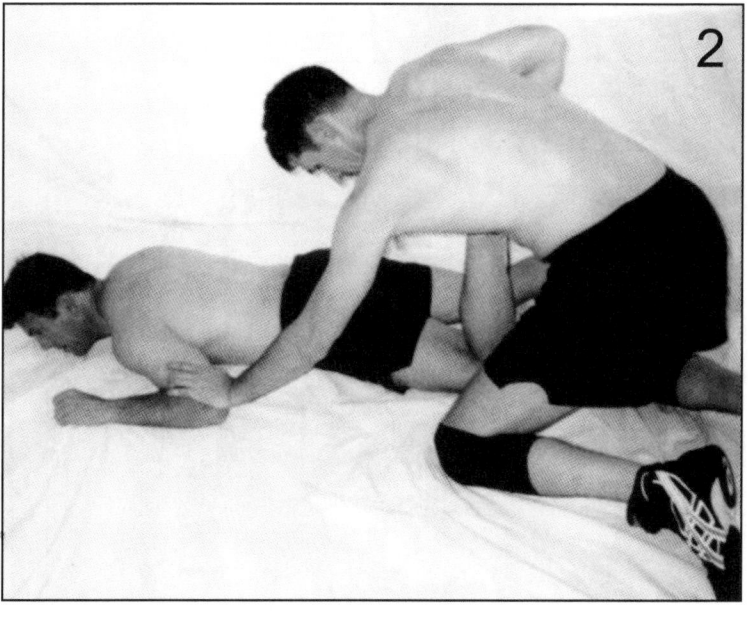

Pick up his foot and drive him forwards, forcing him to the ground. (This picture is from the opposite angle.)

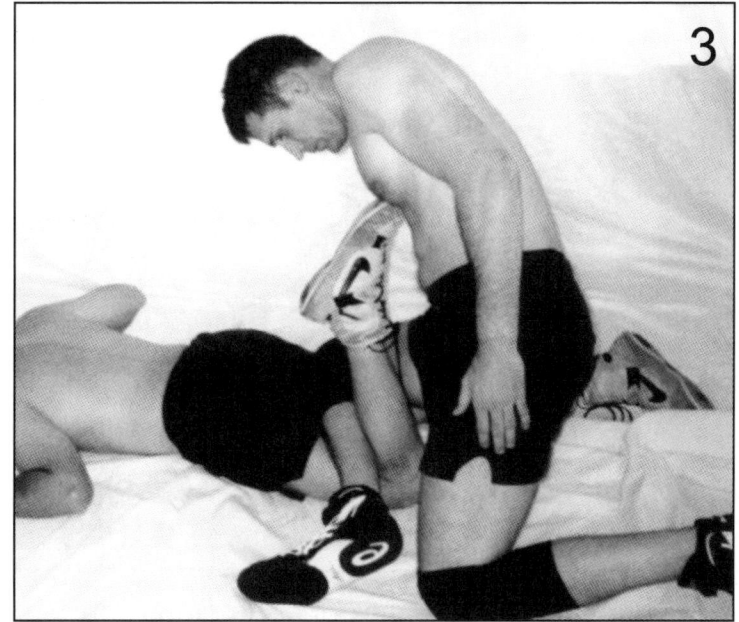

Entangle your leg behind the knee of his targeted leg.

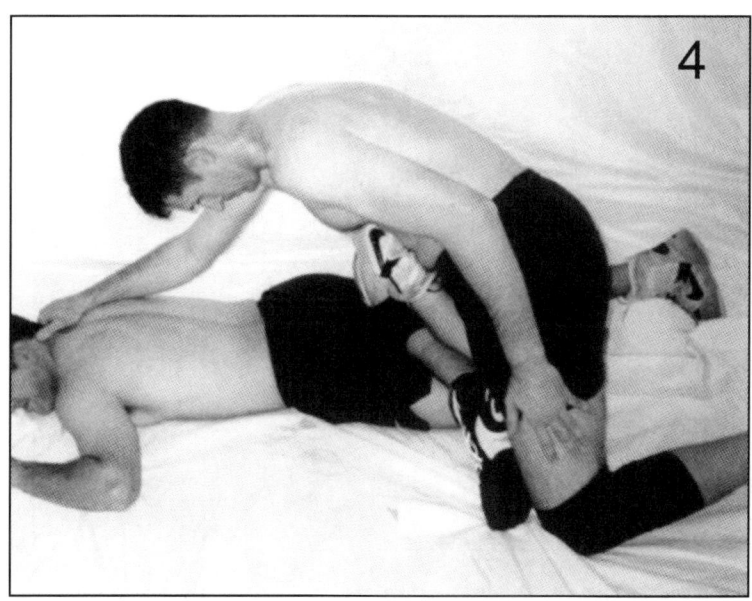

Drive your shin into his knee joint and arch your hips forwards. Try to place his heel on his buttocks for the submission.

KNEE LEVER *With Shin*

You are attacking your opponent from the side. Pin his targeted leg at the foot.

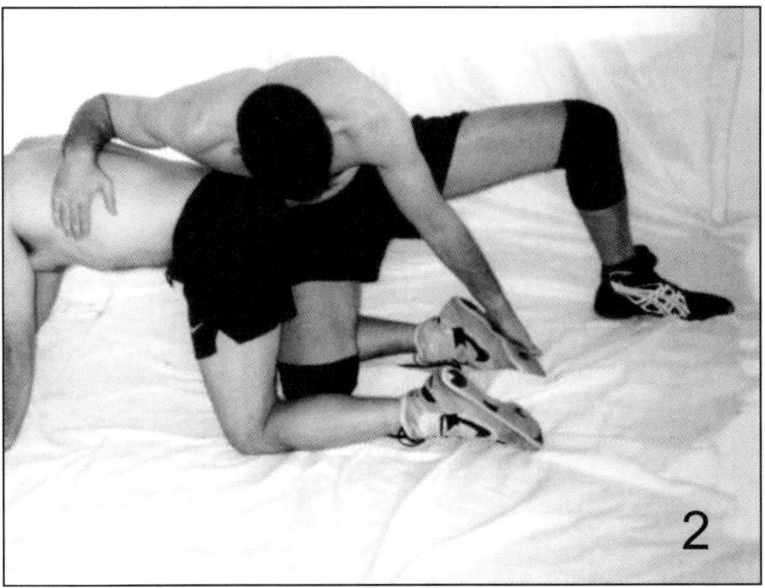

Drive your shin across his calf, deep behind his knee. Secure his foot at the toes.

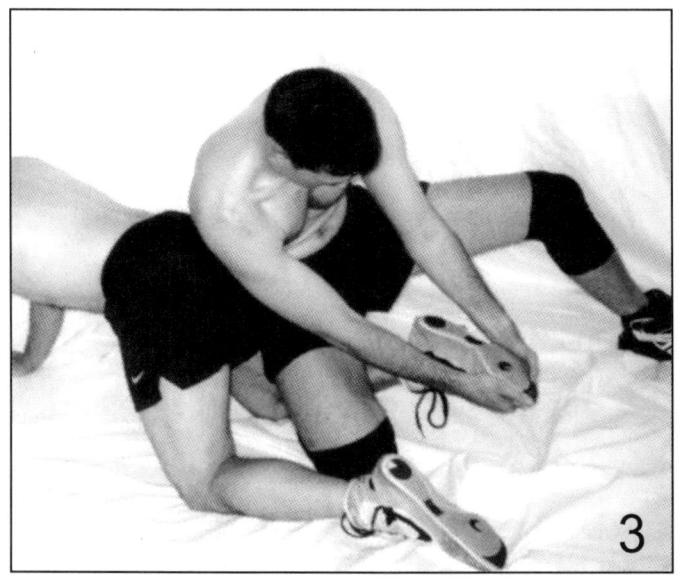

Grab his foot with both hands and place your buttocks against his. Place your free leg out for balance.

Drive your shin into the back of his knee as you pull his foot backwards for the submission. You are in an ideal position to execute a variety of ankle submission techniques as well.

KNEE LEVER *Figure Four Lock*

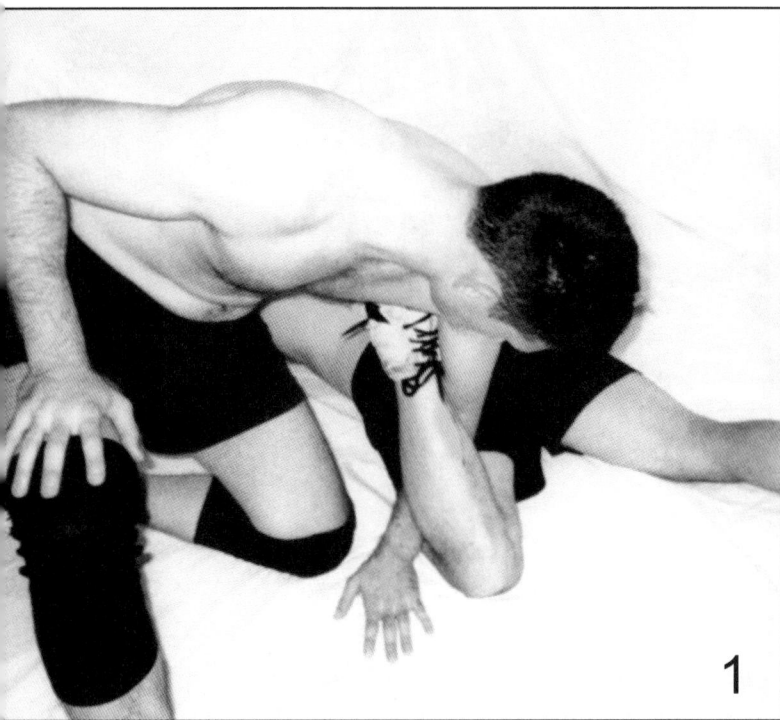

You have broken your opponent down, flat on the ground. Bring your arm over his shin and behind his calf. (Left)

Sit next to his trapped leg and lean backwards into him. Secure his trapped leg at the knee with your other hand. (Right)

Grab your own wrist and secure a figure four lock. Ensure that your attacking forearm is as deep behind his knee as possible. To submit him, lean backwards, driving your forearm into his joint and attempting to place his heel against his buttocks. (Left)

KNEE LEVER

You are attacking your opponent from the rear. You have him secured at his leg in preparation for breaking him down.

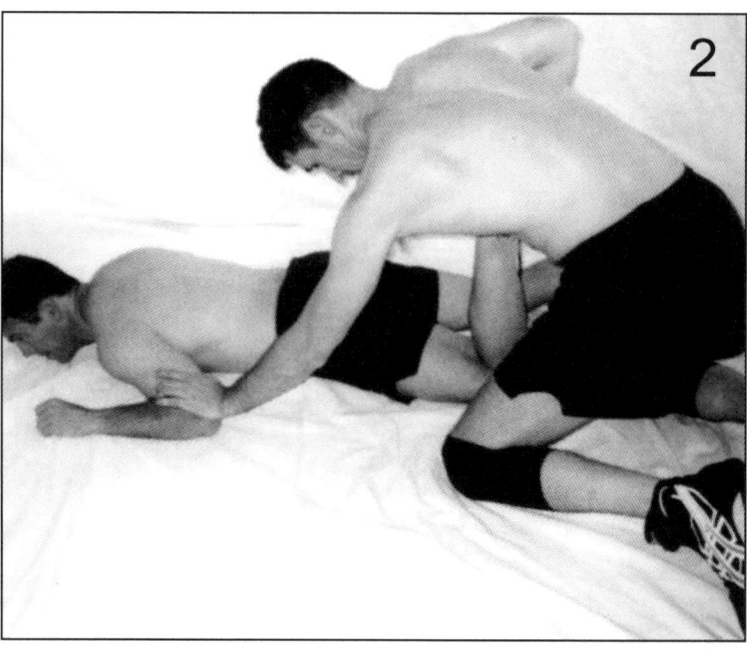

Drive him forwards, forcing him to sprawl. You used his foot to propel him forwards and this foot it is now in your grip and exposed. (This picture is from the opposite angle.)

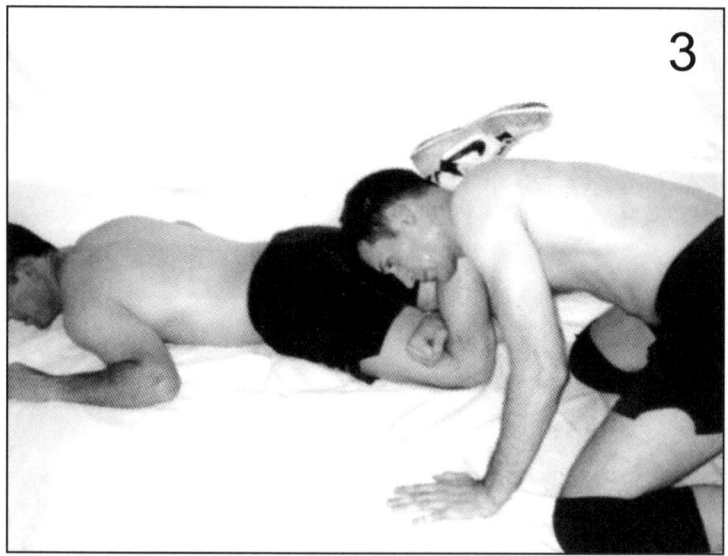

Place your arm behind his knee and place your shoulder against his shin.

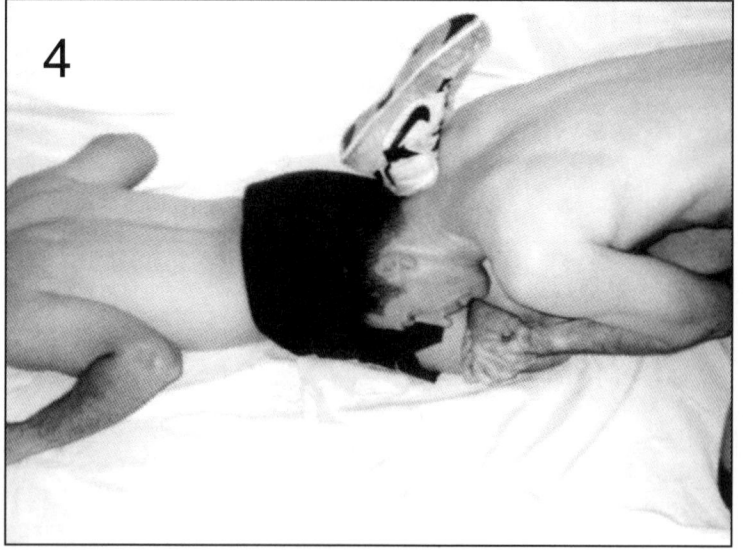

Clasp your hands, keeping your forearm deep in his joint. Drive forwards with your shoulder and attempt to place his heel to his buttocks for the submission.

TOE HOLD

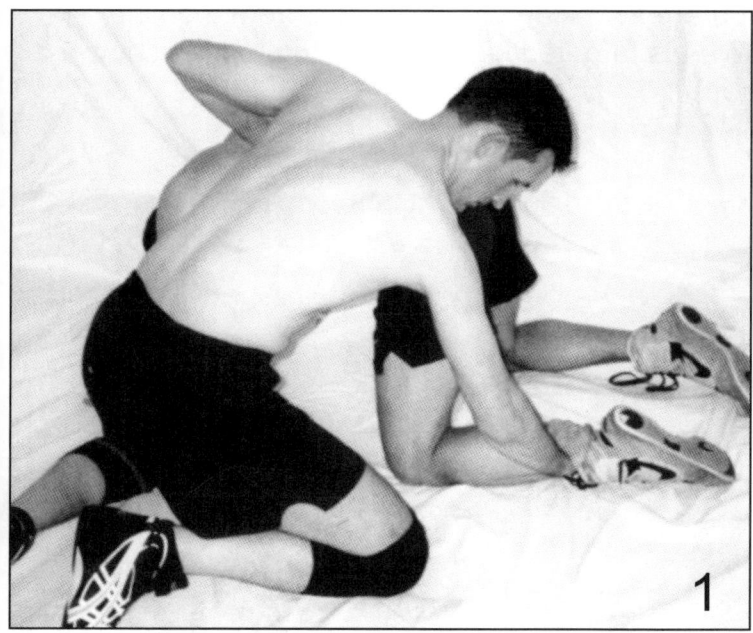

You are attacking your opponent from the side. Secure his targeted leg at the ankle, pinning it to the ground. (Left)

Reach through his legs and grab his foot at the toes. (Right)

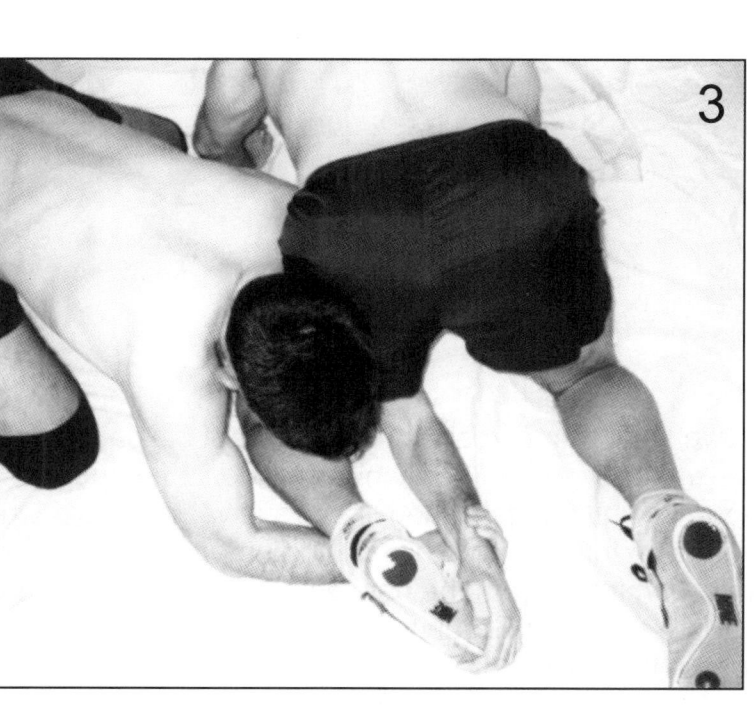

Grab your attacking arm at the wrist. Drive your shoulder into his thigh and pull his toes towards his head, twisting his foot inwards. This move attacks his ankle and threatens to tear the ligaments of his ankle joint. (Left)

TOE HOLD *Shin Assist*

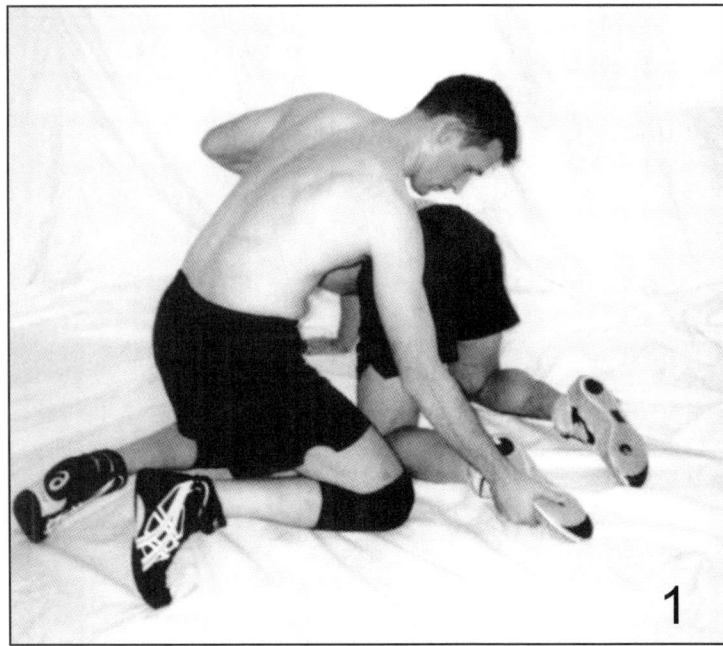

You are attacking your opponent from the side and have his targeted leg pinned at the foot as shown. (Left)

Switch your grip and grab his toes with an overhand grip. (This picture is from the opposite angle) (Right)

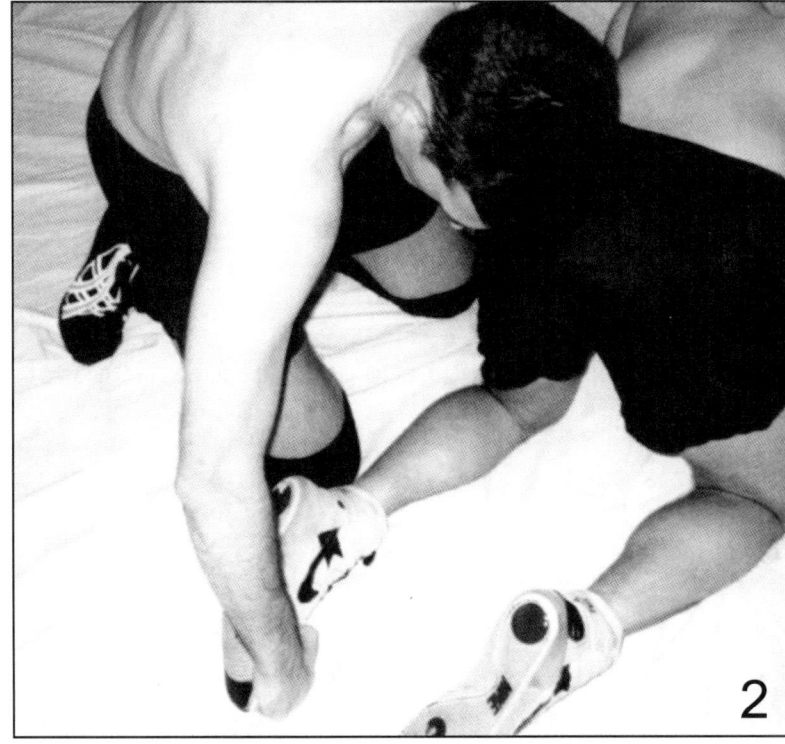

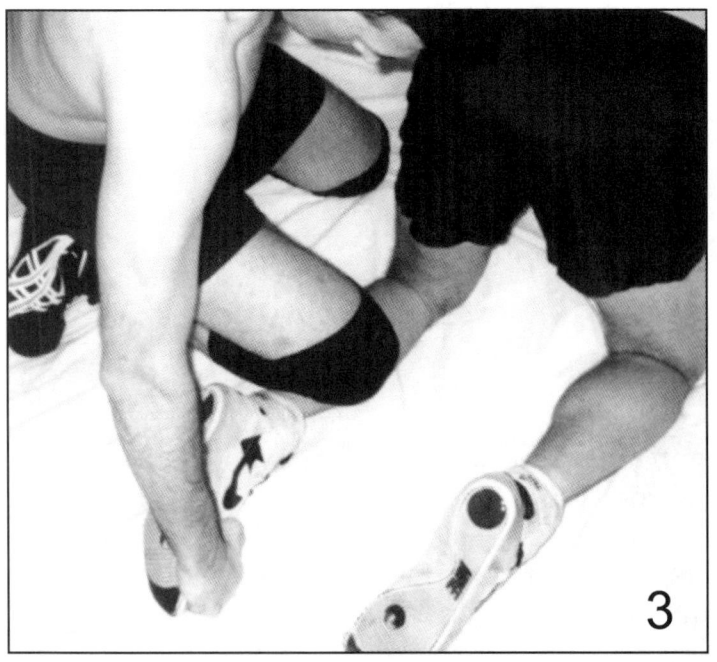

Drive your shin across the lower part of his calf, across the upper portion of his Achilles tendon. Just putting your weight across his leg like this is very painful. Drive your shin into his leg while pulling up on his toes. He will submit first from the pain on his Achilles; if he can endure that, he will submit when you hyper-extend his foot at the ankle. (Left)

ANKLE CRANK *Entangled Legs*

You are attacking your opponent from the side and have his targeted leg secured at the ankle. (Top)

Lift his leg at the ankle and the knee. (Top Right)

Step over his targeted leg. (Right)

Fall backwards and hook your outside leg over his far foot. Your near leg is hooked under his far knee. (Bottom Right)

Secure a figure four lock on his foot and use his foot as a lever to torque his knee for the submission. (Bottom)

217

ANKLE CRANK

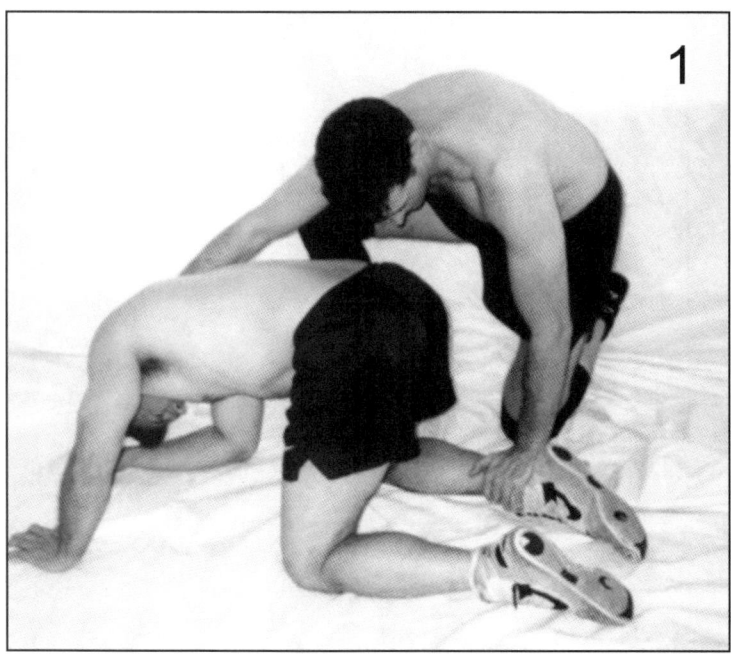

1. You are attacking your opponent from the side. (Left)

Drive your knee deep, across both of his legs and pin his far leg with your shin. (Right)

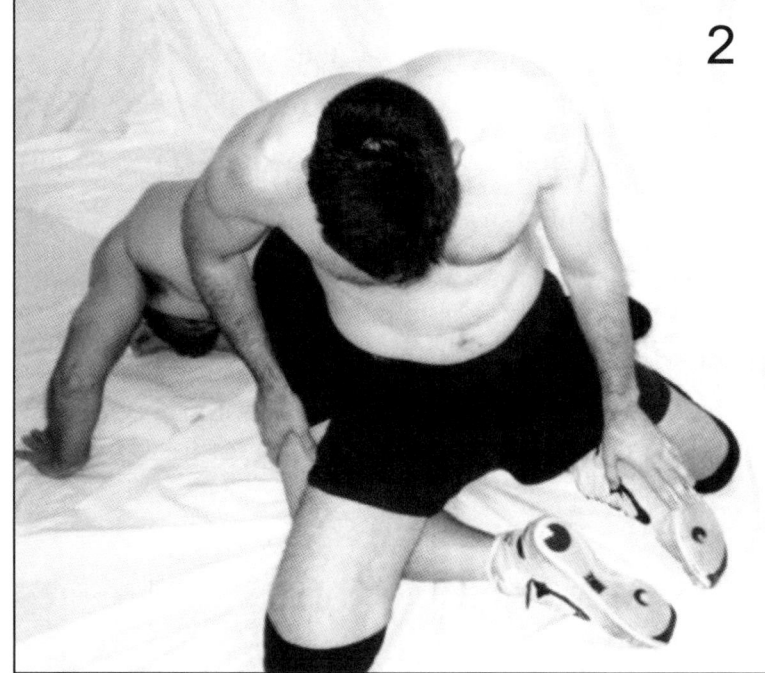

2.

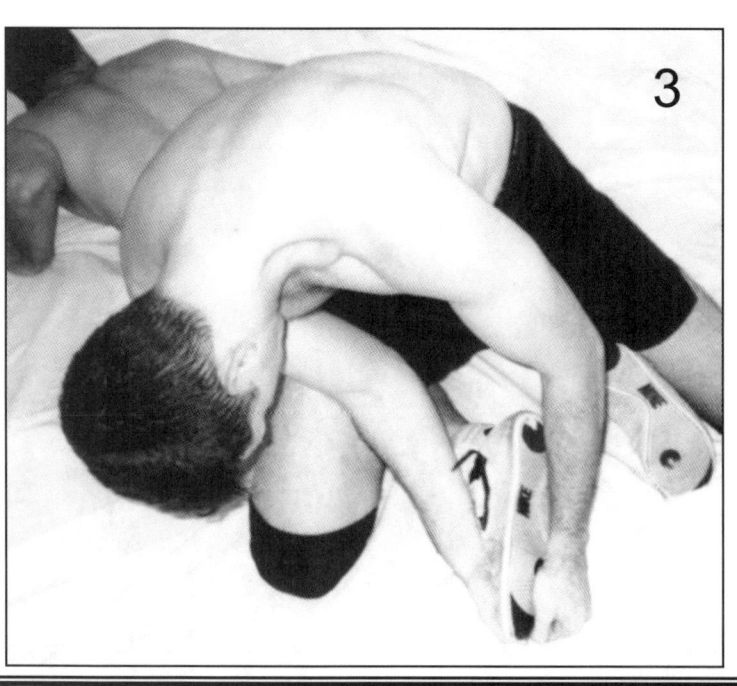

3. Grab his foot on the inside part of his foot, near his toes. Crank his foot, pulling his toes upwards. This uses his foot as a lever to torque his knee for the submission. (Left)

GROIN STRETCH *Banana Split*

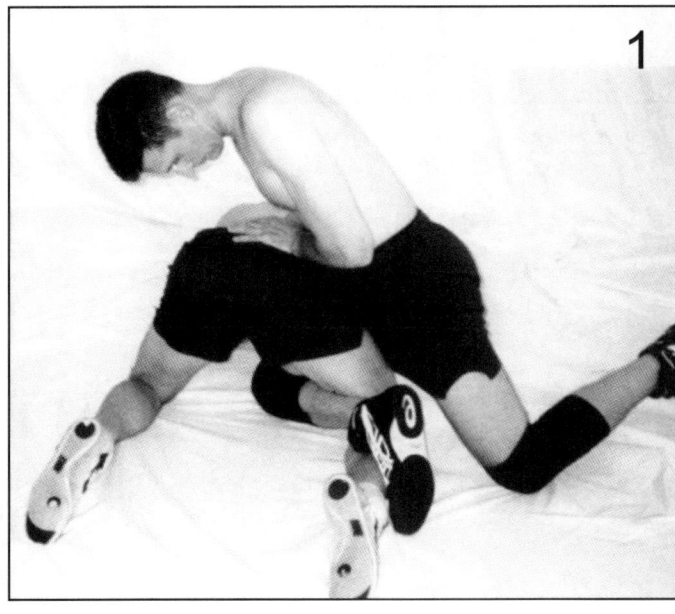

1 You have one leg entangled in his near leg, as if you were going to rear mount or execute a knee lever. (Left)

Hook your legs at the ankles on his near leg. Bear hug his far leg. (Right)

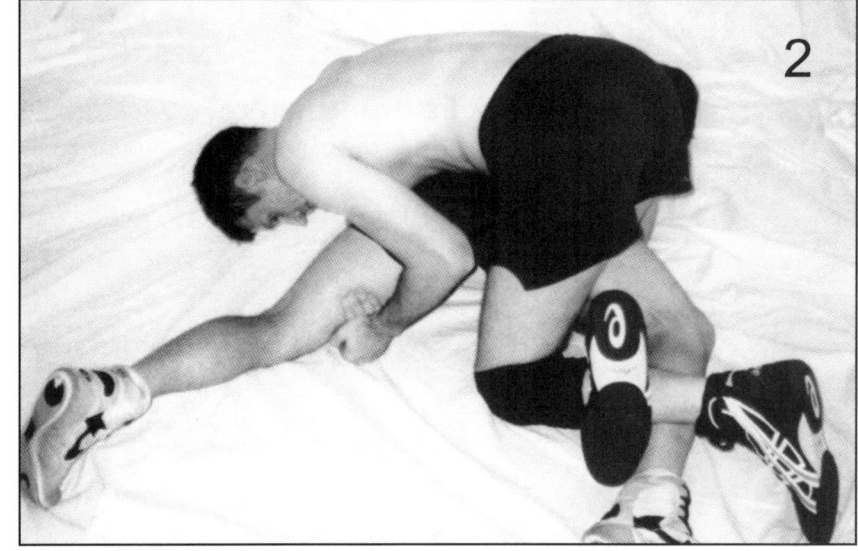

2

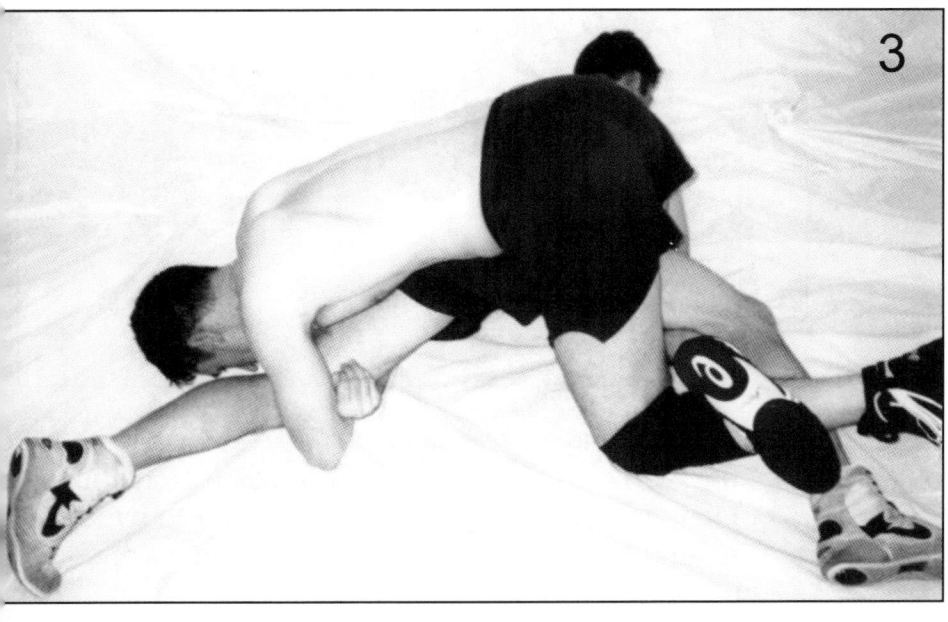

3

Slide your arms to his far knee, straighten your legs, straighten your back, and force his legs apart for the groin stretch. (Left)

ATTACK FROM THE REFEREE *Knee Bar*

Yes! There is an attack from the referee's position! Your opponent has a leg driven between your knees.

Grab his penetrating leg behind the knee.

Maintain a tight grip on his knee and execute a forwards roll, bringing him over you as you roll.

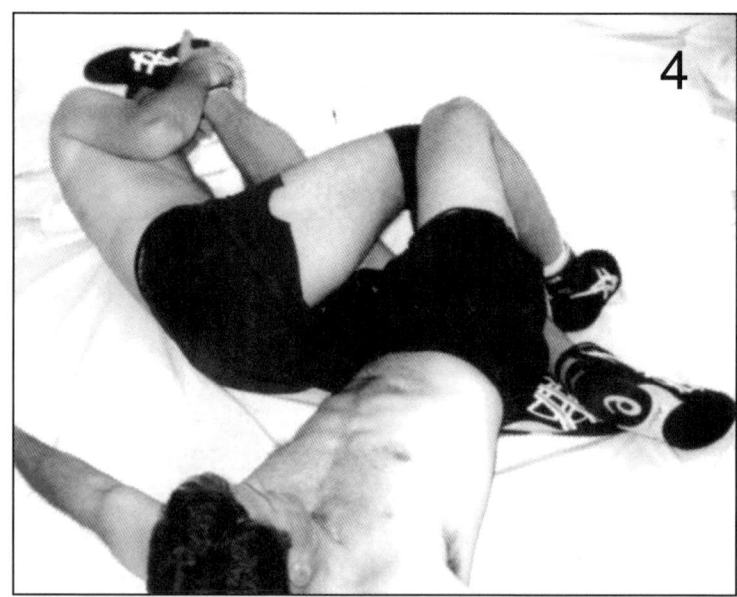

You will end up bear hugging his leg for a knee bar. Drive your feet into his buttocks, arch your hips, and hug his foot to your shoulder to hyperextend his leg at the knee for the submission.

Chapter Sixteen
Submissions From Rear Mount And In Rear Mount

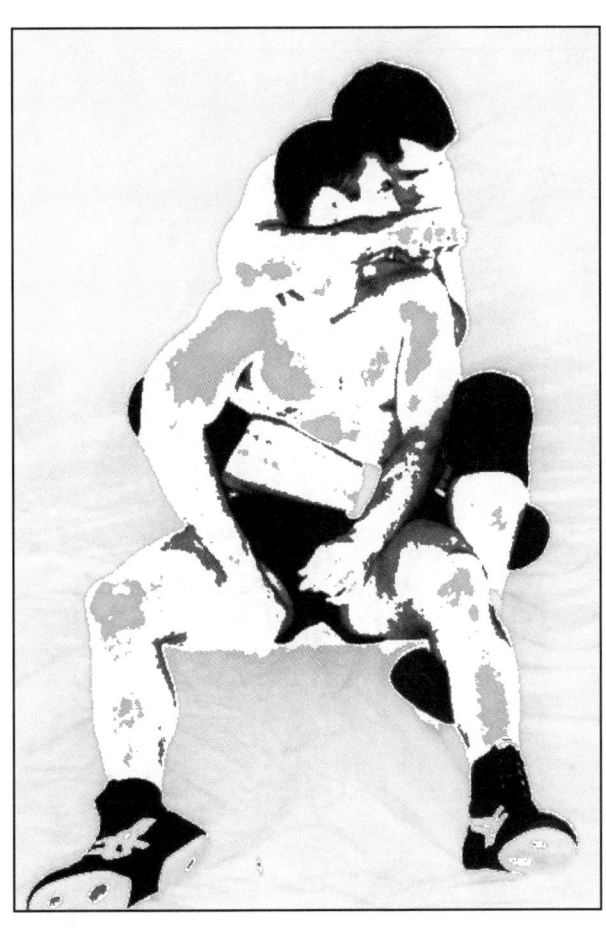

Rear Mount

You have your opponent's back and you can work a variety of attacks including neck cranks, chokes, and shoulder locks. You can under hook his arms and control his upper body.

Control his arm and set him up for arm bars, shoulder cranks, and squeeze locks.

Use your legs and feet to control his legs and prevent him from turning into you and escaping. Crossing your feet or bringing your feet within reach of his arms may leave you open to attack.

NECK CRANK

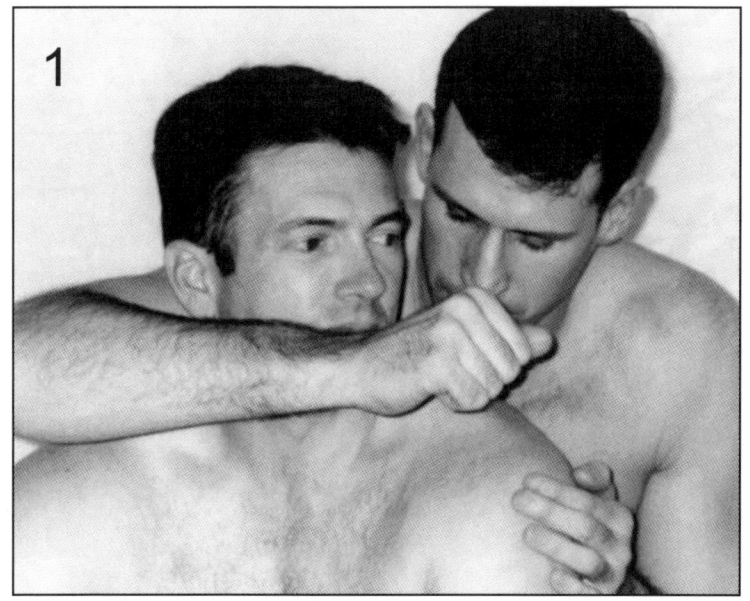

Drive your attacking forearm across his jaw, turning his head to the side. (Left)

Clasp your hands and drive the forearm of your locking arm against his back. Keep your head pressed tightly against his. (Right)

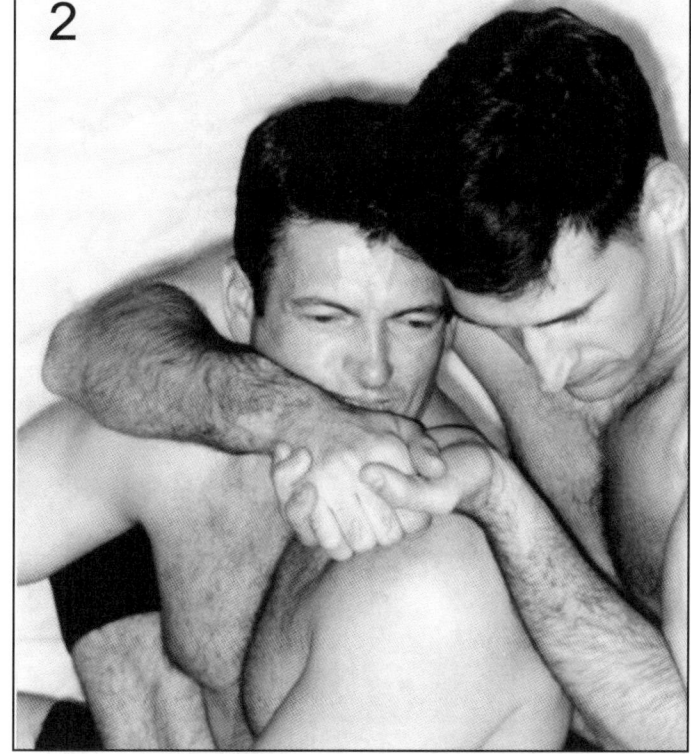

To crank his neck, drive the blade of your attacking forearm into his jaw and force his head backwards. Note possible method of figure four leg control. (Left)

NECK CRANK *Underarm*

Maintain control of your opponent with your legs.

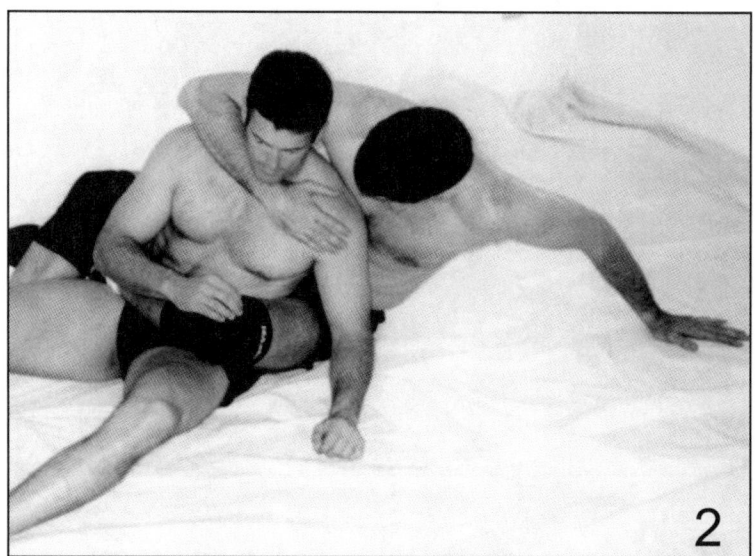

Maintain a secure hold around his neck and post out one arm for balance.

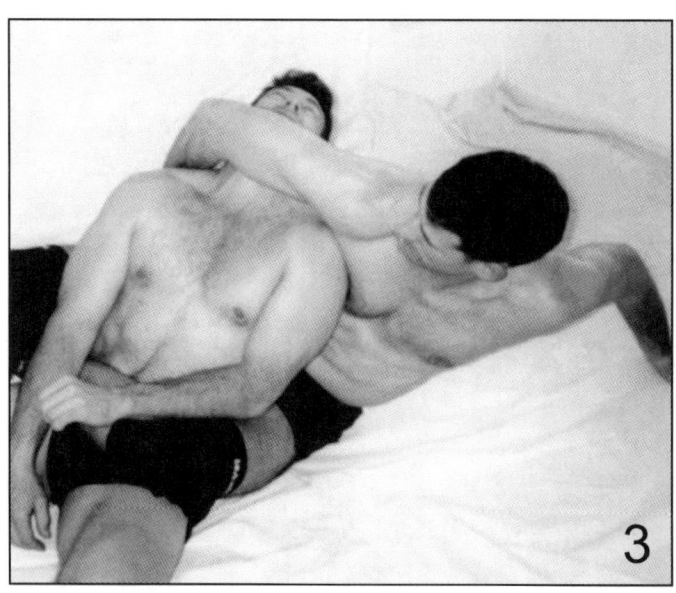

Wrap your attacking arm around his neck and under his chin.

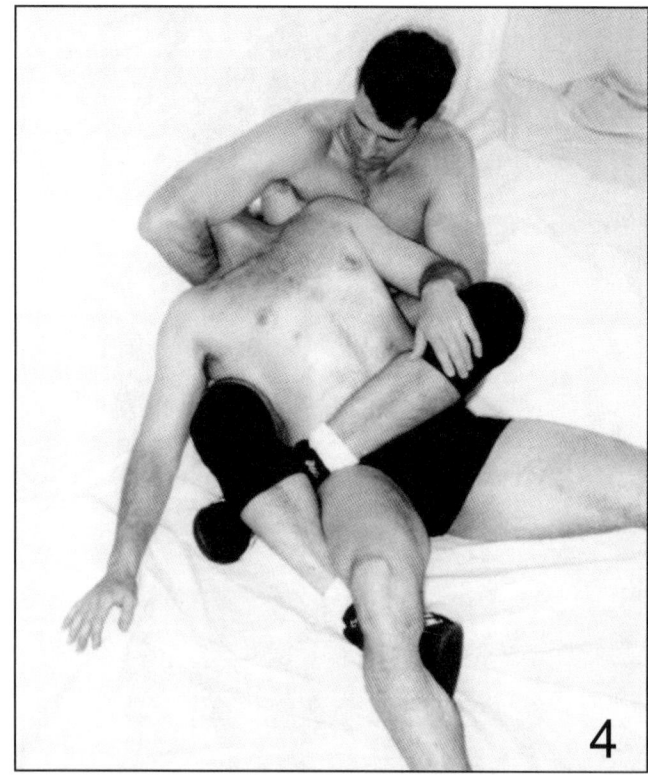

Clasp your hands together and arch your back, hyper-extending his cervical spine backwards until he submits.

NECK CRANKS *Full Nelson*

You are rear mounted on your opponent. You have a half nelson already and are controlling his other arm.

Secure a full nelson, with both hands on the crown of his head. Push his head downwards while pulling back on his arms to hyper-extend his cervical spine for the submission.

Leg Variation

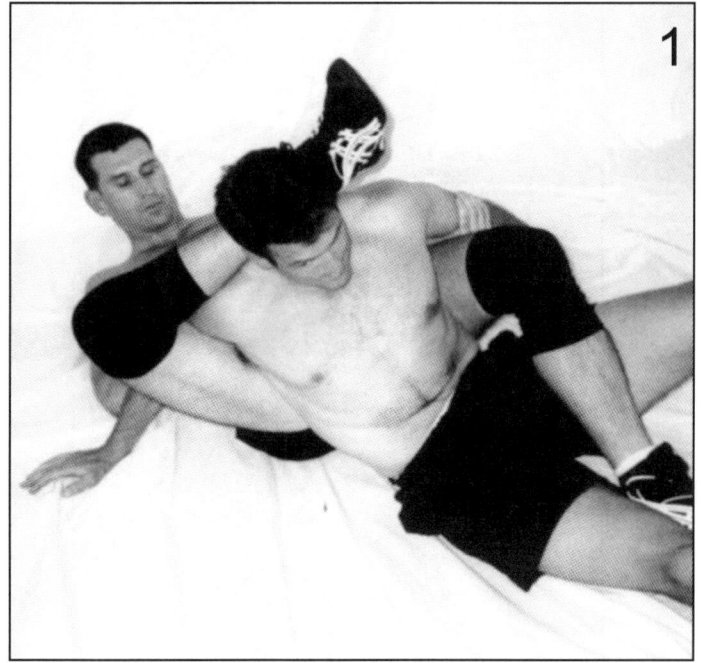

Your opponent has posted out one arm. Place your leg around his arm and behind his neck. Control his other arm.

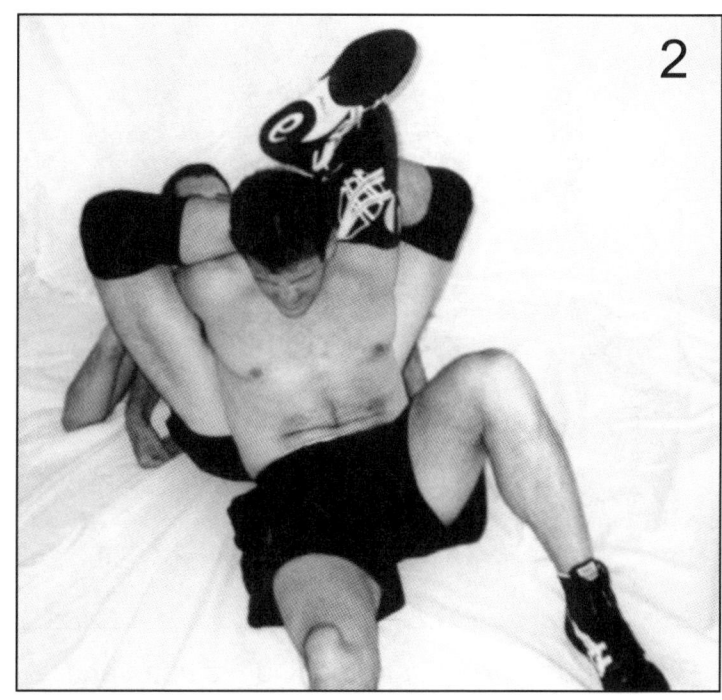

Lock your other leg behind his neck and lock your ankles. Pull his arms back with your own arms and drive your legs straight out to hyper-extend his cervical spine for the submission.

CHOKE *Rear Naked Strangle*

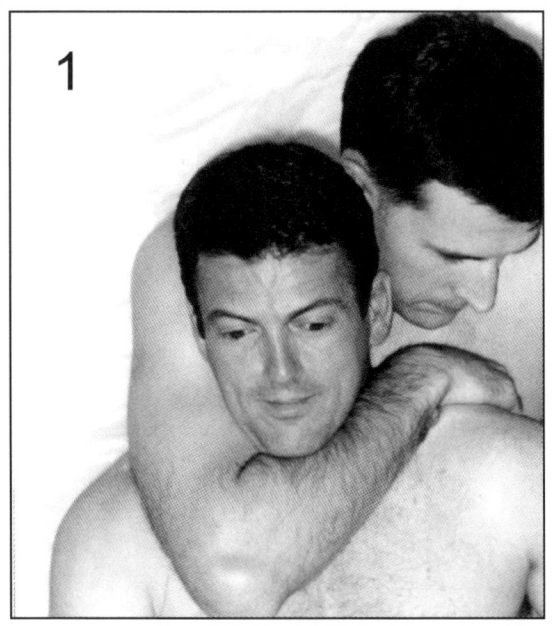

Slide your attacking arm across your opponent's neck and under his chin.

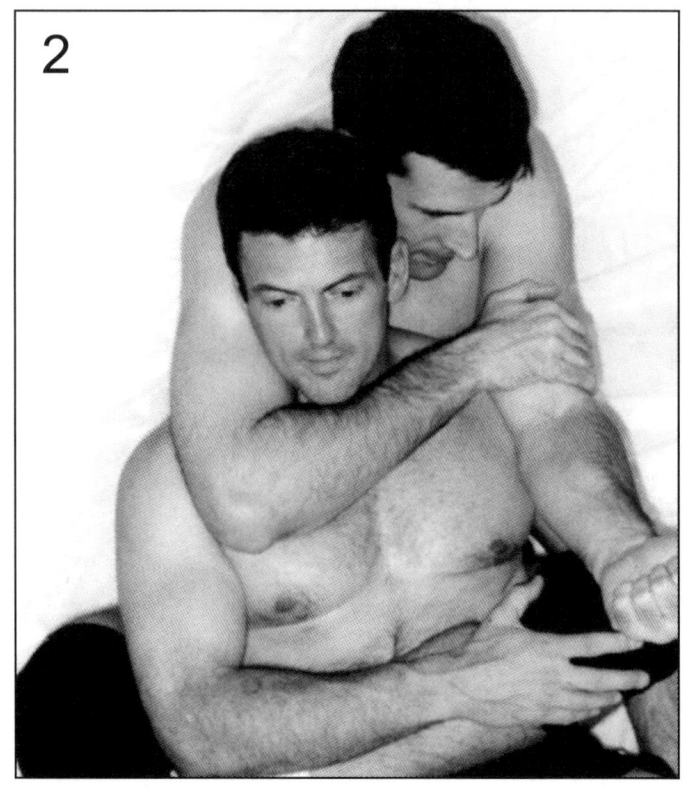

Grab the biceps of your locking arm as shown.

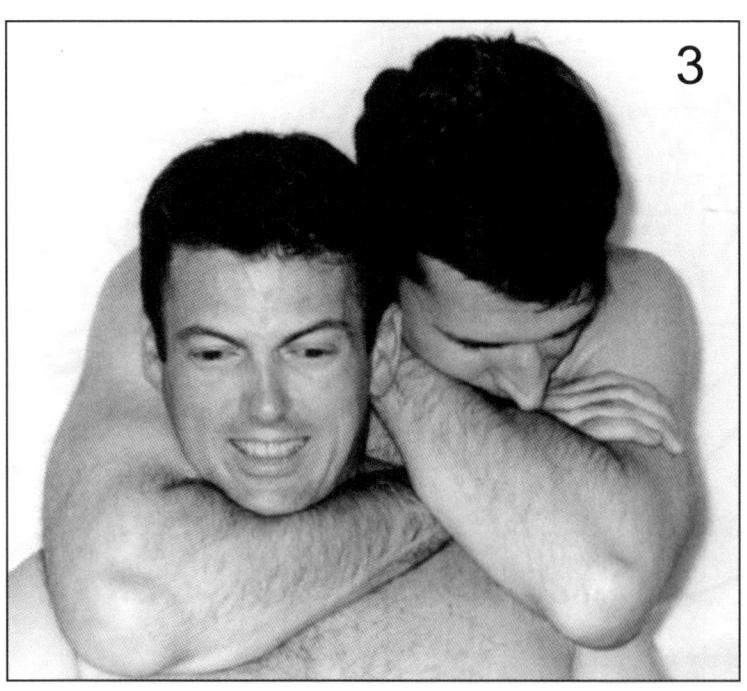

Place your locking hand behind his head and tuck your head tightly against his. To choke, expand your chest and pull your shoulders back as if doing a seated row. When you apply the choke, you want to eliminate any space around his neck.

Even if your opponent gets his hands around your attacking arm, you have enough strength in this technique to choke him.

CHOKE

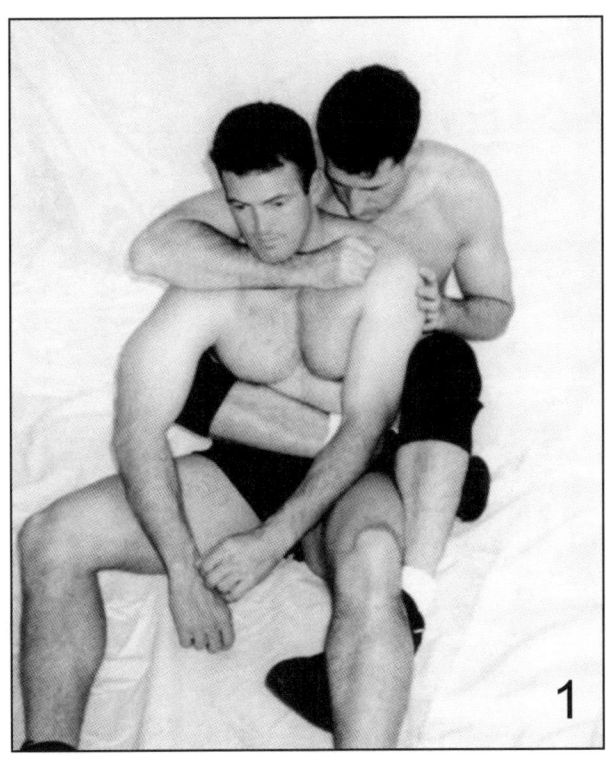

Slide your attacking arm across his throat and under his chin. (Left)

Clasp your hands and place the forearm of your locking arm across his back. (Right)

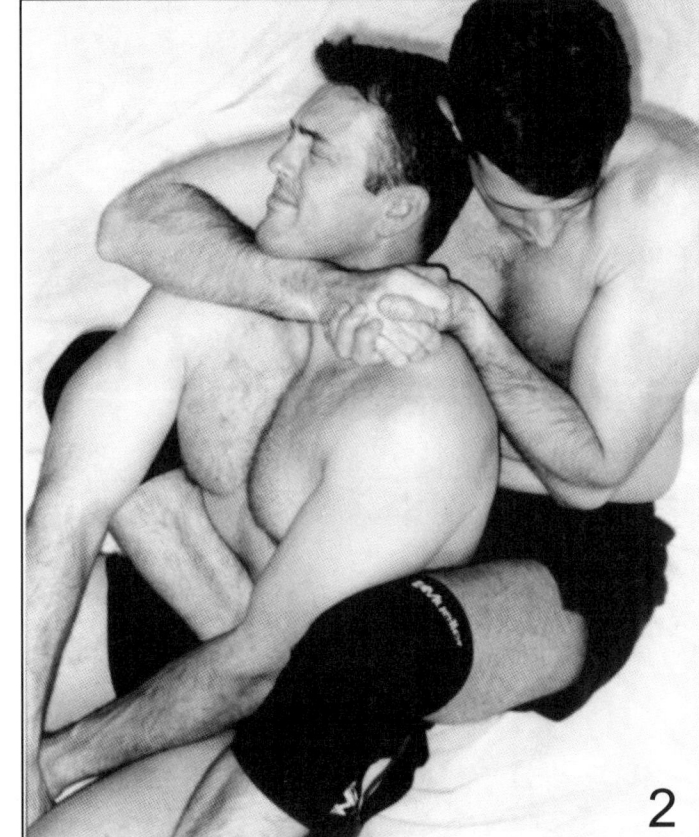

Press your head tightly against his and drive the blade of your attacking forearm into his throat to crush his esophagus for the choke. (Left)

CHOKE *Triangle With Arm Bar*

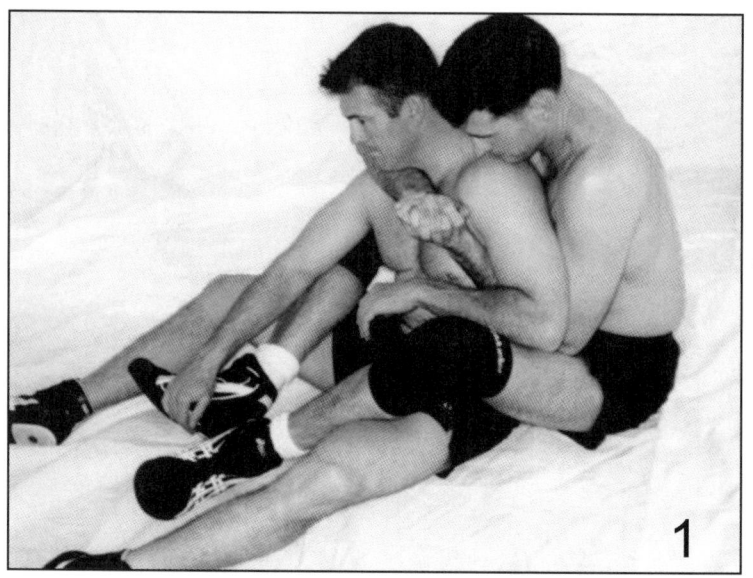

You are rear mounted on your opponent.

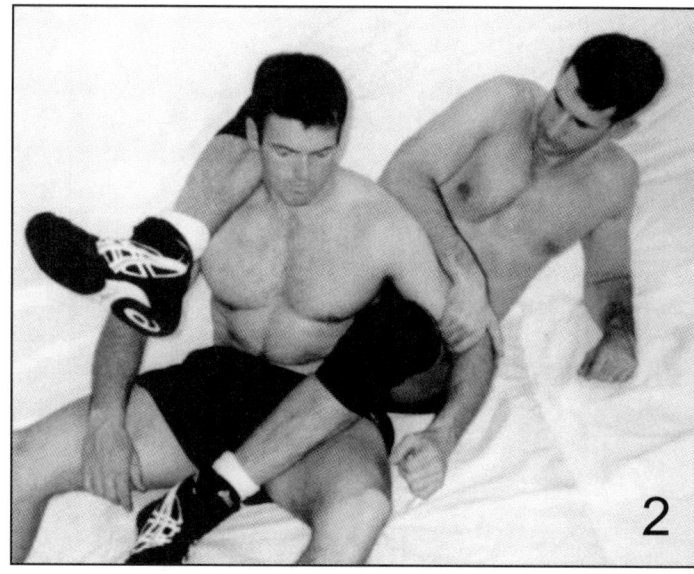

Swing your attacking leg onto his shoulder as shown. Maintain control of his trapped arm.

Hook your attacking leg behind the knee of your locking leg, forming the triangle.

To choke, ensure his arm is straight against his neck and squeeze your knees together. You can also fall backwards, arch your hips and execute an arm bar.

ARM BAR

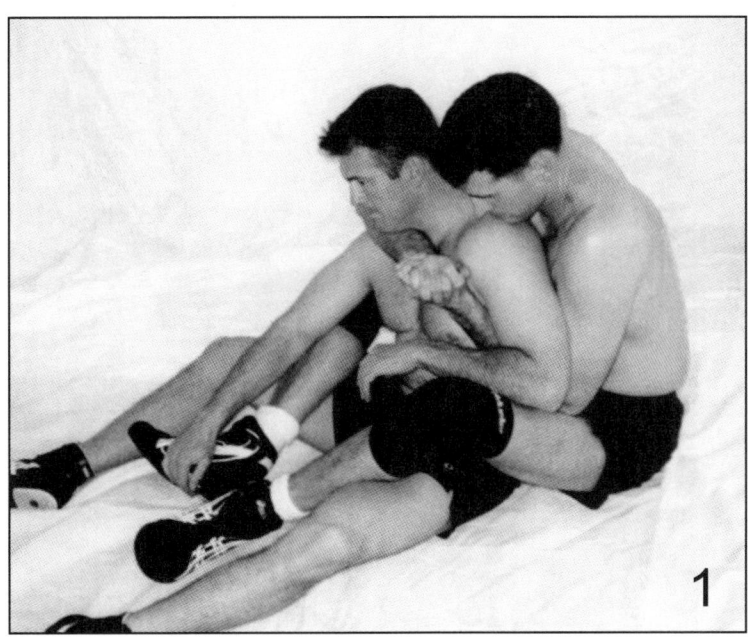

1. You are rear mounted on your opponent.

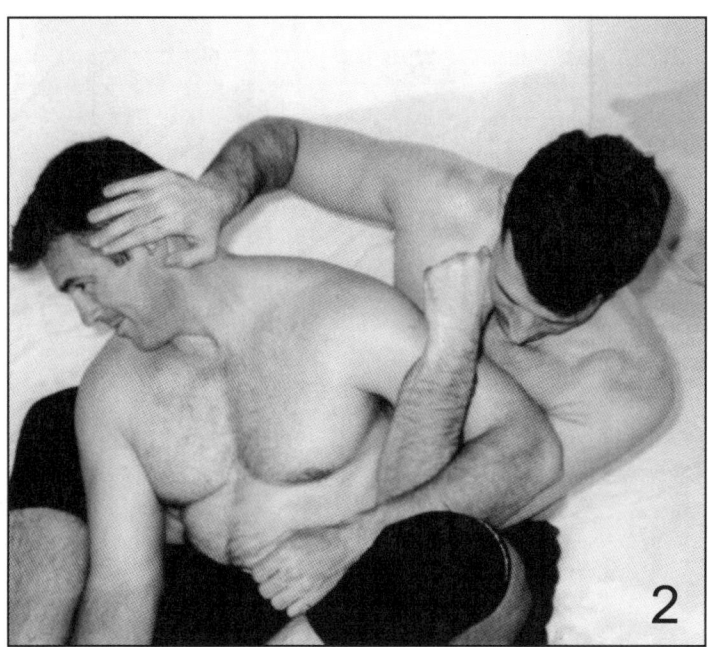

2. Push his head with your free arm and rotate your hips in preparation of swinging your leg over his head.

3. Swing your outside leg over his head and across his throat. Notice how your body has moved perpendicular to his. Maintain a good grip on his targeted arm.

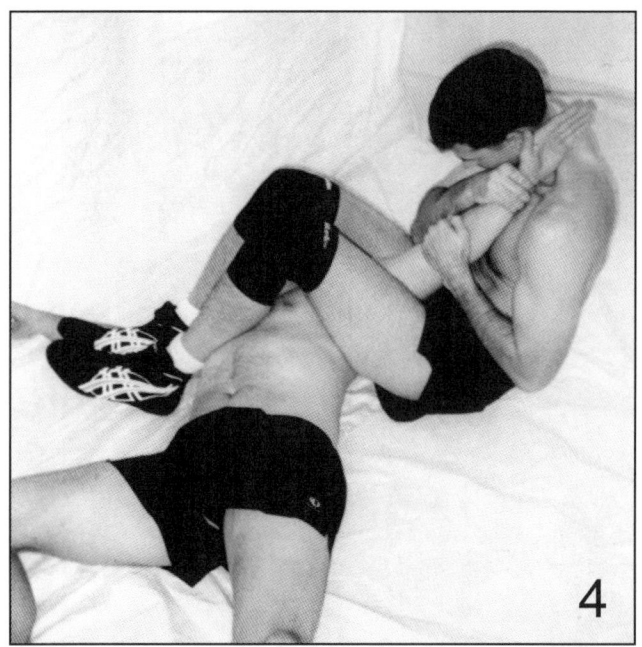

4. Rotate your hips so your leg is across his neck and forces him on his back. Hug his trapped arm, squeeze your knees together and arch your hips upwards to hyper-extend the elbow for the submission.

ARM BAR *Figure Four Lock*

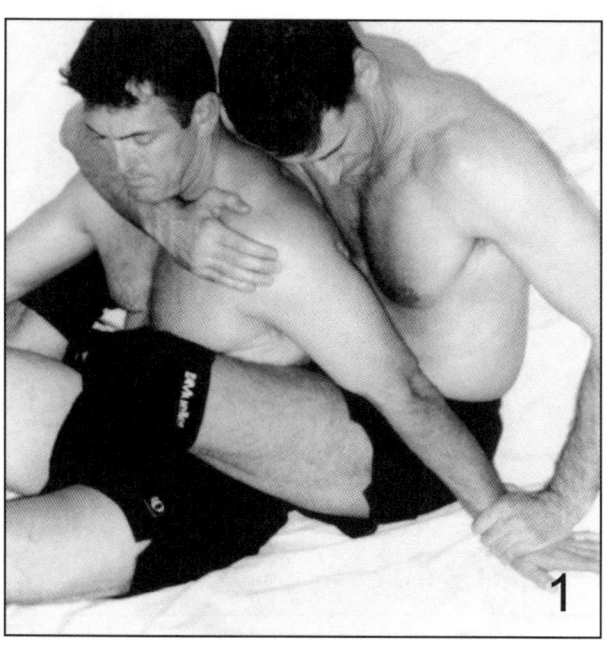

You have your opponent rear mounted. Secure one of his arms as depicted.

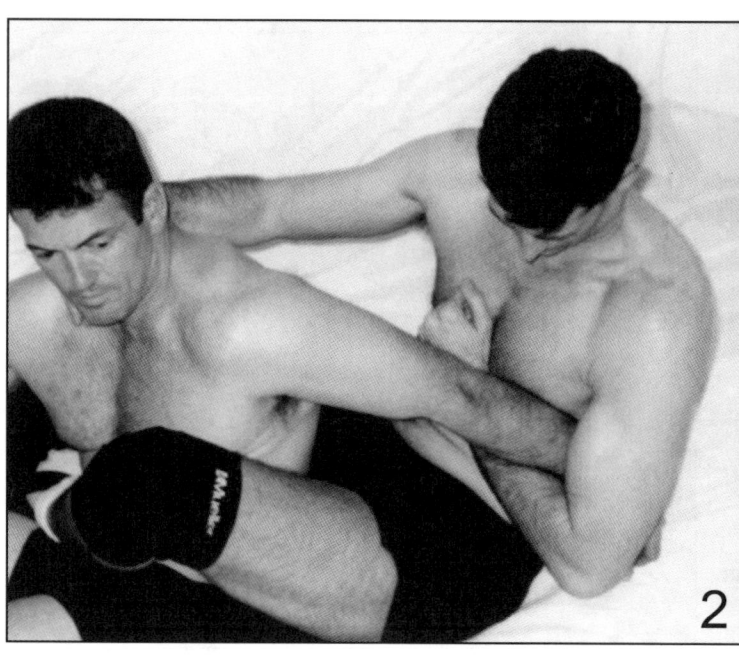

Secure his targeted arm under your armpit.

Place your free arm on his elbow and grab your own wrist. This creates a secure, figure four lock on his targeted arm.

To submit your opponent, push down on his elbow with your figure foured hands and raise his lower arm upwards with your forearm. Curl your body forwards in a crunching motion to increase the pressure and hyper-extend his arm at the elbow for the submission.

SQUEEZE LOCK

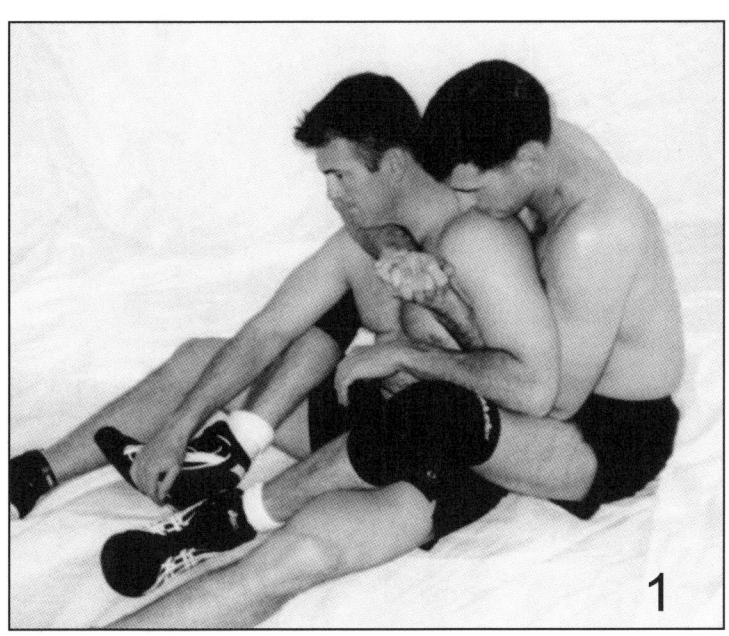

You are rear mounted on your opponent.

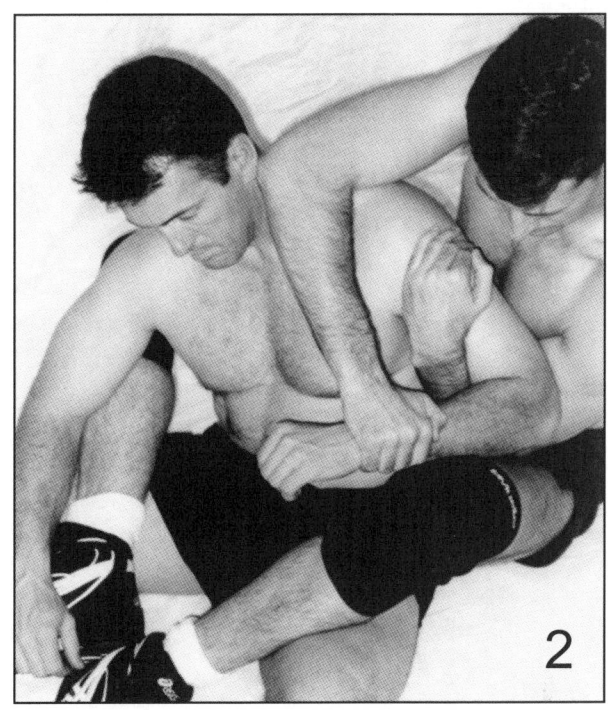

Trap his arm at the biceps with one arm and secure his wrist with your free hand, trapping his arm.

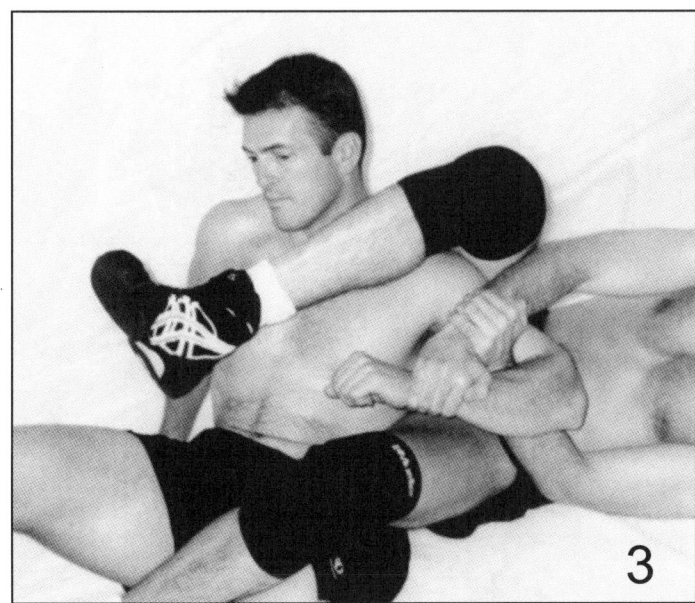

Swing your far leg over his head and across his trapped arm. You can maintain a secure grip on his arm by a figure four lock as shown.

Lock your attacking leg behind your knee, trapping his arm. Clasp your hands to facilitate pulling the blade of your forearm into his biceps. To submit, squeeze your knees together and pull backwards with your arms, forcing your forearm into his elbow joint.

SQUEEZE LOCK *Nutcracker*

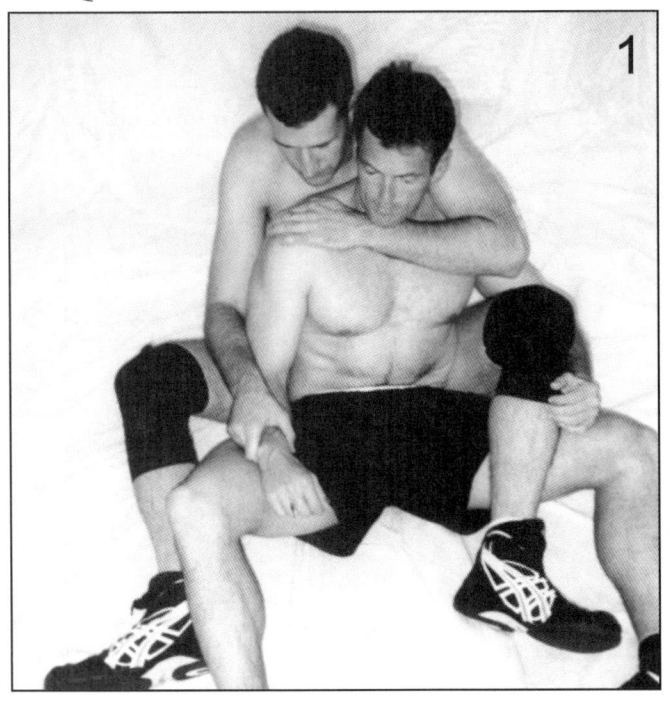

You are rear mounted on your opponent. Secure his arm at the wrist as shown. (Top)

Lock your legs over his arm, trapping it. (Top Right)

Secure his free arm. (Right)

Force his arm behind his neck, like a chicken wing. (Bottom Right)

Bear hug his arm and attempt to make his wrist touch his shoulder, hyper-flexing his arm for the submission. Also, you can twist your upper body towards his head and crank his shoulder. (Bottom)

SHOULDER CRANK *Chicken Wing*

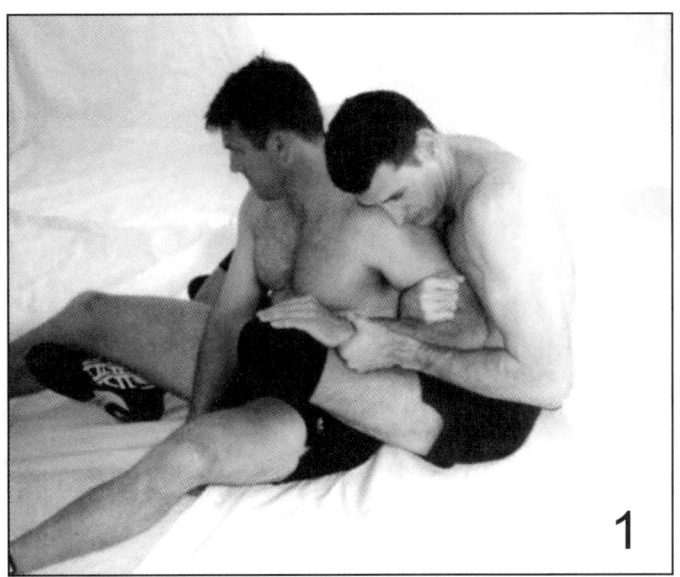

Your have rear mount; secure one of his arms as depicted.

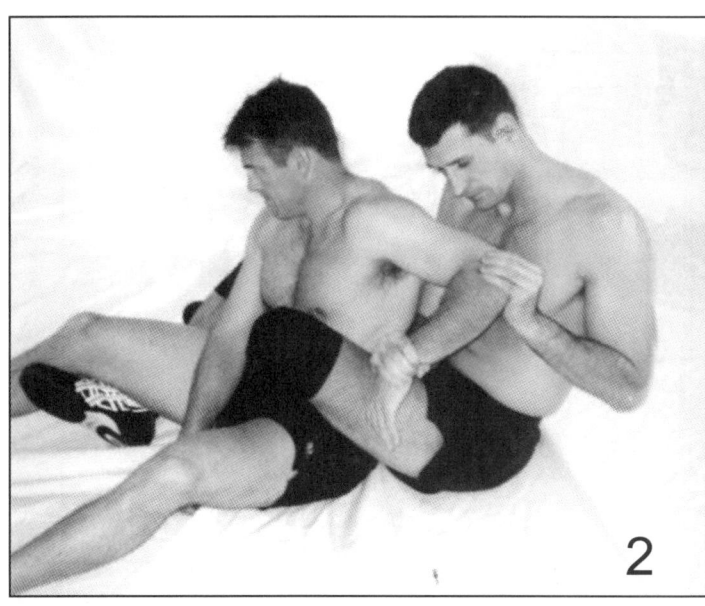

Trap his arm at the elbow with one arm and secure his wrist with your other hand, trapping his arm.

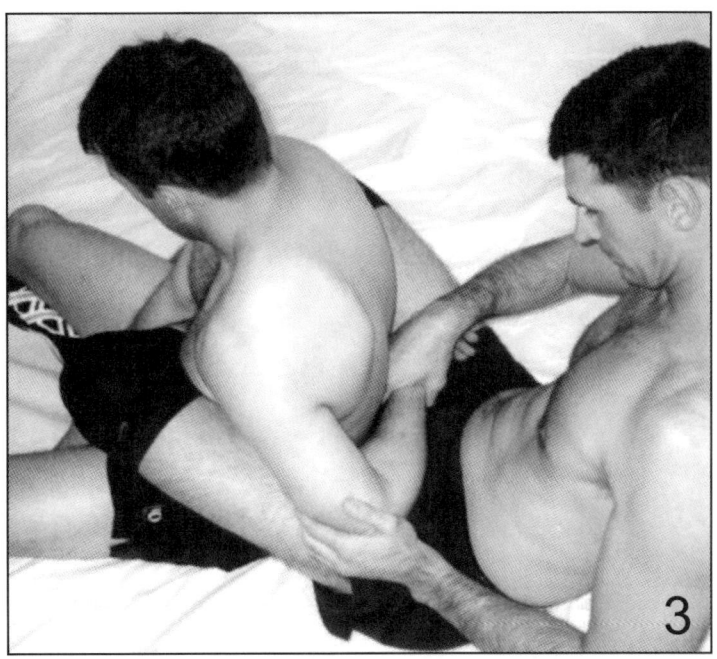

Twist his arm behind his back.

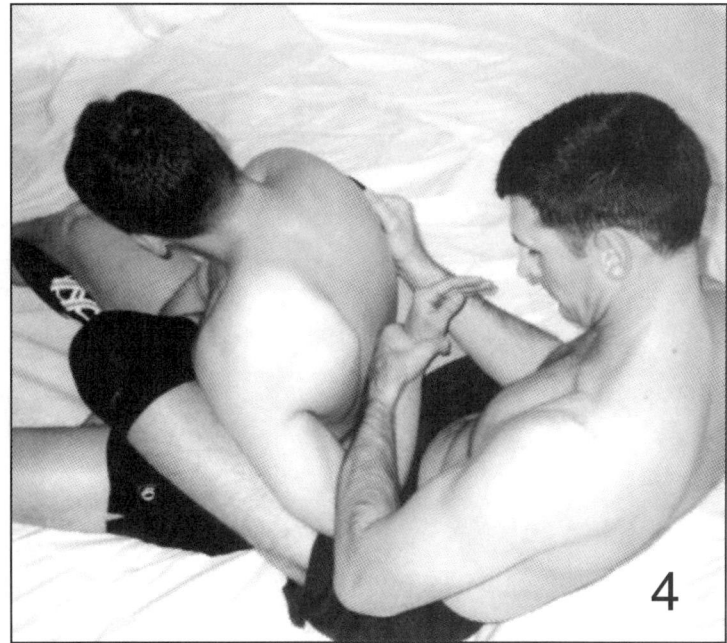

Drive your forearm into his bent elbow to pin his arm and attempt to pull his wrist and place it where his shoulder is. This will crank his shoulder for the submission.

SHOULDER LOCK

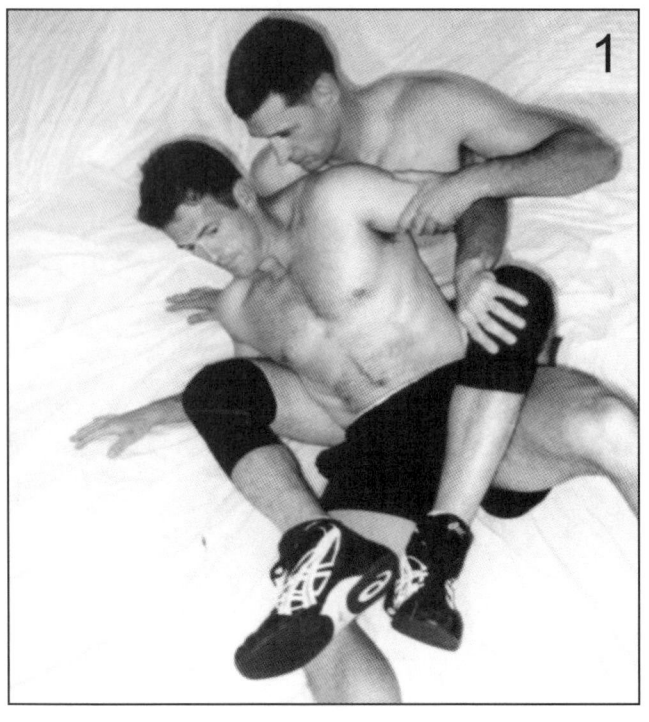

You have your opponent rear mounted. He is posted on one arm.

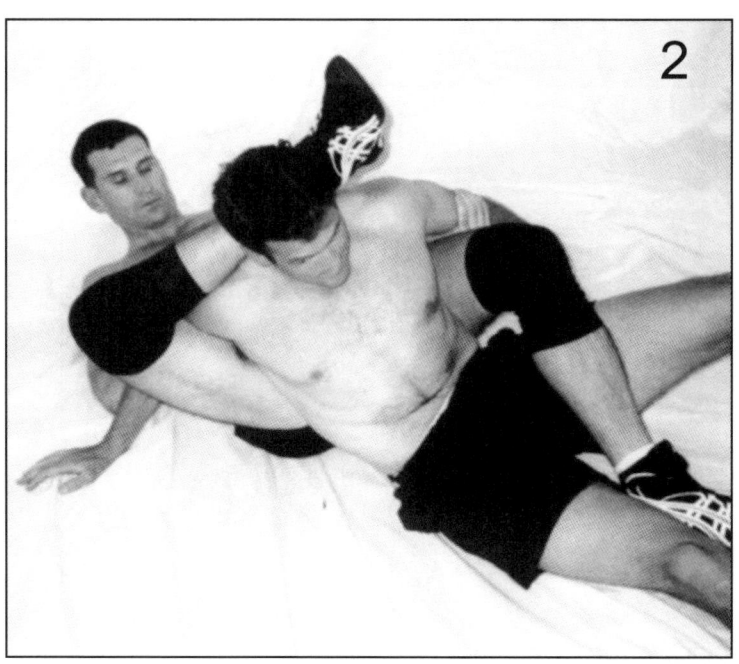

Place your leg across the back of his neck.

Secure his free arm at the wrist with both arms. Driving your entangled leg straight out cranks his neck.

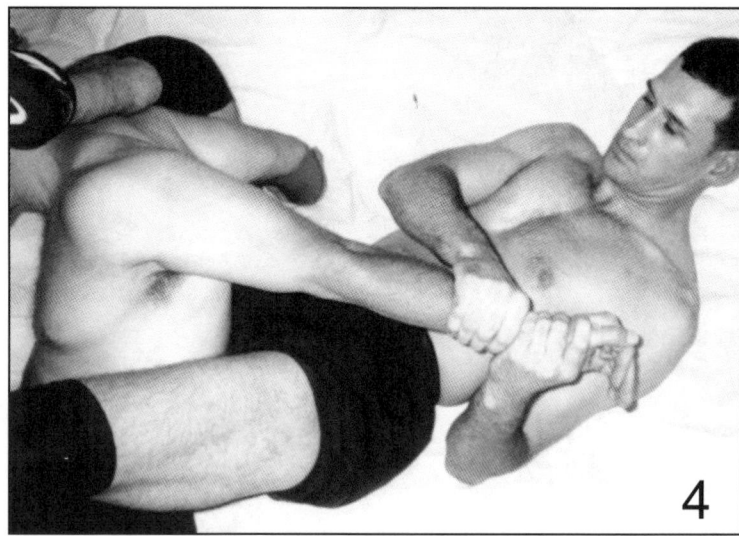

Pull his straightened arm across your chest and his back. This will tear the muscles of his shoulder if he does not submit. (This picture is from the opposite angle.)

ATTACKS IN REAR MOUNT – ANKLE CRANK

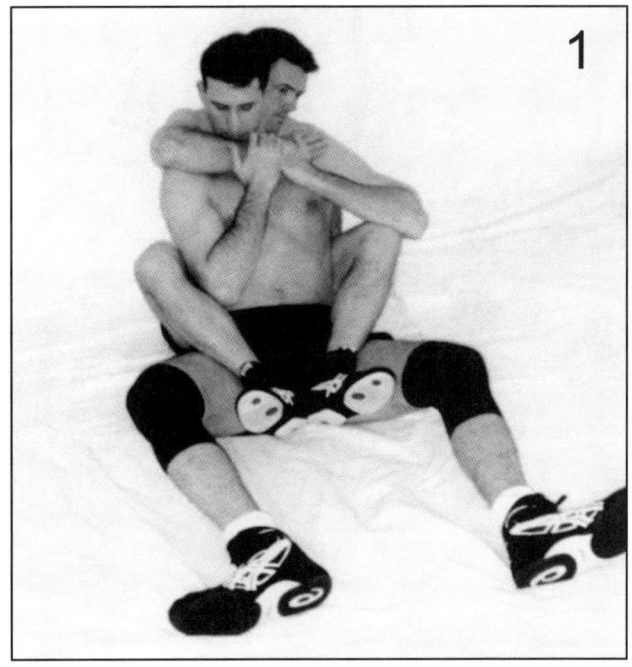

Your opponent is rear mounted as shown. Ensure that you keep your chin tucked to prevent a quick choke by your opponent.

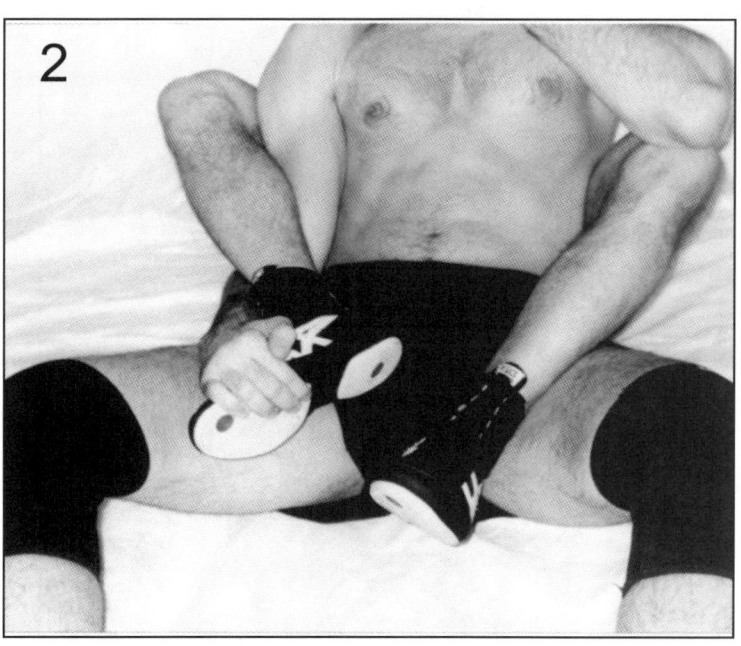

Secure his targeted foot by reaching under his ankle and grabbing his instep. The closer to the end of his foot that you grab, the more torque you can exert on his knee.

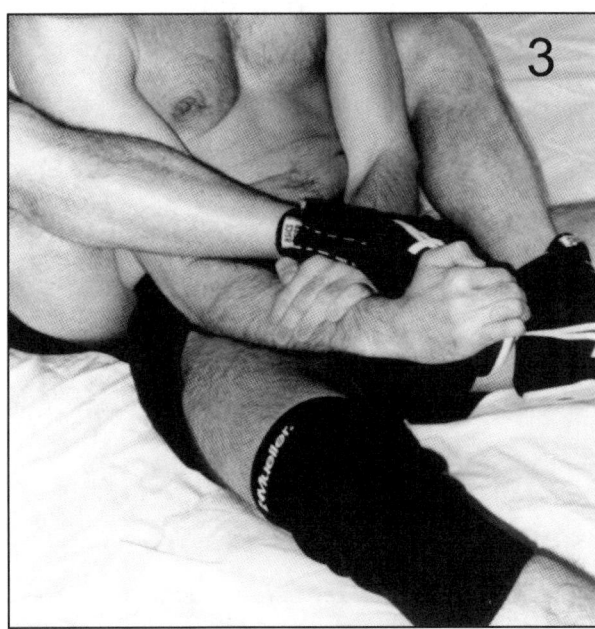

Reach under his ankle with your free, locking arm and grab your attacking arm at the wrist This creates a strong, figure four lock on his foot.

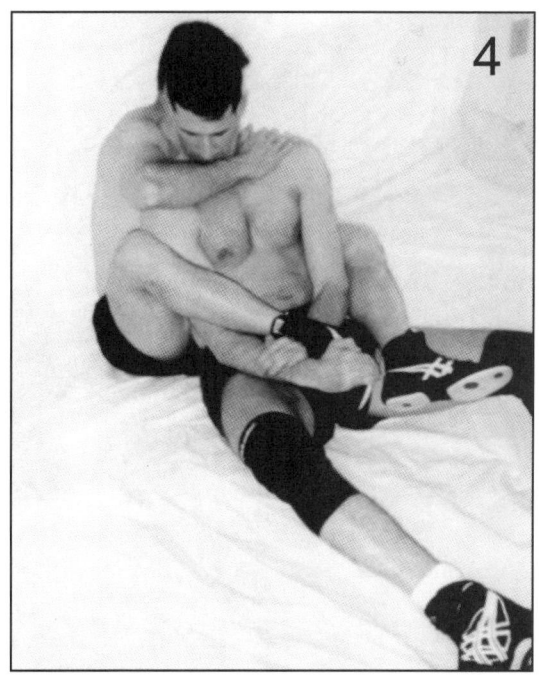

To crank his knee, pull down on his instep with your attacking hand and push his heel upwards with your locking arm. This motion uses his foot as a lever to torque his knee for the submission.

ANKLE CRANK

Your opponent is rear mounted as shown. Ensure that you keep your chin tucked to prevent a quick choke by your opponent.

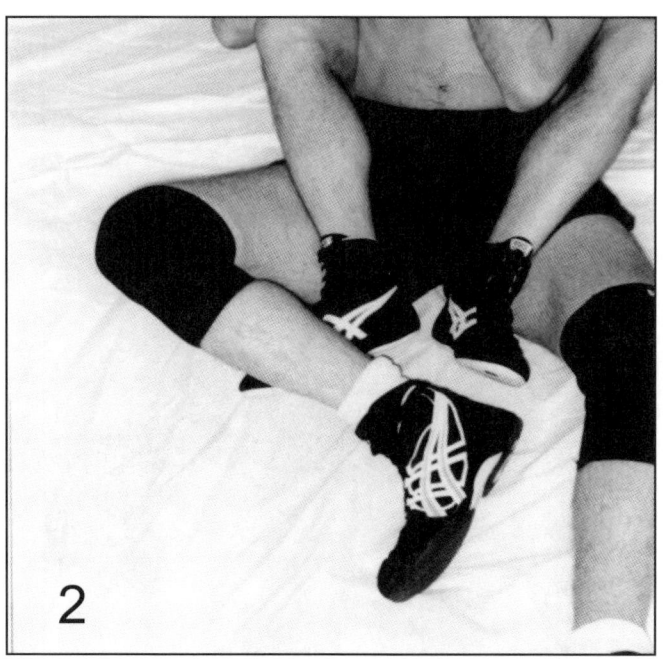

Place your leg over the instep of his his targeted foot. This positioning alone may cause discomfort to your opponent, causing him to reposition himself to ease the pressure on his knee.

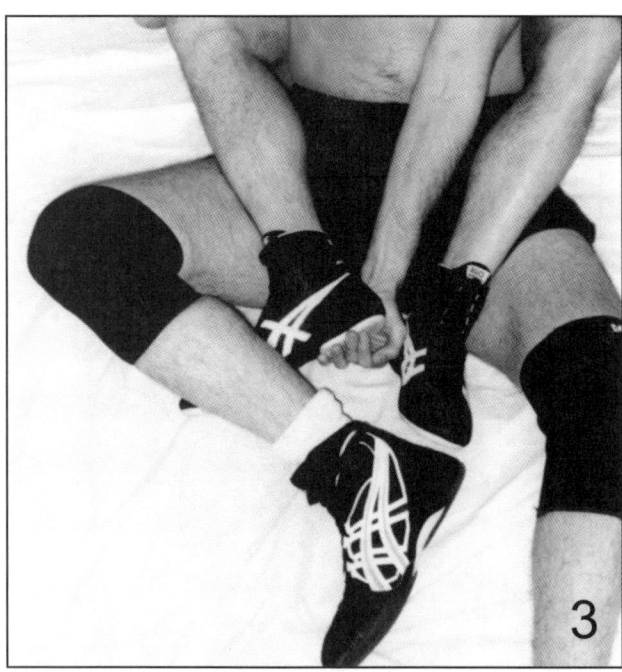

Place the palm of your opposite side hand on the heel of his trapped foot. You can brace the elbow of your attacking arm on your hip to get power for the next step.

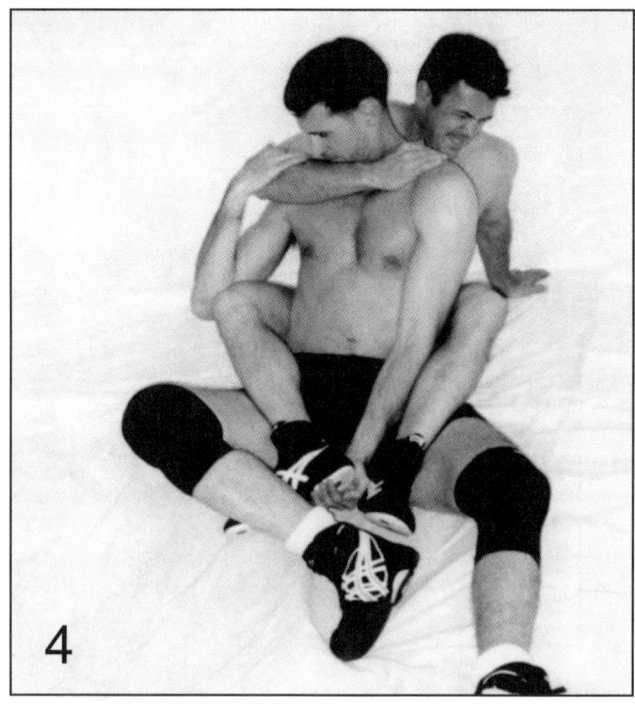

To crank his knee, push out on his heel while keeping his foot pinned to the ground with your leg. This motion uses his foot as a lever to to torque his knee for the submission.

ANKLE CRANK

Your opponent is rear mounted as shown. Ensure that you keep your chin tucked to prevent a quick choke by your opponent.

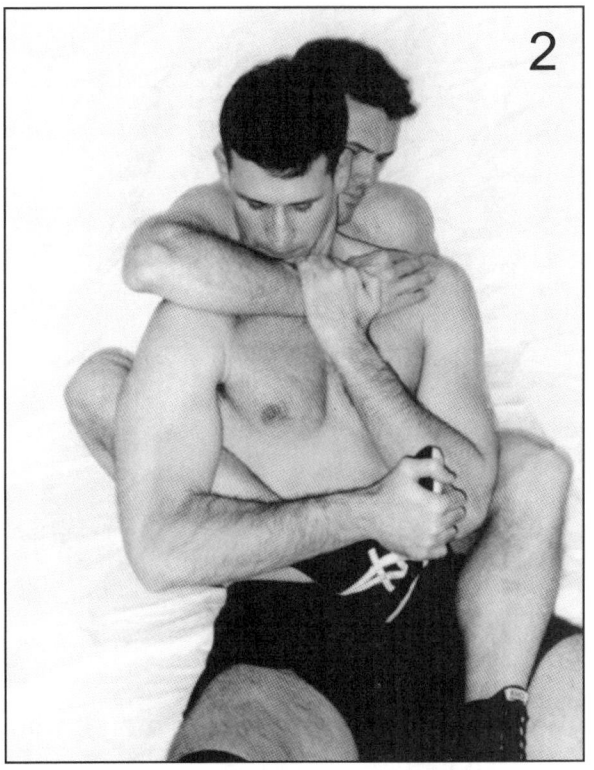

Secure his targeted foot by grabbing the blade of his foot. The closer you are to the end of his foot, the more torque you can exert on his knee.

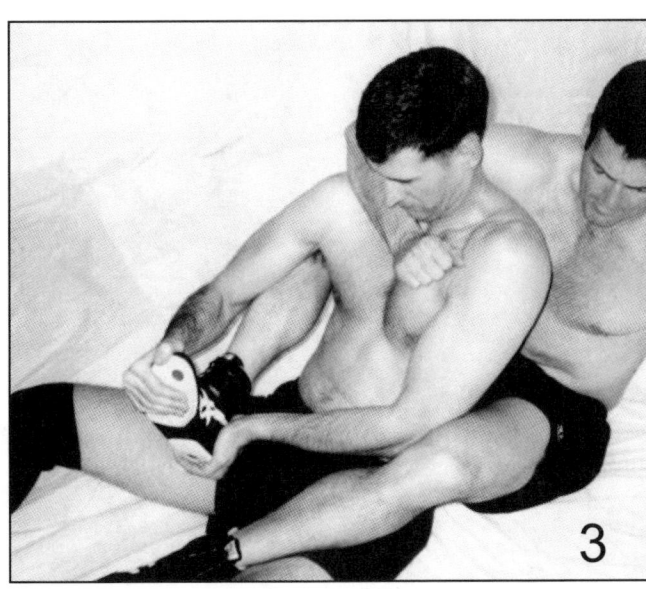

Place the palm of your other hand on his heel. This picture is exaggerated to show you the hand positioning. In reality, his leg will be tight against your body.

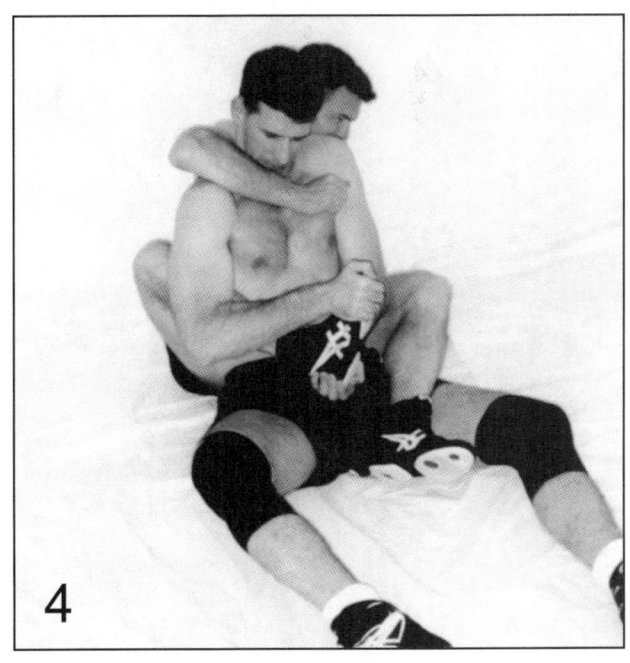

To crank his foot, pull the blade of his foot inwards while pushing out on his heel. This motion uses his foot as a lever to torque his knee for the submission.

ANKLE LOCK *With Legs*

1

Your opponent has the rear mount with his feet crossed.

2

His left foot is crossed over his right; place your right, attacking leg over the top of his left foot.

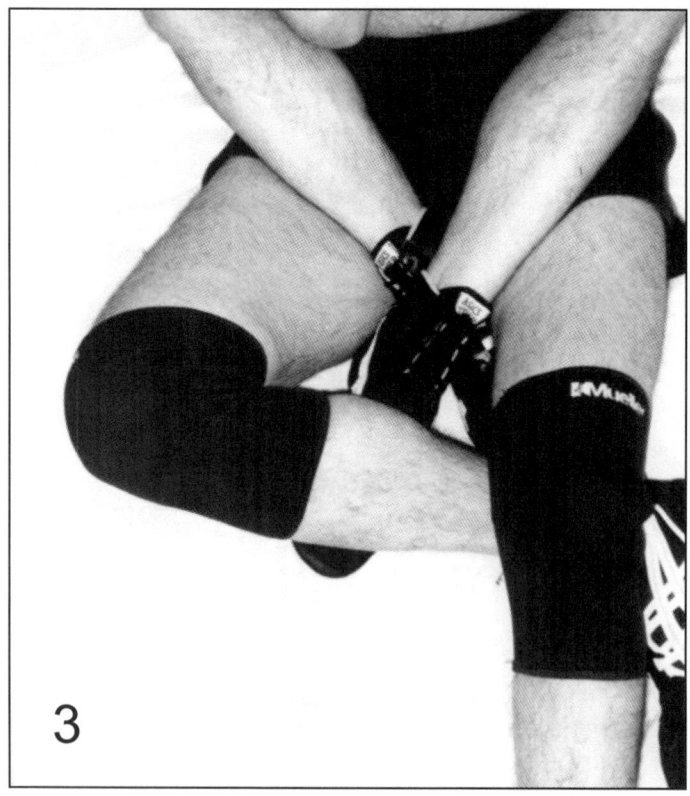

3

Place your free leg over your attacking leg to lock his foot into place.

4

Arch your back, raise your hips, and pull your locked legs downwards in order to hyper-extend his foot for the submission.

Chapter Seventeen
Submissions From North/South And In North/South

North/South

This position allows the attacker's weight to pin his opponent. The attacker can use his arms and knees to overwhelm the defender and the attacker can often submit the defender with rather subtle moves which are difficult to defend against.

Your hips are low giving you a low center of gravity, making it difficult to be reversed. Your hips can pin his head and limit his mobility.

Your body positioning has effectively taken your opponent's hips and legs out of the equation, his attack options are limited.

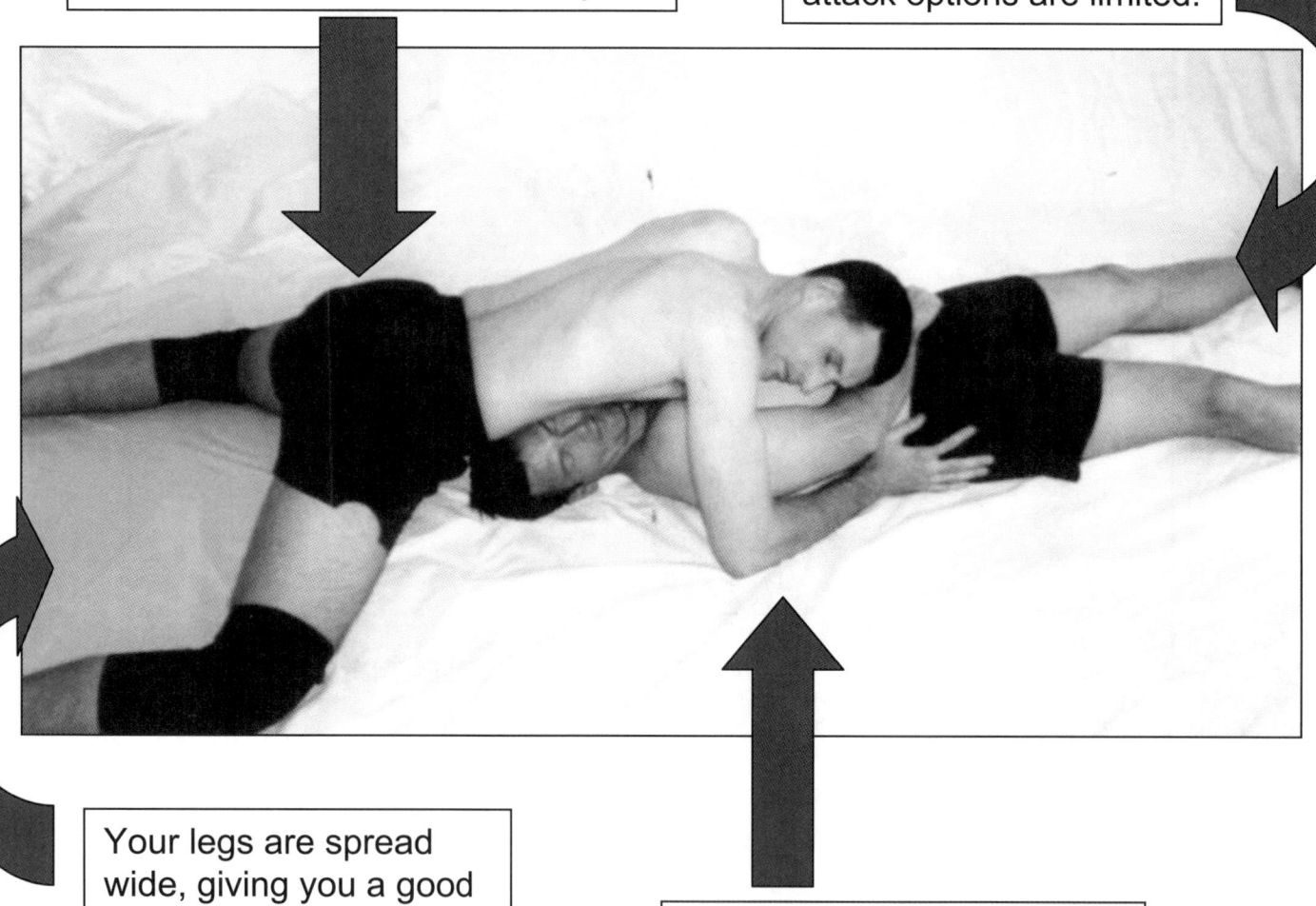

Your legs are spread wide, giving you a good base and making it difficult for you to be reversed.

Your body weight is pinning him to the ground. You can work a variety of attacks targeting his arms and head.

NECK CRANK *Underarm*

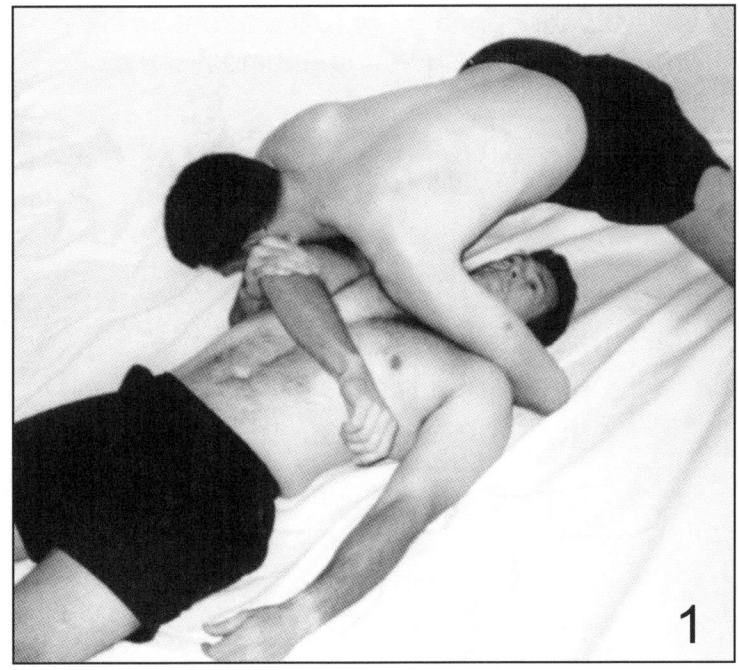

You have one arm wrapped over his neck and under his head. You are controlling his arm at the elbow as shown. (Left)

Maintain secure control of his head and slide your hips and bottom leg under his hips. (Right)

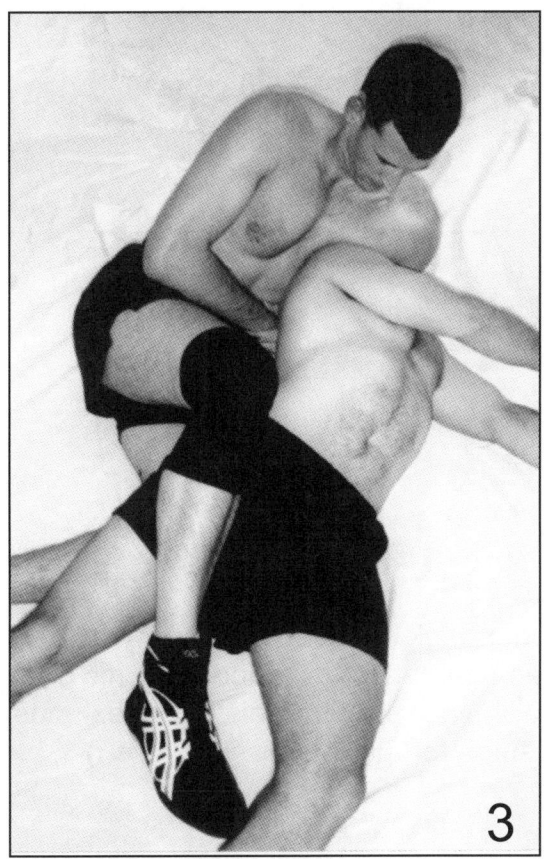

Hook your top leg over his near leg to secure your position. Clasp your hands behind his neck. Arch your back, drive your hands upwards, and push his head backwards with your armpit. This will hyper-extend his cervical spine for the submission. (Left)

NECK CRANK *Underarm*

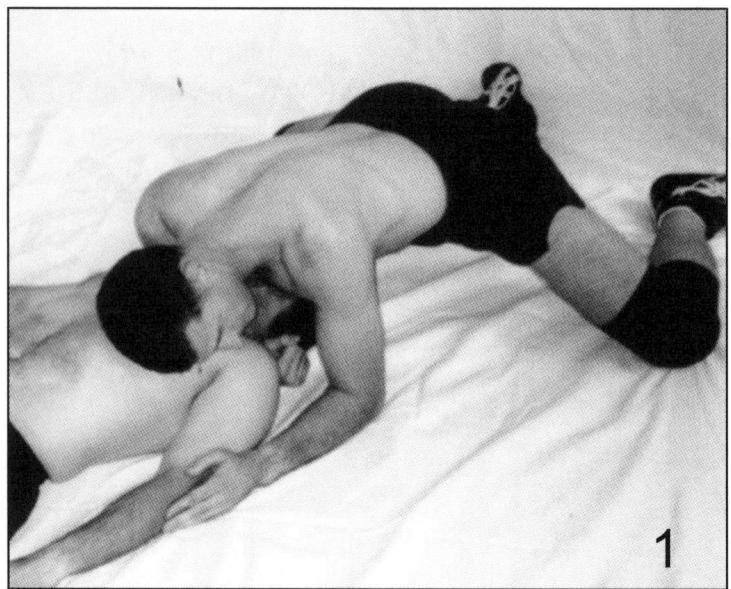

You have your opponent in N/S and one arm is wrapped over his face and behind his neck. (Left)

Clasp your hands behind his neck, trapping his head under your armpit, and come to your knees. (Right)

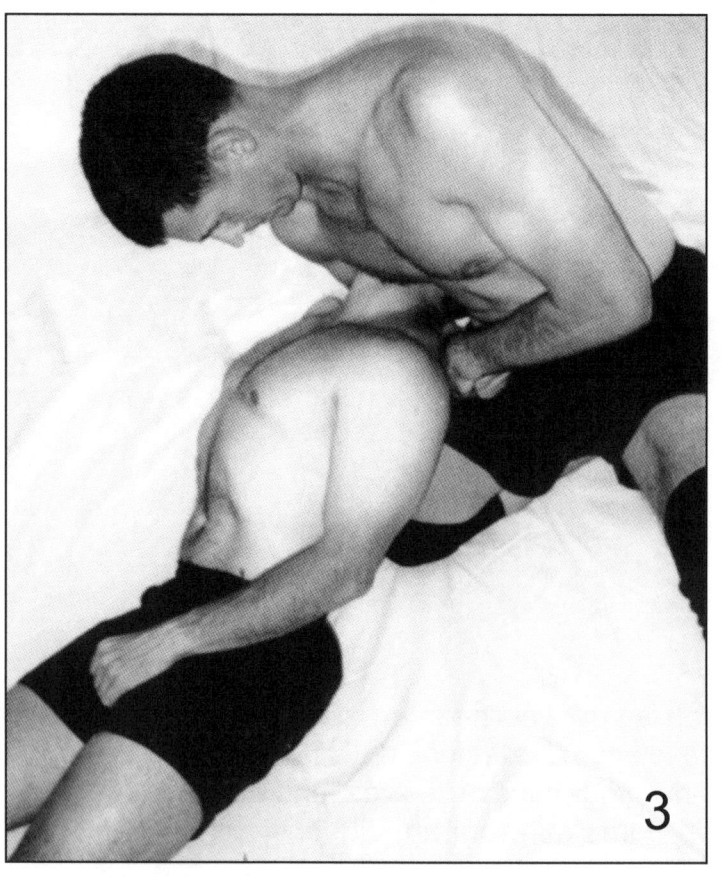

Straighten your back, pull upwards with your hands at the base of his neck, and push his head backwards with your armpit. This hyper-extends his cervical spine for the submission. (Left)

CHOKE *Shoulder*

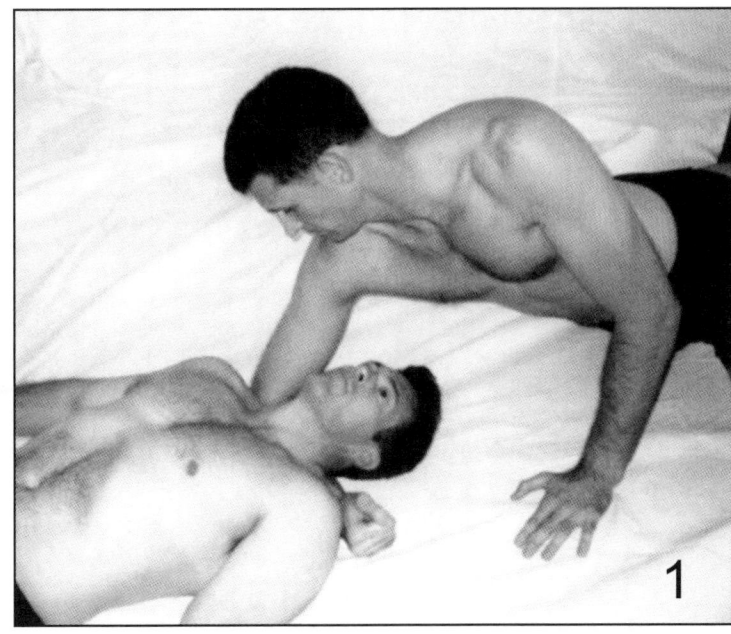

Slide your attacking arm under his head and behind his neck. (Left)

Drive your shoulder into his throat and place the weight of your chest onto his head to pin him down. (Right)

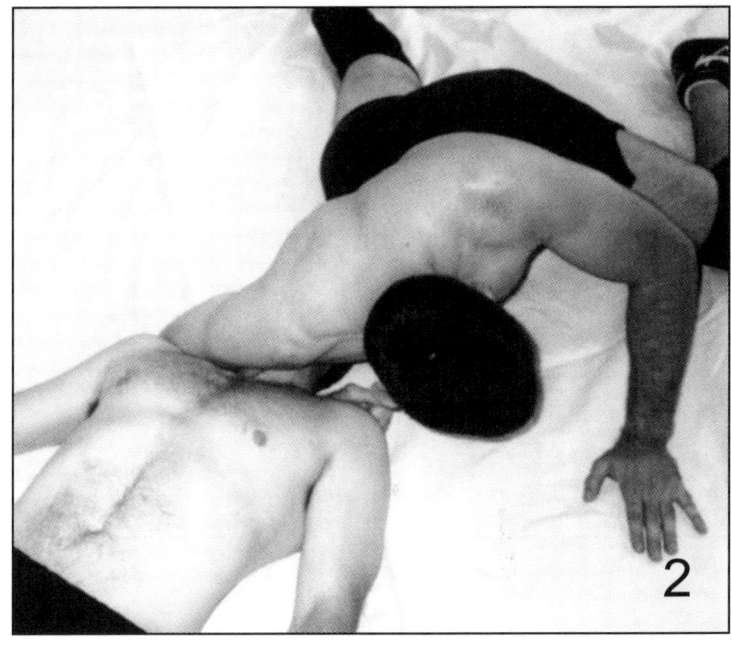

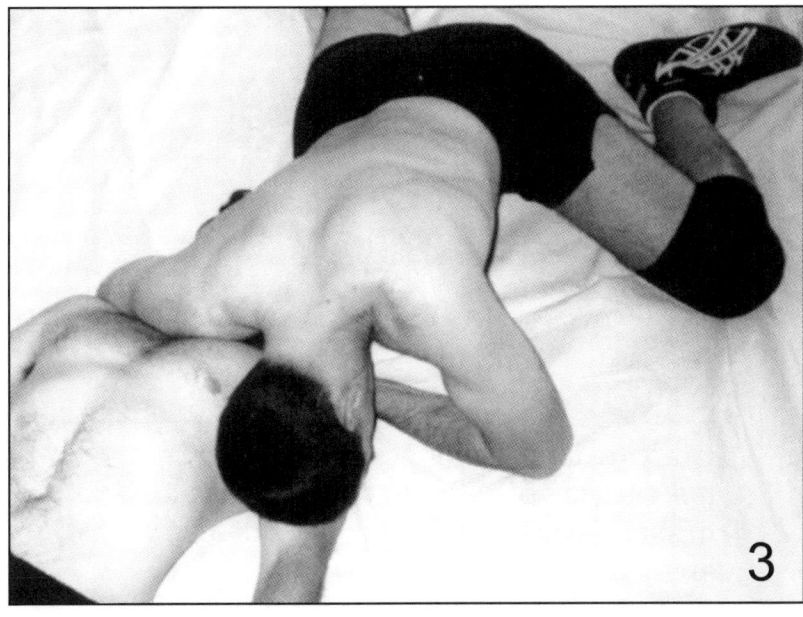

Clasp your hands together to lock in the technique. Pull the blade of your attacking forearm into the base of his neck, raise your hips, and drive your shoulder downwards into his esophagus for the choke. (Left)

CHOKE *Kata Gatame*

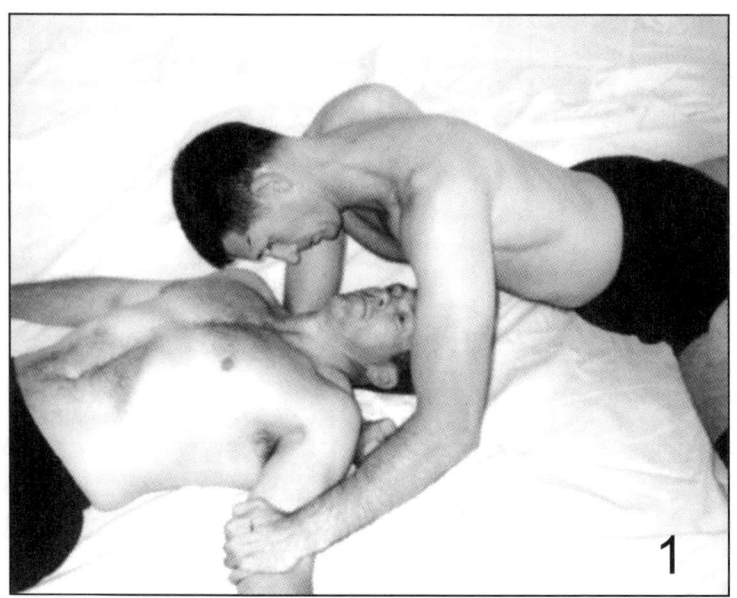

Your attacking arm is wrapped under his neck and you are controlling his arm at the biceps as shown.

Pull his arm straight and push your attacking hand arm under this shoulder.

Grab your locking arm at the biceps and rest your body weight on his head and chest.

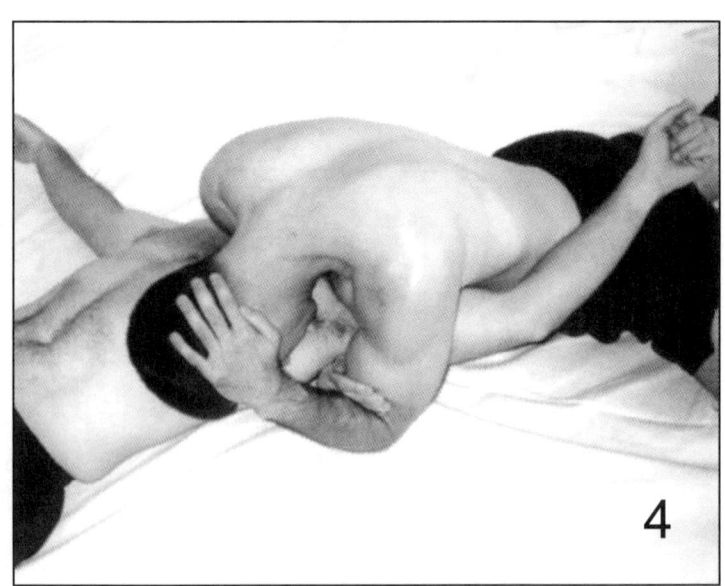

Grab the back of your own head and contract the muscles of your attacking arm for the submission. This move cuts off his carotid arteries.

CHOKE *Leg Scissors*

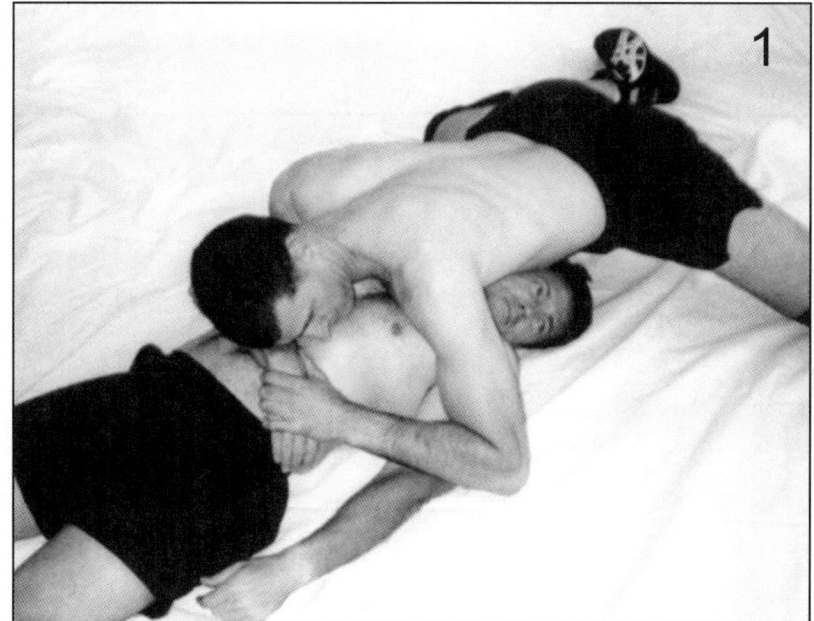

You have your opponent in N/S and have a figure four lock on his exposed arm. (Left)

Maintain your grip on his arm and sit on your side, bringing your leg under his head. (Right)

Place your top leg over your bottom one and hook your ankles. Ensure that the medial, inside portion of your top knee is across his throat and under his chin. Straighten your legs and crush his esophagus for the submission. (Left)

SHOULDER CRANK

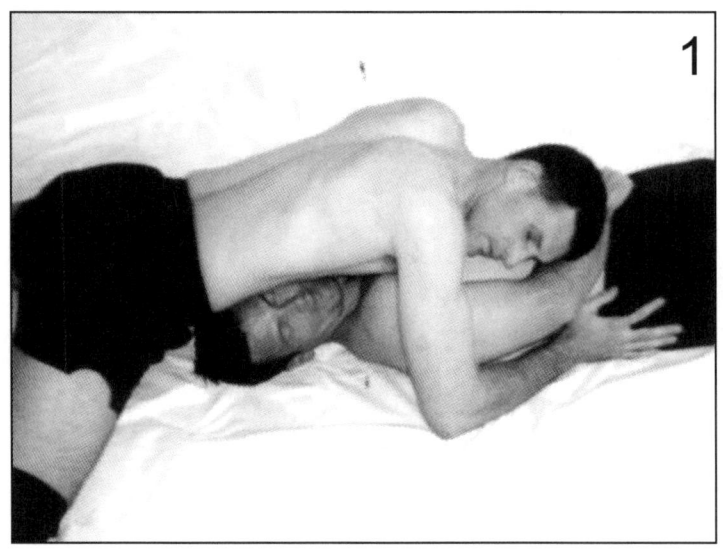

You have your opponent in N/S.

Secure a figure four grip on his exposed arm.

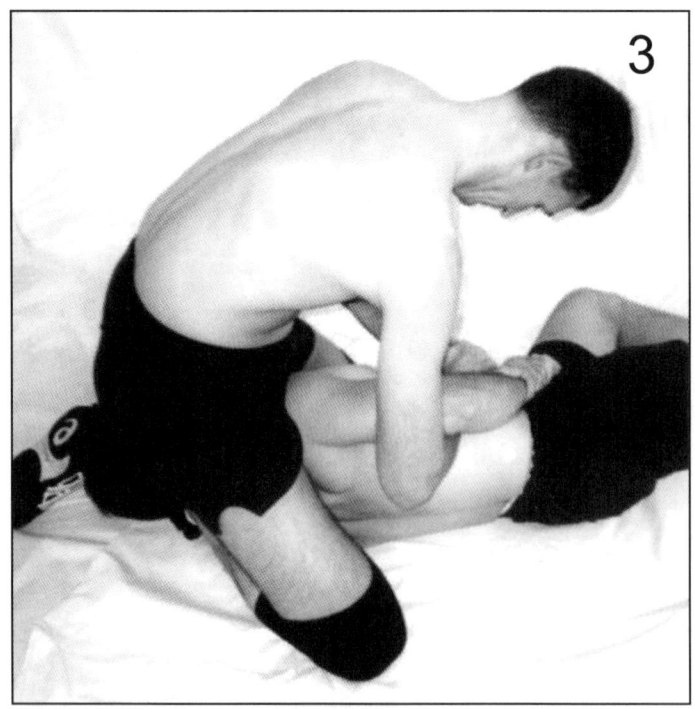

Come to your knees and turn him on his side. You can hook his head under your leg for a reverse mount position.

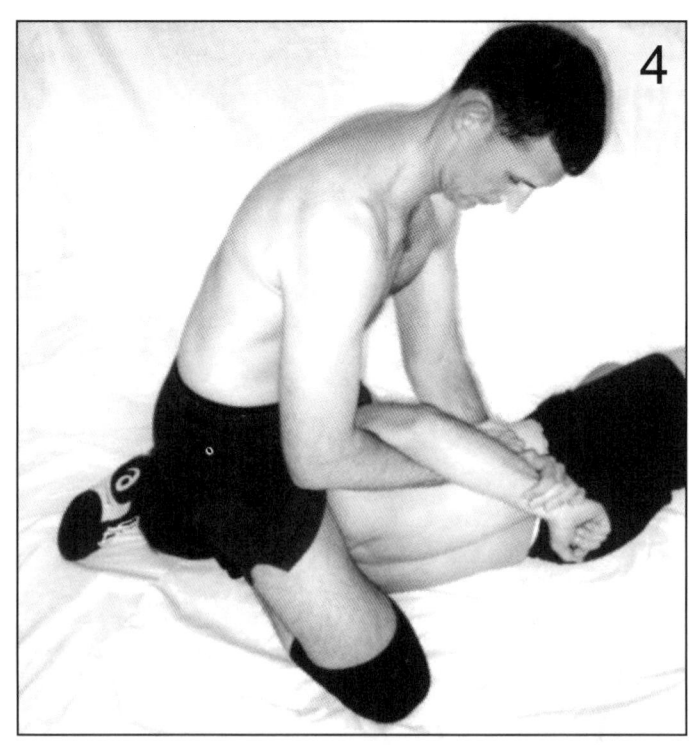

Twist his arm towards his back, using his bent arm as a lever to torque his shoulder for the submission.

ATTACK IN N/S *Arm Bar*

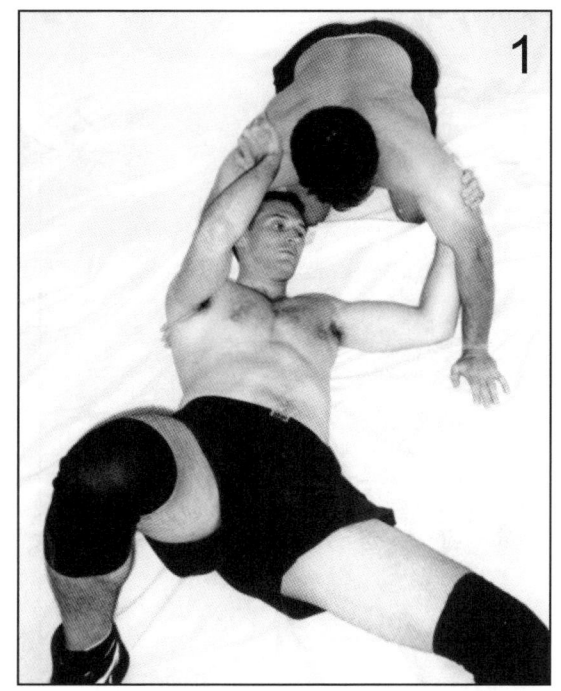

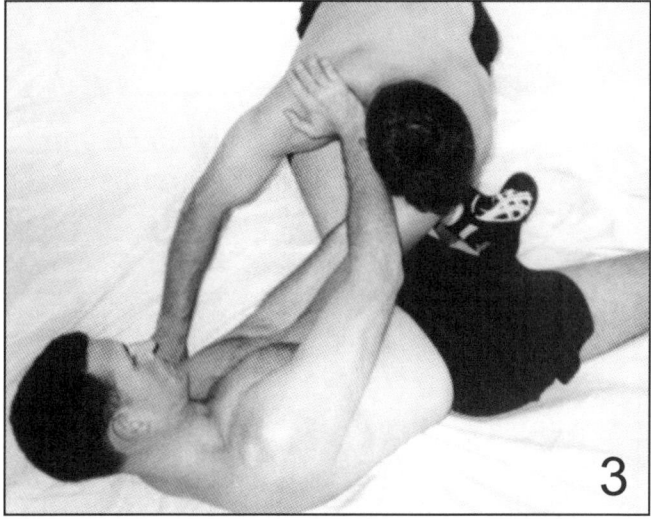

Your opponent has you in N/S. You have created space with your arms. Notice hand positioning. (Top)

Swing your hips towards him and slide your knee under his arm. (Top Right)

Bring your knee under his body and pull his targeted arm towards you. (Right)

Swing your leg over his head and control his trapped arm with both hands. (Bottom Right)

Drive your feet to the ground, squeeze your knees, arch your hips, and hyper-extend his arm at the elbow for the submission. (Bottom)

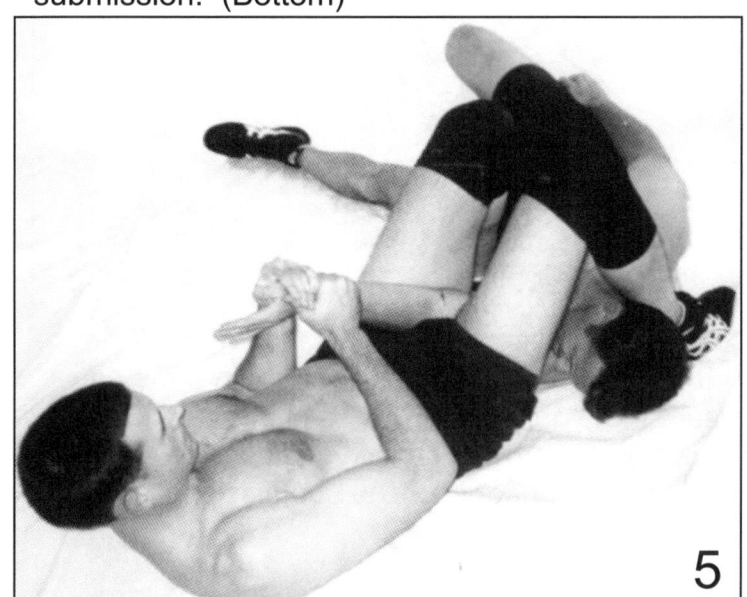

ATTACK IN N/S *Shin Choke*

Your opponent has you in N/S and you have created space with your arms.

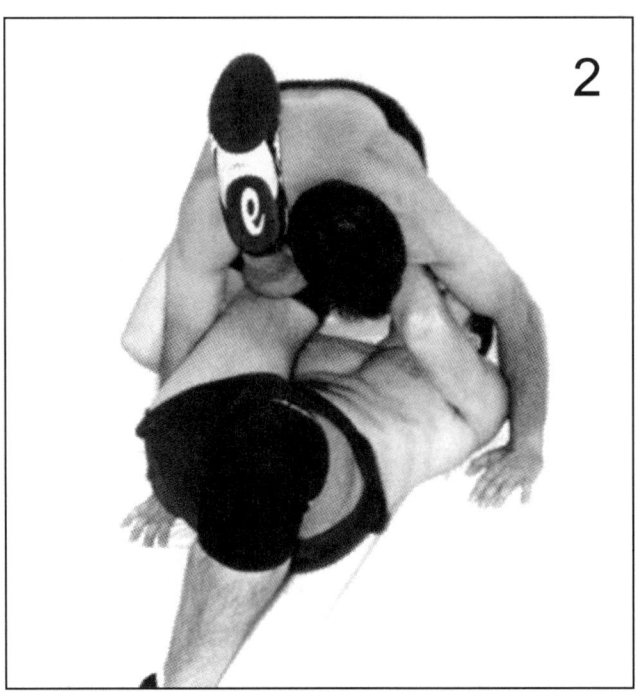

Drive your knee under his shoulder and between your bodies.

Rotate your body so that you are perpendicular to him. Ensure that your foot is over his shoulder and your shin is under his chin.

Grab the back of his head with both arms; ensure that your shin is across his throat. Pull down with both arms while driving your shin into his esophagus for the submission.

Chapter Eighteen
Variations Of Triangle Choke, Arm Bar, Knee Bar, And Foot Attacks

Triangle Choke

You place the foot of your attacking leg behind the knee of your locking leg to secure the technique.

Your attacking leg is tight against his neck, making it difficult for your opponent to stand up; it also forms two of the legs of the triangle.

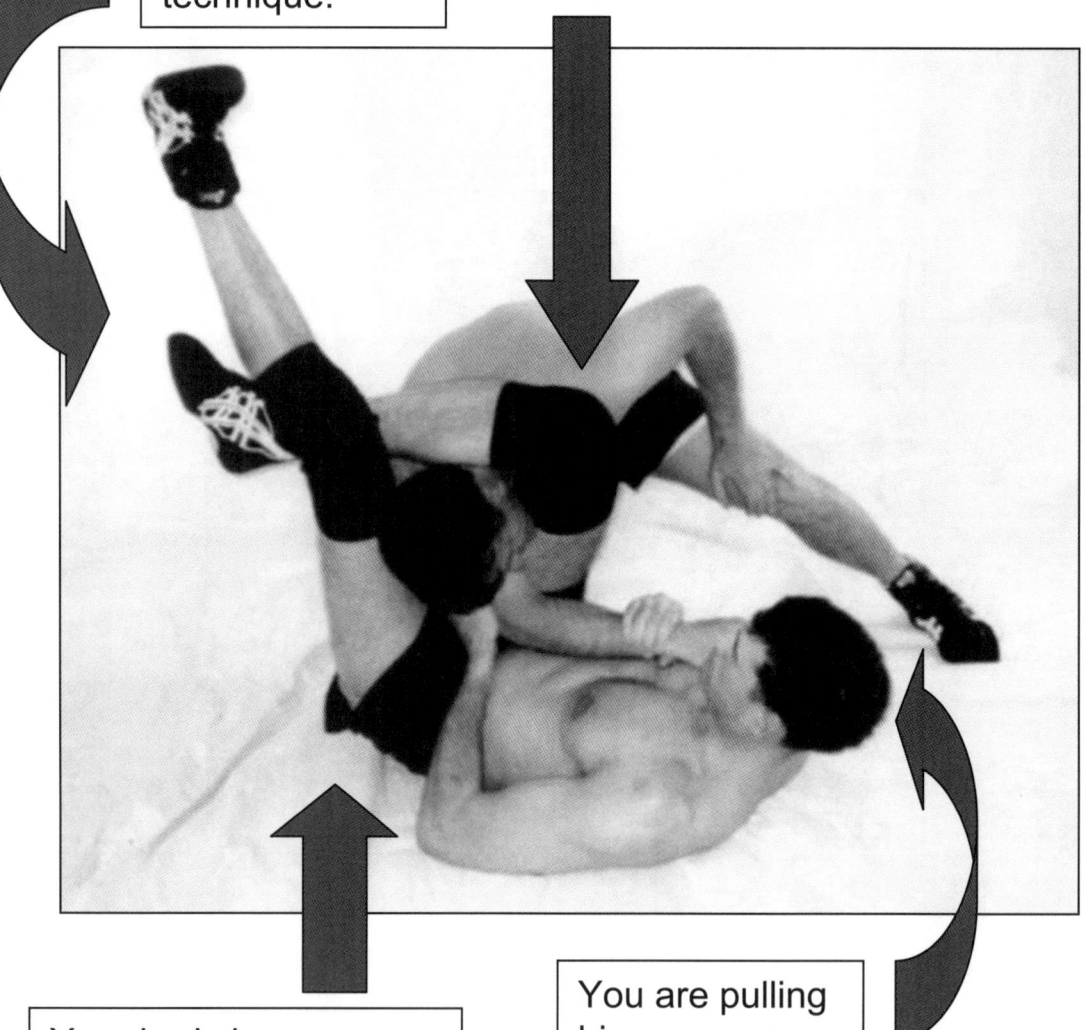

Your body is perpendicular to your opponent's. This allows you to drive your attacking leg tight across the back of his neck.

You are pulling his arm across his neck, forming one of the legs of the triangle.

TRIANGLE CHOKE *Arm Assist Variations*

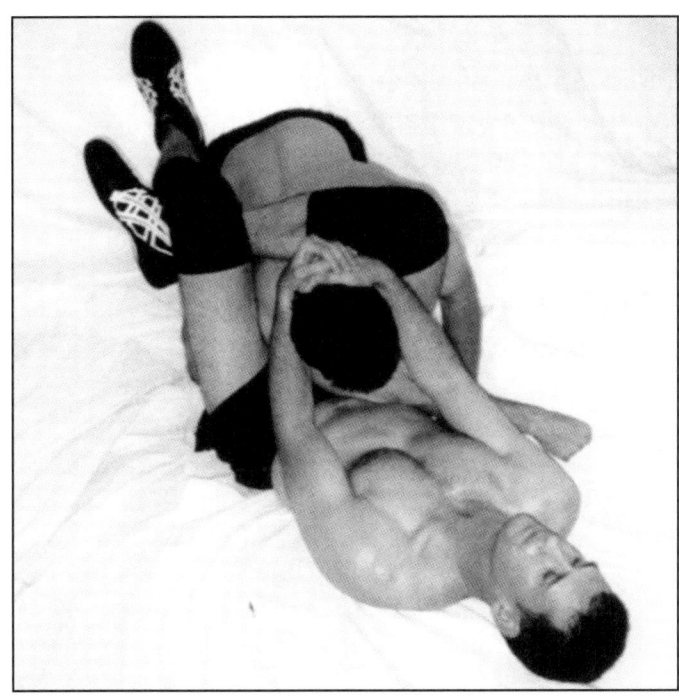

Grab his head with both arms and pull his head forwards, collapsing his esophagus for the choke. (Left)

Reach under your attacking leg with your arm, driving your forearm into the side of his throat for the submission. (Right)

Grab your attacking leg with both hands and lock your attacking leg with your other leg as well. (Left)

TRIANGLE CHOKE *Neck Cranks*

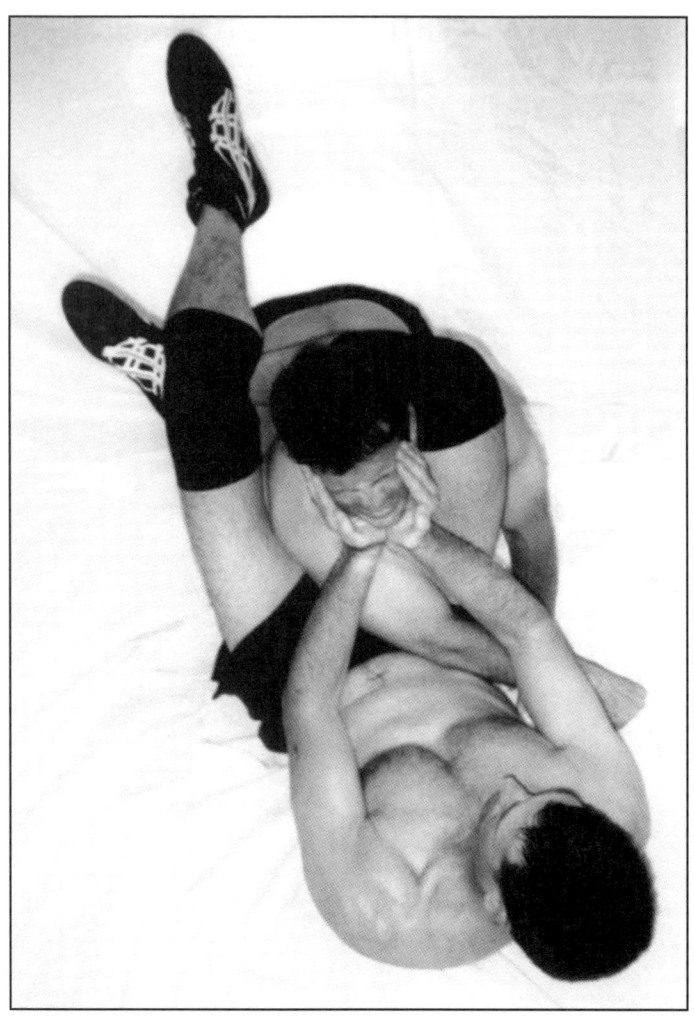

Maintain control of his arm across his throat and plant the palms of both hands on the bottom of his jaw, under his chin. Straighten your arms out and crunch forwards at the abdomen to push his jaw up and his neck back. This is very uncomfortable on his jaw and hyper-extends his cervical spine. (Left)

You can attack his neck with a bottle opener crank, also. Plant one hand on his jaw and the other on the back of his head. Maintain control of his arm across his throat. Twist his head for the neck crank and the submission. (Right)

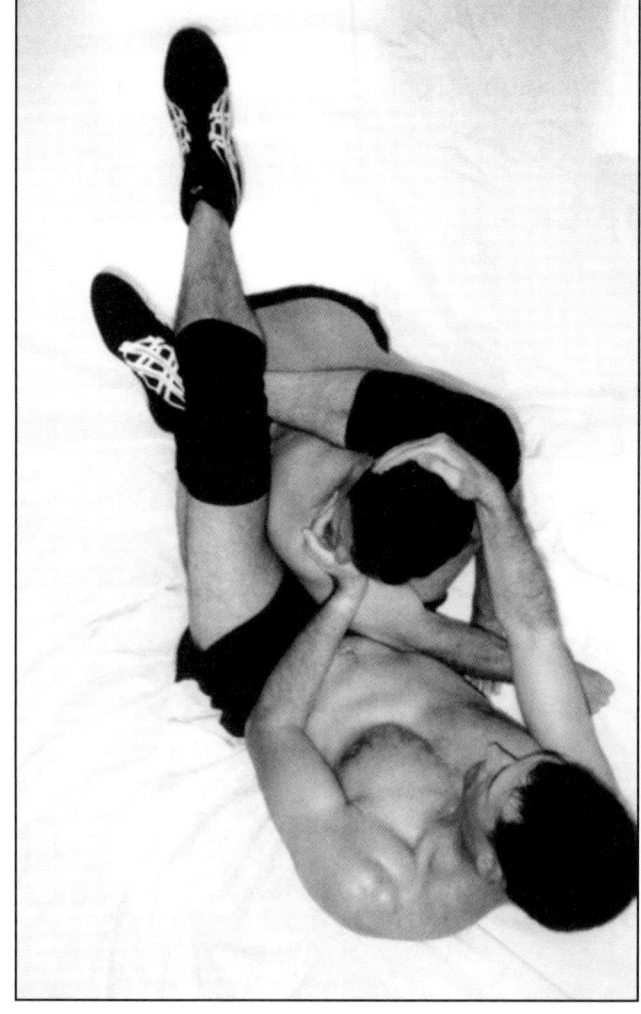

TRIANGLE CHOKE *Shoulder Cranks*

Secure a figure four lock on his near arm and crank his arm forwards to torque his shoulder for the submission. (Left)

Secure a figure four lock on his near arm and crank his arm backwards to torque his shoulder for the submission. (Right)

TRIANGLE CHOKE *Heel Hook*

Secure his near leg and gain control of his foot. Hook his heel and turn his foot to torque his knee for the submission. (Left)

Ankle Attacks

Secure your opponent's near leg and grab him at the foot. You can execute a variety of ankle attacks from this position. Pulling his foot across your chest can put pressure on his lateral knee and his hip. (Right)

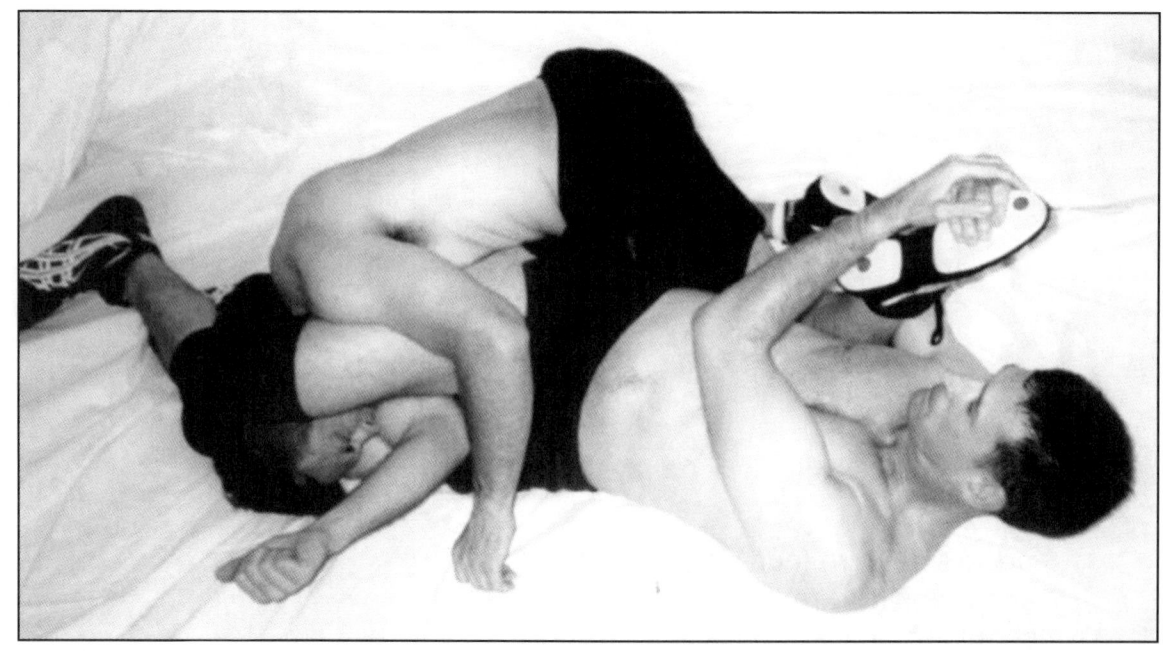

Arm Bar

You are securing him at the wrist with both arms for maximum leverage. His little finger is closest to your chest.

Your leg is across his neck, pinning his head to the ground. Your knees are squeezed together, trapping his arm.

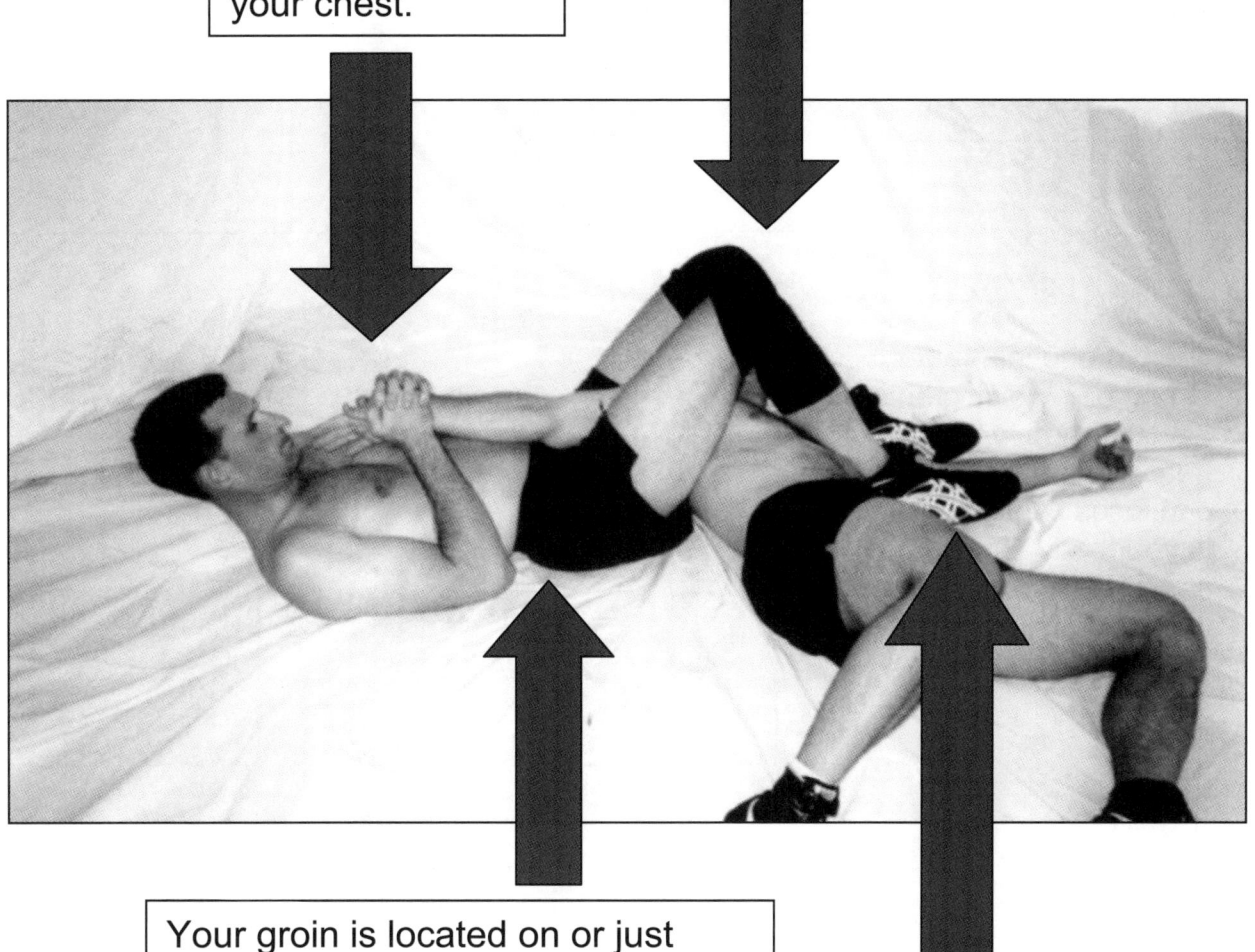

Your groin is located on or just above his elbow, closer to his shoulder. You arch your hips upwards to hyper-extend his arm at the elbow.

Your feet are pressed flat on the ground, preventing him from sitting up and turning into you.

ARM BAR

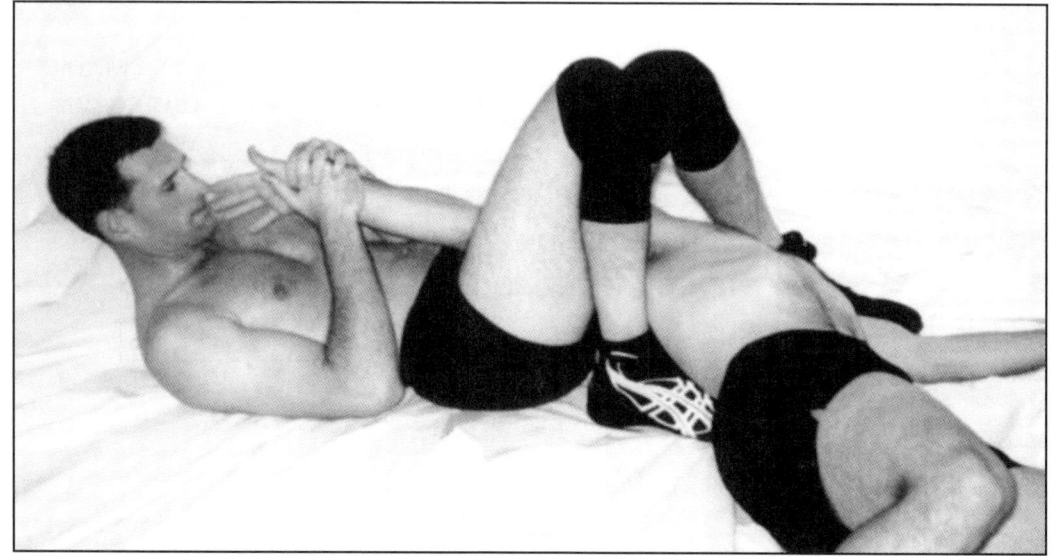

Leg Positioning

Depending on your attack and body positioning, you can place one leg against his ribs. This makes for a very tight hold and forces your opponent on his side, making it difficult for him to turn into you. (Left)

Bear Hug

If your opponent is very strong or is holding onto his other arm, you can bear hug his arm. You can focus every muscle in your body on straightening out his arm for the submission. (Right)

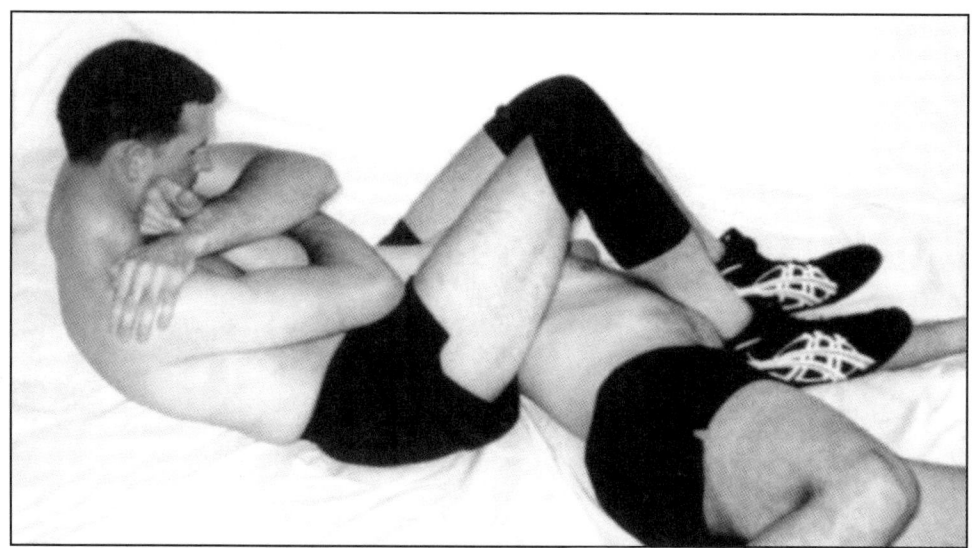

Entangled Legs

Use your imagination and the situation to create different varieties of attack. Here, one leg is entangled in the opponent's far arm and the other is behind his neck, forcing his head forwards in an uncomfortable position. (Left)

ARM BAR *Heel Push*

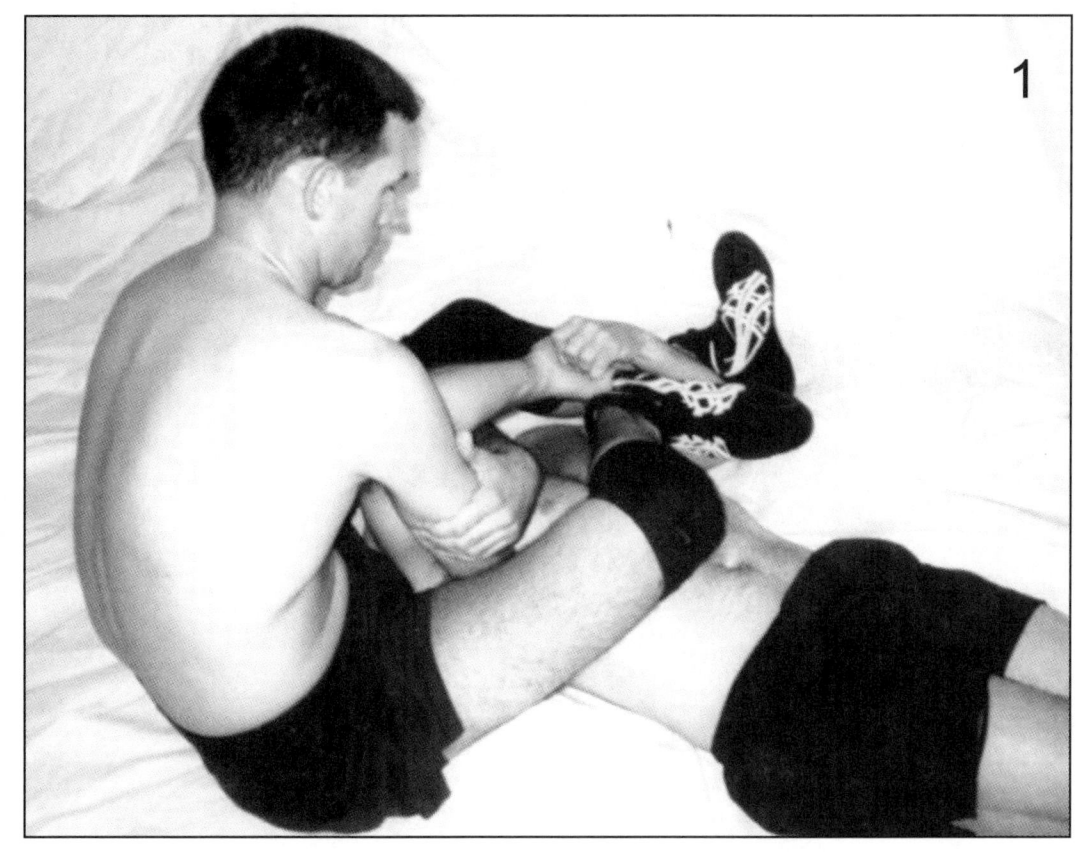

Your opponent may clasp his hands together to protect his trapped arm, so a wrist lock is not effective. Place the heel of your foot on the biceps of his free arm. (Left)

Bear hug his trapped arm. Pull his arm towards you while you push off on his biceps with your foot, breaking his grip. (Right)

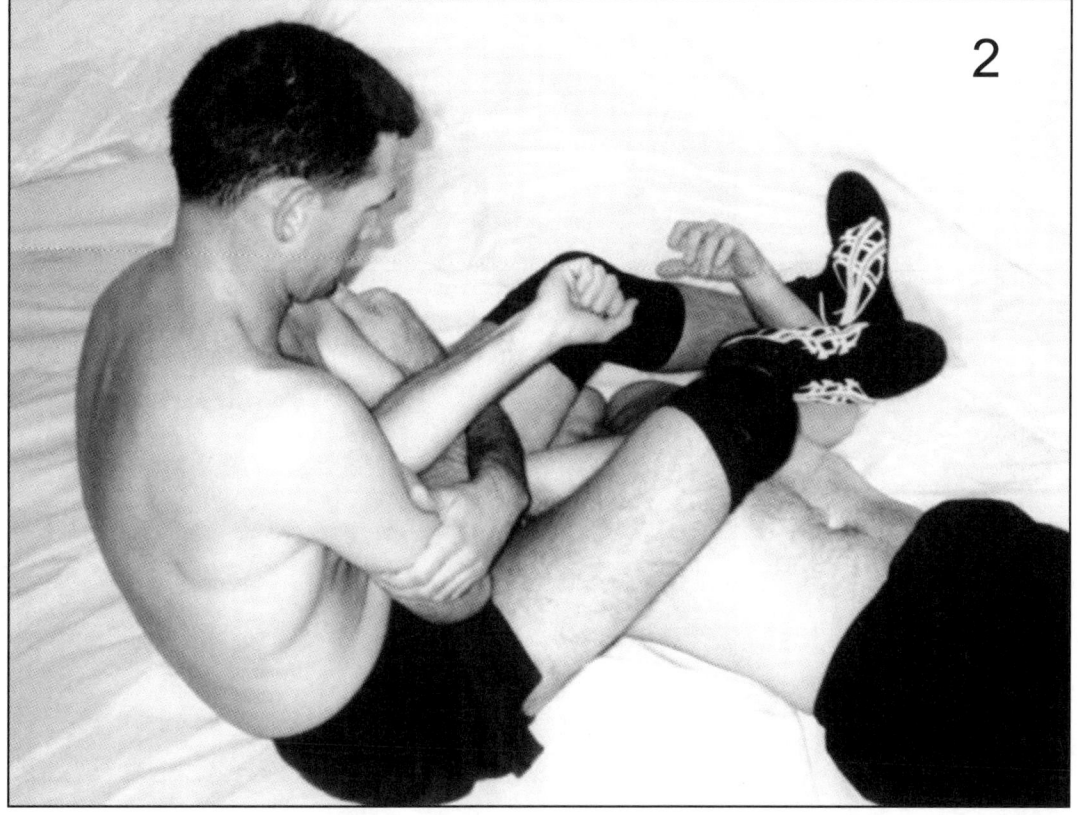

ARM BAR *Wrist Lock*

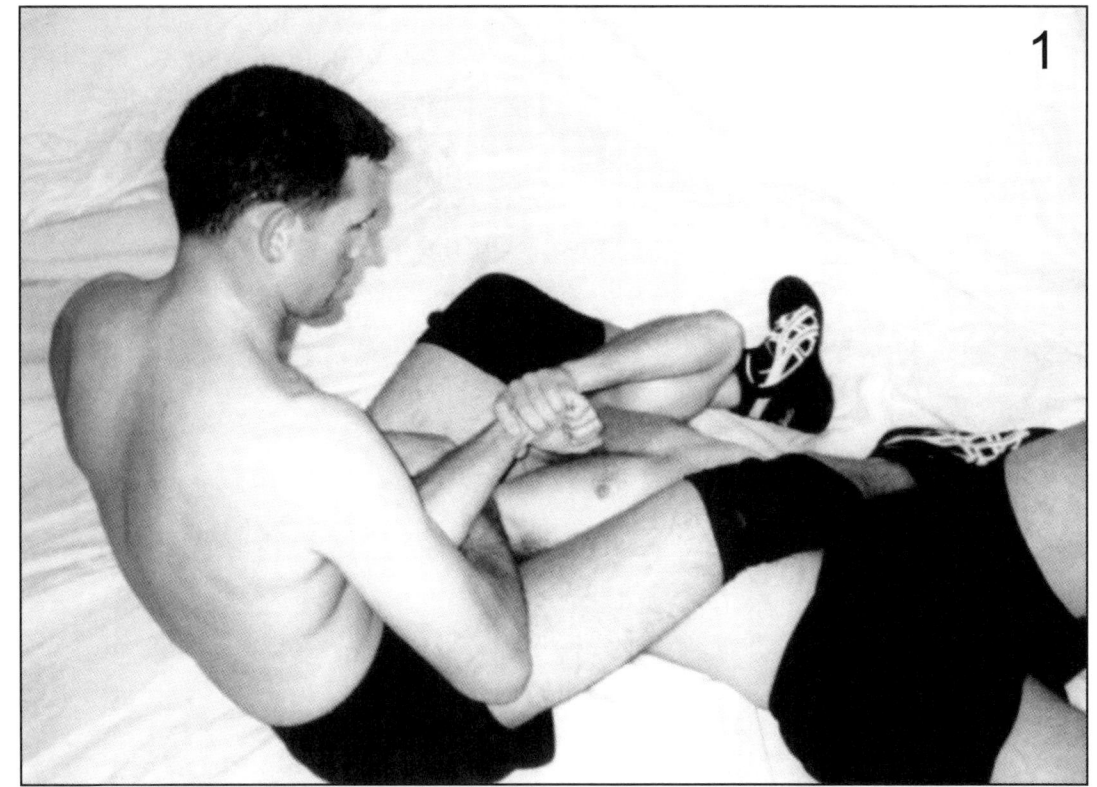

Often times your opponent will secure his targeted arm by grabbing his own wrist. Note that his free arm is grabbing his trapped arm at the wrist. (Left)

Grab his trapped arm at the wrist and bend it back onto itself. This hyper-flexes his wrist for the submission and is very painful. (Right)

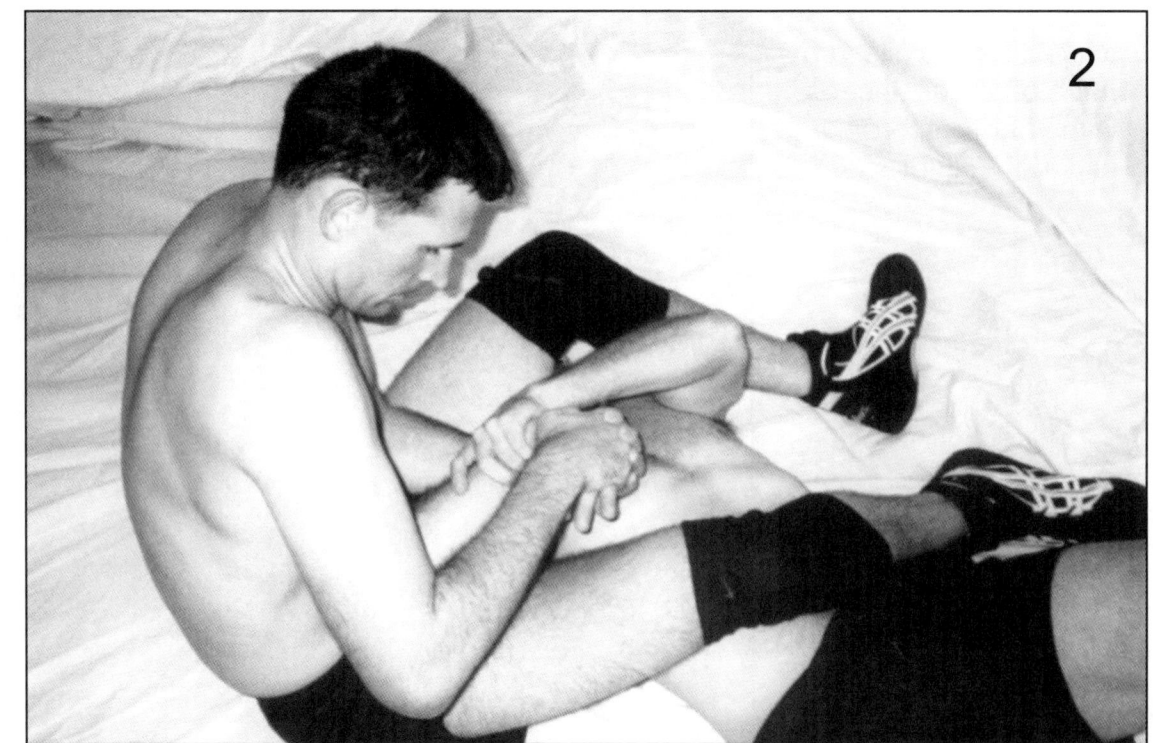

ARM BAR *Shoulder Cranks*

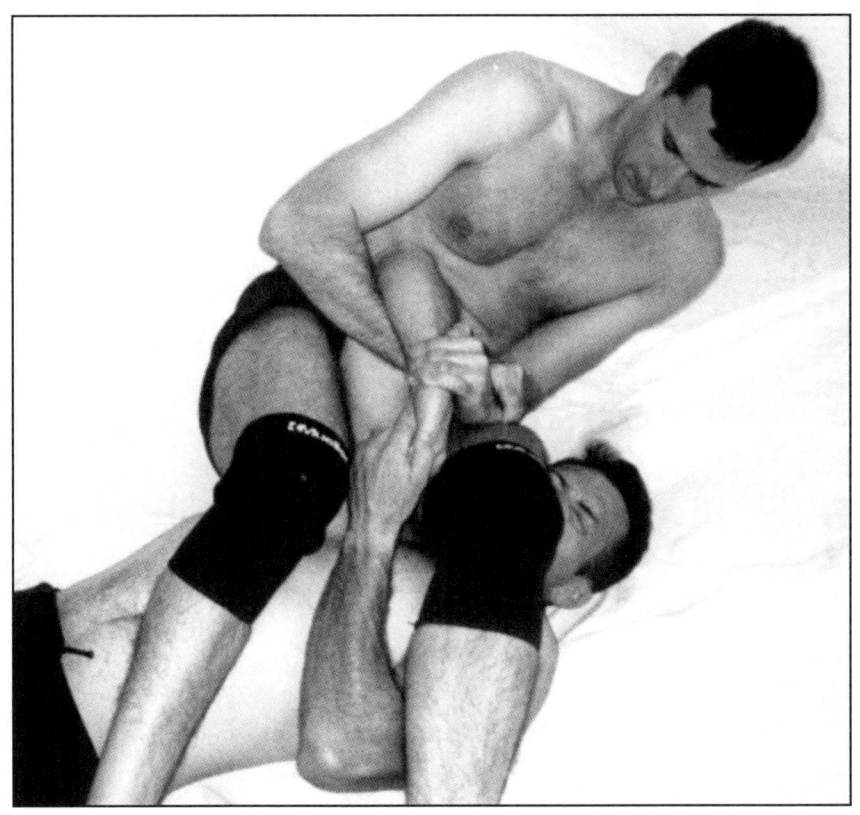

If your opponent is defending your attack, secure a figure four lock on his targeted arm. Lean onto your side, towards his head. If you notice, this is a shoulder crank. He will let go to relieve the pressure on his shoulder. (Left)

Sometimes you may get an opponent's arm trapped under your armpit, but it is not straight and leaning back will not hyper-extend his elbow. With the side that his arm is trapped on, plant the palm of your hand on his elbow. This ensures that as you twist your body, his arm will not straighten out. Reach over and clasp his elbow with your other hand. Pull his elbow in tightly to your side with both arms. Rotate your upper body towards his head, which will crank his shoulder for the submission. (Right)

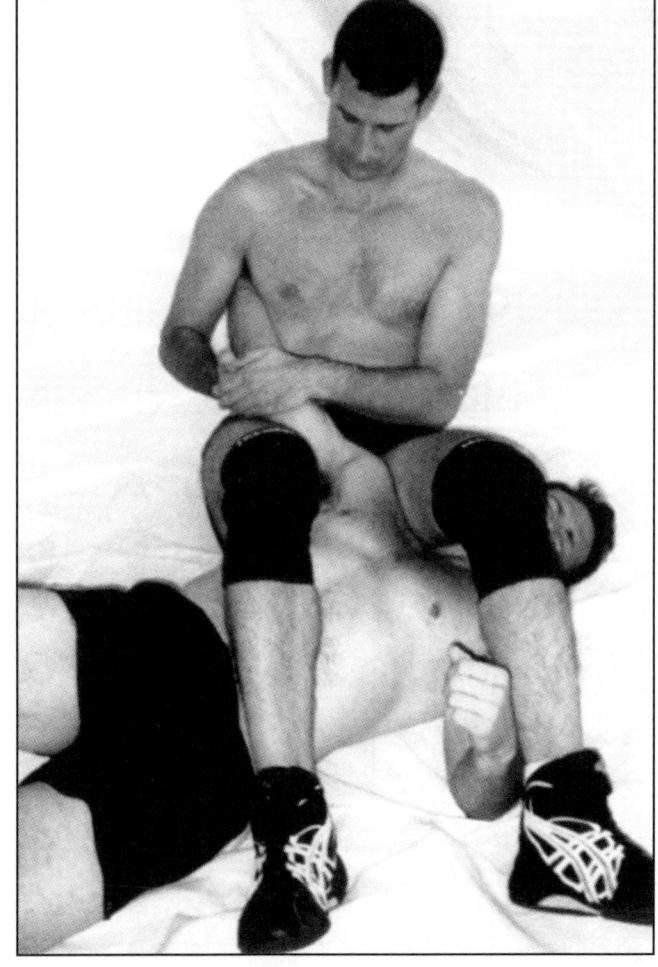

ARM BAR *Squeeze Lock*

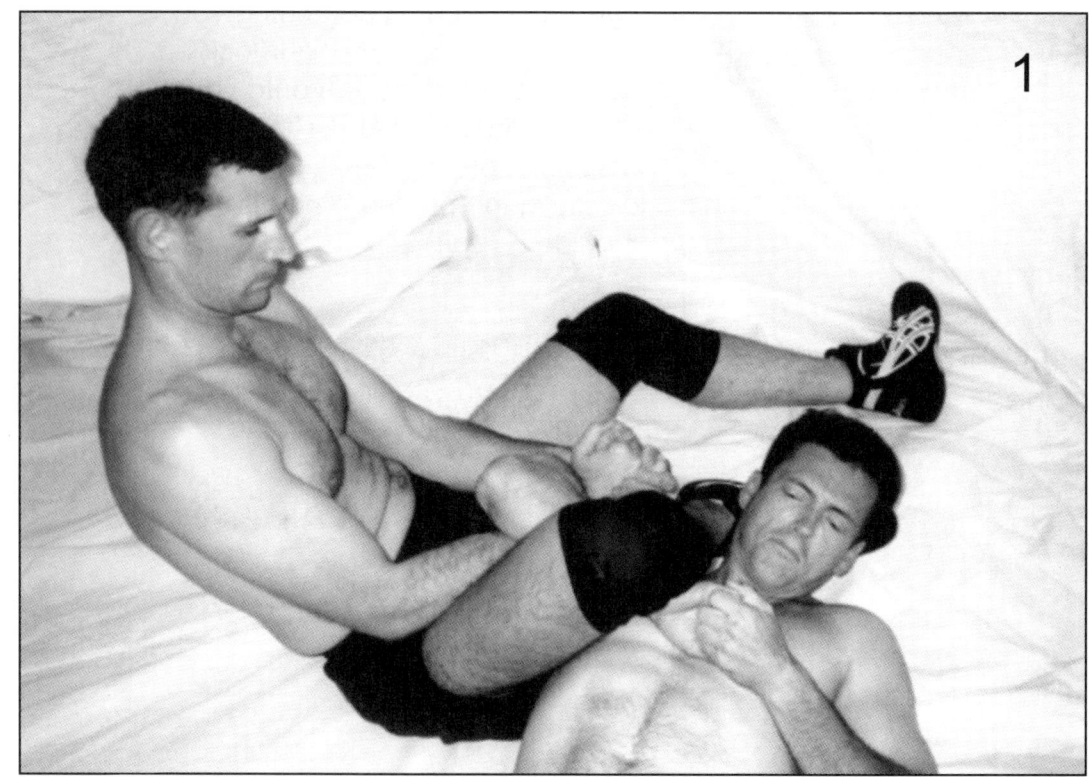

If your opponent tries to protect his trapped arm, he may set himself up for the ideal squeeze lock. Secure his arm so that the blade of your forearm is deep into the joint of his elbow. Swing your leg over his trapped arm and behind his head. (Left)

Lock your other leg over the foot of your attacking leg. Straighten out your back and pull with both arms, forcing the blade of your forearm into his elbow joint for the submission. (Right)

Knee Bar

You have firm control of his foot with both hands. The instep of his foot is facing down and is firmly pulled into your chest.

Your legs are crossed to prevent him from raising his upper body and relieving pressure on his knee. Your heels are pushing downwards, into his buttocks or his back, pinning him to the ground and keeping his trapped leg straight and extended.

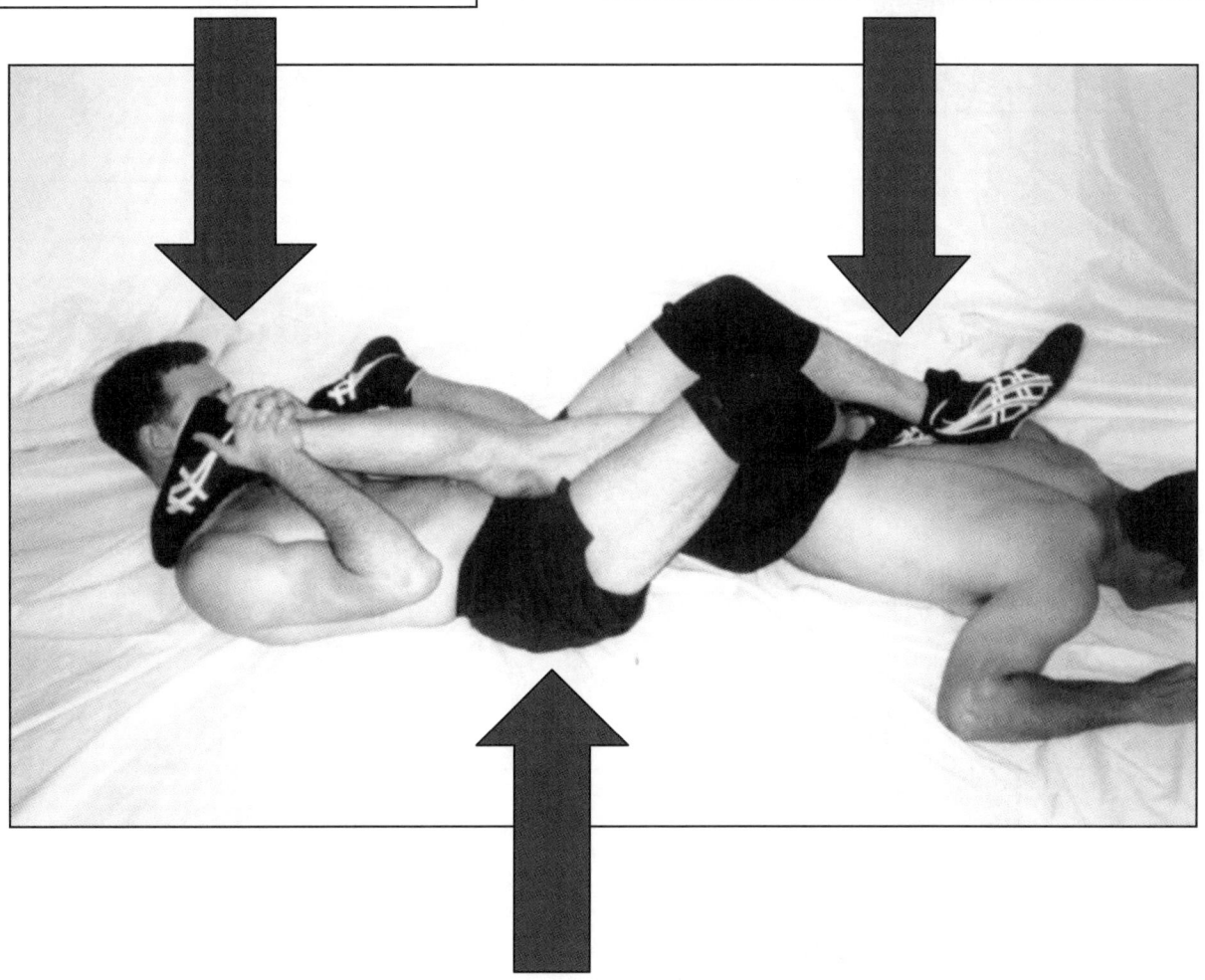

Your groin is located on his knee cap or slightly above it, closer to his groin. You arch your hips to hyper-extend his leg at the knee.

KNEE BAR *Leg Positioning*

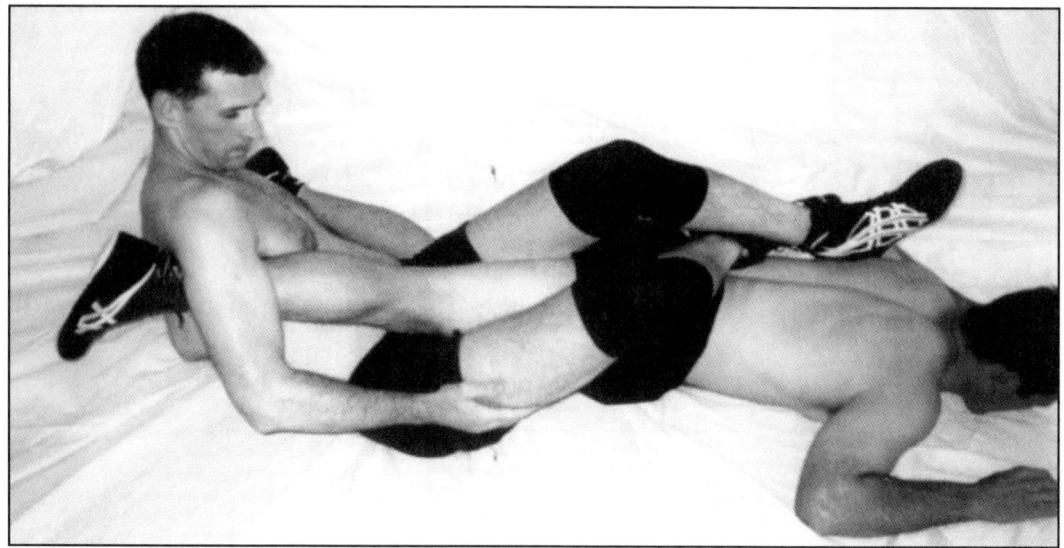

An under arm grip is very effective for implementing the knee bar. This technique uses your body (as you straighten your back) to hyper-extend his knee for the submission. (Left)

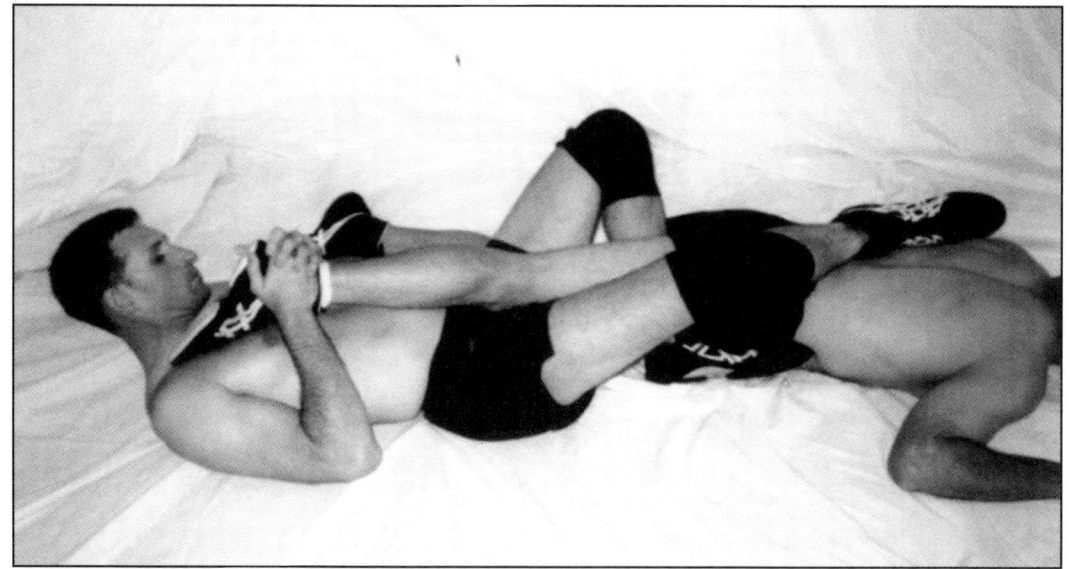

One leg through and posted on his back is sufficient to apply enough pressure on his knee joint for the submission. (Right)

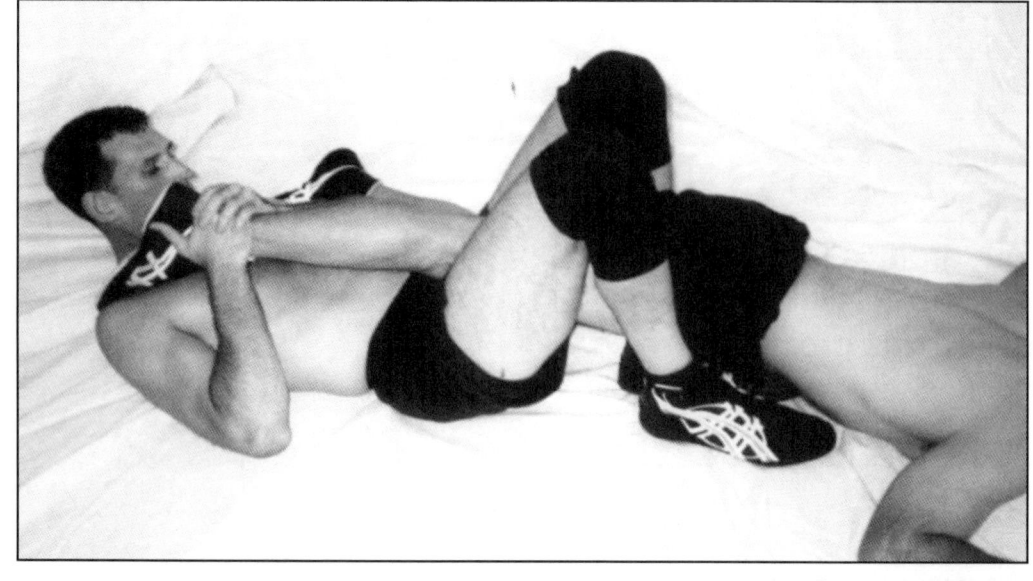

You can have neither leg posted on his body and still execute the technique. Squeeze your knees together to prevent his leg from sliding out and arch your hips for the same results. (Left)

KNEE BAR *Squeeze Lock*

1. Your opponent bends his leg or you can release the hold on his foot in order to bend his leg on purpose. Either way, keep a secure hold on his leg, behind his knee, with your arm. (Left)

Hook your leg over his trapped leg at the shin. This will keep him from straightening his leg and sets up the final step of the technique. (Right)

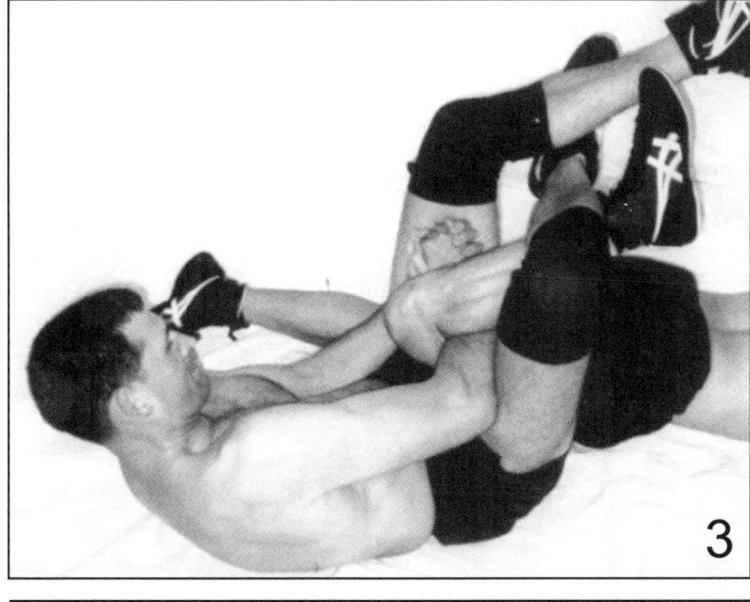

Hook your other leg over your attacking leg's foot, firmly locking his leg into the technique. Clasp your hands together and ensure that your forearm is deep into his knee joint. Squeeze your legs and try to push his heel to his own buttocks. Pull up with both of your arms and straighten your back and drive the blade of your forearm into his knee joint for the submission. (Left)

ANKLE ATTACKS

Secure a figure four lock on your opponent's foot. Keep his heel pinned tightly to your chest and crank his foot towards your chest. This will torque his knee for the submission. (Left)

NOTE: The key to all ankle cranks, which use the foot as a lever to torque the knee, is three-fold. First, you must secure a good grip on his foot. Second, you must have a sufficient range of motion to twist his ankle to apply enough pressure to tear the ligaments in your opponent's knee. Thirdly, you must be able to stop your opponent from repositioning his body, which he will do to relieve pressure on his knee.

Grab under your opponent's foot and grab him on his instep. Pull his toes downwards and torque his knee for the submission. (Right)

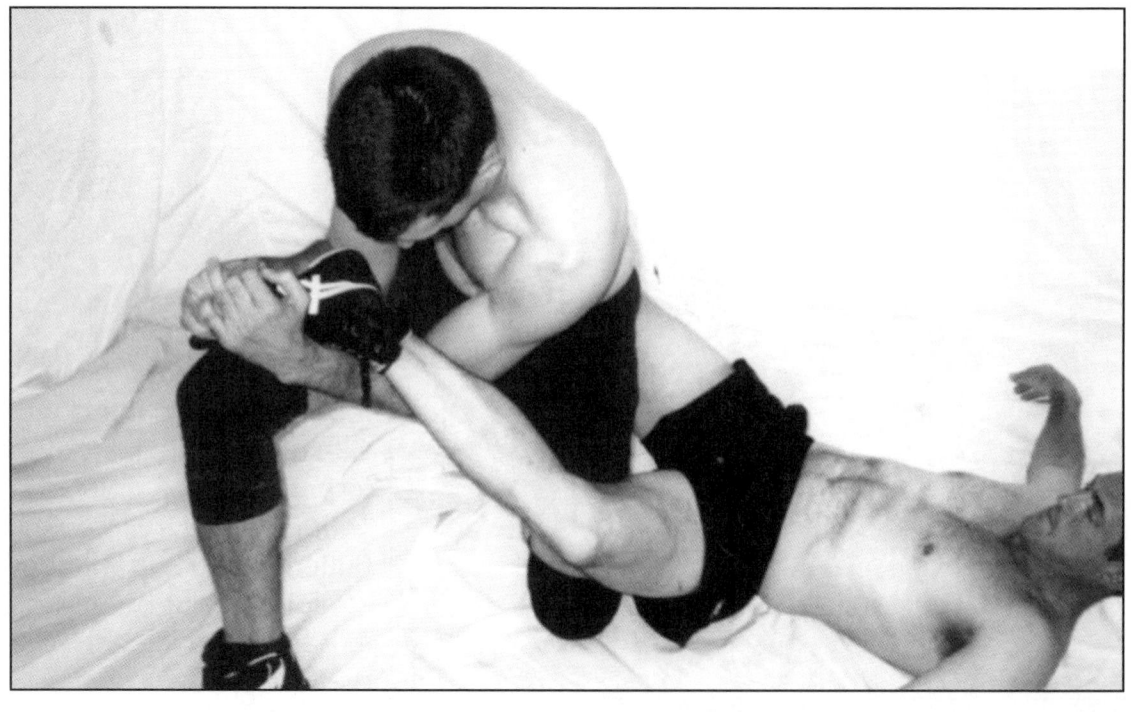

ANKLE ATTACKS *Ankle Locks*

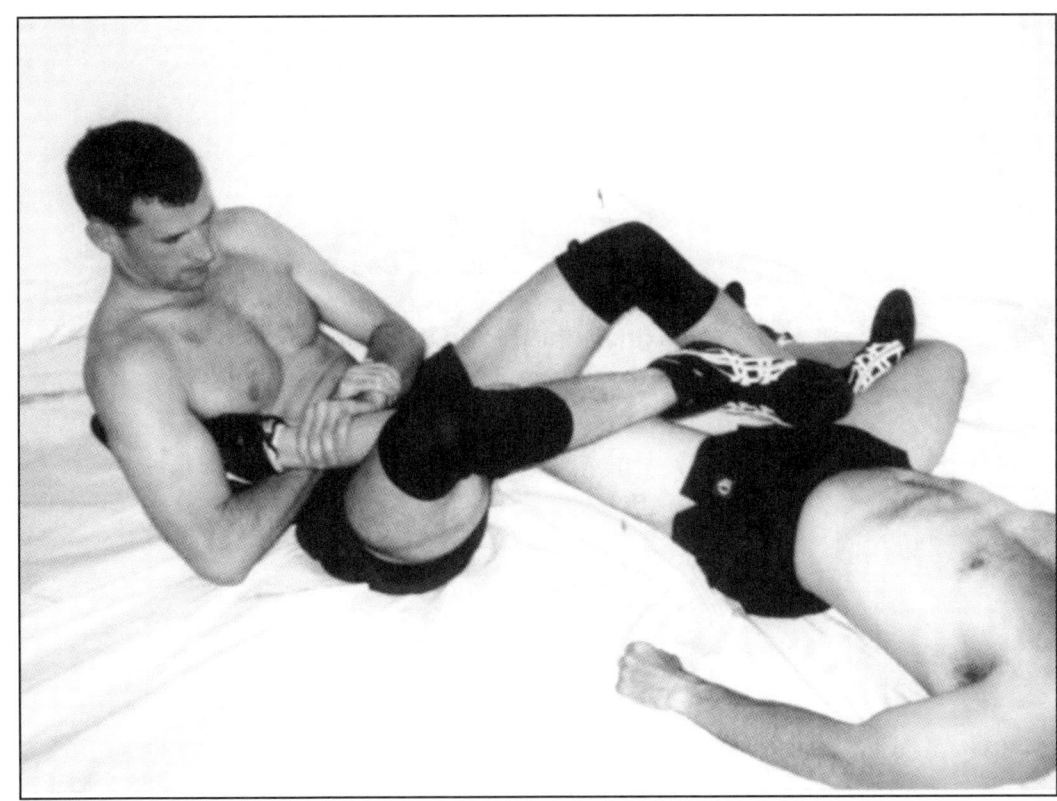

You have his foot secured under your armpit. You have a figure four lock on his foot. Your near leg is hooked over his trapped knee. Your far leg is planted in his far knee, stretching this leg out. This leg/foot positioning prevents your opponent from sitting up into you while you hyper-extend his foot for the submission. (Left)

You have his foot secured under your armpit. Place the same side arm under his ankle and grab your other arm at the wrist. Your other hand is secure on his shin; this forms a figure four lock on his foot. Your knees are squeezed tightly together to control his trapped leg. Press the elbow of your trapping arm against your own side, helping to secure his foot. Arch your back and look upwards to hyper-extend his foot at the ankle for the submission. (Right)

ANKLE ATTACKS *Achilles Locks*

His foot is secured under your armpit. Your attacking arm is hooked under his calf and across his Achilles tendon. Your attacking arm grabs your locking arm at the biceps, ensuring a tight lock on his foot. Arch your back and drive the blade of your attacking forearm into his Achilles for the submission. (Left)

Here is a standard Achilles lock. His foot is secured under your armpit. Your attacking arm is hooked under his calf and across his Achilles tendon. Secure your attacking arm at the wrist. Arch your back and pull up with your arms, driving the blade of your forearm into his Achilles for the submission. (Right)

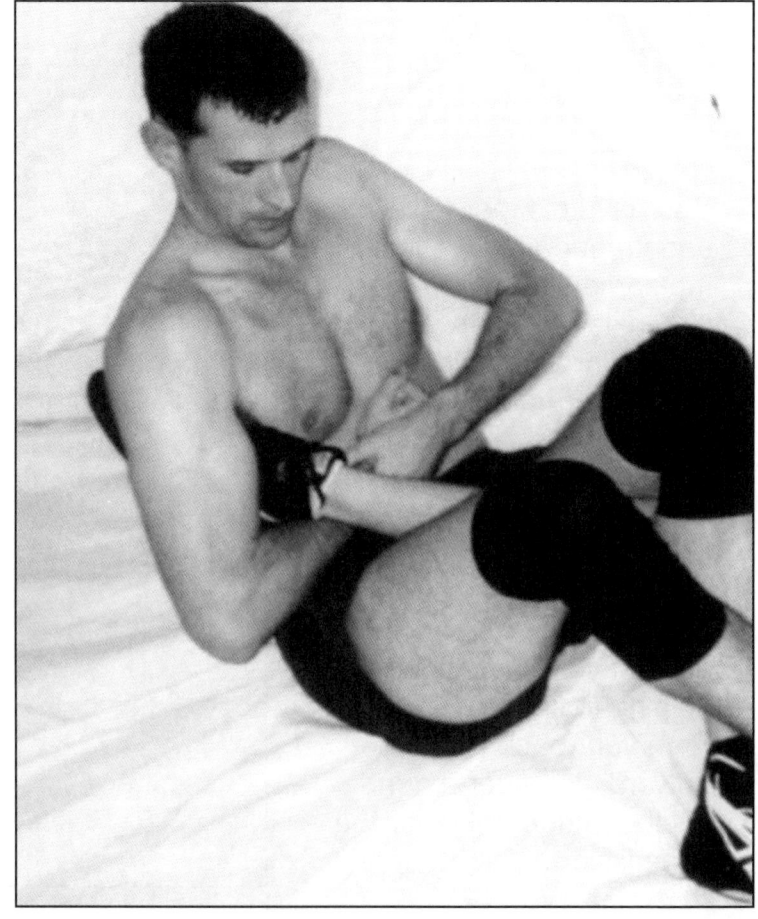

ANKLE ATTACKS

Ankle Crank

You have one leg entangled over his trapped leg and under his far knee. Your other leg is hooked over his far ankle, securing his far leg. Crank his ankle to torque his knee for the submission. (Left)

Heel Hook

Your leg is wrapped over his trapped leg and under the knee of his far leg. Your other leg is pressing down on his foot, securing his far leg. Execute a heel hook to torque his knee for the submission. (Right)

ANKLE ATTACKS

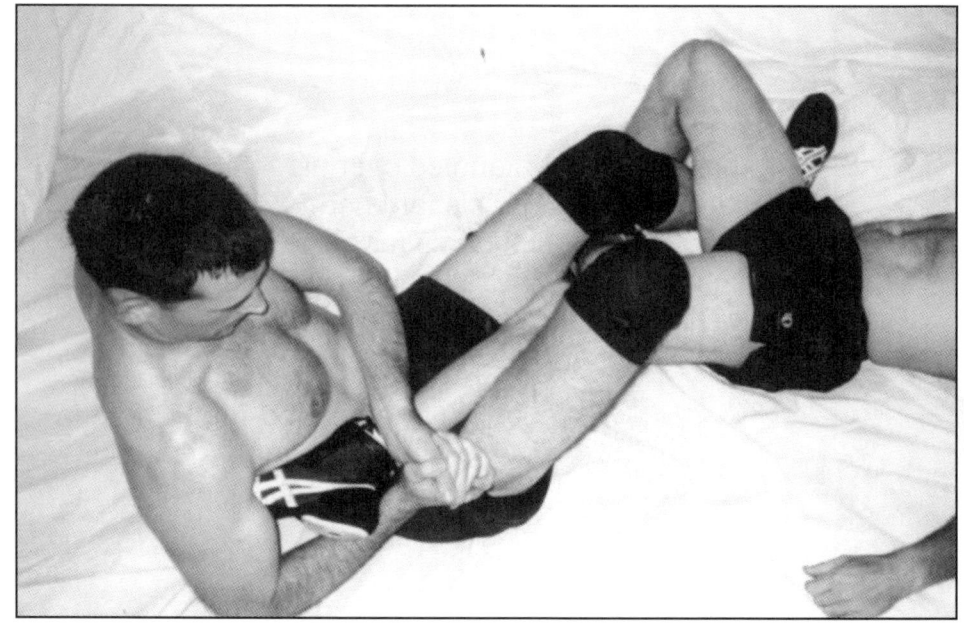

Heel Hook

This is a heel hook but with an entangled leg lock to secure your opponent. Your near leg is hooked over his trapped leg and your foot is behind the knee of your far leg. Your far foot is behind the knee of his far leg. (Left)

Squeeze Lock

Your opponent has your leg in an attempted ankle lock but he has placed his foot near your groin. Drive the blade of your forearm behind his knee and hook your free leg over his targeted leg. Pull the heel of your free leg towards you while you slide your hips forwards, attempting to place the heel of his trapped foot to his buttocks. Pull the blade of your attacking arm into the back of his knee for the submission. (Right)

Bad Leg Positioning

Here is an example of poor foot placement by the attacker. You are attacking his ankle but have allowed him to secure a lock on your own foot. Now, who has who? (Left)

ANKLE ATTACKS

Ankle & Achilles Lock Combo

This is a nice move if you can get it. Secure one of your opponent's legs under your armpit as if in a standard ankle lock. Cross his other leg under this trapped leg and trap his foot in the crook of your elbow. Clasp your hands together, locking his feet in the technique. Arch your back and look upwards as you pull his trapped foot backwards with your hands. This will hyper-extend his foot, under your arm, at the ankle. It will also drive your forearm into the Achilles tendon of his other leg. (Left)

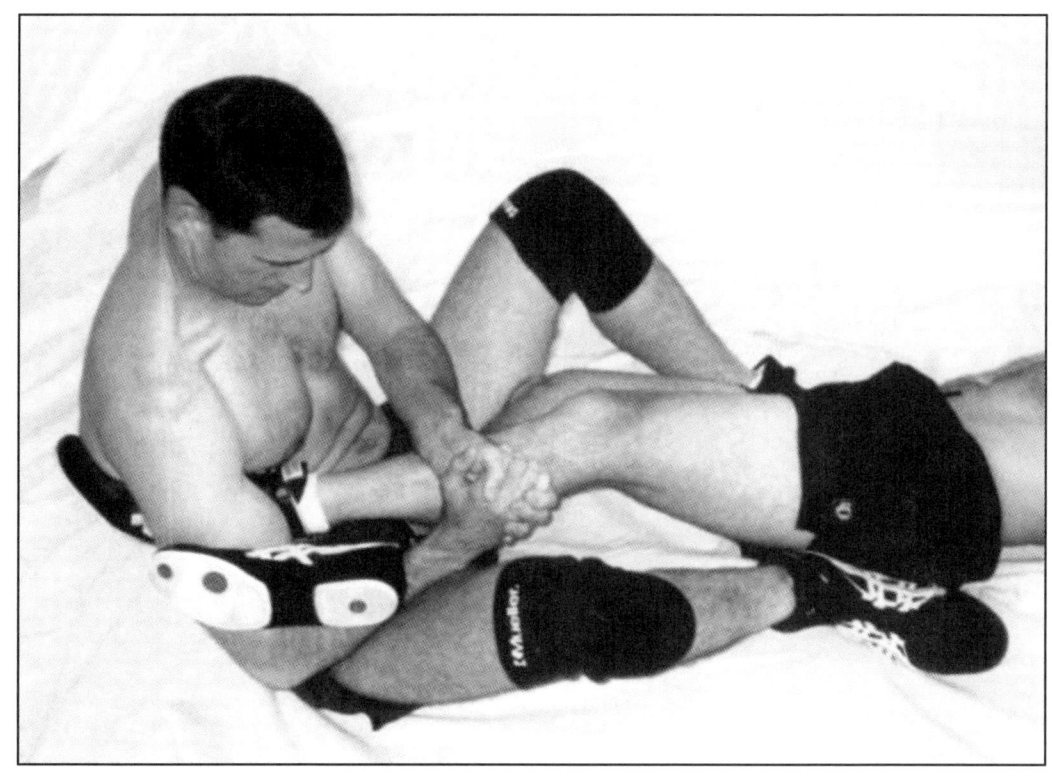

Achilles Lock

Your opponent has placed a foot in your groin area; he may be working on a foot lock against you. Grab his leg behind his calf and pull his instep tight into your groin. Clasp your hands and place the forearm of your attacking arm into the Achilles tendon of his foot. Pull both arms backwards and drive the blade of your forearm into his Achilles tendon for the submission. (Right)

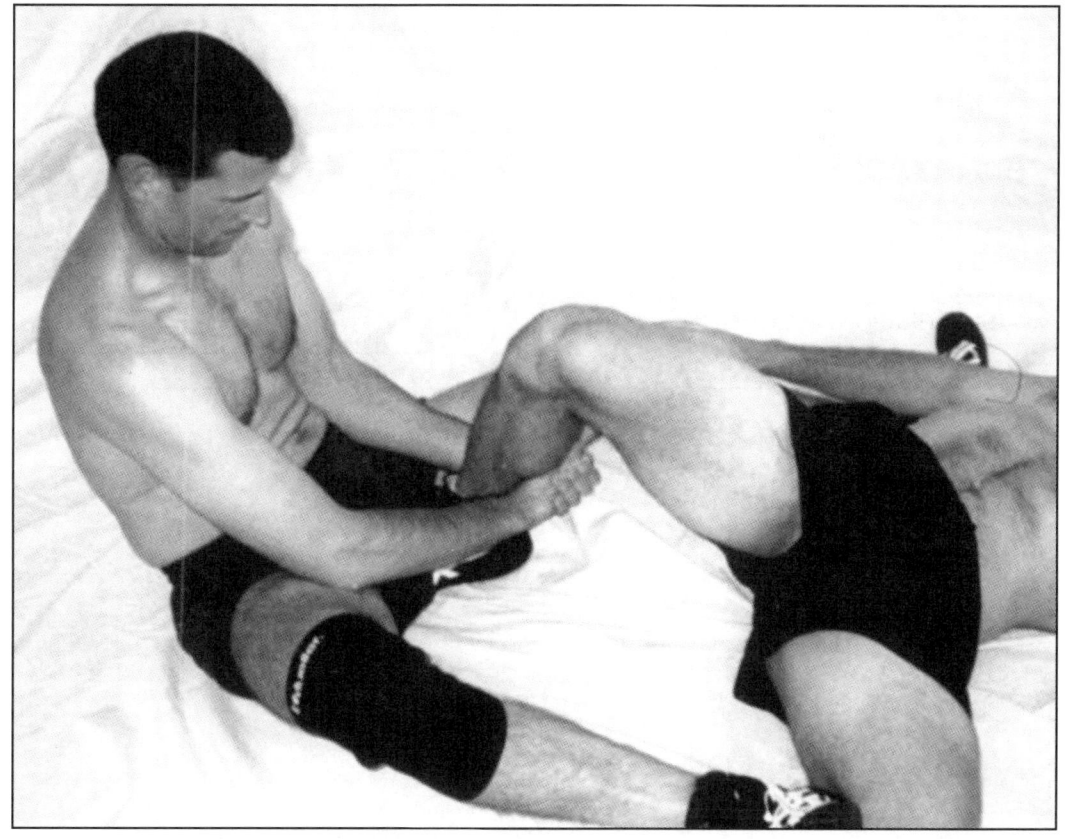

Index

A

Achilles Lock, Crossed Feet, from Side Control, 152

Achilles Lock, Drop, Standing, 8

Achilles Lock, Standing and Sitting, In Open Guard, 71

Achilles Locks, Variations, 266 & 269

Ankle and Achilles Lock, Combination, Variations, 269

Ankle Crank, in Closed Guard, 66

Ankle Crank, Entangled Legs, Referee, 217

Ankle Crank, Far Foot , from Side Control, 151

Ankle Crank, from Half Guard, 85

Ankle Crank, in Half Guard, 86

Ankle Crank, Near Foot, from Side Control, 149 - 150

Ankle Crank, in Open Guard, 74

Ankle Crank, in Rear Mount, 235 - 237

Ankle Crank, Referee, 218

Ankle Crank, Reverse Mount, 129

Ankle Crank, Spin, in Open Guard, 73

Ankle Cranks, Variations, 264 & 267

Ankle Lock, from Ankle Pick, Standing, 9

Ankle Lock, with Legs, in Rear Mount, 238

Ankle Lock, in Mount, 109

Ankle Lock, from Open Guard, 52

Ankle Lock, Roll Out, in Mount, 110

Ankle Lock, Sitting and Standing, in Open Guard, 72

Ankle Lock, Step Over, in Closed Guard, 67

Ankle Lock, from Takedown, from Open Guard, 53

Ankle Locks, Variations, 265

Arm Bar, Bear Hug, Variations, 256

Arm Bar, from Closed Guard, 31

Arm Bar, Double Arm, from Closed Guard, 35

Arm Bar, Elbow Lock, from Closed Guard, 37

Arm Bar, Elbow Lock, Double, from Closed Guard, 36

Arm Bar, Elbow Lock, with Entangled Leg, from Closed Guard, 38

Arm Bar, Elbow Lock, Standing, 17

Arm Bar, Explanation, Variations, 255

Arm Bar, Figure Four Lock, Modified Mount, 117

Arm Bar, Figure Four Lock, from Rear Mount, 230

Arm Bar, Figure Four Lock, from Side Control, 138

Arm Bar, Figure Four Lock, Standing, 16

Arm Bar, Heel Push, Variations, 257

Arm Bar, Hug, Knee On Stomach, 187

Arm Bar, Hug, Modified Mount, 118

Arm Bar, Hug, from Side Control, 139

Arm Bar, Iron Cross, Referee, 205

Arm Bar, Knee Across, Standing, 15

Arm Bar, Knee On Chest, 193

Arm Bar, Knee On Stomach, 185

Arm Bar, with Leg Across, Standing, 14

Arm Bar, with Legs, Referee, 204

Arm Bar, with Leg Scissors, from Closed Guard, 34

Arm Bar, with Leg Scissors, from Open Guard, 58

Arm Bar, with Leg Under Hook, from Closed Guard, 33

Arm Bar, with Leg Under Hook, Modified Mount, 119

Arm Bar, Leg Positioning, Variations, 256

Arm Bar, with Legs, from Scarf Hold, 173

Arm Bar, from Mount, 102

Arm Bar, in North/South, 247

Arm Bar, from Open Guard, 57

Arm Bar, Quarter Nelson, Referee, 207

Arm Bar, Rear Mount, 229

Arm Bar, Reverse Mount, 128

Arm Bar, Roll Over, from Mount, 105

Arm Bar, in Scarf Hold, 176

Arm Bar, Shoulder Cranks, Variations, 259

Arm Bar, in Side Control, 162

Arm Bar, Squeeze Lock, Variations, 260

Arm Bar, Step Across, Knee On Chest, 194

Arm Bar, Step Across, Knee On Stomach, 186

Arm Bar, Step Across, Modified Scarf Hold, 180

Arm Bar, Step Over with Leg, Referee, 206

Arm Bar, Step Over, Modified Scarf Hold, 178

Arm Bar, Step Over, from Scarf Hold, 174

Arm Bar, Step Over, from Side Control, 140

Arm Bar, Straight, with Leg Assist, from Closed Guard, 39

Arm Bar, Straight, from Mount, 103

Arm Bar, Straight, in Side Control, 160

Arm Bar, Underarm, from Closed Guard, 32

Arm Bar, Underarm, from Mount, 104

Arm Bar, Under Hooking Leg, from Closed Guard, 33

Arm Bar, Wrist Lock, Variations, 258

Arm Bar, "X", from Closed Guard, 40

C

Choke, Forearm, in Closed Guard, 62

Choke, Forearm, with Entangled Arm, in Closed Guard, 63

Choke, Forearm, with Entangled Arm, from Mount, 95

Choke, Forearm, from Side Control, 155

Choke, Forearm, with Under Hook, from Mount, 95

Choke, Guillotine, from Closed Guard, 27

Choke, Guillotine, from Knee On Chest, 192

Choke, Guillotine, from Knee On Stomach, 184

Choke, Guillotine, from Mount, 96

Choke, Guillotine, from Side Control, 137

Choke, Guillotine, Standing, 7

Choke, Kata Gatame, from Closed Guard, 28

Choke, Kata Gatame, in Closed Guard, 64

Choke, Kata Gatame, Modified Mount, 115

Choke, Kata Gatame, from Mount, 98

Choke, Kata Gatame, from North/South, 244

Choke, Kata Gatame, Referee, 202

Choke, Kata Gatame, from Scarf Hold, 167

Choke, Kata Gatame, in Scarf Hold, 175

Choke, Kata Gatame, in Side Control, 157

Choke, Kata Gatame, Standing, 5

Choke, Leg Scissors, from North/South, 245

Choke, Modified Kata Gatame, from Closed Guard, 29

Choke, Modified Kata Gatame, in Closed Guard, 65

Choke, Modified Kata Gatame, from Mount, 99

Choke, Modified Kata Gatame, from Scarf Hold, 168

Choke, Modified Kata Gatame, In Side Control, 158

Choke, Paper Cutter, Modified Mount, 115

Choke, Paper Cutter, Referee, 200 - 201

Choke, Paper Cutter, from Side Control, 136

Choke, from Rear Mount, 227

Choke, Rear Naked Strangle, Modified Mount, 114

Choke, Rear Naked Strangle, from Rear Mount, 226

Choke, Referee, 199

Choke, Scissored Arms, from Closed Guard, 26

Choke, Scissored Arms, in Closed Guard, 63

Choke, Scissored Arms, from Mount, 94

Choke, Scissored Arms and Smother, from Scarf Hold, 169

Choke, Shin, from Knee On Chest, 191

Choke, Shin, in North/South, 248

Choke, Shin, from Open Guard, 49

Choke, Shoulder, from North/South, 243

Choke, Shoulder, Standing, 6

Choke, Smother, from Mount, 100

Choke, Triangle, from Closed Guard, 30

Choke, Triangle, Far Arm, from Scarf Hold, 170

Choke, Triangle, Modified Mount, 116

Choke, Triangle, from Mount, 97

Choke, Triangle, Near Arm, from Scarf Hold, 171

Choke, Triangle, from Referee, 203

Choke, Triangle, from Rear Mount, 228

Choke, Triangle, in Side Control, 159

Cradle, Knee On Stomach, 183

F

Forearm Lock, Modified Mount, 123

Forearm Lock, from Side Control, 141

Forearm Lock, Standing, 18

G

Groin Stretch, Banana Split, Referee, 219

Groin Stretch, Banana Split, Standing, 21

Groin Stretch, in Open Guard, 80

Guard, Closed, Explanation, 23

Guard, Half, Explanation, 82

Guard, Open, Explanation, 48

H

Heel Hook, in Mount, 108

Heel Hook, from Open Guard, 50

Heel Hook, in Open Guard, 69

Heel Hook, from Side Control, 154

Heel Hook, from Sweep, in Open Guard, 70

Heel Hook, from Takedown, from Open Guard, 51

Heel Hook, Variations, 267 - 268

Hip Lock, Figure Four Lock, from Side Control, 147

Hip Lock, Modified Mount, 124

Hip Lock, from Side Control, 146

K

Knee Bar, from Ankle Lock, in Open Guard, 75

Knee Bar, Double, in Open Guard, 77

Knee Bar, Drop, Standing, 10

Knee Bar, Explanation, Variations, 261

Knee Bar, Far Leg, Knee On Stomach, 188

Knee Bar, Far Leg, from Side Control, 144

Knee Bar, from Half Guard, 84

Knee Bar, in Half Guard, 87

Knee Bar, Leg Positioning, Variations, 262

Knee Bar, Near Leg, from Side Control, 145

Knee Bar, from Open Guard, 54

Knee Bar, Rolling, in Referee, 220

Knee Bar, Rolling, Referee, 209

Knee Bar, Rolling, Standing, 11 - 12

Knee Bar, Sit Up, in Open Guard, 55

Knee Bar, Sitting, Standing, 13

Knee Bar, Squeeze Lock, Leg, Variations, 263

Knee Bar, Step Over, in Open Guard, 76

Knee Bar, Straight, in Open Guard, 78

Knee Lever, Entangled Leg, Referee, 211

Knee Lever, Entangled Leg, Inside, Referee, 210

Knee Lever, Figure Four Lock, Referee, 213

Knee Lever, from Half Guard, 83

Knee Lever, in Half Guard, 89

Knee Lever, from Mount, 106

Knee Lever, in Mount, 107

Knee Lever, from Open Guard, 56

Knee Lever, Referee, 214

Knee Lever, Shin, Referee, 212

Knee On Chest, Explanation, 190

Knee On Stomach, Explanation, 182

M

Modified Mount, Explanation, 112

Modified Scarf Hold, Explanation, 177

Mount, Explanation, 91

N

Neck Crank, Bottle Cap, Modified Mount, 113

Neck Crank, Can Opener, in Closed Guard, 61

Neck Crank, Can Opener, from Scarf Hold, 166

Neck Crank, Cross Face, Referee, 197

Neck Crank, Crucifix, from Closed Guard, 25

Neck Crank, Crucifix, Knee On Chest, 191

Neck Crank, Crucifix, from Mount, 93

Neck Crank, Crucifix, Standing, 2

Neck Crank, Entangled Arm, from Side Control, 132

Neck Crank, Figure Four Lock, from Closed Guard, 24

Neck Crank, Figure Four Lock, in Closed Guard, 62

Neck Crank, Figure Four Lock, from Mount, 92

Neck Crank, Figure Four Lock, Standing, 3

Neck Crank, Full Nelson, from Rear Mount, 225

Neck Crank, with Legs, from Rear Mount, 225

Neck Crank, Modified Can Opener, Referee, 198

Neck Crank, Modified Can Opener, from Scarf Hold, 165

Neck Crank, from Rear Mount, 223

Neck Crank, Shoulder, from Side Control, 133

Neck Crank, in Side Control, 156

Neck Crank, Step Over, from Side Control, 134

Neck Crank, Underarm, Modified Mount, 113

Neck Crank, Underarm, from North/South, 241 & 242

Neck Crank, Underarm, from Rear Mount, 224

Neck Crank, Underarm, Standing, 4

North South, Explanation, 240

R

Rear Mount, Explanation, 222

Referee Position, Explanation, 196

Reverse Mount, Explanation, 126

S

Scarf Hold, Explanation, 164

Shoulder Crank, Americana, Modified Scarf Hold, 179

Shoulder Crank, Americana, from Mount, 101

Shoulder Crank, Americana, from Side Control, 142

Shoulder Crank, Chicken Wing, from Rear Mount, 233

Shoulder Crank, Head Assist, Modified Mount, 12

Shoulder Crank, High Guard, from Closed Guard, 43

Shoulder Crank, Key Lock, from Closed Guard, 41

Shoulder Crank, Key Lock, Drop, Standing, 19

Shoulder Crank, Key Lock, in Side Control, 161

Shoulder Crank, Knee On Chest, 194

Shoulder Crank, with Leg Assist, from Closed Guard, 42

Shoulder Crank, with Legs, from Closed Guard, 44

Shoulder Crank, with Legs, from Scarf Hold, 172

Shoulder Crank, Modified Mount, 120

Shoulder Crank, from North/South, 246

Shoulder Crank, Reverse Key Lock, from Side Control, 143

Shoulder Crank, Reverse Mount, 127

Shoulder Lock, from Rear Mount, 234

Side Control, Explanation, 131

Squeeze Lock, Arm, from Closed Guard, 45

Squeeze Lock, Arm, Modified Mount, 122

Squeeze Lock, Arm, Nutcracker, from Rear Mount, 232

Squeeze Lock, Arm, Nutcracker, Referee, 208

Squeeze Lock, Arm, Nutcracker, Standing, 20

Squeeze Lock, Arm, from Open Guard, 59

Squeeze Lock, Arm, from Rear Mount, 231

Squeeze Lock, Leg, from Ankle Attack, Variations, 277

Squeeze Lock, Leg, in Half Guard, 88

Squeeze Lock, Leg, in Open Guard, 79

T

Toe Hold, Crossed Feet, from Side Control, 153

Toe Hold, Referee, 215

Toe Hold, from Side Control, 148

Toe Hold, Shin Assist, Referee, 216

Triangle Choke, with Arm Assists, 251

Triangle Choke, Explanation, 250

Triangle Choke, with Heel Hook, 254

Triangle Choke, with Neck Cranks, 252

Triangle Choke, with Shoulder Cranks, 253

W

Wrist Lock, from Closed Guard, 46

About The Author

The author, Steven S. Iverson, was introduced to the martial arts by studying Tae Kwon Do with some exposure to Kung Fu. He then studied American style boxing and Judo while attending college. Several years ago, the author began formal instruction in Jiu-Jitsu and has continued to study this sport to the present day. He has competed in organized Judo, Sambo and Jiu-Jitsu tournaments.